CW01501419

"Brooks is to be congratulated on producing : and comprehensive introduction to key them of education. Threaded throughout the the ments about continuity and change in the contemporary society, supported by a lively range of up-to a distinctively international flavour. A hugely diverse and fascinating range of topics is covered – from epigenetics to home-schooling, sexual harassment in schools and universities, to the ways in which education is implicated in global population flows and projects of nation-building. Highly recommended for students at all levels of their undergraduate and graduate studies as well as seasoned scholars wanting to familiarise themselves with new developments in the sociology of education or looking for fresh insights on familiar themes."

—*Sharon Gewirtz, King's College London, UK*

"Rachel Brooks's *Education and Society* is the sociology of education for the twenty-first century. It is beautifully written, accessible, thoroughly researched and deals with pressing contemporary education issues from multiple sociological perspectives. This book is a must read for all sociologists of education seeking to understand the places, policies and processes of education in our tumultuous globalising times."

—*Bob Lingard, University of Queensland, Australia*

"In a time of increasing inequality and budget cuts to public education, we should all welcome a book like *Education and Society* that provides a clear and accessible sociological overview of education as a social institution. Brooks pays particular attention to the ways in which the education experience has been differentiated by class, race, and gender, as well as the impact neoliberal policies have had on the educational experience of all students. Her attention to power dynamics, even down to the ethics of educational research (who is doing the funding, and with what consequences?) is a refreshing addition to our understanding of the educational field."

—*Allison L. Hurst, Oregon State University, USA*

"A refreshingly up-to-date and much-needed textbook engaging with the complexities of education systems in contemporary society ... beautifully written, authoritative, and highly engaging."

—*Nicola Ingram, Lancaster University, UK*

"*Education and Society* is a highly creative and innovative take on the field of sociology of education ... A fantastic and very valuable contribution to a field that desperately needs an injection of new textbooks. I think it will make an excellent resource for students and lecturers alike."

—*Peter Hemming, Cardiff University, UK*

"This superb book effortlessly combines theoretical reasoning with empirical evidence and offers a breadth, scope and depth that is unrivalled by any text currently available on the complex relationships between education and society."

—*Wolfgang Lehmann, University of Western Ontario, Canada, UK*

"*Education and Society* provides powerful insights into the defining issues of contemporary education, compelling readers to critically consider what it means to think about education through a sociological lens."

—*Glenn Savage, University of Western Australia, Australia*

"This wide-ranging book takes a valuable intersectional approach to understanding how education reproduces and transforms societies, making it a must-read book for students, academics and policy-makers alike"

—*Vikki Boliver, Durham University, UK*

"In *Education and Society*, Brooks skilfully brings together a vast array of theoretical perspectives, critical scholarship and contemporary research to locate key debates and trends in the sociology of education. Written in a clear and accessible manner, and comprehensive in scope, this book is a must-read for anyone interested in the complex relationship between Education and Society."

—*Kim Allen, University of Leeds, UK*

EDUCATION AND SOCIETY

PLACES, POLICIES, PROCESSES

RACHEL BROOKS

macmillan
international
HIGHER EDUCATION

RED GLOBE
PRESS

© Rachel Brooks, under exclusive licence to Springer Nature Limited 2019

All rights reserved. No reproduction, copy or transmission of this publication may be made without written permission.

No portion of this publication may be reproduced, copied or transmitted save with written permission or in accordance with the provisions of the Copyright, Designs and Patents Act 1988, or under the terms of any licence permitting limited copying issued by the Copyright Licensing Agency, Saffron House, 6–10 Kirby Street, London EC1N 8TS.

Any person who does any unauthorized act in relation to this publication may be liable to criminal prosecution and civil claims for damages.

The author has asserted her right to be identified as the author of this work in accordance with the Copyright, Designs and Patents Act 1988.

First published 2019 by
RED GLOBE PRESS

Red Globe Press in the UK is an imprint of Springer Nature Limited, registered in England, company number 785998, of 4 Crinan Street, London, N1 9XW.

Red Globe Press® is a registered trademark in the United States, the United Kingdom, Europe and other countries.

ISBN: 978–1–137–60288–6 hardback
ISBN: 978–1–137–60287–9 paperback

This book is printed on paper suitable for recycling and made from fully managed and sustained forest sources. Logging, pulping and manufacturing processes are expected to conform to the environmental regulations of the country of origin.

A catalogue record for this book is available from the British Library.

A catalog record for this book is available from the Library of Congress.

For my parents, Wendy and Barry Brooks

CONTENTS

ACKNOWLEDGEMENTS

I am grateful to Lloyd Langman at Red Globe Press for persuading me to write this book in the first place, and for the detailed and thoughtful feedback he gave me on each of the chapters. I would like to thank the anonymous reviewers who also sent very useful comments on the entire manuscript. Much of the book is based on the sociology of education course I have taught at the University of Surrey – and I have benefited hugely from the opportunity to learn from all the students who have taken this course over the years. Finally, I would like to thank various colleagues, friends and family for their interest in this book and their support during the time I was writing it – particularly Johanna Waters, Alison Hall, Jude Hussain, Sarah Neal, Andy King, Paul Hodkinson, Jon Garland and Hannah, Martha and Daniel. The book is dedicated to my parents, Wendy and Barry Brooks, with thanks and love.

1 EDUCATION AND SOCIETY: AN INTRODUCTION

Introduction

Education plays a central role in most societies throughout the world. It is a key element of our lives as social beings. This is perhaps most evident to us when we are young and typically have to attend school every day. However, it has become increasingly important at later stages of our lives, too, as we participate in learning in colleges, universities, workplaces and various other contexts. Thus, to understand contemporary society more comprehensively, we need to examine the impact of education and the ways in which it contributes to broader social processes. There are clearly a number of approaches we can take – psychologists, economists and geographers all study education, and apply their own particular disciplinary perspectives. In *Education and Society*, we deploy an explicitly *sociological* approach. In contrast to some other social science disciplines which may focus more on the individual, sociology focuses on *interdependencies* between humans, examining the ways in which human actions are elements of wider figurations or, as Bauman (1990) puts it, a 'non-random assembly of actors locked together in a web of mutual dependency' (p. 7). By this, he means that how we act and the impact of that action are both strongly influenced by the people around us, what they do and/or our anticipation of what they *may* do.

Because of this overriding interest in interdependencies, sociology typically focuses on the groups, societies and institutions of which individuals are part. With respect to education, for example, a sociological approach may examine the extent to which belonging to a particular nation-state may affect an individual's experience of schooling or higher education (HE). A sociological approach also focuses our attention on the ways in which educational experiences may be differentiated by the social groups of which we are a member – for example, a young white man may experience university very differently from an older black woman. In addition, it explores the impact of education itself on the ways in which social groups are formed. The scale of such sociological analyses can differ greatly – from the local level, exploring interactions between two individuals within a classroom, for example, through to the way in which global social processes operate, such as examining cross-national flows of students.

An important emphasis of both sociology in general and sociology of education in particular is the way in which individual experiences often reflect broader issues. C. Wright Mills (1959) expressed this in terms of connections between 'personal troubles' and 'public issues', and argued that a 'sociological imagination' was necessary to identify the interconnections between the two. Part of such a sociological imagination is also the ability to question common-sense beliefs and challenge accepted wisdom. Bauman (1990) describes this as an 'anti-fixating power':

> One could say that the main service the art of thinking sociologically may render to each and every one of us is to make us more sensitive; it may sharpen up our senses, open our eyes wider so that we can explore human conditions which thus far had remained all but invisible. Once we understand better how the apparently natural, inevitable, eternal aspects of ourselves have been brought into being through the exercise of human power and human resources, we will find it hard to accept once more that they are immune and impenetrable to human action – our own action included. (p. 16)

In relation to education, this emphasis on defamiliarising the familiar may focus on what children are taught in school, how they are assessed and the role of the teacher in the classroom. While such scrutiny can sometimes be uncomfortable for those who fall under the researcher's gaze, it nevertheless can often open up 'new and previously unsuspected possibilities of living one's life with more self-awareness, more comprehension – perhaps also with more freedom and control' (Bauman, 1990, p. 15). It is important to note, however, that sociology does not assume that humans are determined by the context in which they are located. Indeed, a focus of much sociological theorising has been the relationship between social structures and individual agency – how society shapes us, but also the capacity we have to shape ourselves.

Underpinned by these various elements of a sociological approach, *Education and Society* engages with important questions about: what 'education' actually is and the purposes it serves; who decides on what formal education includes and what is left out; who gets to participate and who does not; what impact participation has – at both the individual and the societal level; and differences in all these factors across both time and space. This chapter provides an introduction to the 12 chapters that follow. After first outlining the aims and provenance of the book, it then identifies some of the key arguments that are developed across the text as a whole. The subsequent section discusses how researchers have generated knowledge about education, paying attention to differing epistemologies (i.e. theories of knowledge), methodologies and research methods, and how these are influenced by wider intellectual currents, political imperatives and specific institutional contexts. It then explores some of the particular ethical issues raised by conducting research within educational settings before finally outlining the broad structure of *Education and Society*.

Aims and provenance

Education and Society aims to provide a wide-ranging introduction to key debates within the sociology of education that will be of interest to scholars across the globe, sensitive to the *places* in which education occurs, the *policies* that underpin recent initiatives and the social *processes* in which education is implicated. As a result of its detailed engagement with contemporary scholarship and its strong analytical focus, it will be of interest to established scholars, as well as students and researchers at the start of their careers.

Most chapters draw on a wide body of research, which has been conducted in various different national contexts. However, it is important to note that much of the discussion focuses largely on the Global North (i.e. North America, Europe, Australia, New Zealand and developed parts of East Asia that have a disproportionate control of global resources) rather than the Global South. To some extent, this is related to the availability of academic literature. Anglophone nations are also better represented in the examples that are drawn upon than non-English-speaking nations; again, this is primarily because of the availability of material in English-language journals and other texts. While the focus of *Education and Society* is largely on formal education (i.e. that which is conducted in schools, colleges and other institutions), several of the chapters also engage with learning that goes on in other spaces – for example, in the workplace and at home. Different 'stages' of education are also represented well throughout the book – from pre-school learning through to HE, adult education and 'Universities of the Third Age'. Finally, the book aims to speak to a multidisciplinary audience, drawing on relevant work within geography, social policy and youth studies, as well as education and sociology.

Key arguments of the book

While *Education and Society* seeks to evidence the wide variety of research being conducted by scholars across the globe, and the plurality of their theoretical frameworks and substantive positions, it also advances a number of key arguments across the various chapters. First, drawing on some of the themes about the purpose of education that are introduced in Chapter 2, the book suggests that there is compelling evidence that the socially reproductive nature of education remains strong (i.e. that education often helps to perpetuate, rather than lessen, social divisions). This is discussed in relation to social class, for example – by pointing to the ways in which a student's socio-economic status can affect their access to education, experiences while at school and/or university and transitions from education into work (see Chapters 5 and 12). Furthermore, Chapter 5 illustrates the way in which working-class knowledge is often rendered problematic within educational institutions. Similar arguments are made in relation to gender, showing how this patterns students' subject choices and patterns of attainment (Chapter 6). We also explore how gender often impacts parental involvement in processes of learning (with pressure on mothers but rarely fathers to engage in 'intensive parenting', for example – see Chapter 6) and the different opportunities for career progression available to male and female teachers (Chapters 6 and 10). The socially reproductive nature of education is also foregrounded in Chapter 7, which examines how race and ethnicity continue to structure many interactions – both academic and social – in schools through the curriculum, specific forms of assessment, the attitudes of teachers and pupils, and institutional cultures in general (Chapters 7, 9 and 10). In addition, the book considers the impact of age on processes of learning, and how older learners, in particular, can face specific barriers in access to both HE and lifelong learning (Chapters 8 and 12).

In evidencing such processes of social reproduction, *Education and Society* maintains that these social characteristics (and others, such as disability) should not be explored as single variables on their own. Although four of the chapters (Chapters 5–8) each foreground important social characteristics and the impact they have on our experiences of education (as well as education's impact on how we experience these social markers), they also stress the value of an intersectional analysis – that is, an approach in which close attention is paid to the ways in which such social variables interact. Indeed, examples throughout the book demonstrate how exploring the multiple dimensions of an individual's experience is a more adequate means of analysing educational identities and inequalities. Moreover, *Education and Society* provides evidence of how the impact of social characteristics can change across both time and space – demonstrated, for example, by the increase in girls' attainment and participation in post-compulsory education over the past few decades (Chapter 6), the decline of heteronormativity in some particular schools and colleges (Chapter 6) and the progressive impact of some experiments with mixed-age learning (Chapter 8).

Second, the book documents the profound influence of neo-liberalism – a political and economic philosophy that seeks to promote the market and market-like forms of behaviour – across many different national contexts and areas of education. This can be seen in relation to, for example, changes in policymaking (favouring marketisation and 'steering from a distance' rather than direct forms of intervention) (Chapter 3); the increasing involvement of the private sector (Chapter 3 and 12); school choice policies and the emergence of new types of school (Chapter 11); the favouring of neo-liberal values through ostensibly neutral pupil assessments (Chapter 9); and the deprofessionalisation of teachers as a result of a pervasive focus on 'high stakes' tests and standardised curricula (Chapter 10). However, *Education and Society* also suggests that while neo-liberalism is a dominant social force that has wrought considerable change to education worldwide, its effects are often contradictory, leaving gaps and spaces for resistance and alternatives to emerge. This argument is made in a number of the chapters, drawing on literature that has outlined the possibility and power of resisting neo-liberalism – for example, in relation to the actions of teachers' unions in some countries (Chapter 10); the appropriation of school choice policies to promote alternative curricula and more emancipatory practices (Chapter 11); and the use of home-schooling as a means of rejecting the values of competition and individualism that often permeate the state system (Chapter 11). Scholars have also documented the ways in which individual educational programmes can themselves be transformative for students, inculcating, in some cases, a much more critical perspective on society (Chapter 12).

Third, *Education and Society* provides evidence of significant change to the role of the nation-state. It shows how, in some cases at least, influence has shifted away from national governments as a result of the increasing provenance of international organisations and private companies (Chapters 3 and 9); global flows of students, staff and knowledge (Chapter 4); and new forms of international and transnational educational provision (Chapter 4). Chapter 3 suggests that we have witnessed a shift from government to *governance* – in which policy is increasingly formulated and delivered by networks that include a variety of non-state actors including the private sector, civil society, philanthropists and international organisations. Nevertheless, it does not automatically follow that analyses at the level of the nation-state are redundant. Indeed, *Education and Society* documents a wide range of enduring national differences. For example, Chapter 10 discusses in some detail the various ways in which national culture and norms can affect teachers' motivations for joining the profession, while Chapter 6 outlines how such differences can also have a significant impact on what is perceived as an educational 'problem' (and what is not). In addition, neo-liberal models of education are much more firmly established in some countries than others – evident, for example, in the differential attention paid to aspects of the 'global market' such as rankings of HE institutions (Chapter 12). The book also argues that while educational policies may travel around the globe at increasing speed, 'policy borrowing' is multidirectional, and complex processes of local and national policy recontextualisation, enactment and mediation are common (Chapter 3).

Finally, and perhaps most significantly, the following chapters suggest that education remains an important area of policy and social interaction more generally – despite the contention of some scholars that post-modernism has raised fundamental questions about its emancipatory function (Ball, 2004) (see discussion in the section below). This is discussed explicitly in Chapter 12, in relation to the increasing significance of *higher* education in contemporary society, but is implicit in many of the other chapters with respect to other phases of education as well – for example, in relation to the salience of policies of 'school choice' as a means of effecting wider neo-liberal reform (Chapter 3), the associated rise of new school types (Chapter 11) and the close involvement of various international bodies in the way in which education is organised (Chapter 3). The vibrancy of scholarship within the sociology of education underlines the importance of the area to scholars, too. We now go on to consider how knowledge in this area has been generated, noting that there is significant diversity in how a 'sociological approach' has been deployed in practice.

Generation of knowledge

Theoretical shifts

The generation of knowledge about education has been influenced by broad theoretical shifts within the social sciences over the past 50 years or so. In this section, we discuss some of the most significant changes – as they are relevant to the material presented in later chapters. The various studies that are drawn upon in the book adopt different methodologies and do not all share the same theoretical base. Being aware of the traditions that have influenced them is thus important.

Ball (2004) identifies three particular 'turning points' which, he argues, have had a profound influence on the type of knowledge generated and the methods employed by researchers. He argues that, up until the 1970s, sociology of education was dominated by 'naturalism' – that is, the view that the social world is broadly equivalent to the natural world, and thus the same methods of enquiry can be applied to both. Scholars in this period typically used quantitative approaches (e.g. statistical analyses of large-scale datasets), and were interested primarily in the outputs of education (such as qualification level and degree of social mobility) and the structure of educational systems (Lauder et al., 2009).

A well-cited example of this kind of work is what is often called the 'political arithmetic' tradition of educational research, led in the UK by A.H. Halsey and colleagues (1980), which examined how educational expansion affected life chances and social mobility. The underpinning assumptions of this body of scholarship were, however, brought into question with the emergence of various strands of interpretivist research from the 1970s onwards (the first of Ball's turning points). These focused more specifically on social processes within classrooms and the way in which power operated in local contexts – in the belief that reality can only be accessed through shared constructions such as language and the meanings given to objective structures. Interactions between teachers and pupils, and between pupils themselves, became subject to the researcher's gaze, as did the ways in which the curriculum was put together and the particular types of knowledge it privileged. Qualitative methods were considered appropriate to explore these complex issues – with school-based ethnography, for example, becoming popular. In contrast, quantitative methods were rejected by interpretivists on the basis that they tended to reify social phenomena (i.e. treat them as more definite and distinct than they actually are) (Ball, 2004; Hartley, 2007).

The second turning point identified by Ball (2004) is that related to the emergence, in the 1980s, of feminism and other theoretical positions that adopted an anti-essentialist stance (i.e. the belief that particular social groups, such as women, do not have a 'fixed essence'). Extant research was critiqued for perpetuating a fundamentally competitive and masculinist worldview, and simple gender binaries were problematised by black and lesbian feminists (ibid.). As a result, emphasis came to be placed on diversity and the interplay between different social characteristics; qualitative methods were again favoured – seen as the most effective means of both giving voice to historically marginalised groups within education and investigating the experiences of different groups of pupils, teachers and other stakeholders.

The third turning point in Ball's analysis is that associated with the rise of post-modernism from the late 1980s onwards. As part of their critique of 'grand narratives', post-modern scholars brought into question assumptions about the essentially redemptive purpose of education, that is, the idea that, through foregrounding rationality, education could lead to the improvement of human society. Emphasis was placed, instead, on researching educational processes as systems of signs and symbols – predicated on the assumption that language brings objects into being. Consequently, discourse analysis, focusing closely on the language used by social actors, often become the preferred methodological approach (Ball, 2004).

It is important to note, however, that these theoretical shifts have been neither linear nor all-encompassing. In the second decade of the twenty-first century, a pluralist epistemological landscape exists – that is, one in which there remains considerable disagreement about both the nature of knowledge and the most appropriate methods for researching the relationship between education and society (Brooks et al., 2013). This is played out not only in discussions between individual scholars, but also through the broader research landscape – indeed, influential journals in the area exhibit quite different epistemological preferences: for example, research based on post-modern approaches is very common in the journal *Gender and Education*, but relatively rarely in *Sociology of Education* (Brooks et al., 2013). This pluralism is also evident in the later chapters of this book; the work cited draws on a wide range of both qualitative and quantitative methods.

Political and institutional influences

The generation of knowledge is also influenced by the particular political and institutional contexts within which scholars work. Dale (2001) provides a useful analysis of some key ways in which wider political currents have impacted on the sociology of education. Drawing on data from the UK, he argues that during the mid-twentieth century a close relationship was forged between politicians and researchers, which had a positive impact on the resources available to conduct educational research and the social and political impact of new knowledge. Both groups shared an interest in addressing social inequalities and a belief that education systems could bring about significant change (Lauder et al., 2009). They assumed that by implementing research-informed changes to education policy, academic attainment and social justice could both be furthered (Shain and Ozga, 2001). Moreover, in this period a considerable proportion of teacher training moved into HE. As a result, sociologists of education came to make a significant contribution to the curriculum followed by trainee teachers and thus also exerted some influence with school classrooms when their trainees gained employment (Hammersley, 1996). By the 1980s and 1990s, however – across anglophone countries of the Global North at least – such close relationships had broken down. This was largely a consequence of the rise of the 'New Right' (i.e. political parties on the right of the political spectrum, which favoured the introduction of market-based policies and a reduced role for the state). Sociology was squeezed out of teacher training programmes as greater emphasis was placed on practice within schools (Deem, 2004) and, in the UK, severing the link between teachers and the sociology of education became a specific aim of education ministers (Lauder et al., 2009). Moreover, the theoretical developments of the period (see discussion above) raised important questions about the extent to which schools were able to promote social justice, which also contributed to the distancing of researchers and politicians.

A further change in the political environment, which had a substantial impact on those conducting educational research, was the embrace by politicians of what is called 'evidence-based policy'. This had the effect of favouring particular research methods and marginalising others. Two examples of this approach can be found in the 'No Child Left Behind' programme, in place in the USA from 2001 until 2015, and the 'school effectiveness' programme that became dominant in many anglophone nations from the late 1990s. Both were predicated on the assumption that policy should respond to the findings of educational research, but that such research should adopt quantitative methods (e.g. analysing various numerical indicators of schools' success) and a positivist epistemology (i.e. a view of the world that assumes that society, like the natural world, operates according to general laws). Under the 'No Child Left Behind' programme, US politicians advocated the development of a 'scientifically proven' curriculum, while the 'school effectiveness' movement focused on the impact of schools on attainment, once social and other factors had been taken into account. As well as privileging the use of quantitative methods, both also shifted funding away from more sociological and critical approaches to classroom practice and policy formation (Shain and Ozga, 2001; Slee, 1999). This had an impact not only on what type of research was taken seriously by policymakers, but also on recruitment practices within university departments:

> 'School effectiveness' has become the issue of the day. Driven by politicians and policy-makers and their endless critiques of teacher education, faculties of education did not want to employ people who seemed only to have something critical to say, or who wanted to raise bigger questions about what schools were doing. They wanted to leave debates about what particular constructions of curriculum represented out of the discussion, and instead to see schooling and teaching as a technical activity with straightforward aims, and as an activity that could be improved if only it were studied more carefully (that is in more systematic and controlled ways). (Yates, 2009, p. 18)

Nevertheless, sociologists of education have proved relatively resilient in the face of such political imperatives. They have, for example, developed sophisticated critiques of education policy and the impact of this on social mobility (see Chapter 3), and moved into a wide range of other disciplines, including economics, management, social work and youth studies (Hammersley, 1996; Lauder et al., 2009). They have also established new areas of enquiry. There has been considerable growth, for example, in analyses of HE (see Chapter 12) and processes of globalisation as they influence, and are influenced by, education (see Chapter 4). Furthermore, some sociologists of education have been active in advocating new collaborations with researchers working in the areas of data science and computing, and neuroscience and epigenetics (both of these are discussed further in Chapter 13). Moreover, while the number of sociologists of education within education departments may have declined, they have increased their strength within the discipline of sociology, typically having a strong presence at sociological conferences, such as those run by the International Sociological Association and the European Sociological Association, as well as national groups, networks and associations (Brooks et al., 2013). Thus, while challenges still remain – not least the scepticism about the role of 'expert knowledge' expressed recently by high-profile politicians in both the USA and the UK (e.g. Nelson, 2017) – those researching the relationship between education and society have retained considerable strength within academia at least.

Ethical issues

The emergence of new methods to research education as a result of the theoretical shifts discussed in the previous section, as well as various technological developments, has contributed to an increasing emphasis on ethical issues. For example, the use of online research has raised new questions about the extent to which it is necessary, or even possible, to gain informed consent from those who post material on internet fora. However, ethics have also come under greater scrutiny as a result of the increasing regulation of research by funders and the organisations for whom researchers work, and legislative change in many countries that has required researchers to pay more attention to the way data are stored and managed (Brooks et al., 2014). In addition, international conventions have impacted on educational research. The 1989 United Nations Convention on the Rights of the Child, for example, has given more rights to children, which social researchers must respect.

There are several ethical principles that hold across many national contexts and codes of practice. These include ensuring a respect for persons, avoiding harm and promoting justice. Iphofen (2011) has gone as far as to argue that the globalisation of research practices has led to the emergence of various cross-cultural principles about appropriate ethical conduct. Nevertheless, researchers need to be sensitive to the requirements of the particular location in which they are working. There are significant variations, by nation, in the legislative frameworks that apply to research – for example, in some countries mandatory reporting requirements override any commitment made to participants about confidentiality (Brooks et al., 2014). In her account of research in Norwegian schools, Hauge (2013) describes how researchers are required by law to seek to prevent female genital mutilation if they believe a girl is at risk – and how this can sometimes be in tension with promises to research participants of confidentiality. There are also important cultural variations in how research is reported. While it is common practice within many countries of the Global North not to show the faces of participants in any dissemination activities (to ensure that their anonymity is protected), Wood and Kidman (2013) recount how this practice was of concern to the Maori community in New Zealand with whom they worked. To their participants, disguising faces, or not revealing them at all, was disrespectful. The authors thus secured approval from their institutional ethics committee to show participants' faces in outputs from the project. Researchers across all disciplines need to be sensitive to such variations – by both nation and community – and, in countries where there is little in the way of national regulation, be prepared to draw on their own morality and knowledge about local customs to inform their ethical practice (Brooks et al., 2014).

While these ethical principles and approaches to thinking ethically apply equally to all social research, there are a number of ethical issues or dilemmas that are of particular relevance to those conducting *educational* research. Here, we discuss three of these, focusing on the location of much research within educational institutions; power relationships between researcher and researched; and the role of research funders. As will be discussed in more detail later in the book (see Chapters 8 and 12 in particular), educational research does not take place only in schools, colleges and universities; important projects have been conducted in workplaces, playgrounds, homes, youth clubs and a variety of other sites where learning can occur. Nevertheless, a considerable proportion of educational research *is* conducted within institutional locations – not least because such sites can provide an effective means of recruiting a significant number of participants to a study (Denscombe and Aubrook, 1992). While the practical advantages of conducting research in schools and other educational institutions are often clear, the social context presents some potential ethical dilemmas. This is particularly the case with respect to informed consent, that is, the principle that – as part of a commitment to 'respect for persons' – potential participants must be adequately informed about the nature, purpose and methods of the research, and that their decision to take part must be voluntary. In schools, for example, it is common for researchers to approach the head teacher for permission to recruit participants from among the student body. This 'gatekeeper' may prevent his or her students becoming involved in the project by declining the researcher's request. Alternatively, if the head teacher grants permission, then the students may feel some pressure to agree to take part themselves, because they know that their school has assented. Such pressures can be particularly acute in relation to questionnaire surveys – as they may be seen by students as similar to school tests, in which participation is obligatory. Although researchers should take steps to ensure that all participation is consensual, students can sometimes find ways of articulating what Morrow (2005) has called 'informed dissent' – for example, while formally taking part in research, making a minimal contribution – by remaining silent during interviews and/or writing very little in surveys.

Implicit in the discussion above is recognition that there are often important power differentials at play within schools and other educational institutions, which can affect the capacity of children and young people to consent to take part in research. Such differentials can also affect how participants respond as part of research projects, once they have agreed to participate. Some pupils may be concerned that particular responses (e.g. if they are critical of their school or teachers) may get them into trouble or affect the marks they are given for school assignments. This can be a particular problem for 'action research' or other types of research in which teachers research their own practice. The ways in which researchers position themselves can affect such interactions. For example, they may be perceived by pupils – perhaps because of their age, but possibly also because of their social class, ethnicity and/or form of dress – as akin to teachers, which may affect pupils' responses in ways similar to those discussed above. However, researchers may instead try to emphasise their difference from those in power within the institution – through wearing less formal clothes, for example, or emphasising their student status (if they are conducting the research as part of an educational qualification). Power can, however, be exerted in the opposite direction, too; in some situations the researcher may have considerably less influence than those she or he is researching. Walford (2011) discusses some of the ethical dilemmas of researching powerful public figures such as education ministers. These include a possible 'self-censorship' on the part of researchers in reporting data, driven by the need to retain good relations for future research and concerns about possible threats of libel. Walford thus suggests that there may be a tendency for data derived from those in positions of power to be treated differently from that from other types of respondent.

Various resources are available to help think through the ethical issues associated with educational research. Educational research associations often produce their own ethical guidelines – see, for example, the American Educational Research Association's Code of Ethics

Social control

As mentioned previously, in their discussion of the purposes of education, Lauder and colleagues (2006) distinguish between 'consensus' and 'conflict' approaches. While the former (evident in the work of Durkheim and Parsons, for example, discussed above) assumes that people in society have broadly similar interests, all of which can be accommodated through education, the latter argues that social groups often have diametrically opposed interests, which cannot be readily reconciled in this way. Indeed, from this perspective, education is typically seen as advantaging particular groups and disadvantaging others. Some ideas associated with the conflict approach have already been alluded to in this chapter – for example, in relation to different views about what counts as valuable knowledge, and contrasting perspectives about national identity. Various broad theoretical perspectives can be seen to make up the 'conflict' approach – informed by the works of Marx, Weber, Bourdieu and post-modernist scholars, for example. As will be shown below, these all explore the ways in which education has been used not to promote emancipatory ends or foster a healthy democracy, but to achieve social control.

Neo-Marxist approaches are underpinned by a belief that the role of the state and the education system are determined by the nature of economic relations and, in particular, the ownership and control of the means of production. Both serve the interests of the capitalist ruling class by ensuring that its privilege is reproduced, and that the dominant ideology secures legitimacy for the inequalities that follow (Lauder et al., 2006). Thus, for neo-Marxist scholars, the failure of working-class students is seen as inevitable because of the way in which the education system (and the state more generally) is structured. Moreover, the concept of meritocracy is perceived as merely a myth, designed to encourage students to believe their success or failure is a result of their individual efforts rather than a consequence of structural inequalities. One of the clearest articulations of this position is provided by Bowles and Gintis (1976) in *Schooling in Capitalist America*. They argue that there is a close relationship between the social relations of schooling and the social relations of the capitalist economy – expressed through what they term the 'correspondence principle' – and that schools play a key role in preparing pupils for the labour market by stratifying them and inculcating appropriate skills and dispositions. Thus, working-class children are typically socialised for positions in factories, by learning how to be punctual, obedient and docile. Education for these young people generally involves memorisation and following rules. In contrast, those from more privileged backgrounds attend schools or are allocated to classes that place emphasis on autonomy, freedom and leadership, in preparation for them moving into managerial and professional employment. It is notable that, despite the contrast between the 'consensus' and 'conflict' approaches outlined above, there is considerable similarity between Bowles and Gintis' position and that of the structural functionalists discussed above – in relation to, for example, the determinism of the two approaches and their emphasis on the key role of both social structures and processes of socialisation (Gewirtz and Cribb, 2009).

A rather less deterministic neo-Marxist position is evident in the work of Willis. His seminal text, *Learning to Labour: How Working Class Kids Get Working Class Jobs* (1977), places less emphasis on the structures of capital and more on the actions of individuals and social groups. He argues that the young working-class men in his research did not passively conform to the demands of their teachers but were, instead, active in creating a counter-school culture, which rejected authority and school work and valorised both having fun in the present and taking up manual occupations in the future. Willis maintains that while this did, ultimately, lead to their 'entrapment' in manual jobs, they were not passive recipients of structural forces; indeed, it was their own cultural practices that were key to reinforcing wider structural inequalities. This emphasis on cultural practices – of teachers, parents and others involved in education, as well as pupils – is revisited in a number of the chapters that follow, and in relation to a wide range of social inequalities, not just those that pertain to social class (see, for example, Chapter 6 on Gender and Sexuality and Chapter 7 on Race and Ethnicity).

Weberian approaches, while also focusing on the divergent interests of particular social groups, differ from Marxist perspectives in that they assert that exclusionary power can be exerted by various actors – not only those who own and control the means of production (Lauder et al., 2006). The basis of social stratification is thus not seen as solely economic; groups with power can attempt to limit access to resources on the basis of, for example, ethnicity, religion or language – not just social class. In relation to entry to the labour market, for example, Collins (1979) has argued that various professional groups have used their power to limit access, by insisting on particular levels of qualification and/or credential. Similarly, Brown (1997) has shown how a further group of social actors – namely parents – can drive the process of 'credential inflation', by encouraging their children to study for higher levels of qualification as a means of securing distinction, or what he calls 'positional advantage', in an increasingly crowded graduate labour market. (Brown's work is discussed in more detail, in relation to social class and the rise of a 'parentocracy', in Chapter 5.) Thus, Weberian approaches take into account wider forms of power in society. They are also less deterministic than neo-Marxist theories, acknowledging that it is possible for less powerful groups in society to mobilise sufficient resources to enable them to break down particular exclusionary barriers

(Lauder et al., 2006). Both, however, are in agreement that, as Bernstein (1970) famously argued, education cannot 'compensate for society'.

A third and equally influential perspective that views education as a means of social control is that of Pierre Bourdieu. As will be explained in more detail in Chapter 5 on Social Class, Bourdieu argued that different class fractions in a given society possess differing amounts of cultural capital and engage in different parenting practices (Bourdieu and Passeron, 1990). While those from the middle classes are typically more highly educated, make greater use of abstract ideas, and spend more money and time on extra-curricular pursuits for their children, their working-class peers have frequently had a less positive experience of education, tend to make less use of abstract concepts and theoretical ideas in their talk, and often let their children play in autonomous ways by themselves rather than ferry them around to extra-curricular classes (Lareau, 2003; Reay, 1998). These differences, Bourdieussian scholars maintain, have significant effects within the classroom. The kind of skills and ways of thinking inculcated by middle-class families are typically 'misrecognised' by teachers as evidence of innate intelligence, while those from working-class backgrounds are less equipped to adapt to the school's pedagogy (which is based on middle-class norms) (Atkinson, 2015). This, ultimately, Bourdieu contends, has the effect of reproducing inequalities both in educational participation and attainment and, as a consequence, in society more broadly (Bourdieu and Passeron, 1990).

A rather different way of conceptualising the purpose of education is adopted by those whose work is informed by post-modernism. As part of their challenge to the 'deployment of totalising grand narratives' (Ball, 2004, p. 8), post-modern scholars argue that power is not derived simply from the state, economy or specific groups of powerful social actors. Emphasis is placed instead on analysing discourse and narratives, based on the assumption that language brings objects into being which have no prior essence, and that power and oppression are thus cultural phenomena (Brooks et al., 2013; Lauder et al., 2006). Some sociologists of education have argued that this particular theoretical shift has brought about an unhelpful relativism that further distances researchers from those for whom their work should have relevance (Shain and Ozga, 2001). By this they mean that the post-modernist emphasis on discourses and narratives and its rejection of the idea of an objective truth can make it harder for non-academics to engage with educational research, and has led to neglect of the relationship between education as a social institution, state schooling and the production of various social inequalities. Others, however, have welcomed the new possibilities it offers for both academic critique and political struggle (Griffiths, 1995; Kenway, 1997). It has informed, in particular, the work of many scholars of race and gender who have argued that the 'grand theories' of Marx and Weber, for example, tend to marginalise, or ignore completely, the experiences of women and/or people of colour, typically generalising from the experiences of white men. These critiques are discussed further in Chapters 6 and 7, which focus on gender and race and ethnicity respectively.

Conclusion

This chapter has provided an introduction to a number of key themes that will be picked up in various ways throughout the rest of the book. It considered, in some detail, what should constitute the purpose of education, drawing on a wide range of texts from the nineteenth century to the present day – from the cultural critic Matthew Arnold, to educationalists such as John Dewey and Paulo Freire, sociologists including Émile Durkheim and Talcott Parsons, and the political theorist Martha Nussbaum. The chapter interrogated the claims that education should be understood, variously, as a means of generating knowledge for its own sake; promoting solidarity and social integration; preparing workers for the labour market; enabling political participation; fostering national or regional identities; developing global citizens; and achieving social control. In doing so, it has teased out some of the assumptions that underpin these different perspectives, distinguishing, for example, between 'consensual' approaches, which assume that societies progress and develop, often on the basis of commonly held values, and 'conflictual' approaches, which assume instead that the interests of particular social groups are often fundamentally at odds with each other, and that education is frequently used to promote the objectives of more powerful groups. These debates underpin – either implicitly or explicitly – much of the discussion in subsequent chapters of this book.

3 POLICY AND POLICYMAKING

Introduction

This chapter explores what policy is and the ways in which policymaking has changed over the past half-century. In particular, it will consider changes to the role of the state and the emergence of a range of new policy actors, including private companies, philanthropic bodies and international organisations. The chapter will go on to assess whether such changes – evident across the world – mean that policy is converging. Finally, it will examine how policy is taken up by teachers and other staff 'on the ground', and whether there is any space within contemporary education for them to resist dominant (and largely neo-liberal) policy imperatives.

What are policies?

Education policies can often be thought of as rather dry documents, produced by governments and other bodies to articulate the programme of change they intend to implement. From this perspective, policymaking can be seen as a rational and linear activity; indeed, some texts talk of a 'policy cycle' in which policies are produced and implemented in a neat, logical manner, moving through discrete and easy-to-identify stages. Moreover, as Shore and Wright (2011) have argued, a considerable body of literature on policymaking 'continues to be framed within rational choice theories and positivistic models of perfect or bounded rationality in which economic actors pursue purposeful goals, decision-makers make fully informed strategic choices and analysts measure policy effects in terms of calculable costs and benefits' (p. 6). In contrast, however, *sociological* perspectives on education policymaking have tended to problematise this model. Such perspectives typically emphasise that policies rarely have unambiguous goals, and that policymakers rarely choose the most rational, effective means for achieving them. Indeed, they argue that policymaking is an inherently political and human activity, which involves both partisan interests and subjective perceptions (Shanahan et al., 2016).

Developing this more critical stance, Shore (2011) argues that it is helpful to think of policy in three ways: as 'political technology', 'statecraft' and 'method'. In relation to the first, he maintains that while policies are often presented as objective, politically neutral texts and written in fairly bland legal-rational language, they are fundamentally political documents. He goes on to suggest that this 'veiling' of the political, under a cloak of rational neutrality, is a characteristic feature of the way in which power is exerted in contemporary societies. As will be discussed in more detail later in the chapter with respect to the ways in which international organisations have become involved in policymaking, this rendering of the political as technical has profound implications for democratic political ideals. Second, 'policy as statecraft' refers to the way in which policy texts serve to provide legitimacy to particular courses of action. Education policies tend to outline specific interventions or changes, and fix these within a framework of universal principles (such as equality and efficiency). These universalising aspects, Shore argues, help to minimise disagreement – as any challenge to the specific policies can then be seen as also a challenge to the principles on which they are founded (challenges that are likely to be harder to sustain). Finally, 'policy as method' refers to the way in which researchers (and also other people interested in how power is exerted in society) can use policy texts and policy processes to analyse how governing is done. Teasing out connections and observing how policies bring together individuals, discourses and institutions into new formations can help to shed light upon new kinds of governance structures and the networks and relationships upon which they are based (Shore, 2011).

From this more sociological perspective, policies come to be seen not as logical, rational problem-solving devices but as messy and complex processes, involving continual contestation and as 'windows onto political processes in which actors, concepts and technologies interact in different sites, creating or consolidating new rationalities of governance and regimes of knowledge and power' (Shore and Wright, 2011, p. 2). They are important because they are major instruments through which governments (and also, increasingly, other groups and organisations) 'classify and regulate the spaces and subjects they seek to govern' (ibid.). This perspective also emphasises the *contested* nature of policy narratives, and the ways in which they mutate as they migrate into new contexts and settings. This is discussed further below, in relation to what has come to be known as 'policy transfer' or 'policy borrowing' (i.e. the ways in which national governments increasingly look to other nation-states for examples of policies to implement in their own local context), and the processes through which policies are 'enacted' at the local level, which can frequently differ considerably from the policy as articulated in high-level documents (Ball et al., 2011). Moreover, policies can often be

seen as having a 'runaway' effect, actively reshaping the environments in which they are introduced in ways not anticipated by policymakers and other policy actors (Krücken, 2014; Shore and Wright, 2011).

Within this broad framework, it is possible to identify considerable change to both the substantive content of education policies and the methods of policymaking over the past half-century. Indeed, scholars who have explored 'policy as method' have argued that we have witnessed change in two main areas: first, to the role of the state in developing and implementing education policy; and second, to the emergence of new policy actors (including the private sector, philanthropic organisations and, perhaps most significantly, international organisations). These are explored, in turn, in the following two sections of this chapter.

Changes to the role of the state

One of the key changes to policymaking since the 1970s has been the increasing dominance of neo-liberalism – a political and economic philosophy 'dedicated to the extension of the market and market-like forms of governance, rule and control across – tendentially at least – all spheres of social life' (Peck and Tickell, 2006, p. 28). With respect to education, this has led to an emphasis on the choices and actions of individuals (who are assumed to be rational actors); attempts to introduce markets or at least market-like mechanisms across all sectors; and the valorisation of what is known as 'new managerialism' or New Public Management (an approach in which techniques commonly used in the private sector, such as the use of explicit targets and standards of performance, hands-on management and competition for contracts, are instituted within public sector organisations) (e.g. Au and Ferrare, 2015b; Hursh, 2016; Lingard and Rawolle, 2011; Lipman, 2011). The introduction of market-based policies has had significant implications for access to and experiences of education, as will be discussed in many of the chapters that follow. It has also been associated with a substantial change to the role of the state. Indeed, one of the consequences of the shift to neo-liberalism has been the fragmentation of the state and an increasing emphasis on 'steering from a distance' – in which state intervention and prescription are replaced with target-setting, accountability and comparison (Ball, 2007). This does not mean, however, that central control has declined. Rather paradoxically, while the modern state *appears* to be shrinking, in many ways it has come to operate a stronger influence on people's lives (Shore and Wright, 2011) – intervening even in matters of everyday morality and ethics (Pathak, 2013). This is often theorised in terms of the concept of 'governmentality' (as developed by Foucault (1977)) – the idea that New Public Management and other associated reforms tend to deflect attention away from the state itself and onto the

individual through policies that promote individual agency and personal responsibility – for example, the notion of the self-managed worker, who takes responsibility for her own learning throughout her life, to ensure that she remains employable.

The shift to neo-liberalism has also been associated with a change in the temporal patterns of policymaking. The demand for transparency and accountability alongside a 24-hour news cycle and technologically mediated compression of time and space have, Lewis and Hogan (2016) argue, given rise to a highly visible and *fast* form of policy development, supplanting more nuanced, comprehensive and slower approaches. Drawing on Peck and Theodore's (2015) concept of 'fast policy', they contend that new markets for educational research have been opened up (no longer primarily the domain of academics), to inform this new, quicker, 'evidence-based' policymaking. New actors, such as think tanks, corporations, international organisations and voluntary organisations, are now all closely involved in the generation of research for policy purposes. However, such actors typically 'orchestrate' research rather than produce it themselves, publishing simplified and definitive accounts of 'best practice' in short, easy-to-read, glossy publications (Lewis and Hogan, 2016). Emphasis on contextual specificity is abandoned in favour of ready-made examples (often taken from abroad) of 'what works'. In this way, what counts as 'evidence' comes to be refined, and policy processes become faster. One of the examples discussed by Lewis and Hogan (2016) is 'The Learning Curve' (TLC) database developed by Pearson plc (a British multinational publishing and education business). It is populated by data produced by organisations such as the Organisation for Economic Co-operation and Development (OECD), the United Nations, the World Bank and the International Association for the Evaluation of Educational Achievement (IEA), with the espoused aim of helping governments, teachers and individual learners identify the common elements of an 'effective education'. Reflecting on the implications of this, Lewis and Hogan maintain that 'By folding complex policy lessons derived from multiple data sources into one "all knowing" database, Pearson has created an infrastructure that allows unprecedented policy mobility, joining up and condensing data into one easy-to-read format' (p. 10). While the way in which these data are used is likely to differ considerably from place to place, it nevertheless promotes – across all spaces – the idea that 'quick-fix' solutions are readily available and that local, contextual factors (e.g. students' socio-economic characteristics) matter little.

Despite the dominance of neo-liberalism across much of the world for the best part of the last half-century, contemporary scholarship has demonstrated the new forms this can take, and the increasingly complex character of governance, with implications for the role of the state.

One example of this is the increasing importance of policy *networks* involving a range of new policy actors, particularly from business and philanthropy (these are discussed in more detail later in the chapter). Ball (2016) argues that the shift to governing through networks is bringing about a new form of political organisation in which states no longer exert monopolistic control over statework, and polycentric governance has become more common (Ball and Exley, 2010). By this, he means that policy is now increasingly produced through multiple agencies and actors, rather than just the state. Indeed, he contends that this shift is 'a move beyond both bureaucratic and market forms of co-ordination towards more flexible heterarchical relationships, within which responsibility and processes of decision-making are shared by a heterogeneous mix of old and new policy actors, with the effect of re-balancing the governance mix' (Ball, 2016, p. 12). The shift here from *government* to *governance* is significant as the two entail different forms of accountability. *Government* is typically understood as public and structurally connected to democratic forms of accountability (i.e. there is a formal mechanism – through elections – for removing representatives from office). Thus, government bodies that make education policy have some form of public accountability and are required to have some level of public transparency (Au and Ferrare, 2015a). In contrast, *governance*, such as through networks containing non-elected policy actors, has no mechanism for ensuring transparency and holding key actors to account. In network governance, in particular, power is often spread across many different organisations and individuals; it is thus difficult to determine where responsibility lies (ibid.). While such networks can often include powerful private sector players, their complexity is significant. Indeed, some scholars have argued that network governance can be seen as a response to the failures of neo-liberalism and market-based forms of governance, rather than part of the same process (Bevir, 2011). Network governance is discussed further in the subsequent section, in relation to the emergence of a range of new policy actors.

A second example focuses more on the content of education policies (rather than the methods of policymaking), and the way in which some of the key tenets of neo-liberalism are being rethought. Bradbury and colleagues (2013) argue that within UK policy there has been a significant revision to the concept of the rational economic subject – which, as noted above, underpins much neo-liberal thinking. This is evidenced, they contend, through the establishment of a 'Behavioural Insights Team' in the Cabinet Office (a UK government department that supports the prime minister, and acts as a lead in some areas of policy deemed to be high priority) and the adoption of what are commonly referred to as 'nudge' policies. Such policies assume that: (1) individuals do not always make the choices that would benefit them most; (2)

failures to choose well are the result of common cognitive limitations and are thus predictable; and (3) therefore everyday decision-making should be framed in particular ways to encourage ('nudge') people to choose in 'advantageous' ways (ibid.). From this perspective, individuals are understood to be not as rational as had previously been assumed within much neo-liberal education policy (e.g. those that have promoted 'school choice'). The role of policy therefore becomes to model the 'essential irrationality of choosers, to make flaws in their choosing predictable' (p. 250) and to put 'nudges' in place to achieve the outcomes desired by policymakers, knowing the likely patterns of irrationality. This fundamental change in how the individual is understood should not, Bradbury and colleagues (2013) maintain, be viewed as the end of neo-liberalism. On the contrary, they claim that it is necessary to ensure its continuity, citing the example of revisions to school choice policy. By introducing a network of Choice Advisers (from 2006 onwards) to 'nudge' recalcitrant parents into becoming active choosers (i.e. to help to engage parents – who might otherwise just opt for their local school – in the process of school choice), policymakers ensure that the failure of the policy to produce rational subjects is obscured, and opposition to school choice policy in general is more likely to be avoided (because all parents will be helped to become active choosers). Thus, neo-liberalism is reconfigured rather than challenged.

Emergence of new policy actors

As noted above, in many parts of the world policymaking is now typically conducted through network governance. Networks are rarely solely state-based; instead, they commonly involve a wide range of new policy actors across various nation-states. This section of the chapter explores two broad groups of new actors: first, those associated with the private sector and philanthropic and civil society groups; and second, international organisations.

Private sector, philanthropy and civil society

The involvement of the private sector in education policymaking has been usefully delineated by Ball (2009). He identifies three main mechanisms through which private interests exert influence on policymaking across the world. He terms the first 'organisational recalibration'. This refers to the ways in which policy solutions are now 'sold' to schools by a range of private sector companies. Such solutions include professional development programmes, training and support in relation to specific government initiatives. Within the UK context, for example, they offer 'turnaround services' to schools struggling to meet national benchmarks and targets, and often take up positions previously occupied by local education authorities and other public sector bodies. In the UK, and also a range of other counties including the USA, state policies often incentivise schools to purchase such services. (The prevalence of league tables and other means of making relative performance highly public has had a similar effect.) Ball argues that these services – by introducing generic management concepts into schools – have the effect of changing relationships and working practices in education (valorising flexibility and adaptability, for example), making them much more like those that characterise the private sector. The second mechanism identified by Ball (2009) is what he calls 'the colonisation of the infrastructures of policy'. By this, he means the production of policy ideas and texts for and within the state, through the inclusion of consultancies and other education businesses within the networks of policymaking. To take just one case, the firm PriceWaterhouseCoopers has been closely embedded in such policymaking networks at all levels from the international to the local through, for example, conducting research and evaluation projects for governments, writing key government policy documents, drafting outsourcing contracts and acting as auditors for government agencies (ibid.). This has had the effect of normalising business discourse among policymakers and 'inserting into public sector organisations generic organisational relations based on contracts, best value, partnerships, performance monitoring, management, brokering etc.' (Ball, 2009, p. 92). The final mechanism outlined by Ball is 'the global reach of education business'. He describes how educational businesses that typically originated in the Global North have actively pursued new markets abroad – working with international organisations such as the World Bank, and also selling their products directly to national and local education ministries. The work of Pearson plc (discussed above in relation to 'fast policy') is a good example of a private sector company that has become an extremely powerful global policy actor, and which is now involved in all aspects of education policy – from agenda setting to policy production to implementation to evaluation – in diverse countries across the world (Hogan et al., 2015). Such actions help to naturalise Western models of educational management and leadership and thus, Ball (2009) suggests, should be seen as instruments of recolonisation. (Here, there are important links to the 'global flows of knowledge' discussed in Chapter 4.)

The policy networks in which private companies are increasingly located also contain other new actors – such as civil society groups and philanthropists. In the UK context, religious organisations have come to exert considerable power through, for example, the sponsorship of both individual schools and chains of schools; Courtney (2015) contends that this is an example of an 'old' policy actor having successfully reinvented itself through its adoption of market requirements (this is discussed further in relation to faith schools in Chapter 11). Philanthropic influence is illustrated well by the example of the Bill and Melinda Gates Foundation. As Au and Ferrare (2015a) outline in some detail, the Gates Foundation has become a significant policy actor in the USA through the very large sums of money it has invested in specific educational reforms – promoting the 'school choice' agenda (through investment in charter schools), the use of high-stakes standardised tests to evaluate teacher performance and the rolling out of Common Core State Standards (an initiative that seeks to establish consistent standards of educational performance across all US states) (see Chapter 9 for a more detailed discussion of standardised testing). Clearly Bill Gates has strong links to the private sector discussed above and, through the significant influence of the Gates Foundation, has contributed to further engraining neo-liberal norms in the US education system – by prioritising the funding of organisations and projects that align most closely with a neo-liberal agenda (ibid.).

Examples of networks containing a similar range of policy actors can be seen in numerous different parts of the world. Network governance is now common within the EU, for example. Indeed, EU education policy networks typically involve not just policymakers from the member states, but EU officials, experts, representatives of civil society, private sector actors and academics. Souto-Otero (2015) notes that the European Commission 'has succumbed to pressures for greater privatisation of statework' (p. 166) but argues that the involvement of a wider group of actors could be viewed as a means of increasing external legitimacy (i.e. that policy is not now seen as being made by only a small group of EU officials, but the views of a wide range of stakeholders are being sought) and capacity (in a context in which the amount of policy work has increased considerably). However, other scholars have interpreted these changes in a less positive manner, arguing that increasing reliance on non-elected policy actors (whether they are from the private sector, philanthropic groups or academia) should not be seen as a welcome shift towards a more pluralist dialogue but a depoliticisation of the policy process, in which it is increasingly difficult to hold policymakers to account (Lawn and Grek, 2012).

A network that comprises a similarly diverse range of policy actors is identified by Ball (2016) in relation to the Indian Education Reform Movement. This movement focuses on the use of business methods to bring about educational innovation and change in India. Venture philanthropy plays a critical role in the network by, first, funding what are seen as new 'policy solutions' and, second, mobilising policy actors within India and abroad to ensure, through lobbying and persuasion, that 'problems' are recognised and appropriate 'solutions' are validated. Ball argues that bringing coherence to this group of relatively disparate policy actors is a significant challenge but that forging close social relationships often helps. Various face-to-face encounters between network members (such as conferences, workshops and discussion groups) are important occasions for reiterating, reinvigorating and reaffirming discourses and allegiances and developing a shared language (ibid.). In addition, key individuals play a significant role as what Ball calls 'boundary spanners', joining up different sectors and facilitating the mobility of ideas. In the Indian context, he identifies Ashish Dhawan, a venture capitalist who has become a philanthropist and key 'mover and shaker' within the network. The organisation he founded, the Central Square Foundation, funds various high-profile initiatives, such as Teach for India and the India Institute of School Leadership, and also publishes reports on, for example, the advantages of private–public partnerships. (A similar argument is made about the significance of Michael Barber within Pearson plc – an individual with high-level experience in both the state and the private sectors, who is able to initiate policy conversations across different contexts (Hogan et al., 2015).) As with the case of the EU, this policy network can be seen as a means by which more diverse perspectives have been brought into the policymaking process. However, to argue that this has democratised the policymaking process appears unjustified. The difficulty of identifying the various network members (not least because many work internationally, across different national jurisdictions), the informal nature of much of their contact and their reliance on the profits generated by venture capitalism raise serious questions about both transparency and democratic accountability.

International organisations

Another key group of policy actors, who have exerted an increasing influence on education policy from the 1990s onwards, are international organisations such as the OECD, the International Monetary Fund, the World Bank and the World Trade Organization. The World Bank, for example, has been the biggest loan provider for education programmes worldwide and, by attaching specific terms and conditions to these loans, has helped to define the way in which education is developed in recipient nations. Such organisations are clearly not subject to democratic accountability, and are thus another good illustration of the shift from government to governance, as discussed above. Furthermore, the policies they promote typically advance a strong neo-liberal logic, favouring market reforms, privatisation of public bodies, liberalisation of trade and deregulation of national economic activity (Moutsios, 2009). They also tend to engrain power differentials between countries, as decisions within these international organisations are often made by delegates from powerful economies – who commonly promote their own national interests and, sometimes, the interests of large corporations (ibid.). Some scholars have argued that, as a result of such interventions, policymaking should now be considered *transnational*, in the sense that 'national borders are eliminated and mixed up and power flows from the global sphere into nation-states' arenas of power' (Moutsios, 2009, p. 471). This position is, however, contentious. Indeed, this chapter provides various examples of how policy is often enacted differently from place to place, and recontextualised locally. Nevertheless, the influence of international organisations is certainly far-reaching. This section focuses on two specific examples: the EU and the OECD.

The EU can perhaps be viewed more accurately as a regional body rather than an international one. Nevertheless, like the organisations mentioned above, it operates above the level of the nation-state and has become an increasingly important actor with respect to education policy. When the European Community was founded (in the 1950s), little attention was paid to education as it was considered to be a matter for nation-states alone; as Keeling (2006) argues, the field of education is notable by its absence in the EU's founding treaties. This changed in the 1970s, however, with the launch of 'action programmes' in the field of education, followed by the Erasmus programme (to promote student mobility) in the 1980s (Huisman, 2015). By the time the Maastricht Treaty was signed, in 1992, education had assumed an even more prominent role. Article 126 of the treaty stated: 'The Community shall contribute to the development of quality education by encouraging co-operation between Member States and, if necessary, by supporting and supplementing their action' (quoted in Huisman, 2015, p. 147). More recently, the EU's remit has been extended further through its close involvement in the Bologna Process, which seeks to establish a common European Higher Education Area, and its research policy, which has sought to bring about substantial reform of institutional and research management in Europe's universities in order to strengthen the region's 'knowledge economy' (Keeling, 2006) (see also Chapters 8 and 12). This extension of influence has been underpinned by a change in policy aims – moving away from conceptualising education as primarily a means of achieving further European integration and seeing it instead as an important economic driver (Walkenhorst, 2008). As part of this, the EU's focus has shifted from internal matters (such as integration) to external concerns – and, particularly, competition with other regions of the world (ibid.).

Some scholars have argued that this change in focus is closely aligned with the increasing hegemony of neo-liberalism. While the Bologna Process, for example, did originally include a social dimension, Holford (2014) contends that this was not prosecuted with the same intent as other aspects of the reform that were more closely linked to an economic agenda (such as encouraging mobility to Europe). Mitchell (2006) develops a similar argument, maintaining that some of the EU's earlier concerns, that prioritised social liberalism, such as an emphasis on promoting and valuing diversity through education, have been replaced with a market logic that seeks to shape individual behaviours to fit better a competitive knowledge economy. She argues that policies that focus on mobility, lifelong learning and adaptability aim to produce 'a fast-paced, mobile and interchangeable labourer' while simultaneously excluding 'those considered slow, particularist, and/or otherwise "different", who cannot or will not keep up with recent changes' (p. 403). She illustrates this argument by drawing on her research in Marseille in France. She found that very little information about the EU's school exchange programmes had been disseminated to pupils in inner-city schools or their teachers, and none of the school principals she interviewed had heard of the Erasmus programme. Moreover, when she asked staff about the lack of participation in such mobility schemes, they emphasised the difficulties poor pupils had in finding the matched funding required, and also the difficulty of reciprocity – of providing food and accommodation for their exchange counterparts in families where both money and space were severely limited.

The OECD is another international organisation whose influence on education has changed markedly over recent decades. It was founded in 1961 as an intergovernmental organisation of 30 of the world's most developed economies committed to both a market economy and a pluralist democracy. While education has been important to the OECD since its inception, understandings have been contested and have changed over time (Rizvi and Lingard, 2010). In the 1970s and 1980s, for example, European countries within the OECD refused to accept the US view that education should be seen primarily as a tool of economic policy and, instead, sought to promote a social democratic agenda (ibid.). By the mid-1990s, however, the US view came to prevail within the organisation, and a consensual view developed in which education was conceptualised in largely instrumental terms. Moreover, education assumed a more prominent role in the organisation as a whole, evidenced by the establishment of a Directorate of Education in 2002 and the new ways of working that evolved. The OECD's traditional methods of engaging with constituent countries – conducting voluntary reviews of national education systems and encouraging international co-operation – were replaced by the collection and dissemination of comparative performance data (and also the inclusion of non-member economies). Summarising such changes, Rizvi and Lingard (2010) note: 'In the past, the OECD viewed itself as a forum for open dialogue with its members, but it is now clear that it has increasingly become a policy actor in its own right' (p. 133).

The OECD's influence has been perhaps most marked through its Programme for International Student Assessment (PISA), which began in 2000. Under this programme, students in participating countries sit tests at the end of their compulsory schooling (when they are 15 years of age), which assess their ability to apply their knowledge of literacy, maths and science to real-life challenges. They also complete a questionnaire about their own background and schooling. Tests are administered every three years, and the relative performance of countries is disseminated through comparative data, which are quickly converted into international 'league tables' and devoured by politicians, the media and, increasingly, the public at large in participating countries. The impact of PISA has been significant. First, it has helped to develop a 'global education policy space' through establishing common measurements, categories and encoding procedures across diverse nation-states (Desrosieres, 1998; Grek, 2009). This global space has framed education in largely economist terms – as the international comparative measures of student performance are often presented as surrogate indicators of relative economic competitiveness (Lingard and Rawolle, 2011). Second, it has influenced the priorities of policymakers at the national level – not through imposing particular policies, but through countries' desires to be included and perform well in international assessments (Rizvi and Lingard, 2010). It is notable that 43 countries participated in the first PISA tests in 2000; by 2012, the number had grown to 65. In Spain, for example, concern about PISA performance in specific areas – and the policy advice given by the OECD – led to several new initiatives including a national programme to promote reading, measures to promote school autonomy, and the increasing use of ICT in schools (Bonal and Tarabini, 2013). Indirectly, PISA has also been used by the national government in Spain to justify a set of policies that do not seem to be directly related to either the country's performance or OECD advice, for example, the introduction of academic selection early in the education system (arguing that the best PISA performers had such systems in place – despite the lack of a clear pattern in the data) and cuts in the education budget (by arguing that there is no consistent relationship in the PISA data between public expenditure and performance level) (ibid). Third, PISA has influenced various political relationships between and within nation-states, and helped to instantiate 'new spatialities of educational governance' (Lingard and Sellar, 2014). Drawing on the example of Scotland, Lingard and Sellar (2014) argue that the relationship it has forged with the OECD (participating in PISA as a subnational system, separate from the UK, and sending its own observer to meetings of the PISA Governing Board) has helped it to position itself as an independent economy, and thus feed into wider political priorities with respect to independence from the UK. They also cite the example of the short video prepared by the Scottish Department for Education and sent to all schools that were to participate in the 2012 PISA tests. The video, they argue, presents Scotland as a separate nation and assumes that representing Scotland in the PISA sample is equivalent to representing Scotland in sport. Moreover, in the video:

> performance in PISA is taken as a surrogate signifier of future economic prosperity and the attractiveness of a nation/economy to global capital. Here we see a running together of the economic purposes for participating and being seen to perform well in the PISA test and the nationalistic motivations to do one's best for oneself and one's country. (Lingard and Sellar, 2014, p. 16)

Here, PISA is effectively being 'used' by the Scottish government for its own purposes. Nevertheless, it also articulates well with the OECD's desire to work more closely with subnational actors as a means of pursuing new markets, deriving new revenue and extending its influence (ibid.). We return to some of these themes, including the impact of standardised tests, in Chapter 11.

Is policy now the same everywhere?

Much of the preceding discussion may have given the impression that education policy is now the same everywhere as a result of the growing influence of neo-liberalism and the shift from government to governance. There is certainly some evidence of increasing homogeneity in education policy as schools, colleges, HE institutions and providers of lifelong learning all move towards more market-based models of provision (e.g. Musselin, 2014; Teixeira, 2013), the size and significance of the 'global policy field' increases (Moutsios, 2009), and national actors are increasingly willing to draw on the discourses of international organisations to achieve domestic political objectives (Lingard and Rawolle, 2011). Nevertheless, it is important to return to some of the points made at the start of the chapter, and recognise that policy changes as it travels; it is 'recontextualised' as it moves into different national and local contexts. Moreover, while 'policy transfer' or 'policy borrowing' may imply that education policy is being standardised across the world, empirical research has demonstrated that such processes are rarely one-way. Indeed, Forestier and Crossley's (2015) analysis of policy borrowing in England and Hong Kong illustrates this well. They show how, in 2010, England's government gave high priority to learning from Hong Kong and other countries that emphasised didactic approaches to teaching and learning.

High-profile politicians visited Hong Kong, and a new curriculum was introduced in England that foregrounded academic subjects and rote learning in some areas (e.g. guidelines that multiplication tables should be memorised by the age of nine) (ibid.). At the same time, however, Hong Kong was instigating a set of reforms intended to move towards a less pressured and more student-centred approach to learning (that historically had characterised much teaching in England). Here, although policy transfer is much in evidence, very different policies were being borrowed and instantiated; 'desirable' education systems were conceived in very different ways.

It is also the case that various local structures and cultures can have a profound effect on the way in which policy is implemented (and, indeed, the extent to which particular reforms are deemed even possible) (Brooks, 2012). Savage and O'Connor (2015) provide a good example of this in their comparative study of the USA and Australia. Focusing specifically on reforms since the 1980s, they argue that the drivers in both countries were very similar, namely global panics about globalisation, equity and market competitiveness. These underpinned a series of parallel reforms to extend greater central control over the curriculum, which they categorise as: (1) the development of a set of national goals in the late 1980s; (2) failed attempts to impose national standards in the early 1990s; and (3) rejuvenated attempts to instigate national standards (through initiatives such as 'No Child Left Behind' in the USA and the 'Education Revolution' promised by the Australian Labor Party) in the 2000s (see Chapter 11). Nevertheless, despite these apparent similarities, Savage and O'Connor contend that the reforms in each country remained distinct in both scope and form. While the USA ultimately adopted voluntary national standards in a limited range of subjects, in Australia a wide-ranging, national, discipline-based curriculum was successfully implemented. This difference, they suggest, was due to various unique features that informed the national policy space in the two countries. It was harder to introduce a centralised curriculum for the US federal government than its Australian counterpart because it experienced less close relationships with state education ministries; greater public scepticism about the role of central government in formulating schools policy; and more interference/influence from non-governmental organisations, with their own policy priorities. Reflecting on this particular case, Savage and O'Connor conclude that, even when national governments set out to 'borrow' and implement the same policy, reforms do not emerge in a uniform fashion across nation-states. As Peck and Theodore (2015) have argued, policies do not move around the globe in neat bundles but in a much more haphazard and piecemeal fashion. They are recontextualised in particular ways, in particular places, for particular purposes (see also Ball, 2016; Lewis and Hogan, 2016).

Mediation and enactment of policy

As was noted at the start of this chapter, policy and policymaking are not just about the actions of politicians, officials and the range of new policy actors discussed above. They are also about how ideas are taken on – or indeed rejected or modified – by the intended recipients. This section builds on the concept of 'recontextualisation', as discussed above, to show how policies are mediated or 'enacted' through different means in different contexts. It thus suggests that schools, staff, students, parents and others connected to education in a variety of ways can all be considered active agents in the making of policy. Fairclough (1989) has discussed these mediations in terms of what he calls policy 'moves'. He argues that as policy narratives move into new political and social spaces they are translated into new genres at each move. Sometimes, he notes, this movement is initiated from the top (e.g. when a political speech is translated into newspaper articles), but at other times it can be instigated by the intended recipients of policy (e.g. by educational professionals). As each such move entails a 're-translation' from one genre to another, space is opened up for contestation and new voices enter, bringing with them new perspectives and ways of seeing the problem (Shore and Wright, 2011). This conceptualisation of policy has had implications for the way in which it is studied and researched. Wright and Reinhold (2011) advocate 'studying through'. They contrast this with 'studying up' (i.e. researching those with power, perceived to be at the top of the political hierarchy) and 'studying down' (i.e. collecting data from those 'on-the-ground' who are affected by the particular policy) – in that it does not assume a hierarchical relationship between policymakers and those who are governed. It also does not assume that policymaking is a linear process that proceeds neatly from policy definition to policy formulation to implementation (ibid.). Indeed, policymaking is often a ramshackle affair, and policies are often compromises that are 'reworked, tinkered with, nuanced and inflected through complex processes of influence, text production, dissemination and, ultimately, re-creation in contexts of practice' (Ball, 2007, p. 44). Particularly important to this kind of analysis is the way in which language can change (often in quite subtle ways) and how new discourses emerge:

> The aim is to follow a flow of events and their contingent effects, and especially to notice struggles over language, in order to analyse how the meaning[s] of keywords are contested and change, how new semantic clusters form and how a new governing discourse emerges, is made authoritative and becomes institutionalised. What is studied is a process of political transformation through space and time. (Wright and Reinhold, 2011, p. 101)

This approach has much in common with what Ball (2016) has called 'network ethnography', in which policy is 'followed' through processes of mapping, visiting and questioning, in an attempt to identify the paths, pipelines, nodes and activities that guide and shape it.

This view of policy also tends to critique perspectives that argue that individuals' subjectivities (i.e. their sense of self) are determined by policy. Much of the literature on governmentality, for example, assumes that policy conveys a particular rationality which is then converted into technologies of government which, in turn, reframe the subjectivities of the target population (Nielsen, 2011). Similar arguments have been made with respect to neo-liberalism. For example, some scholars who have explored the impact of the introduction of strongly market-orientated HE policies in England and Wales have argued that they have brought about significant change in student identities – with students seeing themselves as consumers and, as a result, adopting a much more passive approach to learning (e.g. Molesworth et al., 2009) and becoming more self-interested in their dealings with other students (Phipps and Young, 2015). Others have argued, however, that this is an overly deterministic stance and that, in practice, political subjects can sometimes resist or at least modify dominant policy prescriptions. For example, the respondents in Brooks and colleagues' (2015) research on student union leadership in the UK accepted market mechanisms if they helped to promote the role of their union but, alongside this activity, they had a desire to pursue partnership working as an alternative to consumerism, and were often critical of their university's focus on profit-generating pursuits. Thus, while students' unions appeared relatively powerless to change the wider political and economic structures around them, they were apparently able to resist the extent to which neo-liberalism 'gets into our minds and our souls, into the ways in which we think about what we do, and into our social relations with others' (Ball, 2012, p. 18). Similarly, Nielsen's (2011) research among international students in Denmark provides evidence that – contrary to the claims made by some policy actors – the introduction of fees for international students did not turn such students into passive consumers. Reflecting on social policy more generally, Clarke (2005) has contended that political subjects are not docile bodies but, instead, reflexive subjects, who can sometimes 'answer back'. These 'sceptical subjects' tend to question how they are constructed within policy, and assumptions made in policy about their relationship to particular institutions (Clarke et al., 2007).

A detailed example of how policy is enacted is provided by Braun and colleagues (2011) in their analysis of four schools in the south-east of England. They show how various school-specific factors (such as intake characteristics, history, staffing, ethos, buildings and budgets) can have a profound effect on the ways in which policy on the ground is shaped and implemented. Furthermore, they contend that individual actors in schools (teachers, teaching assistants, managers, etc.) play an important role in influencing how policy is played out in their particular institutions. In developing this analysis, they offer a typology to differentiate between the different policy positions teachers may occupy. (It is important to note, however, that these positions are not fixed or indeed mutually exclusive, and that one individual may move between two or more positions.) The various types they identify include the following: 'narrators' (typically senior managers) who interpret the policy they receive, and decide and then announce what can be done and what cannot; 'entrepreneurs' who are keen to champion particular policies, and often do so with considerable energy and creativity; 'critics' such as union activists who can monitor policy translations and maintain counter-discourses; and 'receivers', such as newly qualified teachers and teaching assistants, who typically comply with most policy and feel they have little opportunity to interpret it for themselves. An overarching theme of the analysis pursued by Braun and colleagues is that, while teachers can take up a variety of different positions in relation to policy, as outlined above, much of the policy work done in schools can be thought of as 'reconfiguration' – that is, seeking to 'extend the durability of the institution in the face of the de-stabilising effects of … change and of policy' (Braun et al., 2011, p. 637). Thus, their capacity to be creative, introduce new ideas and question current practices is limited. Moreover, they are also constrained by the wider discursive context. Indeed, in the schools that participated in this piece of research, 'other' discourses of education, such as those that foreground democratic or inclusive teaching, were typically marginalised. Thus, while studies such as this provide convincing evidence that policy is not implemented in a simple, top-down fashion, this is not the same as arguing that teachers conceptualised as policy actors and/or 'sceptical subjects' are able to resist policy initiatives in their entirety. We explore this theme further when we consider the changing role of teachers in Chapter 10.

Conclusion

Developing the theme of power, introduced in Chapter 2, this chapter has focused explicitly on the way in which education policies are made. It has suggested that recent years have witnessed considerable changes to processes of policymaking – as the influence of the state has, in many parts of the world, declined quite significantly. Alongside this, new 'policy actors' have come to assume substantial influence. These include private sector companies, philanthropists and international organisations (such as the OECD and the EU) which have become embedded in various policymaking networks. The chapter considered whether, as a result of these changes, education policy has become homogenised. It drew on empirical evidence to suggest that, although education policies now move around the world at great speed, they are 'recontextualised' in different ways in different local contexts. This was illustrated in the final part of the chapter by showing how, at the school level, the stance taken by individual teachers can affect the ways in which national and local policies are enacted.

4 GLOBALISATION AND EDUCATION

Introduction

This chapter builds on some of the themes introduced in Chapter 3 to consider in more detail the extent to which education has changed as a result of globalisation. In many ways education (particularly HE) has been 'global' in its outlook for a long period of time: the student body in medieval universities was typically cosmopolitan in composition; the 'Junior Year Abroad' has been an important element of American HE since the early twentieth century; and colonial relationships, from the late nineteenth century onwards, often facilitated the international mobility of both students and staff. However, the impact of neo-liberal globalisation has wrought more profound change on education – not only in relation to how policy is developed (the focus of the previous chapter), but also with respect to the unprecedented scale of cross-border movement and the development of new forms of educational provision (such as offshore campuses of schools and universities). These latter two developments are the focus of this chapter. Specifically, we consider the 'global flows' of both students and staff – for compulsory schooling as well as HE; the emergence of various forms of international and transnational education; and the implications of both for the ways in which knowledge flows around the world. First, however, we begin by defining what we mean by globalisation, and its relationship with the concept of neo-liberalism, which was discussed in the previous chapter.

What is globalisation?

Globalisation refers, at a fundamental level, to the lateral extension of social relations across time and space. National and regional economies have become more integrated, and political and cultural life has been transformed, as a result of the emergence of global networks of transportation, trade, communication and migration. This has influenced how we conceptualise both space and the boundaries between places:

> Globalisation is understood as blurring distinctions between the international and the domestic, the global and the local and in doing so affects a new spatiality to politics. Its effects are evidenced in core economic activities (where multinationals operate across continents and capital flows across nation states) and in media and electronic communication (which makes the flows of capital possible), in financial markets, the internationalisation of corporate strategies/management, the ecumenical spread of management structures and modes of policy steering across private and public sectors, the spread of worldwide patterns of consumption, the internationalisation of nation states and the diminished capacity of national governments. (Ozga and Lingard, 2007, p. 65)

As the quotation above suggests, it also has political ramifications, by disrupting the sense that the nation-state is the 'natural scale' of politics (ibid.). Indeed, some theorists of globalisation have predicted the end of both national economies and the nation-state as the primary unit of political organisation (A. Green, 2006). This analysis is not, however, shared by all. Other scholars have argued that nation-states remain central – as global capitalism requires strong, reliable nations, which can influence and co-ordinate the actions of their citizens (Rizvi and Lingard, 2010), and state power to create and drive markets (Olssen, 2006).

In much of the academic literature, globalisation is often treated as synonymous with neo-liberalisation – that is, the spread of market mechanisms and principles across all aspects of social life. However, it is important to keep the two analytically distinct (Brooks and Waters, 2013). The emergence of a neo-liberal hegemony is only one possible manifestation of globalisation. As Sklair (2010) contends, the various changes that are commonly associated with globalisation – such as advances in information and communications technology – could have led to radically different forms of political organisation, with significantly greater emancipatory potential. Rizvi and Lingard (2010) develop a similar argument, emphasising that neo-liberalism is only one way of interpreting globalisation, albeit one which 'is designed to steer a particular formation of the subjective or phenomenological awareness of people' (p. 32). They also offer a particularly useful means of theorising globalisation, distinguishing between three ways in which it can be understood: as an *empirical fact*, which describes profound shifts taking place around the world; as an *ideology* that marks various expressions of power and a range of political interests; and as a *social imaginary*, which expresses the sense people have of their own identity, how it relates to the rest of the world, and how it implicitly shapes their aspirations and expectations. This threefold typology captures well both the descriptive and normative aspects to globalisation – that is, that as well as describing the high level of global connectedness that characterises contemporary society, it helps to *prescribe* particular economic formations and ways of being – through its ideological alignment with neo-liberalism.

Global flows of students and staff

Although it was noted previously that the mobility of students across national borders should not be considered a new phenomenon, it is certainly the case that the number of students moving in pursuit of an education has increased very significantly over recent decades, and can be seen as closely bound up with some of the globalising processes discussed above. Indeed, statistics from the OECD (2017) indicate that over 4.6 million students are now enrolled in tertiary education outside their country of citizenship – a number which increased from only 0.8 million in the late 1970s (ibid.). As we will see below, mobility for the purposes of securing a particular kind of education can be seen among pupils and students of all ages. However, it is most common among those wishing to pursue higher-level qualifications. Across OECD countries, over a quarter of students enrolled in doctoral programmes (or their equivalent) are international students, compared to an average of 6 per cent across all levels of tertiary education (OECD, 2017). There are also differences by country, with China, India and Germany sending the largest number of their nationals abroad for HE, and the USA, UK and Australia together receiving over half of all international students (ibid.).

In analysing these global flows of students for HE, Rivza and Teichler (2007) have distinguished between what they term 'vertical mobility' and 'horizontal mobility'. The former relates to movement between two countries that have dissimilar education systems. Here, students typically benefit from an education that is perceived to be of a higher quality or in an area of specialism that would not have been available to them if they had stayed at home. In contrast, the latter refers to mobility to a neighbouring country, with a similar education system. This is typically a less risky option for the students concerned (because of the cultural similarity between country of origin and destination) and one that has a long history – characterising much of the medieval educational migration that was mentioned at the start of the chapter. It is also important to distinguish between 'diploma' and 'credit' mobility: while the former refers to mobility for the whole of a degree, the latter refers to a short-term period abroad, as part of an educational programme in one's home country. An example of credit mobility would be the Erasmus programme that operates across Europe; participating students typically spend one or two semesters in a university in another European country before returning home to complete their studies (see Chapter 2). Here, too, however, there are significant geographical disparities in patterns of movement: the UK and Germany tend to be net recipients of Erasmus students, while countries that have more recently joined the European Union, such as Latvia and Lithuania, typically send relatively large numbers of students and receive relatively few.

While much of the literature on global flows of students focuses exclusively on HE, it is important to note that international mobility is not restricted to this educational sector. Indeed, research in the field of migration studies (rather than education) has shown how mobility for secondary, or even primary, education is common in some parts of the world, and can become the focus of whole family projects. In many cases, these projects, typically undertaken by Asian families, involve a degree of familial separation. For example, some scholars have used the term 'astronaut families' to describe migratory patterns in which the family relocates to the destination country to secure a high-quality education for the children but, subsequently, one parent – usually the father – returns to the home country to continue with the breadwinning (Huang and Yeoh, 2011; Kobayashi and Preston, 2007). This has much in common with the Korean 'kirŏgi' families described by Finch and Kim (2012). In such families, the mother and children move to an English-speaking country for the children's education, while the father remains in Korea to work and support the family financially. Finch and Kim (2012) note that the families who move overseas in this way include those with very high-achieving children, who aim to secure access to the most prestigious universities in the world, but also those with less highly attaining offspring, who seek to gain better credentials than they would have done in Korea. Indeed, they argue that 'kirŏgi' practices are now so widespread that they constitute an important part of the Korean culture: a quarter of Koreans say that they would like to migrate for their children's education, primarily to help them gain cosmopolitan experience (ibid.). Research has also highlighted more extreme cases, in which both parents return to the home country, after settling their children abroad. Ong (1999) describes such children as 'parachute kids' 'who can be dropped off in another country by parents on the trans-Pacific business commute' (p. 19). In these cases, migration is strongly related to educational imperatives. Educational migration can also, however, be a consequence of other factors. Clearly, many students across the world have to adjust to new schools and education systems as a result of their parents' migration for a whole range of other reasons – from 'third culture kids' (Hayden, 2012) who follow parents employed in prestigious areas such as diplomacy, to those in starkly different economic circumstances who may have fled persecution or conflict with their families.

In explaining global flows of students that are driven by education-related factors, scholars have highlighted a range of social, political and economic influences, many of which are related to the increasingly interconnected nature of society described earlier in this chapter. A key line of argument has focused on concerns around 'employability' or labour market success, in a context in which transitions from education into work are seen as significantly more precarious than in previous decades and, as a result of the 'massification' of HE, the graduate labour market has become extremely congested (see Chapter 12 for further discussion). Politicians and policymakers have typically argued that study abroad can enhance employability through the intercultural skills it develops, and the experience of working with those from a variety of different backgrounds (e.g. BIS, 2009; CIHE, 2007). Indeed, many countries have set targets to stimulate international study on the part of their domestic student population (e.g. CEC, 2009). However, research in this area has suggested that the associated advantages tend to be related to the changes brought about in position relative to other graduates. For example, analysis of data from former Erasmus students has indicated that the 'professional value' of participating in the scheme has declined over time, as credit mobility has become more common (Bracht et al., 2006). Some studies have suggested that a degree, obtained as an international student, can itself act as an important mark of distinction that can help distinguish the holder from other graduates of mass HE systems, and thus secure employment advantage (Bodycott, 2009; Singh and Doherty, 2008). Rizvi (2000) has argued, for example, that Malaysian employers attach a particularly high status to overseas qualifications and, thus, the primary objective of many Malaysian students who move to Australia for university is to obtain a well-recognised qualification that will enable them to secure a good job on their return home. Others have maintained that moving abroad for HE is often necessary to secure a place among the 'global elite' or what Sklair (2001) has called the 'transnational capitalist class'. This has been exacerbated by the emergence of a 'global war for talent' (Brown and Tannock, 2009) – a belief among large companies that the pool of suitably qualified graduates is relatively small, and thus a global search for 'the best' is required, often focusing on the most globally prestigious universities. McKinsey (the large global management consultancy company) boasts that it is the largest non-governmental employer of recipients of prestigious Rhodes and Marshall scholarships (awarded to US citizens for study in the UK) (Mazlish and Morss, 2005), while Brown and colleagues (2011) cite the case of a leading financial services company, which targets just eight globally ranked universities, only one of which is in the UK, despite a significant proportion of the company's activities being located in London. It is no surprise that such behaviour then impacts on the decision-making of the affluent middle classes, who 'seek to position their children in the most desirable and prestigious schools and programmes, to become one of the select members of the internationally sought after, high skill elite' (Brown and Tannock, 2009, p. 384). A slightly different argument is advanced by Cairns (2014), which highlights the importance of paying attention to the way in which global flows can be geographically differentiated. While mobility is often seen as the preserve of the rich, Cairns contends that in politically and geographically 'peripheral' regions – such as Portugal and Ireland, where he conducted his research – assumptions about mobility are often rather different. Indeed, being mobile is commonly a normative expectation among young people in the 'periphery' because of the perceived lack of employment opportunities at home. Here, labour market success is conceived of in rather different terms.

Closely related to arguments about securing labour market advantage are others which emphasise the frequently intertwined relationship between educational migration and immigration. Ong (1999) has contended that migration from Hong Kong to countries of the Global North is intimately bound up with notions of what she calls 'flexible citizenship'. She maintains that, 'Although citizenship is commonly thought of as based on political rights and participation within a sovereign state, globalisation has made economic calculation a major element in diasporan subjects' choice of citizenship … seeking to both circumvent and benefit from different nation-state regimes by selecting different sites for investments, work and family relations' (p. 112). In this analysis, acquiring a Western education is part of a broader 'strategy of accumulation' which provides an entry point into Western democracies and the opportunity to both gain citizenship and establish business activities abroad. Ho and Bedford's (2008) analysis of migration from Asia to New Zealand since the 1990s indicates that while 'astronaut' families had been common in the early part of this period, changes to migration policy, which facilitated transition from student to resident, encouraged families to use education as a means of securing residency. Ho and Bedford note that, as a result of these changes, new 'projects' of transnational education have emerged, with many families sending their children to New Zealand as international students with the intention of subsequently applying for residence, and then bringing other family members to join them. Similar arguments have been developed by Robertson (2013) in her analysis of immigration to Australia. She contends that the linkage of international education and skilled migration has been explicitly encouraged by the various policies pursued by the Australian government from the late 1990s onwards, which have favoured international students as potential migrants.

Underpinning arguments about both the labour market and immigration are, in many cases, concerns about securing social mobility and/or social reproduction (Baas, 2006). In this analysis, international education is seen as an important means of accruing both cultural and social capital. Research on mobility for primary or secondary education has typically argued that this form of migration is often pursued in order to enhance the overall status of the family – through helping children to attain prestigious educational credentials. Children are thus seen to play an important role within familial projects of capital accumulation (Yeoh et al., 2005). International education can offer the opportunity to develop highly regarded cosmopolitan sensibilities (Matthews and Sidhu, 2005; Singh et al., 2007), a high-status qualification (Rizvi, 2000; Waters, 2006) and various forms of 'embodied' cultural capital – such as Western forms of deportment, which are highly valued in some South Asian contexts (Waters, 2008). Studying abroad can also offer an alternative means of accessing elite education – particularly when such opportunities have been closed down 'at home'. This has been illustrated well in relation to Hong Kong families concerned about their ability to get their children into highly competitive schools and universities (Waters, 2007); Norwegian students moving to other European countries to study medicine (Wiers-Jenssen, 2008); and UK students, rejected by Oxford and Cambridge, who turned to US institutions such as Harvard and Yale in order to pursue an elite education (Brooks and Waters, 2009). Many of these analyses have drawn on the work of Bourdieu (discussed in Chapters 2 and 5) to argue that such strategies are typically deployed by the middle classes with the explicit aim, in many cases, of advancing, or at least securing, their social position. The class-related nature of much educational decision-making is discussed further in Chapter 5.

While the agency of individuals and their families is clearly a significant focus in understanding educational migration globally, it is also important not to lose sight of the role of HE institutions, national governments and global markets in facilitating such movement. A key driver of international student mobility has been the desire, on the part of individual universities, to maximise their revenue – from fee income – at a time when public funding, in many national contexts, has been cut (see Chapter 12). Indeed, education has increasingly come to be seen, on the part of many governments, as a key export industry (Rizvi and Lingard, 2010; Waters, 2008). Within the UK, for example, recent research has demonstrated the very significant economic contributions made by overseas students, both to individual institutions, through the fees they pay, and to the wider community in which they live. It is estimated that, in 2014/15, international students generated more than £25 billion for the UK economy (UUK, 2017). To sustain the flow of income from international fees, various 'education exporter' (or 'destination') nations target advertising, design quality assurance programmes and even develop immigration programmes to favour international graduates in particular fields of labour shortage (Rizvi and Lingard, 2010;

Sidhu, 2006). While countries such as Australia and the UK have been reliant on such fee income for many years, it is becoming an increasingly important part of HE revenue within other countries of the world, including Singapore, Malaysia, India and Japan (Rizvi and Lingard, 2010), while China has recently begun to pursue various initiatives to increase its own share of students (Brooks and Waters, 2013). As a consequence, many nation-states and individual universities now compete in a relatively aggressive manner for a share of the lucrative international student market.

This sense of a 'global' education market has been entrenched further through the international rankings of universities that are published on a regular basis (particularly by the *Times Higher Education* magazine in the UK and Shanghai Jiao Tong University in China). Such rankings are produced, ostensibly, to help inform student decision-making but, as a result of the way that the metrics used typically favour large, English-speaking universities in the USA and UK, 'tend to reproduce and exacerbate the existing vertical differences in the higher education landscape' (Marginson and van der Wende, 2007, p. 32; see also Jöns and Hoyler, 2013). They have also had a direct impact on national policies in some countries. Germany, for example, introduced a policy to concentrate funding in a small number of HE institutions (as part of what is called the 'Excellence Initiative') because of concern that none of its universities were ranked sufficiently highly in international league tables. Similarly, reforms were introduced in Japan to increase vertical differentiation between its universities, on the assumption that this would help the country to compete more effectively on a global stage (Hazelkorn, 2009).

International student mobility has also been seen as a means of achieving explicitly *political* objectives. As discussed in Chapter 2, at a regional level, the Erasmus mobility programme and the Bologna Process (which has sought to make studying in another European country easier by, for example, standardising the length of undergraduate and postgraduate degrees) have both been underpinned by a desire to inculcate a 'European' identity among students and thus provide legitimacy for the overall project of European integration (King, 2003; Papatsiba, 2005). Such initiatives are also, however, inextricably linked to economic motives – and the assumption that young people who cross national borders for education will be more likely to be prepared to move to take up employment opportunities in the European Union later in their lives (ibid.). More generally, however, it has been argued that the global flows of students that we have witnessed in the late twentieth century and early twenty-first century have helped to reinscribe highly unequal power relations between countries. Indeed, the patterns outlined at the start of this section – about the net 'receivers' and 'senders' – have already hinted at some of these inequalities. Writing about the USA's dominance in attracting students (and also HE staff), Marginson (2008) has contended that 'US university hegemony is akin to US domination of communications and the contents of film, TV and hand-held media; and to American financial and technological might' (p. 311). A similar argument is advanced by Sidhu (2006) on the basis of her analysis of the marketing materials of universities in the USA, UK and Australia. While there were some differences in approach, all three nations emphasised the Global North's history of educating the (international) other. Moreover, she observes that the narratives produced in the marketing materials 'do not foster a vision for reciprocity in learning across cultures, and by default ... continue to reinforce insider-outsider subject positions' (p. 297). It is important to recognise, however, that these relations between countries are not immutable. While the US still dominates world rankings, substantial investment in HE, the recruitment of many more 'international' staff and explicit attempts to raise their global profile have resulted in universities in Malaysia, South Korea, Japan and China improving their international standing and becoming increasingly attractive destinations for mobile students (Brooks and Waters, 2013).

As noted above, the recruitment of 'international' staff has come to assume increasing importance in the global HE market. Kim (2009) contends that, in common with students, academic staff have a long history of moving across national borders (in their case, to teach and conduct research). Indeed, her historical analysis shows how there has been a close relationship between the mobility of academics and the broader international political context. In the early twentieth century, transnational academic mobility often followed the expansion of empires, with British academic expatriates, for example, regarding their entry to the British colonial universities as an entry ticket to the British colonial government service (ibid.). Moreover, the interwar period witnessed the movement of many German and Austrian scientists, most of whom were Jewish, to the USA and the UK to escape Nazi persecution. However, Kim (2009) also argues that, in the contemporary period, the scale and speed of cross-border academic mobility has changed: 'there is a new urgency, new actors, and new ideologies' (p. 387). This new urgency, she suggests, has been brought about by the confluence of several interlinking factors. First, changes in academic labour – particularly the increasing use of short-term contracts and the proliferation of research-only jobs, often linked to specific research projects – have facilitated researcher mobility. Second, there have been equally significant changes with respect to university leadership and governance (see Chapter 12). Across many institutions worldwide, there is now a strong emphasis on entrepreneurial management skills that are deemed to be 'transnational' and 'transferable'. This has led to the recruitment of a growing number of university leaders from abroad (Kim, 2010). Finally, in some parts of the world such as Australia and the USA, new immigration policies have been introduced which favour highly skilled foreign knowledge workers, including mobile university staff. In these contexts, making the transition from an international research student to an international member of academic staff has become more common (ibid.).

It is important to recognise, however, that academic mobility, just like that of students, remains differentiated: not all have an equal chance of securing employment abroad. Indeed, Marginson (2007) argues that a 'global tier' of mobile staff has been imposed on top of national labour markets where the majority of staff continue to be bounded (see also Musselin, 2004). Moreover, there remain important differences by gender. On the basis of her analysis of the characteristics of Humboldt research fellows (who relocated to Germany for the purposes of research), Jöns (2011) argues that female researchers experienced notably less international mobility in their careers than their male counterparts. In large part this was due to prevailing gender differences in domestic work, with women remaining primarily responsible for care of both children and the elderly, and thus faced more constraints on movement than their male peers. Given that such mobility can have a substantial impact on academic careers (Ackers, 2010), this gender gap is significant. Jöns also highlights differences by subject area – the representation of female visiting researchers was much better in the social sciences and humanities than the natural sciences – and by nation. Gender differences among outgoing scholars were much less marked in Denmark, Portugal, France and Spain than in other European countries. This geographical differentiation is a theme pursued by Kenway and Fahey (2007) as part of their wider discussion of 'policy incitements' to mobility. They argue that the flows of research staff across Europe tend to engrain power imbalances across the continent, as 'old Europe' (e.g. the UK, Germany, France) secures advantage over 'new Europe' (nations such as Poland, Estonia and Latvia that have only relatively recently become members of the European Union). They contend that:

> While researchers may be encouraged to undertake cross-cultural and cross-national research, implicitly this runs the risk of being little more than a form of academic 'sight-seeing' through comparative research but with an underlying implicit mission to deliver epistemological homogeneity. (p. 174)

This argument is developed further below, when we focus more specifically on global flows of knowledge.

Transnational and international education

Globalisation has led to a growth in not just the number of pupils, students and, in some cases, their families, who are prepared to cross national borders in pursuit of an education, but also other forms of 'transnational' and 'international' education. While the term 'international education' is typically used to refer to an aspect of education than includes an international, intercultural or global dimension, transnational education is defined as education in which learners are located in a country different from the one in which the awarding institution is based (McBurnie and Ziguras, 2007) – common forms include distance learning programmes, offshore campuses and the delivery of teaching through partner organisations. Transnational education is attractive to providers as it facilitates market expansion and can, in contrast to studying abroad, enhance their international profile. It is also attractive to (some) students as it typically offers a foreign qualification at a reduced cost and, for mature students in particular, can enable them to continue with their work and/or family commitments. Moreover, governments often favour transnational education as a means of meeting local demand for HE without having to build new institutions of their own; such provision can also help reduce the number of students who leave the country for their education (McBurnie and Ziguras, 2007). Attracting inward investment, such as the establishment of branch campuses and other forms of transnational education, has been part of the attempts of some governments to develop 'educational hubs' in their country. This has been particularly marked in Middle Eastern countries such as Dubai, Kuwait and Saudi Arabia, and South Asian nations including Singapore and Malaysia (Olds, 2007; Sidhu, 2009).

The various policy aspirations associated with transnational education are outlined effectively by Geddie (2012) in her analysis of the rapid growth of international branch campuses (IBCs) in the United Arab Emirates (UAE). She notes that:

> First, IBCs are expected to act as a local service industry, potentially developing the country in a student-oriented educational hub. Second, Emirati leaders look to foreign universities as a solution to expand educational capacity and labour training, particularly for the children of the many expatriate workers. Third, high-profile IBCs ... form part of a policy goal to promote the Emirates among global cities as a 'knowledge-capital' and signal the modernization of the UAE economy and society. And lastly, foreign universities are increasingly turned to to develop research infrastructure to encourage the UAE's innovation-driven knowledge economy, transforming their oil and service industry into a post-industrial economy. (pp. 54–55)

Foreign universities, investing in the UAE, also have their own objectives, which relate to their financial and reputational concerns, and their own histories and previous experiences of international working. Geddie (2012) argues that these various motivations can result in a highly diverse field of educational provision, which may not necessarily advantage local students. Although the scale of the educational investment in the region is not in doubt, the quality of the student experience is variable, and local employers are often confused by the wide array of credentials offered by the various providers.

Alongside the development of transnational educational provision are other initiatives to develop more fully the international orientation of educational provision. In part, this can be seen as a response to the growing number of mobile students, discussed above – ensuring that the education offered is perceived as relevant, not just by domestic students, but by those who migrate from other nations. It has also been stimulated, in some parts of the world, by a perceived need to develop the intercultural skills and 'international outlook' of home students, to ensure that – even if they choose not to move abroad for part of their education – they are prepared for jobs that may require them to work abroad, or at least liaise with those from other countries. At one level, this can be seen in the increasingly prevalent attempts to 'internationalise' the curriculum that is offered by both schools and universities. Such initiatives are often strongly encouraged by national governments and international bodies. Indeed, UNESCO suggested that universities, across the world, should be internationalising their curricula in order to adapt to new challenges:

> If the university is to serve well both scholarship and national needs, if it is to prepare graduates for this new era, the university is obligated to modernise and to contribute to the global exchange of knowledge through the movement of people, information and ideas. (UNESCO, 2002, quoted in Rizvi and Lingard, 2010, p. 173)

A very positive account of such developments is given by a number of scholars – often those who discuss initiatives that have taken place within their own institutions to internationalise the curriculum. Jones and Brown (2007), for example, maintain that while in the past international students (in the UK) have often been valued only for their fee income, this has now changed. Instead, they argue, such students are now valued for the diversity they bring to the classroom, which broadens the horizons of both staff and students, 'thus deepening the higher education experience as a whole' (p. 2). In this analysis, international students themselves are seen as making an important contribution to internationalising the curriculum, in ways that benefit all students.

Nevertheless, this interpretation of contemporary HE is not shared by all. Harrison (2015) contends that the concept of 'internationalisation at home' – which encompasses curriculum development (to introduce perspectives from a range of national or cultural contexts) and new, culturally sensitive pedagogic approaches to facilitate greater 'internationalism', alongside the contribution made by the presence of international students – is considerably more problematic than may be imagined. He draws on evidence from across the globe to demonstrate that 'home' students (wherever they may be based) tend to resist intercultural group work and avoid contact with their international peers. Moreover, the advantages of 'internationalisation at home' are often unequally distributed: those students with pre-existing 'cultural interests' are most likely to take advantage of the opportunities offered to them, while those with fewest cultural resources are often least willing (or able) to benefit.

The growth of 'international' education can also be seen in the increasing number of 'international schools' across the world. Many such schools were founded (often several decades ago) to provide an education for globally mobile expatriates. However, as Hayden (2011) has shown, over recent years, such schools have frequently changed their focus and are increasingly catering for affluent *local* populations, who believe that such schools will inculcate the competences and dispositions 'that will allow effortless circulation amongst the international community, its codes and its subjects' (Aguiar and Nogueira, 2012, p. 353), and thus provide their children with a competitive edge in globalised labour markets. As a result, the education offered by the international school has come to be seen as a commodity 'superior to the form of education that would be experienced in local schools' (ibid., p. 218). The number of such schools has also grown, stimulated – in some parts of the world – by national policies. In South Korea, for example, in 2009 a policy change allowed South Korean nationals to establish and operate international schools for the first time, and such schools to recruit up to half their intake from the local population (Song, 2013). In discussing the implications of these trends, Hayden suggests that the Western liberal and Anglo-centric nature of many of these schools raises important questions about the extent to which they promote cultural and linguistic imperialism.

The way in which this internationalising focus is played out does, however, differ by national context. For example, within Brazil, Aguiar and Nogueira (2012) have shown how, in response to perceived demand from the middle and upper classes, private schools are developing international strategies and advertising these clearly in their promotional material. Such strategies typically include international travel, the promotion of bilingualism and additional foreign language learning. Similarly, in South Korea, internationalism is explicitly promoted by many private schools as a means of appealing to parents within a competitive market. Song (2013) provides compelling evidence of how English medium schools, which were initially established to educate foreign residents, have recently transformed themselves into private providers of global education for South Koreans. He contends that these schools have become so popular that they are now able to charge extremely high fees and impose very restrictive admissions criteria. In this way, they have presented themselves to South Korea's privileged classes as 'an optional solution to the latter's need to ensure social reproduction, closure and exclusion in the age of globalisation' (p. 153). For these schools, internationalism is central to their mission and highly visible in their public face. Here, there are clear commonalities with the way in which the International Baccalaureate has been introduced in many schools worldwide, ostensibly as a means of increasing internationalism and developing global citizens. Nevertheless, as noted in Chapter 2, such initiatives have often come to be monopolised by elite social groups – as a means of developing global cultural capital and facilitating access to employment in transnational organisations (Gardner-McTaggart, 2016).

In contrast to the overt promotion of international activity evident in South Korea and Brazil, Brooks and Waters (2015) have shown that while prestigious English schools typically engage in a large number of international activities, often recruit considerable numbers of international students and have strong relationships with elite universities in the USA and elsewhere, these activities are significantly downplayed in the schools' websites, prospectuses and other publicly available materials. Instead, for the schools in their research, emphasis was placed on the maintenance of an *English* identity – firmly located within a local community. In explaining this dissonance, Brooks and Waters suggest that the articulation of an English (rather than global or cosmopolitan) identity is closely linked to the markets from which the schools recruit. 'Englishness' is likely to be strongly desired by those international pupils who cross national borders for their education, by virtue of its association with prestigious and traditional forms of education, access to elite social networks, the value of British educational credentials in the global marketplace and the opportunity to become fluent in a dominant world language. They also contend that, given the spatial disparities in the global field of education and the persistence of neo-colonial influences, 'Englishness' is likely to be valued equally highly by British families seeking an elite schooling for their children – and deemed more desirable than 'international' alternatives. There are thus strong motives for English schools to continue to expand their international activities but also to downplay their internationalism in their public face.

Both transnational and international education initiatives are often promoted as an important national 'industry'. In the UK, for example, at the time of writing, the unit responsible for international education is called 'UK Trade and Investment Education' and is part of UKTI (the government department responsible for trade and investment) and the Department for Business, Energy and Industrial Strategy, rather than the Department for Education. Moreover, the strategy document *International Education: Global Growth and Prosperity*, published by the UK government in 2013, clearly constructs international education primarily as a source of income for the UK; the first line of the foreword states, 'There are few sectors of the UK economy with the capacity to grow and generate export earnings as impressive as education' (BIS, 2013, p. 3). A similar approach to international education has been documented elsewhere. For example, in his analysis of educational provision in New Zealand, Lewis (2011) argues that 'what has changed in the last 20 years is more than simply a proliferation of globalising educational activities and relations. Rather, these activities have become increasingly commercialised, professionalised, institutionalised, and mobilised in political projects' (p. 241). He contends that various practices – such as an emphasis on branding and entrepreneurial activity, and specific forms of governance intended to promote export earnings – have had the effect of normalising market relations (see related discussion in Chapter 3). Education has thus been reshaped, and is now conceived as an industry rather than an emancipatory, nation-building and citizen-shaping project.

As some of the preceding discussion has made clear, a common theme in much of the extant literature in this area is that international and/or transnational education is valued more highly than its domestic equivalent (often to do with assumptions about the associated cultural capital and labour market advantage). However, recent work has highlighted important variation in ascribed value – by both geographical location and type of provider. Sin's (2013) research on Malaysian students, for example, has indicated that while studying in the UK was often valued more highly than attending a Malaysian university, UK institutions located in Malaysia did not have the same appeal (largely because the perceived social and economic rewards were believed to be less). Furthermore, foreign cultural capital was thought sometimes to have negative currency – for example, in organisations that expected a soft, submissive interactional style on the part of their employees, associated with Asian respect for authority and seniority, as one of Lin's interviewees explained:

> [Malaysian employers] want someone who is humble and is pretty down to earth and who is willing to learn, is teachable, as opposed to someone you ... come from [puts on posh Londoner accent], 'Oh, you know, I have a degree from Cambridge and therefore, I can tell you a thing or two about the law'. (Sin, 2013, p. 860)

Similarly, Waters and Leung's (2012) research on UK degrees taught through Hong Kong institutions demonstrates how such qualifications were viewed as significantly less prestigious than those obtained directly from a Hong Kong university or one abroad. Indeed, they suggest that such providers offered an important 'widening participation' function, enabling those without the grades to gain entry to a Hong Kong university and without the money to study abroad to gain a HE. This growing body of work reminds us of the importance of paying attention to the geographical specificity of educational processes, and the ways in which globalising pressures are mediated by local contexts.

Global flows of knowledge

Associated with both the global flows of students and the growth of transnational/international education, discussed above, are debates about the way in which knowledge has been affected by globalisation (this articulates with the wider discussion of knowledge in Chapter 9). Much of the literature in this area has pointed to the methods by which inequalities – between different bodies of knowledge and/or ways of knowing – have been exacerbated. Robinson-Pant (2009), for example, describes how some of the international doctoral students in her research, who had come to the UK to study, intended to become 'change agents' when they returned home – by encouraging a more critical approach and a greater diversity in academic writing styles. However, her research participants also spoke of how they felt they had less opportunity to challenge dominant academic practices during their time in the UK. This echoes the arguments made by Kenway and Fahey, outlined earlier in the chapter, about flows of knowledge within Europe, 'from central points of power in the European university system to more marginal points – from old to new Europe' (p. 172). The increasing dominance of English as the language of instruction – in universities across the world wishing to increase their share of 'international' students (Choi, 2010; Harrison, 2015), as well as 'international' schools orientated towards local populations (Hayden, 2011) – can also be seen as part of such inequalities. Developing this argument further, Naidoo (2010) contends that the particular hegemonic view of knowledge propagated by universities in the USA and Western Europe is particularly disadvantageous for countries in the Global South. Hegemonic knowledge, she suggests, is that which can be used for national competitive advantage. This 'capitalist knowledge regime', as she calls it, drawing on the work of Slaughter and Rhoades (2004) and Foucault (1980), 'operates as a set of norms and practices in which universities find themselves in competition for increased revenues resulting in revenue-generating fields taking on greater relevance'

(p. 79) with 'less profitable' areas of academic life, often associated with the social, political and/or cultural functions of universities, becoming marginalised. While this narrowing of 'valued knowledge' can be seen as detrimental to all societies, it is a particular problem in developing countries, Naidoo (2010) maintains, because of the significant contribution HE makes to non-economic areas of the public good, such as building a strong democracy and cohesive society, and developing expertise that is well-matched with local needs.

However, other scholars have painted a more nuanced picture, arguing that flows of knowledge are not always one-way. While some 'receiving' countries are better than others at integrating international students and ensuring that their voices are heard, some 'countries of origin' are more open than others to the 'new knowledge' brought back by mobile students (Madge et al., 2009). Furthermore, Madge and colleagues (2009) maintain that international students are not passive recipients of hegemonic knowledge but active agents in processes of knowledge flow. This, they argue, can be seen historically – in the way in which international students were influential in shaping the anti-colonial movements of the first half of the twentieth century. Education in the 'mother country' was highly valued but also, they suggest, 'came to spark new spatial imaginaries – including those of an independent nation' (p. 39). Similar effects can be seen in contemporary society. Madge and colleagues note that international students in the UK and other countries of the Global North have influenced the way subjects are taught, by bringing with them their own theories and ways of knowing. However, it is also the case that such influences are often not well-recognised; indeed 'forgetting these contributions has become central to defining and marketing British higher education' (ibid., p. 41).

Conclusion

Although HE, in particular, has long been 'global' in its outlook, in this chapter we have considered the ways in which neo-liberal globalisation (i.e. the form of globalisation associated with market-based reform and the withdrawal of the state from many areas of social provision) has affected how individuals, families and social groups engage with education, and the response of educational institutions. The chapter focused on two specific changes: the unprecedented growth in the number of students moving across national borders to pursue an education (for schooling as well as HE), and the emergence of new forms of international and transnational educational provision. It has argued that both are, to some extent, underpinned by the desire of individuals and families to secure social mobility or reproduction, and of educational institutions and governments to maximise the income associated with international students and achieve various political objectives. Moreover, they often serve to heighten inequalities between both social groups (those who can and cannot afford an international education) and nations. In some cases, these inequalities can be exacerbated by the differences in associated knowledge flows as students move between powerful and less powerful countries. The geography of globalisation is thus important.

5 SOCIAL CLASS

Introduction

The impact of social class on educational destinations and experiences has long been a focus of academic research, dating back to the 1950s. However, this focus has not always been played out in the same way across all nations. Within the UK, social class has been one of the main preoccupations among British sociology of education for decades (Whitty, 2012), evidenced by various seminal texts such as Jackson and Marsden's (1966) *Education and the Working Class*, Willis' (1977) *Learning to Labour* and Reay's (1998) *Class Work*. Although the equally influential examination of the relationship between class and education, *Schooling in Capitalist America* (Bowles and Gintis, 1976), was written by American scholars, in general, differences by race and ethnicity (see Chapter 7) have received significantly more attention in the USA than those by class. By the late twentieth century, however, social class had become an important policy concern in many countries of the Global North, not least because of the comparative data on socio-economic inequalities in educational attainment produced by the OECD through its Programme of International Student Assessment (PISA) (see discussion in Chapter 3). For example, in Germany, the nation's relatively poor showing in the PISA tests led to a new focus within both policy and academic scholarship on how social class inequalities may be reproduced. In general, over recent years, most countries have viewed class differences in education as problematic – usually because of a (at least espoused) commitment to social mobility – but have often struggled to put in place effective policies to remedy them.

In this chapter, we first consider the ways in which social class can impact on access to education, exploring the influence exerted by families, students and educational institutions themselves. We then reflect upon the impact of social class on experiences of education, in relation to both attainment and interactions with other students. Finally, we discuss routes from education into the workplace, and examine how these, too, are often strongly patterned by class position. Social class can be measured in different ways – for example, in relation to occupation, income and/or level of highest educational qualification – and there is a large literature devoted specifically to this topic. The majority of the studies discussed in this chapter define social class in terms of parental education and/or employment and, often associated with both of these, access to specific economic, social and cultural resources. However, social class has been theorised, not just in terms of access to resources, but also in relation to the way in which it is manifest in cultural norms, dispositions to the world and embodied ways of being. These are also considered in the chapter.

Access to education

Participation in education across the globe has risen significantly over recent decades. Indeed, in nearly all OECD countries, the share of younger adults with tertiary-level qualifications is larger than that of older adults with the same level of qualification (OECD, 2015). On average, the difference in tertiary attainment between generations (when 25–34-year-olds are compared to 55–64-year-olds) is 16 per cent (ibid.). However, not all young people have benefited equally from the expansion in post-secondary education. International indicators continue to show stubborn inequalities by social class despite, in some cases, many years of policies aimed at 'widening participation'. For example, of younger adults (i.e. those under 35), OECD data show that 23 per cent of those whose parents did not attain upper secondary education attained tertiary education themselves, compared with 65 per cent of their counterparts whose parents had also attained tertiary education (OECD, 2015). Moreover, there are also differences by social class in the type of institution attended. Students from more privileged backgrounds are much more likely than their less advantaged peers to be found in high-status schools, colleges and universities (e.g. Boliver, 2013; Draelants, 2016; Khan, 2011). For example, at the University of Oxford, only 3 per cent of students come from the most disadvantaged 20 per cent of UK neighbourhoods (Weale, 2016). In explaining this differential access to education, scholars have focused on the actions of individual students (and their families), as well as those of educational institutions. Important to understanding both, however, is the wider political and economic context.

Students and families as choosers

In explaining these patterns of unequal access to and participation within education, scholars have typically pointed to the ways in which families and individuals have responded to two key changes in contemporary society: the expansion of education, and the increasing stratification of educational institutions and qualifications (Atkinson, 2015). As noted above, across the world, a larger percentage of the population now has access to education than in previous decades – as secondary education has been made compulsory, the school leaving age raised and HE 'massified'. Underpinning this expansion has been the assumption that a highly educated workforce is required to fill the increasing number of jobs in the 'knowledge economy' and to enable countries to compete successfully against other nations in a globalised market. Although some of these assumptions have been questioned (e.g. by those who have argued that we need far fewer highly skilled jobs than is commonly thought), they have continued to be used to justify much education policy across the Global North. Some scholars, such as Ulrich Beck and Manuela du Bois-Reymond, have contended that the opening up of educational opportunities to families who have traditionally not participated in post-compulsory education has led to a new age of individualisation in which class background has become much less important in determining outcomes. (Proponents of the 'individualisation thesis' have argued that, as a consequence of various social changes, people are forced to put themselves at the centre of their own plans, and take responsibility for constructing their own social biographies.) Nevertheless, a large body of empirical research has documented the stubbornness of class inequalities, and the ways in which more privileged sections of society have found new ways to reproduce their social advantage within this changing context.

Alongside the mass expansion of education, we have witnessed a growing stratification of educational institutions and, to a lesser extent, qualifications. This is evident at the level of compulsory education – with some national systems channelling young people into different routes at a relatively early age of their schooling. Here, a distinction is often made between 'academic' pathways and more vocational routes (the system in Germany is a good example of this). However, channelling can also occur within individual (ostensibly 'comprehensive') schools, as young people are allocated to different sets or streams. At the level of HE, it is notable that the vertical differentiation of universities has become much more marked over recent decades, as the sector has expanded (see Chapter 12). This differentiation has been stimulated, to some extent, by the appearance and proliferation of university league tables which, as Savage and colleagues (2015) note, have tracked the post-1990 expansion in student numbers very closely. As mentioned in Chapter 4, even Germany, which has historically been committed to an egalitarian HE system with few differences between institutions, has embarked on a series of reforms (comprising what is called the 'Excellence Initiative') to increase vertical differentiation. While such changes are sometimes part of top-down reform (as is the case in Germany), they are frequently exacerbated by the actions of families and individuals keen to secure advantage in what is perceived to be an increasingly competitive environment. It is in this way that class inequalities tend to be reproduced.

Philip Brown (1997) has coined the term 'parentocracy' to describe how parents have responded to changes in the education system such as the process of expansion outlined above. He argues that educational credentials have become more important to the middle classes, in particular, because of the bureaucratisation and rationalisation of the recruitment practices used by large corporations, and also because of increasingly widespread experiences of economic recession and, in some cases, unemployment. Moreover, as 'working one's way up' in an organisation has become less common, externally validated qualifications have assumed new importance as a means of protection against corporate restructuring and global economic downturns. Brown argues that this trend helps explain the growing demand for academic credentials, and also 'the increasingly instrumental attitudes of middle-class parents concerning the education of their children' (p. 402). Thus, the ideals of equality of opportunity or 'meritocracy' (i.e. the idea that people have power in society because of their ability, not as a result of money or social position), which underpinned much education policy in the middle part of the twentieth century in the UK and other countries of the Global North, has been undermined by the actions of new and established middle classes and by the shift, at state level, to an embrace of market principles:

> This form of 'social closure' is the outcome of an evaluation by the middle classes that educational success has become too important to be left to the chance outcome of a formally open competition ... The fact that potentially more able students who do not have the same financial means will lose out just becomes another hard fact of life, because it is not the responsibility of the State to regulate the competition for education in a fair and equal manner, but to ensure the sovereignty of 'parental choice'. (Brown, 1997, p. 402)

Similarly, Ball (2003) has maintained that, because of the interruption to the trajectory of economic growth and patterns of employment that provided the basis for the post-war expansion of the middle classes, 'the imagined futures of the middle classes and those of their offspring are now under threat from the unmanaged congestion in the old and new professions and in management positions' (p. 20). Thus, in response to what is perceived to be increased competition from the working class, middle-class families will either secede from state education (by enrolling in the private sector) or attempt to change the mechanisms of selection and exclusion in education (e.g. what is considered to be a prestigious form of education) (Brown, 1997). The increasing importance placed on the type of university attended (see also Chapters 4 and 12) can be seen as one illustration of the way in which such mechanisms have changed. Prior to the mass expansion of HE in many parts of the world, possession of a degree was itself enough to signal adequate preparation for professional jobs and achievement of a high-status qualification. However, as HE has expanded, and more working-class students have entered, so more emphasis has been placed – in many anglophone countries at least – on the status of the institution attended. As elite universities typically have relatively low numbers of working-class students, such changes have undoubtedly favoured the middle classes. Ball (2003) has argued that cultural change has followed, as the insecure middle classes come to prioritise personal motives over impersonal values, and withdraw their support from progressive pedagogies and other efforts to democratise education.

While the analyses of Brown and Ball are based largely on the UK, similar social processes have been documented in other nations (e.g. Olmedo and Santa Cruz, 2012; Weis and Cipollone, 2013). Waters' (2006) research in Hong Kong, for example, has shown how, as access to education has expanded, so achieving educational 'distinction' has become linked to educational selection. She argues that while the number of HE institutions increased quite considerably in the early 2000s – from three to eleven – the value of obtaining a degree from a 'local' university diminished, and competition to get into one of the 'top three' institutions became fierce. Like Brown, Waters contends that the middle classes now place greater importance on educational 'distinction' than they had done in the past, primarily because of wider economic factors. In Hong Kong, as a result of economic restructuring, middle-class families can no longer depend on the automatic success of their businesses and the enduring value of their financial assets. Instead, obtaining a professional job has come to be seen as a more secure pathway to high social status, and an academic qualification essential to obtaining such a job. Moreover, various 'exclusionary tactics' have been deployed by the Hong Kong middle classes in the ensuing competition for academic recognition and distinction (ibid.). Similar changes to the practices of the middle classes can be seen in France. Draelants (2016) argues that 'highbrow culture' is 'a resource with limited profitability' (p. 151) in society – largely due to the spread of cultural eclecticism. As a result, he suggests the most privileged fraction of society can no longer rely on reproducing their social position merely through access to this culture. Instead, they have come to put much greater emphasis on securing academic credentials in the belief that these are now the key means of accessing high-status jobs and other desirable social positions.

As part of this increased emphasis on education by more advantaged groups in society, the type of school or university attended has become more important – because of the way in which it enables access to particular educational qualifications, and also the status it confers in its own right. Indeed, Ayling (2016) has argued that, in Nigeria, cultural and economic elites typically send their children to English-language boarding schools – believing that such schools' emphasis on manners, deportment and spoken English will help to distinguish them from others. Similar trends have been noted in India (Iyer, 2016), underlining the enduring legacy of colonial relationships. The choice of educational institution is also influenced, for some, by a desire to be educated (or for one's children to be educated) alongside those who are perceived to be similar – which can again help to reinforce class divisions. Ball (2003) has argued that the middle classes, in particular, have a subjective awareness of the cultural and economic interests they hold in common. He contends:

> Despite the centrality of individualism and autonomy in all of this, the judgements and perceptions which parents use and inhabit are collective, they are embedded in and 'carried by the communal practices of one's own immediate group'; they are part of a 'shared intelligibility'. (Ball, 2003, p. 63)

Ziegler (2016) has made similar points in relation to school choice practices among families in Argentina. She argues that the families in her research that chose private schools valued the social segregation such schools were believed to offer. For them, the social homogeneity found in private institutions was seen as a key means of consolidating positions of privilege and guaranteeing membership of desirable social groups. There does, however, remain some variation in the way in which 'social mix' is viewed. For example, while Benson and colleagues (2015) note that it was significant in the choice processes of the families they studied in both London and Paris (and sometimes seen as a proxy for the quality of the school), Parisian parents tended to value a social mix much more than their London counterparts (see also Reay et al., 2011). Moreover, in Norway there remains strong support, among all social classes, for social mixing – and thus comprehensive education (Aarseth, 2016). (See Chapter 11 for a more sustained discussion of different types of school.)

It is also clear that, across many different national contexts, families engage in the 'school choice' process in contrasting ways, which are often closely correlated with their class position. In one of the first studies of such processes, Gewirtz and colleagues (1995) differentiated between three different types of chooser. These are, first, 'skilled' choosers, who are keen to engage in the process of school choice, and have considerable resources to draw upon to help them reach a decision; second, 'semi-skilled choosers', who are happy to take an active role in choosing a school, but have fewer resources to draw upon; and finally, 'disconnected choosers' who have little inclination to compare schools, and are often content with their child attending the local school. These three types map on, quite clearly, to different social classes. 'Skilled choosers' are typically those from more privileged, middle-class families; the 'disconnected' are often working-class families; while the 'semi-skilled choosers' are a mixed-class group. Thus, Gewirtz and colleagues conclude that there are significant differences by social class in both inclination and ability to engage in processes of school choice. Since the publication of this UK-based study, very similar patterns have been identified elsewhere – for example, in France (Benson et al., 2015) and Spain (Olmedo and Santa Cruz, 2012).

These processes have tended to be explained in terms of cultural reproduction theory and the three forms of capital (economic, cultural and social) identified by Bourdieu (1997) (see discussion in Chapter 2). He argues that capital is the 'principle underlying the immanent structures of the social world' (1997, p. 47) and appears in three 'fundamental guises': economic (money, property and other material assets); cultural (dispositions of the mind, and possession of cultural artefacts and educational qualifications); and social (social connections and obligations). Economic capital is significant for middle-class families as it can enable them to access private schooling, move into the catchment area of high-performing state schools and/or afford transport to make the daily journey to and from particular institutions (Coldron et al., 2010). However, as numerous studies have attested, economic resources are rarely sufficient; cultural and social capital often play a key role. In relation to cultural resources, Devine (2004) has argued that middle-class parents mobilise their cultural capital on behalf of their children by making clear their expectations that they will do well at school and secure entry to prestigious HE institutions (and, subsequently, professional employment). Their own, largely successful, educational experiences ensure that they know how to work the system and have both the confidence and the knowledge to intervene effectively on the behalf of their children – when choosing which schools and colleges to apply to, and also during their studies (as will be discussed in more detail below). As Mullen's (2009) work on access to elite universities in the USA has shown, children from such families grow up expecting to 'feel at home' in these institutions rather than harbouring concerns about feeling out of place (a feeling which deters many less privileged students).

Social capital has also been shown to be important in accessing education – in relation to the nature of social networks, and the ways these are used. Ball (2003) draws a clear distinction between the social capital possessed by working-class students, when making decisions about HE, and by their middle-class peers. The former is 'almost exclusively very personal and familial and offered fairly limited descriptive information and bland recommendations and rarely involved other adults and certainly not adults who could be of use in choosing and applying to higher education' (p. 82). In contrast, that invoked by middle-class students is described by Ball as 'effective or operant, high volume social capital, that is, social capital realised through social networks providing direct support and relevant and valued resources' (ibid.). As a result of these particular social relationships, he argues, the middle-class students in his research were able to develop realistic and vivid imagined futures, and draw on useful information when making their HE applications (see also Ball and Vincent, 2001). This middle-class social capital could also be utilised at times of crisis – for example, contacts to draw on to provide private tutoring, and advice about intervening with teachers, if necessary. Furthermore, Devine (2004) has argued that middle-class social networks can also normalise progression to university, and to prestigious institutions in particular. However, her research – conducted in the USA and the UK – suggests that it is not only the privileged middle class who benefit from social capital. Indeed, she maintains that, in her study, working-class students and those from lower middle-class backgrounds spoke of the helpful influence of other academically able students (and also their class teachers) in putting them on the path to HE. Nevertheless, it is important to note that as their contacts were less well-placed, they had less impact on securing advantage within competitive educational markets. Moreover, Reay and colleagues (2005) contend that the meaning attached to personal recommendations and other forms of 'grapevine' knowledge differs significantly by class culture. They argue that the information provided by family and friends (what they term 'hot' knowledge) is of most influence at the two ends of the social spectrum:

> For less privileged and first time applicants [to HE] the importance of soliciting the viewpoint of 'someone like me' led to the prioritising of hot over cold official knowledge; the latter often being seen to be construed for more privileged applicants who are not subject to the same financial, time and distance constraints. Although the privately educated students also gave primacy to hot knowledge, the insider quality of the personal recommendations they were able to access meant their grapevine knowledge was of a totally different order to that of the far less well connected students ... (p. 152)

While more privileged students tend to use multiple sources of information and are able to contextualise personal recommendations within a wide variety of family experiences and other data, in Reay and colleagues' study, those from working-class backgrounds tended to report being significantly influenced by a single personal recommendation, even if it was not supported by any other evidence.

One result of these differential processes of educational choice is that different social fractions end up choosing among relatively limited groups of educational institutions (Brooks, 2003). With respect to schooling, for example, Ball and colleagues (1997) have argued that different social groups choose between three different 'circuits' of school. In their research in London, 'skilled choosers' typically chose from two main 'circuits': cosmopolitan, elite, state schools and private day schools. In contrast, working-class, 'disconnected choosers' were much more likely to associate themselves with only the circuit of local, community, comprehensive schools. Similar class differentiation has occurred in Argentina – evident even *among* elite groups. Indeed, Prosser (2016) has argued that while economic elites in Argentina favour private schooling, cultural elites tend to use academically selective schools instead. Reay and colleagues (2005) have suggested that a similar typology can be applied to HE. In the UK context, for example, while privately educated students tend to dominate Oxford and Cambridge, and middle-class students identify most strongly with older, civic universities, their working-class counterparts feel most at home in institutions that gained university status much more recently. Brooks and Waters (2009) have extended this analysis by adding a fourth circuit. They argue that those from the most privileged backgrounds (across many nation-states) choose within *global* circuits of HE – often choosing to study at elite institutions abroad if they fail to secure access to prestigious institutions in their own country. The growth of an international market for education (as discussed in Chapter 4) has exacerbated such trends.

Studies that have explored the impact of social capital on educational decision-making have also highlighted the ways in which ethnicity can structure social networks, and thus the resources to which young people have access (see also Chapter 7). For example, Archer and Francis (2006) point to the importance of social capital within the British Chinese community and, in particular, the social and educational competitiveness between families which, they argue, furthers academic achievement and a high level of academic aspiration. Similar findings are noted in Pimpa's (2005) research with Thai students: family competition was a strong motivation for pursuing a high-status overseas HE. Some of this work on social capital has raised questions about the extent to which it supports Bourdieu's wider model of social reproduction. For example, both Archer and Francis (2006), on the basis of their work in the UK, and Khattab (2002), drawing on his work among Arabs in Israel, maintain that more consideration needs to be given to the racialised dimension

77

of classed experiences. Both studies suggest that the close social networks of particular ethnic minority groups can help to raise educational aspirations significantly. Indeed, Archer and Francis (2006) argue that among the working-class British Chinese 'familial discourses around mobility appeared to be quite different from popular white working class discourses – where research has identified families discouraging mobility for "getting above your station"' (p. 44). Similar arguments have been made in other countries (e.g. Carolan-Silva and Reyes, 2013). For example, drawing on their research in Canada, Abada and Tenkorang (2009) have argued that it is important to explore the forms of social capital particular to each minority group, and the various ways in which these are utilised within the educational sphere.

The influence of schools and universities

It is important to remember, however, the broader framework within which pupils, students and parents are making their choices. One aspect of this is the expansion of education discussed above, and the various economic and cultural changes that have challenged the traditional means through which those with power in society have been able to maintain their position of advantage. It is also necessary to consider the influence of individual educational institutions – schools, colleges and universities – and how this has some part to play in explaining the inequalities of access by social class.

As noted in Chapter 3, across the world – and particularly in countries of the Global North – 'choice' policies have been introduced in education, to encourage prospective students and their families to act as consumers and thus stimulate a market within education. Such policies are predicated on the assumption that market behaviour, in which institutions are required to compete for pupils and students, leads to higher quality education (see also Chapter 11). Scholars have, however, pointed out various problems with this shift to more market-based forms of education. One line of argument is that such changes advantage the middle classes, but in a much less obvious way than previous policies. In part, this is effected through the actions of schools themselves. Indeed, given the increasing importance of school league tables and performance indicators such as exam results, schools are now incentivised to 'maximise their intake of students who are easy to teach and perform well' (Ball, 2003, p. 33). This can lead to the favouring of those from middle-class backgrounds, although often in rather hidden ways. Research conducted by Gaztambide-Fernandez and Mandhi (2016) in the USA and Canada, for example, has shown how access to high-performing schools is often strongly classed, even in ostensibly 'open enrolment' systems in which prospective students are constructed as empowered consumers. They cite the case of a performing arts school in Canada in which 'exclusion is not operationalised through verifiable markers like high grades or test scores or even money' (p. 63). Instead, subjective criteria, used in the admissions process – such as 'talent' and 'passion' – have the effect of favouring those with the requisite cultural capital. Similarly, they argue that in the context of the high-performing US school in their study, the considerable amount of information required to apply for admission effectively deterred those with fewer cultural resources.

The specific criteria used in admissions processes have also come under critical scrutiny. In the USA, Karabel (2006) has shown how, over the course of the twentieth century, elite HE institutions such as Harvard, Yale and Princeton came to place emphasis on the wider skills and experience of applicants, not only their academic credentials. This, he argues, was a discriminatory change motivated by a concern that assessing only academic performance had resulted in an over-representation of Jewish students in the most prestigious US institutions, and a corresponding decline in the number of students from affluent, white, Protestant families. In exploring contemporary HE practices in the USA, Khan (2011) notes that an emphasis on 'character' remains – although it is now often justified on the grounds that it enables the selection of a more diverse student body. He recognises that US universities are more diverse than in previous decades, but also points to the class inequalities that tend to be engrained by such practices: 'selection based on "character" continues to help students from elite schools as they are given more opportunities to develop "interesting characters" through the wide range of activities that are a central part of their everyday schooling' (p. 177). In the UK, Boliver's (2013) research on access to elite universities (members of the so-called 'Russell Group' of 'research intensive' institutions) has indicated that students from lower social class backgrounds (and also from black and minority ethnic groups) are disadvantaged during the admissions process. Specifically, she shows that applicants from state schools were much less likely to receive offers of admission from Russell Group universities when compared with their counterparts from private schools who had equivalent levels of qualification. Class inequalities within HE are also reinforced, in some countries, by particular relationships between elite schools and elite universities. In the UK, private schools typically provide considerably more support with applications to Oxford and Cambridge than is usually possible within state institutions (Reay et al., 2005) and have been shown to facilitate entry to top universities abroad as well (Brooks and Waters, 2009). Moreover, in France, Buisson-Fenet and Draelants (2013) have documented strong 'institutional linkages' between a small number of secondary schools and the highly selective colleges that offer preparatory classes for the 'Grandes Écoles' (the main HE training for elite professional jobs in engineering, management and politics in France).

Experiences of education

Social class is relevant not just in explaining patterns of access to education. It also influences the ways in which education is experienced, and the qualifications students obtain. Both are discussed in this part of the chapter. We also explore the concept of 'institutional habitus' and consider whether educational institutions themselves can have a 'class disposition'.

Attainment

As noted earlier in this chapter, despite a general expansion in the percentage of people participating in higher levels of education across the world, differences by social class remain. Those from less advantaged backgrounds, when measured by parental education, are less likely to attain a tertiary-level qualification, for example (OECD, 2015). Moreover, data from the 2012 PISA tests, which had a particular focus on mathematics, indicated that in all countries that participated, a student's socio-economic status had a strong impact on her or his performance. Indeed, 15 per cent of the variation in scores obtained in mathematics was attributable to differences in students' socio-economic status (OECD, 2013).

The poorer performance of pupils and students from lower social classes is frequently explained by politicians and other policymakers as the fault of their families – suggesting that they have low aspirations and poor parenting practices (Allen, 2014). Education policy has often been based on similar assumptions, encouraging working-class families to adopt middle-class parenting practices such as monitoring children's progress in school and becoming more active 'choosers' of education (Gewirtz, 2001; Gillies, 2005). However, academic work has played an important role in questioning some of these assumptions, through highlighting the impact of both the material circumstances of families and the cultural and social resources to which families have access. Lupton's (2005) research in four schools in very poor neighbourhoods has provided a vivid account of the numerous ways in which living in poverty can have a direct and deleterious impact on achievement. These include pupil–teacher contact time being diverted from teaching and learning activities by counselling pupils, dealing with major behavioural problems and reinforcing classroom order in the face of frequent minor distractions; a large proportion of senior management time being spent on pupil welfare issues and tasks such as bidding for special funding rather than more standard management activities; and the difficulty of recruiting staff to teach in such schools. Lupton also describes well the often-hidden resourcing problems that such schools face. She gives several examples of these, one of which is homework:

Homework tasks may need to be more carefully designed and differentiated. More guidance may need to be given. It may take longer to mark the work and give feedback, since knowledge of subject may be obscured by problems of writing and presentation. Simply collecting the homework and setting up an expectation that it will be done will demand persistence, reinforcement through the discipline process (with its attendant paperwork), and possibly support in the provision of homework facilities and supervision. All these are possible, but time-consuming. (p. 600)

At the other end of the income scale, economic capital is significant in providing access to, for example, private schooling and private tutoring, both of which have an impact not only on the way in which school is experienced but levels of attainment. Zhang and Bray (2017) have described how a 'shadow' education system has emerged in China, blurring the boundaries between state schooling and private, supplementary schooling. This form of 'micro-neo-liberalism', as they call it, is not unique to China: similar 'shadow' structures have emerged in numerous other nations around the world, including countries as diverse as Cambodia (Bray et al., 2016), Egypt (Hartmann, 2013), Georgia (Kobakhidze, 2014), Greece (Kassotakis and Verdis, 2013) and South Korea (Choi and Cho, 2015).

Family background (and thus social class) is also significant in relation to the 'social gifts' that are passed on, typically from parents to children (Reay, 2017). The work of Bourdieu has again often provided a fruitful framework for theorising these processes. He argued that parents in more privileged social positions, who have significant amounts of cultural capital, socialise their children differently from those in less privileged positions, who have access to less cultural capital. Some of this socialisation is unintentional, such as using an extended vocabulary and complex sentence structure. Other forms of socialisation are more deliberate – for example, enrolling one's child in a wide range of sporting and cultural activities as part of what Lareau (2003) has called a process of 'concerted cultivation' (see also Vincent and Ball, 2007). Moreover, Devine (2004) has noted the particular values that middle-class families often seek to pass on. Writing about her middle-class participants in the USA and the UK, she maintains that:

They sought to inculcate in their children the values of hard work, discipline and deferred gratification and translated these values into how they conducted their everyday family life as they watched their children's educational activities and carefully controlled their free time. (p. 180)

Bourdieu and Passeron (1990) argued that, as a result of such socialisation, children from middle-class families develop what they call 'symbolic mastery' from a very early age, and certainly before they enter school. In contrast, children from working-class families, with less cultural capital, develop 'practical mastery' instead. In school, however, only symbolic mastery is rewarded – thus, children from middle-class backgrounds come to see themselves as intelligent and academically able, while those from working-class backgrounds are often labelled as failures. In this way, and as noted in Chapter 2, Bourdieu and Passeron argue, 'social gifts' are misrecognised as 'natural gifts'.

Some scholars have also argued that children can play an active role in shaping educational inequalities. Based on an ethnography of a diverse state elementary school in the USA, Calarco (2011) has contended that pupils' social class affects their behaviour in the classroom and, in particular, the ways in which they engage with the teacher. She notes that the middle-class children in her research were more likely than their working-class peers to seek help from their teacher and to use more direct approaches when doing so – including interrupting teachers on occasion. Calarco concludes that, as a result of such behaviours, middle-class children are advantaged in the classroom: they spend less time waiting, receive more help and, consequently, are more able to complete their assignments.

Interactions with other students

Education is clearly about much more than academic attainment, and a relatively large body of work has explored the ways in which social class informs interactions between students and other aspects of what can be considered the 'informal' life of educational institutions. A key theme running through scholarship in this area is the propensity for social segregation within education – either through attending different schools, colleges or universities, or by processes that separate students within individual institutions. As has been discussed above, as a result of increased stratification within all sectors of education and across many nations, pupils and students from different class backgrounds often end up studying at different institutions. This inevitably reduces opportunities to mix with those from different social backgrounds, and reinforces relatively homogeneous social norms. Research in more socially mixed institutions has suggested that, here, interacting with those perceived as different (whether that be in terms of social class or other social characteristics) can often be valued highly. Reay and colleagues (2007) have described the way in which middle-class participants in their study, who had chosen to send their children to socially mixed inner-city comprehensive schools, valued the opportunity to 'encounter difference' that such schools offered. Moreover, the young people in Hollingworth and Mansaray's (2012) research, who attended a socially mixed comprehensive school, welcomed what they saw as the 'cosmopolitan canopy' of the institution. Nevertheless, in both studies, when the researchers explored in more depth the actual patterns of interaction between pupils, they found that social mixing was rather less widespread than their participants' celebratory accounts had led them to believe. Hollingworth and Mansaray (2010), for example, note that even among the sixth-formers, who had made a positive choice to stay on at the school, there were relatively few friendship ties across social class. Instead, working-class students tended to maintain ties around their locale – often centred on their family and 'people on my estate' – while middle-class students' ties extended 'across the elite field of private and prestigious state schools across London' (para 5.3). Here, there is evidence that within educational institutions, as in other contexts, processes of 'differential association' (Bottero, 2005) occur: people do not associate with others randomly, or on the basis of arbitrary personal preference. Instead, association tends to be with those who hold similar social resources. While this may have some positive outcomes – particularly for more advantaged groups, who are able to forge links with other advantaged students, but also for other groups (such as the British Indian women discussed by Bhopal (2011)) – differential association may, in some cases, serve to perpetuate the disadvantage of those who come from less privileged backgrounds. Indeed, studies have demonstrated how friendship groups, within HE institutions, are often delineated along class lines, with those from working-class and middle-class backgrounds often remaining distant from one other. Keane (2011), for example, has shown how, in her research in an Irish HE institution, the non-traditional students were aware that they did not have access to the same economic or cultural resources as their middle-class counterparts. They were thus worried about being rejected as interlopers and, as a consequence, 'refused to engage in friendship-building with "other" students' (p. 455). For these students, Keane concludes, feeling subserviently positioned was a common experience.

Similar findings have emerged from US studies, which have pointed to the homogeneity of friendship groups on campus. Aries and Seider (2005), for example, have argued that many of the lower income students in their research 'felt their class backgrounds made it difficult for them to connect to the wealthy students' (p. 428), and frequently expressed feelings of inadequacy, inferiority and intimidation. In Stuber's (2011) research, about half her sample of working-class students felt well-integrated into campus life but the other half had experienced significant feelings of marginality during their time at HE and, for some of this group, such feelings were persistent and debilitating. While such marginality is often the result of dominant middle-class norms within educational institutions, Hurst (2007) has argued that working-class students' own understandings of class and inequality can affect their desire and willingness to integrate with other students. She contrasts those with strong understandings of structural inequality who develop 'loyalist' strategies, through which they retain close ties to their home culture, with those with more individualist understandings of inequality, who develop 'renegade' strategies to seek immersion in the middle-class culture of the college. In China, similar exclusions have been documented. Li (2013) has argued that students from less well-off, rural backgrounds often feel out of place at high-status Chinese universities when compared to their peers from urban areas – because of their lack of access to 'legitimate' cultural forms and their exclusion (and self-exclusion) from high-status societies and social activities.

While such studies from across the globe indicate the prevalence of 'differential association' and exclusion on the basis of social class within education institutions, there is evidence that the mechanisms through which this operates change over time. In his ethnography of an elite private school in the USA, Khan (2011) provides a fascinating account of how the class divide may be manifesting itself in a different way in contemporary education. He argues that the elite students in his study had incorporated some of the cultural attributes and tastes of less advantaged groups. He goes on to claim that this 'omnivorous consumption', as he calls it, develops within groups of elite students (and other elite groups) an ease of position and sense of indifference:

> It is as if the new elite are saying, 'Look! We are not some exclusive club. If anything we are the most democratised of all groups. We are as comfortable with rap as opera. We can dine finely or at a truck stop. We accept all!' Such an attitude makes it appear that privilege is obtained through democratic practices, not aristocratic exclusion. But these practices, this omnivorousness, become their own mark of distinction. (Khan, 2011, p. 152)

It is also worth interrogating the broader assumptions that are made within much of the academic literature on social class. Most scholars – either explicitly or implicitly – assume that social mobility through education is desirable and the social reproduction of the working class is problematic (reflecting the language used by many policymakers – as noted previously). While this does indicate a concern with working-class lives, as Lehmann (2014) observes, it also denies value to working-class perspectives per se. Such perspectives may then be passed on to students. Indeed, Lehmann notes that many of the working-class students in his research in a large Canadian university came to view the working-class friends and family who they had 'left behind' as 'narrow-minded, limiting, racist, sexist, and homophobic' (p. 13). He goes on to argue that:

> In the middle-class hegemony that defines university, we as academics do, of course, contribute to such views of success and failure, by elevating certain forms of cultural capital over others. Thus, rather than finishing university with a more critical understanding of the structural and cultural conditions of their former lives or those of their parents or old friends, the [working-class] students have joined a middle-class chorus that renders working-class knowledge and experience deficient if not pathological. (ibid.)

Similarly, it is notable that while research often documents the advantages that accrue to working-class students who secure access to elite educational institutions, the ways in which such institutions also benefit from the inclusion of such students (such as through increasing the diversity of life experiences and perspectives within the classroom) is rarely discussed (Reay et al., 2009).

Institutional habitus

In exploring how students' experiences of education can be affected by social class, research has also focused on the impact of what has been termed 'institutional habitus'. Reay and colleagues (2001) have defined this as the set of collective dispositions and practices that have been informed by an institution's past experiences, staff and pupils/students, which have an impact on an individual's behaviour. They suggest that institutional habitus is largely determined by intake characteristics (e.g. the social class of the pupils or students who attend the school or college), and so reinforces the class disposition of the majority/dominant group. Others have, however, contended that this relationship is more complex. Research conducted by Donnelly (2014) in three state schools has demonstrated that the collective dispositions and practices of a school can vary considerably, even when their intake characteristics are broadly similar. Drawing on Bernstein's concepts of 'classification' and 'framing', Donnelly argues that the schools in his study differed significantly in, for example, how strongly they framed messages about applying to Oxford or Cambridge: while one of the schools marked out a group of pupils as 'Oxbridge material' and encouraged them to apply, another similar school made no such interventions, and left students to decide for themselves whether they stood a realistic chance of gaining entry to a prestigious university. Thus, Donnelly argues schools can convey their own 'classed messages', which are not straightforwardly determined by the class composition of the student body.

The impact of institutional habitus is also well-illustrated in Ingram's (2009) study of working-class boys in Northern Ireland. She describes the very different habituses of the two secondary schools in which she conducted research (one a comprehensive school, the other an academically selective grammar school), and the influence these had on the working-class pupils who attended them. The grammar school habitus, Ingram contends, 'conveys an academic disposition rooted in middle class values' (p. 432) and did not recognise working-class culture. As a result, the working-class boys who attended this school felt considerable conflict between their own personal habitus and that of the school. They managed this tension by, for example, choosing to socialise with school friends in areas away from their home, to avoid being 'embarrassed' by the people in their local area. Indeed, these boys often came to hold ambivalent views about, or resist completely, their local identity. In contrast, however, the working-class boys who attended the secondary school in the research (who had typically either failed the exam to get into the grammar school or not been selected even to sit the exam) experienced less tension between their habitus and that of the school. This institutional habitus, Ingram notes, was much more accommodating of local culture and 'opposition to schooling was a taken-for-granted disposition' (p. 430). Here, institutional habitus is seen as relating much more closely to the class composition of the student body. It also reflects various previous studies – such as Jackson and Marsden's (1966) seminal study of *Education and the Working Class* – which have demonstrated that working-class culture is often pathologised in schools, particularly those that are academically selective (see also Kulz, 2017).

Transitions and destinations

While a focus on social class has constituted an important part of analyses of what goes on in educational institutions and how they are accessed, over recent years an increasing number of studies have also explored the impact of social class on transitions from schooling and HE into employment (see also Chapter 12). In relation to HE, non-traditional graduates (e.g. those who are the first in their family to have attended university) typically earn less and take longer to secure permanent employment than their peers from more privileged backgrounds (Thomas, 2005). Moreover, research by Macmillan and colleagues (2015) has indicated that there is a large socio-economic gradient in the likelihood of a recent graduate securing access to a managerial or professional job. In their data, 31 per cent of graduates from higher socio-economic groups obtained a 'top job' compared with 27 per cent from lower socio-economic groups. The difference by prior schooling is even starker: 40 per cent of privately educated graduates entered such jobs, compared with only 28 per cent of their state-educated peers. Some of the difference can be explained by educational factors such as level of academic attainment (pre-degree), type of university attended and degree subject. However, other factors are clearly at play. One common assumption is that graduates' social capital is significant. Watters (2016), for example, has argued that the correlation between elite schooling and access to high-status jobs can be explained by the 'old boys' networks' that connect the privately educated, and penetrate professions such as law, medicine, arts and media, finance and property management. Macmillan and colleagues' (2015) research also suggests that social networks are influential. However, they argue that, in their dataset, the kind of educational factors outlined above and differential use of social networks explain only part of the socio-economic difference. In accounting for the remaining difference, they suggest that aspects of cultural capital and economic capital are significant.

Qualitative research has certainly indicated that both forms of capital play an important role in transitions from HE into employment. Economic capital can enable young people to participate in unpaid (or low paid) internships on graduation which can, in turn, open up access to competitive jobs (Leonard et al., 2016). Bathmaker and colleagues (2013), for example, discuss the extent to which the graduates in their sample took up internships after completing their undergraduate degree and argue that there were 'numerous examples of class differences in the capacity to mobilise social and economic capital to considerable advantage' (p. 740). They go on to conclude that:

> Those in dominant and dominated positions are likely to remain so based on the capacity to generate and exploit differing capitals, with middle-class advantage over privileged access to capitals (through economic support from parents, through privileged networks, through long-term investment in leisure activities), meaning they can mobilise these to further weight the game to their advantage (p. 741).

Smetherham (2006) and Brown and Hesketh (2004) have also pointed to the impact of 'personal capital' (such as self-esteem and self-confidence) on securing employment, even for graduates with first-class degrees and from high-status universities. Such differences have been explained in terms of the propensity of graduate employers to recruit from an elite group (Browne, 2010) and the greater resources to which middle-class students have access (when compared to their working-class peers) to pursue various CV-enhancing activities (Stuber, 2009). Similar findings emerged from Rivera's (2015) detailed ethnography of recruitment to high-status graduate positions in the USA (in law, management consulting and investment banking). She shows how the ways in which graduate employers defined and evaluated merit were strong skewed in favour of those from economically advantaged families. Indeed, she argues that there is a 'double filter' on socio-economic status in the competition for top jobs and top salaries – first, because 'top firms' typically recruit only from elite institutions and such institutions are 'overwhelmingly homogeneous socioeconomically' (p. 273) and, second, because of the specific recruitment practices used. Rivera describes the latter in the following way:

> employers sought new hires who were not only capable colleagues but fun and exciting playmates. They distrusted résumés and often privileged their own personal feelings of comfort, validation, and excitement experienced during face-to-face interviews over identifying candidates with superior cognitive or technical skills. They did so not only to reduce uncertainty in a fast-paced, client-service environment but also to increase their personal enjoyment at work. In many respects, they hired in a manner more closely resembling the choice of friends or romantic partners than one resembling the rational model that sociologists typically posit. (p. 270)

Scholars have argued that neo-liberal discourses and practices are central to theorising these processes. In particular, they contend that the emphasis placed, by employers and those preparing young people for employment, upon neo-liberal attributes such as individualism, flexibility and self-sufficiency is strongly classed. Indeed, the neo-liberal self is argued to be not a universal subject position, but one which is 'highly exclusionary, modelled on a middle class, masculinised "rational" and strategising subject' (Allen et al., 2013, p. 434). Skeggs (2004) maintains that this model is 'mainly redundant for the working class' as they rarely have access to the same sites for optimising their own cultural capital. Moreover, while work placements – offered by schools and universities – can been seen as a means of reducing social inequalities, particularly if they are paid (Deakin, 2014), Allen and colleagues' (2013) study of placements offered by UK universities indicated that, for working-class students, some can exacerbate feelings of inferiority and lack of entitlement within the workplace. In their research, negative experiences during placements within creative industries deterred many students from working-class backgrounds from applying to this sector altogether. We return to these themes in Chapter 12.

While such effects by social class have been documented across the HE sector, some differences between institutions are also evident. Leuze (2011), for example, contends that the highly stratified nature of the UK HE system differentiates transitions into work more strongly than in other countries with less stratified systems. Research in other nations with marketised and hierarchical HE systems has also pointed to a relationship between university status and labour market outcome, with those who have attended lower status institutions disadvantaged (Gebel and Baranowska-Rataj, 2012; Li and Miller, 2013). Differences between labour markets are also important – with some nations (such as Germany) placing more emphasis on subject studied rather than institution attended. Waters' (2006) research in Hong Kong has suggested that we also need to pay attention to the transnational dynamics at play in graduate recruitment practices. In common with the argument developed by Rivera (2015), above, she suggests that the way in which educational credentials are evaluated is a subjective process. She shows how, in Hong Kong, the value of a degree obtained abroad depended, to a large extent, on whether or not the graduate was a member of an exclusive network of 'overseas' students and graduates. Within such networks (but not necessarily outside of them), an overseas qualification was seen to guarantee a wide range of embodied characteristics including fluency in English, an innovative approach to learning (rather than a commitment to rote learning) and better communication skills (by virtue of having a more 'free and open' style). Waters (2006) thus concludes that social capital played a key role in the recognition and valuation of cultural capital: 'The spatial proximity of a substantial cohort of overseas-educated graduates within the financial district of Hong Kong has enabled the easy exchange of participants' cultural capital into economic capital' (p. 187). Here, we see various arguments about the impact of globalisation, which were articulated in Chapter 4, played out.

Conclusion

This chapter is the first of four chapters that focus on the impact of particular social characteristics on education. It has explored the way in which class can affect access to education, experiences of education and routes from education into the labour market. Empirical evidence from various countries across the world was drawn upon to show that, despite education being opened up to many more people over the course of the past century, inequalities persist, with students from lower socio-economic backgrounds often facing substantial barriers to participation – commonly as a result of the exclusionary practices of other social groups and/or policies that advantage those with more social, economic and cultural capital. While this chapter has foregrounded differences by class, it is important to recognise the ways in which this particular social character-istic interacts with others, such as gender, ethnicity and age. Such interac-tions have been explored here (e.g. in relation to the ways in which ethnicity can help to structure social networks which, in turn, affect edu-cational decision-making); they will also be discussed explicitly in the fol-lowing three chapters.

6 GENDER AND SEXUALITY

Introduction

The impact of gender on education and learning more generally has been discussed for a considerable period of time. Indeed, during debates in the nineteenth century about the introduction of compulsory schooling, concerns were expressed about the inclusion of girls. In particular, it was believed by some that formal education may weaken girls' physical constitution or encourage them to abandon marriage and motherhood. As this chapter will demonstrate, gender has remained a controversial topic, particularly among policymakers, the media and other social commentators. From the 1970s onwards, it has also constituted an important area of academic enquiry (to the point where there are now whole journals devoted to the topic) – led, in large part, by feminist scholars. The chapter begins by considering the various ways in which gender has been theorised, and then moves on to explore two areas of long-standing concern to both academics and education practitioners – the gendered nature of many of the subject choices taken by pupils, and the links between gender and achievement. Here, the 'moral panic' over the alleged underachievement of boys is discussed in some depth, and similarities and differences across nation-states are identified. The chapter then explores the ways in which school can be considered a key site for the construction of both gender and sexual identities. It suggests that while the pressures of 'compulsory heterosexuality' are experienced by both boys and girls, they are often played out in rather different ways. The final sections of the chapter assess the impact of gender in relation to parents and parenting practices, and also teachers – in both schools and HE.

Theorising gender

Gender has been an important topic of scholarly enquiry since the emergence of second-wave feminism in the 1970s. While first-wave feminism (that occurred in the nineteenth and early twentieth centuries) focused on securing legal rights for women (particularly the right to vote), the emphasis within second-wave feminism was on a broader range of concerns including reproductive rights, family life, the workplace – and schooling. Nevertheless, gender has not always been theorised in the same way. The earliest studies that focused on differences between boys and girls within educational contexts tended to deploy biological explanations – for example, girls' under-representation in mathematics classes was seen largely as a problem residing in girls and their biological constitution, particularly their cognitive abilities (Mendick, 2005). By the 1970s, however, feminist scholars were arguing that gender differences could not be adequately explained on the basis of pupils' physical make-up, and that sociological explanations had to be brought into play. Thus, the concept of 'sex role socialisation' became dominant (Skelton and Francis, 2009). This was based on the idea that a child is taught a particular sex role by his or her parents, which is then reinforced by a range of other social actors – including friends, teachers and the media. Underpinning such theorisation is an understanding of the child as essentially distinct from the social world; someone who is acted *upon* (Mendick, 2005). More recently, post-structural approaches have contested this separation between the child and the social world, and argued that children play more active roles in the construction of gender (and sexual) identities than sex role theory would suggest. From this perspective, masculinity and femininity are viewed as fluid properties of *practices* rather than people (Butler, 1993), and children are seen as playing an active role in these practices (rather than just being socialised into pre-established gender roles). This has been vividly illustrated in Davies' (1989) research with pre-school children in which she read them feminist fairy tales and analysed their responses. The 4–5-year-olds in her study typically saw those characters who took up non-conventional gender roles in the tales (such as the assertive princess) as deviant and thus deserving of punishment. In this way, she argues, young children are actively involved in making gender and producing themselves as male or female. Many of the studies referred to in the rest of the chapter are informed by this post-structural approach in which emphasis is put on the practices of pupils themselves.

Subject choices

A key concern of feminist scholarship on education in the 1970s and 1980s was the gender-differentiated nature of subject choice, both within school and, subsequently, at college and university, with girls tending to choose arts and humanities subjects, and boys, science and mathematics (e.g. Burchell and Millman, 1989). This was seen as a particular concern for girls, as arts and humanities choices typically led to less secure and less well-remunerated careers. While there has been some progress in relation to encouraging young men and young women to pursue non-gender-stereotypical choices in compulsory schooling and beyond – for example, by requiring all students to take both science and arts subjects until they complete secondary education (Arnot et al., 1999) – stubborn differences remain. Perhaps most notably, in many countries of the world, women continue to be significantly less likely than men to pursue science, technology, engineering and mathematics (STEM) subjects beyond compulsory schooling (DiPrete and Buchmann, 2013). Although there are now relatively few differences in the attainment of boys and girls in school science (see discussion below), participation at degree level is strongly differentiated by gender (and also, to some extent, by ethnicity and class) in the Global North: young men from middle-class backgrounds, who are white or have South/East Asian heritage are those most likely to be found on science and engineering programmes (Francis et al., 2017).

In an attempt to explain the under-representation of young women in post-compulsory physics, in particular, Francis and colleagues draw on interviews they conducted with 15–16-year-olds and their parents (in the UK). The interviews indicated the dominance of three main discourses about women's entry to physics. First, just under a third of their student interviewees (and 18 per cent of parents) claimed there was nothing deterring women from pursuing physics, and believed that gender discrimination was a thing of the past; Francis and colleagues label this the 'meritocratic equality' discourse. In contrast, a third of young men and nearly two-thirds of young women thought that there *were* impediments to women's participation in physics, and drew on two main discourses to explain this. A discourse of gender discrimination was common, with many of the respondents believing that gender stereotyping, processes of socialisation, the trope of the 'male scientist' and concerns about 'standing out' because of being in a numerical minority all discouraged women from pursuing post-compulsory physics. Such comments underline the importance of paying attention to the ways in which particular subject areas are represented:

> The relentless repetition of images that present male bodies in association with Physics, and hence work to embody Physics as male in the public psyche, may be identified and critiqued by respondents, but are nevertheless hard to resist – and impact material practices by constituting and reinforcing Physics as masculine. (Francis et al., 2017, p. 168)

Here, Francis and colleagues argue that although young people may be aware of the problems with such images, they are nevertheless affected by them – because of their prevalence in various aspects of everyday life.

The other discourse that was drawn upon to explain why women were less likely than men to pursue physics focused on the construction of the subject as 'quintessentially masculine'. However, as Francis and colleagues explain, this discourse was made up of a number of quite distinct sub-narratives/beliefs, which included the following: certain subjects are gender-stereotyped as masculine or feminine, and thus are appropriate for different genders; men and women are 'naturally' drawn to different subjects; femininity is antithetical to (masculine) manual work (and engineering is associated with manual work); femininity is superficial – women are concerned with their appearance and grooming, and so do not want to get their hands dirty; and, finally, cleverness is masculine, and physics is a subject that can only be pursued successfully by clever people.

The authors note that the construction of physics as 'quintessentially masculine' is not new – it has been identified in previous research studies, and has proved resilient to wider changes to both the composition of the workforce and the patterns of achievement in compulsory education. Moreover, it engrains subject positions in which males are constructed as the subjects and females as 'others' (i.e. people who belong to a subordinate social category). Indeed, Francis and colleagues contend that a number of the sub-narratives listed above are:

> fundamentally intertwined, in turn, with discourses that produce femininity as dim, vane, inane and lacking in substance (Other). The counterside ... is of course the animation of the masculine (Subject) as profound, intelligent, reasoning – in other words, the production of intelligence, or cleverness, as masculine. (p. 169)

Here, Francis and colleagues argue that the way in which physics is talked about, and associated with masculinity and cleverness, has the effect of deterring girls from choosing it as an option. It is also, they suggest, part of a broader discourse in which things that are seen as feminine and/or associated with girls are positioned as of less value than those traditionally associated with boys. Very similar arguments are made in relation to the under-representation of young women in post-compulsory mathematics. Mendick (2005, 2013) maintains that mathematics, too, is discursively positioned as inherently masculine. Within the discourses dominant among her respondents (43 young people all studying post-compulsory maths), mathematics is understood as different from other subjects: 'it is certain, challenging, hard and unrelated to everyday life' (p. 245). Moreover, mathematicians are viewed as different from other people – 'they combine the flattering character of geniuses and heroes with the unflattering character of "nerds"' (ibid.). Thus, young women who pursue maths beyond compulsory schooling experience considerable tension – between, on one hand, engaging in a subject area that is culturally inscribed as masculine and, on the other hand, inhabiting a body that is discursively positioned as feminine.

Clearly, however, there are some young women who *do* pursue STEM subjects at degree-level (just as there are young men who take up subjects that are commonly constructed as feminine). Exploring the characteristics of these 'exceptions' is both interesting and important. The research discussed above, which explored the reasons why some young women are deterred from studying physics beyond compulsory schooling, also examined the characteristics of the relatively small number of young women in the sample (seven out of 70 interviewees – the total sample included a similar number of young men and young women) who did aspire to continue with physics (Archer et al., 2017). These participants were different from the others, Archer and colleagues contend, in both their performance of femininity and their possession and deployment of various capitals. Almost all of these 'exceptional' young women were highly competitive, and proud to be different from their peers. They had high levels of academic attainment, a well-established academic identity and access to considerable 'science capital' within their families. They also attended schools with a well-established science ethos and which provided strong encouragement to girls to pursue physics. They had both a preference for theoretical, rather than applied, physics, and what Archer and colleagues describe as a 'strategic view' about gender distinctiveness in relation to careers – by this they mean that, instead of being put off by the numerical dominance of men, they saw various advantages to being a numerical minority in relation to recruitment and promotion, for example. Together, these resources and identities gave the young women considerable resilience in the face of various challenges to their plans to pursue physics (not least the construction, described previously, of physics as both masculine and difficult). However, as Archer and colleagues make clear, such resources are not equally available to all young women; a 'physics identity' may be particularly hard for those from working-class backgrounds to attain.

Educational achievement

Alongside concerns about the impact of gender on choice of subjects, scholars have been interested in the ways in which gender influences the achievement of girls and boys. In the 1970s and 1980s, feminists highlighted girls' underachievement in relation to maths and science, in particular, and various initiatives were put in place to raise girls' performance in these areas (Skelton and Francis, 2009). At this time, subjects were also identified in which boys were performing less well than girls (most notably, literacy) (e.g. Lee, 1980). By the last decade of the twentieth century, in many countries of the Global North, patterns of both subject choice and educational attainment had changed considerably, with girls and women increasing significantly their participation in post-compulsory education and often 'overtaking' boys in formal examinations across a wide range of subjects. (It is important not to overlook, however, the different patterns of the Global South. Here, girls still lag behind boys in terms of educational participation.) Such changes were brought about, it is argued, by the influence of the women's movement and the greater participation of women in the labour market, as well as specific national reforms. In England and Wales, for example, Arnot and colleagues (1999) argue that although the policy changes introduced in the late 1980s by Margaret Thatcher's Conservative government were driven, in many ways, by Victorian values, they created the conditions for narrowing the gender divide in education. The introduction of a national curriculum required all schools to teach science, arts and a range of craft and design subjects to both sexes, while the shift to a more individualised, competitive system was, Arnot and colleagues contend, more successfully exploited by girls, which led to higher levels of attainment. (Similar arguments have been made in relation to recent reforms in China, and are discussed in more detail below.)

Such changing patterns have not, however, been uncontroversial. Despite the fact that the increased attainment of girls has not, in most parts of the world, resulted in similar 'over-performance' (or even equity) in the labour market (the gender pay gap remains significant), politicians, policymakers and the media have vocally expressed their concern about 'boys' underachievement'. This has been evident in countries as diverse as Australia, Barbados, Canada, Denmark, Germany, Japan, New Zealand and the USA (DiPrete and Buchmann, 2013; Moreau, 2011). In many anglophone countries, this has been aligned with broader concerns about a so-called 'crisis of masculinity', and seen by some as a backlash against feminism, in which boys' interests have been pitted against those of girls (Lingard et al., 2013). The 'underachievement' of boys has been explained by policymakers and the media, variously, as a result of the shortage of male teachers in schools (particularly at primary level); the lack of male role models for boys from single-parent families; and an alleged 'feminisation' of school values (which was said to undermine boys' sense of masculinity) (Epstein et al., 1998). Furthermore, a considerable amount of money has been directed to redressing this 'underachievement' by funding initiatives to, for example, encourage fathers to spend more time reading with their sons, introduce supposedly 'boy-friendly' teaching materials in schools and recruit more men into the teaching profession (see further discussion of this below and in Chapter 10).

There is now a large, international body of evidence, generated in the main by feminist scholars, that has contested many of the assumptions made by policymakers about 'boys' underachievement' and questioned the main parameters of the debate. This has argued that the gendered patterns of differential attainment (with girls 'outperforming' boys) are not as new as we might think – for example, in England, girls typically outperformed boys in the examination (the 'eleven-plus') that was sat to determine access to grammar schools in the 1950s and 1960s, while even during the 1970s and 1980s, more girls than boys secured five or more 'O-level' passes at grades A to C (Arnot et al., 1999; Cohen, 1998). Furthermore, researchers have argued that there is scant evidence that schools have become 'feminised'. Here, they have pointed out that, historically, the number of female teachers has, in most countries, typically been higher than the number of male teachers – but that this was not considered problematic until the 1990s. Women teachers also tend to be concentrated in less prestigious and less well-paid parts of the teaching profession. Moreover, many of the recent reforms to education, associated with New Public Management and high-stakes testing (see Chapters 3 and 9, respectively), are often seen as 'masculinist' in nature (Moreau, 2011), while there is little evidence that pupils look to teachers of the same sex to act as role models (Francis et al., 2008) (see Chapter 10). Perhaps most importantly, researchers have argued that the 'boys' underachievement' discourse draws on essentialist constructions of gender, and thus overlooks important differences between groups of boys and groups of girls. Attainment is differentiated by both social class and ethnicity, for example; thus, not all boys perform poorly, and not all girls do well (e.g. Francis, 2000; Skelton and Francis, 2009).

The socially constructed nature of the 'moral panic' over boys' underachievement is illustrated effectively in Moreau's comparison of policy and media discourse in England and France. She argues that, on the basis of PISA data (see Chapter 3), the performance of boys in the two countries is quite similar. If anything, it is lower in France (both in absolute terms and relative to girls). Nevertheless, the 'boys' underachievement' debate has been prominent only in England; it has not been a topic of concern to either the French media or French politicians. Indeed, Moreau notes that where gender is discussed in French national policy, it is in relation to initiatives to support girls – to help rectify what is perceived to be their disadvantage on entering the labour market and the difficulty of converting their educational capital into success in employment. Moreover, her research in schools indicated that 'boys' underachievement' was totally absent from the narratives of French school teachers, but a very frequent preoccupation of their English counterparts. In explaining the absence of a debate about boys' underachievement in France and yet its prominence in England, Moreau points to differences in national conceptions of citizenship. The British model of citizenship is, she suggests, multicultural, differentialist and liberal, and thus more likely to acknowledge differences between people (such as their gender). From this perspective, treating individuals differently is seen as fairer than treating them as the same. In contrast, the French concept of citizenship is republican and universalist. Individuals are, formally, given equal rights and treated in the same way; it is believed that gender, ethnicity and other social characteristics thus need to be put aside to become a French citizen. These different assumptions, Moreau argues, explain the national differences in relation to 'boys' underachievement'; in France, the universalist discourse has hindered the acknowledgement of individual differences. She notes, however, that other factors are also important – namely the construction of teachers' professional identities, and the function of schools and teachers. In France, because of a strong divide between the public and private spheres, teachers' professional identities are seen as closely related to their subject expertise rather than their personal characteristics (see discussion in Chapter 10). Thus, their gender, with respect to acting as a role model for their pupils, is viewed as irrelevant. In England, however, personal characteristics of teachers are perceived as more important, because their professional identity is considered to be an extension of their personal identity. Moreover, in France, within schools, policies and pedagogic practices 'tend to resist differentiation as part of a dominant vision of equality which associates fairness with "sameness"' (pp. 173–174). In summary, Moreau presents a compelling case to demonstrate how the construction of particular questions as 'policy problems' often bears little relation to what happens on the ground, and can often be explained, instead, by the broader societal context.

Somewhat similar arguments are made, with respect to Australia, by Lingard and colleagues (2013). They describe the impact of wider society and, in particular, the political allegiances of policymakers, on the (government-funded) research they conducted on the educational needs of boys. They argue that their research was commissioned, in the first place, as part of a strategy to 'contain' academic expertise that took a more socially critical perspective on boys, masculinity and schooling than that adopted by the government. They then go on to catalogue a variety of interventions from government officials intended to challenge the main arguments being developed by the researchers on the basis of their empirical data. These interventions included asking them to use more of the language of the original tender document (written by the government) in their reports; not publishing the literature review they produced (despite an initial commitment to do so); in advisory board meetings, treating media discourses (about boys' underachievement) as equivalent to rigorous, academic research (which contested many of the media claims); and asking them to take out of their final report specific evidence. Reflecting on this experience, Lingard and colleagues contend that at the heart of these challenges was a fundamental contestation about boys' education, and government officials' concern that their research was contrary to the 'feminisation of teaching' position, and the 'recuperative masculinity politics' (namely the desire to return to a 'golden time' before feminism) endorsed by the bureaucracy.

Gender and sexual identities

As noted above, one of the key critiques made by scholars of the moral panic over 'boys' underachievement' is that it fails to acknowledge differences *between* boys (e.g. related to social class and/or ethnicity) and, similarly, treats girls as a homogeneous group. Many boys (particularly those from white, middle-class families) continue to attain highly, while particular groups of girls (often those from working-class backgrounds) have performed markedly less well. Gender scholars have made a particular contribution in this area, by showing how pupil identities are affected by a range of social characteristics, which interact in complex ways, to effect experiences of education. Thus, it is highly problematic to assume that all girls' experiences of education are the same, just as it is erroneous to assume that all boys 'underachieve'. A very clear example of this complexity is provided by Reay (2001) in her ethnography of a primary class at a school in London. She argues that the girls in the class took up varied positions in relation to traditional femininities, which provided the basis for their friendship groups, and also had a profound effect on how teachers and other pupils saw them (and thus their experiences of the school). The 'nice girls' were mostly middle class, hardworking and well-behaved, while the 'girlies' were working class, emphasised their femininity and were active in reinforcing heterosexual norms within the classroom through, for example, writing love letters and flirting. (These two groups were named by other members of the class, not the girls themselves.) Reay maintains that, despite their differences, both groups were subject to discourses of denigration: the boys and some of the girls positioned the 'nice girls' as boring and the 'girlies' as stupid. Reay notes that the 'working class discourse of conventional femininity within which [the "girlies"] were enmeshed operated to elide their academic achievement within the peer group' (p. 159). The third group of girls, who called themselves the 'spice girls', were similar in many ways to the 'girlies' but were feistier and not afraid to challenge some of the boys within the class. However, while similar behaviour on the part of boys was, Reay suggests, not seen by teachers as problematic, the activities of the 'spice girls' were viewed as inappropriate and counterproductive to learning. Finally, Reay identifies the 'tomboy' in the class, arguing that her performance of a 'surrogate masculinity' (e.g. playing football, climbing trees) was accorded prestige in the classroom – thus solidifying rather than challenging the gender divide. While Reay's ethnography illustrates well the different subject positions girls can take up within education – and how they are often informed by social class – it also demonstrates how femininity is frequently denigrated and being a boy is commonly viewed as a preferable subject position.

The importance of heterosexual norms, mentioned by Reay above, is explored further by Renold (2000, 2001, 2002) in a series of papers on primary school children and their sexual identities. She argues that the primary school is a key site for the production of such identities – and that hegemonic forms of both masculinity and femininity involve the presumption of heterosexuality. Moreover, children should be understood as active agents in processes of gender identity construction. On the basis of ethnographic research, she maintains that both boys and girls within the primary school are subject to the pressures of compulsory heterosexuality, but that it is played out in different ways for the two groups. Like the 'girlies' and 'spice girls' in Reay's study, the majority of the girls observed and interviewed by Renold also produced their femininity through dominant notions of heterosexuality – 'policed through surveillance of their own and others' bodies and behaviours' (2000, p. 323). Moreover, she notes that the girls who rejected 'girlie' hyper-femininity – wearing, for example, trainers rather than high heels, and shorts rather than mini-skirts – appeared to be successful in being seen as sufficiently feminine only when they engaged in competent heterosexual performances and relationships:

> Girls who resisted hyper-feminine discourses but who did not engage in heterosexual practices or who were not positioned as heterosexually desirable were denigrated and rendered 'non-girls', signified by insults such as 'weirdo' and even 'boys'. (p. 317)

While the boys in Renold's research were subject to the same pressures to conform to heterosexual norms, they had a wider variety of routes available to them to achieve this; playing football and fighting other boys were both seen as alternative signifiers, for example. Nevertheless, the pressures on them were not insignificant. Those who did not engage in football or fighting often received heterosexist and homophobic insults, and were ostracised from the other boys.

Constructions of hegemonic masculinity are often related, not just to compulsory heterosexuality, but also particular orientations to school work. Various studies have shown how boys frequently have to negotiate the often-competing demands of masculine peer group cultures, on one hand, and 'good student' subjectivities, on the other (Mac an Ghaill, 1994; Willis, 1977). Those who choose to prioritise the former – engaging in 'lad' behaviours (Jackson, 2002), for example – can end up in conflict with teachers. Renold's (2001) work has shown how these tensions emerge early on in schooling, and are frequently associated with assumptions about hegemonic masculinities. She documents a wide range of strategies that were used by the 10–11-year-old boys in her ethnography to avoid what were perceived as 'non-masculine' behaviours and/or disguise their academic success. These included teasing or even bullying other boys who were not investing in hegemonic masculinities, playing down their own academic achievement, and devaluing girls' school work by labelling their achievements as failures. She contends that while, on the surface, many of the boys in her research displayed what appeared to be a coherent and consistent masculinity, they were often 'engaged in an ongoing struggle to negotiate playground and class room hierarchies' (p. 381). Such tensions become particularly acute in secondary school, when academic demands typically step up. The 'academic achievers' in Mac an Ghaill's (1994) research, for example, were positioned as effeminate and bullied by other boys because of their commitment to school work and investment in non-hegemonic masculinities. Moreover, in Renold's (2001) study, high-achieving boys increased their involvement in dominant masculine pursuits such as football and fighting at this time as a means of ensuring they were not seen by peers as 'sissies'. Indeed, researchers from across the world have shown how pupils who do not conform to hegemonic sexual and gender identities can experience both harassment and bullying. For example, drawing on a survey of over 1,300 students in California schools, Thompson and colleagues (2013) argue that 'the vast majority of students are subject to some form of gender harassment at some time (sexual harassment, homophobic epithets, etc.), that the vast majority of such attacks are witnessed by other students, and that they are a regular occurrence' (p. 163). Thus, they conclude, they should be not viewed as isolated experiences but rather part of the everyday fabric of school life.

As some of the discussion above attests, schools can often be seen as homophobic spaces, in which homosexuality is constructed by some pupils as a deviant form of masculinity (Epstein and Johnson, 1998). However, there is now some evidence of change, albeit from a relatively small number of studies. McCormack and Anderson (2010), for example, have argued that within the school sixth-form in which they conducted research there was considerable evidence of inclusive practices among the boys. These young men (aged 16–18) typically espoused pro-gay attitudes and had eliminated homophobic language from their conversations. McCormack and Anderson contend that this permitted 'an expansion of heteromasculine boundaries', enabling the boys to be physically tactile with one another and express emotional intimacy without 'being homosexualised' by their behaviours. However, they also note that, even in this more inclusive context, processes of heteronormativity remain – for example, because of the lack of homophobia in the school, boys were perceived as gay only if they identified as such – thus it was assumed that all other boys were heterosexual.

Change in gender/sexual identities has also been noted in relation to some (but not all) high-achieving girls. Kim and colleagues (2017) have maintained that, in China, as a result of economic restructuring (primarily the shift to a service economy, in which flexibility is valued highly) and the country's One Child Policy (which encouraged families with a single daughter to invest heavily in her education and preparation for employment), many young women have taken on more flexible gender identities. They are thus, Kim and colleagues contend, more open to taking jobs in male-dominated sectors of the economy, and following their own interests rather than limiting themselves to gender-stereotyped jobs. Men's gender identities and career pathways have not undergone a similar degree of change. Within the Welsh context, Renold and Allan (2006) distinguish between two ways in which the high-achieving girls in their study negotiated their identity. The first approach, which they call the 'feminine-ization' of success, is largely in line with some of the findings discussed above. Here, the girls were concerned to ensure that their academic success did not interfere with their performance of normative femininity. However, the second approach – the '(post) feminist-ization' of success – is rather different. Girls in this group appeared happy to either abandon normative conceptions of femininity or rework traditional feminine traits and incorporate, for example, 'girliness' and hyper-femininity, as part of a new 'super girl' identity (see also Harris, 2004, with respect to the Australian context).

Many of the issues discussed above, in relation to school pupils, are reflected within HE. For example, although women now outnumber men in most HE sectors (Eurostudent, 2015), universities can still be experienced as 'masculinist' spaces (Read and Kehm, 2016). Dominant discourses within HE, across many countries, have tended to construct the 'ideal learner' in limited and masculinist terms – as 'male, white, middle class and able-bodied, an autonomous individual, unencumbered by domestic responsibility, poverty or self-doubt' (Leathwood and O'Connell, 2003, p. 599). These constructions are often then internalised by those who are positioned as 'other' within the discourse (Burke, 2006; Read et al., 2003). Moreover, it is argued that the academic culture which often follows from this view of the 'ideal learner' frequently privileges traits commonly seen as 'masculine' such as boldness, individualism and competitiveness (Read et al., 2003) (this is discussed further in Chapter 12).

Sexual harassment and sex education

Masculinised academic cultures can also give rise to the sexual harassment of female students (by male staff and fellow students). In the UK context, this has been evidenced by the work of Phipps and Young (2015). Over two-thirds of the women HE students who responded to their survey had been subject to conduct such as banter, wolf-whistling, catcalling and groping, and at least half of these specified that this had caused discomfort. Phipps and Young argue that such behaviour is shaped, at least in part, by the economistic discourses that are now dominant in UK HE (see Chapter 12). More specifically, they suggest that the environment of the marketised university is based on a culture that foregrounds 'having' or 'getting' (grades and/or jobs) and such values have been taken up by students and informed their wider beliefs and behaviours. Reflecting on their interviews with women students, Phipps and Young write, 'Ideas about "having" – mainly related to [men having] women – were central, with [one] interviewee relating how girls were "passed round friendship groups" and "everyone [had] a go", and describing a "concept of ownership" which meant that once a girl had slept with a "lad", he automatically had "a right to sleep with her again" regardless of whether she wanted to' (Phipps and Young, 2015, p. 314). Such evidence is not confined to the Global North. Indeed, Morley's (2011) research in Ghana and Tanzania has argued that gender and status inequalities are such that some male academics consider it a right to demand sex from female students in return for grades. Moreover, she shows how the construction of female sexuality as a commodity in this way produces negative female learner identities. If female students fail, their performance is attributed to their lack of academic ability; if they succeed, it is seen as a result of their 'favoured' position in commodified academic markets. Morley concludes that:

> Sexual harassment marks out the territory as male, and regulates female agency and visibility. It appears to be a low-risk, high reward activity [for men] that validates masculinity and patriarchal power relations. It also re-inscribes and reduces women's identities as bodies when they dare to enter the life of the mind. (p. 113)

Some scholars – and others who work in the HE sector – have called for educational interventions to address such issues, as well as broader rethinking of institutional cultures. Nevertheless, sex and relationship education (SRE) is not always a panacea. Research has shown how, in some cases, such interventions can serve to further entrench gender inequalities. Sundaram and Sauntson (2016), for example, argue that the SRE curriculum in England tends to construct sex as risky and dangerous, particularly for young women, positioning women as objects of sexual pleasure and men as recipients and enactors of sexual pleasure. Young women are thus encouraged to see themselves as potential victims and sexual objects, rather than as sexual subjects who have a right to seek pleasure in the same way as their male counterparts –

with serious implications, Sundaram and Sauntson suggest, for young people's understandings of sexual choices, rights, consent, harassment and violence.

Parents and parenting

Gender is also relevant to an analysis of parenting practices, with respect to education. Although there is now robust evidence that fathering practices have changed, and many men are considerably more involved with their own children than their fathers were with them (e.g. Dermott, 2008), a large number of studies have indicated that a significant proportion of 'educational labour' continues to fall to mothers, rather than fathers. While fathers are now often keen to have an emotionally close relationship with their children, they are more reluctant to take on the work of organising and managing their children's lives (including liaising with teachers and overseeing homework), and so such activities are typically picked up by mothers (Miller, 2011: Vincent, 2017) (although see Posey-Maddox (2017) for an interesting example of the close involvement of some black fathers in their children's education). Such enduring gender differences have been noted in relation to processes of school choice, and also of providing support throughout a child's education. In relation to the former, various studies of secondary school choice have indicated that, in both working-class and middle-class families, it is mothers who typically take responsibility for collecting information about local schools, organising visits and talking to children about their preferences (Brantlinger et al., 1996; Reay and Ball, 1998). Similar patterns have emerged with respect to both pre-school provision and primary schools (e.g. Vincent and Ball, 2001). Scholars have pointed out, however, that while mothers appear to be carrying out the majority of the 'labour', fathers often retain considerable power in relation to the final choice of school (Reay and Ball, 1998). There is some evidence that similar gender disparities remain at later stages of education, too (although see Brooks (2004) for a different perspective). Indeed, Ball (2003) has argued that middle-class mothers, in particular, play an important role in maintaining their class advantage. He contends that nearly all the middle-class mothers in his research on university choice:

> were involved in visiting universities with their children. They also telephoned higher education institutions on behalf of their children and collected brochures and various kinds of 'hot knowledge'. Mothers and daughters, less so mothers and sons, represented choosing as a joint exercise. (p. 105)

Drawing on data from the same study, David and colleagues (2003) note that there were clear differences between the close and detailed involvement of the mothers and the more distant role of the fathers.

When we turn to parental involvement in education, once a child has started at a particular school, gender differences are again evident (e.g. Lareau, 1989; Vincent, 2000). Indeed, Walkerdine and colleagues (2001) have argued that the degree of congruence between the mothering practices of different social classes and the dominant culture of schools has a strong bearing on the likelihood of educational success. They write: 'it is a woman's domestic labour that produces what counts as natural and normal development and that women have been regulated very strongly as mothers, having the responsibility to produce normality, correct development and educational success' (p. 114). Reay (1998) has developed a similar argument, maintaining that it is women who 'make cultural capital work' for their children, by playing an active role in making links between the home and what goes on in the classroom. They, rather than fathers, are also the ones who take on responsibility for monitoring their child's progress, and for initiating contact with teachers, when they consider it to be necessary. (However, important class differences are played out in such practices, with middle-class mothers more likely than their working-class peers to have the social and cultural resources to facilitate such interventions – see Chapter 5.)

These types of mothering practice – evident across many countries of the Global North – have often been discussed in relation to the rise of 'intensive mothering' (Wall, 2010). This form of parenting 'requires the mother to take on complete responsibility for all aspects of children's cognitive, emotional and physical development. It requires a centring of children and their needs in family life, accompanied by a considerable degree of maternal self-sacrifice' (Braun et al., 2008, p. 545). It has been associated with what Lareau (2003) has called the 'concerted cultivation' of a child through not only intervening in their formal education, but ensuring they have access to a wide range of extra-curricular learning opportunities – for example, through sports, music and art lessons (producing what Vincent and Ball (2007) have termed the 'Renaissance child'). In many affluent countries, intensive mothering is commonly positioned not just as one of several possible approaches to parenting, but the moral choice, the way one *ought* to parent (Vincent, 2017). Vincent (2017) has argued that, across the Global North, intensive mothering has become normalised as a parenting strategy for all – pervading TV programmes, parenting guides and a whole range of child-focused services, as well as education policy. It is underpinned, she contends, by neo-liberal norms, in which parents are expected to act in individualised and competitive ways, to produce children who are self-sufficient and self-regulating, and who achieve highly both in school and in a range of extra-curricular pursuits. Gambles' (2010) analysis of the popular TV programme *Supernanny* supports this thesis – showing how the problems parents face are typically individualised, and mothers, in particular, are expected to work on themselves and their parenting practices in order to improve outcomes for their children. While all women can be adversely affected by such discourses, those who are working class may find it virtually impossible to adhere to such norms – often lacking the money to take their children to extra-curricular activities, and the time to be physically present at their child's school (Gambles, 2010; Vincent, 2017).

Similar issues have been raised in relation to (HE) students who are themselves parents. Research has indicated that while female 'student-parents' typically experience considerable difficulties combining study with looking after their children, their male counterparts, while far fewer in number, appear to face a significantly smaller number of problems (Brooks, 2012). In large part, this disparity was due to the different expectations of the men and women: while many of the men (and their families) appeared to treat study as akin to work and thus devoted long hours to their degrees, the women typically had to juggle their studies alongside care for their children – and so experienced considerable guilt at not spending enough time with their children and/or on their academic work (Brooks, 2015). While similar findings about the pressures on student-mothers have emerged from various anglophone nations, including the USA (Lynch, 2008), New Zealand (Longhurst et al., 2012) and the UK (Brooks, 2012, 2015; Marandet and Wainwright, 2010), there is some evidence of variation by welfare regime. For example, the experiences of male and female student-parents in Denmark – where childcare is cheap and plentiful, and there no strong societal expectations that mothers of young children will stay at home to care for them – were much more similar (Brooks, 2013). Moreover, none of the Danish student-mothers reported any feelings of guilt at not spending more time with their children (Brooks, 2015). While discourses of 'intensive mothering' are common across the Global North, this evidence suggests they are not yet played out in all geographical contexts.

Teachers

Gender is relevant, not just to the identities, experiences and choices of pupils and students, but also to those of teachers (see Chapter 10). Indeed, the discussion above about 'boys' underachievement' made reference to perceptions of policymakers and the media that the teaching workforce has become more 'feminised'. In the ensuing debates, conducted across numerous anglophone nations, the gender of teachers has been a particularly prominent theme. However, as Mills and colleagues (2004) have argued, the way in which gender has been discussed by policymakers and social commentators has often been highly problematic. Their analysis of an Australian policy document, ostensibly focused very directly on gender – the state of Queensland's 'Male Teachers' Strategy' – highlights how many key issues relating to how gender is played out in schools (particularly, in relation to the disadvantage of women) remained unaddressed, and the ways in which essentialist readings of both femininity and masculinity are propagated. For example, they argue that the promotion of male role models within the document is driven by both a misogynist culture of blame that attributes boys' lack of success in school to female teachers and 'feminised' forms of pedagogy and 'recuperative masculinity politics'. Furthermore, they maintain that the implication in the document that only male teachers can discipline boys effectively promotes a deficit view of female teachers in which their behaviour management skills are brought into question. The document's more general emphasis on men's responsibility for bringing up sons, rather than for child-rearing per se, tends, Mills and colleagues assert, to shore up the hegemony of traditional masculinities rather than help to construct new ones. Such essentialist assumptions about gender 'are unlikely to construct a re-culturing of the school environment that enables men to perform non-traditional masculinities or to slow down the escalation of men out of the classroom into management' (p. 365).

Similar arguments have also been made in relation to the culture inhabited by HE staff. Female academics remain under-represented in higher status jobs in the academy – including more senior academic positions (such as full professor) and in senior management (Read and Kehm, 2016). Masculinist discourses operate in relation to staff, too – for example, normalising high workloads and assuming total commitment to the workplace, and thus overlooking the caring responsibilities of many female (and some male) staff (Acker and Armenti, 2004). Because of the strong construction of the university as a meritocracy, and the adoption of 'gender-blindness' in the name of fairness, individuals are commonly judged solely on their performance, and differences in their capacity to perform (as a result of caring responsibilities, time taken on maternity leave, etc.) are discounted (ibid.). Reflecting the discussion about 'student-parents' above, Raddon (2002) has described how the discourses of 'good mother' and 'successful academic' are in many ways contradictory – as they make very different assumptions about how women should spend their time. Moreover, research has indicated that female staff can be discriminated against in measures used to evaluate performance – particularly when students are asked to rate their teaching (MacNell et al., 2015; Wagner et al., 2016). As will be discussed again in Chapter 10, research has suggested that students tend to give male lecturing staff higher scores, irrespective of the actual quality of their teaching. Gendered assumptions also affect access to leadership positions. Cross-national research, conducted by Read and Kehm (2016), indicated that women were more likely to be promoted to the most senior management positions (such as vice-chancellor or rector) in smaller and less prestigious institutions than in bigger, elite universities – largely, they suggest, because of the way the 'prestige' economy within HE is gendered: women are much less likely to be perceived as an 'acceptable fit' in higher status institutions. Their research also emphasises some of the constraints faced by women who do secure senior leadership positions. All of their (female) respondents, who were vice-chancellors in either the UK or Germany, believed that it was harder for them than their male peers to become accepted as leaders, and that their dress, behaviour and general image were all scrutinised more intently. While Read and Kehm note that none of their respondents implied an essentialised relationship between leadership and gender, they highlighted the challenges they faced 'due to the interpretation of their practices as "other" to the discursively constructed norm of the embodied male leader' (p. 825). Further issues relating to the gender of teachers are covered in more detail in Chapter 10.

Conclusion

In this chapter, we considered the extent to which inequalities in access to and experiences of education are influenced by gender. The chapter argued that educational attainment and subject choice are both strongly patterned by gender. However, the nature of these patterns has changed over time – young women, in particular, have increased both their participation in education and their average level of attainment over recent decades. The chapter also explored the 'moral panic' which emerged in some countries (although not all) in relation to the alleged underachievement of boys, and noted the important questions raised by scholars about the validity of some of the associated claims about boys' performance. A key contention of researchers working in this area is that it is problematic to assume that all boys have similar experiences and/or that the experiences of all girls are homogeneous. Instead, they have pointed to the significant ways in which education is differentially experienced (and attainment differentially patterned) by ethnicity and class as well as gender. The means by which schools and other educational institutions can act as sites for the construction of particular gender and sexual identities were also discussed in some detail, with a particular focus on the pressures of what has been termed 'compulsory heterosexuality' evident even in primary schools. The chapter then shifted the focus from pupils to parents and teachers, and investigated the ways in which gender can affect the engagement of both groups with education. The impact of gender on the day-to-day work of teachers is developed further in Chapter 10.

7 RACE AND ETHNICITY

Introduction

Building on the previous two chapters, which explored social class and gender respectively, this chapter focuses specifically on race and ethnicity and their impact on experiences of education and patterns of attainment. The chapter first defines the terms race and ethnicity, and introduces the concept of Critical Race Theory (CRT), which underpins much recent scholarship. It then considers a number of particular areas in which experiences of education have been patterned by race, including the curriculum and methods of assessment; processes of teaching; and the training that is made available to teachers (both before they take up their first post and subsequently). The chapter next considers processes of ethnic mixing within educational institutions by exploring how these are affected by the perspectives of students and the processes of 'educational choice'. The chapter then assesses the extent to which practices of racialisation may be played out differently for 'domestic' and international students, before finally examining the experiences of *staff* who come from black and minority ethnic backgrounds.

The chapter draws primarily on material from nations in the Global North as it is here that the scholarship on race and ethnicity is most extensive. In large part, this is related to the dominance of white groups in such parts of the world. As will be discussed below, white privilege has had a profound effect on educational experiences, frequently working to disadvantage those from black and minority ethnic backgrounds. Research has played an important role in highlighting and challenging such forms of inequality. The literature on race and education is particularly extensive in the USA and has long been a key focus of American sociology of education. This is related closely to the nation's history and, in particular, the central role played by educational institutions in the segregation of ethnic groups from the nineteenth century to the second half of the twentieth century. In relation to contemporary concerns, however, there are strong similarities between social processes played out in the USA and elsewhere; a number of these are highlighted in this chapter.

Defining race and ethnicity

The term 'race' has a long history. Indeed, Biddis (1979, quoted in Meer, 2014) has noted that:

> Before 1800 race was used generally as a rough synonym for 'lineage'. But over the first half of the 19th [century] race assumed an additional sense that seemed, initially, tighter and more scientific. This usage was evident, at its simplest, in the growing conviction that there was a finite number of basic human types, each embodying a package of fixed and mental traits whose permanence could only be eroded by mixture with other stocks. (p. 114)

However, such biological approaches have now been undermined, not least through scientific research (Meer, 2014). Most sociological studies that have explored the ways in which educational experiences are differentiated by race have theorised race as a social construct, often drawing on the seminal work of Stuart Hall (1992). Thus, it is understood as an unstable concept, subject to transformation by political struggle, but having very real material and symbolic consequences (Archer and Francis, 2007). Such a perspective assumes that what we mean by 'racial differences' are socially constructed, perpetuated and reinforced by society (Rollock et al., 2015); it also informs much of what follows in the rest of the chapter. Alongside race, the chapter refers to the concept of ethnicity. This is understood as denoting real or imagined features of group membership, such as language, culture, religion and dress (Meer, 2014).

Research on race and education conducted from the latter part of the twentieth century onwards has been strongly influenced by CRT. This approach originated among legal scholars in the USA who believed that the campaign for racial equality had lost momentum, and the US legal system (and broader system of government) did not have either the capacity or the will to bring about substantial change. Instead, they offered a more profound critique of society, based on the following assumptions: racism is endemic to social life; power structures in society are based on white supremacy and white privilege; elites will support the advancement of blacks only if it furthers white self-interest; claims of neutrality, objectivity, meritocracy and colour-blindness should be treated sceptically; and eliminating racial oppression is part of a broader goal of ending all forms of oppression (Matsuda et al., 1993). Indeed, CRT suggests that the majority of racism is not noticed by most people, with only the crudest forms deemed problematic (Rollock et al., 2015). It was subsequently taken up across many disciplines and different national contexts and, within education, it became influential following the publication of an article by Ladson-Billings and Tate in *Teachers College Record* in 1995, entitled 'Toward a critical race theory of education'.

CRT also introduced the concept of 'whiteness' to analyses of race and ethnicity. This is a racial discourse that refers to a set of assumptions, beliefs and practices that place the interests and perceptions of white people at the centre of what is considered normal, but also avoids identifying with any racial experience or group – thus, unlike other racial groups, white people are not perceived and do not identify in terms of their race (Gillborn, 2005; Rollock et al., 2015). A key claim made by critical race theorists is that whiteness is associated with the power to exclude. As Ladson-Billings and Tate (1995) note in their seminal article, such exclusions can operate in different ways across different time periods and contexts. They write:

> In schooling, the absolute right to exclude was demonstrated initially by denying blacks access to schooling altogether. Later, it was demonstrated by the creation and maintenance of separate schools. More recently it has been demonstrated by white flight and the growing insistence on vouchers, public funding of private schools, and schools of choice. Within schools, absolute right to exclude is demonstrated by resegregation via tracking. (p. 60)

Here, they suggest that, by the end of the twentieth century, some of the neo-liberal reforms (discussed in Chapters 3 and 11) that aimed to promote a more market-based system, by encouraging parents to 'shop around' by using vouchers to fund schooling, for example, had a particularly adverse effect on black students. Since Ladson-Billings and Tate's work in the mid-1990s, a substantial literature has developed in the area of whiteness studies. This has shown how 'whiteness', like 'blackness', is a heterogeneous category, often riddled with diversity.

Many contemporary accounts that have explored the role of race within schooling have demonstrated how numerous recent policies have sustained racial inequalities. This can be seen in relation to school choice reforms, discussed explicitly later in this chapter, but also various initiatives introduced in the wake of terrorist attacks in the Global North. Students of Pakistani heritage, and others assumed to be Muslim, have come under increasing surveillance in schools and other educational institutions across Europe, the USA and Australia, while multicultural curricula in these countries have often been sidelined (Harris, 2013; Mirza and Meetoo, 2014; Shain, 2012). As noted in Chapter 2, in the UK, all teachers in state schools have, since 2014, been required to teach their pupils 'fundamental British values', supposedly to reduce the risk of pupils turning to radical Islam (Tomlinson, 2015). Although, as noted above, the majority of this chapter focuses on processes of racialisation within Western nations, and many studies discussed here focus on specific national contexts, Leonardo (2002) has argued that whiteness and the problem of white privilege transcend the nation-state, often allied to the global spread of capitalism. Strong commonalities can be seen across much of the empirical material discussed below.

Curriculum, assessment and attainment

As will be explored in more detail in Chapter 9, scholars from across the world have shown how inequalities by race and/or ethnicity have often been perpetuated through the curricula that is taught in schools, colleges and HE institutions, and the ways in which learning is assessed. In many cases, these have led to significant differences in attainment by ethnic group. Curricula have tended to favour dominant ethnic groups and marginalise the histories and contemporary experiences of those from non-dominant groups. One such example is the positioning of Aboriginal peoples within Canadian curricula. Despite an explicit call, in 2015, by Canada's Truth and Reconciliation Commission for Aboriginal contributions to Canadian society (in both the past and the present) to be made clear within textbooks and other curricular materials, analyses of texts carried out by Godlewska and colleagues (2016) suggest that, while there has been some reform, in general the curriculum still suffers from 'silences and lack of context, problematic placement and associations, the intrusion of settler perspectives' (p. 1) as well as various inconsistencies and contradictions with respect to the lives of First Nations, Métis and Inuit peoples. Similar findings have been documented with respect to other national contexts. Williams (2016), for example, argues that the physical education curriculum offered in many Australian schools is highly Eurocentric, despite the stipulation in national policy directives that Indigenous perspectives must be included. For example, in one of the schools in which he conducted his research, the importance of students participating in 'Australian cultural activities' was emphasised, including football, swimming and annual carnivals. Moreover, the state-produced list of 40 sports considered 'essential and worthwhile' to teach in schools, analysed by Williams, was made up entirely of non-Indigenous sports and physical activities. Aboriginal games such as buroinjin (running and ball passing) and jillora (ball spinning) were notable by their absence.

In England, research on black history has made similar arguments, contending that it fundamentally fails to meet the needs of black and minority ethnic students. Despite an official requirement that all schools should provide a broad and balanced history curriculum that responds to the diverse needs of children from different backgrounds, there is compelling evidence that this vision is rarely realised (e.g. Doharty, 2015; QCA, 2005). Doharty (2015) argues that an explicit commitment to improve the teaching of black history (on the part of the public body responsible for the school curriculum) became overshadowed by wider political fears about multiculturalism, Islamist infiltration of British schools and 'home-grown' terrorists. As a result of such concerns, the history curriculum came to be seen by politicians as a key means of promoting the 'fundamental British values' mentioned previously. A very traditional history curriculum was thus developed, 'promoting an exclusivist version of British history, culture and identity' (Doharty, 2015, p. 51). Doharty also contends that, when black history does appear in the curriculum of English schools, it tends to fall into one of two camps: it is positioned either in opposition to whiteness (e.g. compared negatively with white 'advancement' during the Enlightenment), or as part of a celebratory and congratulatory story (such as about the abolition of slavery and the success of the civil rights movement in the USA). Moreover, she argues that the way in which black history is taught differs significantly from white history. Here, she draws on her fieldwork in English schools to show how black history was often 'performed' (e.g. through children having to act out being part of a slave auction), and thus not afforded the same respect, tolerance or depth as white history (the Holocaust, in contrast, was taught through sombre reflection, not dramatic performance). Similar arguments have been made in relation to the curriculum offered by HE institutions – articulated particularly clearly in the UK by students who have campaigned under the slogan 'Why is my curriculum white?' (Hussain, 2015). (Chapter 9 provides other examples of how particular groups can remain marginal to, or even wholly absent from, formal curricula.)

Differential rates of educational attainment by ethnic groups have been evident in many countries of the world, and concerns about these have often driven changes to assessment practices – including the 'high-stakes testing' that has been introduced in the USA, the UK, Australia and various other nations (see Chapter 9 for further details). (It is interesting to note that in France, however, data are not collected on academic performance by ethnic group on the basis of the belief that individuals should not be judged on the basis of their skin colour.) For example, in the USA, black and Hispanic students generally score lower than white students (National Center for Education Statistics, 2011). Indeed, in 2011 national mathematics assessments carried out during Grade 8 (when students are around 13 years old), black students scored on average 31 points lower than their white counterparts, and Hispanic students 23 points lower (on a 500-point scale) (ibid.). The 'No Child Left Behind' programme, which was introduced in the USA in 2002, focused explicitly on the differential performance of ethnic groups and introduced a raft of measures intended to close the racial/ethnic achievement gap. These included providing strong incentives to encourage schools to focus more closely on the test scores of *all* their pupils; requiring higher levels of teacher qualification; and facilitating school choice (Darling-Hammond, 2007) (see Chapter 9 for further details). However, research from across the USA has shown how these measures were often counter-productive, harming the very children they were intended to help. For example, an increased focus on test scores led to a narrowing of the curriculum (making it less likely that black history, for example, would be taught), while schools became more likely to exclude low-performing students so as to maximise their average score. Moreover, the 'No Child Left Behind' programme failed to redress inequalities in schools' resources and staffing – with those serving poor children and minority ethnic groups typically having fewer resources and less well-qualified staff than other schools (Darling-Hammond, 2007).

In England, pupils of Indian and Chinese heritage have consistently outperformed their white counterparts for many years, and the performance of black Caribbean and Pakistani groups has improved significantly over the past decade (Alexander et al., 2015). Nevertheless, the average performance of those from a black Caribbean or Pakistani background remains lower than that of most other ethnic groups (DfE, 2015). There is also variation by ethnic group in relation to academic progress over time, which shows rather different patterns. For example, Burgess (2015) has explored the progress pupils make between the age of 11 and 16. He notes that Indian and Chinese students do well – as they also do in relation to absolute levels of attainment at 16. However, various groups that perform less well in absolute terms at 16, score highly in terms of their progress. These include those of Bangladeshi, Pakistani and black African heritage. The worst performing group according to this measure is white British. Thus, he concludes, most black and minority ethnic children start secondary school, on average, some way below white children but, over their secondary education, catch up totally or partially, or overtake white students. Burgess suggests that these patterns are likely to be explained by, first, the high aspirations held by non-white groups. Drawing on longitudinal survey data, he argues that much higher fractions of non-whites typically want to stay on at school beyond compulsory education than would be expected from their prior attainment levels. Second, he suggests that some of the progress may be related to immigrants (who constitute a significant number of some minority ethnic groups) improving their English language over the course of their secondary education.

An alternative perspective on this English attainment data is provided by Gillborn (2015). He argues that media stories about the improvements in educational performance by some black and minority ethnic groups have constructed whites as victims, which have fed into wider discourses about the failure of the 'white working class'. He argues that government attention has typically focused on the (relatively) poor performance of whites at GCSE (the exams taken by all 16-year-olds in England and

Wales) rather than the groups that do even less well (such as Pakistani, black Caribbean and Mixed Race). Moreover, Gillborn is also critical of the government's use of the performance of those entitled to 'free school meals' (FSM) as a key indicator. He contends that while only about 14 per cent of the school population (in England and Wales) is eligible for FSM, the government frequently assumes an equivalence between being working class and in receipt of FSM. Thus, 'By referring to FSM data as if it described the working class … an enormous mis-representation is taking place. Up to 60 per cent of the population will read the headlines about "white working class failure" and imagine incorrectly that it means their children' (p. 7). Constructing white people as victims in this way, he argues, has a clear impact on policy: concerns about race equality can come to be seen as irrelevant, damaging or even racist, informing decisions to cut funding for race equality initiatives and programmes to recruit more black and minority ethnic teachers.

While the educational performance of black and minority ethnic pupils in England may have improved over recent years, it is not the case that this always converts into labour market advantage. Lee (2015) has shown that although, in the UK, minority ethnic groups are not behind whites in degree-level education (e.g. those of black African, Indian and Chinese heritage are more likely than whites to have a degree), they suffer a double disadvantage in the labour market – finding it more difficult to both secure jobs and advance within them. Lee cites data on unemployment from the 1980s to early 2010s to show that, for example, Chinese men were twice as likely as white men to have degree-level education, and yet had unemployment rates 5 per cent higher than their white peers. Furthermore, black and minority ethnic groups are also under-represented at high-status universities in the UK and on apprenticeship schemes (Alexander et al., 2015; Boliver, 2016).

Schools, teachers and teaching

There is evident diversity in school responses to issues related to race and ethnicity – even among those who set out to adopt an explicitly anti-racist approach. Doharty's (2015) research highlights the limited way in which some English institutions have approached anti-racism. One of the schools in her sample, for example, produced diversity statements and anti-racist policies, but saw them as the only necessary measure of equality within the school. She notes that, in this school, 'racism is falsely believed to be one-dimensional and the result of ignorance, rather than multi-faceted, multi-layered and deeply embedded within the school environment – including the curriculum' (p. 53). In the American school that is the focus of Meshulam and Apple's (2014) analysis, there was evidence of a more thorough-going understanding of racism, and an attempt to instil anti-racist approaches across all activities. Indeed, the school was well-known for its attempt to build and sustain a socially transformative education that challenged historical patterns of dominance and subordination along racial lines. It ran two flagship programmes: one focused on promoting English and Spanish bilingualism, the other critical multiculturalism (allied to overtly anti-racist goals). However, as Meshulam and Apple describe, the school's anti-racist work became increasingly hard to sustain as a result of the changing policy context. More specifically, following budget cuts (introduced as part of a drive to improve 'efficiency' in the local area), the funding the school received was reduced and it had to make difficult choices about which activities it would sustain. The school decided to prioritise its bilingual programme rather than its multicultural initiatives because of the popularity of the former among middle-class parents who valued the cultural capital that would accrue from their children learning Spanish. As a result, jobs associated with the bilingual programme were ring-fenced, while some on the multicultural programme were lost. Priority was given to employing bilingual teachers and, as the school found it near-impossible to find African-American staff fluent in Spanish, African-Americans became marginalised among the staff, ultimately occupying only low-wage positions, such as cook and cleaner. These changes also affected the school's enrolment: the number of African-American pupils declined considerably, while the number of white English-speakers and native Spanish-speakers rose. Meshulam and Apple (2014) conclude by observing that 'the needs of two-way bilingualism … effectively stripped the African-American community of its recognition as a distinct political and cultural … group at the school' (p. 664). This example also illustrates well Leonardo's (2002) point about the ways in which whiteness and capitalism are often intertwined: 'efficiency' cuts became translated, quite quickly, into the marginalisation of black students.

Research has indicated that racial inequalities are, in addition, often played out because of the practices of individual teachers at classroom level. Some teachers adopt a 'colour-blind' perspective, which assumes that all students should be treated the same way irrespective of their race/ethnicity. However, such approaches tend to compound teachers' ignorance about racism, the ways in which it operates and how policy and practice can serve to embed dominant, and often discriminatory, discourses (Lander, 2015). For example, Uy (2016) describes how ethnic identity was very important to the experiences of the Southeast Asian Americans in her research, who often focused on the language, religion and food that differentiated them from other Americans. However, they were frequently overlooked or ignored by teachers, who typically thought ethnic identities were not relevant in the classroom – leading the students to feel considerable frustration with their education, as they believed key elements of their identity were not valued.

There is now also a large body of evidence from the USA, the UK and other countries that has demonstrated how teachers have often underestimated the level of academic performance of black and minority ethnic pupils. In the USA, Leonardo and Grubb (2014) have argued that as a result of separation into different-ability 'tracks' (often based on teacher judgements), 'Whites and Asian Americans have upwardly mobile educational experiences, whereas Latinos and Blacks find themselves in lower tracks where they and their teachers have both lower social status and less access to higher-status knowledge' (p. xi). In the UK, black children have been disproportionately placed in lower ranked teaching groups – because, it is argued, teachers are unduly influenced by stereotypes about 'black underachievement', and make judgements about black pupils on the basis of behavioural and attitudinal issues rather than their academic ability (Crozier, 2005; Maylor, 2014). Assumptions are frequently (and erroneously) made that black and minority ethnic students come from families that lack cultural capital and are not supportive of education (Maylor, 2014). Moreover, in the USA and the UK, increasing forms of segregation over recent years have disproportionately affected black pupils, as they are less likely than their white peers to gain access to groups for the 'gifted and talented' and schools that select by aptitude (Gillborn, 2015; Leonardo and Grubb, 2014). Moreover, black pupils tend to be disciplined more severely than their white peers, and their behaviour more heavily policed (Kulz, 2014). They are also more likely than whites to be expelled from school (Gillborn, 2015; Leonardo and Grubb, 2014). Relatedly, black and minority ethnic pupils with special educational needs have often found it hard to gain formal recognition of their difficulties within schools. Research has shown that even relatively advantaged middle-class groups can face substantial hurdles. Rollock and colleagues (2015) argue that 'disability' 'continues to operate as a racialised barrier to equity in English schools' (p. 95). Many of the black parents in their study recounted experiences in which their concerns about their child were dismissed. Even in cases where they had secured specialist assessment of special educational needs from external sources, their respondents described how teachers often discounted such evidence, arguing instead that the child was not working hard enough or just had limited talents. Two exceptions to this general pattern emerged in their dataset – here, the schools in question initiated special educational needs assessments after the child had been racially harassed by white peers. In these cases, the authors suggest, the schools' actions were driven by a desire to shift attention away from institutional failings (with respect to the harassment) and onto the supposed deficit in the individual child.

Such racialised practices can prevail even when there are very few white pupils in a class. Weiner (2015) carried out research in a Dutch primary school class in which there was only one white Dutch child. She observed that, despite the multi-ethnic composition of the class, and the school's situation in an ethnically diverse part of Amsterdam, the teacher drew extensively on discourses that reflected white cultural norms. For example, he made frequent reference to the importance of time – doing things faster, good and bad uses of time, and the time left to complete particular activities. These time-related discourses, Weiner argues, 'mimic those of colonial missionaries' paternalistic efforts to teach indigenous people about European conceptions of time, with the students rarely ever measuring up to their teacher's culturally derived demands' (p. 365). The teacher placed similar emphasis on cleanliness, a work ethic, order and observing Christian festivals – all of which are associated with dominant white Dutch culture. Moreover, he made explicit claims about Dutch supremacy, contrasting life in the Netherlands with the poverty and disorder found in the (mainly non-European) countries from where the pupils and their families had migrated. Together, these had the effect, Weiner contends, of explicitly racialising diverse pupils while also promoting the supremacy of Dutch culture.

Teachers do not, however, always treat all non-white pupils in the same way. This is illustrated well in research on British-Chinese pupils conducted by Archer and Francis (2007). They show how teachers typically focused on the high achievement of this particular group, emphasising the value they accorded to education, and the considerable support they had from their parents. However, this emphasis on educational success was, Archer and Francis suggest, unwittingly framed as problematic. For example, British-Chinese parents' unwavering support for the school was seen by teachers as antithetical to notions of the 'engaged parent' – associated instead with a more questioning approach, and more critical interactions with school staff. Furthermore, the parents' underrepresentation at home-school activities, such as events organised by the parent-staff association, was seen as evidence that they were not fully participating in the life of the school. With respect to the pupils themselves, Archer and Francis maintain that, despite their typically high attainment, they were very rarely seen as 'ideal' pupils. They develop the concept of a 'trichotomy' to explain the ways in which these students (and also those from other minority groups) were positioned with respect to white pupils. (Their framework is also attentive to the disparities by social class and gender, discussed in Chapters 5 and 6, respectively.) Their central contention is that the normalised pupil is white, male and middle class, and that the trichotomy 'operates through a splitting and projection of undesirable qualities into other groups, which serves to preserve the privileged identity of the ideal pupil' (p. 67). Thus, black pupils and those from white working-class backgrounds are seen as 'demonised pupils', and those from Asian and Oriental backgrounds as 'other' or 'pathologised'. They go on to argue that this then 'provides a way for understanding how minority ethnic success is always-already positioned as "abnormal"/other and as potentially undesirable – a "wrong" sort of approach to learning' (ibid.). It also helps explain why the educational success of minority ethnic groups (and also that of female students and those from working-class backgrounds) is seen as precarious. Students' abilities, achievements and behaviours are thus read differently (by teachers, but also a range of other actors, including policymakers and the media) according to their social characteristics (ibid.).

Teacher training

Teacher training may seem an obvious place for some of the problems with classroom practice, identified by research and discussed above, to be addressed. And, indeed, the provision of high-quality sociology of education as part of initial teacher education is likely to increase teachers' awareness of many of the issues covered so far in this chapter. However, evidence suggests that teacher training as it is practised in many countries today is rarely effective in encouraging teachers to explore processes of racialisation within education and confront their own preconceptions. Arday (2015) suggests that, within the English context, many teachers are afraid of addressing issues of race and racism because of a fear of making assumptions that may lead to perpetuating racial stereotypes and inequalities. As such fears are not addressed in their initial teacher training, they can linger throughout a teacher's career. Moreover, none of the teachers who participated in his research had received any training at all on racial stereotyping within the education system and how to challenge it (see also Lander, 2015). Maylor (2014) argues that the standards for qualifying as a teacher in England place greater emphasis on not undermining 'fundamental British values' than developing teaching skills that facilitate effective education of pupils within multi-ethnic classrooms. Training in anti-racist initiatives has also been adversely affected by the shift, in the UK at least, of a significant proportion of initial teacher training from universities into schools (Lander, 2015) (see Chapter 10 for further discussion).

Other studies have shown that even when pre-service teachers are exposed to good-quality training on multiculturalism and anti-racism, it can remain hard to disturb long-held attitudes and dispositions. Indeed, the ways in which teachers can act to maintain dominant understandings of race is illustrated well by research on white pre-service teachers in the USA, conducted by Picower (2009). She argues that the respondents in her study had gained hegemonic understandings about race and difference through their previous life experiences. When these understandings were challenged, through taking a pre-service course on multicultural education, they deployed what she calls various 'tools of whiteness' to protect their understandings. She distinguishes between emotional, ideological and performative tools. The first – emotional tools – were used to obfuscate the concepts that were introduced during the course. The teachers sought to protect themselves and their prior understandings by responding in emotional ways. For example, she contends that participants' comments such as 'stop trying to make me feel guilty' reinforced the idea that learning about historical racism is a personal attack against white people. The second type of tool – ideological – encompasses various beliefs that participants evoked to avoid exploring the themes introduced during the course. These included attributing racism to personal ignorance rather than institutional practice, and asserting that an individual teacher could do little to change wider social structures – thus, they argued, there was little point in them adopting multicultural approaches within the classroom. Finally, Picower discusses performative tools – referring to the ways in which participants' behaviour was consistent with their hegemonic understandings. These included being silent about issues of race, and believing that just 'being there' was enough to address racism (absolving them from changing anything within their classrooms). These tools, Picower maintains, protected not just her participants' previous understandings of race and difference, but also positions of white supremacy within society more generally. Very similar findings have emerged from other studies, including Solomona and colleagues' (2005) research with 200 applicants to the teaching profession in Canada. Like their US counterparts, they deployed various strategies to avoid addressing whiteness and its associated privileges in Canadian society, including drawing heavily on discourses of individual endeavour and meritocracy.

Students' perspectives

Learning contexts are considered by some as important sites for multicultural mixing. While numerous other spaces in society are already 'territorialised' by particular ethnic groups, it is argued that schools, colleges and universities 'can operate as neutral and destabilising zones where encounter is required and difference negotiated through shared tasks and new solidarities can be formed accordingly' (Harris, 2013, p. 58). They provide the context for mundane, everyday exchanges between members of diverse communities (Ho, 2011; Noble, 2009). Indeed, much early research on race and education focused on schools as sites for easing racial tensions and promoting assimilation (Byrne, 2009). However, more recent scholarship has problematised some of these claims, by exploring the views pupils have of one another, and the extent to which social mixing happens, in practice, in educational institutions. Research in three diverse urban primary schools, conducted by Iqbal and colleagues (2016), provides evidence of some mixing across ethnic groups. Indeed, they note that the children in their study were able to mix competently, without either major tensions or recourse to processes of racialisation or othering. However, they also contend that this mixing process was partial – limited by their own affinity towards those ethnically (and socially) more similar to themselves, and also their parents' interventions (with respect to out-of-school interactions). Studies of secondary schooling have provided even stronger evidence of some of the barriers to social mixing. Australian research has indicated that such schools are becoming increasingly ethnically polarised, not least because of school choice policies (Ho, 2011), which are discussed further below. Hollingworth and Mansaray (2012) argue that, in their case-study school, which celebrated its ethnic mix in a wide variety of public statements, both ability grouping and differences by ethnic group in subject choice had the effect of restricting mixing. Black students (and those from working-class backgrounds) were effectively 'filtered out' from 'top sets' and the sixth form. They argue that as the lower ability groups became spaces for black 'undesirable learners', they simultaneously became desirable black *social* spaces. As Youdell (2003) has noted, in racialised school spaces, because of the way in which blackness is often associated with a disengagement with learning, it can be extremely difficult for black students to retain both high-status subcultural affiliations and the identity of a successful learner. Kulz (2014) describes how one of the African-Caribbean students she encountered in her school ethnography deliberately moved from an ethnically mixed social group to a white middle-class one in order to accrue future benefits – he believed that socialising with white high achievers would make it more likely that he would be invited to join the head teacher's 'special club' which visited elite universities.

Judgements about others, on the basis of race, are also highlighted in Pettigrew's (2012) study of a diverse secondary school in the south-west of England. Here, the multi-ethnic composition of the school was used by pupils to differentiate it from the whiter, posher, 'more boring' private schools or 'posh' state schools nearby, but also the 'rougher', 'bad schools' attended by largely white working-class pupils. Social class and ethnicity were thus closely intertwined in the pupils' narratives and meaning-making. Interestingly, Pettigrew claims that, in identifying with their diverse school, 'students could temporarily deny or obscure their own ethnic or racial and class positionings' (para. 4.6). Other studies have been rather more explicit in discussing overt racism in schools and other learning contexts (e.g. Lander, 2015). Rollock and colleagues (2011) have argued that, for their black middle-class participants in the UK, school represented a site where they came to learn how they were perceived by wider society – through their interactions with white pupils (and also staff members).

They cite the case of Vanessa, one of their interviewees, who – through her interactions with other pupils – 'begins to understand and examine her racial identity in relation to those aspects of her otherness that are picked out and met with intrigue by white peers. She becomes intrigued at their intrigue, shocked at their questions and confused by their lack of understanding' (p. 1082). Rollock and colleagues go on to claim that interactions between pupils within the spaces of the school can be seen as part of a process of 'zoologising' the black body, through subjecting it to 'dehumanising acts of curiosity and inspection' (ibid.). Furthermore, they suggest that it is through participating in middle-class educational institutions such as universities that their respondents learnt what forms of cultural capital have status and legitimacy within white British society – which they subsequently deployed to distinguish themselves from the black working class. It is important to note, however, that racism can be played out in different ways for different ethnic groups. For example, while racism is often an everyday experience for British-Chinese school pupils (Archer and Francis, 2007), it typically takes on a different form from that experienced by black pupils, discussed above. Indeed, Archer and Francis (2007) contend that it is frequently culturally grounded and expressed through what they call 'negative-positives'. British-Chinese boys and girls are positioned by other pupils (as well as their teachers, as noted previously) as clever, diligent, passive and hard-working. While in some ways these traits can be seen as positive, they also carry negative connotations; indeed, the participants in Archer and Francis' research were concerned that they constructed them as weak, powerless, effeminate and victim-like. Furthermore, they were often called upon by others to conform to a particular kind of heterosexual desirability – for boys, this was through a requirement to perform a 'hard' type of Chinese masculinity associated with martial arts.

While the respondents in several of the studies discussed above appeared to be conscious of the way in which racial difference was played out in the schools and other educational institutions they attended, in other contexts, students can find it harder to name ethnic inequalities. This is illustrated well in research in Jewish schools in Israel carried out by Mizrachi and colleagues (2009). Various studies have indicated that there are considerable educational disparities between Mizrahim (Jews of Middle Eastern and north African origin) and Ashkenazim (Jews of European origin), with the latter group significantly more likely to secure access to higher academic tracks. Nevertheless, Mizrachi and colleagues argue that students themselves are extremely reluctant to acknowledge any ethnic (or class) basis to such patterns. Instead, they adhere strongly to the notion of meritocracy, which is underpinned, the authors suggest, by three deeply engrained discourses. The first is psychological, which designates the autonomous individual as the only legitimate point of reference. This is closely aligned to the second discourse, neo-liberalism, which frames students as 'free agents' engaged in the pursuit of academic credentials as valuable commodities. The third discourse is related to the Zionist national ethos. This, they argue, maintains a strict boundary between 'culture' and 'politics' in the Jewish-Israeli context. Ethnic differences (such as those between Mizrahim and Ashkenazim) are allowed to be expressed only in non-politicised forms, and are rejected as the foundation of claims to collective political rights. They explain this by pointing to the wider political situation, arguing that 'the political chasm between Jewish- and Arab-Israelis casts a heavy shadow over, and censors, any acknowledgement of internal Jewish ethnic divides' (p. 1205). Acknowledging or claiming discrimination on the basis of ethnic origin within the education system would be seen as a political statement and thus, Mizrachi and colleagues maintain, is avoided. Furthermore, they suggest that deploying notions of meritocracy and free choice may also help students in lower tracks maintain a sense of dignity and self-worth.

Educational 'choice'

While many of the issues discussed above have a long history within education, scholars have shown how the specific form racialisation has taken has often changed with the broader policy context – indeed, the impact of some policy influences, such as neo-liberal imperatives to become more 'efficient', has already been noted. Policies of 'educational choice' (see Chapters 3 and 11) have been particularly influential – not just in increasing social class inequalities (as explored in Chapter 5), but also in furthering polarisation in the racial make-up of schools. Ho and colleagues (2015), for example, provide compelling evidence of the way in which school choice policies, introduced in Australia over the last two decades of the twentieth century, combined with processes of gentrification (i.e. the movement of the middle classes into inner-city areas) to reshape the composition of Sydney schools. The two neighbouring schools in their research, 'Cooper Hill' and 'Cooper Creek' (pseudonyms), both had long histories of serving disadvantaged, multicultural communities in a specific Sydney suburb. However, by the time Ho and colleagues conducted their study, the school populations had become ethnically polarised: Cooper Creek had become a highly desirable school for white middle-class gentrifiers, while Cooper Hill had come to be seen as the 'poor cousin' school and continued to have a high proportion of students defined as 'Language Background other than English' (LBOTE). Sixty-four per cent of students at Cooper Hill were designated as LBOTE, compared with only 29 per cent at the neighbouring Cooper Creek. Ho and colleagues argue that as the schools were so close geographically (just one kilometre apart) and their catchment areas were virtually identical on all major indicators, the polarisation of the school communities reflects an active choice on the part of white middle-class families to send their children to Cooper Creek. This thesis is supported by their interview data, which demonstrate that, in deciding which school to send their children to, white parents were concerned to avoid contexts where there were what they perceived to be 'too many' children from minority ethnic backgrounds.

Very similar accounts of parental choice have emerged from other national contexts. The USA, for example, has had a long history of racial segregation in schooling – extending from the 1870s to the 1960s. However, civil rights legislation, passed in Congress in 1968, required that schools were desegregated, and an era of 'bussing' followed, in which children were transported across cities and other areas by bus, to ensure that schools contained an ethnic mix. More recently, however, ethnic segregation has again become more common – related, in part, to the impact of school choice policies and the rise of 'charter schools' (i.e. independent schools that are funded directly by the state rather than through local administrations). For example, in her analysis of the growth of charter schools in New Orleans, Buras (2015) shows how such schools became increasingly segregated and often oppressed both black students and their teachers (this is discussed further in Chapter 11). Similarly, in Spain, as a result of school choice policies, minority ethnic students (and those from economically disadvantaged families) tend to be concentrated in declining state schools, while white students (and those from wealthier backgrounds) commonly dominate the most popular schools (of which many are in the private sector) (Kelly, 2009). Moreover, research in the Netherlands (another country that has adopted wide-ranging choice policies) has indicated that parental decisions are influenced by the ethnic and social mix of schools, as well as the perceived quality of their education (ibid.). UK-based studies have similarly shown how consideration of ethnic mix can be important to the middle classes when choosing schools and universities. Reay and colleagues' (2007) work on the urban white middle classes has indicated that while some parents put material and cultural distance between themselves and ethnic (and classed) 'others' by moving into elite enclaves, others make use of the 'conveniently accessible and acceptably valuable ethnic other' (p. 1053) to gain useful global multicultural capital. They conclude by arguing that 'attending multi-ethnic urban comprehensives becomes yet another, if slightly risky, exciting way of resourcing the middle class self' (ibid.). (Similar motivations are also noted in Ho and colleagues' (2015) Australian study.) The choices of the *black* middle classes are, unsurprisingly, played out differently. Rollock and colleagues (2015) distinguish between two main groups: the 'academic choosers' who prioritise educational achievement, and accept the absence of an ethnic mix in favour of apparently better opportunities for advancement, and the 'social choosers', who foreground a 'good mix' as a matter of principle, believing it will support their children's social, emotional and psychological development.

In relation to HE, research has shown that the ethnic profile of institutions differs quite considerably (Gamsu and Donnelly, 2017), and students from ethnic minority backgrounds sometimes favour universities with more ethnically diverse populations – in a belief that they will fit in better and not be defined primarily in terms of their ethnicity (Ball et al., 2002). More generally, Gamsu and Donnelly (2017) have shown that UK students growing up in the least diverse neighbourhoods tend to attend the least diverse universities, while those who grow up in diverse neighbourhoods in large cities are disproportionately concentrated in the most diverse universities, which are largely 'newer', lower status institutions.

Migrant and international students

Much of the preceding discussion has focused on 'domestic' students, that is, those who are permanently resident in a particular country. However, issues of race and racism are relevant also to international students. Research has documented how particular groups of such students can face open hostility and even racist violence (e.g. Baas, 2014; Kim, 2011), as well as difficulties integrating within school and university classrooms (e.g. Rienties et al., 2015). This is a particular concern for refugee students – or those whose migration has been motivated by a desire to escape specific political and/or economic hardship at home (Bloch and Hirsch, 2017; Correa-Valez et al., 2017). However, racism can also affect those who migrate for less pressing reasons, including a desire to pursue what is perceived to be a more prestigious education abroad (see Chapter 4). For example, international students, particularly those moving from the East to the West, are often positioned as passive and as in need of tutelage from the West within institutional and national marketing materials (Sidhu, 2006), or absent from such representations altogether (Brooks and Waters, 2015). Collins' (2006) analysis of media coverage of Asian international students in New Zealand demonstrates the dominance of three main discourses, which position such students, variously, as 'exotic others', economic objects and social problems. Collins argues, however, that these constructions also have implications for Asian domestic students in New Zealand. He contends that:

> all the representations are mimetically fixated upon a fantasy of the geographical origin of Asian students. By fixing so strongly on the process of constructing this racial identity, such discourses

> are indeed not simply about Asian international students but ... about Asian students, or perhaps more accurately young Asian bodies and their effect upon Auckland [in New Zealand]. (p. 218)

However, such processes are inflected by national context. Brooks' (2017) research on media representations of East Asian students in the UK (in both compulsory schooling and tertiary education) has contrasted the positive way in which East Asian international students are constructed with the much more problematic treatment of their domestic counterparts – with, for example, concerns about 'ethnic mix' articulated in relation to the latter group only. This, she suggests, can be explained by the differing economic status of the two groups (with non-British East Asians paying significantly larger amounts for their UK education), and also assumptions related to their citizenship status (with non-British East Asians assumed to be only temporary residents in the UK).

Black and minority ethnic teachers

The majority of this chapter has focused on the experiences of black and minority ethnic *students*. However, it is important to consider how the experiences of teachers may also be racialised. Research has documented how black and minority ethnic groups are significantly under-represented among academic staff in HE in some countries (Henry et al., 2016), particularly in more senior roles (Equality Challenge Unit, 2015), and also in many parts of schooling systems (Farinde et al., 2016). As will be discussed in Chapter 10, there have been various attempts to increase the number of black teachers in schools, on the assumption that they will act as positive role models for black pupils. However, there is also a considerable body of literature that attests to the racism experienced by black and minority ethnic staff (e.g. Bhopal, 2015). Burgess' (2016) research with early career Aboriginal teachers in Australian schools explores the ways in which her respondents felt positioned by dominant discourses about their ethnic and cultural background. Assumptions were made by their colleagues that, for example, they had a 'natural' connection to Aboriginal communities, they would be able to solve Aboriginal 'problems' and that 'Aboriginal work' (i.e. dealing with perceived Aboriginal problems in the school) was not real work, and peripheral to schools' main business. They also spoke about being positioned as 'other' within school contexts. One of the Aboriginal teachers interviewed by Burgess spoke of the alienation she felt from other staff in her school, and believed that this was a result of her challenging the normative views held by her colleagues of non-Aboriginal people. She confided to Burgess that "'my reputation for questioning schools on Aboriginal issues meant that they were wary of me ... maybe they feel threatened by an educated

Aboriginal woman"' (p. 8). Burgess surmises that this kind of positioning tends to limit both the spaces that Aboriginal teachers can occupy and their opportunities to articulate diverse identities that better reflect how they wish to be recognised. Similar findings emerged from Henry and colleagues' (2016) research in Canadian HE institutions. On the basis of their four-year national study, they argue that Indigenous and minority ethnic lecturing staff occupy only a relatively small number of positions, earn less than their white colleagues and are able to exert little power or influence within their organisations. They maintain that the failure of Canadian universities to diversify can be explained partly by structural barriers and discriminatory practices that have resulted in the exclusion of Indigenous and minority ethnic staff. However, they contend that it is also a result of: 'the inadequately examined preference for sameness that leads to practices of replication … Change has also eluded universities because of the subtle workings of unacknowledged biases that privilege affinity and the needs of dominant insider groups' (p. 12). A more positive perspective is provided by black and minority ethnic trainee teachers interviewed by Bhopal (2015). While they also reported experiencing racism (in this case from students rather than staff), they were keen to teach in largely white schools as a way of challenging hegemonic knowledge and negative black role models. Bhopal writes:

> The majority of respondents felt that an ethnocentric experience of teaching was the norm and so used their own identities to reinforce aspects of BME [black and minority ethnic] history in their teaching. Consequently, they felt their role was to ensure that aspects of race and ethnicity were acknowledged and celebrated in their teaching curriculum. (p. 207)

These themes are discussed further in Chapter 10 in relation to the role of teachers, more generally, and also in Chapter 9, with respect to the capacity of non-dominant groups to challenge the knowledge that is taught in educational institutions.

Conclusion

The various social characteristics that are discussed in *Education and Society* should not be viewed as isolated variables. The ways in which they interact has been of considerable interest for scholars over recent years. The experiences of black working-class boys are often considerably different from those of black middle-class girls, for example. While recognising these important intersections, this chapter has analysed the impact of race and ethnicity on education. It examined how a wide variety of aspects of education – the curriculum, methods of assessment, pedagogies and teacher training – have all been patterned by race and/or ethnicity, and the impact of this on pupils of different racial and ethnic groups. Although there are important differences by group (e.g. teachers often respond to students of Chinese heritage in a very different way to black students), the patterning tends, in general, to disadvantage those from black and minority ethnic backgrounds. The chapter also explored the extent to which 'ethnic mixing' happens within educational institutions – and the impact of recent policies (particularly pertaining to 'school choice') on such processes – before turning to the experiences of teachers, demonstrating how these too are often differentiated along the lines of race and/or ethnicity. Themes introduced in this chapter are returned to in later chapters, notably when we consider curricula and assessment (Chapter 9), the social characteristics of teachers (Chapter 10) and the impact of particular types of school (Chapter 11).

8 AGE

Introduction

While discussed less in the research on education than other social characteristics such as class, gender and ethnicity, age is an important variable in terms of how education is structured in many countries, and also how it is experienced. This chapter begins by considering different perspectives on age, suggesting that chronological age is not the only meaningful way of thinking about how 'age differences' are played out in education. It then goes on to consider how age is relevant to the educational experiences of 'younger learners'. The age at which children start and leave school are both discussed, as is the impact of education itself on the conceptualisation of age and life stage (particularly in relation to who we consider to have achieved adult status). The second part of the chapter explores the experiences of 'older learners', focusing on formal settings, such as further education and HE, as well as the University of the Third Age (U3A) and non-formal contexts. Finally, the chapter considers the relatively limited body of work on education in mixed-age contexts, in which learners of different chronological ages are brought together.

Perspectives on age

Age difference has been theorised in a number of different ways (e.g. Eisenstadt, 1956; Mannheim, 1952; Pilcher, 1995), which has a bearing on the arguments developed in this chapter. A particularly useful framework is provided by Aapola (2002) on the basis of her empirical research with secondary school students in Finland. She analysed autobiographical essays written by 88 15–16-year-olds and argues that, across the dataset, her respondents constructed the concept of age difference in four distinct, although often overlapping, ways. First, some deployed a *chronological* discourse of age. Aapola notes that this discourse is well-established in the public sphere and is probably the most well-known dimension of age. For the young people in her sample, chronological age was important because it was a clear signal of the rights they were entitled to (such as voting and entering age-limited spaces such as bars), and also their responsibilities. Aapola argues that there are two sub-discourses, linked to the concept of chronological age: that of *institutional* age and of *developmental* age. The former is engrained in the education system in most parts of the world, such that pupils who do not follow the 'normal' pattern of study (i.e. moving up one year group each calendar year) are sometimes considered deviant (ibid.). Developmental age tends to be informed by psychological theories which delineate a linear, highly normative, 'universal' course of development, which all children and young people are expected to follow. Those deviating from these stages can be seen as problematic (by teachers and other professionals).

The second main discourse Aapola highlights is what she calls the discourse of *physical* age. By this, she means the assessments made on the basis of an individual's bodily condition, outward appearance and ability to carry out a range of physical tasks. Here, she distinguishes between two sub-discourses: *biological/medical* age and *contextual* age. The idea of biological age refers to the importance attached to physical change over time. Within the essays analysed by Aapola, physical age was often discussed in terms of the associated social changes. For example, one respondent made reference to her own 'shortness' (meaning that she had not yet gone through puberty) as an indication of why she was 'too young' to date boys. Contextual age, Aapola maintains, refers to estimates made about an individual's chronological age on the basis of contextual markers – most commonly, an individual's physical appearance. Third, Aapola outlines what she calls the discourse of *experiential* age – defined as the age a person subjectively attributes to him/herself. Many of the young people in her research identified with adulthood and an older chronological age, reflecting, Aapola suggests, the social power typically attached to this life stage. However, as will be discussed later in this chapter, it is also common for older adults to identify with younger chronological ages – sometimes directly as a result of engaging in particular forms of education and/or mixing with younger learners. Aapola's final discourse is that of *symbolic* age. This refers to the expectations (about appropriate behaviour and dress, for example) attached to various life stages. She distinguishes between the sub-discourse of *functional* age – in which achievement of particular skills can affect how one is seen – and that of *ritual* age – here, taking part in a particular ceremony or other ritual is viewed as conferring a particular age. The Finnish matriculation examinations at the end of secondary school are one example of such a ritual. Although these exams are no longer used for university entry, Aapola argues that they are still seen as marking the transition to membership of adult society: the graduates' names are published in local and national newspapers, they often receive valuable gifts from family and friends and typically celebrate when their results arrive.

As will be evident from the rest of this chapter, many researchers have argued that age distinctions between students are highly relevant to understanding contemporary education. However, it is important not to overlook the body of work that has suggested that age-related boundaries are perhaps not as clear-cut and significant as Aapola's analysis would suggest. The European Group for Integrated Social Research (2001), for example, has identified three ways in which the distinction between youth and adulthood may be blurred, and in which people are able to combine both youthful and adult behaviours. First, they suggest that some young adults experience aspects of youth and adult life simultaneously and live 'divided lives' (e.g. following a training course but experiencing freedom in their personal lives). Second, they identify 'pending lives', experienced by those who perceive themselves as neither youths nor adults. This, they argue, is a result of the youth status of transition having 'lost its clear and attainable destination of a completely integrated adult' (p. 103). Finally, they outline the 'swinging lives' of those who consciously alternate between classic biographical phases (such as childhood, youth and adulthood). Here, they cite the examples of young parents who cling to youth culture and professionals who continue to take part in raves.

Other writers have argued that emphasising the distinctiveness of age-groupings may overlook significant differences between people of the same chronological age, as well as important continuities across age groups. Wyn and White (1997), for example, argue that much theorising about young people's lives has been tied to a horizontal frame of reference 'in which youth as a life stage is emphasised at the expense of seeing that the experiences and perspectives of young people are integrally related to those of other people who share their social location' (p. 97). They go on to argue for the inclusion of a vertical frame of reference that would take account of continuities between generations, women, men, local geographical communities and cultural groups, for example. Their argument is premised on the assumption that, although young people do have some things in common because of their age, social divisions and geographical location have the effect of placing young people in close proximity to older adults who share the same social circumstances. Thus, as has been suggested in other chapters, it is important to adopt an intersectional lens when exploring the impact of various social characteristics – remaining aware that the experiences of a black, working-class, 16-year-old boy may be significantly different from those of a white, middle-class girl of the same chronological age.

The following two sections of this chapter focus, respectively, on 'younger learners' and 'older learners'. This division reflects some of the constructions of age in Aapola's typology (e.g. in relation to chronological age, institutional age and symbolic age) – with younger learners taken to include those within compulsory education and who have made the transition from school or college straight to HE. The section on older learners, in contrast, refers to those who have had some break from formal education and who are of an older chronological age. However, these categorisations are clearly not always straightforward and uncontested; indeed, as will be discussed below, the education system itself can help shape who are seen as 'younger' and 'older' learners, and thus definitions can change over time.

Younger learners

Until the start of the twentieth century, education was very age-heterogeneous; it was common for students of different chronological ages to learn alongside one another (Aapola, 2002). This changed gradually, as schooling was opened up to a greater proportion of the population, and psychologists and educationalists began to differentiate between different 'developmental ages' (ibid.). Now, in many parts of the world, children are typically grouped according to their chronological age and 'move up' one school year per calendar year. Although this type of age-stratification is relatively uncontroversial (although see the section on age-mixing at the end of this chapter), there is considerable debate about the age at which children should start school. Within Europe, for example, some pupils start school at the age of four (in Northern Ireland), others start at five (Cyprus, England, Malta, Scotland and Wales), the majority start at six and some start at seven (including Bulgaria, Croatia, Estonia, Finland, Latvia, Lithuania, Poland and Sweden) (Eurydice, 2016). Advocates of a starting age of four or five tend to emphasise the educational benefits of beginning formal education early. However, the academic evidence does not provide unambiguous support for such claims. Indeed, those countries who have a later starting age cite the educational benefits of a longer period of play, prior to commencing formal education, and the positive impact it has on children's physical, intellectual and emotional development (Whitebread, 2012).

In the UK, there is an ongoing discussion about whether children who are relatively 'young' when compared to others in their cohort group are disadvantaged in the first few years of school, and possibly thereafter, too. A report published in 2013 called for the exam marks of children born in the summer (which is towards the cut-off date for the cohort) to be boosted, to compensate for these pupils being among the youngest in their year group when they are assessed (Crawford et al., 2013). There is now a body of evidence that suggests there is an association between month of birth, structure of schooling and academic (and social) outcomes. Reviewing the literature in this area, Campbell (2014) argues that pupils who are younger in the school year tend consistently, throughout their compulsory schooling, to score lower on tests of academic ability than their relatively older peers. She also notes that such children are more likely than others to be diagnosed with special educational needs, experience bullying and have low levels of self-confidence. They are also less likely than their older counterparts to report that they enjoy school, and to progress to post-compulsory education. There is considerable debate about the reasons for these patterns. Teachers' perceptions about children's relative ability have been shown to correlate quite strongly with month of birth: older children are more likely to be judged as 'above average' by their teachers (Crawford et al., 2011). Given the evidence about the impact of teachers' perceptions on pupils' performance and educational trajectory (see discussion in Chapter 9), some scholars have argued that teachers' assumptions about younger children's 'relative immaturity' (the 'developmental age', in Aapola's typology) may explain the differential attainment (Campbell, 2014). The impact of such judgements may be exacerbated in primary schools which group children by ability (within their year group). Campbell's (2014) analysis of data from the UK's Millennium Cohort Study (a sample of 5,481 English seven-year-olds and their teachers) suggests that in-class grouping may contribute to the creation of systematic birth month differentials in pupil attainment. She contends:

> Among children who are in-class ability grouped, autumn-summer variation in teacher perceptions of *ability and attainment* is greater than among pupils who are *not* grouped. The already disproportionate tendency of autumn-born favourably to be judged 'above average' is amplified among grouped children. (p. 762, italics in original)

This suggests that because autumn-born children (the oldest in the cohort) are often placed in the top group when in-class ability grouping takes place, 'they are advantaged through a heightening of teachers' judgements of their *ability and attainment* which is related to this group placement' (ibid., italics in original). (It should be noted that there is significant national variation in the school calendar and starting age cut-offs; thus, 'autumn-born' children will not necessarily be the oldest in their year group in other countries.)

Alongside debates about the age at which children should start school and whether those who are relatively young in their year should be compensated in some way, are those that focus on the age of pupils when they *leave* formal schooling (Green and Navarro Paniagua, 2012; Woodin et al., 2013). While the rationale for raising the school leaving age has often been justified by various governments on economic grounds (e.g. in order to increase the skill level of the workforce and thus improve national competitiveness) (Woodin et al., 2013), political motives have often also been significant (Simmons, 2008). Simmons (2008) argues that the most recent reform to the school leaving age in England – in which, from 2015 onwards, participation in some kind of education or training up to the age of 18 became compulsory – was aimed primarily at engaging young people 'not in education, employment or training', commonly referred to as 'NEETs'. He suggests that the government rhetoric associated with the policy, which emphasised economic competitiveness and social inclusion, was misleading; instead, the reform was intended to provide certain employers with a continuing supply of cheap labour (as, under the policy, young people who do not want to stay on at school or college are able to pursue government-funded training within the workplace, through an apprenticeship or traineeship). Here, we see played out the view that a primary purpose of education is to prepare young people for the labour market (see Chapter 2).

A small number of research studies have suggested that the education of younger learners is also affected by the age of their parents. Research conducted by Powell and colleagues (2006) using longitudinal data from the USA (the National Education Longitudinal Survey) indicated that having older parents was, on average, an advantage to young people. More particularly, they found that the older a child's parents, the greater the transmission of education-related economic, social and cultural resources. Such resources included involvement in school events and close association with their child's friends and their parents (examples of social capital); taking their child to museums and galleries, and enrolling them in out-of-school classes (cultural capital); and the amount of money saved for the child's college education and the number of 'educational objects' around the home (economic capital). These patterns held even when factors such as social class were controlled for. Powell and colleagues also found that older parents were more likely than their younger counterparts to have high educational expectations of their children. While they note that the effects of parental age are not as powerful as those of parental income or education, they conclude that the strength of the association should encourage 'greater attention to age as a component of stratification that affects the life experiences and prospects not only of the incumbent [i.e. the individuals concerned] but also of family members' (p. 1376).

While the studies discussed so far have explored whether chronological age (of parents or young learners themselves) has an impact on education, research has also considered the extent to which educational structures, processes and transitions have themselves affected our conceptualisation of age. Here, the main focus has been on the experiences of those reaching the end of compulsory education. Youth has traditionally been understood as a period of transition – from the parental home into independent housing, from 'the family of origin' into 'the family of destination' and from education into employment. In this analysis, adulthood is typically seen as the state reached once these transitions have been made and young people have moved from dependence to independence. Recent years have, however, witnessed significant rethinking of this model as a result of quite profound changes to the lives of young men and women. As post-compulsory training and education have expanded very considerably (OECD, 2016), young people are now entering the labour market later, and thus are considerably older when they achieve financial independence. This, in turn, has increased the average age at which people get married and have children (Furlong and Cartmel, 2007). Alongside the expansion of educational opportunities, in some parts of the world (although not all), the funding of education has changed, so that individual learners and their families are expected to carry more of the cost. This is particularly the case in countries with high university tuition fees, such as the USA and the UK, and where there is little in the way of maintenance support to cover the living costs of students, such as Italy and Greece (Brooks, 2018) – although Antonucci (2016) has argued that, across Europe, we are seeing similar trends, in which families are increasingly expected to support their children financially through their post-compulsory education. This clearly has implications for the relationships between students and their parents, frequently increasing the dependency of younger learners.

Scholars have argued that these trends are evidence of 'delayed adulthood'. For some, such as du Bois Reymond (1998), this is a largely positive development, offering young people opportunities to experiment with different lifestyles. Others, however, have taken a different view, arguing that identity formation becomes more difficult the longer the period between physical maturation (biological age in Aapola's typology, discussed above) and attainment of adult status (symbolic age) (Côte and Allahar, 1994). A further group of scholars have argued that, as a result of educational expansion and other changes to the lives of young people, transitions to adulthood have undergone a more profound shift, not merely a delay. Reflecting some of the discussion above, Stokes and Wyn (2007) have argued that young people are now 'engaged simultaneously in adult and youth practices, blurring the boundaries of youth, adult, student and worker' (p. 508). Moreover, Arnett (2004) has suggested that researchers should recognise a new and distinct life stage: that of 'emerging adulthood' between the early and late twenties, during which time young people engage in self-focused exploration, trying out different types of relationships and jobs. While these theorists evaluate the nature of recent changes in different ways, they share an assumption that institutional age and ritual age (see discussion above) are significant in young people's transitions to adulthood, and that educational institutions play key roles in both. Implicit in this analysis is a rejection of the view that education should be understood as simply a mechanism for social integration (see Chapter 2); instead, it is positioned as an institution that helps to shape new forms of social relationships and structures.

Older learners

Higher (and further) education

One of the areas in which there has been most sustained scholarly enquiry with respect to age and learning is in relation to the experiences of older learners within formal, post-compulsory education (mainly HE but also, although to a lesser extent, further education) (see discussion in Chapter 12). Here, they are often called 'mature' or 'adult' students, to distinguish them from their younger counterparts who have moved straight from school or college. While Saar and colleagues (2014) note that defining an adult (HE) student is not necessarily straightforward, they identify the following criteria which are commonly employed within research: (1) chronological age (usually defined as 25 years or over); (2) having had a major break in one's educational path, prior to entering HE; (3) having gained significant life experience through work, family and/or community involvement; and (4) having responsibility for others (e.g. as a parent). Nevertheless, it is important also to recognise national variation in these distinctions (and, more broadly, in the construction of age). The average age of HE students differs quite considerably across Europe, for example – from 20.7 in Russia and Greece to 29.1 in Sweden (Eurostudent, 2015) – related to differing national norms about working alongside a degree and taking breaks from study, as well as the way in which HE is funded.

Adult learners have come to play an important role within HE in many nation-states. In Australia, mature-aged students comprise a significant proportion of the sector – often more than a third of all students are over 21 years of age (Tones et al., 2009). In the UK, mature students were foregrounded in government plans to expand and reform the sector from the late 1980s onwards (González-Arnal and Kilkey, 2009; Reay, 2002). The proportion of mature students among those graduating from HE in England and Wales rose from 10 per cent in 1980 to over 30 per cent only a decade later (ibid). Although this level of growth has not been sustained (and, indeed, the number of adult students declined from 2011 onwards as a result of substantial increases in tuition fees (UUK, 2015)), Europe-wide reforms have also given prominence to adult learners. Within the Bologna Process, which has sought to reconfigure HE across the continent to ensure comparability in the standards and quality of HE qualifications (see Chapters 3 and 12), lifelong learning has been given considerable prominence (Jakobi and Rusconi, 2009). As part of this reform agenda, universities have been asked to develop flexible learning pathways, establish alternative routes to HE, create opportunities for the recognition of prior learning and provide programmes relevant to a diverse student population (Saar et al., 2014). Underpinning these various initiatives is a belief that institutions need to do more to enable adult access to HE (ibid).

While much of lifelong learning policy (and other reforms targeted at adult learners specifically) is driven by economic imperatives, namely the desire to ensure that there is a good match between the skills of adults and those required by the labour market (Roberts, 2015) (see discussion of the labour market in Chapter 2), research that has explored the motivations of adult learners themselves has revealed considerable diversity. Osborne and colleagues (2004), for example, identify six different categories of adult learner. While two of these relate directly to the workplace – the 'careerists', who were in employment and sought a qualification to make progress in their career, and the 'escapees', who wanted a qualification as a means to move out of a job they disliked – the other four categories relate to wider aspirations. These comprised 'delayed traditional students'; 'late starters' (who had undergone a life-transforming event such as divorce and sought a 'new start'); 'single parents' (who wanted to provide a positive role model for their children); and 'personal growers' (who pursued learning for its own sake). These broader motivations are evident in various other studies of adult learners (e.g. González-Arnal and Kilkey, 2009; Reay, 2002), and often distinguish such students from their younger counterparts who are more likely to see HE as simply part of the normal life course (Reay, 2002).

Differences by age are also evident in the way students experience HE. A prominent theme in the literature on adult students is the way in which wider aspects of their lives can impinge upon the process of learning. This is particularly marked for those with responsibility for children, who often have to juggle competing demands on their time and, for women students in particular, a tension between societal expectations of a 'good mother' (who is, for example, always available for her children) and the academic demands of a university course (Brooks, 2013; Lee, 2013; Osborne et al., 2004) (see also discussion in Chapter 6). Alsop and colleagues (2008) note that 'the fact that women have been traditionally the carers in the family, and that students have been conceptualised as male and non-carers, influences … the ways in which they are perceived by others, and also the manner in which their own identity is reconstructed' (p. 629). It is argued that such tensions result in complex identity practices, as women downplay their mother role in academia and their student role when they are outside the university (Lynch, 2008). González-Arnal and Kilkey (2009) draw on the experiences of adult students with children to critique the philosophy of the 'rational economic man', which often underpins HE policy. They argue that caring responsibilities influence where such students study (often having to choose an institution close to where they live), the quality of the degree obtained, their future career paths and sometimes also their attitudes to debt (and thus the extent to which they perceive it feasible to take out loans to fund their studies). Previous educational encounters can also influence how adult students (particularly those from working-class backgrounds) experience HE. Drawing on interviews with adult students in a further education college, who were making decisions about university, Reay (2002) argues that many of her respondents had 'often negative, frequently disrupted, and sometimes fragmented, educational histories' (p. 411), which made their university decisions difficult. They felt different from the 'traditional' HE student in relation to both their class and their age. As a result, they often sought safety rather than transformation in their HE choices – opting for the security and comfort that they believed less prestigious institutions would offer.

The challenges faced by students as a result of both their previous educational experiences and caring responsibilities can often be exacerbated by the practices and policies of the institutions at which they study. Saar and colleagues (2014) usefully differentiate between institutional and structural barriers that can adversely affect adult students. The former include problems related to timetabling, transport to the institution, enrolment procedures, lack of timely information and the fees charged. The latter are broader in focus, and relate to the following: the extent to which different types of institution encourage the participation of adults; admission arrangements; available modes of study (e.g. part-time and distance); financial and other support; the extent of institutional flexibility with respect to course content and organisation; and the availability of short courses that can help to engage adult learners. Analyses indicate that there is considerable variety, by nation-state, in the extent to which such impediments to HE are present. Focusing on only the institutional barriers, Saar and colleagues (2014) contend that, within Europe, they are most evident in post-socialist/communist countries (such as Slovenia, Estonia and Russia), and least present in social democratic countries (such as Norway) and liberal countries (such as England and Ireland). However, even in England, qualitative research has indicated that institutional barriers can be significant. Marandet and Wainwright (2009), for example, have shown how student-parents are often disadvantaged by the late availability of timetables, a lack of nearby childcare facilities and policies that prohibit children from coming onto campus (see discussion in Chapter 6). Nevertheless, despite these barriers, it is clear that many adults who enrol in post-compulsory education derive huge benefit and enjoyment from their experiences. As will be discussed below, some older learners draw on them to contest negative age stereotyping (Isopahkala-Bouret, 2015), while others report gaining in self-confidence and developing new social networks (Busher et al., 2014; Lee, 2013). There is also evidence to suggest that adult students are advantaged, in comparison to their traditional-age peers, when it comes to securing paid employment (and, in particular, graduate-level employment) at the end of their studies (Woodfield, 2011).

University of the Third Age

During the second half of the twentieth century, various institutions emerged, worldwide, to cater specifically for the learning needs of older adults. One of the most successful is what came to be known as the 'University of the Third Age' (U3A), founded in 1972. Formosa (2014) suggests that U3As 'can be loosely defined as socio-cultural centres where older persons acquire new knowledge of significant issues, or validate the knowledge which they already possess, in an agreeable milieu and in accordance with easy and acceptable methods' (pp. 42–43). The 'third age' in its title is intended to refer to the 'third age' of life, subsequent to employment. U3As first emerged in France, following legislation in the late 1960s, in which responsibility for lifelong learning was given to universities. A summer programme of lectures and other educational activities, put on in 1972 by the University of Toulouse for retired people, was so popular that the initiative was repeated the following year, with an extended programme. It was subsequently taken up by universities in other areas of France – and also in Belgium, Switzerland, Poland, Italy, Spain and Canada – with a commitment to enabling older learners to access high-quality university-level programmes and receive teaching from university staff. The curriculum remained the responsibility of academics, and learners were expected to show deference to the professors who taught them (Formosa, 2014).

A second model of the U3A was developed a decade later in the UK. In contrast to the deferential, 'top-down' model established in France, in which university staff retained considerable power and authority, the British model 'embraced a self-help approach based on the principle of reciprocity, of mutual giving and taking' (Formosa, 2014, p. 45). Emphasis was placed on students learning from each other rather than eminent university staff. They typically adopted an anti-authoritarian stance and had no formal connection to the university sector (Jarvis, 2014). However, the British model was also informed by the wider political context, and particularly the failure of UK universities to commit themselves to comprehensive programmes of adult education (Formosa, 2014). While many contemporary U3As follow the French or British model, other types have also emerged. Formosa (2014) identifies a distinct Chinese model, for example, which promotes a holistic perspective on learning, emphasising 'the maintenance and development of citizenship, cultural consolidation, philosophical reflection and bodily harmony' (p. 47). In recognition of this diversity, some scholars have argued that the U3A should be conceptualised as a global network, rather than an organisation. Indeed, various U3A associations, usually operating on a regional basis, have facilitated the global spread of the movement through online newsletters, websites and discussion fora (Ratana-Ubol and Richards, 2016).

U3As are typically argued, by their proponents, to offer a range of benefits to those who participate in them – and also to society more generally. These include the democratisation of lifelong learning – by extending opportunities to those who would otherwise be excluded; health benefits (from continued mental stimulation); improved levels of self-esteem, self-assurance and satisfaction; and a means of easing the transition from employment to retirement (through developing new social networks and new interests) (Formosa, 2014; Wilińska, 2012). However, the movement also faces a number of challenges. These range from the practical – such as securing adequate space and funding to be able to run activities – to concerns about access and power relationships. Researchers have documented, for example, the middle-class bias in U3A membership. Reflecting some of the arguments made in Chapter 5 on social class, studies have shown how middle-class elders often perceive the U3A as a familiar and non-threatening environment, similar to those they have studied in previously. In contrast, their working-class counterparts are more likely to feel alienated by the word 'university' in its title, the curriculum offered (which often focuses on 'liberal arts' subjects, rather than those with a more practical focus) and the social characteristics of other participants (Formosa, 2014; Morris, 1984). Within the French model, in particular, learners can also experience a lack of agency, as university staff typically determine the curriculum and general ethos of all learning activities (Formosa, 2014). Some scholars have suggested that the orientation of the U3A, underpinning both the French and the British models, is based on assumptions prevalent in the Global North which are not necessarily relevant in other parts of the world. Ratana-Ubol and Richards (2016) argue that focusing on *returning* to learning, as they suggest the U3A does, overlooks the fact that many older people outside the Global North may never have received any formal education, and may thus be most interested in basic literacy provision – and a wider embrace of non-formal means of tuition. They suggest that this is why in some countries, such as Thailand (the focus of their analysis), U3As have yet to be established.

A fascinating analysis of the U3A in Poland has been conducted by Wilińska (2012). She explores the 'stories told about ageing' by the

U3A in the context of wider societal discourses. The U3A is popular in Poland: at the time she conducted her research, there were 180 different U3As in the country (based primarily on the French model, but also incorporating ideas about self-help and voluntarism from the British variant), with over 60,000 members. Perhaps counter-intuitively, Wilińska argues that, far from countering the ageism prevalent in wider society, Polish U3As help to reinforce dominant ideologies and, in particular, the idea that old age is a time of decline. They do this, she contends, through conveying the message that U3A participants learn and enjoy their life *in spite of* their age. For example, one of the discourses she identifies in the U3A publications and other promotional materials, is the idea of the U3A as a place of refuge. She writes:

> Members of the U3A feel a sense of shared experience and refer to themselves as a special social category, distinct from old people in the general population. The U3A becomes a sanctuary that protects people from the harshness of social reality. (p. 299)

A second discourse she identifies constructs the U3A as a place in which ageing does not happen. She notes that when she first entered a U3A to talk about her research, she was greeted with the comments "'If you are interested in ageing and older people in Poland, this is not a good place; walk the streets of the city, visit some care centres … '" (p. 294). She goes on to maintain that this denial of ageing was central to both the ways in which members saw themselves and the stories of ageing produced by the organisation. Becoming engrossed in learning activities was presented as an effective means of 'battling old age'. Such ways of talking, Wilińska argues, reinforce widespread ageist discourses that see the process of ageing as fundamentally negative and associated with decline.

Non-formal learning

Clearly, much adult learning goes on outside formal contexts. Indeed, that is part of the critique of the U3A movement made by those in Thailand, as mentioned above. Seddon (2014) has argued that learning now occurs in a range of new settings – which operate on different scales – such as the lifelong learning city or region. Her broader point is that while the development of formal, national systems of education during the twentieth century can be seen as part of the territorialisation of state power (see discussion in Chapter 2), various de- and re-territorialising processes have affected education in the current century with emphasis on, for example, subnational and transnational scales. The transnational focus is evident in Guo's (2014) work on the relationships between migration and lifelong learning. In critiquing the common construction, within Canadian policy, of migrants as passive citizens, he shows how Chinese immigrants were actively involved in the support of other immigrants (to Canada), and also how this voluntary activity constituted an important source of informal, community-based learning. While Guo's research demonstrates how non-formal learning can be a means of establishing social solidarity, it can also – like various other types of learning discussed throughout this book – be a site in which exclusionary practices can be played out. Schuller and colleagues (2004), for example, discuss the case of Susan, one of the participants in their research on non-formal learning in the UK. They maintain that her strong desire to learn alongside people she perceived to be similar to herself (white and middle class) was both 'an internalisation of class and a realisation of class in terms of replicating homogeneous, middle class, white civic associations' (p. 145). They go on to contend that, in the aggregate, such actions constitute a class strategy, 'showing how adult education creates social capital but not necessarily the conditions for social inclusion' (p. 145). Similar processes were evident in Brooks' (2006) research with adults in their mid-twenties: decisions about post-university learning opportunities, even in non-formal contexts, were inflected by social class and influenced by concerns about social positioning. Here, we see many of the themes discussed previously, in Chapter 5, being played out.

Age-mixing within education

As noted at the start of this chapter, it is now typical for education systems across the world to be stratified by age; thus, learners rarely interact within the classroom with those of a different chronological age (other than the teacher). Even within HE systems, in many countries, 'mature' students typically constitute only a minority of students and can often be concentrated within particular institutions and/or on particular courses (e.g. Archer et al., 2003; Merrill, 1996). Jones and Wallace (1992) have argued that one consequence of the strong age focus in much UK education policy is that all sense of dynamic within the life course is lost: 'each age group or age grouping … becomes static and membership within each group is frozen, so that within each age group no process is involved – all sense of process is channelled into the transition from one age grouping to another' (pp. 148–149). Nevertheless, while relatively rare, age-mixing in education *does* occur. This final part of the chapter focuses on three different contexts in which learners of different ages have come into contact with one another: in an Australian pre-school, Finnish HE institutions and English further education colleges.

While pre-schools typically have a relatively narrow age range (from 0 to the age at which children start school), in many countries further age-related grouping occurs within individual institutions. In Australia, for example, children tend to be grouped according to whether they are infants (0 to 12–18 months), toddlers (12–18 months to 3 years) or pre-schoolers (3–5 years). Rouse's (2015) study, which explored the impact on children and staff when children of all ages in one particular pre-school setting were brought together, highlights numerous benefits associated with this approach. In particular, many children enjoyed being able to interact with their siblings during the day, while those who did not have any siblings gained experience of learning how to negotiate with children of a different age. Moreover, the educators involved believed that by bringing together children of different ages a more familial and community-orientated environment was established which, in turn, helped to foster more pro-social behaviours. However, Rouse (2015) also notes the enduring dispositions of many of the educators involved. She argues that their overriding concern with 'protecting' the younger children – and thus their tendency to age-differentiate the learning activities even when the children were all in the same physical space – undermined the agency of the learners. She concludes by arguing that those working with pre-school children need to reposition their thinking – away from focusing on children through a developmental lens (one of the sub-discourses of 'chronological age' in Aapola's (2002) typology), seeing them instead as knowledgeable experts who are able to support the learning of others.

At the other end of the age spectrum, Isopahkala-Bouret's (2015) research explores the experiences of older learners (defined as aged 50 or above) as they engage with significantly younger counterparts within the Finnish HE system. The participants in her study were all pursuing master's-level courses as a means of furthering their professional development. Isopahkala-Bouret argues that, for these Finnish professionals, studying for a postgraduate degree provided them with resources from which to develop new cultural constructions of ageing. While some of these resources were related to studying per se – for example, embarking on something new, and demonstrating their capacity to perform well – others were related more specifically to the age-mixing that occurred on their courses. Indeed, Isopahkala-Bouret notes that:

> Aging workers positioned themselves as 'not-old' by emphasizing the similarities they shared with their younger colleagues. They adopted a non-authoritarian and humble attitude, and did not underline their superior experience and know-how. This was a form of strategic and situational resistance through which aging professionals differentiated themselves from cultural stereotypes. (p. 8)

In contrast to some of the experiences of mature students discussed above, her respondents believed that, within their interactions with younger students on their particular course, rigid age boundaries were not experienced. While Isopahkala-Bouret frames these experiences as entirely positive (reflecting the views of the students themselves), there are interesting parallels with the study of the University of the Third Age in Poland, discussed previously. In both cases, ageing is constructed as something associated with decline and to be resisted. Moreover, the education pursued in both contexts appears to provide a resource to *individuals* to enable them to distance themselves from negative age-related stereotypes, rather than to contest these stereotypes in an explicit manner. There is also evidence that access to such cultural resources is not available to all. The middle-class orientation of the U3A has been noted previously. Similarly, Isopahkala-Bouret argues that the opportunities offered by Finnish HE are socially circumscribed: the older learners in her study all had access to sufficient cultural and economic capital to facilitate their smooth movement into the university environment.

Research conducted on mixed-age learning in the UK (in a sample of six further education colleges) has also highlighted some of the ways in which those who were involved in such intergenerational interactions considered themselves to be advantaged (Brooks, 2005). First, both students and the lecturers who taught them believed that, typically, mixed-age classes engendered a very positive learning environment. This was seen as stemming from the commitment of the older learners (who had often made a very definite decision to return to education) and what was perceived to be their more mature attitude to learning. One of the younger students who was interviewed claimed:

> If it was a group of all 18 year-olds, we'd probably behave differently because you want to fit in, don't you? We probably wouldn't get any work done because we'd be talking all the time. It would be really disruptive. (18-year-old administrative procedure student, quoted in Brooks, 2005, p. 62)

Staff believed that older learners benefited, too – with the often more relaxed attitude of the younger learners encouraging them to be less anxious about their studies. Being able to share different life experiences and bring different perspectives to bear on the subjects of study were also identified as pedagogic benefits of mixed-age classrooms. In addition, respondents noted various social benefits – several younger students described, in appreciative terms, how they had been 'looked after' by older classmates, while a student in her seventies was extremely grateful for the lift home that some of the younger students provided (Brooks, 2005). The most commonly cited 'wider benefit' of mixed-age groups, however, was that such groups prepared students well for other parts of their life in which they would be likely to mix with people of a different age.

Respondents believed that working with older or younger students not only helped to overcome age-related stereotypes, but enabled learners to develop interpersonal skills that could be used in other contexts, and particularly the workplace. More generally, a considerable number of those interviewed believed that mixed-age learning could play an important role in helping to increase intergenerational learning and respect (ibid.).

It is important to note, however, that although the students and staff interviewed in Brooks' (2005) research made frequent reference to 'older' and 'younger' learners, age differences were not always understood in the same way. Indeed, the boundary between the two groups was drawn in different places and on the basis of different criteria. The vast majority of the age-related differences identified by respondents corresponded, broadly, to what they considered to be a dichotomy between 'youth' and 'adulthood'. In line with other discourses connected to adolescence (e.g. Raby, 2002), the former was typically associated with less responsible and independent attitudes to learning, while 'older/adult' learners were commonly seen as self-motivated and strongly committed to their studies. Beyond this, however, different markers were brought into play. Some of these related to traditional markers of adult status (such as moving out of the parental home and gaining full-time employment), but others did not. One common means of differentiating between older and younger learners was by making reference to work experience. Numerous students across the six case-study colleges emphasised the importance of full-time work experience in conferring adult status. In some cases, even one year of such employment was considered sufficient. One head of department described how a 17-year-old student had made a request to be enrolled on what the college termed an 'adult' course (i.e. one not comprised only of 16–19-year-olds) on the grounds that she had little in common with the students who had come straight from school because of the year she had spent in full-time work. (Interestingly, part-time work pursued while a full-time student appeared not to have the same value to respondents.) Other markers included experience of post-compulsory education. Some respondents, for example, distinguished between 16–17-year-olds who had come straight from school and – it was believed, were used to being 'spoon fed' – and those aged 18 and above, who had had more experience of post-school education and had developed more independent approaches to learning as a result. A third means by which respondents differentiated between 'younger' and 'older' learners was on the basis of specific life events and domestic transitions. Leaving the parental home, committing to a long-term relationship with a partner and having children were all thought to be significant here. Thus, while most respondents believed that age was an important dimension in explaining differences between students and their orientations to learning, chronological age appeared to be seen as a poor proxy for other, more profound changes in one's life that may affect the process of learning (Brooks, 2005). Discourses of 'functional age' (Aapola, 2002) were more readily drawn upon.

Conclusion

The chapter first considered the various ways in which 'age difference' can be conceptualised – including, for example, 'institutional age', 'contextual age' and 'symbolic age', as well as the more common 'chronological age'. It then explored a range of issues that impact particularly on 'younger learners', including the age at which one starts and finishes school, and examined the influence that education itself can have on how we think about age (in relation to when a young person becomes an adult, for example). Here, the potential of education to shape social structures and relationships, rather than just reproduce them, is illustrated. The chapter then considered the experiences of 'older learners' within both formal spaces of learning (such as further and higher education) and informal settings. Although such learners have come to play an increasingly important role in post-compulsory education, their experiences often vary considerably from those of younger learners. Some of this variation is explained by the particular life experiences of older learners (e.g. having caring responsibilities); however, it is often exacerbated by the policies and practices of educational institutions that assume that all students are of a 'traditional age'. Finally, the chapter examined the relatively limited body of work that has analysed those who learn within 'mixed-age' settings. Returning to the discussion at the start of the chapter, scholarship in this area has suggested that there are more fruitful means of conceptualising age difference than merely 'chronological age'.

9 CURRICULUM AND ASSESSMENT

Introduction

This chapter focuses specifically on what is taught in educational institutions and how learning is assessed. Both were relatively neglected areas within academic enquiry throughout a large part of the twentieth century, as scholars chose to focus on issues relating to access to education and transitions from education into the labour market, rather than what was going on in individual classrooms. Nevertheless, since the 1970s, research on both the curriculum and assessment has grown considerably. This has been stimulated by 'the new sociology of education' which ushered in relativist understandings of knowledge, that is, the idea that knowledge is not absolute, but exists in relation to culture, society and historical context (associated, for example, with the work of Apple in the USA, and Bernstein and Bourdieu in Europe) and more recent debates about 'powerful knowledge' (articulated by Young). Both of these are explored in detail in the first half of the chapter, making links to some of the themes introduced in Chapter 2 in relation to the 'contested purposes of education'. Alongside these, we explore the idea of 'twenty-first-century skills' and the questions this raises about traditional approaches to the curriculum. The second half of the chapter considers assessment – both as a social process, which can have a key role in informing the identities of learners, for example, and as a policy tool, which can be used to effect considerable change in classroom practices. The latter is discussed with respect to the introduction of 'high-stakes' standardised testing across many countries of the world from the late twentieth century onwards.

Curriculum

The emergence of the 'new sociology of education'

The 1970s marked a significant turning point in the sociology of education, as scholars' attention came to focus on the ways in which the curriculum, and associated teaching practices, may be implicated in the reproduction of inequalities. Previously, attention had centred, primarily, on questions of access to education rather than the processes taking place within classrooms (Lauder et al., 2009). This change was stimulated by the publication in 1971 of *Knowledge and Control: New Directions for the Sociology of Education*, edited by Michael Young (Young, 1971). The various contributions to this book (by Basil Bernstein and Pierre Bourdieu among others) outlined a relativist approach to knowledge. Together, they claimed that school curricula did not have a secure epistemic foundation (i.e. were not based purely on agreed-upon knowledge) but, instead, should be seen as the product of power relationships and, more specifically, class domination. Bourdieu's two chapters in the book emphasised the ways in which knowledge is structured by social class (Bourdieu, 1971a, 1971b). This theme was developed further in his work with Passeron (*Reproduction in Education, Society and Culture*, 1990), in which he argued that schools help to impose what he called the 'cultural arbitrary' – an arbitrary form of culture, associated with dominant social groups, which is 'misrecognised as objective truth' (p. 22). Thus, he contends that there is no intrinsic reason why certain cultural forms should be considered 'better' or higher value than others; their positioning in this way is merely a result of unequal power relations. The cultural arbitrary, he went on to argue, provided consistency between the experiences and socialisation of middle-class children as they moved between home and school, but exposed those from working-class backgrounds, who did not share the same culture as their more privileged peers, to 'symbolic violence' (i.e. 'the violence which is exercised upon a social agent with his or her complicity' (Bourdieu and Wacquant, 1992, p. 167)). Bernstein's contribution to *Knowledge and Control* made similar arguments but with a strong emphasis on the ways in which knowledge was selected, classified and framed (Bernstein, 1971). Those adopting the agenda laid out in *Knowledge and Control* were strong advocates of change. They argued that, by altering what they taught in their classrooms, teachers could bring about greater equality for pupils. This required a significant shift in how teachers thought about their work; instead of seeing teaching as a progressive force for greater equality, they were encouraged by the book's authors to view it as deeply implicated in processes of social reproduction (Lauder et al., 2009). This 'new sociology of education' represented a clear articulation of the belief that education often acts as a form of social control, and a rejection of the notion that it straightforwardly passes on to the next generation 'knowledge for its own sake' (see discussion in Chapter 2).

The ideas developed almost half a century ago have remained highly influential in studies of the curriculum across the world up to and including the present day. Here, two examples are drawn upon to demonstrate this ongoing relevance. The first focuses on the concept of the 'absent curriculum' and how, in English schools, this has served to disadvantage Muslim pupils, in particular. Wilkinson (2014) explains that the absent curriculum refers to what *could have been taught*, but has not been, and is made up of three elements: the 'null curriculum', the 'unselected curriculum' and the 'un-enacted curriculum'. The null curriculum focuses on national-level policy, and directs our attention to topics that could have been included in the formal curriculum, but which were omitted by policymakers. Drawing on his empirical research on the ways in which the English history curriculum was taught in secondary schools, Wilkinson argues that Muslim contributions were left out from various places where they naturally and easily could have been introduced. For example, in an optional module entitled 'From Aristotle to the atom: scientific discoveries that changed the world?' there was no mention of the contribution made by Islamic civilisation (particularly the Islamic 'Golden Age' from around 700–1450) to the progress of the natural sciences. Wilkinson notes that this 'represented a damaging gap both in the quality of *all* pupils' historical learning of the development of empirical science and potentially in terms of the feelings of self-worth and intellectual participation of Muslim children' (p. 430). Shifting focus to the level of the school, the unselected curriculum refers to topics which appear in the formal curriculum but which are not selected by the school for its own scheme of work. Wilkinson observes that none of the four schools in his sample, despite having significant numbers of Muslim students, chose to teach any of the optional modules that focused specifically on Muslim history (such as 'What were the achievements of the Islamic states, 600–1600?'). These decisions were justified by teachers on the grounds that they had insufficient knowledge and resources within the school to teach them effectively, could not see where such units 'fitted in' with the rest of the curriculum and believed there was not sufficient interest from pupils. Finally, Wilkinson discusses the un-enacted curriculum. This refers to topics that are included in the school or department's scheme of work, but which are not taught by teachers in the classroom. Here, he argues that, during a unit on the First World War, the opportunity was missed by the teachers in his research to link the topic to the Muslim heritage shared by many of the pupils in the class. He contends that 'This was a serious omission considering that the contemporary Muslim-majority world was shaped in large part by outcomes of the First World war in the demise of the Ottoman Empire and the creation of European-style nation-states across the Middle East' (p. 434). Taken together, these aspects of the absent curriculum had a negative impact on the pupils he interviewed, weakening their interest in and sense of connection to both history in general and British history in particular. (Here, there are clear parallels to some of the themes discussed in Chapter 7, in relation to race and ethnicity.)

Although the arguments about the relative nature of knowledge were articulated first in relation to schools, similar analyses have followed with respect to other sectors of education (see, for example, the discussion of global flows of knowledge in Chapter 4). The second example focuses more specifically on the ways in which knowledge is approached within universities. Pereira (2015) outlines effectively how changing power relationships within Portuguese HE have affected the ways in which different types of knowledge and specific disciplines are valued. Drawing on the example of women's, gender and feminist studies (WGFS), she argues that the traditional questioning of the epistemic value of the discipline (i.e. the value of the knowledge it generates) changed when its financial value was recognised. She writes:

> In Portugal, the increased orientation towards profitability has helped expand space for WGFS in a community that was for long openly hostile to it. Because many Portuguese WGFS scholars are highly performing, well-networked academics with good track records of securing funding, and WGFS courses and degrees attract students, university administrators became more supportive of WGFS in the face of significant cutbacks. (p. 287)

Interestingly, this change in status was described publicly only in terms of epistemic (knowledge-related) factors. Playing down the relationship between profitability and disciplinary status is necessary, Pereira maintains, to ensure that universities continue to be seen as institutions concerned primarily with knowledge, rather than profit.

The 'new sociology of education' focused attention not only on curricula and the status of particular types of knowledge, but also on the role of textbooks as cultural artefacts. Michael Apple (2004), who was instrumental in developing a relativist perspective in the USA, argues that textbooks should not be viewed as simply delivery systems of facts but as the result of political, economic and cultural activities, battles and compromises. These negotiations operate at a variety of points in time – when a text is conceived and authored, when publishing decisions are made, and when teachers and students engage with the text. In all stages, different power relationships, perspectives on the world and political commitments are brought into play. While textbooks can be seen as reflecting the 'official knowledge' or 'cultural arbitrary' discussed by Bourdieu and the other contributors to *Knowledge and Control*, Apple contends that they are important objects in themselves, signifying through their content and form particular constructions of reality. There are now numerous examples, from across the world, which demonstrate how textbooks have changed in line with shifting political realities (see, for example, Takayama's (2009) analysis of the impact of changing international relationships on the content of Japanese textbooks), providing good illustrations of the ways in which education is often used to shape national or regional identities (see Chapter 2). Korbits (2015) shows how such changes are often evident in the language employed, as well as the specific content. He notes the different forms of persuasion used in Estonian history textbooks during and after the Soviet occupation (from the 1940s until 1991). While political ideologies were communicated clearly in both periods, the Soviet textbooks are written in a much more direct style, and are 'largely declarative in their rhetoric' (p. 788). They draw on little evidence and rely largely on praising the Russian people. In contrast, those from the post-Soviet era, written in and for a democratic society, use 'more indirect ways of persuading the audience of the rightness of the Western way' (ibid.), moving the Estonian narrative closer to dominant discourses in the West. Emotional tones are replaced by more academic, fact-based writing.

Textbooks are also important *economic* objects, as they generate considerable revenue for publishers. Apple (2004) demonstrates how politics and economics often become intertwined in publishing decisions in the USA. As nearly half of US states have textbook adoption committees – which decide which texts will be allowed to be sold to schools – publishers devote considerable effort to gaining a place on these lists. As a consequence, Apple notes, the texts made available to the whole nation are those determined by what will be attractive to only those states with adoption committees. Such processes are now often played out on an international scale. As a result of the dominance of a small number of large publishing conglomerates, the textbooks sold to many nations across the world often reflect the 'official knowledge' of the USA and the UK, rather than more local forms. Changes in educational ideology in the USA (such as the foregrounding of high-stakes testing, as will be discussed later in this chapter) can thus have a significant impact on the knowledge that is taught in schools around the world, reflecting some of the arguments made about 'global flows of knowledge' in Chapter 4.

It is important to note, however, that Apple does not suggest that textbooks reflect only the knowledge of socially dominant groups, or that the material contained within textbooks is interpreted in a uniform way in all classrooms. His concept of 'cultural incorporation' has highlighted the often-complex processes involved, suggesting that there is a constant 'remaking and relegitimisation' of a country's 'plausibility system' (p. 187). He argues that these processes of rebuilding hegemonic control rely, at least to some extent, on incorporating within textbooks some of the knowledge and perspectives of less powerful social groups – although without any 'substantive elaboration of the world as seen from their perspective' (ibid.). In societies where old regimes have successfully been overthrown (such as former colonial countries that have gained independence), educational texts become crucial means of constructing the new reality and communicating the emerging 'official knowledge'. Change is also possible through the way in which teachers and pupils respond to textbooks and other written materials. Indeed, individuals accept, reject or reinterpret what counts as legitimate knowledge selectively, and are active constructors of meaning within classrooms. The role of the educator, Apple thus suggests, is to foster 'the conditions necessary for all people to participate in this creation and re-creation of meanings and values' (p. 192). Here, we see a more nuanced articulation of the 'education as means of social control' perspective discussed in Chapter 2.

Powerful knowledge

Over the past decade, a rather different argument about the curriculum and the sociology of knowledge has been advanced by Michael Young and various colleagues. Indeed, despite Young's seminal contribution to developing a more relativist understanding of school knowledge, he has recently been highly critical of 'new sociologists of education' for collapsing questions of knowledge entirely into those of power. He argues that, in its most extreme form, the perspective held by such sociologists suggests that, because we have no objective way of making knowledge claims, the curriculum should be based on the learner's experiences and interests – which are equated with the interests of society (Young and Lambert, 2014). In this way, the curriculum becomes primarily an instrument of politics (e.g. for expanding access or developing workplace skills) and only secondly an instrument for achieving educational goals (ibid.). Moreover, Young argues that this kind of perspective leaves no stable criteria upon which to develop an alternative curriculum from the one the relativists critiqued. Instead, he argues that in all areas there is 'better' knowledge – knowledge which is more reliable, and 'nearer to the truth about the world we live in and what it is to be human' (Young and Muller, 2016, p. 142).

In developing their arguments, Young and Muller (2016) distinguish between what they maintain are two very different forms of knowledge: context-dependent and context-independent. The former, they argue, is developed over the course of solving problems in everyday life. It can be practical or procedural but in either case tells an individual how to do things. In contrast, context-independent knowledge is more theoretical knowledge. It has been developed to provide generalisations and makes claims to universality. This knowledge Young and Muller term 'powerful knowledge' because of its role in furthering life chances and promoting social equality. They argue:

> For children from disadvantaged homes, active participation in school may be the only opportunity they have to acquire powerful knowledge and to be able to move, intellectually at least,

> beyond their local and particular circumstances. It does them
> no service to construct a curriculum around their experience on
> the grounds that it needs to be validated, and as a result leave
> them there. (p. 111)

Making specific reference to some of the arguments advanced by
Bourdieu, they note that pedagogy informed by the ideas of 'powerful knowledge' will always involve an element of symbolic violence – as
pupils are taught to move away from everyday, particular knowledge and
towards understanding generalisable principles. Furthermore, Young
and Muller (2016) maintain that powerful knowledge is *specialised* – in
how it is both produced and transmitted. This specialisation is expressed
through the boundaries between disciplines and subjects, which define
their focus and objects of study. From this perspective, a subject-based
curriculum is seen as significantly more preferable than one based on
topics or cross-curricular themes (Young and Lambert, 2014).

Such debates about the nature of knowledge and its place in the
school curriculum have also been played out within policy and among
policymakers. Various international organisations, such as the World
Bank, have been highly critical of the kind of subject-based curriculum advocated by Young and colleagues on the basis that – because of
its emphasis on the primacy of information and (often) memorisation
and rote learning – it is not adequate to meet the needs of a knowledge
economy in which, it is argued, employees are required to work crea-
tively across disciplinary divides (Winter, 2012). Instead, the OECD has
encouraged the adoption of skills-based educational policies, contending
that more (subject- and information-based) traditional approaches will
further the skills deficit and do nothing to address socio-economic
inequalities (ibid.).

At the national level, empirical work that has aimed to test some
of Young's contentions has indeed concluded that knowledge is often
downplayed in contemporary school curricula. Analysis of Scotland's
'Curriculum for Excellence' and New Zealand's 'Curriculum Framework' conducted by Priestley and Sinnema (2014) has indicated that
although both documents accord considerable importance to knowledge
in their statements of intent, they contain mixed messages about the role
of knowledge and fail to advance a coherent position. For example, they
note that in neither document is content heavily prescribed, and desired
knowledge is typically expressed as broad ideas or conceptual understandings that teachers should develop. While Priestley and Sinnema
note that this could be seen positively, as a shift towards higher levels of professional trust, they observe that it presents risks to curricular
practice – as teachers may choose to downgrade knowledge (placing more
emphasis on skills development, for example) and/or specify content for
the wrong reason (e.g. to meet the demands of assessment rather than

build an appropriate curriculum). However, these policy positions have not been taken up uniformly. In England, the Conservative-led Coalition government, in power from 2010 to 2015, explicitly moved away from the kind of curriculum recommended by the OECD and other international organisations. Influenced by Hirsch's (1988) concept of 'cultural literacy', which attempts to make explicit the knowledge 'every child should have', it reintroduced a more knowledge-based, academic and discipline-orientated curriculum. In many ways, this has much in common with the more specialist, differentiated approach to 'powerful knowledge' outlined above. However, Young has also critiqued this curriculum policy in England, arguing that it assumes an overly static, unchangeable view of knowledge and does not acknowledge that it is fallible and always open to change (Young, 2011). In Australia, 'powerful knowledge' has also been discussed, although the Australian curriculum has tended to emphasise both knowledge and skills as related but distinct parts of the curriculum (e.g. Yates, 2017).

The concept of powerful knowledge has been controversial – among policymakers, educational practitioners as well as scholars. Critics have questioned, for example, whether the distinction between everyday knowledge and disciplinary knowledge is as clear-cut as Young and his colleagues suggest. Priestley and Sinnema (2014) ponder whether high-level knowledge should be understood as the skill of being able to differentiate between concepts, while Jones (2015) argues that experiential knowledge can be complex – and not always limited, local and prone to error, as in Young's account. Reflecting assumptions made by the OECD and other international organisations discussed above, critics have also questioned why it should be seen as problematic that schools teach everyday knowledge to prepare students for everyday life. Moreover, it is far from clear that even when school knowledge is disciplinary it always constitutes *powerful* knowledge – it can, for example, be taught in a superficial manner without bringing about any deep learning (Priestley and Sinnema, 2014). Finally, it is argued that the concept of powerful knowledge fails to acknowledge the wider social relations that are at play in many schools across the world – for example, the pressures of performativity, the tendency towards the 'Taylorisation' of educational work (i.e. the process of breaking down tasks into their constituent parts, with the aim of improving productivity), and the impact on both curricula and pedagogy of high-stakes testing.

Twenty-first-century skills

An alternative, but perhaps equally significant, influence on contemporary curricula has been the concept of 'twenty-first-century skills' put forward by Zhao (2012). In contrast to the arguments proffered by Young, Zhao has argued that current educational reforms that promote a common and standardised educational experience for all children are actively harmful and fail to prepare them for a changing world. Reflecting some of the points made about 'global citizens' in Chapter 2, he contends:

> Environmental degradation and destruction are no longer confined to one place. With over seven billion people living [in] different economic, social and cultural settings, some of which do not necessarily share the same values or interests, we must be concerned about how to get along and what we can equip our children with to make the world they will occupy peaceful and sustainable. They have to be educated as citizens of the world beyond citizens of a nation. A global perspective and genuine concern about the well being of others are essential for citizens in the age of globalisation. (Zhao, 2015, p. 130)

Zhao contrasts what he calls the 'employee-orientated' paradigm, within which much traditional education is located, with the 'entrepreneur-orientated' educational paradigm that he believes is necessary in the contemporary world. The former is characterised, he contends, by an emphasis on transmitting a body of knowledge and skills defined on the basis of what is thought to be useful to society and the economy, and preparing pupils to fit existing jobs. The latter focuses – not on the transmission of knowledge – but on developing the potential of each individual child, and on preparing pupils to assume responsibility to *create* jobs. Such arguments have been taken up by some policymakers. For example, the OECD has recently announced that it will be including a new 'global competences' test as part of its Programme for International Student Assessment (see Chapter 3) to help assess respect for other cultures, tolerance and engagement with issues such as racism, cultural identity and prejudice. It is notable, however, that not all countries that take part in PISA have chosen to participate in the new global competence test: Denmark, England, Finland, France, Germany, Ireland, the Netherlands and the USA have all opted out.

Assessment

Assessment as a social process

While educational assessment can be perceived as an entirely objective process – and is often presented as such by policymakers and teachers – sociological analyses have demonstrated convincingly that it is instead a value-laden social activity, which, rather than measuring what is already in existence, creates and shapes what is measured (Stobart, 2008). For example, while some forms of assessment can be useful in raising awareness of inequalities between different social groups (e.g. Singh, 2014), they can also serve to legitimise such inequalities. Liu (2013) makes this argument in relation to the very competitive university entrance exam, the Gaokao, in China. She contends that the exam tends to favour students from professional families, who live in urban areas and attend good secondary schools. However, the commonly held understanding of the assessment as strongly meritocratic helps to justify the privileges of urban residents and advantaged families, and further consolidates their advantage by enabling access to elite universities (Liu, 2013). (These arguments will be returned to later in the chapter.)

Assessment can also have a direct impact on the identities of learners. Reay and Wiliam's (1999) interviews with primary school children in English classrooms revealed how the standardised ability tests (commonly known as SATs), which all children are required to take at the age of 11, had a profound effect on how the children thought about themselves as learners. One young girl, Hannah, described herself to the researchers as a 'nothing' (referring to the numerical score given to pupils on the basis of their SATs) because of her perception that her performance in spelling and times tables (two of the main foci of the tests) was below that of her peers. Her high level of attainment in areas such as writing, problem-solving, art and dancing were seemingly overlooked and irrelevant to her sense of self as a learner because they were not measured by the school tests. A further example of how assessment policies can help shape understandings of what it means to be a successful learner is provided by Bradbury (2013) in her analysis of the statutory form of assessment – the 'Early Years Foundation Stage Profile' – used in the first year of primary schools in England. The profile sets out a model of a 'good learner' through 117 statements, such as 'Forms good relationships with adults and peers' and 'Uses phonic knowledge to read simple, regular words'. The assessment is teacher-based; primary teachers collect evidence throughout the year to demonstrate attainment with respect to each of the statements, and each child ends the year with a score out of 117. These statements are not, however, value-neutral. As Bradbury shows, they reflect a strong neo-liberal discourse, in which rational choice, taking responsibility for one's own learning, and self-promotion are valorised. They also serve to position children differently. Because much of the assessment relies on verbal responses from pupils as evidence of learning, quiet, shy children and those who speak English as an additional language may find it harder to meet the criteria than their peers (and thus be constructed as failing) (Bradbury, 2013). Social class differences are also played out. Bradbury notes that children from middle-class backgrounds are more likely than their working-class counterparts to arrive at school enthusiastic about and flexible in their approach to learning – because of the extra-curricular activities in which they will typically already have taken part. Such children are thus likely to have few problems meeting statements such as 'Selects and uses activities and resources independently' and 'Continues to be interested, motivated and excited to learn'. In contrast, Bradbury asserts, 'it seems reasonable to assume that children who do not have experience of a wide range of activities will find it more difficult to cope with choosing between an array of different activities involving unfamiliar resources' (p. 16).

While in this case, national assessment policy played a key role in defining 'successful learner identities', the practices of teachers can also be influential (Morgan et al., 2002). Drawing on data from a Texan primary school in the USA, Booher-Jennings (2008) argues that teachers first reinforced a strong achievement ideology, in which desert was linked with outcome – thus, 'passing students were able to justify their privileged social position, while failing students learned not to question the social order because they only had themselves to blame' (p. 158). Second, teachers' messages to pupils, about assessment, were often (unwittingly) differentiated by gender. For example, teachers tended to explain boys' failure to pass the Texan Assessment of Knowledge and Skills test (required to progress to the next grade) in terms of poor behaviour and attitude, while girls' failures were attributed to low self-esteem. Girls were thus told that doing their best was good enough, while boys were chided to work harder and improve their behaviour. Booher-Jennings argues that this message was particularly problematic for boys who were trying their best and yet still failed the test. Indeed, for some, their teacher's message led them to question the legitimacy of schooling. She surmises, 'While girls who did not succeed … still won their teachers' affirmation for trying hard, boys lacked this reinforcement. Absent both substantive and symbolic rewards, these boys began to doubt the utility of their investment in schooling' (p. 159). It is important to note that pupils were also, to some extent, active agents in constructing social categories and identities around assessment results. In the Texan study, the girls who passed the test were particularly judgemental about those who had failed. Therefore, in order to protect their place within female friendship groups, girls who failed had to work hard to distance themselves from the failing boys, to demonstrate that they were different. They did this by becoming some of the strongest advocates of the achievement ideology, as a consequence strengthening this discourse within the classroom.

Bound up with questions about achievement are issues related to intelligence and ability, which are also often strongly socially patterned. Intelligence testing, as measured through IQ tests and the like, has been widely discredited – not least because of the way in which it was used to create a construct, which was then reified and used to justify the social position of those with power in society (Stobart, 2008). As Broadfoot

(1979) has argued, 'Intelligence testing, as a mechanism for social control, was unsurpassed in teaching the doomed majority that their failure was the result of their own inbuilt inadequacy' (p. 44). Nevertheless, there remains a widespread assumption that individuals are born with fixed amounts of intelligence – and that ability or aptitude tests can be used effectively to predict future educational outcomes, irrespective of current levels of educational attainment. Sociologists (and other assessment experts) have argued, however, that intelligence and ability should be seen as a *consequence* of our learning and wider experiences, rather than causal factors. Moreover, they have shown how ability scores can affect both the identity of individual learners and the way in which they are perceived by teachers (Stobart, 2008). Recent initiatives, popular in many schools – including testing for 'multiple intelligences', 'emotional intelligence' and 'learning styles' – although often intended to resist the claim of a central, single intelligence and recognise differences between children in a positive manner, make similar assumptions about innateness and fixity. The social and situated nature of intelligent behaviour and learning is thus again overlooked (ibid.).

The allegedly objective nature of assessment is further problematised when we explore changes to the ways in which it has been understood over time. These have varied quite considerably in line with the broader social, political and economic context. There are three main purposes of educational assessment: to select people and certify the knowledge, skills and competencies they have; to specify, and then raise, standards (often referred to as the 'accountability' function); and to improve learning (commonly referred to as formative assessment) (Stobart, 2008). The emphasis that has been placed on specific purposes has differed over time. As Stobart (2008) notes, the development of assessment systems was well-intentioned, as its original aim was to replace systems of patronage with fairer selection mechanisms, and to improve standards of teaching and learning. Over time, however, certification has, in many parts of the world, become an end in itself, with relatively little importance attributed to what is learnt in the process. Dore (1976) has referred to this as the 'diploma disease' – arguing that as competition for jobs has intensified, credential inflation has occurred, with learning seen in increasingly instrumental terms and primarily as a means of differentiating oneself from others (see also Chapters 2 and 12). In contemporary society, the accountability function of assessment has tended to be prioritised as policymakers have come to see testing as a powerful tool in educational reform (Stobart, 2008). As will be discussed in detail in the section below, so called 'high-stakes' testing has been implemented across the world – often conceived by policymakers as a faster and cheaper route to changing educational practice than introducing curricular and pedagogical reform.

High-stakes tests

'High-stakes' tests are standardised tests used widely by governments to hold teachers, schools and local districts to account for the education they provide. Since the 1980s, as noted above, they have become a key means for reforming educational systems – often supported by a wide range of stakeholders from across the political spectrum who see them as a neutral, fair and accurate means of assessing the performance of both individuals and schools (and, in some cases, whole educational systems) (Au, 2009). Stobart (2008) argues that there are four key features of such test-based accountability systems: goals (which are commonly referred to as 'standards'); targets (typically set for both annual and longer-term performance); measures (the tests by which achievement in relation to goals is judged); and consequences. It is the final feature (the consequences) that make the tests high-stakes: results are commonly linked to a series of punishments and rewards – for example, the future of a school may be determined by its performance in the tests. High-stakes testing is associated with an Anglo-American model of educational reform that has now been rolled out on a global scale, based on top-down initiatives (such as the central prescription of tests) and also the involvement of the private sector (Lingard et al., 2016). The edu-business Pearson (discussed in some detail in Chapter 3), for example, is responsible for marking the writing element of the standardised tests used in New South Wales, Australia and, in addition, manages the testing of students in New York in the USA (ibid.). High-stakes testing is also linked closely to the work of international organisations such as the OECD and the growth of broader data infrastructures: school tests can, for example, now be linked to other national administrative datasets, and the results of international testing programmes. Indeed, the Programme for International Assessment (PISA) tests run by the OECD (see Chapter 3) are integrated into the National Assessment Programme of Australia (Lingard et al., 2016). As a consequence of these various interests, Lingard and colleagues (2016) argue:

> Testing programs must be understood as one important element of a broader assemblage of national and international policy agendas that are being enacted in education systems around the world and in relation to the global fields of educational assessment and policy making. (p. 3)

Standardised tests can also be seen as closely aligned with a 'production' model of education as they allow for efficient categorisation and sorting of pupils; commodify pupils (their value comes to be seen primarily through their test score); enable greater surveillance and monitoring of educational processes; and support a meritocratic ideology (by claiming to measure all pupils objectively) (Au, 2009).

The origins of high-stakes testing can be traced back to the early 1980s in the USA. A key moment was the publication of a report entitled 'Nation at risk: the imperative for education reform'. The report argued that the American education system was substandard, had been over-taken by other countries and was consequently a risk to national security (Au, 2009). Its publication had a significant impact – stimulating com-prehensive reform across many states in the years that followed, including the introduction of standardised testing. Such policies were reinforced in the twenty-first century, as high-stakes testing assumed a central place in the 'No Child Left Behind' legislation that was passed in 2002. This required all students in grades 3–8 (between the ages of 8 and 13) to be tested in reading and mathematics, and at least once in science in each of elementary, middle and high school (ibid.) (see also discussion in var-ious other chapters). If schools do not show consistent improvement in these tests, as specified in Annual Yearly Progress targets, they can face various 'corrective actions' such as the offer of technical assistance, a requirement to give students the option of moving to another school and demands that they replace some teaching staff. If after five years a school has still not demonstrated adequate progress, more severe penalties come into play, such as a requirement that the school reopens as a charter school and/or the majority of staff are replaced (Stobart, 2008). Reflect-ing concerns raised two decades previously, the NCLB tests are officially promoted as a means of enhancing human capital and thus ensuring the USA is able to compete effectively with other nations (ibid.).

A very similar testing regime has been instigated in Australia – commonly referred to as NAPLAN (National Assessment Program – Literacy and Numeracy). In 2008, the Australian Curriculum, Assessment and Reporting Authority was established with the aim of overseeing a new educational agenda – specifically, developing and administering a national curriculum and national assessments, and collecting and ana-lysing data relating to comparative school performance (Lingard et al., 2014). Since 2008, all pupils in years 3, 5, 7 and 9 in Australian schools (ages 8–15) have sat tests in reading, writing, language conventions and numeracy, with school performance measured against national mini-mum standards of attainment. Results (at school rather than individual level) are made available on a dedicated website called 'MySchool' and an Index of Community Socio-educational Advantage has been developed to facilitate comparisons between schools serving similar populations (ibid.). Strong commonalities can be seen in other countries, too. Eng-land adopted a national curriculum in 1988, and standardised national tests were subsequently introduced in English, mathematics and science (taken by all pupils at specific points throughout compulsory schooling) –

primarily for accountability and standards-raising purposes. Outside of the anglophone world, Chile also introduced standardised tests as part of a raft of market-driven policies. These were first sat by pupils in 1988, and results have been publicly available (and published in the media) since 1996. At the start of the twenty-first century, a system was introduced to classify schools into high, intermediate or low performance groups based on their pupils' attainment and social characteristics (Falabella, 2016). The group to which a school is assigned determines both the degree of autonomy they have (with higher performing schools being given more) and the amount of state support received (ibid.).

The impact of high-stakes testing has been considerable. In various ways such tests have helped to shape the space in which education policy is made and the means through which it is carried out. In Australia, for example, prior to the introduction of NAPLAN, education was conceived of as a state-level activity. While schooling does still remain, officially, the responsibility of states and territories, the nation-wide comparison of schools made possible (and indeed encouraged) by the MySchool website has reconfigured Australian schooling as a *national* field (Hardy, 2014; Lingard et al., 2014). Furthermore, Gorur (2016) argues that the MySchool website fundamentally altered relationships between governments (national and state), schools, students and parents by creating a 'collective imaginary' based around the ideals embedded in the standardised tests. Similarly, and as discussed in more detail in Chapter 3, the OECD's PISA tests, which can be seen as an international form of high-stakes testing, have helped to create a global space of educational measurement and comparison, in which distinct national systems of education are positioned as proximate and equivalent. As Lingard and colleagues (2014) have contended, 'Similarly to NAPLAN's elision of differences between schools, PISA elides the geographical, cultural, historical, demographic, political and economic specificities of particular nations and assumes a degree of curricula isomorphism' (p. 723). Educational policy and practice have also been reconfigured by a shift of power to the national (or even international) level; through high-stakes testing, policymakers now have much greater influence on what happens at the classroom level – what Au (2009) and others have described as 'steering at a distance'. Decision-making typically moves from teachers to bureaucrats and technical experts, who are often divorced from local contexts (Ravitch, 2010). The implications of this for curriculum content and pedagogy is discussed further below.

While the academic analysis of high-stakes testing has generally problematised its impact on classroom practice and broader aspects of education, some positive effects have also been noted. One such effect is the way in which expectations of year-on-year improvement, particularly in relation to traditionally low-performing groups of pupils, have challenged conceptions of intelligence and/or ability as fixed and innate (see discussion above). Moreover, there is evidence that the clear targets set for schools have encouraged some teachers to work harder and more effectively, and stimulate whole-school efforts to ensure students are prepared well for assessment (Stobart, 2008). Improvements in data quality have made it easier to track student progress, while national benchmarks can enable schools and departments to evaluate their own programmes and identify their strengths and weaknesses more effectively (Hardy, 2014). Hardy (2014) argues that NAPLAN test results 'were not simply valued capitals in and of themselves, but were instead employed diagnostically by teachers, and in association with other programmes, to improve students' understanding' (p. 14). Standardised tests also offer the numerous stakeholders in education a common language with which to communicate (Lingard et al., 2016). Furthermore, the increased transparency about educational attainment has been used by activist groups (at least in Australia) to show that government schools have been able to achieve the same results as their private counterparts, despite lower levels of funding (ibid).

Nevertheless, the majority of research on high-stakes testing – across a wide variety of national contexts – has pointed to the distorting effect the policies have had on teaching, learning and conceptions of education more broadly (Ravitch, 2010; Zhao, 2012). Scholars have provided detailed evidence of how classroom practices have changed, sometimes quite profoundly, in response to standardised testing. As noted previously in this chapter, high-stakes tests have often led to a narrowing of curriculum context as teachers focus on what will be examined, in order to maximise the scores of their pupils. For example, within the UK, the introduction of testing into the early years (i.e. pre-school and the first year of compulsory schooling) has led to the adoption of a more formal curriculum, with greater emphasis on the specific cognitive skills and knowledge that are assessed at the end of the early years. Roberts-Holmes' (2015) research indicated that early years teachers were spending a disproportionate amount of time on mathematics and literacy, on the grounds that they believed it was harder for pupils to score well in these areas. Very similar findings have emerged from Australian studies on the impact of NAPLAN. Polesel and colleagues (2014), for example, sought the views of 8,000 teachers from across Australia. Around three-quarters of their sample believed that the testing regime had reduced the importance of curriculum areas not covered by the tests and a similar proportion believed that the time devoted to other subjects had been reduced. Pedagogy has been similarly affected. Although there is evidence that teachers, in some contexts, are able to appropriate actively the language and prescription of high-stakes test for their own ends (Hardy, 2014), a more common reaction appears to be to tailor one's teaching more closely to the test. In Roberts-Holmes' (2015) early years study this was evidenced in a shift away from child-centred pedagogies to more formal approaches, while over half the respondents in Polesel and colleagues' (2014) Australian research stated that they had narrowed the range of teaching strategies they used since the introduction of NAPLAN (see also Barrett (2011) in relation to the use of summative assessment in low-income countries). There is also strong evidence that, under high-stakes testing regimes, teachers are incentivised to focus more attention on those just below the pass mark – what Gillborn and Youdell (2000) called 'educational triage' – and/or to supress entry levels of attainment when progress is used as a key measure of school success (Bradbury and Roberts-Holmes, 2016). Furthermore, data from Chile have shown how high-stakes tests can sometimes provoke defensive strategies from schools, inimical to the school improvement strategies they are intended to incentivise. Schools in Falabella's (2016) research were engaged in producing narratives of success (however large or small the actual success) while also excusing themselves from poor results by, for example, blaming pupils and their families.

There is strong evidence to suggest that the impact of high-stakes testing is not experienced equally (Lipman, 2004; Valenzuela, 2005). Although many such systems were introduced with the specific aim of addressing inequalities in education, very little attention is typically paid by policymakers to the various structural factors that may help to explain differential academic performance (Barrett, 2011; Lingard et al., 2014). Moreover, Au (2009) argues that, in the USA at least, students with 'non-standard identities' are trapped in a 'triple bind'. First, as the school curriculum becomes more closely matched to the tests, it typically becomes less diverse and less likely to represent the histories and experiences of non-standard groups. Second, this narrowing of the curriculum works against a diversity of identities in the classroom. Third, because of differential test performance (with black students and those from low socio-economic status backgrounds commonly doing less well, for example), students with non-standard identities can feel more intense pressure to do well.

Finally, high-stakes testing has had a significant impact on broader discourses of education – what is valued, how good and bad schools are defined, and how successful and unsuccessful learners are understood, for example (Ravitch, 2010; Thompson et al., 2016). Drawing on the Chilean example, Falabella (2016) maintains that standardised, high-stakes tests have further engrained a logic of competition, which is played out in relation to both schools and leaners, and provides only a very narrow conceptualisation of the purpose of education. She writes: 'Schools are subjectivised and recognised through hierarchically ranked identities, according to who is above and below them. Individuals, then, employ a positional discourse and, based on a competitive matrix, schools are compared and contrasted' (p. 756). In line with the arguments made earlier in this chapter, such discourses can impact on learner identities – and also those of teachers. As Au (2009) notes, with respect to high-stakes tests in the USA, the categories constructed around the test scores to interpret what they mean (e.g. good/bad school/teacher, passing/failing student) encourage individuals to think of themselves and their institutions in these terms, often provoking feelings of anxiety and shame on the part of both teachers and pupils (Howell, 2016; Polesel et al., 2014; Rice et al., 2016). Reflecting the arguments developed throughout this part of the chapter, this underlines clearly the very *social* impact of what are often portrayed as neutral and objective measures.

Conclusion

In this chapter, we charted how research on the curriculum has increased substantially over the past 50 years, stimulated by both what is commonly referred to as the 'new sociology of education', which encouraged scholars from the 1970s onwards to thinking more critically about what was being taught in schools, and more recent writing about so-called 'powerful knowledge' and 'twenty-first-century skills'. All three aim to address some of the inequalities outlined in earlier chapters of the book, but offer very different solutions. The second part of the chapter focused on assessment. Drawing on a range of recent evidence from different national contexts, it showed how assessment practices can have a profound effect on pupils' identities. It also demonstrated how assessment has become a key policy tool used by both international organisations and national governments to effect change in classroom practice. Reflecting some of the points made in previous chapters, it argued that these changes have not affected all learners equally and have, in some cases, served to exacerbate inequalities.

10 TEACHERS AND TEACHING

Introduction

Teachers are clearly key actors in processes of education. Nevertheless, it is only relatively recently that their work has become the focus of (sociological) academic enquiry. Dale (2001) has argued that this is largely because of the institutional location of sociologists of education. Typically, they have worked within departments of education rather than sociology – an institutional context that made it difficult for them to critique the work of classroom teachers (as they were often their colleagues, engaged in teacher training and working alongside them in the same department). In the twenty-first century, however, the research base has grown significantly, influenced, at least in part, by the shifting policy context, which has increasingly positioned teachers as central to raising educational attainment and, in some cases, broader societal reform. The shift in teacher training, in many countries, away from universities and into schools, may also have made it easier for scholars to subject the work of teachers to critical scrutiny.

This chapter starts by exploring the changing role of the teacher from the early twentieth century onwards. It then examines the different ways in which teachers enter the profession, how they are trained, and the ways in which their day-to-day work has altered over time. The chapter subsequently considers the social characteristics of teachers, and policies that have aimed to 'match' the social characteristics of teachers and pupils. Finally, the chapter focuses on the relationship between teachers and parents, examining the claim that schools can sometimes constitute a 'site of struggle' between the two groups. Throughout, the focus is primarily on school teachers, rather than those who teach in HE or elsewhere. However, many of the arguments made in the chapter apply to teachers in a range of different contexts, and in the section on the changing nature of teachers' work we draw out these similarities in a more explicit manner.

Changing role of the teacher

Teachers have occupied an important place within most societies for a very long time. However, their numbers expanded greatly during the twentieth century, when compulsory schooling was introduced by nation-states across the world. Moreover, since the mid-twentieth century, the social significance and role of the teacher has changed quite considerably. Indeed, Hargreaves (2006) distinguishes between four different 'ages of (teacher) professionalism'. Although such ages are not, he acknowledges, universal, they are relatively common across anglophone nations at least. Non-English-speaking countries are now also engaging with the four ages, although not necessarily in the order Hargreaves outlines. He argues:

> The ages should … be seen as a contingent history of anglophone nations that now contribute a collage of opportunities with which other cultures engage, rather than being viewed as discrete stages with an evolutionary necessity that all other cultures must follow. (p. 674)

The first age he identifies is the 'pre-professional' age, dominant in anglophone countries prior to the 1960s. During this period, Hargreaves maintains, teaching was perceived as managerially demanding (in terms of keeping large classes under control, for example) but technically simple. Learning to become a teacher was undertaken through a practically focused apprenticeship, and teachers in general were viewed as enthusiastic people with good subject knowledge and communication skills. Little emphasis was placed on training, and budget cuts, which reduced contact between teachers outside the classroom, were believed by policymakers and others to have little impact on the quality of teaching within the classroom. During the second age of professionalism identified by Hargreaves – what he calls the 'age of the autonomous professional' (running from the 1960s until the 1980s) – the status of the profession increased, as teachers were expected to hold a degree, and they gained more autonomy over the curriculum they taught. Curriculum innovation was encouraged through government funding, and a variety of different approaches to pedagogy was evident in schools (e.g. child- and subject-centred approaches, open and closed classrooms, and progressive and traditional methods). However, as Hargreaves notes, 'professional autonomy might have stimulated many innovations, but with no support structures for teachers, few innovations moved beyond adoption to successful implementation, and fewer still became institutionalised throughout the system as a whole' (p. 680).

The third of Hargreaves' ages, 'the age of the collegial professional', spans the period from the mid- to late-1980s until the end of the twentieth century. During this time, he argues, central governments typically prescribed particular forms of teaching and promoted collaboration between teachers as a means of delivering this policy change. Thus, while teacher professionalism became more collegial and extended in some ways, in other ways professional autonomy was curtailed. Alongside these changes, teachers were expected to take on more pastoral responsibilities, and to respond in a constructive manner to the growing ethnic and religious diversity of their classrooms. Finally, Hargreaves describes the 'post-professional' or 'post-modern professional' age which, he suggests, characterises contemporary teaching in many anglophone nations. This period, he contends, has witnessed various assaults on professionalism (which have been conducted across the public sector, and are not unique to teaching) as market principles have been adopted by governments across the world. Centralised curricula have been imposed alongside 'high-stakes' testing regimes (see Chapter 9). The status of teachers has been lowered through both a widespread 'discourse of derision' (Ball, 1990) and the relocation of much training from universities to schools. Hargreaves concludes his typology by suggesting that there are some strong commonalities between this 'post-professional' age and the 'pre-professional' age of almost a century earlier.

Hargreaves' chronology is helpful in emphasising the contested nature of what it means to be a teacher, and also the historical contingency of some of these ideas. A similar argument is developed by Larsen (2010). While Hargreaves focused on the changing nature of professionalism and the teacher's professional identity, Larsen's emphasis is on the extent to which teachers are positioned as central to student success and societal reform. She argues that there have been two particular occasions in which teachers have been viewed in this way – the first during the nineteenth century, when they were understood as central to the project of establishing national education systems (and thus cohesive societies), and the second in the twenty-first century, when teachers have come to be seen by policymakers, the media and teachers themselves as critical to establishing effective schools and ensuring students reach their potential. For example, in the USA, the No Child Left Behind Act of 2002 claimed that the quality of the teacher is one of the most important determinants of how well children achieve, while both the 'Teachers for the 21st Century' strategy paper published by the Australian federal government in 2005, and the UK white paper 'The Importance of Teaching' published in 2010, both aimed to improve teacher quality as a means of maximising student attainment. The media have tended to construct similar discourses about the powerful role teachers play in their students' lives. Larsen (2010) notes the examples of films such as the *The History Boys, Mr Holland's Opus* and *Half Nelson* – all of which are 'stories of idealistic, inspirational, primarily male teachers committed to saving disadvantaged students through their personal charisma and commitment to teaching' (pp. 212–213) – while female teachers are typically represented by the media as selfless, caring and completely dedicated to their students (ibid.). Alhamdan and colleagues' (2014) research has demonstrated the similarity of media representations of teachers across quite different national contexts – Saudi Arabia, South Africa, Oman, Bangladesh and Australia. They note that in all five countries, teachers are depicted in newspapers as honest and caring role models, who represent the nation's aspirations and are accountable for the preparation of students (in a holistic way) for their future.

While, on one hand, this construction of the teacher as central to student success can be seen as a welcome contrast to the frequent marginalisation of teachers within processes of educational reform, on the other hand, it tends to decontextualise teaching (ignoring the impact of social, economic and political factors) and reduce the complex phenomena associated with schooling to a few simplified generalisations (Larsen, 2010; Skourdoumbis, 2014). Furthermore, policy reforms that have been intended to improve teaching quality (such as those outlined in the various government documents cited above) have often, through their emphasis on measuring performance and individual accountability, had the effect of tightening controls on teachers, thereby increasing levels of stress and anxiety (ibid.). Academic research has also fed into this agenda. The 'school effectiveness' movement, which has been hugely influential across many anglophone countries, has produced lists of 'characteristics of effective teachers' (e.g. Sammons et al., 1995) – predicated on the assumption that good teaching consists of a set of skills and competencies that can be taught to all. The OECD (discussed in more detail in Chapter 3) has also helped drive this agenda. Its *Teachers Matters* report, for example, published in 2005, argued that, after family background, teacher quality made the greatest different to schooling outcomes, and adopted a very technocratic approach (Connell, 2009). The impact of this repositioning of the teacher has been contradictory: while the new emphasis on the importance of the teacher has brought about increased pride and status, the associated rise in accountability-based reforms can be seen as a form of deprofessionalisation, akin to what Hargreaves describes in his account of the 'post-professional' (see also Ishumi, 2013 in relation to the African context). These themes are developed further later in the chapter, when the changing nature of teachers' day-to-day work is discussed.

Entering the profession

Motivations

Teaching is often viewed as a 'vocation' – that is, a career that individuals feel a 'calling towards', and assess as particularly worthwhile. As Moreau (2015) has argued, this construction of teaching feeds neatly into ideas about the 'neo-liberal project of the self', notably in the emphasis placed on individual choice and free will. However, comparative research has helped to reveal how motivations for entering the teaching profession are often socially structured. Moreau's interviews with relatively experienced secondary school teachers in England and France demonstrate how national norms can play a key role in defining how teaching is understood and, as a result, the type of people it attracts. She notes that, for her French respondents, interest in their subject was a key motivation. This relates closely to the wider context in France in which teachers are recruited primarily on the basis of their subject expertise. The status of teachers as civil servants was also important to her French respondents – because of the job security it was thought to offer, and also the way it signalled that they were contributing to a wider public good. In addition, autonomy was a key motivating factor – indeed, French teachers have considerable flexibility in how they organise their work, are rarely required to carry out administrative or pastoral duties and there is no expectation that they will remain on school premises outside their contracted teaching hours (Moreau, 2015). In contrast to their English counterparts, very few of the French teachers described a desire to work with children as motivation for entering the profession – although some did describe it as a positive aspect of the job that they came to appreciate after they had started teaching.

The narratives of Moreau's English respondents were significantly different. For them, working with children was the main motivation for entering teaching. They were much less likely than the French teachers to mention their passion for or expertise in the subject they taught, and were considerably more likely to focus on the attraction of the wider aspects of the job, including the social and/or pastoral dimensions. As with the French sample, the influence of the wider societal context appears to be strong. In England, both the training and the selection of teachers places considerable emphasis on teaching practice rather than subject expertise. Moreover, since the 1960s and 1970s, when child-centred pedagogies became very influential in England, teachers have tended to focus on the development of the 'well-rounded child' – including their physical and moral progress, as well as intellectual development (Moreau, 2015). Moreau argues that the differences in motivation between English and French teachers are related to the wider ethos of the nation-state:

> This concern for the well-rounded individual also appears related to a more individualist Anglo-Saxon tradition, in which teachers aim to 'reach the potential' of each individual and put forward their desire to 'make a difference' in children's lives … while, on the contrary, their French colleagues are concerned with the equal treatment of all children, with equality equated with sameness. (p. 412)

The motivations of English teachers thus reflect the marketised, diversified and individualist nature of the school system in general, while those of their French counterparts are more in line with the universalist and centralist approach that characterises French education in which homogeneity is valued highly (ibid.). (Here, there are strong parallels with the differences in understanding of boys' educational attainment in England and France, as discussed in Chapter 6.)

Recruitment schemes

As part of the reforms to teaching in the twenty-first century, outlined above, governments across the world have sought to change the profile of those entering the profession. Various schemes have been tried including financial incentives such as 'golden handshakes' for new entrants, reimbursement of tuition fees and assistance with housing (Hirsch et al., 2001). One initiative, which has gained traction in several different nation-states, is the 'Teach for All' programme. This is an umbrella organisation of about 35 teacher education projects that are funded by public sources and/or private philanthropy (Ellis et al., 2016). These aim to recruit 'the most promising future leaders' to teach (usually for a relatively short period of time – often a couple of years) and thus help to raise attainment in schools. Such teachers are typically deployed in areas where there are particular social inequalities, such as inner cities. Ellis and colleagues (2016) analysed the marketing materials and other forms of publicity produced by four of these schemes: Teach for America, Teach First (the UK version), Teach for China and Teach First Norway. They show how various tropes were common across the four different national contexts, which constructed both teaching and teacher education in particular ways. First, all four schemes positioned teaching as a short-term commitment, something participants take up for a few years only, and which acts as a stepping stone to elite leadership positions. (Data from participants themselves have shown that recruits also saw the schemes as only short-term commitments (Gottfried and Straubhaar, 2015)). Indeed, Teach for America actively encourages its recruits to leave the classroom after a two-year appointment through its Graduate School and Employer Partnership Program. Here, there is a significant contrast with traditional views of teaching, which have understood it as a long-term career, strongly linked to cultures of professionalism and commitment. Second, the schemes are constructed as primarily about leadership. Recruits are expected to 'lead learning' in challenging classrooms, lead students towards an economically successful life and then go on to lead further societal change in their subsequent (elite) positions. Third, as a consequence of this emphasis on recruits as leaders, teacher education becomes repositioned as essentially about leadership development; the traditional focus of teacher education on concepts such as curriculum development and pedagogy are thus marginalised or erased completely. Finally, the four Teach for All schemes implicitly offer quite particular solutions to the problem of social inequality and public sector under-investment. They suggest that dynamic leadership, when combined with social entrepreneurship and philanthropic investment, can play a key role in addressing deep-seated social and economic disadvantage. Ellis and colleagues (2016) maintain that there are also some important national inflections to the scheme. Teach for China, for example, has particular historical resonance. Describing its website, they write:

> The image of the young leaders teaching in the remote but beautiful southern areas of China evokes memories of the Christian missionaries who preached in the coastal areas of the country over 100 years ago. Time and place may vary, but mission it is and one with an echo of colonization, this time by a travelling reform idea entering a culture of teacher professionalization. (p. 71)

Research that has explored the impact of the various Teach for All schemes has indicated that recruiting teachers in this manner can have a positive impact on pupils' attainment – at least as measured by standardised tests (Xu et al., 2011). Nevertheless, it has suggested that in other respects, it may be serving to further social and economic inequalities. Drawing on data from the UK scheme, Teach First, Smart (2009) argues that while the participants clearly tried very hard on an individual level to combat educational disadvantage, their actions had the effect of entrenching middle-class advantage through enhancing their own social and cultural capital (e.g. through the various networking events and business coaches that were laid on for them); reproducing middle-class values (e.g. through the kind of negative judgements they made about the pupils they taught (and their families), and the absence of any sense that they could learn anything from them); and reinforcing discourses that justified middle-class privilege (e.g. encountering publicity materials that emphasised how Teach First participants were 'naturally excellent teachers', with 'innate abilities' and 'outstanding personal qualities').

Alongside an attempt to attract 'high-flying graduates' into teaching (albeit for a short period of time) via the Teach for All programmes, some nations have also devoted significant resources to attracting other groups of potential teachers. Men and those of black ethnicity have been particular targets, and are discussed further below. Ex-service personnel have also been targeted – in both the USA and the UK – through 'Troops to Teachers' initiatives. The USA first introduced such a scheme in 1984 with the aim of relieving staff shortages in particular subject areas; recruiting to 'problem' inner-city areas, to work with children from low-income backgrounds; and providing employment for those who had previously worked in the armed services (Dermott, 2011). A similar rationale lay behind the UK equivalent, outlined in 'The Importance of Teaching' white paper of 2010, which enabled ex-service personnel to be 'fast-tracked' into teaching positions (Tipping, 2013). In her analysis of the UK scheme, Dermott (2011) argues that it is often in tension with other espoused aims of teacher reform – such as repositioning teaching as a career choice for high academic achievers. Others have argued that, through its focus on inner-city areas, it helps to legitimise the view that (contrary to the evidence) there is a pervasive underclass responsible for an academic and disciplinary crisis in UK schools and urban areas (Tipping, 2013). Moreover, it renders initial teacher education virtually irrelevant, as those entering the profession through this route are not expected to be subject specialists but provide military-style discipline – and to bring the requisite skills with them (Chadderton, 2014). Reflecting on some of the themes discussed previously, the Troops to Teachers initiative also casts teaching as a practical, mechanistic trade, rather than a profession with deep intellectual foundations (Tipping, 2013).

Teacher education

As will have been clear from the preceding discussion, many of the recent changes to teachers and teaching have had implications for teacher education – in terms of both its content and place of delivery. The dominant policy construction of teaching as a set of skills and competencies (discussed above) has been particularly influential. As Larsen (2010) has argued, courses now tend to be based on the assumption that teaching is a scientific, practical and predictable profession. As a consequence, 'the idea of a teacher who thinks critically about the social contexts of education and acts as an advocate for social change is almost entirely absent from compulsory initial teacher education curricula' (p. 218). Universities have also lost their pre-eminent role in teacher education as result of these changes: practical experience, craft and skills (typically developed in schools) are now valued over and above a critical understanding of the historical, philosophical and sociological underpinnings of education (a common focus of university education). There is, however, significant geographical variation. A shift to skills-based training has been easier to bring about in England than in other European countries partially because in this particular context teacher education has never enjoyed parity of esteem with other disciplines or professions. Indeed, Maguire (2014) argues that in England:

> Teacher education has always existed in an uneasy alliance between the classroom and the lecture theatre; it has always existed in a contained relationship with the state lying

> somewhere between a pattern of total domination to strong
> indirect influence at different moments in time. (p. 782)

However, across many countries, we have witnessed the rise of explicit, competence-based standards for teachers and forms of teacher evaluation, which have come to underpin various forms of teacher education and professional development. Connell (2009), for example, details how a 'good teacher' in Australia has been defined in terms of statements about what teachers do or should do – such as 'Develop a calm and approachable demeanour' and 'Initiate or lead the implementation of policies or processes to integrate ICT into the learning environment'. She contends that although such statements are in some respects very traditional, in that they refer to the 'background knowledge, pedagogical skills, organizational know-how, ideology and social conformity that has always been expected of the workforce of a mass school system, since the nineteenth century' (p. 219), they are also strongly influenced by corporate managerialism. The language used in the statements – focusing, for example, on efficiency and flexibility – constructs the teacher as an entrepreneur, concerned primarily about personal advancement through a marketised system. While such standards have been welcomed by some as articulating clearly the complex work undertaken by teachers, they have also been criticised for promoting a highly individualised, neo-liberal view of the teacher and ignoring the social context within which teaching takes place (Connell, 2009). New forms of teacher evaluation have grown up alongside these competences. These are often related to students' performance in high-stakes tests (see Chapter 9) but, in some countries, also include assessment of teacher performance by pupils, parents and colleagues (Elstad et al., 2015; Looney, 2011). Again, however, research has shown that there are notable differences in teachers' capacity to resist such initiatives. For example, teachers in South Korea, with secure contracts of employment, have been much more vociferous in their opposition to teacher evaluation than their American peers, whose jobs can often depend on such assessments (Kim and Youngs, 2016).

In the Global South, different patterns are evident. Although teacher education has also been seen as relatively low status, initial teacher education has tended to remain within universities because this currently constitutes a cheaper form of delivery (Ishumi, 2013). Here, resource constraints have had a significant impact on both initial teacher education and continuing professional development. In East Africa, for example, pre-service teachers spend relatively little time practising in classrooms and, once qualified, rarely have access to a supportive probationary system and/or ongoing development opportunities (Ishumi, 2013).

While there are clearly important differences here between the Global North and the Global South – for example, in the extent to which emphasis is placed on skills acquisition and practical experience during initial teacher education – there are also commonalities, not least in the extent to which governments are keen to intervene in teacher training programmes. In relation to Africa, Ishumi (2013) contends that various national governments (in Lesotho, Malawi, Tanzania and Uganda, for example) have frequently experimented with teacher training programmes and introduced a myriad of changes, often driven by political imperatives. He notes that even as late as the first decade of the twenty-first century, governments were frequently employing as teachers students straight from their secondary education and after only six months of training – driven partially by international pressure to increase universal primary education. Maguire (2014) has made similar points in relation to England, arguing that teacher education has been regarded by successive governments as a suitable case for reform. In exploring why it has been much more susceptible to intervention than the training of other professional groups such as lawyers and doctors, she suggests that it is because of the ongoing debates about the relative value of theory and practice (see discussion above) and the fluctuation of teachers' social status over time. In addition, she argues that the power of teacher educators to resist policy initiatives (and/or propose their own) has been compromised by the diversity of the sector in England (the now-numerous routes into teaching) and the hierarchy of status and prestige that marks teacher education (in terms of both institutions and specific programmes of study). The political nature of debates about teacher education is illustrated well by Schneider's (2014) account of the training offered by the Teach for America programme. He argues that, over time, the short but intensive teacher training given to Teach for America recruits has become increasingly similar to university-based initial teacher education. However, this similarity has not been publicised primarily, Schneider maintains, because it undermines the broader entrepreneurially focused policy context. In this context, 'leaders at TfA [Teach for America] have had every incentive to differentiate their training model from that of "conventional" teacher education, even as their practices become increasingly similar' (p. 439).

Changing nature of teachers' work

Alongside changes to dominant understandings of the role of the teacher, routes into teaching and the nature of teacher education, we have also witnessed – unsurprisingly – changes to the day-to-day work of teachers in schools, colleges, universities and other educational settings. One of the main shifts, which has already been referred to in an earlier part of this chapter, is the increased accountability of teachers, associated with their positioning as key to raising educational attainment and bringing about social reform. This has been driven by a dominant neo-liberal and new managerialist agenda, which has sought to increase the central regulation and surveillance of teachers, and develop quasi-markets in education based upon ideas of choice and competition (Lipman, 2009; Page, 2017; see also Chapters 3 and 11). Broader social changes have also fed into this agenda, including an increasing public scepticism of professional authority, a culture of consumerism and demands for public services that are more responsive to increasingly diverse cultural and social identities (Clarke and Newman, 2009; Gewirtz et al., 2009). It is important to note, however, that such policies have not been rolled out in an identical way across all national contexts. Teachers in the Global South face different pressures (e.g. related to political imperatives about universal education, as discussed above). Even within Europe, however, policies are 'recontextualised' (see Chapter 3) in different ways. As Gewirtz and colleagues (2009) note, in France and Italy, teacher unions and other social movements have been strong enough to block some aspects of neo-liberal reform, whereas the weaker unions of Spain, Germany and England have had much less success (see also Giersch, 2014). There is also diversity in how national governments with broadly similar objectives have gone about restructuring teaching. For example, Gewirtz and colleagues argue that while Norwegian teachers' day-to-day working lives are tightly prescribed by a national curriculum, in neighbouring Sweden, a softer form of regulation has been implemented, in which the national curriculum specifies only broad 'goals', thereby allowing teachers more autonomy. Nevertheless, they note that the overall policy shift is a global one – and one which has brought about fundamental change to both teachers' practices and their identities.

Pedagogy is one area in which practice has been affected. Based on his large empirical study of teaching in the state of Queensland in Australia, Lingard (2009) argues that the neo-liberal and managerialist policies outlined above have had the effect of 'thinning out' pedagogies in schools. By this, he means that, because of a range of structural pressures (such as a crowded curriculum and the privileging of basic skills and teaching to the test over intellectual depth), teachers were not valuing sufficiently the diversity within their classrooms nor connecting their teaching to the world beyond the school, and only rarely making substantial intellectual demands of their students (see also Polesel et al., 2014). Nevertheless, he also maintains that policy does not always impact all teachers in the same way – his study revealed a number of 'productive pedagogies', typically in smaller schools, where local policies had encouraged ongoing conversations about professional practice. Lipman (2009) similarly notes some diversity in the impact of neo-liberal reforms on US teachers' practice. She argues that new forms of inequality have been produced as those teaching in higher performing schools have typically been subject to fewer accountability pressures than their counterparts in schools where attainment was lower: 'across the school district surveillance was differentiated by race and class. Schools in low-income neighbourhoods of colour were the ones on probation and thus least in charge of their own destiny' (p. 73). Lipman's research in Chicago schools found widespread evidence, among lower performing schools, of teachers eschewing conceptual, enquiry-based mathematics in favour of procedures to solve quickly problems in standardised tests, and putting away literature texts and projects in order to focus on test preparation using the booklets supplied by the test makers.

The impact of neo-liberal and managerial reform on teachers' identities has been equally marked. Woods and Jeffrey (2002) provide a compelling account of the changes to the identities of English primary school teachers. They note that the social identities of this group of teachers were remarkably consistent throughout the 1970s and 1980s, and were based upon two sets of values: first, humanism, with an emphasis on person-centredness and warm, caring relationships, and second, vocationalism, in which teachers were wholly dedicated to their job, and had a strong moral and political commitment to the work they were doing. However, during the 1990s, such values came under sustained attack from the changes brought about by managerialism and marketisation (Woods and Jeffrey, 2002). Teachers faced pressure from government and school inspectors to abandon child-centred teaching in favour of using more measurable criteria that could be assessed easily by external agencies. Furthermore, the shift to 'audit accountability' tended to undermine the local trust that had sustained relationships between teachers (and also those between teachers and parents). Instead, trust was redefined as something that was established through the implementation and monitoring of centrally defined strategies and practices. The construction of what constituted a 'good teacher' also changed. Instead of being based on personal qualities, it came to be associated with teacher competencies such as subject expertise and management abilities. The 'human element' thus gave way to a 'commodified experience' (ibid.).

Many of the teachers in Woods and Jeffrey's research found it hard to negotiate consistency between their self-concept – based on the principles of humanism and vocationalism – and the new social identity of teachers that was being forged through these changes to the profession. Most adopted some form of strategic compliance, in which they accepted the changes in their day-to-day lives, but held on to their (substantial) private reservations. Inevitably, however, such practices resulted in more fragmented identities. Very similar accounts of identity change have emerged from other countries that have been subject to neo-liberal reform, including the USA (e.g. Croft et al., 2016) and Australia (e.g. Hardy, 2015). They have also been evident among teachers in the post-compulsory sector. On the basis of her interviews with young academics, Archer (2008) argues that at the micro-level there are important spaces in which HE staff can resist neo-liberal imperatives. However, she also charts the difficulty, expressed by her respondents, of maintaining collegiate, principled projects in an environment that values (or even demands) competitive, individualistic behaviours. She argues that neo-liberalism infiltrated her interviewees' bodies and minds and 'made it difficult for them to speak about what was happening to them and the injustices and losses they experienced' (p. 282). As in the schools sector, the impact of neo-liberal reform has not been experienced the same way by all teachers – those working in higher status institutions have tended to be more protected (Naidoo et al., 2011), while there are also differences by social characteristic. MacNell and colleagues (2015) have shown that – in student evaluations of teaching (an increasingly important metric with respect to teacher performance) – males typically fare considerably better than their female counterparts (see also Wagner et al., 2016). After online instruction, in which individual instructors operated under two different gender identities, students in MacNell and colleagues' study rated the male identity significantly higher than the female identity, regardless of the instructor's actual gender.

Teachers' social characteristics: gender, ethnicity and class

As will have been evident from some of the previous chapters of this book, when social characteristics – such as class, gender and ethnicity – have been discussed within the academic literature, analysis has tended to focus on the characteristics of pupils, students and other learners, rather than those of teachers. Similar trends are evident in policy. Moreover, as some of the discussion below will illustrate, even when policy has addressed the social characteristics of teachers, it has typically been driven by concern about pupils rather than teachers per se (Moreau, 2014). Nevertheless, as educational institutions are places of work for teachers, not merely sites of learning, it is instructive to consider the teaching workforce and how this is structured by key social variables. Within many countries across the world, there are significant imbalances by gender – with women usually comprising a considerably larger proportion than men (Trent, 2015). As might perhaps be expected, there is some differentiation, with men better represented in higher levels of education (e.g. secondary and post-compulsory), mathematics and science subjects, and management positions (Moreau et al., 2007). Research has demonstrated, however, that these gender imbalances are evaluated in rather different ways. For example, there has been considerable concern on the part of policymakers and social commentators at the so-called 'feminisation' of teaching (this is discussed further below; see also Chapter 6); indeed, the low (or at least ambiguous) status of the profession in many countries can be understood as both a function and an effect of its conceptualisation as feminised (Braun, 2015). In contrast, however, there has been much less anxiety at the under-representation of women in leadership positions, as a result of dominant discourses about the meritocratic nature of schools, and a belief that such patterns merely reflect the gendered division of labour within the home, with women less willing to take on management positions because of their family responsibilities (Chan, 2014; Moreau et al., 2007).

Although, as noted above, the social composition of the teaching workforce is often overlooked in policymaking (and sometimes also in educational research), a notable exception is the way in which both male and black teachers have been sought out, specifically to act as role models in primary and secondary schools. Across many anglophone countries, policies have been introduced to increase the number of men entering teaching. Such policies are, in part, a response to concerns about the alleged 'feminisation' of teaching. Those adhering to this perspective argue that not only do women teachers outnumber men teachers in many schools, but that the contemporary teaching environment is more suited to females than males, which has the effect of promoting the learning and ultimate success of girls rather than boys (Martino and Rezai-Rashti, 2010). Increasing the number of male teachers in schools is thus seen as an important component of addressing 'boys' underachievement' and 'laddish cultures' (Francis, 2008) (see Chapter 6). The male teacher has been positioned as 'central to the project of re-masculinisation that is designed to rehabilitate boys' damaged or failing masculinities, as a consequence of the feminisation of … schooling' (Martino and Rezai-Rashti, 2010, p. 249). (It is interesting to note, however, that similar discourses do not pertain across all national contexts. In Hong Kong, for example, over three-quarters of the primary school workforce is female, and the profession is frequently labelled as 'feminised', and yet this is not seen as problematic (Trent, 2015). Discourses of femininity remain prevalent within Hong Kong primary teaching – seeing it as closely allied to practices of 'mothering', 'serving' and 'caring' (ibid.).) Policies have also been put in place in many countries across the Global North, including the USA, the UK, Finland, Australia and New Zealand, to increase the number of black school teachers. These policies typically aim to reflect better the increasing number of pupils from black and minority ethnic groups, and to help improve both the behaviour and the attainment of pupils from these groups by encouraging black staff to operate as role models.

Both sets of 'role modelling' policies have come under sustained critique by scholars. With respect to the recruitment of male teachers, sociologists have argued that the assumptions upon which such policies are based – that is, that men teachers behave and teach differently from their female colleagues, in ways that are more appealing to boys – are flawed. Indeed, they have argued that this understanding of gender identity as fixed, unitary and replicable has been thoroughly undermined by the empirical evidence (as well as critiqued by both social constructionist and post-modern theories of identity) (Francis, 2009). Francis (2009) draws on case studies of a small number of male teachers (drawn from a large, qualitative research project) to demonstrate the significant diversity in their teaching practice and relationships with pupils. She notes that Mr Bentham's 'reflexive, slightly anxious and unconfident subjectivity produces characteristics social ascribed as feminine rather than masculine' (p. 115) while, in contrast, Mr Adams projects what she calls 'authentic authority'. On the basis of this evidence, she argues that masculinity is not the exclusive province of those discursively sexed as male, nor femininity the exclusive domain of those constructed as female. She also notes the fluid and changing nature of gender constructions – citing the apparent paradox of Mr Adams' espoused feminism and somewhat 'feminine' dress, alongside his strict approach to teaching and authoritarian classroom manner. Moreover, research that has sought the views of primary pupils themselves has suggested that they do not perceive gender to be a salient factor in their relationships with teachers, prioritising instead what they see to be the abilities of individual teachers (Francis et al., 2008). Reflecting on the findings of this study, Francis and colleagues note that the pupils' rejection of the importance of gender in this way is intriguing, given what prior research has shown about how children draw on gender discourses from an early age (see Chapter 6 for a more detailed discussion). Indeed, they argue that it may reflect the pupils' 'limited understanding of teachers' pedagogical practices, and their innocent belief in the fairness of systems' (p. 33) rather than necessarily demonstrating that gender does not affect classroom relations. Nevertheless, at the very least, such responses challenge common-sense assumptions that biological sex informs boys' (and girls') relationships to their teachers (Francis et al., 2008). A further critique of policies to promote male role modelling focuses on their failure to address fundamental gender inequalities in schools by remaining silent about the privileges of men and boys at the expense of women and girls, and not engaging with issues related to misogyny and gender discrimination (Martino and Rezai-Rashti, 2010; Mills et al., 2004).

With respect to policies to increase the number of black teachers in schools, Maylor (2009) demonstrates how two key assumptions of such policies are not supported by the available empirical evidence. First, she notes that the policies assume that black teachers regard themselves as role models and want to perform such a role within schools. In contrast, however, her focus groups and individual interviews with black teachers suggested that they did not want to be perceived in this way. While all her respondents agreed that more black teachers should be recruited to address their under-representation in schools, they saw their role as being a teacher, not a role model. Some also believed that such policies engrained unequal expectations of staff, based on their ethnicity: more was expected of black staff, they claimed, because of the assumption that they would act as role models. Second, Maylor maintains that policy-makers assume that black pupils will automatically see black teachers as role models and make a connection between the behaviour they model and their own behaviour, aspirations or achievement. The empirical data suggested, however, that this was not always the case. Respondents described how some pupils found it hard to relate to them because of differences in their social class and/or age. Moreover, broader social constructions also militated against black teachers automatically being seen as role models by pupils; as Maylor notes, 'at a societal level Black people are not regarded as "authority" figures and are invariably depicted as "failures"' (2009, p. 16). Critics have argued that role modelling policies deflect attention away from the complex dynamics of racism that impact on teachers' identities, practices and pedagogical relationships with students (Martino and Rezai-Rashti, 2010). More generally, the role model discourse can be seen, some scholars argue, as a subtle critique of black families and communities – as it assumes that black underachievement is a result of problematic family relations (such as the absence of a father-figure) rather than long-term structural and institutional practices of racism that have sustained inequalities in learning opportunities (Brown and Brown, 2014). (See Chapter 7 for a fuller discussion of some of these issues.)

The literature on the social class of teachers is considerably smaller than that relating to their gender and ethnicity. Moreover, the majority of work in this area has tended to focus on those teaching in HE, rather than at earlier stages of education. School-based studies that have foregrounded class have tended to focus on the middle-class identity of teachers as part of broader arguments about the difficulties faced by many working-class parents in liaising with the school (e.g. Reay, 1998) (see discussion below). With respect to HE, there are now a number of studies that have detailed the experiences of working-class academics, stretching from the 1980s to the present day (e.g. Hurst and Nenga, 2016; Mahony and Zmroczek, 1997; Ryan and Sackrey, 1984). An analysis of eight edited collections of auto-ethnographic essays written by working-class academics identifies some strong commonalities over both time and space (Warnock, 2016). These include feelings of alienation from what are viewed as middle-class HE institutions, being subject to classist language, and experiencing both 'imposter syndrome' and 'survivors' guilt'. Prevalent also was a belief that their own forms of cultural capital did not match that which was dominant among their peers; indeed, Warnock argues that the working-class academic 'must learn a new and different language and way of communicating while often being taught that their own natural style is inferior and not welcome or effective' (p. 31). For those entering the profession more recently, such difficulties were compounded by the high levels of debt they brought with them from their own HE, and the increasingly precarious nature of many of the jobs they had taken up.

Relationships between teachers and parents

The relationship between teacher and parents has, like the role modelling discussed above, also been the focus of policy intervention. Various national governments have tried to initiate closer contact between the two, based on the assumption that pupils achieve more highly when what they learn at school is reinforced at home. In Norway, for example, although the historical relationship between teachers and parents has been weak, recent reforms have strengthened parents' formal rights – through increasingly their representation on school decision-making bodies, for example. Parents have also been described within policy documents as partners (with teachers) in promoting their child's learning (Baeck, 2010). Furthermore, home-school agreements are now common, through which, it is claimed, teachers aim to enforce parental subordination to the school (Vincent, 2000). Moreover, many of the 'choice' policies introduced by governments of the Global North (see Chapters 3 and 5) have been intended to engage parents as consumers of education. Gewirtz (2001) has argued that such policies have also attempted to 'produce' a particular kind of parent – one who monitors their child's progress closely, is not afraid to challenge teachers if they believe their son or daughter is not making adequately progress and provides a range of stimulating learning opportunities within the home. These attributes, she suggests, have a strong class inflection, and tend to reproduce middle-class norms. She contends that policies intended to reconfigure relationships between parents and schools in this way overlook the reasons why working-class parents do not behave like middle-class parents in the first place. Poverty, ill health and precarious employment can all make it difficult for families to prioritise education. Furthermore, in low-income families where parents work long hours, there is often very little time available for taking children on educational outings and/or monitoring progress in any detail. Finally, Gewirtz questions whether the values that underpin the parental practices promoted by policy, such as individualism and competitiveness, are socially desirable. This argument is also made by Kwan and Wong (2016) with respect to Hong Kong schooling. They argue that Hong Kong parents view involvement in the child's schooling as 'an additional battlefield in which they compete with each other to enable their children to get ahead' (p. 100).

While some (working-class) families may be resistant to calls to establish closer relations with their child's school (or not have sufficient time and/or money to do so), teachers themselves are not necessarily enthusiastic about greater parental involvement. Baeck's (2010) research with school teachers in Norway, for example, demonstrates how the school can sometimes be a site of struggle between parents and teachers. The teachers involved in her study were typically positive about parents who supported what they were trying to achieve and gave practical help to their children. They were critical, however, of those parents (commonly from high socio-economic groups, and well-educated) whom they perceived as overstepping the 'supporter' role – by, for example, monitoring teachers, intervening in the school and expressing their own opinions about pedagogy. Moreover, they took steps to distance themselves from such parents by emphasising their own professionalism. This, Baeck argues, 'is part of their defensive discourse of orthodoxy, and thus serves as a conservation strategy that undermines increased involvement and influence of parents in schools' (p. 334). Thus, parents may experience conflicting pressures from policy on one hand and some teachers on the other hand about the extent to which their close involvement in the life of the school is desirable.

Conclusion

In this chapter, we examined how the role of the teacher has changed in many national contexts since the start of the twentieth century. We considered the recruitment of teachers, the training offered to them, as well as their day-to-day work. Although there are some broad commonalities across nation-states (e.g. in the popularity, among policymakers, of the 'Teach First' scheme), we also examined some enduring national differences in the way in which teaching is understood. The chapter then moved on to consider the social characteristics of teachers, drawing on some of the themes that had already been raised in Chapters 5–7 in particular, and policies that had aimed to 'match' the gender and ethnicity of teachers and pupils – highlighting that they are often based on rather problematic assumptions. The final part of the chapter explored the relationship between teachers and parents, suggesting that it is not always harmonious.

11 TYPES OF SCHOOL

Introduction

Various aspects of schooling have been addressed by previous chapters in this book. Schools, for example, play an important role with respect to the construction of gender and sexual identities (as Chapter 6 has shown), and are also key sites for the reproduction of inequalities by social class (Chapter 5) and ethnicity (Chapter 7). The activities that go on in schools are strongly associated with the way in which the teaching profession and the day-to-day work of teachers are understood (Chapter 10) and the extent to which particular curricula and forms of assessment are prescribed (Chapter 9). This chapter focuses more specifically on the different types of school that have emerged in particular areas of the world, how they are linked to broader social and political processes, and the influence they exert.

An important part of the 'school choice' policies that have been introduced in many countries (and which were discussed in Chapters 3 and 5) has been the creation of new types of school – in the belief that increasing the diversity of provision will enable more parents to find a school that suits their child, and that competition between schools of different types will improve educational standards. This is largely consonant with the neo-liberal logic outlined in Chapter 3. However, diversity in school type is not necessarily new. The first part of the chapter discusses some of the different types of school that emerged from the late nineteenth century onwards. Here, we consider co-educational and single-sex schools; religious schools of various denominations; those funded privately and by the state; international schools (see Chapter 4) as well as those that are nationally funded and focused; and various 'alternative' schools. After providing a relatively brief overview of these different types, the chapter then explores in more detail three specific formations, which have particular contemporary relevance: faith schools in England; independent state-funded schools in the USA and Sweden (known as charter schools and free schools, respectively); and home-schooling in a number of countries across the world. It considers how such schools and forms of schooling have emerged, their characteristics and the impact they have on both those who attend them and wider society.

Variety of provision

While many analyses of schooling treat schools as relatively homogeneous entities, there is significant variation by type – both currently and certainly over time. In part, this is related to the historical development of education systems in many parts of the world, which were initially reliant on a variety of non-state providers. In the UK, for example, this goes some way to explaining the dominance of religious schools within publicly funded education, and is discussed further in the section on 'faith schools' below. Variations in school type are also related to differing views of the purpose of schooling (linked to some of the debates covered in Chapter 2). This is illustrated well by the role single-sex schools are believed, by some, to play in society. Many of the first schools to be set up in many nations catered exclusively for boys – as girls were deemed not to need a formal education because of their assumed future role as wives and mothers. Moreover, when views changed and the formal education of girls became more socially acceptable, schooling them separately was often advocated – on the basis that either they required a different curriculum (focusing, for example, on languages, arts and domestic skills) or that they needed their own space, away from boys, in order to develop self-confidence and not be limited by gender stereotypes (particularly in relation to performance in maths and science – see discussion in Chapter 6) (Elwood and Gipps, 1999). The latter position is often held by those who advocate single-sex schooling in contemporary society – that is, that schools provide a safe environment, away from the prejudices of everyday life, in which girls can pursue traditionally 'male' subjects without fear of teasing or pressure to conform to traditional gender norms. Nevertheless, there is no consensus within the academic literature on the actual impact of such schools (e.g. Pahlke et al., 2014; Park et al., 2013). Sikora's (2014) research in Australia has suggested that while students in all-girls schools are more likely to take physical science subjects than their peers who attend co-educational schools, and show more interest in careers in science and engineering, these differences are explained by a variety of other factors (such as differences in academic attainment, parental characteristics, number of qualified teachers and time spent studying) rather than the single-sex nature of their schooling (see also Elwood and Gipps, 1999). She thus concludes that single-sex schooling by itself fosters few non-traditional subject choices. The debate about the relative merits of single-sex schooling is, in some ways, mirrored in disputes about the extent to which schools that cater for particular religious groups offer protection from discrimination, or merely serve to exacerbate religious tensions (Jackson, 2003).

A further key difference between schools is whether they are academically selective or not. While many private schools require prospective pupils to sit an entry exam before they are offered a place, academic selection within state systems is often more controversial. Indeed, the 'tripartite system' (of grammar schools, secondary moderns and technical schools) established in England and Wales in the 1940s – to cater for what were thought to be 'different kinds of mind' – lasted only a few decades after it was shown to reproduce inequalities by both social class and gender. Girls typically had to score higher than boys in the entry exams to secure a place in the academically selective grammar schools (Goldstein, 1986), while working-class students were less likely than their middle-class peers to gain entry because of the way in which the selection procedure advantaged those with more economic, social and cultural capital (Crook et al., 1999). Although England and Wales had moved largely to a comprehensive school system by the mid-1960s, grammar schools do still exist in some counties – and have been subject to the same ongoing critique of their role in social reproduction (e.g. Coldron et al., 2010).

As noted above, many academically selective schools operate outside of the state system. However, it is not the case that entry to all private schools is on the basis on academic ability. Maxwell and Aggleton (2016) have documented the increasing variety of private schools and the distinct markets for which they cater. While some of the schools in their sample focused on the education of elites, others responded to an increasingly competitive market by choosing to differentiate themselves from their competitors by, for example, concentrating on preparing girls for entry to high-status universities, or offering an international education by teaching the International Baccalaureate. Over recent years, we have witnessed the boundaries between state and private education becoming more porous and blurred. This is related, to some extent, to the increasing involvement of private sector actors within the state system (as discussed in Chapters 3 and 12). However, blurring also occurs through the increasing use of private tutoring (sometimes delivered through large tutoring schools or franchises) by pupils who attend state schools (Jerrim, 2017); the funding of private schools by the state (as seen in Chile, for example (Carrasco, 2012)); and incentives for state schools to take on some of the 'independence' usually found within the private sector. This latter point is pursued in further detail in a subsequent section of this chapter. Moreover, most international schools are also located within the private sector. As noted in Chapter 4, such schools are increasingly used by local populations rather than solely expatriate groups – as a means of accessing 'global' cultural capital. Furthermore, over recent years, private schools from anglophone nations have begun to establish campuses abroad, ostensibly to help meet demand for an English-language education from communities in the Middle East and East Asia (Brooks and Waters, 2015).

Finally, a number of schools define themselves not in terms of their selection policy or pupil composition, but with respect to their particular educational philosophy. Montessori schools, for example, pursue a child-centred philosophy in which children are encouraged to lead their own learning, have free movement within the classroom and learn alongside those of different ages. While such 'alternative' schools are often found in the private sector, some elements of their pedagogy have been adopted by state schools. The principles of 'forest schools', for example, first introduced in Scandinavia, have been adopted by primary schools in other countries – providing pupils with an opportunity to learn outdoors in a wooded environment, and encouraging them to focus on aspects of learning not frequently covered in the classroom, such as risk-taking and teamwork. Indeed, Pimlott-Wilson and Coates (2017) have argued that forest schools can offer pupils some relief from the neo-liberal demands of much contemporary schooling (see Chapter 9). Home-schooling is perhaps the most distinct version of alternative education – albeit one that is not underpinned by a single pedagogy or educational philosophy – and is discussed in some detail in the final part of the chapter.

Faith schools

There is significant variation across nations with respect to the place of religion within education. In Europe, for example, although the European Convention on Human Rights enshrines in law parents' rights to educate their children in line with their religious beliefs (and other convictions), it does not guarantee a right to state financial support for such schooling. Thus, while many religious schools in the UK are publicly funded, across the Channel in France, religious schools can be found only in the private sector and a strong secular ethos pervades the state system (this is discussed in relation to the work of teachers in Chapter 10). In this part of the chapter, England is used as a case study to explore one context in which religious schools have been important both historically and in relation to contemporary policy and practice.

Religious organisations have long played a key role in educating English pupils. The Church of England, for example, has for many centuries educated English elites within its private schools and, in 1811, established the National Society for the Education of the Poor as a means of extending its reach to less privileged communities. In part, this was a reaction to the activities of other Christian churches, which had launched educational initiatives in poor communities (Allen and

West, 2011). The Roman Catholic Church was also active at this time, establishing a large number of schools from 1847 onwards, in response to mass Irish immigration into the UK (ibid.). During the nineteenth century, the state provided some financial support to religious schools – first to the Church of England and various other Protestant schools (in 1833) and then, by mid-century, to Roman Catholic schools and a small number of Jewish schools (Grace, 2012; Miller et al., 2016). The state became more fully involved in funding church schools in the twentieth century, most notably after the 1944 Education Act when all religious schools were offered the opportunity of becoming 'voluntary controlled' – in these cases, the state would provide funding for the school and assume control. Alternatively, schools could accept funding through the 'voluntary aided' route. Here, the church was required to make a significant contribution to a school's capital costs but, in return, retained a majority on the governing body – thus giving it effective control of all major functions in the school. All Jewish and Roman Catholic schools opted for voluntary aided status, but many Church of England schools chose to become voluntary controlled (Allen and West, 2011). The two models remain in place today.

Some have argued that the later post-war period in the UK (the 1960s–1980s) is notable for its emphasis on secularism and multiculturalism within education (Walford, 2008). Although never articulated explicitly in government policy, less emphasis came to be placed on Christian teaching, and there was large-scale abandonment of the (formally compulsory) daily act of worship (ibid). Moreover, Church of England schools in particular had become used to accommodating the religious needs of children of many different faiths (ibid). This approach changed markedly towards the end of the twentieth century, when the New Labour government (elected in 1997), decided to fund a greater range of schools for religious minorities. This policy to expand 'faith schools', as they came to be called, was underpinned by Prime Minister Tony Blair's belief that such schools have a distinct ethos, which encourages both academic success and moral development. It was also linked closely to the 'school choice' agenda (discussed in Chapter 3 and above), in which providing more options for parents was seen as a means of stimulating a market in education and thus improving educational outcomes (Patrikios and Curtice, 2014). In an attempt to encourage Muslim, Hindu and Sikh schools into the state system, the government made it easier for private schools to convert to voluntary aided status, by reducing the required capital contribution (ibid). At the same time, it encouraged faith groups to become sponsors of its new 'academy' schools (independent state-funded schools, a type which is discussed further below). Although sponsors were required to contribute to the capital costs of establishing such schools, many faith groups considered this to be an economical use of resources. For example, the Church Schools Trust (formerly the Church Schools Company, founded in 1883 to run Church of England private schools) set up a subsidiary, the United Learning Trust, specifically to sponsor academies (Walford, 2008). By 2010, over a quarter of all the newly established academies had a religious character (Allen and West, 2011). Nevertheless, the faith schools policy was controversial, relating to broader debates about the place of religion in an increasingly secular society and concerns about some schools exacerbating social segregation, promoting intolerant views and limiting the personal autonomy of pupils (Clements, 2016; Jackson, 2003; Walford, 2008).

Research that has explored people's attitudes to faith schools, within England, has revealed considerable variation. For example, Clements' (2010, 2016) analysis of data from the British Social Attitudes survey has evidenced clear differences by religious affiliation. Catholics and those of non-Christian religions were much more likely to support the policy than those who identified with the Church of England or other Christian religions, or who had no religious beliefs. Moreover, those who were religiously committed themselves were more likely than others to approve of funding for all faith schools. Clements suggests that such views may be based on 'a sense of having common cause in defending the role played by faith schools in religious socialisation and protection of minority identities, in a society where the proportion of the population with no affiliation has clearly increased over recent years' (p. 9). Valins' (2003) research indicates that there can also be variation in the meanings attached to faith schooling – even by those who are closely involved. On the basis of his study of Jewish schools in England, he argues that the parents of pupils held markedly different views about the purpose of such schools from the religious leaders who ran the schools. While the latter believed that the key function of Jewish schools was to strengthen the cultural identity of Jewish children, and thus prevent further assimilation and the decline of a Jewish identity, the parents viewed the schools as primarily about academic excellence. Many of the mothers and fathers Valins interviewed saw them as low-cost alternatives to private schools. Moreover, although they welcomed the promotion of a Jewish ethos by the schools, they understood this in largely social and cultural terms; in contrast, school and community leaders placed much greater emphasis on the religious nature of this ethos.

In relation to substantive impact, pupils at faith schools do obtain better qualifications than their peers at non-religious schools. However, this is largely due to the schools' composition (Walford, 2008). Research conducted by Allen and West (2009) in London indicated that secondary schools with a religious character catered predominantly for pupils from particular religious and ethnic groups, and were populated largely by those from more affluent backgrounds who had higher than average levels of prior attainment. Moreover, faith schools in general tend to have more privileged intakes than the neighbourhoods in which they are located, with fewer than average pupils in receipt of free school meals (Allen and West, 2011). Allen and West argue that, on the basis of their data, there appear to be some 'elite' Church of England and Roman Catholic schools that 'select out' low-income families through particular admissions practices (such as interviews and school-administered ability banding). They suggest that self-selection is also likely to occur, as low-income families judge that they have little chance of getting in to such schools and/or believe they are not places where children like theirs would fit in (Allen and West, 2009). It is also possible that parents from higher socio-economic backgrounds are better able to negotiate the often-complex admissions processes and understand how to demonstrate they have met specific admissions criteria (Allen and West, 2011). As noted previously, faith schools are often valued highly by (typically middle-class) parents as a low-cost alternative to private schools. In relation to Jewish schools in particular, Miller and colleagues (2016) argue that 'They provide an exclusive social and academic environment for parents who would prefer for their children not to take their chances in the state system' (p. 552).

The expansion of faith schools in England can be seen, as discussed above, as part of the broader 'school choice' agenda, in which offering parents a greater variety of schools to choose from is believed to stimulate a competitive educational market and incentivise schools to improve the quality of their teaching. Drawing on detailed research in East London, Butler and Hamnett (2012) have contended that being drawn into the mainstream discourse of school choice has had a profound effect on the composition and nature of faith schools:

> the faith schools which once served a non-geographic sub-regional catchment are increasingly coming to serve more narrowly-defined catchment areas in which perceptions of good behaviour, standards, the reproduction of social privilege and educational attainment rather than religious faith have become their main attraction. (p. 1243)

They note that in multi-ethnic areas such as East London, faith schools typically allocate a significant number of non-faith places. Although such practices were introduced to ensure a more representative Asian presence, the places have often been taken up by the middle classes who have been more successful than other groups in demonstrating that their familial 'ethos' is similar to that of the school (an emphasis on complementary 'ethos' is often used as part of selection criteria). Thus, Butler and Hamnett conclude that the faith schools in their study had come to be seen as a refuge for those wanting to avoid schools that they perceived as 'too mixed' (normally meaning dominated by one or more black and minority ethnic groups) or 'insufficiently mixed' (meaning dominated by white working-class pupils). Here there are strong links to some of the arguments made in Chapter 5. It seems likely, however, that the impact of school choice policies differs by school type. For example, research on both Roman Catholic schools (Patrikios and Curtice, 2014) and their Jewish counterparts (Miller et al., 2016; Valins, 2003) has suggested that such schools are often valued more as a means of expressing and affirming a collective group identity than pursuing individual advantage. Indeed, Patrikios and Curtice write: 'Rather than a means of enabling individual parents to express household preferences, it could be argued that such schools are designed primarily to accommodate the interest of a collective social group' (p. 519). Similarly, the leaders of the Jewish schools in Valins' research valued the role their schools played in drawing clear spatial boundaries between Jews and non-Jews, in the hope that 'through the construction of educational boundaries, identities can … be formed and institutionalised' (p. 238). However, as discussed above, such views were not necessarily shared by the families who attended these Jewish schools, who placed more emphasis instead on the schools' perceived academic excellence. In the parents' accounts – which also valued the Jewish ethos offered by the schools – the convergence of individual and collective interests is notable.

Independent state-funded schools

Independent state-funded schools have been introduced in various countries across the world as part of a broader package of market-based reforms underpinned by a neo-liberal ideology (see Chapter 3 for further discussion of this) and, within the USA specifically, as a response to libertarian pressures. Their funding is provided by the state and they are accountable to central government, but function outside of local government control. Some of the most prominent examples of these schools – American charter schools and Swedish free schools – are discussed in more detail below. However, they have also been introduced in Australia, Chile, Colombia, England (the academies discussed above, for example) and New Zealand. Such schools typically have a higher degree of autonomy than other schools, with fewer restrictions on curriculum, staffing, and enrolment practices (Chapman and Salokangas, 2012). They also often have stronger links with business, and may have a particular curriculum specialism or ideological function (e.g. serving a specific religious or ethnic community) (ibid.). Such schools are underpinned by a common set of beliefs: first, that schools rather than the government know best how to use resources; second, that autonomy from local government leads to an increase in educational standards; and third, that increasing the number of providers drives competition which, in turn, has a positive impact on the quality of education received by pupils (ibid). While some of these schools now have a relatively long history – Swedish free schools were introduced in 1992, for example – their form is changing. In particular, it is now more common for independent state-funded schools to be part of larger groups or chains (Berends, 2015).

Wells and colleagues (1999) have argued that US charter schools have a paradoxical nature (and the same argument could be applied to other types of independent state-funded school). By this they mean that, on the one hand, they can be seen as disparate, local projects that celebrate difference and often fight for cultural recognition of traditionally marginalised groups. On the other hand, however, 'they are conceptualised within and connected to larger global trends of less redistribution and more privatisation, greater inequality between the rich and the poor, and of increased commodification of culture via images of mass marketing' (ibid.). This paradoxical nature is now explored in more detail with reference to independent state-funded schools in the USA and Sweden.

US charter schools

As noted above, the American version of the independent state-funded school is the charter school. Such schools are named after the charter (or contract) that is drawn up between state education officials and the leaders of the proposed school, and which specifies the goals and metrics for which the school will be held accountable. Charter schools are typically given up to five years to establish themselves; if, after this time, they are not meeting the required standards (usually state and federal targets for pupils' test scores), their charter is unlikely to be renewed. The state of Minnesota was the first to introduce charter schools in 1991, followed by California in 1992. Currently, 43 of the 50 states have adopted policies allowing such schools. By 2017, there were more than 6,800 charter schools in the USA, educating almost 3 million children (National Alliance for Public Charter Schools, 2017). Around two-thirds (67 per cent) of these are single-site schools run on a non-profit basis, one-fifth (20 per cent) are run by a non-profit organisation that runs more than one charter school, and the remaining 13 per cent are run by for-profit organisations (ibid.). Although the schools have their roots in progressive education, they have been vigorously championed by corporate elites and politicians as part of a platform of market reform, aimed to improve standards through introducing more competition into the system (Kretchmar et al., 2014; Lee, 2014) and have been supported by both Republican and Democrat governments (Reckhow et al., 2015).

Under the Obama administration, for example, charter school reform was promoted as a means of increasing states' competitive advantage in securing significant discretionary funds made available through the federal government's 'Race to the Top' Programme (Berends, 2015). As a result, several states introduced new legislation to remove the cap on the number of charter schools allowed (Reckhow et al., 2015). There remain, however, some differences between states in the regulation of charter schools – for example, they vary in relation to the proportion of their staff who are required to be certified by the state; whether or not schools of a religious character are prohibited; and whether appeals are allowed with respect to application decisions. While a pro-charter consensus has dominated the top levels of national politics in the USA for some time, such views are not shared by all. Indeed, some Democrat politicians operating at state and local levels have opposed charter school policy and, in 2013–2014, anti-charter school protests occurred in several predominantly Democrat cities including Chicago, Newark, New Orleans and Philadelphia (Reckhow et al., 2015). However, the most vocal opposition has come from teacher unions – on the grounds that charter schools represent the privatisation of public education and have reduced both accountability and transparency (ibid.).

Drawing on extensive data collection in the state of California in the early days of the charter school policy, Wells and colleagues (1999) provide a comprehensive typology of what they call different charter school 'composites'. First, they identify what they call 'urban, ethno-centric and grassroots' charter schools. These were typically founded by parents, educators and community members who wished to create a 'safe place' for students of particular racial or ethnic groups. Wells and colleagues argue that these schools represent localised social movements, in which people of colour fight for greater independence from what they see as a hegemonic state-run system. They are thus 'born of the frustration that parents and educators in marginalised communities often feel toward an education system that has failed to take their knowledge, their history and their experiences seriously' (pp. 156–157). However, they also note that, on visiting the schools in this group, there was little evidence of the redistribution of material resources, with many housed in makeshift, poor-quality facilities. The second composite they identify is 'home-schooling/independent study programmes'. Charter schools in this group tend to cover wide geographical areas, often using technology to enable distance learning, and draw together families who had been home-schooling before the charter school opened. Such schools are typically loosely organised and can include both extremely conservative and progressive families. Wells and colleagues argue, however, that most are populated by white, middle-class students. Many of the teachers attached to such schools are employed on a part-time basis, and there is significant variation in the quality of teaching received by students. The schools can be viewed by their founders as a way of making money – because of the relatively low costs of teaching students for only a few hours a week.

The third composite in Wells and colleagues' typology are those charter schools founded by 'charismatic educational leaders'. Such people are commonly motivated by a desire to secure more autonomy from the local school district in terms of pedagogy, the curriculum and/or the budget. One of the leaders identified by their research had used the autonomy that came with charter school status to introduce a new mathematics programme, for example. Generally, schools in this group valued highly the professional knowledge of teachers and were often 'converted' public schools. In some ways, these schools were similar to those in the fourth composite – 'teacher-led charter schools'. Such schools also tended to have converted from public schools, and had pursued charter status as a means of developing a particular pedagogical approach (e.g. progressive, mixed-age, open classroom or a traditional 'classic' curriculum). Those teaching in such schools were typically very committed to public education as long as teachers had sufficient freedom to exercise their own professional judgement. The fifth composite Wells and colleagues identify is the 'parent-led charter school'. These were most likely to be found in wealthy areas, and to have been set up by well-educated and well-off parents with plenty of social connections. They were attractive to other professional, middle-class families but varied considerably in their pedagogic focus (from those focusing on a highly traditional curriculum to others that favoured a much more progressive approach). The final composite in the typology is the 'entrepreneur-initiated charter school'. These schools were often located in urban areas and served students deemed to be 'at risk' – that is, those from poor families, of colour and/or who had been excluded from school. They were typically founded by people from outside the local community who had a strong view about how schools should be run; such views often placed little value on the professional knowledge of educators and emphasised, instead, the utility of implementing business models. The curriculum in these schools was often driven by textbook publishers and, compared to the other types of charter school, pupils spent relatively little time with teachers. Teachers themselves were often employed on part-time contracts, with few benefits.

This evident variety in charter schools makes judging their overall impact a complex task. With respect to academic achievement, there is little consistent evidence of widespread improvement. Some studies have shown a positive impact, but these have focused on charter schools in a small number of specific US cities (Berends, 2015); others have suggested that there has been a positive impact with respect to reading but not in mathematics (CREDO, 2013). There have, however, been some positive results in terms of progression to college (ibid). Research has also focused on charter schools' wider social, political and educational influence. Wells and colleagues argue that they do offer some emancipatory potential – for example, by enabling those who have been marginalised by the public education system to have a say in how their children are educated and to offer curricula that recognise cultural difference, and facilitating more collective decision-making in which teachers and parents can become more involved. However, returning to the paradox discussed previously, they also note the regressive tendencies of charter schools. In particular they emphasise the increasing atomisation of the education system, and the way in which poor communities become isolated – from both one another and more affluent groups, and the consolidation of middle-class power. Moreover, they suggest that charter schools can provide a means for privileged parents to resist redistributive state policies (i.e. opting out of a local system in which a proportion of the budget is ring-fenced for bilingual education and special educational needs provision, for example) (see also Kretchmar et al., 2014). Social sorting can also occur through some schools' requirements that parents volunteer (despite a legal requirement that schools are non-discriminatory). Regressive tendencies are also highlighted in more recent qualitative studies. Buras' (2015) detailed ethnographic study of the huge growth in the number of charter schools in New Orleans over the past ten years has argued that black families have been significantly disadvantaged by the changes as a result of the location of many new schools in white rather than black communities; the exclusion of local people from many of the decisions about schools and curricula; and the replacement of black veteran teachers with young, white teachers employed through the Teach First scheme (see Chapter 10 for fuller discussion of this scheme and Chapter 7 for more detail about black students' experiences of education).

Swedish free schools

Free schools were established in Sweden around the same time as their counterparts in the USA and have many features in common. In explaining how such schools came to be introduced in a system that has, historically, been strongly comprehensive, Wiborg (2010) points to the impact of the decline of export markets (particularly in the mining and ship-building industries) in the 1970s, which led to a general economic decline in Sweden. In this context, education fell victim to the general criticism of the public welfare system and, by the mid-1980s, there was, for the first time in post-war Swedish history, collective opposition to the social democratic principles of universal welfare (ibid.). Neo-liberal policies were thus pursued by the Conservative-led coalition government that came to power in 1991. In 1992, a voucher system was introduced and privately operated schools were allowed to compete for pupils on an equal financial basis as their public counterparts. Wiborg notes that these reforms changed Sweden's education system dramatically – from a virtually all-public system with little room for parental choice to one of the world's most liberal public education systems. Reflecting the various 'composites' in the US system, outlined above, the Swedish free school sector is also characterised by diversity – with schools run by small parent co-operatives, subject specialists and large for-profit companies (Wiborg, 2010). However, in contrast to the USA, the most common type of free school is that run by for-profit organisations (West, 2014). Nevertheless, West (2014) argues that, despite allowing schools to run on a for-profit basis, a strong commitment to equality of opportunity remains in the Swedish system; schools are allowed to use only a very limited number of admission criteria and selection on the basis of religion is prohibited, for example.

Assessing the impact of Swedish free schools is as complex and politi-cally fraught as in the USA, and there has been profound public criticism of the policy. Opponents have argued that for-profit companies are inter-ested primarily in generating revenue rather than promoting pedagogical innovation and preparing pupils for democratic citizenship, and are mak-ing money at the expense of the Swedish taxpayer (Wiborg, 2010). There is evidence of overall costs having risen as a result of overcapacity in some local areas that have a large number of free schools (ibid.). In addition, free schools are seen as exacerbating social segregation, by both social class and ethnicity (West, 2014). More generally, some contend that the dominant educational discourse has shifted profoundly – from one that emphasises the role of schools in preparing young people, in an inclusive manner, for civic participation, to one that foregrounds the instrumental role of education, primarily as preparation for work (Wiborg, 2010) (see Chapter 2 for a fuller discussion of these contested purposes). Schools are less likely to collaborate now that they have to compete for pupils, and teachers, it is suggested, have adopted more market-oriented behaviours (ibid.). With respect to academic attainment, the data indicate that chil-dren attending free schools achieve slightly more highly than their peers in public schools, but this is explained largely by their socio-economic status: those attending free schools are more likely to come from highly educated families (Bunar, 2010).

Home-schooling

What is home-schooling?

From a historical perspective, the institution of the school is a relatively recent phenomenon. Indeed, prior to the late nineteenth century, chil-dren were usually educated at home, their learning the sole responsibility of their parents; it was only with the rise of industrialisation that schools came to take on this responsibility. Thus, the increasing popularity of 'home-schooling' in many parts of the world from the middle of the twentieth century can be seen, in some ways, as a return to earlier forms of education. In other ways, however, it is closely related to contemporary practices, including the call from many politicians and policymakers for parents to be much more closely involved in their children's education in general (see discussion in Chapters 3 and 10). (Neuman and Aviram, 2003). Home-schooling is usually considered to be a form of 'alternative education' in that practitioners tend to distance themselves from mainstream provision – similar to those who become involved in other alternative forms such as Montessori and Steiner schools. However, as Kraftl (2013) argues, home-schooling is considered an alternative practice only in countries in which it is expected that all students attend a school of some sort. There is also significant diversity of practice and policy even among countries of the Global North. Although the number of families choosing to educate their children at home has grown considerably since the 1970s, the legal status of home-schooling, and the involvement of the state, is varied. In Germany, for example, home-schooling is illegal; parents found to be educating their children at home can face fines and a prison sentence of up to six months (Spiegler, 2009). In the USA, however, home-schooling was legalised in 1993, and home-schoolers have gained increasing freedoms over time. A similar pattern has emerged in Israel, where parents are able to ask for exemptions from formal schooling. Here, home-schooling was considered very unusual until the 1990s, but then grew in popularity and gained greater political acceptance (Neuman and Aviram, 2003). In the UK, home-schooling is legal but, during the twenty-first century, has come under increasing government scrutiny (Kraftl, 2013). In contrast, in some remote parts of Australia where it is physically impossible to attend school, home-schooling is a necessity rather than a choice – and is supported by the state through distance education programmes and daily radio lessons (N. Green, 2006).

Data on the number of home-schoolers are rarely very accurate, because in many countries families are either not required to formally register as home-schooling, or choose not to anyway. Nevertheless, estimates suggest the number of children being educated at home is around 2 million in the USA – at least 2.2 per cent of the school-age population – and between 50,000 and 150,000 in the UK (Hanson Thiem, 2007; Kraftl, 2013). The US numbers are particularly significant since, even as recently as 1980, home-schooling was illegal in 30 states. The substantial increase in the number of families pursuing home-schooling in the late twentieth century was accompanied by a similar shift in public attitudes. In the USA, for example, the number of Americans who were actively opposed to home-schooling (i.e. who considered it a 'bad thing') fell from 73 per cent in 1988 to 57 per cent in 1999 (Cooper and Sureau, 2007).

The rise of home-schooling

A key question, which is explored in a number of studies of home-schooling, is why did this particular form of education become popular, across many countries of the Global North, in the second half of the twentieth century? Most analyses focus on the USA, in particular, and attempt to explain both the numerical growth in home-schooling and its institutionalisation. Scholars agree that the origins of home-schooling are in the counter-culture movements of the 1960s and early 1970s, when parents rejected what they perceived to be the rigidity and inflexibility of state education. They were influenced by a range of ideas from the political left, including progressive pedagogies and the alternative schools movement (Gaither, 2009; Hanson Thiem, 2007). Home-schooling was also taken up by those on the political right as a solution to their own concerns about state education. Evangelical Christians, in particular, were critical of the growing secularisation of schools, and the increasing difficulty of accessing Christian schools. They adopted home-schooling in considerable numbers as a means of reintegrating religious training, and protecting their children from peer influence (Gaither, 2009; Hanson Thiem, 2007). Gaither (2009) suggests that the rise of home-schooling was also related to the increasing number of educated women in the population; for those who believed they should stay at home rather than enter paid employment, teaching their children was seen as a means of putting their own education to good use. Finally, in the second half of the twentieth century, in the USA and elsewhere, people's homes became bigger and more comfortable, thus providing a more amenable environment for home education (Gaither, 2009).

Various scholars have argued that the rise of home-schooling is associated with the increasing dominance of neo-liberal policies worldwide which (as explained in Chapter 3) are broadly pro-market and anti-state in their orientation. Apple (2000), for example, contends that those who choose to home-school are often motivated by the belief that the welfare state is an active agent in national decline, as well as a drain on their own family's resources. However, this position is not shared by all. Indeed, drawing on their research in Canada, Aurini and Davies (2005) maintain that many of the home-schoolers in their study had withdrawn their children from mainstream schools (or not enrolled them in the first place) *because of* what they perceived to be damaging neo-liberal reform. They do acknowledge, however, that neo-liberalism may play a role in home-schooling by legitimising it through the logic of 'school choice' that is now well-embedded in many nation-states (see above). They go on to argue that many of their respondents were driven by what they call an 'expressive logic' – that is, the belief that their child was too important to be entrusted to others and that s/he needed both personal attention and a tailored pedagogy, neither of which could be provided by mainstream schools. Here, there are strong links to the idea of 'intensive mothering' discussed in Chapter 6.

The impact of home-schooling

In a fascinating account of families who home-school in the UK, Kraftl (2013) argues that the decision to take a child out of mainstream education and teach them at home represents three key changes in the practices of education. First, he notes that most of the parents in his study discussed their choices in terms of a shift in pedagogy – towards a more child-centred and flexible approach. Second, he argues that this change in practice also represents a significant physical shift – in terms of the places that are used for learning. Many of his respondents described how their child now spent much more time learning outdoors – and also 'on the move', during shopping trips, for example. Developing his analysis of these new spaces of learning, Kraftl contends that, for home-schoolers, learning becomes embedded in the material, and often quite banal, details of a child's experience – exploring, for example, the salt left on a windowsill after saltwater had accidentally been spilt there. He reflects that while school-based learning often values highly (and sometimes exclusively) a 'rationalised form of order', his respondents valorised instead 'mess, clutter, stuff and disorganisation' (p. 443). Third, he identifies the temporal change that is often associated with learning at home rather than at school. Home-schooling tends, he argues, to be associated with both slowness and spontaneity. Slowness was emphasised by parents in relation to ensuring that their children had sufficient time to play, and were able to follow their own interests at a pace that suited them and relaxed in their approach to learning. Often this was (implicitly or sometimes explicitly) contrasted favourably with the more relentless pace of learning in schools. Nevertheless, a faster tempo was also valued at times by the home-schoolers. Many spoke of enjoying the freedom to follow up particular interests of their child in a spontaneous manner.

Drawing similarly on the theme of change, Mazema (2016) describes how home-schooling had a significant impact on the African-American children in her research. Although there was considerable diversity in the practices of the 74 families she interviewed, she notes that all of them were implementing a curriculum that was inclusive of African or African-American history and culture as part of a conscious attempt to foster a new narrative for their children. This was motivated, at least in part, by the parents' own experience of the (mainstream) school curriculum as a site of racial and cultural oppression, with a near-exclusive focus on European history and culture (see Chapters 7 and 9). Mazema concludes by arguing that 'many Black home-schoolers are redefining for themselves what counts as curriculum by claiming that the history and culture of their people are significant' (p. 38). Home-schooling has also been pursued in the UK by Traveller families (Romany gypsy families and showmen) as a response to what they perceive to be a lack of respect for their cultures within formal schooling and frequent racist bullying (D'Arcy, 2014). However, in contrast to the experiences of the African-American families discussed above, D'Arcy's (2014) research suggests that home-schooling can often exacerbate the inequalities experienced by Traveller children. Many of the families she interviewed had difficulty affording books and other educational resources and, because of the lack of support for home-educating parents, were unsure whether what they were doing was right, especially in the case of children who had special educational needs.

Some scholars have suggested that home-schooling also has a wider impact – affecting society in general, not just the families who choose to educate in this way. Lubienski (2000), for example, maintains that it should be seen as the ultimate form of privatisation and antithetical to the common good. The discourse of home-schooling, in his analysis, focuses on individual rights and private benefits, and is thus part of a broader trend in which private goods are elevated above their public counterparts. He argues that the common good is denied in two ways. First, as both children and social capital are withdrawn from state schools, those remaining behind are adversely affected. Second, by leaving the system altogether, rather than working with schools to address their weaknesses, home-schooling families deny schools the opportunity to improve and become more responsive as democratic institutions. Thus, Lubienski concludes, home-schooling is not only a reaction to, but a cause of, decline in state schools. Similar arguments are made by Apple (2000), who contends that religiously motivated home-schoolers, in particular, are 'engaged in exploiting public funding in ways that are not only hidden but ... that raise serious questions about the drain on economic resources during a time of severe budget cuts' (p. 268). He cites the example of virtual charter schools in California that give money to enrolling home-schooling families, which is then used by the parents to buy conservative religious teaching materials (despite the legal prohibition of public money being used for religious purposes). Moreover, Apple argues that home-schooling in the USA is an extension of what he calls the 'suburbanisation' of everyday life – that is, akin to the privatisation of neighbourhoods (through 'gated communities'), parks and other open spaces. It is, he maintains, a microcosm of an increasingly segmented American society, in which families seek to 'cocoon' themselves from others. These differing analyses of home-schooling reflect, in some respects at least, those discussed above in relation to the paradoxical nature of independent state-funded schools.

Conclusion

This chapter focused on the variety of new school types that have been introduced in many parts of the world over recent decades. It noted that, historically, there has been significant variation in school type – including those funded by the state or privately; religious and non-religious schools; selective and non-selective schools; and single-sex and co-educational institutions. However, it examined in more detail three particular types of schooling that have been promoted particularly in some nations over the last couple of decades. It considered the high political priority given to religious (or 'faith') schools in England, before documenting the rise of independent, state-funded schools in both the USA and Sweden (where they are called charter schools and free schools, respectively). Finally, it explored the rise of home-schooling in various countries – and the motivations of those parents who choose to educate their children in this way. Links were made both to Chapter 3, in relation to dominant policy imperatives, and to Chapters 5 to 7, with respect to the impact of these school types on particular groups of pupils.

12 HIGHER EDUCATION AND BEYOND

Introduction

Over recent decades, HE has expanded significantly in many parts of the world and has become an increasingly common experience for young people before they enter full-time employment. It is also seen in some nations as an important means of re-engaging older learners, and ensuring that skills and knowledge are kept up to date. This chapter begins by considering some of the changes to HE over the past 10 to 20 years, including the new significance it has taken on in the context of putative wider economic shifts. It then focuses more specifically on processes of learning and assessment in HE, and the ways in which HE students have been conceptualised (e.g. as consumers, political actors and workers, as well as learners). The chapter moves on to explore routes out of HE into the graduate labour market, and the relationship between HE and life-long learning more generally.

Changing nature of higher education

Universities have a long history, with the first having been established in the eleventh and twelfth centuries. Medieval universities were made up of groups of scholars – committed to the pursuit of knowledge – who formed themselves into self-governing guilds; they were subsequently recognised as formal foundations with the power to award degrees (Bathmaker, 2003). The focus on self-government and the pursuit of knowledge continued to underpin the universities of the nineteenth century; emphasis was placed on exposing students to the best knowledge and thinking in the world (ibid.). Such ideals have also informed understandings of the modern university – which foreground ideas about respect for others, tolerance of rival views, a willingness to be self-critical and the importance of the quest for truth (Barnett, 2000; Bathmaker 2003). There have, however, been various differences in the model of the university that has been adopted in particular nation-states. A commonly made distinction is between Humboldtian, Napoleonic and Anglo-Saxon models (Sam and der Sijde, 2014). The Humboldtian (or German) model was influenced by the ideas of the nineteenth-century Prussian philosopher, diplomat and civil servant, Wilhelm von Humboldt, who founded the University of Berlin. It places emphasis on research-based learning, the primacy of 'pure' science (over professional training), and the freedom of lecturers to decide what and how to teach. In contrast, the Napoleonic (or French) model focuses on the role of HE in preparing graduates for a rapidly changing labour market, by providing professional education and high-level vocational training. The Anglo-Saxon model, which emerged in the universities of Oxford and Cambridge in the nineteenth century, foregrounds the importance of personality development through a 'liberal education' (ibid.). While some such differences remain (see discussion later in the chapter), we have witnessed an increasing convergence of HE systems. Indeed, Sam and der Sijde (2014) have argued that the three traditional models have been replaced by a single Anglo-American model, characterised by, for example, competition, marketisation, decentralisation and a focus on entrepreneurial activity. Until the mid-twentieth century, universities, whichever model they followed, typically taught only a small proportion of the population. In the UK, as late as 1950, only 3.4 per cent of young people went on to HE – very much an elite system (Trow, 1973). In the second half of the twentieth century, however, the HE sector in many parts of the world changed fundamentally – in relation to its societal function and significance, size, and relationship with the private sector. Each of these are now discussed in turn.

New significance within a knowledge economy

HE has, in many different locations, taken on a new significance and meaning in contemporary society. In large part, this has been related to the concept of a global 'knowledge economy' and the belief that future economic prosperity will rest on the ability of nations to produce highly skilled graduates to engage in 'knowledge work'. Universities have thus been positioned as key sites for economic production – through educating knowledge workers and also by creating knowledge products to enable private sector growth (Shear and Hyatt, 2015). Although one purpose of formal education has always been to support economic development (see discussion in Chapter 2), many scholars have argued that the changes to HE witnessed over recent years have been particularly profound, and have encompassed far-reaching changes to institutions' goals and practices and, in many cases, their relationship with the state. Indeed, as Hazelkorn (2015) notes, 'higher education has been transformed from being considered a social expenditure to being an essential component of the productive economy' (pp. 4–5). The consequence of this, she goes on to argue, is that the way in which HE is managed and governed has, in many nations, become a significant policy issue (this will be discussed further, in relation to privatisation, below).

One way in which this new significance has been played out is in the increasing involvement within HE of supranational and/or regional bodies. In Europe, for example, a large number of nation-states (currently 48) have come together to develop a European Higher Education Area – often referred to as the 'Bologna Process' (taking its name from the place where the initial declaration was signed in 1999) (see discussion in Chapters 3, 4 and 8). This process has sought to standardise various aspects of HE across signatory countries, including the introduction of comparable degree programmes, based on two main cycles (under-graduate and postgraduate); a common system of credits for courses, to facilitate student (and staff) mobility; similar criteria and methodologies for quality assurance; and a 'European dimension' in HE – through, for example, curriculum development, collaboration between HEIs, and closer integration across the continent of study and research programmes (Holford, 2014). The Bologna Process is not, however, restricted to members of the EU and, as Birtwistle (2007) has noted, encompasses 'the wider Europe, stretching from Azerbaijan to Iceland' (p. 182). While an important aim of the European Higher Education Area has been to promote mobility – and thus employability and economic competitiveness – within Europe, it is also an outward-facing policy, seeking to strengthen the attractiveness of European HE relative to other parts of the world, and encourage other regional HE systems to follow the model set by Europe (Robertson, 2009). The Erasmus-Mundus programme, for example, established in 2004, aims to encourage mobility between EU and non-EU countries of both students and staff through funding scholarships and partnerships between institutions. This outward-facing emphasis has been particularly strong since 2003, Robertson (2009) contends, related to a more explicitly globalising strategy on the part of the EU, with the intention of legitimising the European Commission as a state-like actor, and providing a more solid springboard for competition with the USA.

Although politicians and policymakers across Europe have generally spoken positively about the Bologna Process, these sentiments have not always been shared by all those working (and indeed studying) in HE. With respect to Austria, for example, Pechar and Wroblewski (2012) argue that the reforms have been introduced in a largely superficial manner due to widespread objections to the perceived emphasis on employ-ability within the European Higher Education Area. These objections, they maintain, are closely related to the Humboldtian tradition that tends to reject the notion that universities should be concerned, to any extent, with practical and applied knowledge (see also Wolter, 2012). They also note that many Austrians are committed to the Humboldtian idea of 'unity of teaching and research' within HE, and are thus resistant to undergraduate degrees that contain little or no research focus:

> In the German-speaking countries, the idea of 'unity of teaching and research' is still regarded as the essence of any kind of higher education. Any move towards a more structured curriculum with explicit obligations for both students and teachers is pejoratively called 'Verschulung' – a move towards a school-like curriculum that eliminates the differences in the learning cultures of schools and universities. (p. 29)

Austrian employers (including, rather ironically, the government) have also been sceptical about the new bachelor's degree introduced as part of the Bologna reforms, and still tend to prefer those with a master's degree; indeed, the bachelor's degree is often not regarded as a degree in its own right (ibid.). Thus, the emphasis on developing common HE 'regions' has achieved only partial success.

Massification

A second major change relates to the significant expansion of HE across the world, or what is commonly called 'massification'. Trow (1973) has usefully distinguished between elite, mass and universal national HE systems. According to his typology, elite systems typically cater for under 15 per cent of the eligible population, mass systems for between 15 and 40 per cent, and universal systems for over 40 per cent. Since the early 1960s, many countries of the Global North have moved from elite to mass systems. Indeed, across OECD countries, an average of 40 per cent of young people now progress to HE. Similar patterns have more recently been played out in other parts of the world, too. Since the 1980s, Asia Pacific countries such as China, Taiwan, Japan and South Korea have all witnessed substantial growth in their HE population – with demand often outstripping the supply of places available within the public sector (Mok, 2016). China, for example, has devoted significant energy and resource to expanding its own HE system, in the belief that HE growth is necessary to bolster national competitiveness. In 1988, the Chinese government published an 'Action Plan to Vitalize Education in the 21st Century', which aimed to achieve a gross enrolment rate of 15 per cent by 2010, later adjusting the goal when it was reached five years early (Mok and Jiang, 2016).

Alongside an expansion in student numbers has been an emphasis – in some countries although not all – on ensuring that a wider cross-section of the population has access to HE. Such initiatives have been stimulated in part by data that have indicated that more privileged groups in society have tended to benefit most from processes of massification. In the UK, for example, Crawford and colleagues (2017) have shown that the university entry rate of students from non-manual backgrounds increased from around 10 per cent at the end of the Second World War to nearly 50 per cent by the end of the century. In contrast, the comparable increase among their peers from manual backgrounds was to a level that remained below 20 per cent by 2000. This pattern is not unique to the UK; there are many other countries in which a young person's likelihood of progressing to HE is strongly influenced by their family background (Crawford et al., 2017). Inequalities also endure in *experiences* of HE and degree outcomes, not just access – patterned by variables such as race, ethnicity, gender and age, as well as social class, as discussed in Chapters 5–8.

While many people have welcomed the opening up of HE to a significantly larger proportion of the population, in some nations the sector has changed considerably as a result (Trow, 1973). First, and as discussed in Chapters 2 and 9, a process of 'credential inflation' (Collins, 1979) has occurred, in which a first degree has come to be seen as no longer sufficient to secure entry into well-paid professional employment (graduate destinations are discussed further below). Students now increasingly seek higher-level qualifications as a means of differentiating themselves from other graduates of a mass HE system (Brooks and Everett, 2009). Other forms of distinction are also sought, including taking up internships, work experience and relevant extra-curricular activities, and studying overseas (Brown and Hesketh, 2004; Roulin and Bangerter, 2013; Waters, 2008; see also Chapters 4 and 5). Second, in many nations, more emphasis has come to be placed on the reputation of the HE institution attended (Reay et al., 2005), with newer institutions (which have, in part, enabled the expansion of student numbers) typically regarded less favourably than their older counterparts. This increasing stratification of institutions has been exacerbated by the introduction of market mechanisms into the sector (explored in more detail below). Finally, the expansion of HE has prompted many governments to introduce new ways of funding an increasingly expensive sector. These have typically involved students paying a larger share of the costs themselves, and the taxpayer (via government subsidies to HE) correspondingly less (Heller and Callender, 2013).

Privatisation

Universities and other HE institutions have not been immune from the various neo-liberal pressures that were outlined in some detail in Chapter 3. Indeed, the funding shifts described above have also been related to an increasing reluctance, on the part of many national governments, to use public money to pay for public services (Deem, 2001). Moreover, like various other educational establishments, HEIs have been expected to take on market-like behaviours, adopting the practices and values of the private sector (ibid). Some of these changes have been closely linked to shifts in government support. For example, the reduction in public funding for HE, in many countries of the world, has led to an increasing reliance on the (often very high) fees paid by international students. Universities have been required to adopt more 'efficient' approaches (such as teaching larger numbers of students through distance education) and new organisational forms (to provide a better interface with industry, for example), and strengthen central management (Clark, 1998). HE has thus come to be positioned as a largely private rather than public good (Shear and Hyatt, 2015) – contributing to what Clark (1998) has called the emergence of the 'entrepreneurial university'. As discussed in Chapter 10, these changes have impacted on the work of HE staff who have had to adopt competitive behaviours themselves, to secure funding for their research, for example (Slaughter and Leslie, 1997).

The privatisation of HE is closely bound up with many of the processes of internationalisation discussed in detail in Chapter 4 and elsewhere. For example, Chapter 4 explored how the emergence of global 'rankings' of individual HEIs has helped to create a global education market, which has, in turn, encouraged some countries to embark on thorough-going reform of the HE system in order to improve their international standing. However, the example of rankings can also provide a useful lens for exploring some of the enduring heterogeneity of HE systems – despite a general tendency for most HE systems to be influenced, in some way, by encroaching neo-liberalism. In her detailed analysis of national responses to global rankings, Hazelkorn (2015) distinguishes between two main models. The neo-liberal model, she maintains, aims to create a small number of world-class universities by fostering greater vertical differentiation, in order to compete globally. Germany and Japan are good examples of countries that have adopted this approach – attempting to increase the research performance of individual HEIs by instigating national competitions for centres of excellence and graduate schools (France, Russia, China and South Korea are other examples). In contrast, the social democratic model focuses on the *system* rather than individual institutions, and aims to support a diverse range of high-performing HEIs, with teaching and research excellence spread geographically. Norway, for example, has explicitly stated that it has chosen not to build elite institutions, while Australia and Ireland have taken a comparable approach. A similar argument, albeit with reference to HE more generally, is made by Deem (2001). Reflecting on the diversity of types of HE that remained evident at the start of the twenty-first century, she contends that 'the notion of hybridisation of a range of organisational forms, practice and cultures may actually present a more useful account of what is happening to higher education than attempts to document convergence across different countries' (p. 13). It thus remains important to pay attention to variation and differentiation at both the national and the subnational level.

Learning and assessment in higher education

Studying in HE can, for many students, be a transformative experience. A compelling example of this is provided by McLean and colleagues (2015) in their three-year study of students learning sociology and other related social science subjects at four different UK HEIs (with different market positions). They argue that the majority of the students in their research developed a strong disciplinary identity, which was characterised by 'thinking in open-minded ways about human behaviour, by questioning the relationship between individuals and the conditions they find themselves in and being oriented to improving society' (p. 181). This identity, they go on to suggest, benefited both the students – through broadening their horizons and enabling them to participate in a specialised group – and wider society – by giving them the skills, knowledge and motivation to play an active role in civic life. Moreover, they found that these benefits were reaped by students at all four of the institutions in their research. The curricula in all the institutions were similar, covering the same ideas and methodologies, and projecting the same disciplinary identity. On the basis of this evidence, McLean and colleagues argue that this form of learning, at least, can provide an important means of disrupting the social order: students from lower socio-economic groups, attending lower status HEIs accrued the same benefits as their peers with more social resources and/or who attended higher status institutions. There may well, however, be important differences in such effects by discipline. Muddiman (2017), for example, has shown – drawing on her research in Singapore and Wales – that while sociology students in both countries emphasised the importance of developing empathy and critical thinking, and were able to identify civic and non-economic benefits to their learning (as in McLean and colleagues' research), their peers studying business were focused much less on learning, and more on gaining individual advantage and enhancing their competitiveness in the labour market.

Despite the evidence that some courses can be transformative, as previous chapters have demonstrated, HE can also help to reproduce social inequalities – through the admissions process and experiences during the degree (see Chapters 5–8, which have explored differences by class, gender, race and age, respectively). Research that has focused on learning, in particular, has shown how the knowledge that is taught within HE institutions often privileges the perspectives of dominant groups, and curricula are increasingly influenced by economic imperatives (see the discussion of the changing status of women's studies in Portugal in Chapter 9). Practices of assessment, speaking and writing in HE are also affected in a similar way. Drawing on detailed studies of how HE staff go about marking students' work, Leathwood and Read (2009) have argued that behaviours and approaches typically understood as male (such as boldness, individualism and competitiveness) are often favoured (see also Francis et al., 2001). They also note, however, that in many cases female students have become quite adept at conforming to this particular style of writing:

> Both men and women lecturers rate most highly the forms of 'masculinised' academic language favoured in the academy, and women students' success seems to be primarily related to [their] hard work at adapting to the masculinised cultural discourses relating to speaking, writing and assessment in the academy rather than signs that academic practices are themselves becoming feminised. (p. 156)

Here, the authors suggest that female students have taken on particular styles of writing that are often traditionally seen as 'masculine' – such as being dispassionate and self-confident in their claims.

Chapter 10 noted how assessments of HE lecturers' teaching are themselves often gendered, with students rating male instructors higher than their female counterparts. Indeed, the validity of student assessments of teaching in HE has been brought into question by a number of studies. Shevlin and colleagues (2004), writing well over a decade ago, indicated that student evaluations were strongly influenced by perceptions of charisma, rather than any more objective assessment of teaching quality. More recently, Sabri (2013) has explored the impact of evaluations of teaching that are implemented on a national basis. Countries such as Australia, the Netherlands and the UK all have national student surveys of teaching with near universal participation at the institutional level. Germany also has a similar survey, but this is administered every two to three years and includes only a relatively small number of universities (ibid.). Sabri contends that these evaluations of teaching should be considered social objects in their own right, in that they structure processes of production and consumption in HEIs, 'with the potential to transform the way prospective and current students think about HE and to reconfigure the nature of HE work' (para 1.2). In developing this argument, she draws on the example of the National Student Survey (NSS) in the UK. The NSS, she maintains, serves to structure the 'student experience' by determining what 'counts' and what does not.

For example, it contains no questions about students' relationships with their peers or curriculum content and design – despite both being important to the students in the focus groups she ran. Moreover, the only question about the curriculum (which asks students about the extent to which they agree with the statement 'The course is intellectually stimulating') positions students as passive receivers of education, failing to acknowledge their own role in knowledge creation, and the fact that meaningful learning can often be hard and challenging. Instead, it asks about whether students are, overall, satisfied with their course – and more specific questions about, for example, assessment and feedback, organisation and management, and the learning resources that have been made available to them. Such limited foci encourage institutional managers – who typically take NSS performance very seriously because it feeds directly into most national league tables – to be equally narrow in their conceptualisation of learning, and can inform academics' sense of their own value as teachers (Sabri, 2013). (Here, there are some similarities with the evaluations of school teachers discussed in Chapter 10.) The impact of the NSS in the UK is largely dependent on the extent to which institutions are insulated from league table vulnerability and reliant on non-teaching streams of funding (ibid.). In other countries, however, national evaluations have had less pernicious consequences – largely because they have used broader concepts of teaching and learning. In the USA and Australia, for example, measures such as level of student engagement and involvement, time spent on task, quality of student effort and degree of academic and social integration are used to assess the quality of the student experience (ibid.). National differences thus again remain important.

Dominant understandings of higher education students

Research has suggested that, although learning is obviously often a primary focus for a large majority of those who participate in HE, students are not always understood – by themselves, their institutions and/or society more generally – as simply 'learners'. Taking a historical perspective, Williams (2013) has argued that while the student as an individual committed above all else to the pursuit of knowledge was one of two dominant constructions prior to the middle of the twentieth century, it existed alongside a rather different construction – which understood students as young men from wealthy families, engaged in hedonistic, rather than intellectual, endeavours. Studies that have focused on contemporary HE have recognised similar complexity. On the basis of an analysis of university websites, Leathwood and Read (2009) have argued that while some students are understood by institutions as 'independent learners' (often linked to assumptions about the characteristics of white, middle-class, autonomous and able-bodied men), an equally common trope is that of the 'needy student'. They argue that this construction is often associated with non-traditional students who are typically seen not as autonomous adults, but as dependent pupils. They contend that such students are frequently pathologised, feminised and seen as 'an interloper in the academy who arrives without the required academic, financial, social or cultural capital to succeed independently at university, and whose physical embodiment positions them in terms of emotional need rather than intellectual autonomy' (p. 103). The heterogeneity of HE learners is also emphasised by Reay and colleagues (2010). However, they argue that the learner identities that students are able to take up are frequently – in the UK at least – differentiated by institution, and are strongly influenced by students' wider lives (and, often, their social characteristics). They contend that 'where students have to manage competing demands of paid work and family responsibilities with being a student, the students only partially absorb a sense of themselves as students, and their learner identities remain relatively fragile and unconfident' (p. 115). In contrast, they maintain that students without these commitments develop a much stronger sense of themselves as academic learners. In their study, they found the former group was more likely to attend newer, less prestigious institutions, while the latter group was more likely to be found in older, higher status universities.

Since the middle of the twentieth century, students have been understood not merely as learners (or even as hedonists). A review of the literature on dominant constructions of students (Brooks, 2018) has suggested that, across Europe at least, students are often seen as political actors, consumers and/or future workers. The idea that students are important political players is frequently invoked in public debate, with commentators in many countries of the Global North often lamenting the alleged political apathy of contemporary students when compared to previous generations (Brooks, 2016). However, as Williams (2013) has argued, this particular understanding was only really foregrounded in the 1960s – with the terms 'student activist' and 'student revolt' both being used in print for the first time in 1969. From this point onwards, however, constructions of the student changed, and 'an emotional commitment to political principle was considered by many students to be more important a statement of their identity than the conclusions of dedicated and painstaking scholarship' (ibid., p. 108).

Another common understanding of the student – in many anglophone countries at least – is as a consumer. This is associated with the increased marketisation and privatisation of many HE systems across the world, as discussed above. Indeed, various scholars have argued that not only are students positioned as consumers by policymakers intent on introducing thorough-going 'choice' policies into the HE sector (see Chapters 3 and 11 for a discussion of such policies in relation to education more generally), but students themselves have come to understand their relationship to HE in this way. Molesworth and colleagues (2009), for example, have suggested that the market discourse prevalent in the UK promotes a mode of existence whereby students seek to *have* a degree rather than *be* learners. Nevertheless, the prevalence of consumerist constructions is differentiated by nation-state. Within continental Europe, although many national governments have implemented policies to increase competition between institutions and promote 'student choice' (Tavares and Cardoso, 2013; Willemse and de Beer, 2012), it is less apparent that this has led to a strong consumerist discourse (Modell, 2005; Tomlinson, 2016).

In relation to the construction of HE students as workers, recent changes to the funding of HE, in many countries of the world, in which students and/or their families have come to shoulder a greater proportion of the costs, have led many students to engage in paid work alongside their studies. This is, however, patterned differently between and within nations (Brooks, 2018). Students from less privileged backgrounds, and in countries in which less state support is provided for HE, are more likely to have to engage in paid employment. For these students, work can take up considerable time and energy, and distract them from their studies. While this may not be of much consequence in some countries – such as Estonia and Russia – in which labour market participation appears to provide better signals than educational qualifications to future employers (Apokin and Iudkevich, 2008; Beerkens et al., 2011), in other nations, long hours of paid work can adversely affect academic progress and restrict opportunities to develop wider parts of 'traditional' student identities associated with, for example, extra-curricular pursuits and other types of informal learning outside the classroom (Brooks et al., 2016).

Routes out of higher education and into the labour market

As discussed above, the concept of a 'knowledge economy' has been used by successive governments in many nations of the Global North to justify the mass expansion of HE. A key assumption of this 'knowledge economy' discourse is that there is a growing amount of 'knowledge work', which requires an increasingly highly educated workforce (Roberts, 2013). Over the past decade, however, such assumptions have been subjected to critical scrutiny by scholars from across the social sciences. Although in many parts of the world there has been a decline in manufacturing jobs and a corresponding increase in those in the service sector, researchers have raised questions about whether the number of 'knowledge-focused' jobs is as great as governments often suggest. Indeed, there is a substantial literature indicating that many graduates are often forced into 'flexible' positions with low wages and few training opportunities (Bertrand-Cloodt et al., 2012; Green and Zhu, 2010) and feel overqualified for the jobs they are doing (Brown et al., 2011; Smetherham, 2006). Moreover, there appears little prospect of the graduate labour market expanding in line with the increased supply of graduates (Aston and Bekhradnia, 2003; Brown et al., 2011). While a small number of studies have suggested that the substitution of graduates for nongraduates has itself led to the upgrading of jobs (Purcell and Elias, 2004), this view is not widely shared. Indeed, Mason (2002) contends that this 'burden of adjustment' falls more heavily on individual graduates than employers, and thus contributes to a widening divergence of salaries and career prospects across the graduate labour market.

The oversupply of graduates has led, it is argued, to increasing competition for jobs within a congested labour market. As discussed above, many students now go to considerable lengths to 'distinguish themselves' from other graduates of a mass HE system. Brown and colleagues (2011) have described this change in the graduate labour market as an 'opportunity trap', maintaining that there is now a worldwide battle to secure access to good middle-class jobs, which – at an individual level – involves almost every aspect of one's public life and private self. They write:

> [the] opportunity trap ... forces people to spend more time, effort and money on activities that may have little intrinsic purpose in an attempt to fulfil one's opportunities. The trap is that if everyone adopts the same tactics, such as getting a bachelor's degree or working longer hours to impress the boss, no one secures an advantage. (p. 12)

Not all graduates are, however, affected in the same way. Research by sociologists, educationalists and economists has highlighted the various inequalities that pattern graduate participation within the labour market. Rafferty (2012), for example, has demonstrated that, despite their levels of academic attainment, penalties exist for those from several specific ethnic minority groups. Differences have also been identified with respect to age – with older graduates tending to fare better than their younger counterparts (Woodfield, 2011). There are also differences by nation, which relate to the nature of the HE system. For example, as discussed in Chapter 5, highly stratified systems are often associated with more stratified transitions from HE to work (e.g. Li and Miller, 2013). Variation is also evident *within* individual nations. In the UK, for example, graduates located within, or able to move to, London and the south-east of England have relatively more labour market opportunities than their counterparts elsewhere (Faggian et al., 2013). Recent research has also shown how there are often quite significant differences by employment sector. Although, as discussed in Chapters 4 and 5, in many nations of the world, overseas qualifications can provide a significant advantage within the graduate labour market, within particular sectors domestic qualifications may be valued more highly. For example, as noted in Chapter 4, Malaysian students who had chosen to study at home rather than overseas, believed that they had certain advantages over their overseas-educated peers when seeking employment in Malaysia (Sin, 2013). These included a 'willingness to adopt a softer, more submissive interaction style, indicative of Asian reverence for authority and seniority' (ibid., p. 860), which they believed was valued by Malaysian employers, although not necessarily by transnational organisations. Similarly, in the UK, some graduate employers have been suspicious about those with overseas qualifications, on the basis that they assumed UK degrees to be inherently superior (Brooks et al., 2012).

The most striking social inequalities, however, have been identified in relation to social class (Brown et al., 2011). Non-traditional graduates (e.g. those who are the first in their family to have attended HE) typically earn less and take longer to secure permanent employment than their peers from more privileged backgrounds (Crawford et al., 2016). Indeed, Grayson (2004) has argued that variables viewed as measures of cultural capital have a statistically significant effect on graduates' incomes, net of social capital and human capital gained at university. He concludes that, overall, his study shows that 'even in an economy based on knowledge, some job outcomes are related to broader social dynamics in addition to the acquisition of human capital in universities' (p. 625). Extant research in this area has shown how social, cultural and economic capital play a key role in these processes of social reproduction. This has focused on both the resources to which graduates have access (within their families and wider networks) and the activities of graduate employers. In relation to the former (and as discussed in detail in Chapter 5 on social class), UK studies have shown that graduates from middle-class families often have extensive social networks that they can draw upon to gain internships, work experience and secure professional jobs, and the economic capital to allow them to pursue a range of unpaid or low-paid CV-building activities that are frequently necessary to gain access to jobs in particular areas of the economy (e.g. Allen et al., 2013; Bathmaker et al., 2013). It is important to note, however, that the impact of social capital, at least, can be quite complex. Drawing on research conducted in Germany, Weiss and Klein (2011) contend that it is important to distinguish between different types of social network (e.g. those established while working during one's studies, and those more dependent on family and friends), as they appear to have different influences on destinations. They also suggest that the impact of social networks differs by type of employment being sought. Similarly, Martin's (2009) research in the USA emphasises differences between types of social tie and labour market sector. He argues that:

> Having extensive ties to campus positions [i.e. members of staff within the HEI] appears to be more important for students pursuing careers that typically involve graduate or professional study, such as college professors and especially medical doctors. Conversely, the use of family and personal contacts for post-graduation plans is associated with working full-time after graduation and plans to become a lawyer. These results suggest that the resources contained in within-college networks are more readily convertible into future advantages for students pursuing careers that have stronger links to postsecondary institutions and typically involve graduate study. Off-campus, personal networks likely have more immediate returns for students who transition directly into the workforce after graduation. (p. 199)

He concludes by suggesting that students' particular investment strategies (both of an instrumental and a relatively unconscious nature) result in the accumulation of social resources that facilitate distinct high-status career pathways.

The actions of employers are also important when considering the nature of graduates' transitions from education into work. Various examples of these were given in Chapter 5, when exploring the impact of social class – for example, a focus in recruitment practices on various subjective criteria such as 'personal capital' and 'polish', which tend to advantage those from privileged families who have had the money and time to invest in a range of extra-curricular activities, and who feel socially comfortable interacting with other privileged young people (Brown and Hesketh, 2004; Rivera, 2015). Similarly, a discourse analysis of the recruitment material of top international employers such as Google and PWC has indicated that although emphasis is often placed on concepts such as meritocracy and inclusivity, a concomitant focus on individual 'traits' such as resilience, self-confidence, polish and passion tends to promote social reproduction – in which middle class-ness (and also youthfulness, male-ness and white-ness) are privileged (Allen and Ingram, 2017).

Thus, it appears that while HE has ostensibly become more open and accessible, with over a third of young people now progressing to HE in most countries across the world, inequalities by social class remain, and continue to pattern educational decision-making, the experiences of those who do progress to HE and, as discussed in this section, routes from HE into the labour market.

Higher education and lifelong learning

The relationship between HE and lifelong learning has already been examined to some extent in Chapter 8 (in relation to older learners). While this suggested that much recent lifelong learning policy has been driven by economic imperatives, this has not always been the case. The concept of lifelong learning was widely promulgated, over a period of many decades, by a range of international organisations including UNESCO, the OECD and the EU (Field, 2006). Slowey and Schuetze (2012) argue that, at its core, it is built around two axes:

> a vertical one which relates to the truism that people learn not just while they are young, but over the whole of their lives; and a horizontal axis which relates to the fact that active and purposeful learning takes place not only in formal educational institutions such as schools or universities, but also in the workplace, in the community, in different social environments, as well as through individual non-formal study. (pp. 3–4)

They also note significant changes in the meaning of the term over time. In its original conception, in the 1970s, it was closely allied to the radical traditions of adult education – which critiqued the elitist nature of traditional education and advocated 'deschooling' in its place. It was thus associated with an emphasis on social justice and inclusion, and the promotion of 'second chance' opportunities for those returning to education as adults. Participation in education was viewed as the bedrock for participation in civic and political life, and thus of critical importance for a healthy democracy, as well as preparation for employment (Slowey and Schuetze, 2012). By the 1990s, however, lifelong learning became imbued with a rather different meaning. It came to be seen as a key means of fostering a 'knowledge economy' through the training and education of an adaptable and flexible workforce, in which individuals were expected to take on responsibility for their own learning and 'employment-readiness'. The OECD, EU and World Bank all continued to promote such learning but, unlike their pronouncements of the 1970s, emphasis was placed on its utility in preparation for employment, rather than personal development or civic engagement. Such international organisations have also played an important role in monitoring participation in lifelong learning, and thus facilitating 'governance by numbers' (see Chapter 3). The OECD, for example, presents data on participation by country in its annual 'Education at a Glance' reports, while the EU uses the Labour Force Survey to assess progress towards its own lifelong learning goal (i.e. that 15 per cent of all adults between the ages of 25 and 64 participate in at least one formal or informal learning activity for at least a four-week period) (Boeren, 2017).

Despite such activities on the part of international organisations, participation in lifelong learning varies quite considerably between nation-states. Within the Global North, Nordic countries tend to have the highest rates, followed by English-speaking nations and nations in continental Western Europe, while Southern European countries have the lowest rates (Boeren, 2017; Slowey and Schuetze, 2012). Such differences are typically explained in terms of differences in the strength of national economies, the welfare system in place, benefits offered to the unemployed and the level of national investment in research and development (Boeren, 2017). Data about participation in the Global South are less robust, and thus comparisons are more difficult to draw. Moreover, some scholars have raised questions about the appropriateness of the term 'lifelong learning' in such parts of the world. For example, in relation to South Africa, Slowey and Schuetze (2012) write:

> from an educational perspective, what does it mean to be an 'adult learner' when life expectancy is low, and when a young person of 12 years of age may have to take on responsibility as head of a family due to the impact of a disease such as AIDS? In such circumstances, education has to be extended over a longer period of time as it fits around work and domestic responsibilities ... (p. 283)

While the national context is clearly important in explaining differential rates of participation in lifelong learning, so too are individual- and organisational-level factors (just as they are for the other forms of learning discussed in this book). As discussed in Chapter 8, adults' propensity to participate in learning activities is often affected by their previous experiences of education, which can serve to exacerbate inequalities – as those with positive experiences are more likely to engage in subsequent learning than their peers who found formal education alienating (Reay, 2002). These differences are often aligned with social class, but gender, race and ethnicity can also help shape responses to lifelong learning (Leathwood and Francis, 2006), as can individuals' own motivations (see Chapter 8). At the organisational level, various structural factors are significant. For example, in relation to learning at work, Fuller and Unwin (2003) have distinguished between what they call 'restricted' and 'expansive' learning environments. While in the former, emphasis is placed primarily on ensuring that employees are adequately equipped to carry out the specific work tasks for which they are responsible, in the latter, more attention is paid to the wider development of the employee. Workplaces can also differ significantly in the resources they make available for learning, and the range of opportunities they offer (in this respect, larger employers typically have sufficient economies of scale to provide a wider range – often through a dedicated training or development unit) (Boeren, 2017). Similarly, and as discussed in previous chapters, formal educational institutions can differ in the extent to which they are able to facilitate lifelong learning – through, for example, being flexible about entry routes and modes of study (Saar et al., 2014).

In relation to HE, in particular, various studies have indicated that HEIs have been slow to facilitate lifelong learning, and that some of the recent changes to HE, evident across the globe, have made it harder for adult students to enrol. In Germany, for example, although the rhetoric of policymakers suggests that there is high-level commitment to opening up HE to lifelong learners, in practice, this is not often translated well into the activities of individual universities (Wolter, 2012). Wolter argues that this is related to an inflexible admissions process, in which undue emphasis continues to be placed on the Abitur (the academically focused school-leaving certificate), and the enduring distinction in German culture between what is seen as two different types of knowledge – theoretical/cognitive and practical/experimental – with universities viewed as catering only for the former (this relates to the Humboldtian ideal, discussed previously). Similarly, with respect to Austria, Pechar and Wroblewski (2012) maintain that university staff have only a limited conception of lifelong learning – seeing it primarily as continuous education for those who have already completed successfully their initial education. Thus, provision tends to focus on academically orientated courses, many of which are aimed at those who already possess a degree. Recent reforms have sometimes exacerbated these problems. For example, many of the priorities that have dominated the quest for 'world-class' status (see discussion above) have resulted in initiatives to promote lifelong learning – such as widening participation, learner support and an emphasis on teaching quality – becoming marginalised (Slowey and Schuetze, 2012). Indeed, as Wolter (2012) notes with respect to Germany, 'adopting lifelong learning structures, opening up HE for non-traditional students and promoting continuing education have often been eyed suspiciously as detrimental to the achievement of academic excellence' (p. 47). Moreover, financial pressures on many HEIs have encouraged them to focus more sharply on full-time students rather than those pursuing study on a part-time basis, and ensure that students complete their degrees in a timely fashion – rather than dropping in and dropping out, as had sometimes been the case in the past, to suit their learning requirements (Pechar and Wroblewski, 2012).

Conclusion

In many parts of the world, HE has taken on a new significance as it has expanded to cater for significantly larger numbers of students and been positioned as key to skill development in what is frequently called a 'knowledge economy'. The chapter first charted some of the ways in which HE has changed, focusing on processes of 'massification' and privatisation. It then went on to examine learning in the sector, and the different ways in which the HE student is understood (e.g. as a consumer and future worker, as well as (or instead of) a learner). The chapter also considered transitions from HE into full-time employment, and the relationship between HE and lifelong learning. As with many other chapters in the book, although commonalities across countries were identified, some enduring national differences were also discussed. This suggests that claims that HE systems worldwide have now converged into a single Anglo-American model are a little premature.

13 NEW DIRECTIONS IN EDUCATIONAL RESEARCH

Introduction

This final chapter of the book turns to the future and considers some of the new directions for researchers committed to analysing the relationship between education and society. Although there are a wide variety of topics that could have been included in this chapter, we focus on two in particular, because of their strongly interdisciplinary orientation and current salience. The first topic, that of education and the biosciences, addresses an area that has traditionally been largely neglected by sociologists of education but, more recently, has become an important focus of enquiry (for example, a recent special issue of the journal *Discourse: Studies in the Cultural Politics of Education* was devoted to the theme of 'new biological rationalities in education'). As Gulson and Baker (2018) have argued, academic biology has historically had a difficult relationship with sociologically informed education research – often critiqued for the way in which it has legitimated particular prejudices (for example, through genetically determinist accounts of skills and aptitudes, and family transmission of intelligence). Nevertheless, as will be explored in more depth below, new fields such as epigenetics and neuroscience have been seen – by some scholars at least – as offering the potential for biological life to be shaped in particular ways which, in turn, may facilitate the involvement of sociologists. More generally, however, new biological research has been used as the pretext for a wide variety of educational interventions – from the early years through to professional development in the workplace. Educational research is increasingly playing an important role in subjecting such interventions to critical scrutiny. The second topic addressed in this chapter, that of new technologies, has a more established position within sociologically focused educational research (although, until recently, quite low profile). Nevertheless, the rapid development of technologies over recent years – not least the growth in 'learning analytics' and the increasing availability of big data – has posed new challenges for teachers and learners, and also for those researching this area. New tools, knowledges and collaborations are often necessary. The first part of the chapter explores these two areas, highlighting some of the innovative research that has been conducted. It then draws on these new fields of enquiry, as well as the preceding chapters, to identify some of the key challenges for educational research in the years ahead.

Biological sciences

Neuroscience, epigenetics and educational research

Neuroscience has assumed a significant place within educational research over the recent past. It is seen by many scientists, policymakers and educationalists as having a key role to play in generating new knowledge about how the brain works and the ways in which humans learn. Substantial funding has been allocated to the field of 'neuroeducation' by governments in the USA and the UK; the OECD has called for educators to develop a better understanding of the brain science that underpins learning; and, in 2015, *Nature* launched a new journal called *Science of Learning*, which aims to promote the transfer of neuroscientific findings into the classroom (Pykett, 2013; Rose and Rose, 2016). Research in this area has typically focused on numeracy and literacy skills; the best ways to care for the brain in order to optimise learning; critical periods of brain development (particularly the age range of 0–3); methods of cognitive enhancement; the learning needs of specific groups who have been diagnosed with development disorders; and emotional and behavioural issues (Pykett, 2017). While many policymakers, teachers and educational leaders have enthusiastically embraced the findings of neuroscience and their supposed implications for educational practice, social scientists have adopted a more critical stance. In general, they have suggested that neuroscientific approaches to education are often underpinned by behavioural assumptions; pay insufficient attention to the cultural, social and political contexts that shape decision-making; and promote a form of biological determinism, through leaving little room in their accounts of how humans function for ethical deliberation, notions of responsibility or social and political debate. Moreover, they have argued that such approaches are firmly allied to late capitalist modes of production – as a result of the close relationship between neuroscientists and the pharmaceutical industry, and governments' interests in producing self-governing individuals who are able to care for their own bodies and minds without having to call on the resources of the state (Pykett, 2013).

Emergent findings from the field of epigenetics are also drawn on frequently by policymakers, particularly in relation to parenting practices and government-sanctioned interventions in the first few years of a child's life (Wastell and White, 2017). Epigenetics is the study of the biological mechanisms through which gene expression is turned on and off (without a change to the DNA sequence), and focuses attention on the particular circumstances that cause chemical modifications around genes that, in turn, cause the genes to either become active or dormant. Epigenetics is significant in demonstrating that the genome itself does not determine how a human (or other animal) will behave. As Youdell (2017) notes, 'the genome provides a resource that, in interaction with other influences, is embroiled in the action of molecules, cells and the creatures these make up. The potentialities of a body are vastly greater than the genome' (p. 5). A wide variety of factors have been shown to relate to such chemical modifications including an individual's diet, age, social context, sleep and amount of exercise. Many of the critiques that have been made by social scientists about the transfer of findings from epigenetic studies to social policy are similar to those noted above in relation to neuroscience. However, in addition, scholars have noted that the majority of epigenetic research has been conducted on animals in laboratories, and questioned whether the results of such experiments can be straightforwardly transferred to humans who operate in much more complex social environments (Wastell and White, 2017). These critiques are explored in more detail below with reference to three specific areas of learning: 'early years' interventions, school-based initiatives and workplace training.

Intervention in the early years

Within the UK, findings from both neuroscience and epigenetics have been particularly influential with respect to children who have not yet begun compulsory education – a phase that is often referred to in policy as the 'early years' (see the discussion of early years' assessment in Chapter 9, for example). Policymakers have argued that neuroscientific evidence demonstrates that the quality of parental nurturing and attachment in the first few years of a child's life is crucial in terms of whether the brain is set up for success or failure. Pregnant women and new mothers have thus been targeted with a range of educational initiatives, ostensibly to improve their parenting skills. These have typically focused on encouraging them to adopt more 'sensitive' mothering approaches, on the basis that these are more likely to produce more richly networked brains in their infants, and to avoid stress, because of assumptions that babies in stressful environments are more likely to produce cortisol, which can damage the brain (Edwards et al., 2015; Rose and Rose, 2016). Such initiatives have also been informed by epigenetic research which has shown that among rats at least, differences in the nurturing behaviour of mothers can affect the epigenetic code of their offspring. High levels of positive maternal intervention, such as licking, are associated with calmer, less anxious behaviour on the part of baby rats (Youdell, 2017).

Early intervention policies are often framed as progressive – because they are typically focused on poor communities, with the aim of breaking cycles of disadvantage and thus promoting social mobility. Such framings have, however, been strongly contested by various social scientists. Edwards and colleagues (2015), for example, have argued that far from being progressive, such policies tend to essentialise relationships between mother and child, biologise ideas about cycles of deprivation, and reproduce 'classed value judgements about the means of achieving the "right sort" of brain development' (p. 168). They also, the authors contend, mispresent neuroscientific findings – pointing to the lack of evidence between an individual's synaptic profile in infanthood and their future performance – and overlook entirely the impact of wider environmental factors beyond the family. They conclude by suggesting that early intervention policy and practice 'is basically arguing that the poor are underdeveloped, that there is something missing in their brains, that they do not experience "normal" emotions, and most powerfully that they do not love their children like "we" [i.e. middle-class policymakers] do' (p. 183). Thus, despite the newness of the underpinning science, when we explore the ways in which the biosciences have been appropriated by some policymakers, well-established inequalities (such as those discussed in Chapter 5 with respect to class) are again evident.

'Brain training' in schools

Similar critiques have been made by social scientists of the various brain-orientated initiatives that have been widely introduced within schools. Such initiatives have focused on specific approaches to teaching and learning (such as mind-mapping); 'learning styles' (such as visual, auditory and kinaesthetic); ingestion and the brain (for example, an emphasis on the positive impact of fish oils – which draws on epigenetic research as well as neuroscience); 'growth mindsets'; and emotional intelligence (Pykett, 2017). As noted above, many of these interventions have been criticised for promoting a sense of biological determinism. Indeed, Busso and Pollack (2015) note that the popular 'Brain-Based Workshops' sold by the US-based Jensen Learning Corporation include one that focuses specifically on 'Enriching the Brain of Students in Poverty'. This describes to teachers four ways in which poor children's brains supposedly differ from those of their more privileged peers, and suggests various teaching strategies to remedy this alleged deficit. Busso and Pollack argue also that the ways in which neuroscience has been appropriated within classrooms have important implications for how we understand the goals and purpose of education more generally (see Chapter 2). They write:

> To say that a teacher … is a kind of social stimulus acting upon regions of a student's brain presents an impoverished view of what really goes on in classrooms. Teachers can inspire,

empower and engage individuals, not just their brains, not only inviting them to have experiences but to reflect on them too, nurturing their moral sensibilities and fostering their aesthetic preferences. (p. 178)

Here, there are important links to the way in which the 'good teacher' is understood, discussed in Chapter 10. The wider implications of 'neuroeducation' are also explored by Gagen (2015) in her analysis of educational programmes to promote emotional literacy. Such programmes include the UK government's 'Social and Emotional Aspects of Learning' (SEAL), which was introduced in English primary schools in 2005 and secondary schools in 2007. The SEAL programme is based on the assumptions, derived from neuroscience, that individuals can shape themselves through the conscious management of neurochemicals; emotions play a key role in how we think and act; and intelligence is fundamentally determined by our emotional faculties (Gagen, 2015). Thus, as part of the SEAL programme Gagen analysed, students were required to develop 'neurochemical awareness' – by, for example, learning how to change uncomfortable feelings through exercise, breathing and thinking positive thoughts, and manage impulses by means of distraction techniques and visualisation. Gagen argues that, through such initiatives, SEAL prescribed particular forms of self-governance and helped to construct new forms of (neo-liberal) citizenship. Indeed, she contends that implicit in the SEAL programme is the message that to be a good citizen young people must learn to manage their neurochemical impulses so they can respond in more measured and productive ways. Citizenship is thus transformed 'from a subjectivity performing specific civic duties to one requiring the close management of neurologically defined emotional behaviours' (p. 141).

Workplace training

Neuroscience has also been drawn upon with respect to education and training within the workplace. Pykett and Enright (2016) have shown how a raft of programmes have been introduced into organisations with the intention of promoting a culture of 'optimism and optimal functioning' (p. 51). These typically aim to engender, both within individuals and organisations, a range of positive emotions – through, for example, an emphasis on mindfulness and positive psychology. Reflecting some of the arguments made by Gagen with respect to schools, Pykett and Enright suggest that such training programmes bring about new forms of governance, which are informed by the neo-liberal orientation of workplaces. They argue that the way in which responsibility is placed on the individual (rather than their employer or indeed society more generally) for their own emotional state is concurrent both with the individualised nature of lifelong learning (see Chapter 12) and the spread of individualised practices of performance management within many workplaces (particularly in the UK and the USA). The focus on brains in workplaces, like in schools, directs our gaze inward rather than outward. As Pykett (2017) observes, through neuroeducation, 'we are incited to know more about our brain than our world; to train our habits rather than change our spaces' (p. 156). It thus has important political consequences.

Contribution of the social sciences

Despite the various critiques of the ways in which findings from epigenetics and neuroscience have been translated into education policies and practices, there remain calls (from sociologists) for closer working relationships between biological scientists and their social science counterparts. Youdell (2017), for example, argues that the strengthening evidence of the impact of the social on the biological – in both epigenetics and neuroscience – provides an important point of connection. In relation to neuroscience, evidence about the plasticity of the brain and the observed changes to its structures and networks over an individual's lifetime open up, Youdell maintains, a broad field of potential interface between the brain and the social world. Educational researchers could, she suggests, consider the neurological impact of a wider range of relationships than just the mother–child dyad and close family (as has typically been the case in the early years intervention programmes discussed above) – exploring, for example, relationships with teachers and peers within school classrooms. Similarly, with respect to epigenetics, she suggests that gene adaptations may be affected by everyday processes played out in schools and classrooms, not just early experiences of nurture. Thus, she contends that the 'conceptual tools and research accountabilities' that the sociologist of education brings with them 'have the potential to transform life sciences' understanding of environment and its potential influences and, therefore, the questions it asks and the hypotheses it moves from' (2017, p. 11).

New technologies

Technology and educational research

Despite being more established than the biosciences, the study of technology has generally had a relatively low profile within the sociology of education and related areas (Facer and Selwyn, 2013). Moreover, within the field of educational research more generally, social accounts of technological development and use have often had to vie with those that have taken a more positivist perspective. The latter is typically associated with a deterministic position, which holds that technologies have properties independent of the observer, which then act on people and/or situations and bring about change (Oliver, 2013). In contrast, social accounts place emphasis on the way in which technologies are produced, made sense of and, even, in some cases, rejected – by a range of human actors. Furthermore, they reposition 'technology as a site of contestation in which different groups try to advance their own interests about how it should be used and understood' (Oliver, 2013, p. 35). Various studies have indeed emphasised that access to technology does not necessarily determine usage. Australian research, for example, has highlighted the different ways in which families interact with the internet at home, which are often patterned by social class (Angus et al., 2004). In Angus and colleagues' study, while the middle-class families in their sample tended to take advantage of a variety of educationally focused online resources, their working-class counterparts spent the majority of their time online on 'un-school-like' activities, including chatting with others, downloading music and searching for information about consumer products. Thus, in this example, the use of technology reflects the differential relationships families have with formal education, rather than determining these relationships in any straightforward manner.

Facer and Selwyn (2013) argue that developing a more thoroughgoing analysis of the relationship between society and new technology should be a key objective of educational researchers in the future. They suggest that:

> One of the key strengths of a sustained and deliberate sociology of education and technology would be its willingness to approach the understanding of technological change in education as a contested political project rather than as a matter for technocratic debate over efficiency. (p. 220)

They then go on to outline four specific debates to which they believe the social study of technology and education can make an important contribution. First, they suggest that it can help generate new knowledge about the 'virtualisation' of knowledge and the development of personalised learning. Here, they are referring to the ways in which various new technologies are being used to 'disaggregate' educational institutions, through the promotion of distance learning, massive online open courses (MOOCs) and other initiatives that enable individuals to learn on their own, often following their own independent pathways. They suggest that the libertarian tradition of computing and ostensibly 'democratic narratives of co-production' (p. 222) through digital networks have helped to promote both individualisation and de-institutionalisation. Scholars approaching the study of education and technology from a social perspective need, they contend, to establish the extent to which 'the promise of online connectivity to (m)any place(s) and people obscures the continued importance of immediate "local" contexts in framing learning processes and practices' (p. 223).

Second, and as will be discussed further below, they call for research that addresses the ways in which institutional technologies are used to promote data-driven accountability through, for example, 'learning analytics'. Attention needs to be focused, they maintain, on the values that underpin these technologies and the extent to which they may disempower both teachers and pupils – through publicly accessible 'data profiles', for example – and promote a form of 'predictive surveillance' in which data about past performance are used to inform expectations about future behaviour (to which individuals are then held to account). Third, Facer and Selwyn encourage a focus on the increased forms of commercialisation and privatisation that are often associated with educational technology – in terms of selling digital products to schools, as well as the provision of entire educational programmes. Such trends raise important questions about the values that are being instantiated within education as a result, and the extent to which such transactions are further entrenching marketisation. Finally, Facer and Selwyn point to the enduring inequalities in usage of new technologies, noting, for example, that those from more advantaged backgrounds are more likely to be actively involved in the *production* of online content, rather than merely its consumption. On the basis of these four issues, they call on researchers both to problematise the relationship between education and technology, and give greater thought to the ways in which digital technologies can be used to promote fairer futures. They write:

> an engaged sociology of education would take advantage of its understanding of the inherently political and social processes of technology production and use. It would detail and then test the opportunities available to educators, learners and other interested parties to intervene in the processes of commissioning, developing, design and appropriation of technologies to tip the balance of these processes to more equitable and democratic outcomes. (p. 229)

To develop such an 'engaged sociology of education', however, those conducting research may need to develop new skills and knowledge. Writing in relation to sociology more broadly, Beer and Burrows (2007) have argued that the discipline needs to 'technologise itself' in order to understand and analyse many new social challenges. Similarly, Williamson (2015) has contended that a new field of 'educational data science' is being opened up, with which researchers based in HE settings need to engage, otherwise it will be taken over by technical specialists in big data labs and commercial organisations. Indeed, he notes that a range of new 'data careers' have become available across a variety of organisations – including Pearson and the OECD – for those with the expertise to turn educational data into forms which hold meaning for policymakers, educational leaders and classroom teachers (ibid.).

In the remaining parts of this section, various examples are provided of some of the ways in which educational researchers have responded to this kind of challenge, focusing on learning analytics; the impact of digital 'datafication' on processes of governance; the increasing use of technologies for surveillance within educational institutions; and students' own engagement with new technologies. Finally, and drawing on the previous part of the chapter, it considers the ways in which new technologies and developments in the biological sciences have been brought together in the analyses of some scholars.

Learning analytics

'Learning analytics' is one way in which 'big data' (i.e. extremely large datasets that can be analysed computationally to reveal patterns and associations) have been put to use within education. It can be seen as a manifestation of what is often called 'datafication', namely the quantification of various aspects of human behaviour and social interactions. It relies on a variety of information about students – derived from, for example, institutional student information systems, virtual learning environments, attendance records, security records and computer logins – to model their behaviour and thus, its advocates contend, better understand and predict students' needs, and produce corrective educational interventions, particularly for those deemed to be at-risk (Oliver, 2016). Government proponents of learning analytics suggest that the agency of students can also be activated by the use of such data by, for example, empowering them to work with their institution to formulate personalised curricula and learning trajectories (ibid.). It is thus often positioned (in a rather determinist manner) as a key means of improving processes of teaching and learning, particularly within HE. Nevertheless, scholars have argued that there are also various problems associated with the adaption of this particular approach. First, they have highlighted concerns over privacy. There are, as Oliver (2016) has cogently argued, ethical questions that arise in relation to the creation of a 'data double' which can be shared publicly. He asks who should be allowed to 'gaze' at which parts of an individual's technologically mediated and distributed body, and whether there are any areas where institutions can reasonably be expected not to look. Second, there are often 'blind spots' in the data – things we cannot measure – which may be forgotten in the subsequent interpretation or deemed to be less important precisely because they are not amenable to measurement (ibid.). Finally, learning analytics has been conceptualised by some scholars as a new form of governance in which learners are regulated through self-measurement, tracking and the use of predictive data. This particular theme is common to analyses of various other new technologies, and is developed in more detail below.

Datafication and governance

The new form of governance, brought about through processes of datafication, is described by Williamson (2016b) in the following way:

> In a statistical regime of datafication, the state seeks to shape its citizens into an enumerable form in order to fit them to classificatory systems, undertake constant and real-time audits of their behaviours, make probabilistic predictions and allocate services that might reshape the ways that they act and conduct themselves – a process of 'database government' that is increasingly being delegated to automated algorithmic systems. (p. 138)

As in the example of learning analytics, data are collected from individuals on a large scale, analysed computationally and then fed back into classrooms and other learning spaces 'in the shape of pedagogic prescriptions intended to sculpt learners' conduct to fit algorithmically inferred global norms' (ibid., p. 139). In this way, Williamson suggests, data come to shape the learner as much as the learner produces the data. Scholars have identified numerous ways in which this kind of digital governance is practised in contemporary society. Ozga (2016), for example, has argued that the method through which schools in England and Wales are inspected has shifted from being an embodied process, dependent – at least partially – on the professional judgements made by inspectors on the basis of interactions in classrooms, to one in which digitised data are now foregrounded. Software devices produced by commercial contractors measure, categorise and rank school data according to preset algorithms. Moreover, the use of school 'data dashboards' and the national interactive database which schools can use themselves to analyse their performance (from July 2017 called the 'Analyse School Performance' service) have produced, Ozga contends, new kinds of governing knowledge in which problems come to be identified not from the external environment, but from the statistical data. Schools themselves can sometimes drive these new forms of governance. Selwyn and colleagues (2015) have shown, for example, that the Australian schools in their research responded to the ever-increasing external demands for data by collecting *more* data of their own. Indeed, the teachers interviewed as part of the study hoped to redress the 'mandated' requirements of national testing (such as NAPLAN, discussed in Chapter 9) and information required for purposes of accountability by generating more individualised data about their own pupil population. Selwyn and colleagues thus note that 'rather than ameliorating the disciplinary effects of external "compliance data" regimes, these shadow arrangements could be seen as equally controlling' (p. 779). They go on to suggest that the localised forms of data collected by the schools produced an incomplete and 'de-socialised' picture of their communities, as the focus was exclusively on individual pupils and their current circumstances. Moreover, they tended to reinforce traditional power relationships as school leaders and managers held considerable sway over how the data were used and to whom they were made available.

Commercial organisations play an increasingly important role in such processes of governance. Chapter 3 discussed 'The Learning Curve' database, produced by Pearson plc, which contains educational data from a wide variety of international and national organisations, with the aim of helping educators to identify the constituents of an 'effective education'. Williamson (2016b) cites this database as an example of how processes of datafication can promote new forms of governance. He argues that by configuring the user as a participant (by encouraging them to manipulate the data by performing their own analyses and creating data visualisations), they shift from being merely a passive consumer of data to a more active 'prosumer' (i.e. someone who produces content as well as consumes it). Such devices are not, however, he contends, value-neutral. They are forms of social control, in which users are attracted to participate in the logics of global competition. More specifically, The Learning Curve 'reinforces a view of education as made up of elements that can be compared and correlated through statistical analyses' (p. 133). By encouraging users to manipulate educational data in much the same way as they would monitor their own social media profile, such statistical analyses are both normalised and depoliticised (ibid.).

Technologies of surveillance

Technologies have also been implicated in new forms of surveillance in schools. While educational institutions have long been theorised as spaces in which bodies are closely monitored, scholars have suggested that technological developments have facilitated more invasive surveillance practices. Hope (2016) discusses these in relation to the operation of what he calls 'biopower'. Such practices include the use of biometric data for purposes of identification and screening, for example, the use of automated fingerprint scanning systems for daily registration, borrowing library books and paying for lunches. While this form of data is often introduced by schools to increase the efficiency of administrative systems, it has the effect of producing compliant bodies – through normalising invasive surveillance procedures. Similarly, the increasing use of electronic detection devices, such as metal detectors used to prevent pupils taking guns and knives to school, has a 'clear disciplinary aspect' (Hope, 2016, p. 890), by treating the body as a carrier and object of information, rather than a subject of communication (ibid.). Hope also describes how fitness devices are increasingly used in schools, citing the example of a school in Minneapolis in the USA where pupils were given step-tracking wristbands, to ensure that they completed at least 1,500 moves per day. While often associated with 'fun' and leisure, such trackers (and a range of other fitness devices) typically promote an ideal, 'Western' body type, and may socialise pupils into viewing the body as a site for discipline and work rather than of pleasure (ibid.). CCTV cameras are perhaps the new surveillance technology closest to the 'panopticon' described by Foucault (1977), often used as part of school security systems (Taylor, 2013). Because pupils are not sure if they are being filmed, but aware of the possibility that they may be, some are likely to adopt self-policing behaviours (Hope, 2016). CCTV can also be focused more specifically on the behaviour of teachers – used in nurseries so that parents can check that their children are being cared for appropriately (Hope, 2016), and in Russian schools to ensure that staff implement the national standardised tests in an objective manner (Paittoeva, 2016).

Some of the processes of 'datafication' discussed above – for example, the use of learning analytics, and the capture of school performance data for the purposes of inspection and/or self-evaluation – can also be viewed as new technologies of surveillance or 'dataveillance' (Lupton and Williamson, 2017), which stretch across institutional and even national borders. While Hope (2016) notes that such processes may foster resistance on the part of students – for example, through gaming the system by producing data doubles that increase their academic and economic prospects – in general, scholars have tended to point to rather more pernicious consequences. At the institutional level, they may dehumanise relationships between pupils and teachers, as the latter 'shift from social to informational ways of knowing' (Hope, 2016, p. 895), and the embodied and subjective voices of children are replaced by the 'supposed objectivity provided by technological mouthpieces of data' (Lupton and Williamson, 2017, p. 790). They also further entrench the commodification of education, through the close involvement of private companies in the provision of data services, while providing students few opportunities (if any) to challenge the predictions that are made about them on the basis of algorithmic calculations (ibid.). Through processes of dataveillance, information about children's bodies and behaviours becomes converted into a form of 'biocapital' and classrooms are transformed into small-scale digital economies in which personal data have exchange value and utility (Lupton and Williamson, 2017).

Students' engagement with technology

A further body of work has examined the way in which students themselves engage with technologies as part of everyday learning practices. While various positivist accounts have assumed that the emergence of new technologies will usher in new forms of learning significantly different from their traditional, 'analogue' counterparts, scholars who have adopted a more socially informed perspective have questioned this binary, pointing out that assuming such a 'digital dualism' mispresents the ways students learn. Gourlay and colleagues (2015), for example, explored the textual practices of students and staff in HE, and found a constant shifting on the part of students between digital and print forms. Indeed, they contend that transitions between the two often constituted important stages in the authoring process. These transitions included 'the printing of text that had been skim read on screen to allow for close engagement; the move from handwritten notes to a first word-processed draft; [and] the highly symbolic printing and binding of the definitive dissertation at the point of submission' (p. 270). Furthermore, other studies, which have also rejected a determinist view of technology, have shown how various social characteristics have a clear impact on pupils' engagement with technology within learning contexts – see, for example, Schilhab's (2017) discussion of the impact of age on Danish pupils' use of school-provided iPads.

Nevertheless, rejecting technological determinism is not the same as assuming that new technologies have no role in shaping learning practices. Selwyn (2003) has provided a detailed account of the ways in which the characteristics of what he calls the 'mobile generation' (i.e. pupils who have grown up with mobile technologies around them) have important implications for education. In particular, he argues that they disrupt two functions that have, traditionally, been important to schools – the normalisation of human subjects (through categorising and differentiating between pupils), and the normalisation of knowledge (through retaining tight control of the curriculum). By accessing both people and information outside the physical walls of the school through the internet, pupils are, he argues, able to resist these forms of regulation – and assume greater autonomy in how they learn, where they learn and what they learn – with significant implications for the traditional learning environment of the school.

Technologies and the biological sciences

Scholarship has also started to explore the ways in which technological developments have become interlinked with new areas of interest within the biological sciences, discussed previously in this chapter. William-son (2016a), for example, has argued that the ways in which children and their education are being digitally analysed increasingly involves focusing on their biological, psychological and neurological make-up, drawing together expertise and practices from statistics, computing and the biological sciences. He differentiates between three main areas of growth – what he terms 'biopedagogies', 'psychopedagogies' and 'neuropedagogies' – some of which are closely related to the types of surveillance outlined above.

Biopedagogies refers to the ways in which the physiological body of a child is translated into biophysical data through, for example, health-tracking devices worn on the body (increasingly made available via schools); these data are then used to inform new forms of instruction to encourage children to undertake 'data-driven practices of bodily opti-misation' (Williamson, 2016a, p. 402) and induct them into habits of self-quantification and body-monitoring (Lupton, 2016). Psychopeda-gogies operate in a similar manner, but focus instead on pupils' emotional state. Emotion-sensing devices, such as webcams, can be used to capture facial expressions, while various apps operate a reward system for the display of 'positive emotions and behaviours' such as perseverance, grit and helping others (Williamson, 2016a). These initiatives have much in common with wider government agendas, such as the promotion of indi-cators for national happiness and well-being (Davies, 2015), and some of the forms of school-based surveillance discussed previously. Indeed, Williamson (2016a) notes that such interventions 'ultimately educate children to inhabit a wider milieu in which constant psychological sur-veillance is undertaken for the purpose of monitoring and ordering the mood of the population as a whole' (p. 410). Drawing on the ideas about the brain's plasticity, noted above, the third area of growth identified by Williamson – neuropedagogies – aims to develop knowledge of the brain which can inform new technologies which will, in turn, enhance pupils' cognitive functioning through reshaping the neural structure of the brain itself. Williamson gives the example of the 'cognitive classroom' project, being pursued by scientists at IBM, as part of their 'Cognitive Comput-ing for Education' programme. Such classrooms are intended to provide environments modelled on learners' brains and interventions that will improve their neural structures:

> The cognitive classroom promises personalisation of the learn-ing experience, real-time feedback on learner performance, adaptive learning software that can learn from and adapt to the learner, and intelligent software tutors that can automate reme-dial intervention or even prescribe appropriate curricular con-tent or automate pedagogic tasks. (Williamson, 2016a, p. 411)

Such aspects of 'educational data science' should not be considered solely areas of intellectual enquiry and research. Instead, because of their pedagogical orientation and aim to change the bodies, minds and brains of pupils, they constitute a field of *biopolitical intervention* (Williamson, 2016a).

Challenges for the future

Implicit, and at times explicit, in the discussion above of the 'new directions' offered by the biological sciences and new technologies are a number of challenges for those who conduct research on the relationship between education and society. These include being prepared to work constructively across disciplines; developing a range of new skills and knowledge to be able to collaborate with, for example, biologists, psychologists and computer scientists; and – recognising that the translation of findings from these areas of science into policy and practice are often problematic – being willing to subject such translations to critical scrutiny. The preceding discussion has also highlighted that educational research is being conducted in a variety of new places, such as within private sector data labs, which may constitute competition for the scholar located within HE – in terms of both securing funding for her or his endeavours and remaining at the forefront of new knowledge generation.

Challenges can also, however, be identified in the wider social and political environment. Notwithstanding the points made in various chapters about the persistence of national differences with respect to some areas of education, *Education and Society* as a whole has demonstrated the value of exploring movements across national borders – of policies, people, knowledge and institutions. A challenge for contemporary researchers is thus to be sensitive to the transnational character of many educational processes and to develop the necessary tools, networks and perspectives to be able to engage in data collection and analysis beyond the confines of their own nation-state.

In many parts of the world, those researching the relationship between education and society – in common with other scholars – have had to respond to changes in the way funding for research is allocated. In nations such as Denmark, the USA and the UK, government investment in research has increasingly become tied to areas of enquiry perceived to be of strategic importance. This is also the case, at a supranational level, for much of the research funding made available by the European Union. Such prioritisation has, in some cases, been to the detriment of the social sciences in general, while in others it has channelled money to only a limited number of areas of educational research. Recent calls from the UK's main social science funder, the Economic and Social Research Council, have prioritised, for example, projects focusing on neuroscience and education and the analysis of 'big data' held by government within the National Pupil Database. Moreover, educational researchers who wish to access government funds also have often to accommodate the methodological preferences of politicians and policymakers. Typically, and as noted in Chapter 1, over recent years, this has meant the use of quantitative rather than qualitative methods. Indeed, Luke (2010) has argued that as part of a shift towards so-called 'evidence-based policy' in many anglophone nations of the Global North, a binary division has been created:

> between qualitative 'critical work' which has been portrayed as scientifically 'soft', politically correct and ideological by the press, politicians and educational bureaucrats – and empirical, quantitative scientific research, which is presented as unbiased, truthful and the sole grounds for rational policy formation. (p. 178)

In the USA, for example, randomised control trials (RCTs) have been promoted since the turn of the twenty-first century, with funding for specific educational interventions frequently tied to the condition that RCTs would be used for the associated evaluation (Ong-Dean et al., 2011). Such imperatives create significant challenges for researchers who wish to pursue topics not obviously allied with strategic priorities and/or deploy non-quantitative methods.

These problems can be exacerbated in a political climate in which 'expert knowledge' – irrespective of topic or method – is derided by politicians and the media alike (Nelson, 2017). Certainly it is the case that sociologists of education do not now have the close relationship with policymakers that they had, in some countries at least, in the middle of the twentieth century (Dale, 2001; Lauder et al., 2009). Nevertheless, such scholars do still play an important role in, what Whitty (2012) has termed, 'inoculating' the public mind against inappropriate policies. Moreover, given the significant place education has assumed across the contemporary world, sociologists of education can offer fundamentally important insights into the relationship between the routes through which learning becomes institutionalised and the broader processes of social transformation. By explicating the links between their discipline and the everyday experiences of students in classrooms and other spaces of learning, they can also play a critical role in demonstrating the ongoing relevance of rigorous scholarship and informed debate. Educational researchers thus need to rise to the challenges outlined here and ensure that their own position in society is as salient as that of the object of their analysis.

REFERENCES

Aapola, S. (2002) Exploring dimensions of age in young people's lives, *Time and Society*, 11, 2–3, 295–314.

Aarseth, H. (2016) A sound foundation? Financial elite families and elite schooling in Norway, in: Maxwell, C. and Aggleton, P. (eds) *Elite Education: International Perspectives*, London, Routledge.

Abada, T. and Tenkorang, E. (2009) Pursuit of university education among the children of immigrants in Canada: The roles of parental human capital and social capital, *Journal of Youth Studies*, 12, 2, 185–207.

Acker, S. and Armenti, C. (2004) Sleepless in academia, *Gender and Education*, 16, 1, 3–24.

Ackers, L. (2010) Internationalisation and equality: The contribution of short stay mobility to progression in science careers, *Recherches Sociologiques et Anthropologiques*, 41, 1, 83–103.

AERA (American Educational Research Association) (2011) Code of ethics, *Educational Researcher*, 40, 3, 145–156. Available at: www.aera.net/Portals/38/docs/About_AERA/CodeOfEthics(1).pdf (Accessed 17/07/17).

Aguiar, A. and Nogueira, M. (2012) Internationalisation strategies of Brazilian private schools, *International Studies in Sociology of Education*, 22, 4, 353–368.

Alexander, C., Weekes-Bernard, D. and Arday, J. (2015) Race and education – contemporary contexts and challenges, in: Alexander, C., Weekes-Bernard, D. and Arday, J. (eds) *Race, Education and Inequality in Contemporary Britain*, London, The Runnymede Trust.

Alhamdan, B., Al-Saadi, K., Baroutsis, A., Du Plessis, A., Hamid, O. and Honan, E. (2014) Media representation of teachers across five countries, *Comparative Education*, 50, 4, 490–505.

Allen, K. (2014) 'Blair's Children': Young women as 'aspirational subjects' in the psychic landscape of class, *The Sociological Review*, 62, 4, 760–779.

Allen, K. and Ingram, N. (2017) *'Talent Spotting?' Inequality, Cultural Sorting and Constructions of the Ideal Graduate in Elite Professions*. Presentation to British Sociological Association Annual Conference, University of Manchester, 4 April 2017.

Allen, K., Quinn, J., Hollingworth, S. and Rose, A. (2013) Becoming employable students and 'ideal' creative workers: Exclusion and inequality in higher education work placements, *British Journal of Sociology of Education*, 34, 3, 431–452.

Allen, R. and West, A. (2009) Religious schools in London: School admissions, religious composition and selectivity, *Oxford Review of Education*, 35, 4, 471–494.

Allen, R. and West, A. (2011) Why do faith secondary schools have advantaged intakes? The relative importance of neighbourhood characteristics, social background and religious identification amongst parents, *British Educational Research Journal*, 37, 4, 691–712.

Alsop, R., Gonzalez-Arnal, S. and Kilkey, M. (2008) The widening participation agenda: The marginal place of care, *Gender and Education*, 20, 6, 623–637.

Angus, L., Snyder, I. and Sutherland-Smith, W. (2004) ICT and educational (dis)advantage: Families, computers and contemporary social and educational inequalities, *British Journal of Sociology of Education*, 25, 1, 3–18.

Antonucci, L. (2016) *Student Lives in Crisis: Deepening Inequality in Times of Austerity*, Bristol, Polity Press.

Apokin, A. and Iudkevich, M. (2008) Analysis of student employment in the context of the Russian labour market, *Voprosy Ekonomiki*, 6, 98–110.

Apple, M. (2000) The cultural politics of home schooling, *Peabody Journal of Education*, 75, 1–2, 256–271.

Apple, M. (2004) Cultural politics and the text, in: Ball, S. (ed) *The RoutledgeFalmer Reader in the Sociology of Education*, London, Routledge.

Archer, L. (2008) The new neoliberal subjects? Young/er academics' constructions of professional identity, *Journal of Education Policy*, 23, 3, 265–285.

Archer, L. and Francis, B. (2006) Challenging classes? Exploring the role of social class within the identities and achievement of British Chinese pupils, *Sociology*, 40, 29–49.

Archer, L. and Francis, B. (2007) *Understanding Minority Ethnic Achievement: Race, Gender, Class and 'Success'*, Abingdon, Routledge.

Archer, L., Hutchings, M. and Ross, A. (2003) *Higher Education and Social Class: Issues of Exclusion and Inclusion*, London, Routledge.

Archer, L., Moote, J., Francis, B., De Witt, J. and Yeomans, L. (2017) The 'exceptional' physics girl: A sociological analysis of multimethod data from young women to explore gendered patterns of post-16 participation, *American Educational Research Journal*, 54, 1, 88–126.

Arday, J. (2015) Considering mentoring among Black and minority ethnic learners and issues concerning teacher training, in: Alexander, C., Weekes-Bernard, D. and Arday, J. (eds) (2015) *Race, Education and Inequality in Contemporary Britain*, London, The Runnymede Trust.

Aries, E. and Seider, M. (2005) The interactive relationship between class identity and the college experience: The case of lower income students, *Qualitative Sociology*, 28, 419–443.

Arnett, J.J. (2004) *Emerging Adulthood: The Winding Road from the Late Teens Through the Twenties*, New York, Oxford University Press.

Arnold, M. (2006) *Culture and Anarchy*, Oxford, Oxford University Press.

Arnot, M., David, M. and Weiner, G. (1999) *Closing the Gender Gap?*, Cambridge, Polity.

Aston, L. and Bekhradnia, B. (2003) *Demand for Graduates: A Review of the Economic Evidence*, Higher Education Policy Institute http://www.hepi.ac.uk/downloads/3DemandforGraduatesAreviewoftheeconomicevidence.pdf

Atkinson, W. (2015) *Class*, Cambridge, Polity Press.

Au, W. (2009) *Unequal by Design: High-Stakes Testing and the Standardization of Inequality*, New York, Routledge.

Au, W. and Ferrare, J. (2015a) Introduction: neoliberalism, social networks and the new governance of education, in: Au, W. and Ferrare, J. (eds) *Mapping Corporate Education Reform: Power and Policy Networks in the Neoliberal State*, New York, Routledge.

Au, W. and Ferrare, J. (eds) (2015b) *Mapping Corporate Education Reform: Power and Policy Networks in the Neoliberal State*, New York, Routledge.

Aurini, J. and Davies, S. (2005) Choice without markets: Homeschooling in the context of private education, *British Journal of Sociology of Education*, 26, 4, 461–474.

Ayling, P. (2016) 'Eliteness' and elite schooling in contemporary Nigeria, in: Maxwell, C. and Aggleton, P. (eds) *Elite Education: International Perspectives*, London, Routledge.

Baas, M. (2006) Students of migration: Indian overseas students and the question of permanent residency, *People and Place*, 14, 1, 9–24.

Baas, M. (2014) Victims or profiteers? Issues of migration, racism and violence among Indian students in Melbourne, *Asia Pacific Viewpoint*, 55, 2, 212–225.

Baeck, U.-D.K. (2010) '*We* are the professionals': A study of teachers' views on parental involvement in school, *British Journal of Sociology of Education*, 31, 3, 323–335.

Ball, S. (1990) *Politics and Policymaking in Education*, London, Routledge.

Ball, S. (2003) *Class Strategies and the Education Market*, London, Routledge.

Ball, S. (2004) The sociology of education: A disputational account, in: Ball, S.J. (ed) *The RoutledgeFalmer Reader in Sociology of Education*, London, RoutledgeFalmer.

Ball, S. (2007) Big policies/small world. An introduction to international perspectives in education policy, in: Lingard, B. and Ozga, J. (eds) *The RoutledgeFalmer Reader in Education Policy and Politics*, London, Routledge, pp. 36–47.

Ball, S. (2009) Privatising education, privatising education policy, privatising educational research: Network governance and the 'competition state', *Journal of Education Policy*, 24, 1, 83–99.

Ball, S. (2012) Performativity, commodification and commitment: An I-Spy guide to the neo-liberal university, *British Journal of Educational Studies*, 60, 1, 17–28.

Ball, S. (2016) Following policy: Networks, network ethnography and education policy mobilities, *Journal of Education Policy* (Advance online access).

Ball, S., Bowe, R. and Gewirtz, S. (1997) Circuits of Schooling: A sociological exploration of parental choice of school in social-class contexts, in: Halsey, A., Lauder, H., Brown, P. and Wells, A.S. (eds) *Education: Culture, Economy, Society*, Oxford, Oxford University Press, pp. 409–421.

Ball, S. and Exley, S. (2010) Making policy with 'good ideas': Policy networks and the 'intellectuals' of New Labour, *Journal of Education Policy*, 25, 2, 151–169.

Ball, S., Reay, D. and David, M. (2002) 'Ethnic choosing': Minority ethnic students, social class and higher education choice, *Race Ethnicity and Education*, 5, 4, 333–357.

Ball, S., Maguire, M., Braun, A. and Hoskins, K. (2011) Policy actors: Doing policy work in schools, *Discourse: Studies in the Cultural Politics of Education*, 32, 4, 625–639.

Ball, S. and Vincent, C. (2001) 'I heard it on the grapevine': 'Hot knowledge' and school choice, *British Journal of Sociology of Education*, 19, 3, 377–395.

Barnett, R. (2000) *Realizing the University in an Age of Super-Complexity*, Buckingham, Society for Research into Higher Education and Open University Press.

Barrett, A. (2011) A millennium learning goal for education post-2015: A question of outcomes or processes, *Comparative Education*, 47, 1, 119–133.

Bathmaker, A.M. (2003) The expansion of higher education: A consideration of control, funding and quality, in: Bartlett, S. and Burton, D. (eds) *Education Studies: Essential Issues*, London, Sage, pp. 169–189.

Bathmaker, A.M., Ingram, N. and Waller, R. (2013) Higher education, social class and the mobilisation of capitals: Recognising and playing the game, *British Journal of Sociology of Education*, 34, 5–6. 723–743.

Bauman, Z. (1990) *Thinking Sociologically*, Oxford, Blackwell.

Beer, D. and Burrows, R. (2007) Sociology and, of and in Web 2.0: Some initial considerations, *Sociological Research Online*, 12, 5. Available online at: www.socresonline.org.uk/12/5/17/html (Accessed 20/06/16).

Beerkens, M., Magi, E. and Lill, L. (2011) University studies as a side job: Causes and consequences of massive student employment in Estonia, *Higher Education*, 61, 679–692.

Benson, M., Bridge, G. and Wilson, D. (2015) School choice in London and Paris: A comparison of middle class strategies, *Social Policy and Administration*, 49, 1, 24–43.

Berends, M. (2015) Sociology and school choice: What we know after two decades of charter schools, *Annual Review of Sociology*, 41, 159–180.

Bernstein, B. (1970) Education cannot compensate for society, *New Society*, 15, 387, 344–347.

Bernstein, B. (1971) On the classification and framing of educational knowledge, in: Young, M. (ed) *Knowledge and Control: New Directions for the Sociology of Education*, London, Collier-Macmillan.

Bertrand-Cloodt, D., Corvers, F., Kriechel, B. and Thor, J. (2012) Why do recent graduates enter into flexible jobs? *De Economist*, 160, 2, 157–175.

Bevir, M. (2011) Governance and governmentality after neo-liberalism, *Policy and Politics*, 39, 4, 457–471.

Bhopal, K. (2011) 'We tend to stick together and mostly we stick to our own kind': British Indian women and support networks at university, *Gender and Education*, 23, 5, 519–534.

Bhopal, K. (2015) Race, identity and support in initial teacher training, *British Journal of Educational Studies*, 63, 2, 197–211.

Biesta, G. (2009a) Good education in an age of measurement: On the need to reconnect with the question of purpose in education, *Educational Assessment, Evaluation and Accountability*, 21, 1, 33–46.

Biesta, G. (2009b) What kind of citizenship for European higher education? Beyond the competent active citizen, *European Educational Research Journal*, 8, 2, 146–158.

Birtwistle, T. (2007) European and European Union dimensions to mobility, in: Jones, E. and Brown, S. (eds) *Internationalising Higher Education*, London, Routledge, pp. 181–192.

BIS (Department of Business, Innovation and Skills) (2009) *Higher Ambitions: The Future of Universities in a Knowledge Economy*, London, Department of Business, Innovation and Skills.

BIS (Department of Business, Innovation and Skills) (2013) *International Education: Global Growth and Prosperity*, London, Department of Business, Innovation and Skills.

Bloch, A., and Hirsch, S. (2017) The educational experiences of the second generation from refugee backgrounds, *Journal of Ethnic and Migration Studies* (Advance online access).

Bodycott, P. (2009) Choosing a higher education study abroad destination: What mainland Chinese parents and students rate as important, *Journal of Research in International Education*, 8, 3, 349–373.

Boeren, E. (2017) Understanding lifelong learning participation as a layered problem, *Studies in Continuing Education* (Advance online access).

du Bois Reymond, M. (1998) 'I don't want to commit myself yet': Young people's life concepts, *Journal of Youth Studies*, 1, 1, 63–79.

Boliver, V. (2013) How fair is access to more prestigious UK Universities? *British Journal of Sociology*, 64, 2, 344–364.

Boliver, V. (2016) Exploring ethnic inequalities in admission to Russell Group universities, *Sociology*, 50, 2, 247–266.

Bonal, X. and Tarabini, A. (2013) The role of PISA in shaping hegemonic educational discourses, policies and practices: The case of Spain, *Research in Comparative and International Education*, 8, 3, 335–341.

Booher-Jennings, J. (2008) Learning to label: Socialisation, gender and the hidden curriculum of high-stakes testing, *British Journal of Sociology of Education*, 29, 2, 149–160.

Bottero, W. (2005) *Stratification: Social Division and Inequality*, London, Routledge.

Bourdieu, P. (1971a) Intellectual field and creative product, in: Young, M. (ed) *Knowledge and Control: New Directions for the Sociology of Education*, London, Collier-Macmillan.

Bourdieu, P. (1971b) Systems of education and systems of thought, in: Young, M. (ed) *Knowledge and Control: New Directions for the Sociology of Education*, London, Collier-Macmillan.

Bourdieu, P. (1997) The three forms of capital, in: Halsey, A., Lauder, H., Brown, P. and Wells, A.S. (eds) *Education: Culture, Economy, Society*, Oxford, Oxford University Press.

Bourdieu, P. and Passeron, J.-C. (1990) *Reproduction in Education, Society and Culture* (second edition), London, Sage.

Bourdieu, P. and Wacquant, L. (1992) *An Invitation to Reflexive Sociology*, Chicago, IL, University of Chicago Press.

Bowles, S. and Gintis, H. (1976) *Schooling in Capitalist America*, Boston and London, Routledge and Kegan Paul.

Bracht, O., Engel, C., Janson, K., Over, A., Schomburg, H. and Teichler, U. (2006) *The Professional Value of Erasmus Mobility*, Final report presented to the European Commission, Directorate-General Education and Culture.

Bradbury, A. (2013) Education policy and the 'ideal learner': Producing recognisable learner-subjects through early years assessment, *British Journal of Sociology of Education*, 34, 1, 1–19.

Bradbury, A., McGimpsey, I. and Santori, D. (2013) Revising rationality: The use of 'Nudge' approaches in neoliberal education policy, *Journal of Education Policy*, 28, 2, 247–267.

Bradbury, A. and Roberts-Holmes, G. (2016) Creating an OFSTED story: The role of early years assessment data in schools' narratives of progress, *British Journal of Sociology of Education* (Advance online access).

Brantlinger, E., Majd-Jabbari, M. and Guskin, S. (1996) Self-interest and liberal educational discourse: How ideology works for middle-class mothers, *American Educational Research Journal*, 33, 3, 571–597.

Braun, A. (2015) The politics of teaching as an occupation in the professional borderlands: The interplay of gender, class and professional status in a biographical study of trainee teachers in England, *Journal of Education Policy*, 30, 2, 258–274.

Braun, A., Ball, S.J., Maguire, M. and Hoskins, K. (2011) Taking context seriously: Towards explaining policy enactments in the secondary school, *Discourse: Studies in the Cultural Politics of Education*, 32, 4, 585–596.

Braun, A., Vincent, C. and Ball, S. (2008) 'I'm so much more myself now, coming back to work' – working class mothers, paid work and childcare, *Journal of Education Policy*, 23, 5, 533–548.

Bray, M., Kobakhidze, M., Liu, J. and Zhang, W. (2016) The internal dynamics of privatised public education: Fee-charging supplementary tutoring provided by teachers in Cambodia, *International Journal of Educational Development*, 49, 291–299.

Broadfoot, P. (1979) *Assessment, Schools and Society*, London, Methuen.

Brooks, R. (2003) Young people's higher education choices: The role of family and friends, *British Journal of Sociology of Education*, 24, 3, 283–297.

Brooks R. (2004) 'My mum would be pleased as punch if I went, my dad seems more particular about it': Paternal involvement in young people's higher education choices', *British Educational Research Journal*, 30, 4, 495–514.

Brooks, R. (2005) The construction of age and the impact of 'age-mixing' within UK further education colleges, *British Journal of Sociology of Education*, 26, 1, 55–70.

Brooks, R. (2006) Young graduates and lifelong learning: The impact of institutional stratification, *Sociology*, 40, 6, 1019–1037.

Brooks, R. (2007) Young people's extra curricular activities: Critical social engagement – or 'something for the CV'? *Journal of Social Policy*, 36, 417–434.

Brooks, R. (2012) Student-parents and higher education: A cross-national comparison, *Journal of Education Policy*, 27, 3, 423–437.

Brooks, R. (2013) Negotiating time and place for study: Student-parents and familial relationships, *Sociology*, 47, 3, 443–459.

Brooks, R. (2015) Social and spatial disparities in emotional responses to education: Feelings of 'guilt' among student-parents, *British Educational Research Journal*, 41, 3, 505–519.

Brooks, R. (ed) (2016) *Student Politics and Protest: International Perspectives*, London, Routledge.

Brooks, R. (2017) Representations of East Asian students in the UK media, *Journal of Ethnic and Migration Studies* 43, 14, 2363–2377.

Brooks, R. (2018) Understanding the higher education student in Europe: A comparative analysis, *Compare* 48, 4, 500-517.

Brooks, R., Byford, K. and Sela, K. (2015) Students' unions, consumerism and the neo-liberal university, *British Journal of Sociology of Education* (Advance online access).

Brooks, R., Byford, K. and Sela, K. (2016) The spaces of UK students' unions: Extending the critical geographies of the university campus, *Social and Cultural Geography*, 17, 4, 471–490.

Brooks, R. and Everett, G. (2009) Post-graduation reflections on the value of a degree, *British Educational Research Journal*, 35, 3, 333–349.

Brooks, R., McCormack, M. and Bhopal, K. (2013) Contemporary debates in the sociology of education: An introduction, in: Brooks, R., McCormack, M. and Bhopal, K. (eds) *Contemporary Debates in the Sociology of Education*, Basingstoke, Palgrave.

Brooks, R., te Riele, K. and Maguire, M. (2014) *Ethics and Education Research*, London, Sage.

Brooks, R. and Waters, J. (2009) A second chance at 'success': UK students and global circuits of higher education, *Sociology*, 43, 6, 1085–1102.

Brooks, R. and Waters, J. (2013) *Student Mobilities, Migration and the Internationalization of Higher Education*, Basingstoke, Palgrave (New foreword).

Brooks, R. and Waters, J. (2015) The hidden internationalism of elite English schools, *Sociology*, 49, 2, 212–228.

Brooks, R., Waters, J. and Pimlott-Wilson, H. (2012) International education and the employability of UK students, *British Educational Research Journal*, 38, 2, 281–298.

Brown, A. and Brown, K. (2014) Panacea and liberator: Racial formation and the Black teacher in the United States, in: Moreau, M.-P. (ed) *Inequalities in the Teaching Profession: A Global Perspective*, Basingstoke, Palgrave.

Brown, P. (1997) The 'third wave': Education and the ideology of parentocracy, in: Halsey, A., Lauder, H., Brown, P. and Wells, A.S. (eds) *Education: Culture, Economy, Society*, Oxford, Oxford University Press.

Brown, P. and Hesketh, A. (2004) *The Mismanagement of Talent*, Oxford, Oxford University Press.

Brown, P. and Lauder, H. (2006) Globalisation, knowledge and the myth of the magnet economy, *Globalisation, Societies and Education*, 4, 1, 25–57.

Brown, P., Lauder, H. and Ashton, D. (2011) *The Global Auction: The Broken Promises of Education, Jobs and Income*, New York, Oxford University Press.

Brown P. and Tannock, S. (2009) Education, meritocracy and the global war for talent, *Journal of Education Policy*, 24, 4, 377–392.

Brown, S. and Jones, E. (2007) Introduction: Values, valuing and value in an internationalised Higher Education context, in: Jones, E. and Brown, S. (eds) *Internationalising Higher Education*, London, Routledge, pp. 1–6.

Browne, L. (2010) As UK policy strives to make access to higher education easier for all, is discrimination in employment practice still apparent? *Journal of Vocational Education and Training*, 62, 3, 313–326.

Buisson-Fenet, H. and Draelants, H. (2013) School-linking processes: Describing and explaining their role in the social closure of French elite education, *Higher Education*, 66, 39–57.

Bunar, N. (2010) Choosing for quality or inequality: Current perspectives on the implementation of school choice policy in Sweden, *Journal of Education Policy*, 25, 1, 1–18.

Bunnell, T. (2015) The rise and decline of the International Baccalaureate Diploma programme in the United Kingdom, *Oxford Review of Education*, 41, 3, 387–403.

Buras, K. (2015) *Charter Schools, Race and Urban Space: Where the Market Meets Grassroots Resistance*, New York, Routledge.

Burchell, H. and Millman, V. (1989) *Changing Perspectives on Gender: New Initiatives in Secondary Education*, Milton Keynes, Open University Press.

Burgess, C. (2016) 'Having to say everyday … I'm not black enough … I'm not white enough': Discourses of aboriginality in the Australian education context, *Race Ethnicity and Education* (Advance online access).

Burgess, S. (2015) Aspirations, language and poverty: Attainment and ethnicity, in: Alexander, C., Weekes-Bernard, D. and Arday, J. (eds) (2015) *Race, Education and Inequality in Contemporary Britain*, London, The Runnymede Trust.

Burke, P.-J. (2006) Men accessing education: Gendered aspirations, *British Educational Research Journal*, 32, 5, 719–733.

Busher, H., James, N., Piela, A. and Palmer, A.-M. (2014) Transforming marginalised adult learners' views of themselves, *British Journal of Sociology of Education*, 35, 5, 800–817.

Busso, D. and Pollack, C. (2015) No brain left behind: Consequences of neuroscience discourse for education, *Learning, Media and Technology*, 40, 2, 168–186.

Butler, J. (1993) *Gender Trouble: Feminism and the Subversion of Identity*, London, Routledge.

Butler, T. and Hamnett, C. (2012) Praying for success? Faith schools and school choice in east London, *Geoforum*, 43, 1242–1253.

Byrne, B. (2009) Not just class: Towards an understanding of the whiteness of middle class schooling choice, *Ethnic and Racial Studies*, 32, 3, 424–441.

Cairns, D. (2014) *Youth Transitions, International Student Mobility and Spatial Reflexivity*, Basingstoke, Palgrave.

Calarco, J. (2011) 'I need help!' Social class and children's help-seeking in elementary school, *American Sociological Review*, 76, 6, 862–882.

Campbell, T. (2014) Stratified at seven: In-class ability grouping and the relative age effect, *British Educational Research Journal*, 40, 5, 749–771.

Carolan-Silva, A. and Reyes, R. (2013) Navigating the path to college: Latino students' social networks and access to college, *Educational Studies*, 49, 4, 334–359.

Carrasco, A. (2012) Voucher system and school effectiveness: Reassessing school performance differences and parental choice decision-making, *Estudios de Economia*, 39, 2, 123–141.

CEC (Commission of the European Communities) (2009) *Promoting the Learning Mobility of Young People* COM (2009) 329 Final. Brussels, Commission of the European Communities.

Chadderton, C. (2014) The militarisation of English schools: Troops to Teachers and the implications for initial teacher education and race equality, *Race, Ethnicity and Education*, 17, 3, 407–428.

Chan, A. (2014) Making sense of their career pathways: The work narratives of women primary school principals in Hong Kong, in: Moreau, M.-P. (ed) *Inequalities in the Teaching Profession: A Global Perspective*, Basingstoke, Palgrave.

Chapman, C. and Salokangas, M. (2012) Independent state-funded schools: Some reflections on recent developments, *School Leadership and Management*, 32, 5, 473–486.

Cho, H.S. and Mosselson, J. (2017) Neoliberal practices amidst social justice orientations: Global citizenship education in South Korea, *Compare* (Advance online access).

Choi, J. and Cho, R. (2015) Evaluating the effects of governmental regulations on South Korean private cram schools, *Asia Pacific Journal of Education*, 36, 4, 1–23.

Choi, P.K. (2010) 'Weep for the Chinese university': A case study of English hegemony and academic capitalism in higher education in Hong Kong, *Journal of Education Policy*, 25, 2, 233–252.

CIHE (Council for Industry and Higher Education) (2007) *Global Horizons for UK Students: A Guide for Universities*, London, CIHE.

Clark, B. (1998) *Creating Entrepreneurial Universities: Organizational Pathways of Transformation*, Oxford, Pergamon Press.

Clarke, J. (2005) New labour's citizens: Activated, empowered, responsibilised, abandoned? *Critical Social Policy*, 25, 4, 447–463.

Clarke, J. and Newman, J. (2009) Elusive publics: Knowledge, power and public service reform, in: Gewirtz, S., Mahony, P., Hextall, I. and Cribb, A. (eds) *Changing Teacher Professionalism: International Trends, Challenges and Ways Forward*, London, Routledge.

Clarke, J., Newman, J., Smith, N., Vidler, E. and Westmarland, L. (2007) *Creating Citizen-Consumers*, London, Sage.

Clements, B. (2010) Understanding public attitudes in Britain towards faith schools, *British Educational Research Journal*, 36, 6, 953–973.

Clements, B. (2016) Attitudes towards faith-based schooling amongst Roman Catholics in Britain, *British Journal of Religious Education* (Advance online access).

Coffey, A. (2004) *Reconceptualising Social Policy: Sociological Perspectives on Contemporary Social Policy*, Maidenhead, Open University Press.

Cohen, M. (1998) 'A habit of healthy idleness': Boys' underachievement in historical perspective, in: Epstein, D., Elwood, J., Hey, V. and Maw, J. (eds) *Failing Boys? Issues in Gender and Underachievement*, Buckingham, Open University Press.

Coldron, J., Cripps, C. and Shipton, L. (2010) Why are English secondary schools socially segregated? *Journal of Education Policy*, 25, 1, 19–35.

Collini, S. (2012) *What are Universities For?*, London, Penguin Books.

Collins, F.L. (2006) Making Asian students, making students Asian: The racialisation of export education in Auckland, New Zealand, *Asia Pacific Viewpoint*, 47, 2, 217–234.

Collins, R. (1979) *The Credential Society: An Historical Sociology of Education and Stratification*, New York, Academic Press.

Connell, R. (2009) Good teachers on dangerous ground: Towards a new view of teacher quality and professionalism, *Critical Studies in Education*, 50, 3, 213–229.

Cooper, B. and Sureau, J. (2007) The politics of home schooling: New developments, new challenges, *Educational Policy*, 21, 1, 110–131.

Correa-Valez, I., Gifford, S., McMichael, C. and Sampson, R. (2017) Predictors of secondary school completion among refugee youth 8 to 9 years after resettlement in Melbourne, Australia, *Journal of International Migration and Integration*, 18, 3, 791–805.

Côte, J. and Allahar, A. (1994) *Generation on Hold: Coming of Age in the Late 20th Century*, New York, New York University Press.

Courtney, S. (2015) Mapping school types in England, *Oxford Review of Education*, 41, 6, 799–818.

Crawford, C., Dearden, L. and Greaves, E. (2011) *Does When You Are Born Matter? The Impact of Month of Birth on Children's Cognitive and Non-cognitive Skills in England*, London, Institute for Fiscal Studies. Available online at: (Accessed https://www.ifs.org.uk/publications/5736 on 24/02/17).

Crawford, C., Dearden, L. and Greaves, E. (2013) *When You Are Born Matters: Evidence for England*, London, Institute for Fiscal Studies. Available online at: https://www.ifs.org.uk/comms/r80.pdf (Accessed 24/02/17).

Crawford, C., Dearden, L., Micklewright, J. and Vignoles, A. (2017) *Family Background and University Success*, Oxford, Oxford University Press.

Crawford, C., Gregg, P., Macmillan, L., Vignoles, A. and Wyness, G. (2016) Higher education, career opportunities, and intergenerational inequality, *Oxford Review of Economic Policy*, 32, 553–575.

CREDO (2013) *Charter School Growth and Replication* Stanford, C.A., CREDO. Available online at: https://credo.stanford.edu/research-reports.html (Accessed 02/05/18).

Croft, S., Roberts, M. and Stenhouse, V. (2016) The perfect storm of education reform: High stakes testing and teacher evaluation, *Social Justice*, 42, 1, 70–92.

Crook, D., Power, S. and Whitty, G. (1999) *The Grammar School Question: A Review of Research on Comprehensive and Selective Education*, London, Institute of Education Publications, University of London.

Crozier, G. (2005) 'There's a war against our children': Black educational underachievement revisited, *British Journal of Sociology of Education*, 26, 5, 585–598.

Dale, R. (2001) The sociology of education over 50 years, in: Demaine, J. (ed) *Sociology of Education Today*, Basingstoke, Palgrave.

D'Arcy, K. (2014) Home education, school, travellers and educational inclusion, *British Journal of Sociology of Education*, 35, 5, 818–835.

Darling Hammond, L. (2007) Race, inequality and educational accountability: The irony of 'No Child Left Behind', *Race Ethnicity and Education*, 10, 3, 245–260.

David, M., Ball, S., Davies, J. and Reay, D. (2003) Gender issues in parental involvement in student choices of higher education, *Gender and Education*, 15, 1, 21–36.

Davies, B. (1989) *Frogs and Snails and Feminist Tales*, London, Allen and Unwin.

Davies, W. (2015) *The Happiness Industry: How the Government and Big Business Sold Us Wellbeing*, London, Verso Books.

Deakin, H. (2014) The drivers to Erasmus student work placement mobility: A UK student perspective, *Children's Geographies*, 12, 1, 25–39.

Deem, R. (2001) Globalisation, new managerialism, academic capitalism and entrpreneurialism in universities, *Comparative Education*, 37, 1, 7–20.

Deem, R. (2004) Sociology and the sociology of higher education: A missed call or a disconnection? *International Studies in Sociology of Education*, 14, 1, 21–44.

Denscombe, M. and Aubrook, L. (1992) 'It's just another piece of schoolwork': The ethics of questionnaire research on pupils in schools, *British Educational Research Journal*, 18, 2, 113–131.

Dermott, E. (2008) *Intimate Fatherhood*, London, Routledge.

Dermott, E. (2011) 'Troops to teachers': Solving the problem of working class masculinity in the classroom? *Critical Social Policy*, 32, 2, 223–241.

Desrosieres, A. (1998) *The Politics of Large Numbers: A History of Statistical Reasoning*, Cambridge, MA, Harvard University Press.

Devine, F. (2004) *Class Practices: How Parents Help Their Children Get Good Jobs*, Cambridge, Cambridge University Press.

Dewey, J. (2006) The democratic conception in education, in: Lauder, H., Brown, P., Dillabough, J. and Halsey, A. (eds) *Education, Globalization and Social Change*, Oxford, Oxford University Press, pp. 91–100.

DfE (Department for Education) (2014) *Promoting Fundamental British Values as Part of SMSC in Schools*, London, Department for Education.

DfE (Department for Education) (2015) *Statistical First Release: GCSE and Equivalent Attainment by Pupil Characteristics, 2013 to 2014 (Revised)*, London, DfE. Available at: https://www.gov.uk/government/uploads/system/uploads/attachment_data/file/399005/SFR06_2015_Text.pdf (Accessed 23/12/16).

DiPrete, T. and Buchmann, C. (2013) *The Rise of Women: The Growing Gender Gap in Education and What it Means for American Schools*, New York, Russell Sage Foundation.

Doharty, N. (2015) 'Hard time pressure inna Babylon': Why Black history in schools is failing to meet the needs of BME students at Key Stage 3, in: Alexander, C., Weekes-Bernard, D. and Arday, J. (eds) (2015) *Race, Education and Inequality in Contemporary Britain*, London, The Runnymede Trust.

Donnelly, M. (2014) The road to Oxbridge: Schools and elite university choices, *British Journal of Educational Studies*, 62, 1, 57–72.

Dore, R. (1976) *The Diploma Disease: Education, Qualification and Development*, London, Allen and Unwin.

Draelants, H. (2016) The Insiders: Changing forms of representation in education, in: Koh, A. and Kenway, J. (eds) *Elite Schools: Multiple Geographies of Privilege*, New York, Routledge.

Durkheim, E. (2006) Education: Its nature and role, in: Lauder, H., Brown, P., Dillabough, J. and Halsey, A. (eds) *Education, Globalization and Social Change*, Oxford, Oxford University Press, pp. 76–87.

Edwards, R., Gilles, V. and Horsley, N. (2015) Brain science and early years policy: Hopeful ethos or 'cruel optimism'? *Critical Social Policy*, 35, 2, 167–187.

Eisenstadt, S.N. (1956) *From Generation to Generation: Age Groups and Social Structure*, London, Free Press of Glencoe Collier-Macmillan Ltd.

El-Haj, T.R.A. (2010) 'The beauty of America': Nationalism, education and the war on terror, *Harvard Educational Review*, 80, 2, 242–275.

Ellis, V., Maguire, M., Trippestad, T., Liu, Y., Yang, X. and Zeichner, K. (2016) Teaching other people's children, elsewhere, for a while: The rhetoric of a travelling educational reform, *Journal of Education Policy*, 31, 1, 60–80.

Elstad, E., Lejonberg, E. and Christophersen, K.-A. (2015) Teaching evaluation as a contested practice: Teacher resistance to teaching evaluation schemes in Norway, *Education Inquiry*, 6, 4, 375–399.

Elwood, J. and Gipps, C. (1999) *Review of Recent Research on the Achievement of Girls in Single-Sex Schools*, London, Institute of Education.

Epstein, D., Elwood, J., Hey, V. and Maw, J. (eds) (1998) *Failing Boys? Issues in Gender and Underachievement*, Buckingham, Open University Press.

Epstein, D. and Johnson, R. (1998) *Schooling Sexualities*, Buckingham, Open University Press.

Equality Challenge Unit (2015) *Equality in Higher Education Statistical Report 2015. Part 1: Staff*. Available online at: http://www.ecu.ac.uk/publications/equality-higher-education-statistical-report-2015/ (Accessed 20/12/16).

European Group for Integrated Social Research (2001) Misleading trajectories: Transition dilemmas of young adults in Europe, *Journal of Youth Studies*, 4, 1, 101–118.

Eurostudent (2015) *Social and Economic Conditions of Student Life in Europe 2012–2015. Synopsis of Indicators*. Available online at: http://www.eurostudent.eu/download_files/documents/EVSynopsisofIndicators.pdf (Accessed 27/01/17).

Eurydice (2016) *Compulsory Education in Europe – 2016/17. Eurydice Facts and Figures*, Luxembourg, Publications Office of the European Union.

Facer, K. and Selwyn, N. (2013) Towards a sociology of education and technology, in: Brooks, R., McCormack, M. and Bhopal, K. (eds) *Contemporary Debates in the Sociology of Education*, Basingstoke, Palgrave.

Faggian, A., Comunian, R., Jewell, S. and Kelly, U. (2013) Bohemian graduates in the UK: Disciplines and location of determinants of creative careers, *Regional Studies*, 47, 2, 183–200.

Fairclough, N. (1989) *Language and Power*, London, Longman.

Falabella, A. (2016) Do national test scores and quality labels trigger school self-assessment and accountability? A critical analysis in the Chilean context, *British Journal of Sociology of Education*, 37, 5, 743–760.

Farinde, A., Allen, A. and Lewis, C. (2016) Retaining Black teachers: An examination of Black female teachers' intentions to remain in K-12 classrooms, *Equity and Excellence in Education*, 49, 1, 115–127.

Field, J. (2006) *Lifelong Learning and the New Educational Order* (second edition), London, Trentham Books.

Finch, J. and Kim, SK. (2012) *Kirŏgi* families in the US: Transnational migration and education, *Journal of Ethnic and Migration Studies*, 38, 3, 485–506.

Forestier, K. and Crossley, M. (2015) International education policy transfer – borrowing both ways: The Hong Kong and England experience, *Compare*, 45, 5, 664–685.

Formosa, M. (2014) Four decades of Universities of the Third Age: Past, present and future, *Ageing and Society*, 34, 42–66.

Foucault, M. (1977) *Discipline and Punish: The Birth of the Prison*, New York, Random House.

Foucault, M. (1980) *Power/Knowledge: Selected Interviews and Other Writings 1972–1977*, New York, Pantheon.

Francis, B. (2000) *Boys, Girls and Achievement: Addressing the Classroom Issues*, London, RoutledgeFalmer.

Francis, B. (2009) Teaching manfully? Exploring gendered subjectivities and power via analysis of men teachers' gender performance, *Gender and Education*, 20, 2, 109–122.

Francis, B., Archer, L., Moote, J., De Witt, J., MacLeod, E. and Yeomans, L. (2017) The construction of physics as a quintessentially masculine subject: Young people's perceptions of gender issues in access to physics, *Sex Roles*, 76, 156–174.

Francis, B., Robson, J. and Read, B. (2001) An analysis of undergraduate writing styles in the context of gender and achievement, *Studies in Higher Education*, 26, 3, 313–326.

Francis, B., Skelton, C., Carrington, B., Hutchings, M., Read, B. and Hall, I. (2008) A perfect match? Pupils' and teachers' views of the impact of matching educators and learners by gender, *Research Papers in Education*, 23, 1, 21–36.

Freire, P. (2017) *Pedagogy of the Oppressed*, London, Penguin.

Fuller, A. and Unwin, L. (2003) Learning as apprentices in the contemporary UK workplace: Creating and managing expansive and restrictive participation, *Journal of Education and Work*, 16, 4, 407–426.

Furlong, A. and Cartmel, A. (2007) *Young People and Social Change: Individualization and Risk in Late Modernity* (second edition), Buckingham, Open University Press.

Gagen, E. (2015) Governing emotions: Citizenship, neuroscience and the education of youth, *Transactions of the Institute of British Geographers*, 40, 140–152.

Gaither, M. (2009) Homeschooling in the USA: Past, present and future, *Theory and Research in Education*, 7, 3, 331–346.

Gambles, R. (2010) Supernanny, parenting and a pedagogical state, *Citizenship Studies*, 14, 6, 697–709.

Gamsu, S. and Donnelly, M. (2017) *Diverse Places of Learning? Home Neighbourhood Ethnic Diversity and the Ethnic Composition of Universities*, University of Bath, Institute for Policy Research.

Gardner-McTaggart, A. (2016) International elite, or global citizens? Equity, distinction and power: The International Baccalaureate and the rise of the South, *Globalisation, Societies and Education*, 14, 1, 1–29.

Gaztambide-Fernandez, R. and Mandhi, J. (2016) 'Private schools in the public system': School choice and the production of elite status in the USA and Canada, in: Maxwell, C. and Aggleton, P. (eds) *Elite Education: International Perspectives*, London, Routledge.

Gebel, M. and Baranowska-Rataj, A. (2012) New inequalities through privatisation and marketization? An analysis of labour market entry of higher education graduates in Poland and Ukraine, *European Sociological Review*, 28, 6, 729–741.

Geddie, K. (2012) Constructing transnational higher education spaces: International branch campus developments in the United Arab Emirates, in: Brooks, R., Fuller, A. and Waters, J. (eds) *Changing Spaces of Education: New Perspectives on the Nature of Learning*, London, Routledge.

Gewirtz, S. (2001) Cloning the Blairs: New Labour's programme for the re-socialization of working-class parents, *Journal of Education Policy*, 16, 4, 365–378.

Gewirtz, S., Ball, S. and Bowe, R. (1995) *Markets, Choice and Equity in Education*, Maidenhead, Open University Press.

Gewirtz, S. and Cribb, A. (2009) *Understanding Education: A Sociological Perspective*, Cambridge, Polity Press.

Gewirtz, S., Mahony, P., Hextall, I. and Cribb, A. (2009) Policy, professionalism and practice: Understanding teachers' work, in: Gewirtz, S., Mahony, P., Hextall, I. and Cribb, A. (eds) *Changing Teacher Professionalism: International Trends, Challenges and Ways Forward*, London, Routledge.

Giersch, J. (2014) Aiming for giants: Charter school legislation and the power of teacher unions, *Education and Urban Society*, 46, 6, 653–671.

Gillborn, D. (2005) Education policy as an act of white supremacy: Whiteness, critical race theory and educational reform, *Journal of Education Policy*, 20, 4, 485–505.

Gillborn, D. (2015) The monsterisation of race equality: How hate became honourable, in: Alexander, C., Weekes-Bernard, D. and Arday, J. (eds) (2015) *Race, Education and Inequality in Contemporary Britain*, London, The Runnymede Trust.

Gillborn, D. and Youdell, D. (2000) *Rationing Education: Policy, Practice, Reform and Equity*, Buckingham, Open University Press.

Gillies, V. (2005) Raising the 'meritocracy': Parenting and the individualization of social class, *Sociology*, 39, 5, 835–853.

Godlewska, A., Rose, J., Schaefli, L., Freake, S. and Massey, J. (2016) First Nations, Métis and Inuit presence in the Newfoundland and Labrador curriculum, *Race Ethnicity and Education* (Advance online access).

Goldstein, H. (1986) Gender bias and test norms in educational selection, *Research Intelligence* (British Educational Research Association), 23, 2–4.

González-Arnal, S. and Kilkey, M. (2009) Contextualizing rationality: Mature student carers and higher education in England, *Feminist Economics*, 15, 1, 85–111.

Gorur, R. (2016) The performative politics of NAPLAN and MySchool, in: Lingard, B., Thompson, G. and Sellar, S. (eds) *National Testing in Schools: An Australian Assessment*, New York, Routledge.

Gottfried, M. and Straubhaar, R. (2015) The perceived role of the Teach for America program on teachers' long-term career aspirations, *Educational Studies*, 41, 5, 481–498.

Gourlay, L., Lanclos, D. and Oliver, M. (2015) Sociomaterial texts, spaces and devices: Questioning 'digital dualism' in library and study practices, *Higher Education Quarterly*, 69, 3, 263–278.

Grace, G. (2012) Faith schools: Democracy, human rights and social cohesion, *Policy Futures in Education*, 10, 5, 500–505.

Grayson, J.P. (2004) Social dynamics, university experiences and graduates' job outcomes, *British Journal of Sociology of Education*, 25, 5, 609–628.

Green, A. (2006) Education, globalization and the nation-state, in: Lauder, H., Brown, P., Dillabough, J. and Halsey, A. (eds) *Education, Globalization and Social Change*, Oxford, Oxford University Press, pp. 192–197.

Green, A. (2013) *Education and State Formation: Europe, East Asia and the USA* (second edition), Basingstoke, Macmillan.

Green, C. and Navarro Paniagua, M. (2012) Does raising the school leaving age reduce teacher effort? Evidence from a policy experiment, *Economic Inquiry*, 50, 4, 1018–1030.

Green, F. and Zhu, Y. (2010) Overqualification, job dissatisfaction, and increasing dispersion in the returns to graduate education, *Oxford Economic Papers*, 62, 740–763.

Green, N. (2006) Everyday life in distance education: One family's home schooling experience, *Distance Education*, 27, 1, 27–44.

Grek, S. (2009) Governing by numbers: The PISA 'effect' in Europe, *Journal of Education Policy*, 24, 1, 23–37.

Griffiths, M. (1995) Making a difference: Feminism, post-modernism, and the methodology of educational research, *British Educational Research Journal*, 21, 2, 219–235.

Gulson, K. and Baker, B. (2018) New biological rationalities in education, *Discourse; Studies in the Cultural Politics of Education*, 39, 2, 159–168.

Guo, S. (2014) Immigrants as active citizens: Exploring the volunteering experience of Chinese immigrants in Vancouver, *Globalisation, Societies and Education*, 1, 1, 51–70.

Hall, S. (1992) New ethnicities, in: Donald, J. and Rayyansi, A. (eds) *'Race', Culture and Difference*, London, Sage.

Halsey, A.H., Heath, A. and Ridge, J. (1980) *Origins and Destinations*, Oxford, Clarendon Press.

Hammersley, M. (1996) Post-mortem or post-modern? Some reflections on British sociology of education, *British Journal of Educational Studies*, 44, 394–406.

Hammond, C. and Keating, A. (2017) Global citizens or global workers? Comparing university programmes for global citizenship education in Japan and the UK, *Compare* (Advance online access).

Hanson Thiem, C. (2007) The spatial politics of educational privatisation: Re-reading the US homeschooling movement, in: Gulson, K. and Symes, C. (eds) *Spatial Theories of Education: Policy and Geography Matters*, New York and London, Routledge.

Hardy, I. (2014) A logic of appropriation: Enacting national testing (NAPLAN) in Australia, *Journal of Education Policy*, 29, 1, 1–18.

Hardy, I. (2015) Education as a 'risky business': Theorising student and teacher learning in complex times, *British Journal of Sociology of Education*, 36, 3, 375–394.

Hargreaves, A. (2006) Four ages of professionalism and professional learning, in: Lauder, H., Brown, P., Dillabough, J. and Halsey, A. (eds) *Education, Globalization and Social Change*, Oxford, Oxford University Press.

Harris, A. (2004) *Future Girl: Young Women in the 21st Century*, New York, Routledge.

Harris, A. (2013) *Young People and Everyday Multiculturalism*, New York, Routledge.

Harrison, N. (2015) Practice, problems and power in 'internationalisation at home': Critical reflections on recent research evidence, *Teaching in Higher Education*, 20, 4, 412–430.

Hartley, D. (2007) Bringing knowledge back in: From social constructivism to social realism in the sociology of education (Review Essay), *British Journal of Sociology of Education*, 28, 6, 817–822.

Hartmann, S. (2013) Education 'home delivery' in Egypt: Private tutoring and social stratification, in: Bray, M., Mazawi, A. and Sultana, R. (eds) *Private Tutoring Across the Mediterranean*, Rotterdam, Sense.

Hauge, M. (2013) Research with young people on female circumcision: Negotiating cultural sensitivity, law and transparency, in: Te Riele, K. and Brooks, R. (eds) *Negotiating Ethical Challenges in Youth Research*, New York, Routledge, pp. 137–148.

Hayden, M. (2011) Transnational spaces of education: The growth of the international schools sector, *Globalisation, Societies and Education*, 9, 2, 211–224.

Hayden, M. (2012) Third culture kids: The global nomads of transnational spaces of learning, in: Brooks, R., Fuller, A. and Waters, J. (eds) *Changing Spaces of Education: New Perspectives on the Nature of Learning*, London, Routledge.

Hazelkorn, E. (2009) Rankings and the battle for world class excellence: Institutional strategies and policy choice, *Higher Education Management and Policy*, 21, 1, 1–22.

Hazelkorn, E. (2015) *Rankings and the Reshaping of Higher Education* (second edition), Basingstoke, Palgrave.

Heller, D. and Callender, C. (2013) *Student Financing of Higher Education: A Comparative Perspective*, New York, Routledge.

Henry, F., Dua, E., Kobayashi, A., James, C., Li, P., Ramos, H. and Smith, M. (2016) Race, racialization and indigeneity in Canadian universities, *Race Ethnicity and Education* (Advance online access).

Hirsch, E.D. (1988) *Cultural Literacy: What Every American Needs To Know*, New York, Vintage Books.

Hirsch, E., Koppich, J. and Knapp, M. (2001) *Revisiting What States Are Doing to Improve the Quality of Teaching: An Update on Patterns and Trends*, Seattle, WA, Centre for the Study of Teaching and Policy, University of Washington.

Ho, C. (2011) Respecting the presence of others: School micropublics and everyday multiculturalism, *Journal of Intercultural Studies*, 32, 6, 603–619.

Ho, C., Vincent, E. and Butler, R. (2015) Everyday and cosmo-multiculturalisms: Doing diversity in gentrifying school communities, *Journal of Intercultural Studies*, 36, 6, 658–675.

Ho, E. and Bedford, R. (2008) Asian transnational families in New Zealand: Dynamics and challenges, *International Migration*, 46, 4, 41–62.

Hogan, A., Sellar, S. and Lingard, B. (2015) Network restructuring of global edu-business: The case of Pearson's *Efficacy Framework*, in: Au, W. and Ferrare, J. (eds) *Mapping Corporate Education Reform: Power and Policy Networks in the Neoliberal State*, New York, Routledge.

Holford, J. (2014) The lost honour of the social dimension, Bologna, exports and the idea of the university, *International Journal of Lifelong Education*, 33, 1, 7–25.

Hollingworth, S. and Mansaray, A. (2012) Conviviality under the cosmopolitan canopy? Social mixing and friendships in an urban secondary school, *Sociological Research Online*, 17, 3, 2 http://www.socresonline.org.uk/17/3/2.html(Accessed 15/9/17)

Hope, A. (2016) Biopower and school surveillance technologies 2.0, *British Journal of Sociology of Education*, 37, 7, 885–904.

Howell, A. (2016) Exploring children's lived experiences of NAPLAN, in: Lingard, B., Thompson, G. and Sellar, S. (eds) *National Testing in Schools: An Australian Assessment*, New York, Routledge.

Huang, S. and Yeoh, B. (2011) Navigating the terrains of transnational education: Children of Chinese 'study mothers' in Singapore, *Geoforum*, 42, 394–403.

Huisman, J. (2015) Higher Education Experts and Commissioned Research: Between Stability, Fragility and Ambiguity? In: Souto-Otero, M. (ed) *Evaluating European Education Policy-Making*, Basingstoke, Palgrave.

Hursh, D. (2016) *The End of Public Schools: The Corporate Reform Agenda to Privatize Education*, New York, Routledge.

Hurst, A. (2007) Telling tales of oppression and dysfunction: Narratives of class identity reformation, *Qualitative Sociology Review*, 3, 2, 82–104.

Hurst, A. and Nenga, S. (eds) (2016) *Working in Class: Recognising How Social Class Shapes Our Academic Work*, Lanham, Rowman and Littlefield.

Hussain, M. (2015) *Why Is My Curriculum White?* Available online at: https://www.nus.org.uk/en/news/why-is-my-curriculum-white/ (Accessed 07/09/17).

Ingram, N. (2009) Working class boys, educational success and the misrecognition of working class culture, *British Journal of Sociology of Education*, 30, 4, 421–434.

Iphofen, R. (2011) *Ethical Decision Making in Social Research: A Practical Guide*, Basingstoke, Palgrave.

Iqbal, H., Neal, S. and Vincent, C. (2016) Children's friendships in super-diverse localities: Encounters with social and ethnic difference, *Childhood* (advance online publication).

Ishumi, A. (2013) The teaching profession and teacher education: Trends and challenges in the 21st century, *Africa Education Review*, 10, 1, S89–S116.

Isopahkala-Bouret, U. (2015) Graduation at age 50+: Contest efforts to construct 'third age' identities and negotiate cultural stereotypes, *Journal of Aging Studies*, 35, 1–9.

Iyer, R. (2016) Exclusive consumers: The discourse of privilege in elite Indian school websites, in: Koh, A. and Kenway, J. (eds) *Elite Schools: Multiple Geographies of Privilege*, New York, Routledge.

Jackson, B. and Marsden, D. (1966) *Education and the Working Class*, Harmondsworth, Pelican Books.

Jackson, C. (2002) 'Laddishness' as a self-worth protection strategy, *Gender and Education*, 14, 1, 339–360.

Jackson, R. (2003) Should the state fund faith-based schools? A review of the arguments, *British Journal of Religious Education*, 25, 2, 89–102.

Jakobi, A.P. and Rusconi, A. (2009) Lifelong learning in the Bologna process: European development in higher education, *Compare*, 39, 1, 51–65.

Jarvis, P. (2014) From adult education to lifelong learning and beyond, *Comparative Education*, 50, 1, 45–57.

Jerrim, J. (2017) *Extra Time: Private Tuition and Out-of-School Study, New International Evidence*, London, The Sutton Trust. Available online at: https://www.suttontrust.com/wp-content/uploads/2017/09/Extra-time-report_FINAL.pdf (Accessed 08/09/17).

Jones, K. (2015) Knowledge politics, *British Journal of Sociology of Education*, 36, 3, 495–504.

Jones, G. and Wallace, C. (1992) *Youth, Family and Citizenship*, Buckingham, Open University Press.

Jöns, H. (2011) Transnational academic mobility and gender, *Globalisation, Societies and Education*, 9, 2, 183–209.

Jöns, H. and Hoyler, M. (2013) Global geographies of higher education: The perspective of world university rankings, *Geoforum*, 46, 45–59.

Karabel, J. (2006) *The Chosen: The Hidden History of Admission and Exclusion at Harvard, Yale and Princeton*, New York, Mariner Books.

Kassotakis, M. and Verdis, M. (2013) Shadow education in Greece: Characteristics, consequences and eradication efforts, in: Bray, M., Mazawi, A. and Sultana, R. (eds) *Private Tutoring Across the Mediterranean*, Rotterdam, Sense.

Keane, E. (2011) Distancing to self-protect: The perpetuation of inequality in higher education through socio-relational dis/engagement, *British Journal of Sociology of Education*, 32, 3, 449–466.

Keeling, R. (2006) The Bologna Process and the Lisbon Research Agenda: The European Commission's expanding role in higher education discourses, *European Journal of Education*, 41, 2, 203–223.

Kelly, A. (2009) Juxtaposing some contradictory findings from research on school choice, *Magis: Revista Internacional de Iinvestigación en Educación*, 2, 3, 261–274.

Kenway, J. (1997) Having a post-modern turn or post-modern angst: A disorder experienced by an author who is not yet dead or even close to it, in: Halsey, A.H., Lauder, H., Brown, P. and Stuart Wells, A. (eds) *Education: Culture, Economy, Society*, Oxford, Oxford University Press.

Kenway, J. and Fahey, J. (2007) Policy incitements to mobility: Some speculations and provocations. In: Epstein D, Boden R, Deem R, Rizvi F, and Wright S. (eds) *Geographies of Knowledge, Geometries of Power: Framing the Future of Higher Education World Yearbook of Education 2008*, New York: Routledge.

Khan, S. (2011) *Privilege: The Making of an Adolescent Elite at St Paul's School*, Princeton, NJ, Princeton University Press.

Khattab, N. (2002) Social capital, students' perceptions and educational aspirations among Palestinian students in Israel, *Research in Education*, 68, 77–88.

Kim, J. and Youngs, P. (2016) Promoting educational improvement or resistance? A comparative study of teachers' perceptions of teacher evaluation policy in Korea and the USA, *Compare*, 46, 5, 723–744.

Kim, S., Brown, K.-E. and Fong, V. (2017) How flexible gender identities give young women advantages in China's new economy, *Gender and Education* (Advance online access).

Kim, T. (2009) Shifting patterns of transnational academic mobility: A comparative and historical approach, *Comparative Education*, 45, 3, 387–403.

Kim, T. (2010) Transnational academic mobility, knowledge and identity capital, *Discourse: Studies in the Cultural Politics of Education*, 31, 5, 577–591.

Kim, Y. (2011) *Transnational Migration, Media and Identity of Asian Women*, London, Routledge.

King, R. (2003) International student migration in Europe and the institutionalisation of identity as 'Young Europeans', in: Doomernik, J. and Knippenberg, H. (eds) *Migration and Immigrants: Between Policy and Reality*, Amsterdam, Askant, pp. 155–179.

Kobakhidze, M. (2014) Corruption risks of private tutoring: Case of Georgia, *Asia Pacific Journal of Education*, 34, 4, 455–475.

Kobayashi, A. and Preston, V. (2007) Transnationalism through the life course: Hong Kong immigrants in Canada, *Asia Pacific Viewpoint*, 48, 2, 151–167.

Korbits, K. (2015) The representation of the cold war in three Estonian textbooks, *Compare*, 45, 5, 772–791.

Kraftl, P. (2013) Towards geographies of alternative education: A case study of UK home schooling families, *Transactions of the Institute of British Geographers*, 38, 436–450.

Kretchmar, K., Sondel, B. and Ferrare, J. (2014) Mapping the terrain: Teach for America, charter school reform and corporate sponsorship, *Journal of Education Policy*, 29, 6, 742–759.

Krücken, G. (2014) Higher education reforms and unintended consequences: A research agenda, *Studies in Higher Education*, 39, 8, 1439–1450.

Kulz, C. (2014) 'Structure liberates?': Mixing for mobility and the cultural transformation of 'urban children' in a London academy, *Ethnic and Racial Studies*, 37, 4, 685–701.

Kulz, C. (2017) *Factories for Learning*, Manchester, Manchester University Press.

Kwan, P. and Wong, Y.-L. (2016) Parental involvement in schools and class inequality in education: Some recent findings from Hong Kong, *International Journal of Pedagogies and Learning*, 11, 2, 91–102.

Ladson-Billings, G. and Tate, W. (1995) Toward a critical race theory of education, *Teachers College Record*, 97, 1, 47–68.

Lander, V. (2015) 'Racism, it's part of my everyday life': Black and minority ethnic pupils' experiences in a predominantly white school, in: Alexander, C., Weekes-Bernard, D. and Arday, J. (eds) (2015) *Race, Education and Inequality in Contemporary Britain*, London, The Runnymede Trust.

Lareau, A. (1989) *Home Advantage*, Langham, MD, Rowman and Littlefield.

Lareau, A. (2003) *Unequal Childhoods: Class, Race, and Family Life*, Berkeley, CA: University of California Press.

Larsen, M. (2010) Troubling the discourse of teacher centrality: A comparative perspective, *Journal of Education Policy*, 25, 2, 207–231.

Lauder, H., Brown, P., Dillabough, J. and Halsey, A. (eds) (2006) *Education, Globalization and Social Change*, Oxford, Oxford University Press.

Lauder, H., Brown, P. and Halsey, A.H. (2009) Sociology of education: A critical history and prospects for the future, *Oxford Review of Education*, 35, 5, 569–585.

Lawn, M. and Grek, S. (2012) *Europeanising Education*, Oxford, Symposium Books.

Leathwood, C. and Francis, B. (eds) (2006) *Gender and Lifelong Learning: Critical Feminist Engagements*, London, Routledge.

Leathwood, C. and O'Connell (2003) 'It's a struggle': The construction of the 'new student' in higher education, *Journal of Education Policy*, 18, 6, 597–615.

Leathwood, C. and Read, B. (2009) *Gender and the Changing Face of Higher Education. A Feminized Future?*, Maidenhead, Open University Press.

Lee, A. (1980) 'Together we learn to read and write': Sexism and literacy, in: Spender, D. and Sarah, E. (eds) *Learning to Lose: Sexism and Education*, London, The Women's Press.

Lee, J. (2014) The mechanisms of charter school policy adoption: The case of American states, *International Journal of Public Administration*, 37, 20–34.

Lee, S. (2013) Gender, power and emotion: Towards holistic understanding of mature women students in South Korea, *Gender and Education*, 25, 2, 170–188.

Lee, Y. (2015) Ethnic education and labour market position in Britain (1972–2013), in: Alexander, C., Weekes-Bernard, D. and Arday, J. (eds) (2015) *Race, Education and Inequality in Contemporary Britain*, London, The Runnymede Trust.

Lehmann, W. (2014) Habitus transformation and hidden injuries: Successful working-class university students, *Sociology of Education*, 87, 1, 1–15.

Leonard, P., Halford, S. and Bruce, K. (2016) 'The new degree?' Constructing internships in the third sector, *Sociology*, 50, 2, 383–399.

Leonardo, Z. (2002) The souls of white folk: Critical pedagogy, whiteness studies and globalization discourse, *Race, Ethnicity and Education*, 5, 1, 29–50.

Leonardo, Z. and Grubb, W.N. (2014) *Education and Racism*, New York, Routledge.

Leuze, K. (2011) How structure signals status: Institutional stratification and the transition from higher education to work in Germany and Britain, *Journal of Education and Work*, 24, 5, 449–475.

Lewis, N. (2011) Political projects and micro-practices of globalising education: Building an international education industry in New Zealand, *Globalisation, Societies and Education*, 9, 2, 225–246.

Lewis, S. and Hogan, S. (2016) Reform first and ask questions later? The implications of (fast) schooling policy and 'silver bullet' solutions, *Critical Studies in Education* (Advance online access).

Li, H. (2013) Rural students' experiences in a Chinese elite university: Capital, habitus and practices, *British Journal of Sociology of Education*, 34, 5–6, 829–847.

Li, I. and Miller, P. (2013) The absorption of recent graduates into the Australian labour market, *Australian Economic Review*, 46, 1, 14–30.

Lingard, B. (2009) Pedagogising teacher professional identities, in: Gewirtz, S., Mahony, P., Hextall, I. and Cribb, A. (eds) *Changing Teacher Professionalism: International Trends, Challenges and Ways Forward*, London, Routledge.

Lingard, B., Martino, W. and Mills, M. (2013) Managing oppositional masculinity politics: The gendering of a government-commissioned research project, *International Journal of Qualitative Studies in Education*, 26, 4, 434–454.

Lingard, B. and Rawolle, S. (2011) New scalar politics: Implications for education policy, *Comparative Education*, 47, 4, 489–502.

Lingard, B. and Sellar, S. (2014) 'Representing your country': Scotland, PISA and new spatialities of educational governance, *Scottish Educational Review*, 46, 1, 5–18.

Lingard, B., Sellar, S. and Savage, G. (2014) Re-articulating social justice as equity in schooling policy: The effects of testing and data infrastructures, *British Journal of Sociology of Education*, 35, 5, 710–730.

Lingard, B., Thompson, G. and Sellar, S. (2016) National testing from an Australian perspective, in: Lingard, B., Thompson, G. and Sellar, S. (eds) *National Testing in Schools: An Australian Assessment*, New York, Routledge.

Lipman, P. (2004) *High Stakes Education*, London, Routledge.

Lipman, P. (2009) Paradoxes of teaching in neo-liberal times: Education 'reform' in Chicago, in: Gewirtz, S., Mahony, P., Hextall, I. and Cribb, A. (eds) *Changing Teacher Professionalism: International Trends, Challenges and Ways Forward*, London, Routledge.

Lipman, P. (2011) *The New Political Economy of Urban Education: Neoliberalism, Race and the Right to the City*, New York, Routledge.

Lister, R. with Smith, N., Middleton, S. and Cox, L. (2005), Young people and citizenship, in: Barry, M. (ed) *Youth Policy and Social Inclusion*, Abingdon, Routledge.

Liu, Y. (2013) Meritocracy and the Gaokao: A survey study of higher education selection and socio-economic participation in East China, *British Journal of Sociology of Education*, 34, 5–6, 868–887.

Longhurst, R., Hodgetts, D. and Stolte, O. (2012) Placing guilt and shame: Lone mothers' experiences of higher education in Aotearoa New Zealand, *Social and Cultural Geography*, 13, 3, 295–311.

Looney, J. (2011) Developing high-quality teachers: Teacher evaluation for improvement, *European Journal of Education*, 46, 4, 440–455.

Lubienski, C. (2000) Whither the common good? A critique of home schooling, *Peabody Journal of Education*, 75, 1–2, 207–232.

Luke, A. (2010) Documenting reproduction and inequality: Revisiting Jean Anyon's 'Social class and school knowledge', *Curriculum Inquiry*, 40, 1, 167–182.

Lupton, D. (2016) *The Quantified Self*, Cambridge, Polity Press.

Lupton, D. and Williamson, B. (2017) The datafied child: The dataveillance of children and implications for their rights, *New Media and Society*, 19, 5, 780–794.

Lupton, R. (2005) Social justice and school improvement: Improving the quality of schooling in the poorest neighbourhoods, *British Educational Research Journal*, 31, 5, 589–604.

Lynch, K. (2008) Gender roles and the American academe: A case study of graduate student mothers, *Gender and Education*, 20, 6, 585–605.

Mac an Ghaill, M. (1994) *The Making of Men*, Buckingham, Open University Press.

McBurnie, G. and Ziguras, C. (2007) *Transnational Education: Issues and Trends in Offshore Higher Education*, London, Routledge.

McCormack, M. and Anderson, E. (2010) 'It's just not acceptable anymore': The erosion of homophobia and the softening of masculinity at an English sixth form, *Sociology*, 44, 5, 843–859.

McLean, M., Abbas, A. and Ashwin, P. (2015) 'Not everybody walks around and thinks "That's an example of othering or stigmatisation"': Identity, pedagogic rights and the acquisition of undergraduate sociology-based social science knowledge, *Theory and Research in Education*, 13, 2, 180–197.

Macmillan, L., Tyler, C. and Vignoles, A. (2015) Who gets the top jobs? The role of family background and networks in recent graduates' access to high-status professions, *Journal of Social Policy*, 44, 3, 487–515.

MacNell, L., Driscoll, A. and Hunt, A. (2015) What's in a name? Exploring gender bias in student ratings of teaching, *Innovation in Higher Education*, 40, 291–303.

Madge, C., Raghuram, P., and Noxolo, P. (2009) Engaged pedagogy and responsibility: A postcolonial analysis of international students, *Geoforum*, 40, 34–45.

Maguire, M. (2014) Reforming teacher education in England: 'An economy of discourses of truth', *Journal of Education Policy*, 29, 6, 774–784.

Mahony, P. and Zmroczek, C. (eds) (1997) *Class Matters: Working Class Women's Perspectives on Social Class*, Abingdon, Taylor and Francis.

Mannheim, K. (1952) *Essays on the Sociology of Knowledge*, London, Routledge and Kegan Paul.

Marandet, E. and Wainwright, E. (2009) Discourses of integration and exclusion: Equal opportunities for university students with dependent children?, *Space and Polity*, 13, 2, 109–125.

Marandet, E. and Wainwright, E. (2010) Invisible experiences: Understanding the choices and needs of university students with dependent children, *British Educational Research Journal*, 36, 5, 787–805.

Marginson, S. (2002) Nation-building universities in a global environment: The case of Australia, *Higher Education*, 43, 3, 409–428.

Marginson, S. (2007) Have global academic flows created a global labour market?, in: Epstein, D., Boden, R., Deem, R., Rizvi, F. and Wright, S. (eds) *Geographies of Knowledge, Geometries of Power: Higher Education in the 21st Century. (World Year Book of Education 2008)*, New York, Routledge, pp. 305–318.

Marginson, S. (2008) Global field and global imagining: Bourdieu and worldwide higher education, *British Journal of Sociology of Education*, 29, 3, 303–315.

Marginson, S. and van der Wende, M. (2007) To rank or to be ranked : The impact of global rankings in higher education, *Journal of Studies in International Education*, 11, 3–4, 306–329.

Martin, N. (2009) Social capital, academic achievement, and postgraduate plans at an elite, private university, *Sociological Perspectives*, 52, 2, 185–210.

Martino, W. and Rezai-Rashti, G. (2010) Male teacher shortage: Black teachers' perspectives, *Gender and Education*, 22, 3, 247–262.

Mason, G. (2002) High skills utilisation under mass higher education: Graduate employment in service industries in Britain, *Journal of Education and Work*, 15, 4, 427–456.

Matsuda, M., Lawrence, C., Delgado, R. and Crenshaw, K. (eds) (1993) *Words that Wound: Critical Race Theory, Assaultive Speech and the First Amendment*, Boulder, CO, Westview Press.

Matthews, J. and Sidhu, R. (2005) Desperately seeking the global subject: International education, citizenship and cosmopolitanism, *Globalisation, Societies and Education*, 3, 1, 49–66.

Maxwell, C. and Aggleton, P. (2016) Schools, schooling and elite status in English education – changing configurations?, *L'Année sociologique*, 66, 147–170.

Maylor, U. (2009) 'They do not relate to Black people like us': Black teachers as role models for Black pupils, *Journal of Education Policy*, 24, 1, 1–21.

Maylor, U. (2014) *Teacher Training and the Education of Black Children: Bringing Colour into the Difference*, London, Routledge.

Mazema, A. (2016) African American homeschooling practices: Empirical evidence, *Theory and Research in Education*, 14, 1, 26–44.

Mazlish, B. and Morss, E. (2005) A global elite? in: Chandler, A. and Mazlish, B. (eds) *Leviathans: Multinational Corporations and the New Global History*, Cambridge, Cambridge University Press, pp. 167–186.

Meer, N. (2014) *Key Concepts in Race and Ethnicity*, London, Sage.

Mendick, H. (2005) Mathematical stories: Why do more boys than girls choose to study mathematics at AS level in England?, *British Journal of Sociology of Education*, 26, 2, 235–251.

Mendick, H. (2013) Choosing subjects: Sociological approaches to young women's subject choices, in: Brooks, R., McCormack, M. and Bhopal, K. (eds) *Contemporary Debates in the Sociology of Education*, Basingstoke, Palgrave.

Merrill, B. (1996) *Gender, Change and Identity, Mature Women Students in Universities*, Aldershot, Ashgate.

Meshulam, A. and Apple, M. (2014) Interrupting the interruption: Neoliberalism and the challenges of an antiracist school, *British Journal of Sociology of Education*, 35, 5, 650–669.

Miller, H., Pomson, A. and Wolf, H. (2016) Secondary school choice as a window on Jewish faith schools in contemporary British society, *Journal of School Choice*, 10, 4, 537–559.

Miller, T. (2011) Falling back into gender? Men's narratives and practices around first-time fatherhood, *Sociology*, 45, 6, 1094–1109.

Mills, C.W. (1959) *The Sociological Imagination*, Harmondsworth, Penguin.

Mills, M., Martino, W. and Lingard, B. (2004) Attracting, recruiting and retaining male teachers: Policy issues in the male teachers debate, *British Journal of Sociology of Education*, 25, 3, 355–369.

Mirza, H.S. and Meetoo, V. (2014) Gendered surveillance and the social construction of young Muslim women in schools, in: Bhopal, K. and Maylor, U. (eds) *Educational Inequalities: Difference and Diversity in Schools and Higher Education*, London, Routledge.

Mitchell, K. (2006) Neoliberal governmentality in the European Union: Education, training and technologies of citizenship, *Environment and Planning D*, 24, 389–407.

Mizrachi, N., Goodman, Y. and Feniger, Y. (2009) 'I don't want to see it': Decoupling ethnicity and class from social structure in Jewish Israeli high schools, *Ethnic and Racial Studies*, 32, 7, 1203–1225.

Modell, S. (2005) Students as consumers? An institutional field-level analysis of performance measurement practices, *Accounting, Auditing and Accountability Journal*, 18, 4, 537–563.

Mok, K.H. (2016) Transnationalizing and internationalizing higher education in China: Implications for regional cooperation and university governance in Asia, in: *Internationalizing Higher Education in Korea: Comparative Perspectives*, Stanford, CA, AsiaPacific Research centre, Stanford University.

Mok, K.H. and Jiang, J. (2016) *Massification of Higher Education: Challenges for Admissions and Graduate Employment in China*, Centre for Global Higher Education working paper series. Available online at: http://www.researchcghe.org/perch/resources/publications/wp5.pdf (Accessed 24/04/17).

Molesworth, M., Nixon, E. and Scullion, E. (2009) Having, being and higher education: The marketization of the university and the transformation of the student into consumer, *Teaching in Higher Education*, 14, 3, 277–287.

Moreau, M.-P. (2011) The societal construction of 'boys' underachievement' in educational policies: A cross-national comparison, *Journal of Education Policy*, 26, 2, 161–180.

Moreau, M.-P. (2014) Introduction: Theorising and mapping inequalities in the teaching profession, in: Moreau, M.-P. (ed) *Inequalities in the Teaching Profession: A Global Perspective*, Basingstoke, Palgrave.

Moreau, M.-P. (2015) Becoming a secondary school teacher in England and France: Contextualising career 'choice', *Compare*, 45, 3, 401–421.

Moreau, M.-P., Osgood, J. and Halsall, A. (2007) Making sense of the glass ceiling in schools: An exploration of women teachers' discourses, *Gender and Education*, 19, 2, 237–253.

Morgan, C., Tsatsaroni, A. and Lerman, S. (2002) Mathematics teachers' positions and practices in discourses of assessment, *British Journal of Sociology of Education*, 23, 3, 445–461.

Morley, L. (2011) Sex, grades and power in higher education in Ghana and Tanzania, *Cambridge Journal of Education*, 41, 1, 101–115.

Morris, D. (1984) Universities of the Third Age, *Adult Education*, 57, 2, 135–139.

Morrow, V. (2005) Ethical issues in collaborative research with children, in: Farrell A. (ed), *Ethical Research with Children*, Maidenhead, Open University Press, pp. 150–165.

Moutsios, S. (2009) International organisations and transnational education policy, *Compare*, 39, 4, 469–481.

Muddiman, E. (2017) *Disengaged Instrumentalism: How it Damages Students' Capacity to Engage with Social Issues, and Why Studying Sociology Could be the Answer ...*, Presentation to British Sociological Association Annual Conference, University of Manchester, 5 April 2017.

Mullen, A. (2009) Elite destinations: Pathways to attending an Ivy League university, *British Journal of Sociology of Education*, 30, 1, 15–27.

Musselin, C. (2004) Towards a European labour market? Some lessons drawn from empirical studies on academic mobility, *Higher Education*, 48, 55–78.

Musselin, C. (2014) Research issues and institutional prospects for higher education studies, *Studies in Higher Education*, 39, 8, 1369–1380.

Naidoo, R. (2010) Global learning in a neo-liberal age: Implications for development, in: Unterhalter, E. and Carpentier, V. (eds) *Global Inequalities and Higher Education* Basingstoke, Palgrave.

Naidoo, R., Shankar, A. and Veer, E. (2011) The consumerist turn in higher education: Policy aspirations and outcomes, *Journal of Marketing Management*, 27, 11–12, 1142–1162.

National Alliance for Public Charter Schools (2017) *Facts about Charters*. Available online at: http://www.publiccharters.org/get-the-facts/public-charter-schools/faqs/ (Accessed 14/03/17).

National Center for Education Statistics (2011) *The Nation's Report Card: Mathematics 2011 (NCES 2012-458)*, Washington, DC, Institute of Education Sciences, U.S. Department of Education.

Nelson, F. (2017) Michael Gove was (accidentally) right about experts: Pronouncements from wonks are no substitute for proper political argument, *The Spectator*, 14 January. Available online at: https://www.spectator.co.uk/2017/01/michael-gove-was-accidentally-right-about-experts/ (Accessed 20/06/16).

Neuman, A. and Aviram, A. (2003) Homeschooling as a fundamental change in lifestyle, *Evaluation and Research in Education*, 17, 2–3, 132–143.

Nielsen, G. (2011) Peopling policy: On conflicting subjectivities of fee-paying students, in: Shore, C., Wright, S. and Però, D. (eds) *Policy Worlds: Anthropology and the Analysis of Contemporary Power*, New York, Berghahn Books.

Nixon, J. (2011) *Higher Education and the Public Good: Imagining the University*, London, Continuum.

Noble, G. (2009) Everyday cosmopolitanism and the labour of intercultural community, in: Wise, A. and Velayutham, S. (eds) *Everyday Multiculturalism*, London, Palgrave, pp. 46–65.

Nussbaum, M. (2010) *Not for Profit: Why Democracy Needs the Humanities*, Princeton, NJ, Princeton University Press.

OECD (2013) *PISA 2012 Results: Excellence Through Equity: Giving Every Student the Chance to Succeed (Volume II)*, Paris, OECD Publishing.

OECD (2015) *Education at a Glance*, Paris, OECD Publications.

OECD (2016) *Education at a Glance*, Paris, OECD Publications.

OECD (2017) *Education at a Glance*, Paris, OECD Publications.

Olds, K. (2007) Global assemblage: Singapore, foreign universities and the creation of a 'global education hub', *World Development*, 35, 6, 959–975.

Oliver, M. (2013) Learning technology: Theorising the tools we study, *British Journal of Educational Technology*, 44, 1, 31–43.

Oliver, M. (2016) *Self-Control? Students' Quantified Self in the Digital University*, Presentation to the SRHE annual conference, Newport, Wales, December 2016.

Olmedo, A. and Santa Cruz, L.E. (2012) 'Being middle class is not enough': Social class, education and school choice in Spain, in: Weis, L. and Dolby, N. (eds) *Social Class and Education: Global Perspectives*, New York, Routledge.

Olssen, M. (2006) Neoliberalism, globalization, democracy: Challenges for education, in: Lauder, H., Brown, P., Dillabough, J. and Halsey, A. (eds) *Education, Globalization and Social Change*, Oxford, Oxford University Press, pp. 261–287.

Ong, A. (1999) *Flexible Citizenship: The Cultural Logics of Transnationality*, Durham, Duke University Press.

Ong-Dean, C., Hofstetter, C. and Strick, B. (2011) Challenges and dilemmas in implementing random assignment in educational research, *American Journal of Education*, 32, 1, 29–49.

Osborne, M., Marks, A. and Turner, E. (2004) Becoming a mature student: How adult applicants weight the advantages and disadvantages of higher education, *Higher Education*, 48, 291–315.

Ozga, J. (2016) Trust in numbers? Digital education governance and the inspection process, *European Educational Research Journal*, 15, 1, 69–81.

Ozga, J. and Lingard, B. (2007) Globalisation, education policy and politics, in: Lingard, B. and Ozga, J. (eds) *The RoutledgeFalmer Reader in Education Policy and Politics*, London, Routledge, pp. 65–82.

Pais, A. and Costa, M. (2017) An ideology critique of global citizenship education, *Critical Studies in Education* https://www.tandfonline.com/doi/abs/10.1080/17508487.2017.1318772

Paittoeva, N. (2016) The imperative to protect data and the rise of surveillance cameras in administering national testing in Russia, *European Educational Research Journal*, 15, 1, 82–98.

Pahlke, E., Hyde, J.S. and Allison, C.M. (2014) The effects of single-sex compared with coeducational schooling on students' performance and attitudes: A meta-analysis, *Psychological Bulletin*, 140, 4, 1042–1072.

Page, D. (2017) Conceptualising the surveillance of teachers, *British Journal of Sociology of Education* 38, 7, 991–1006.

Papatsiba, V. (2005) Political and individual rationales of student mobility: A case-study of ERASMUS and a French regional scheme for studies abroad, *European Journal of Education*, 40, 2, 173–188.

Park, H., Behrman, J. and Choi, J. (2013) Causal effects of single-sex schools on college entrance exams and college attendance: Random assignment in Seoul high schools, *Demography*, 50, 2, 447–469.

Parmenter, L. (1999) Constructing national identity in a changing world: Perspectives in Japanese education, *British Journal of Sociology of Education*, 20, 4, 453–463.

Parsons, T. (1961) The school class as a social system, in: Halsey, A.H., Floud, J. and Anderson, C. A. (eds) *Education, Economy and Society: A Reader in the Sociology of Education*, New York, Free Press.

Pathak, P. (2013) Ethopolitics and the financial citizen, *The Sociological Review*, 62, 90–116.

Patrikios, S. and Curtice, J. (2014) Attitudes towards school choice and faith schools in the UK: A question of individual preference or collective interest? *Journal of Social Policy*, 43, 3, 517–534.

Pechar, H. and Wroblewski, A. (2012) Austria: Non-traditional students in the 2000s, in: Slowey, M. and Schuetze, H. (eds) *Global Perspectives on Higher Education and Lifelong Learners*, London, Routledge.

Peck, J. and Theodore, N. (2015) *Fast Policy: Experimental Statecraft at the Thresholds of Neoliberalism*, Minneapolis, MN, University of Minnesota Press.

Peck, J. and Tickell, A. (2006) Conceptualising neoliberalism, thinking Thatcherism, in: Leitner, H., Peck, J. and Sheppard, E. (eds) *Contesting Neoliberalism: Urban Frontiers*, New York, Guilford Press, pp. 26–50.

Pereira, M. (2015) Higher education cutbacks and the reshaping of epistemic hierarchies: An ethnography of the case of feminist scholarship, *Sociology*, 49, 2, 287–304.

Pettigrew, A. (2012) Confronting the limits of antiracist and multicultural education: White students' reflections on identity and difference in a multi-ethnic secondary school, *Sociological Research Online*, 17, 3.

Phipps, A. and Young, I. (2015) Neoliberalisations and 'lad cultures' in higher education, *Sociology*, 49, 2, 305–322.

Picower, B. (2009) The unexamined whiteness of teaching: How White teachers maintain and enact dominant racial ideologies, *Race, Ethnicity and Education*, 12, 2, 197–215.

Pilcher, J. (1995) *Age and Generation in Modern Britain*, Oxford, Oxford University Press.

Pimlott-Wilson, H. and Coates, J. (2017) *Are We Really Learning? Forest School Programmes from the Perspective of Children*, Presentation to the Royal Geographical Society annual conference 2017, 30 August 2017.

Pimpa, N. (2005) A family affair: The effect of family on Thai students' choices of international education, *Higher Education*, 49, 431–448.

Polesel, J., Rice, S. and Dulfer, N. (2014) The impact of high-stakes testing on curriculum and pedagogy: A teacher perspective from Australia, *Journal of Education Policy*, 29, 5, 640–657.

Posey-Maddox, L. (2017) Schooling in suburbia: The intersections of race, class, gender and place in black fathers' engagement and family-school relationships, *Gender and Education* (Advance online access).

Powell, B., Steelman, L. and Carini, R. (2006) Advancing age, advantaged youth: Parental age and the transmission of resources to children, *Social Forces*, 84, 3, 1359–1390.

Priestley, M. and Sinnema, C. (2014) Downgraded curriculum? An analysis of knowledge in new curricula in Scotland and New Zealand, *The Curriculum Journal*, 25, 1, 50–75.

Prosser (2016) The economy of eliteness: Consuming educational advantage, in: Koh, A. and Kenway, J. (eds) *Elite Schools: Multiple Geographies of Privilege*, New York, Routledge.

Purcell, K. and Elias, P. (2004) *Seven Years On: Graduate Careers in a Changing Labour Market*, London, The Higher Education Careers Services Unit.

Pykett, J. (2013) Neurocapitalism and the new neuros: Using neuroeconomics, behavioural economics and picoeconomics for public policy, *Journal of Economic Policy*, 13, 845–869.

Pykett, J. (2017) *Brain Culture: Shaping Policy through Neuroscience*, Bristol, Policy Press.

Pykett, J. and Enright, B. (2016) Geographies of brain culture: Optimism and optimisation in workplace training programmes, *Cultural Geographies*, 23, 1, 51–68.

QCA (Qualifications and Curriculum Authority) (2005) *History 2004/05 Annual Report on Curriculum and Assessment*, London, QCA.

Raby, R. (2002) A tangle of discourses: Girls negotiating adolescence, *Journal of Youth Studies*, 5, 4, 425–448.

Raddon, A. (2002) Mothers in the academy, *Studies in Higher Education*, 27, 4, 387–403.

Rafferty, A. (2012) Ethnic penalties in graduate level over-education, unemployment and wages: Evidence from Britain, *Work, Employment and Society*, 26, 6, 987–1006.

Ratana-Ubol, A. and Richards, C. (2016) Third age learning: Adapting the idea to a Thailand context of lifelong learning, *International Journal of Lifelong Education*, 35, 1, 86–101.

Ravitch, D. (2010) *The Death and Life of the Great American School System*, Pennsylvania, PA, Basic Books.

Read, B., Archer, L. and Leathwood, C. (2003) Challenging cultures? Student conceptions of 'belonging' and 'isolation' at a post-1992 university, *Studies in Higher Education*, 28, 3, 262–277.

Read, B. and Kehm, B. (2016) Women as leaders of higher education institutions: A British-German comparison, *Studies in Higher Education*, 41, 5, 815–827.

Reay, D. (1998) *Class Work*, London, UCL Press.

Reay, D. (2001) 'Spice girls', 'nice girls', 'girlies' and 'tomboys': Gender discourses, girls' cultures and femininities in the primary classroom, *Gender and Education*, 13, 2, 153–166.

Reay, D. (2002) Class, authenticity and the transition to higher education for mature students, *The Sociological Review*, 50, 5, 398–418.

Reay, D. (2017) *Miseducation*, Bristol, Policy Press.

Reay, D. and Ball, S. (1998) 'Making their minds up': Family dynamics of school choice, *British Educational Research Journal*, 24, 4, 431–448.

Reay, D., Crozier, G. and Clayton, J. (2009) Strangers in paradise: Working class students in elite universities, *Sociology*, 43, 6, 1103–1121.

Reay, D., Crozier, G. and Clayton, J. (2010) 'Fitting in' or 'standing out': Working class students in UK higher education, *British Educational Research Journal*, 36, 1, 107–124.

Reay, D., Crozier, G. and James, D. (2011) *White Middle Class Identities and Urban Schooling*, Basingstoke, Palgrave.

Reay, D., David, M. and Ball, S. (2001) 'Making a difference?': Institutional habituses and higher education choice, *Sociological Research Online*, 5, 4.

Reay, D., David, M. and Ball, S. (2005) *Degrees of Choice: Social Class, Race and Gender in Higher Education*, London, Trentham Books.

Reay, D., Hollingworth, S., Williams, K., Crozier, G., Jamieson, F., James. D., and Beedell, P. (2007) A darker shade of pale: Whiteness, the middle classes and inner city schooling, *Sociology*, 41, 6, 1041–1060.

Reay, D. and Wiliam, D. (1999) 'I'll be a nothing': Structure, agency and the construction of identity through assessment, *British Educational Research Journal*, 25, 3, 343–354.

Reckhow, S., Grossman, M. and Evans, B. (2015) Policy cues and ideology in attitudes toward charter schools, *Policy Studies Journal*, 43, 2, 207–227.

Renold, E. (2000) 'Coming out': Gender, (hetero)sexuality and the primary school, *Gender and Education*, 12, 3, 309–326.

Renold, E. (2001) Learning the 'hard' way: Boys, hegemonic masculinity and the negotiation of learner identities in the primary school, *British Journal of Sociology of Education*, 22, 3, 369–385.

Renold, E. (2002) Presumed innocence. (Hetero)sexual, heterosexist and homophobic harassment amongst primary school girls and boys, *Childhood*, 9, 4, 415–434.

Renold, E. and Allan, A. (2006) Bright and beautiful: High-achieving girls, ambivalent femininities and the feminisation of success, *Discourse: Studies in the Cultural Politics of Education*, 27, 4, 547–473.

Rice, S., Dulfer, N., Polesel, J. and O'Hanlon, C. (2016) NAPLAN and student wellbeing: Teacher perceptions of the impact of NAPLAN on students, in: Lingard, B., Thompson, G. and Sellar, S. (eds) *National Testing in Schools: An Australian Assessment* New York, Routledge.

Rienties, B., Johan, N. and Jindal-Snape, D. (2015) A dynamic analysis of social capital-building of international and UK students, *British Journal of Sociology of Education*, 36, 8, 1212–1235.

Rivera, L. (2015) *Pedigree: How Elite Students Get Elite Jobs*, Princeton, NJ, Princeton University Press.

Rivza, B. and Teichler, U. (2007) The changing role of student mobility, *Higher Education Policy*, 20, 457–475.

Rizvi, F. (2000) International education and the production of global imagination, in: Burbules, N. and Torres, C. (eds) *Globalisation and Education: Critical Perspectives*, New York, Routledge, pp. 205–225.

Rizvi, F. and Lingard, B. (2010) *Globalizing Education Policy*, London, Routledge.

Roberts, S. (2015) We know what they earn, but what do they learn? A critique of lifelong learning through the lens of workplace learning at the bottom of the service sector, in: Brooks, R., McCormack, M. and Bhopal, K. (eds) *Contemporary Debates in the Sociology of Education*, Basingstoke, Palgrave.

Roberts-Holmes, G. (2015) The 'datafication' of early years pedagogy: 'If the teaching is good, the data should be good and if there is bad teaching, there is bad data', *Journal of Education Policy*, 30, 3, 302–315.

Robertson, Shanthi (2013) *Transnational Student-Migrants and the State*, London, Palgrave.

Robertson, S. (2009) Europe, competitiveness and higher education: An evolving project, in: Dale, R. and Robertson, S. (eds) *Globalisation and Europeanisation in Education*, Oxford, Symposium Books, pp. 65–83.

Robinson-Pant, A. (2009) Changing academies: Exploring international PhD students' perspectives on 'host' and 'home' universities, *Higher Education Research and Development*, 28, 4, 417–429.

Rollock, N., Gillborn, D., Vincent, C. and Ball, S. (2011) The public identities of the Black middle classes, *Sociology*, 45, 6, 1978–1093.

Rollock, N., Gillborn, D., Vincent, C. and Ball, S. (2015) *The Colour of Class: The Educational Strategies of the Black Middle Classes*, London, Routledge.

Rose, H. and Rose, S. (2016) *Can Neuroscience Change Our Minds?* Cambridge, Polity Press.

Roulin, N. and Bangerter, A. (2013) Students' use of extra-curricular activities for positional advantage in competitive job markets, *Journal of Education and Work*, 26, 1, 21–47.

Rouse, E. (2015) Mixed-age grouping in early childhood – creating the outdoor learning environment, *Early Child Development and Care*, 185, 5, 742–751.

Ryan, J. and Sackrey, C. (1984) *Strangers in Paradise: Academics from the Working Class*, Boston, MA, South End Press.

Saar, E., Täht, K. and Roosalu, T. (2014) Institutional barriers for adults' participation in higher education in thirteen European countries, *Higher Education*, 68, 691–710.

Sabri, D. (2013) Student evaluations of teaching as 'fact-totems': The case of the UK National Student Survey, *Sociological Research Online*, 18, 4.

Sam, C. and de Sijde, P. (2014) Understanding the concept of the entrepreneurial university from the perspective of higher education models, *Higher Education*, 68, 891–908.

Sammons, P., Hillman, J. and Mortimore, P. (1995) *Key Characteristics of Effective Schools: A Review of School Effectiveness Research*, London, Office for Standards in Education (OFSTED).

Savage, G. and O'Connor, K. (2015) National agendas in global times: Curriculum reforms in Australia and the USA since the 1980s, *Journal of Education Policy*, 30, 5, 609–630.

Savage, M., Cunningham, N., Devine, F., Friedman, S., Laurison, D., Mckenzie, L., Miles, A., Snee, H. and Wakeling, P. (2015) *Social Class in the 21st Century*, London, Pelican Books.

Schilhab, T. (2017) Impact of iPads on break-time in primary schools – a Danish context, *Oxford Review of Education*, 43, 3, 261–275.

Schneider, J. (2014) Rhetoric and practice in pre-service teacher education: The case of Teach for America, *Journal of Education Policy*, 29, 4, 425–442.

Schuller, T., Preston, J., Hammond, C., Brassett-Grundy, A. and Bynner, J. (2004) *The Benefits of Learning: The Impact of Education on Health, Family Life and Social Capital*, London, RoutledgeFalmer.

Seddon, T. (2014) Making educational spaces through boundary work: Territorialisation and 'boundarying', *Globalisation, Societies and Education*, 12, 1, 10–31.

Selwyn, N. (2003) Schooling the mobile generation: The future for schools in the mobile-networked society, *British Journal of Sociology of Education*, 24, 2, 131–144.

Selwyn, N., Henderson, M. and Chao, S.-H. (2015) Exploring the role of digital data in contemporary schools and schooling – '200,000 lines in an Excel spreadsheet', *British Educational Research Journal*, 41, 5, 767–781.

Shain, F. (2012) Intersections of 'race', class and gender in the social and political identifications of young Muslims in England, in: Bhopal, K. and Preston, J. (eds) *Intersectionality and 'Race' in Education*, London, Routledge.

Shain, F. and Ozga, J. (2001) Identity crisis? Problems and issues in the sociology of education, *British Journal of Sociology of Education*, 22, 1, 109–120.

Shanahan, T., Axelrod, P., Trilokekar, R. and Wellan, R. (2016) Policy-making in higher education: Is a 'theory of everything' possible?, in: Case, J. and Huisman, J. (eds) *Researching Higher Education: International Perspectives on Theory, Policy and Practice*, London, Routledge/SRHE.

Shear, B. and Hyatt, S. (2015) Higher education, engaged anthropology and hegemonic struggle, in: Hyatt, S., Shear, B. and Wright, S. (eds) *Learning Under Neoliberalism: Ethnographies of Governance in Higher Education*, New York, Berghahn.

Shevlin, M., Banyard, P., Davies, M. and Griffiths, M. (2004) The validity of student evaluation of teaching in higher education: Love me, love my lectures? In: Tight, M. (ed) *The RoutledgeFalmer Reader in Higher Education*, London, Routledge.

Shore. C (2011) Espionage, policy and the art of government, in: Shore, C., Wright, S. and Però, D. (eds) *Policy Worlds: Anthropology and the Analysis of Contemporary Power*, New York, Berghahn Books.

Shore, C. and Wright, S. (2011) Conceptualising policy: Technologies of governance and the politics of visibility, in: Shore, C., Wright, S. and Però, D. (eds) *Policy Worlds: Anthropology and the Analysis of Contemporary Power*, New York, Berghahn Books.

Sidhu, R. (2006) *Universities and Globalization: To Market, to Market*, Mahwah, NJ, Lawrence Erlbaum Associates Ltd.

Sidhu, R. (2009) Running to stay still in the knowledge economy, *Journal of Education Policy*, 24, 3, 237–253.

Sikora, J. (2014) Gender gap in school science: Are single-sex schools important? *Sex Roles*, 70, 9–10, 400–415.

Simmons, R. (2008) Raising the age of compulsory education in England: A NEET solution? *British Journal of Educational Studies*, 56, 4, 420–439.

Sin, I.L. (2013) Cultural capital and distinction: Aspirations of the 'Other' foreign student. *British Journal of Sociology of Education*, 34, 5–6, 848–867.

Singh, A. (2014) Test score gaps between private and government sector students of school entry age in India, *Oxford Review of Education*, 40, 1, 30–49.

Singh, M., Rizvi, F. and Shrestha, M. (2007) Student mobility and the spatial production of cosmopolitan identities, in: Gulson, K. and Symes, C. (eds) *Spatial Theories of Education: Policy and Geography Matters*, New York, Routledge, pp. 195–214.

Singh, P. and Doherty, C. (2008) Mobile students in liquid modernity: Negotiating the politics of transnational identities, in: Dolby, N. and Rizvi, F. (eds) *Youth Moves: Identities and Education in Global Perspective*, New York, Routledge, pp. 115–130.

Skelton, C. and Francis, B. (2009) *Feminism and 'the Schooling Scandal'*, London, Routledge.

Skeggs, B. (2004) *Class, Self, Culture*, London, Routledge.

Sklair, L. (2001) *The Transnational Capitalist Class*, Oxford, Blackwell.

Sklair, L. (2010) *The Emancipatory Potential of Generic Globalisation*, Presentation to the Sociology Department, University of Surrey, January.

Skourdoumbis, A. (2014) Teacher effectiveness: Making the difference to student achievement? *British Journal of Educational Studies*, 62, 2, 111–126.

Slaughter, S. and Leslie, L. (1997) *Academic Capitalism: Politics, Policies and the Entrepreneurial University*, Baltimore, MD, Johns Hopkins University Press.

Slaughter, S. and Rhoades, G. (2004) *Academic Capitalism and the New Economy: Markets, State and Higher Education*, Baltimore, MD, Johns Hopkins University Press.

Slee, R. and Weiner, G. with Tomlinson, S. (eds) (1999) *School Effectiveness for Whom? Challenges to the School Effectiveness and School Improvement Movements*, London, Falmer Press.

Slowey, M. and Schuetze, H. (eds) (2012) *Global Perspectives on Higher Education and Lifelong Learners*, London, Routledge.

Smart, S. (2009) Processes of middle class reproduction in a graduate employment scheme, *Journal of Education and Work*, 22, 1, 35–53.

Smetherham, C. (2006) Firsts among equals? Evidence on the contemporary relationship between educational credentials and the occupational structure, *Journal of Education and Work*, 19, 1, 29–45.

Solomona, R.P., Portelli, J.P., Daniel, B.-J. and Campbell, A. (2005) The discourse of denial: How white teacher candidates construct race, racism and 'white privilege', *Race Ethnicity and Education*, 8, 2, 147–169.

Song, J.J. (2013) For whom the bell tolls: Globalisation, social class and South Korea's international schools, *Globalisation, Societies and Education*, 11, 1, 136–159.

Souto-Otero, M. (2015) Conclusion: Who benefits from EU policy-making in education: The European commission' and the privatisation of education policy, in: Souto-Otero, M. (ed) *Evaluating European Education Policy-Making*, Basingstoke, Palgrave.

Spiegler, T. (2009) Why state sanctions fail to deter home education: An analysis of home education in Germany and its implications for home education policies, *Theory and Research in Education*, 7, 3, 297–309.

Stobart, G. (2008) *Testing Times: The Uses and Abuses of Assessment*, London, Routledge.

Stokes, H. and Wyn, J. (2007) Constructing identities and making careers: Young people's perspectives on work and learning, *International Journal of Lifelong Education*, 26, 5, 495–511.

Stuber, J. (2009) Class, culture and participation in the collegiate extra-curriculum, *Sociological Forum*, 24, 4, 877–900.

Stuber, J. (2011) Integrated, marginal and resilient: Race, class and the diverse experiences of white, first-generation college students, *International Journal of Qualitative Studies in Education*, 24, 1, 117–136.

Sundaram, V. and Sauntson, H. (2016) Discursive silences: Using critical linguistic and qualitative analysis to explore the continued absence of pleasure in sex and relationships education in England, *Sex Education*, 16, 3, 240–254.

Takayama, K. (2009) Globalising critical studies of 'official' knowledge: Lessons from the Japanese history textbook controversy over 'comfort women', *British Journal of Sociology of Education*, 30, 5, 577–589.

Tavares, O. and Cardoso, S. (2013) Enrolment choices in Portuguese higher education: Do students behave as rational consumers? *Higher Education*, 66, 297–309.

Taylor, E. (2013) *Surveillance Schools: Security, Discipline and Control in Contemporary Education*, Basingstoke, Palgrave.

Teixeira, P. (2013) *The Tortuous Ways of the Market: Looking at the European Integration of Higher Education from an Economic Perspective*. LSE Europe in Question Working Paper 56/2013. Available online at: http://www.lse.ac.uk/europeanInstitute/LEQS%20Discussion%20Paper%20Series/leqspaper56.pdf (Accessed 09/09/16).

Teichler, U. (1996) Student mobility in the framework of ERASMUS: Findings of an evaluation study, *European Journal of Education*, 31, 2, 153–179.

Thomas, L. (2005) *Progression Beyond Higher Education*, Paper presented at the British Educational Research Association Annual Conference, 15–17 September, Glamorgan University.

Thompson, E., Sinclair, K., Wichins, R. and Russell, S. (2013) It's how you look or what you look like: Gender harassment at school and its association with student achievement, in: Brooks, R., McCormack, M. and Bhopal, K. (eds) *Contemporary Debates in the Sociology of Education*, Basingstoke, Palgrave.

Thompson, G., Sellar, S. and Lingard, B. (2016) The life of data: Evolving national testing, in: Lingard, B., Thompson, G. and Sellar, S. (eds) *National Testing in Schools: An Australian Assessment*, New York, Routledge.

Tipping, A. (2013) 'Troops to teachers': Implications for the coalition government's approach to education policy and pedagogical beliefs and practices, *Educational Studies*, 39, 4, 468–478.

Tomlinson, M. (2016) Students' perceptions of themselves as 'consumers' of higher education, *British Journal of Sociology of Education* (Advance online access).

Tomlinson, S. (2015) Fundamental British values, in: Alexander, C., Weekes-Bernard, D. and Arday, J. (eds) *Race, Education and Inequality in Contemporary Britain*, London, The Runnymede Trust.

Tones, M., Fraser, J., Elder, R. and White, K. (2009) Supporting mature-age students from a low income background, *Higher Education*, 58, 505–529.

Trent, J. (2015) The gendered, hierarchical construction of teacher identities: Exploring the male primary school teacher voice in Hong Kong, *Journal of Education Policy*, 30, 4, 500–517.

Trow, M. (1973) *Problems in the Transition for Elite to Mass Higher Education*, Berkeley, CA, Carnegie Commission on Higher Education.

Universities UK (UUK) (2015) *Patterns and Trends in UK Higher Education 2015*, London, Universities UK.

Universities UK (UUK) (2017) *The Economic Impact of International Students*. Available online at: http://www.universitiesuk.ac.uk/policy-and-analysis/reports/Documents/2017/briefing-economic-impact-international-students.pdf (Accessed 28/08/17).

Uy, P.S. (2016) Unpacking racial identities: The salience of ethnicity in Southeast Asian-American youth's schooling experience, *Race Ethnicity and Education* (Advance online access).

Valenzuela, A. (ed) (2005) *Leaving Children Behind*, Albany, NY: State University of New York Press.

Valins, O. (2003) Defending identities or segregating communities? Faith-based schooling and the UK Jewish community, *Geoforum*, 34, 235–247.

Vincent, C. (2000) *Including Parents? Education, Citizenship and Parental Agency* Buckingham, Open University Press.

Vincent, C. (2017) 'The children have only got one education and you have to make sure it's a good one': Parenting and parent-school relations in a neo-liberal age, *Gender and Education* (Advance online access).

Vincent, C. and Ball, S. (2007) 'Making up' the middle class child: Families, activities and class dispositions, *Sociology*, 41, 6, 1061–1077.

Wagner, N., Rieger, M. and Voorvelt, K. (2016) Gender, ethnicity and teaching evaluations: Evidence from mixed teaching teams, *Economics of Education Review*, 54, 79–94.

Walford, G. (2008) Faith-based schools in England after ten years of Tony Blair, *Oxford Review of Education*, 34, 6, 689–699.

Walford, G. (2011) *Researching the powerful*, British Educational Research Association on-line resource. Available online at: https://www.bera.ac.uk/wp-content/uploads/2014/03/Researching-the-Powerful.pdf (Accessed 17/07/17)

Walkenhorst, H. (2008) Explaining change in European Union education policy, *European Journal of Public Policy*, 15, 4, 567–587.

Walkerdine, V., Lucey, H. and Melody, J. (2001) *Growing Up Girl: Psychosocial Explorations of Gender and Class*, Basingstoke, Palgrave.

Wall, G. (2010) Mothers' experiences with intensive parenting and brain development discourse, *Women's Studies International Forum*, 33, 253–262.

Warnock, D. (2016) Paradise lost? Patterns and precarity in working-class academic narratives, *Journal of Working-Class Studies*, 1, 1, 28–44.

Wastell, D. and White, S. (2017) *Blinded by Science: The Social Implications of Epigenetics and Neuroscience*, Bristol, Policy Press.

Waters, J. (2006) Geographies of cultural capital: Education, international migration and family strategies between Hong Kong and Canada, *Transactions of the Institute of British Geographers*, 31, 2, 179–192.

Waters, J. (2007) 'Roundabout routes and sanctuary schools': The role of situated educational practices and habitus in the creation of transnational professionals, *Global Networks*, 7, 4, 477–497.

Waters, J. (2008) *Education, Migration and Cultural Capital in the Chinese Diaspora: Transnational Students between Hong Kong and Canada*, New York, Cambria Press.

Waters, J. and Leung, M. (2012) Young people and the reproduction of disadvantage through transnational higher education in Hong Kong, *Sociological Research Online*, 17, 3.

Watters, S. (2016) Old Boy network: The relationship between elite schooling, social capital and positions of power in British society, in: Koh, A. and Kenway, J. (eds) *Elite Schools: Multiple Geographies of Privilege*, New York, Routledge.

Weale, S. (2016) Universities told to raise numbers of working-class and black students, *The Guardian*, 11 February. Available online at: http://www.theguardian.com/education/2016/feb/11/universities-told-to-raise-numbers-of-working-class-and-black-students (Accessed 20/05/2016).

Weiner, M. (2015) Whitening a diverse Dutch classroom: White cultural discourses in an Amsterdam primary school, *Ethnic and Racial Studies*, 38, 2, 359–376.

Weis, L. and Cipollone, K. (2013) 'Class work': Producing privilege and social mobility in elite US secondary schools, *British Journal of Sociology of Education*, 34, 5–6, 701–722.

Weiss, F. and Klein, M. (2011) Social networks and tertiary graduates' job search: The impact of network type on monetary return and job adequacy, *Zeitschrift für Soziologie*, 40, 3, 228–245.

Wells, A.S., Lopez, A., Scott, J. and Holme, J. (1999) Charter schools as postmodern paradox: Rethinking social stratification in an age of deregulated school choice, *Harvard Educational Review*, 69, 2, 172–204.

West, A. (2014) Academies in England and independent schools (friståande skolor) in Sweden: Policy, privatisation, access and segregation, *Research Papers in Education*, 29, 3, 330–350.

Whitebread, D. (2012) *The Importance of Play*. Available online at: http://www.importanceofplay.eu/IMG/pdf/dr_david_whitebread_-_the_importance_of_play.pdf (Accessed 26/01/18).

Whitty, G. (2012) A life with the sociology of education, *British Journal of Educational Studies*, 60, 1, 65–75.

Wiborg, S. (2010) *Swedish Free Schools: Do they Work?* LLAKES Working Paper, London UCL-Institute of Education.

Wiers-Jenssen, J. (2008) Does higher education attained abroad lead to international jobs? *Journal of Studies in Higher Education*, 12, 2, 101–130.

Wilińska, M. (2012) Is there a place for an ageing subject? Stories of ageing at the University of the Third Age in Poland, *Sociology*, 46, 2, 290–305.

Wilkinson, M. (2014) The concept of the absent curriculum: The case of the Muslim contribution and the English National Curriculum for history, *Journal of Curriculum Studies*, 46, 4, 419–440.

Willemse, N. and de Beer, P. (2012) Three worlds of educational welfare states? A comparative study of higher education systems across welfare states, *Journal of European Social Policy*, 22, 2, 105–117.

Williams, J. (2013) *Consuming Higher Education: Why Learning Can't Be Bought*, London, Bloomsbury.

Williams, J. (2016) 'I didn't even know that there was such a thing as aboriginal games': A figurational account of how Indigenous students experience physical education, *Sport, Education and Society* (Online advance access).

Williamson, B. (2015) Digital governance: An introduction, *European Educational Research Journal*, 15, 1, 3–13.

Williamson, B. (2016a) Coding the biodigital child: The biopolitics and pedagogic strategies of educational data science, *Pedagogy, Culture and Society*, 24, 3, 401–416.

Williamson, B. (2016b) Digital education governance: Data visualisation, predictive analytics and 'real time' policy instruments, *Journal of Education Policy*, 31, 2, 123–141.

Willis, P. (1977) *Learning to Labour: How Working Class Kids Get Working Class Jobs*, London, Gower Publishing.

Winter, C. (2012) School curriculum, globalisation and the constitution of policy problems and solutions, *Journal of Education Policy*, 27, 3, 295–314.

Wolter, A. (2012) Germany: From individual talent to institutional permeability: Changing policies for non-traditional access routes in German higher education, in: Slowey, M. and Schuetze, H. (eds) *Global Perspectives on Higher Education and Lifelong Learners*, London, Routledge.

Wood, B. and Kidman, J. (2013) Negotiating the ethical borders of visual research with young people, in: Te Riele K. and Brooks, R. (eds) *Negotiating Ethical Challenges in Youth Research*, New York: Routledge, pp. 149–162.

Woodfield, R. (2011) Age and first destination from UK universities: Are mature students disadvantaged? *Studies in Higher Education*, 36, 4, 409–425.

Woodin, T., McCulloch, G. and McCowan, S. (2013) Raising the participation age in historical perspective: Policy learning from the past? *British Educational Research Journal*, 39, 4, 635–653.

Woods, P. and Jeffrey, B. (2002) The reconstruction of primary teachers' identities, *British Journal of Sociology of Education*, 23, 1, 89–106.

Wright and Reinhold (2011) 'Studying through': A strategy for studying political transformation. Or sex, lies and British politics, in: Shore, C., Wright, S. and Però, D. (eds) *Policy Worlds: Anthropology and the Analysis of Contemporary Power*, New York, Berghahn Books.

Wyn, J. and White, R. (1997) *Rethinking Youth*, London, Sage.

Xu, Z., Hannaway, J. and Taylor, C. (2011) Making a difference? The effects of Teach for America in high school, *Journal of Policy Analysis and Management*, 30, 3, 447–469.

Yates, L. (2009) From curriculum to pedagogy and back again: Knowledge, the person and the changing world, *Pedagogy, Culture and Society*, 17, 1, 17–28.

Yates, L. (2012) *My School, My University, My Country, My World, My Google, Myself …* What is education for now? *Australian Educational Researcher*, 39, 259–274.

Yates, L. (2017) Schools, universities and history in the world of twenty-first century skills. 'The end of knowledge as we know it?', *History of Education Review*, 46, 1, 2–14.

Yeoh, B., Huang, S. and Lam, T. (2005) Transnationalizing the 'Asian' family: Imaginaries, intimacies and strategic intents, *Global Networks*, 5, 4, 307–315.

Youdell, D. (2003) Identity traps or how black students fail: The interactions between biographical, sub-cultural and learner identities, *British Journal of Sociology of Education*, 24, 1, 3–20.

Youdell, D. (2017) Biosciences and the sociology of education: The case for biosocial education, *British Journal of Sociology of Education* (Advance online access).

Young, M. (ed) (1971) *Knowledge and Control: New Directions for the Sociology of Education*, London, Collier-Macmillan.

Young, M. (2011) The return to subjects: A sociological perspective on the UK Coalition government's approach to the 14–19 curriculum, *The Curriculum Journal*, 22, 2, 265–278.

Young, M. and Lambert, D. (2014) *Knowledge and the Future School: Curriculum and Social Justice*, London, Bloomsbury.

Young, M. and Muller, J. (2016) *Curriculum and the Specialisation of Knowledge: Studies in the Sociology of Education*, London, Routledge.

Zhang, W. and Bray, M. (2017) Micro-neoliberalism in China: Public-private interactions at the confluence of mainstream and shadow education, *Journal of Education Policy*, 32, 1, 63–81.

Zhao, Y. (2012) *World Class Learners: Educating Creative and Entrepreneurial Students*, Thousand Oaks, CA, Corwin.

Zhao, Y. (2015) A world at risk: An imperative for a paradigm shift to cultivate 21st century learners, *Society*, 52, 129–135.

Ziegler, S. (2016) Schools and families: School choice and formation of elites in present-day Argentina, in: Koh, A. and Kenway, J. (eds) *Elite Schools: Multiple Geographies of Privilege*, New York, Routledge.

INDEX

Printed by Printforce, the Netherlands

CW01512313

Captives and Companions

JUSTIN MAROZZI

Captives and Companions

A History of Slavery and the Slave Trade in the Islamic World

ALLEN LANE
an imprint of
PENGUIN BOOKS

ALLEN LANE

UK | USA | Canada | Ireland | Australia
India | New Zealand | South Africa

Allen Lane is part of the Penguin Random House group of companies
whose addresses can be found at global.penguinrandomhouse.com.

Penguin Random House UK
One Embassy Gardens, 8 Viaduct Gardens, London SW11 7BW

penguin.co.uk

First published in Great Britain by Allen Lane 2025

001

Copyright © Justin Marozzi, 2025

Penguin Random House values and supports copyright.
Copyright fuels creativity, encourages diverse voices, promotes freedom
of expression and supports a vibrant culture. Thank you for purchasing
an authorized edition of this book and for respecting intellectual property
laws by not reproducing, scanning or distributing any part of it by any
means without permission. You are supporting authors and enabling
Penguin Random House to continue to publish books for everyone.
No part of this book may be used or reproduced in any manner for the
purpose of training artificial intelligence technologies or systems. In accordance
with Article 4(3) of the DSM Directive 2019/790, Penguin Random House
expressly reserves this work from the text and data mining exception.

The moral right of the author has been asserted

Set in 10.5/14pt Sabon LT Std
Typeset by Six Red Marbles UK, Thetford, Norfolk
Printed and bound in Great Britain by Clays Ltd, Elcograf S.p.A.

The authorized representative in the EEA is Penguin Random House Ireland,
Morrison Chambers, 32 Nassau Street, Dublin D02 YH68

A CIP catalogue record for this book is available from the British Library

ISBN: 978-0-241-52215-8

Penguin Random House is committed to a sustainable future
for our business, our readers and our planet. This book is made from
Forest Stewardship Council® certified paper.

For the voices lost.

Contents

List of Illustrations

Every effort has been made to contact copyright holders. The author and publisher would be glad to amend in future editions errors or omissions brought to their attention.

COLOUR PLATES

1. Glass painting of the warrior-poet Antara ibn Shaddad. Public domain, via Wikimedia Commons.
2. Miniature from a 1595 edition of *Siyer-i Nabi*, the fourteenth-century Ottoman epic on the life of the Prophet. Public domain, via Wikimedia commons.
3. Salman al Farsi – the Persian. Miniature from *Siyer-i Nabi*, 1595. Courtesy of the Public Domain Archive, New York Public Library.
4. Illustration by Yahya ibn Mahmud, from a 1207 edition of *Maqamat al Hariri* (Arabic tales told in rhymed prose), an illuminated manuscript by the poet Al Hariri of Basra. Public domain, via Wikimedia Commons
5. Illustration from the illuminated *Kitab al Hayawan* (*Book of Animals*) by the Iraqi polymath Al Jahiz. Public domain, via Wikimedia Commons.
6. Portrait of the Kapi Agha, from the studio of Jean Baptiste Vanmour, *c*.1720. Image courtesy: Album.
7. Portait of the Kizlar Agha, from the studio of Jean Baptiste Vanmour, *c*. 1720. Image courtesy: Album.
8. Photograph of Saeed Adam Omar in Medina, 2013. Adel al Quraishi, via The Park Lane Gallery, London.
9. Interior of the Ottoman sultan's imperial harem engraved by François Denis Née (1732–1817) after Antoine Ignace Melling. Public Domain, via Wikimedia Commons.

INTEGRATED IMAGES

List of Maps

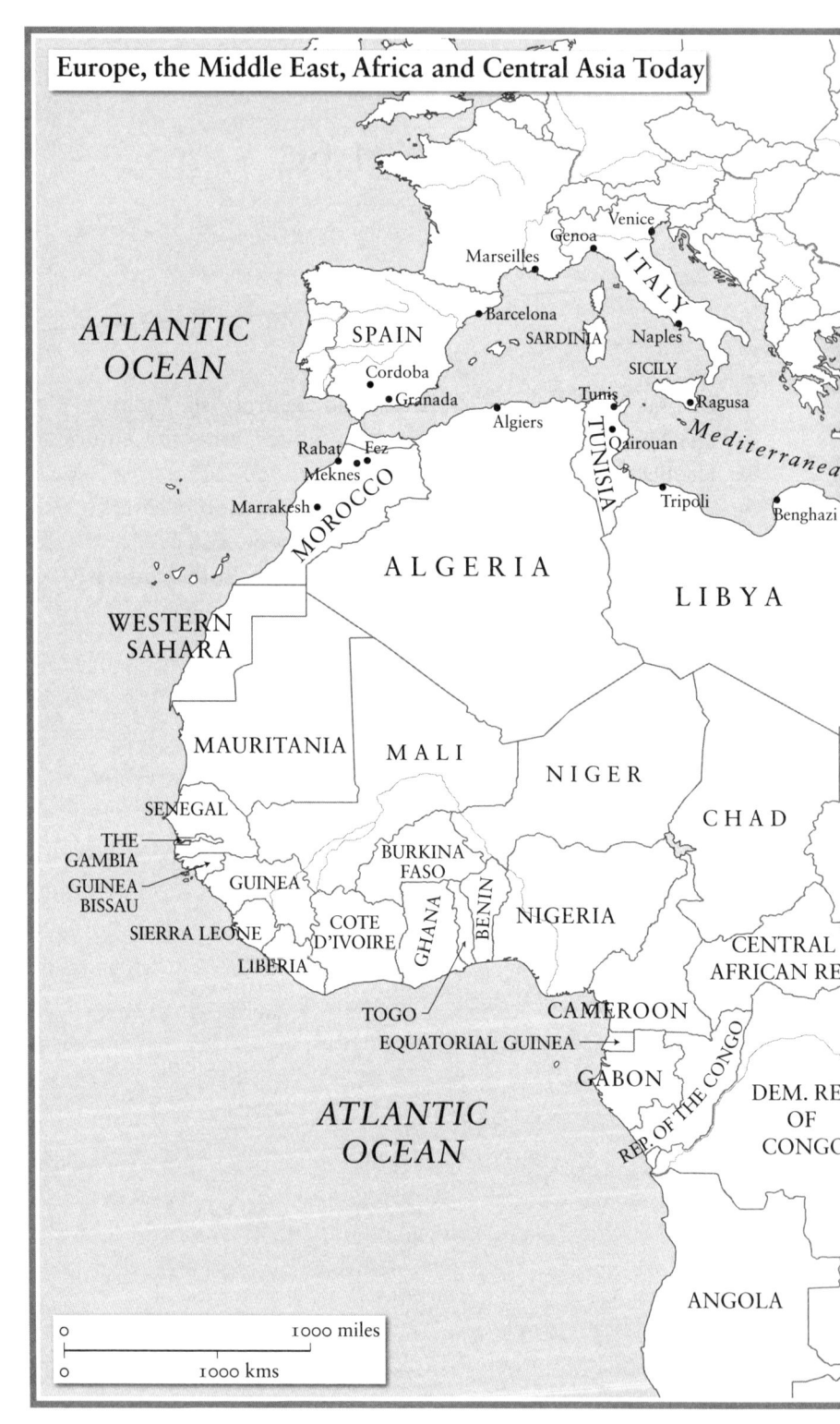

Europe, the Middle East, Africa and Central Asia Today

ATLANTIC OCEAN

SPAIN

Marseilles

Genoa

Venice

ITALY

Barcelona

SARDINIA

Naples

Cordoba

SICILY

Granada

Tunis

Ragusa

Algiers

Qairouan

Mediterranean

Rabat

Fez

Meknes

MOROCCO

Tripoli

Benghazi

Marrakesh

ALGERIA

LIBYA

WESTERN SAHARA

MAURITANIA

MALI

NIGER

CHAD

SENEGAL

THE GAMBIA

BURKINA FASO

GUINEA BISSAU

GUINEA

BENIN

NIGERIA

CENTRAL AFRICAN RE

SIERRA LEONE

COTE D'IVOIRE

GHANA

LIBERIA

TOGO

CAMEROON

EQUATORIAL GUINEA

GABON

REP OF THE CONGO

DEM. RE OF CONGO

ATLANTIC OCEAN

ANGOLA

0   1000 miles

0   1000 kms

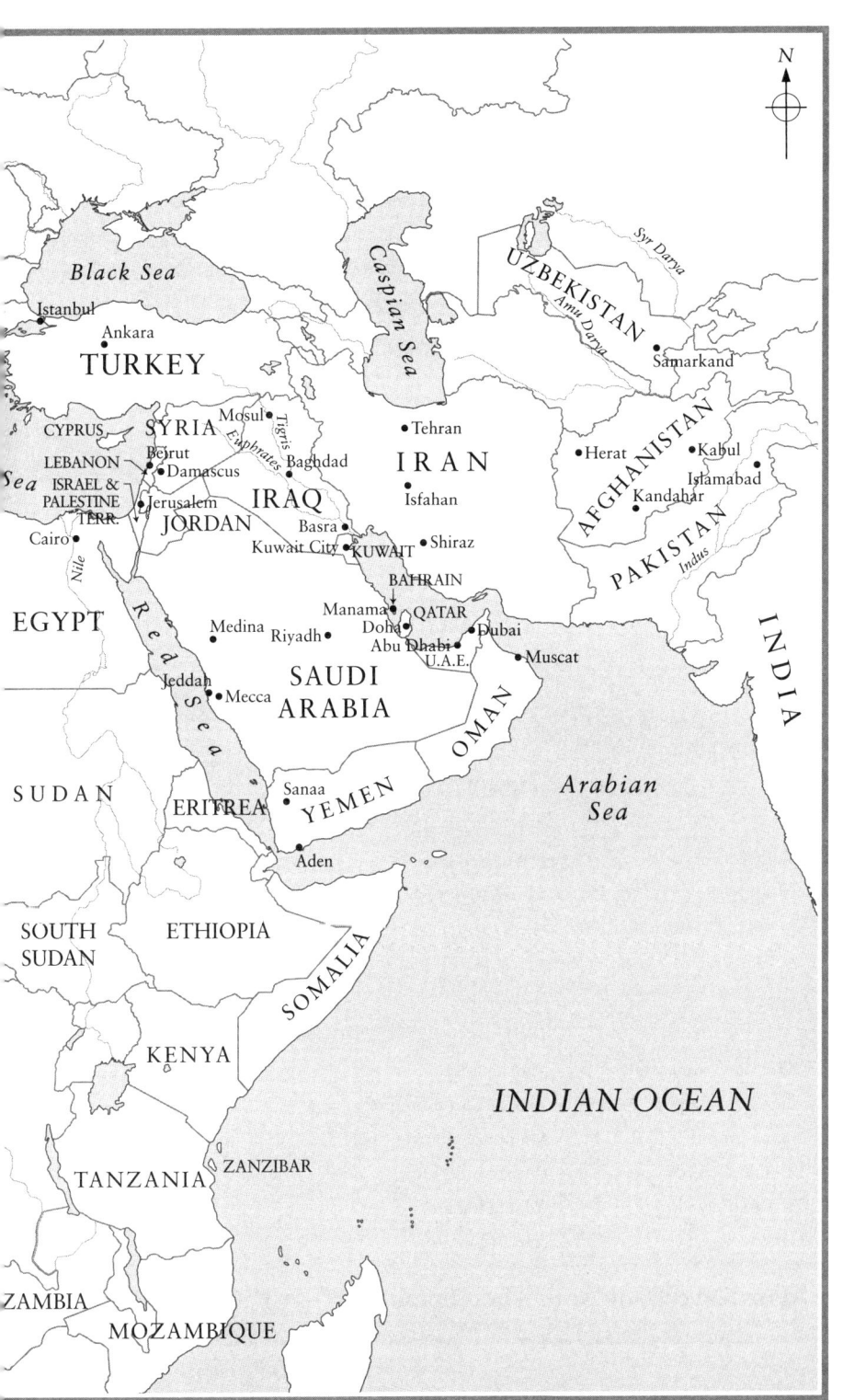

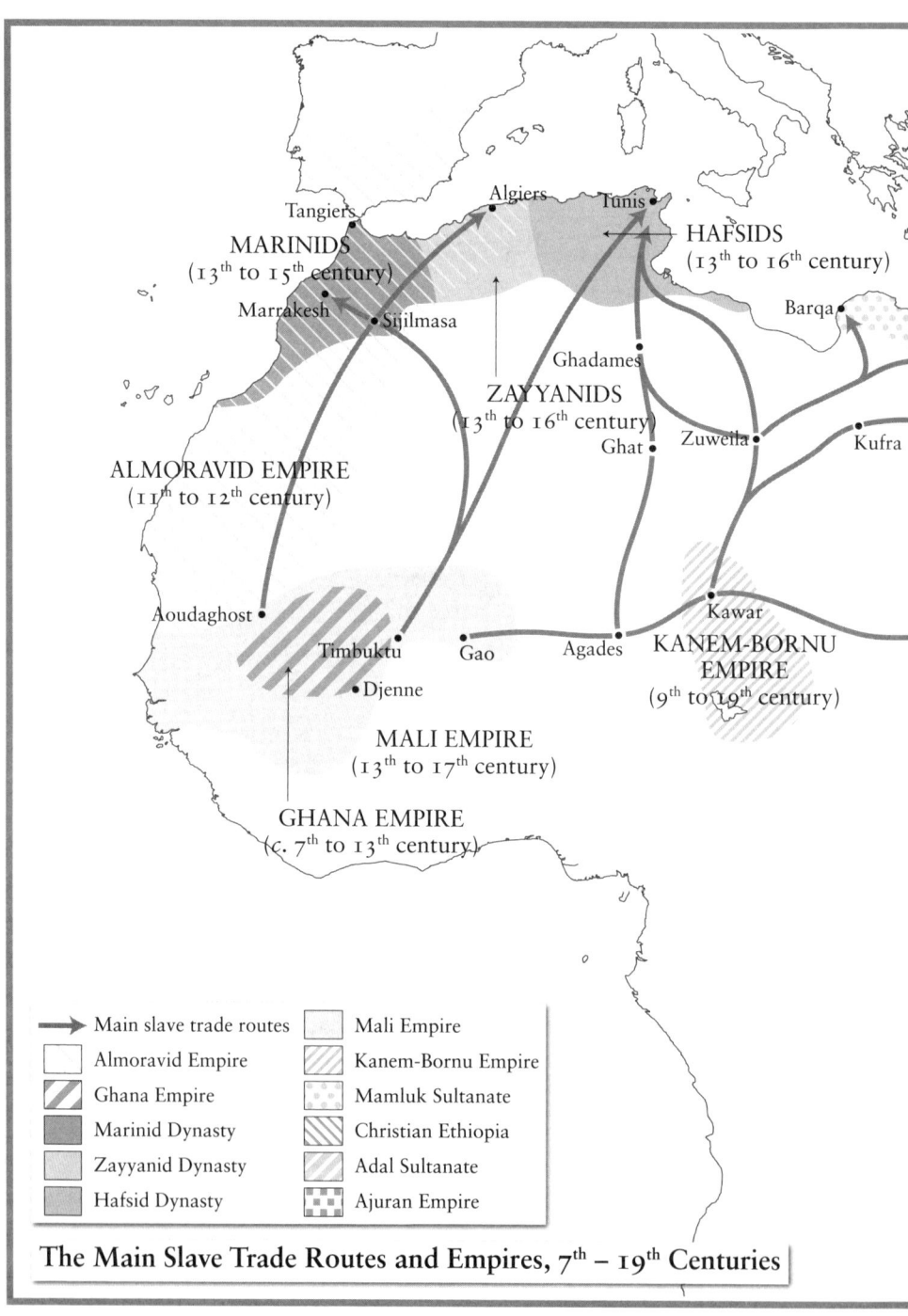

The Main Slave Trade Routes and Empires, 7th – 19th Centuries

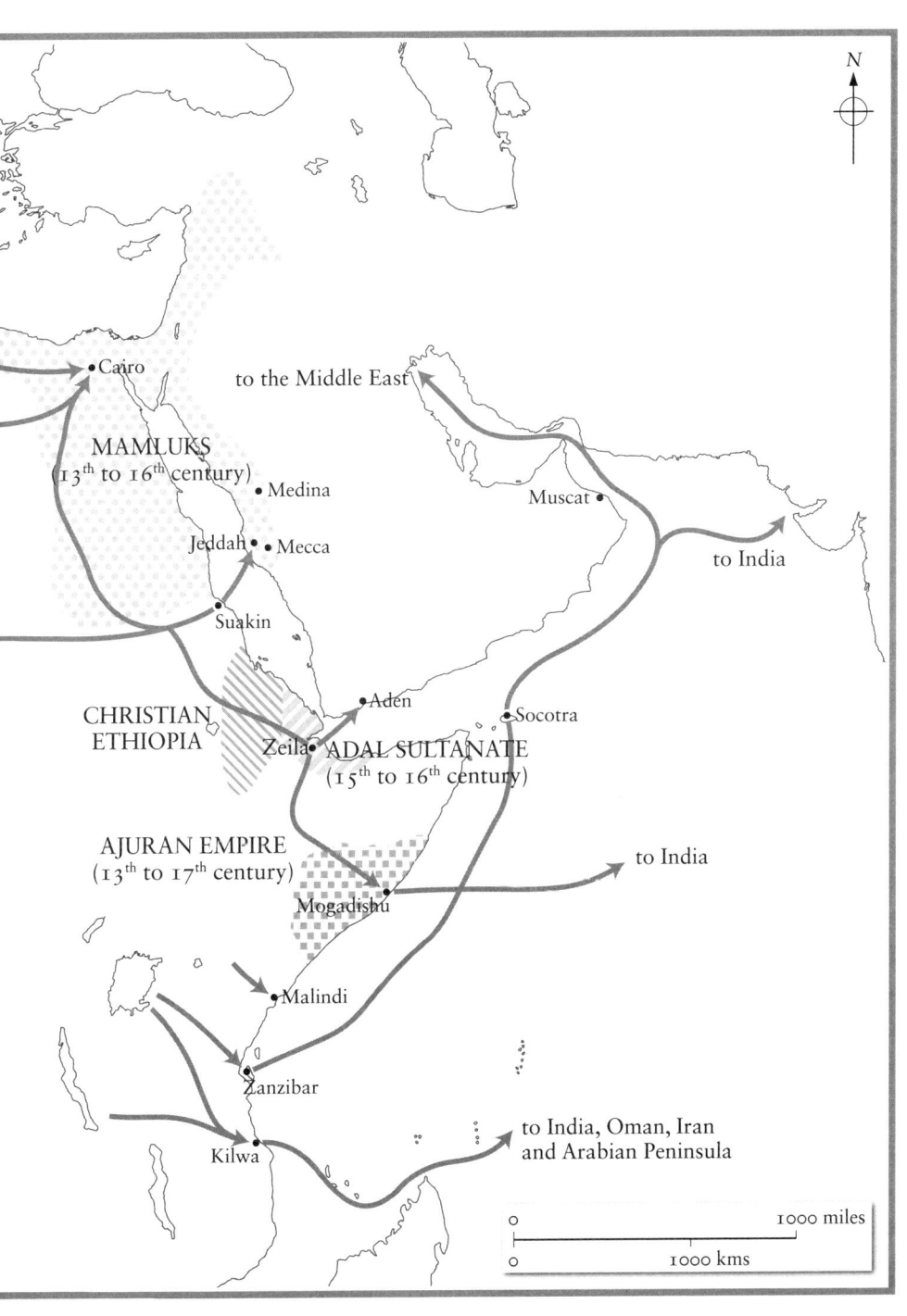

N

to the Middle East

•Cairo

MAMLUKS
(13th to 16th century)   •Medina

Jeddah• •Mecca   Muscat •

Suakin   to India

CHRISTIAN
ETHIOPIA   •Aden
          Zeila• ADAL SULTANATE   •Socotra
                  (15th to 16th century)

AJURAN EMPIRE
(13th to 17th century)
                  Mogadishu•   to India

                  •Malindi

              •Zanzibar

                                  to India, Oman, Iran
Kilwa•   and Arabian Peninsula

0   1000 miles

0   1000 kms

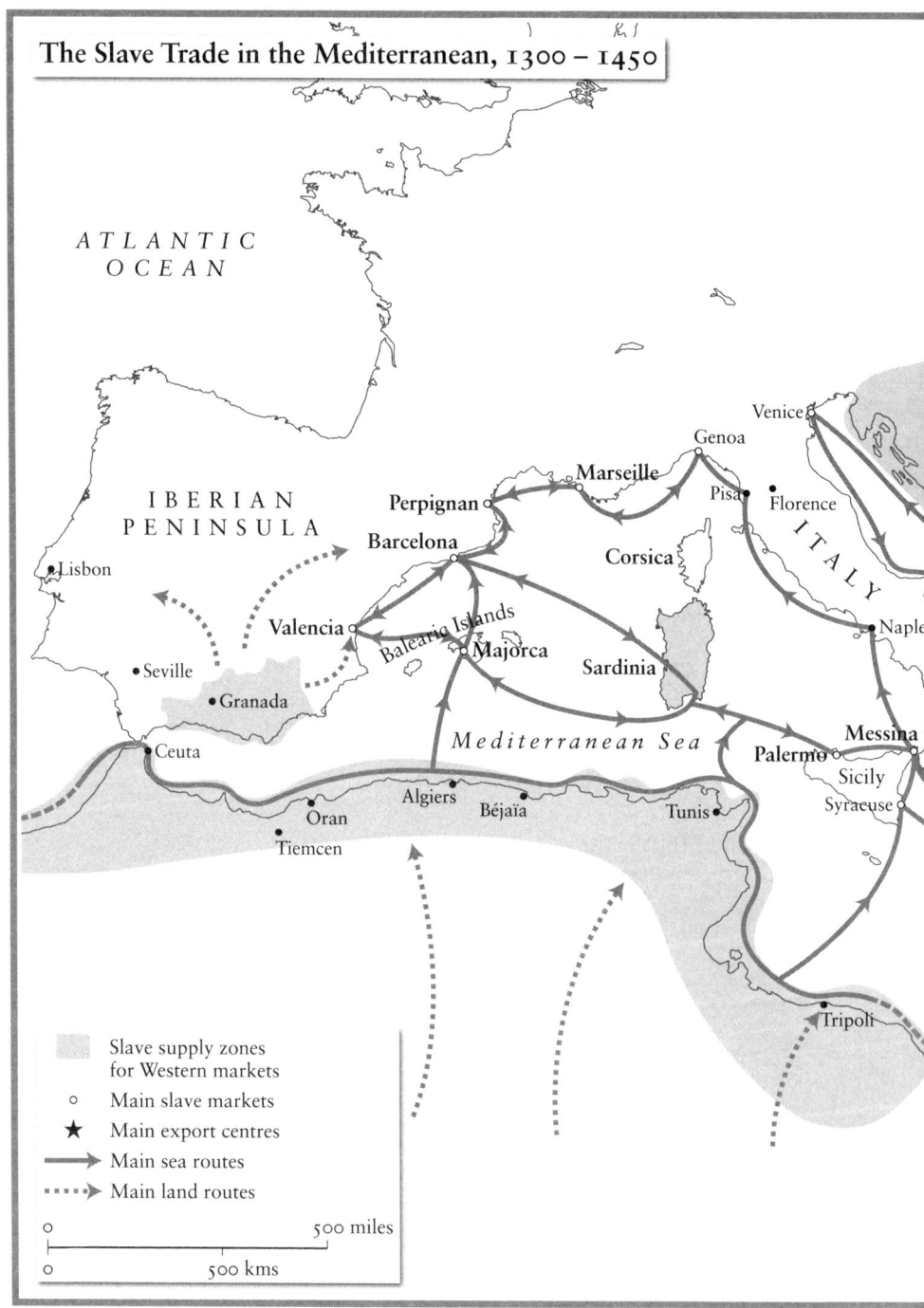

The Slave Trade in the Mediterranean, 1300 – 1450

ATLANTIC OCEAN

IBERIAN PENINSULA

Mediterranean Sea

ITALY

- Lisbon
- Seville
- Granada
- Ceuta
- Valencia
- Barcelona
- Perpignan
- Marseille
- Genoa
- Pisa
- Florence
- Venice
- Naple[s]
- Corsica
- Sardinia
- Balearic Islands
- Majorca
- Messina
- Palermo
- Sicily
- Syracuse
- Oran
- Tiemcen
- Algiers
- Béjaïa
- Tunis
- Tripoli

Slave supply zones for Western markets
○ Main slave markets
★ Main export centres
→ Main sea routes
····▶ Main land routes

500 miles

500 kms

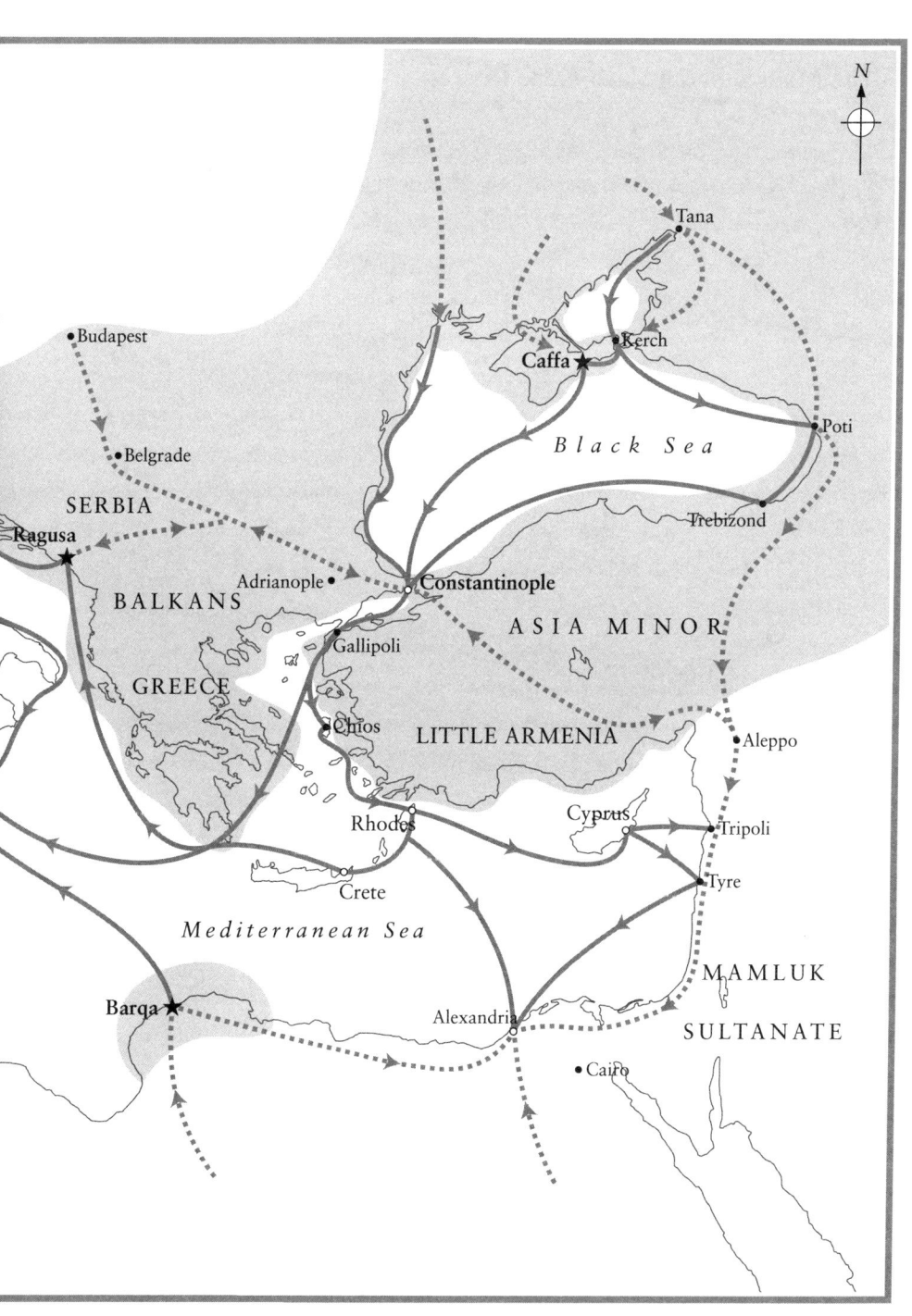

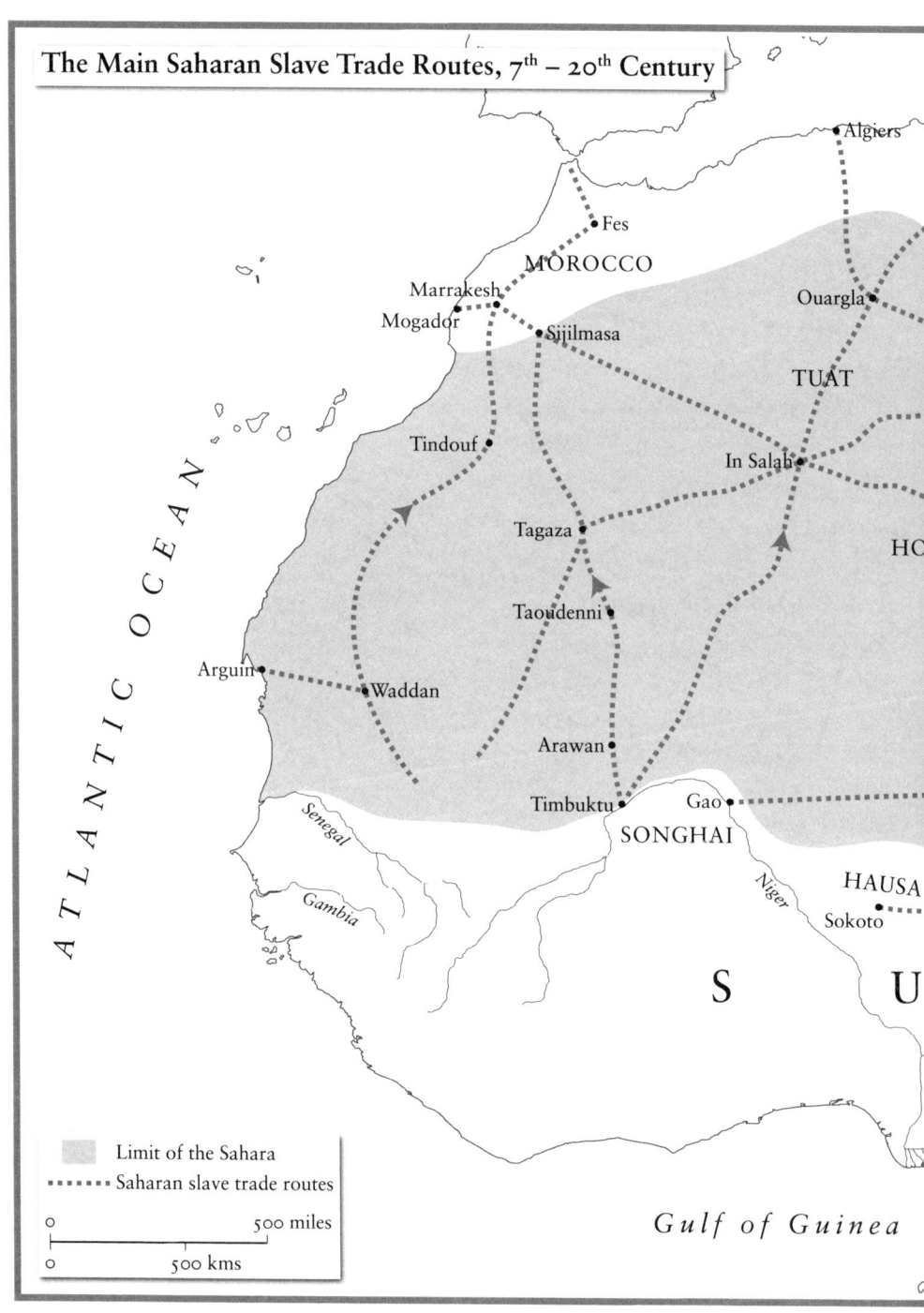

The Main Saharan Slave Trade Routes, 7ᵗʰ – 20ᵗʰ Century

Algiers

Fes

MOROCCO

Ouargla

Marrakesh

Mogador

Sijilmasa

TUAT

Tindouf

In Salah

HO

Tagaza

Taoudenni

A T L A N T I C   O C E A N

Arguin

Waddan

Arawan

Timbuktu

Gao

SONGHAI

Senegal

Niger

HAUSA

Gambia

Sokoto

S

U

Gulf of Guinea

Limit of the Sahara

Saharan slave trade routes

500 miles

500 kms

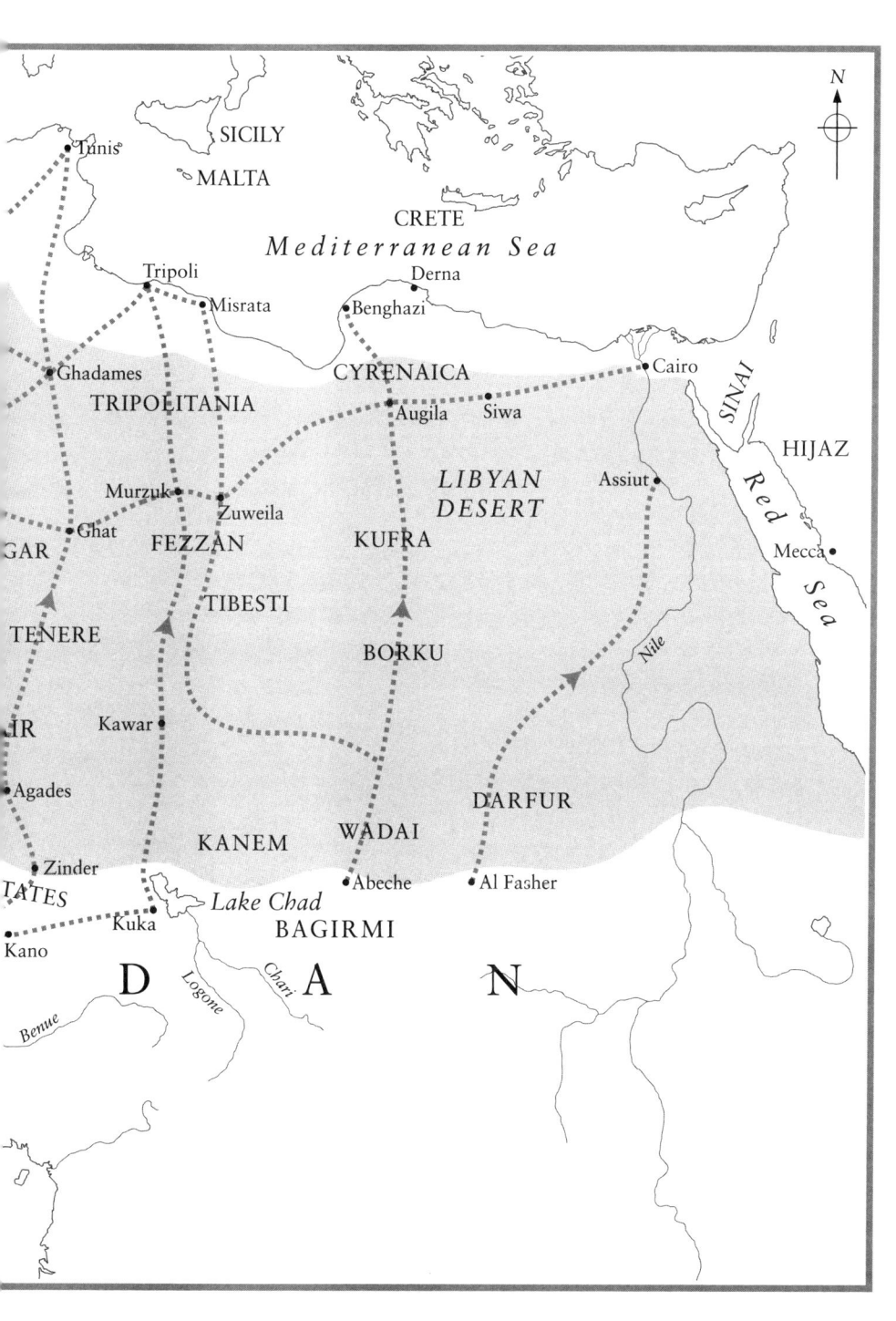

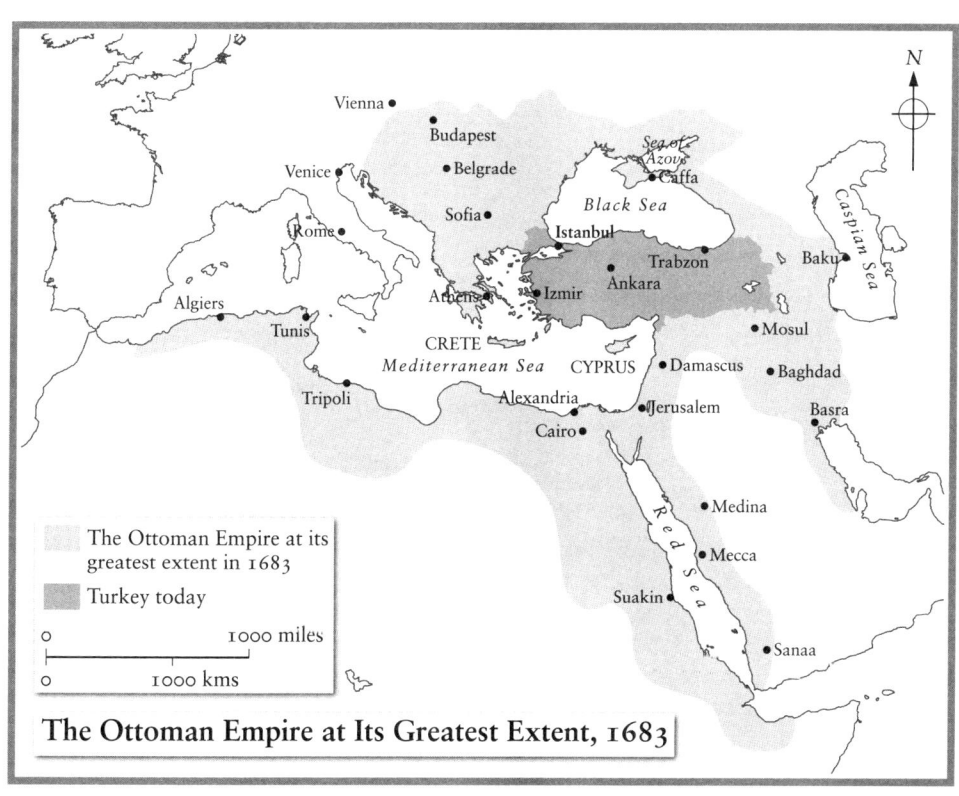

N

Vienna

Budapest

Belgrade

Venice

Sofia

Rome

Sea of Azov

Caffa

Black Sea

Istanbul

Trabzon

Baku

Caspian Sea

Algiers

Athens

Izmir

Ankara

Tunis

CRETE

Mediterranean Sea

CYPRUS

Damascus

Mosul

Baghdad

Tripoli

Alexandria

Jerusalem

Basra

Cairo

Medina

Mecca

Suakin

Red Sea

Sanaa

The Ottoman Empire at its greatest extent in 1683

Turkey today

0   1000 miles

0   1000 kms

The Ottoman Empire at Its Greatest Extent, 1683

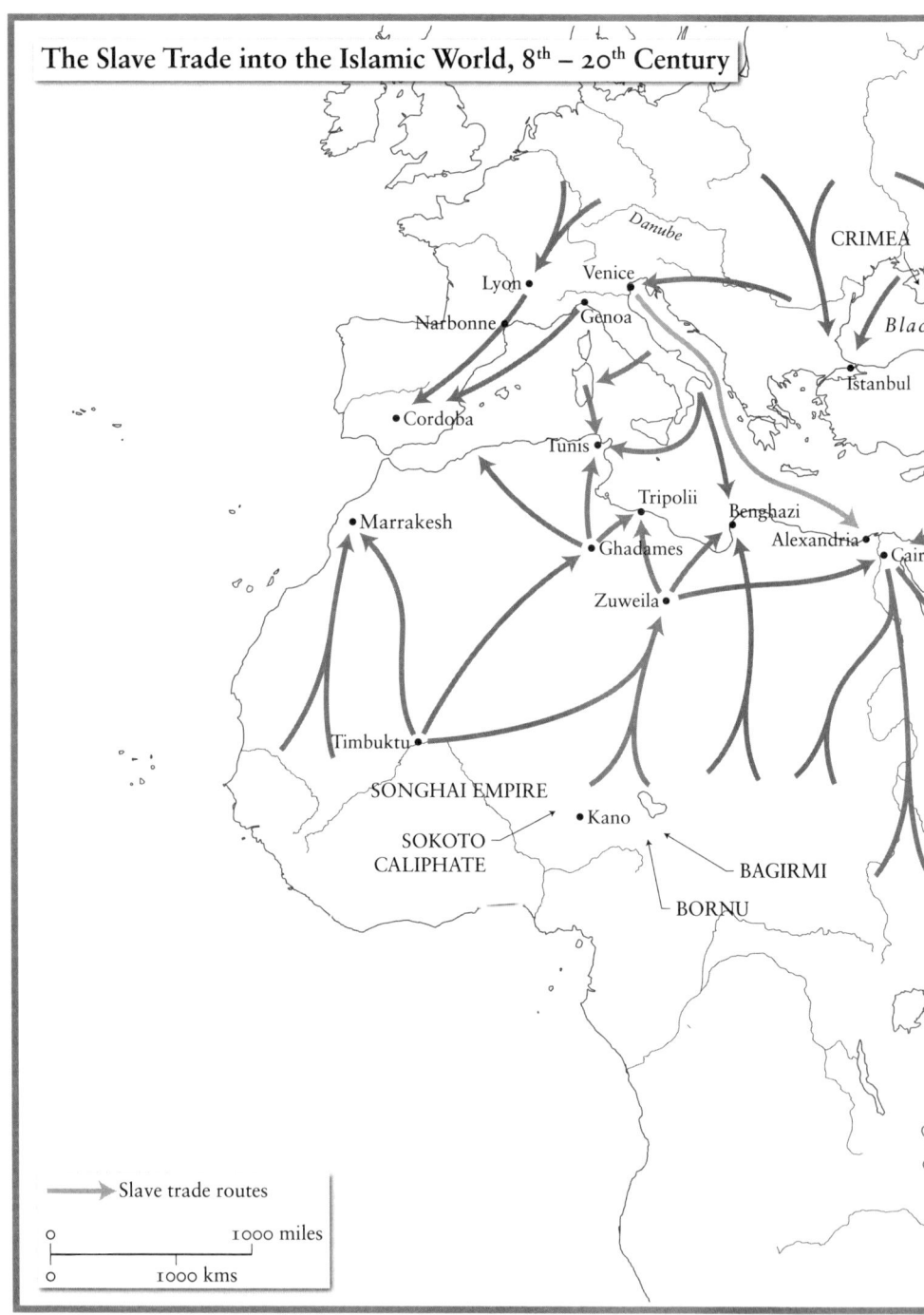

The Slave Trade into the Islamic World, 8th – 20th Century

Danube

CRIMEA

Lyon

Venice

Blac

Narbonne

Genoa

Istanbul

Cordoba

Tunis

Tripoli

Benghazi

Marrakesh

Ghadames

Alexandria

Cair

Zuweila

Timbuktu

SONGHAI EMPIRE

Kano

SOKOTO
CALIPHATE

BAGIRMI

BORNU

Slave trade routes

| | 1000 miles |
| 1000 kms |

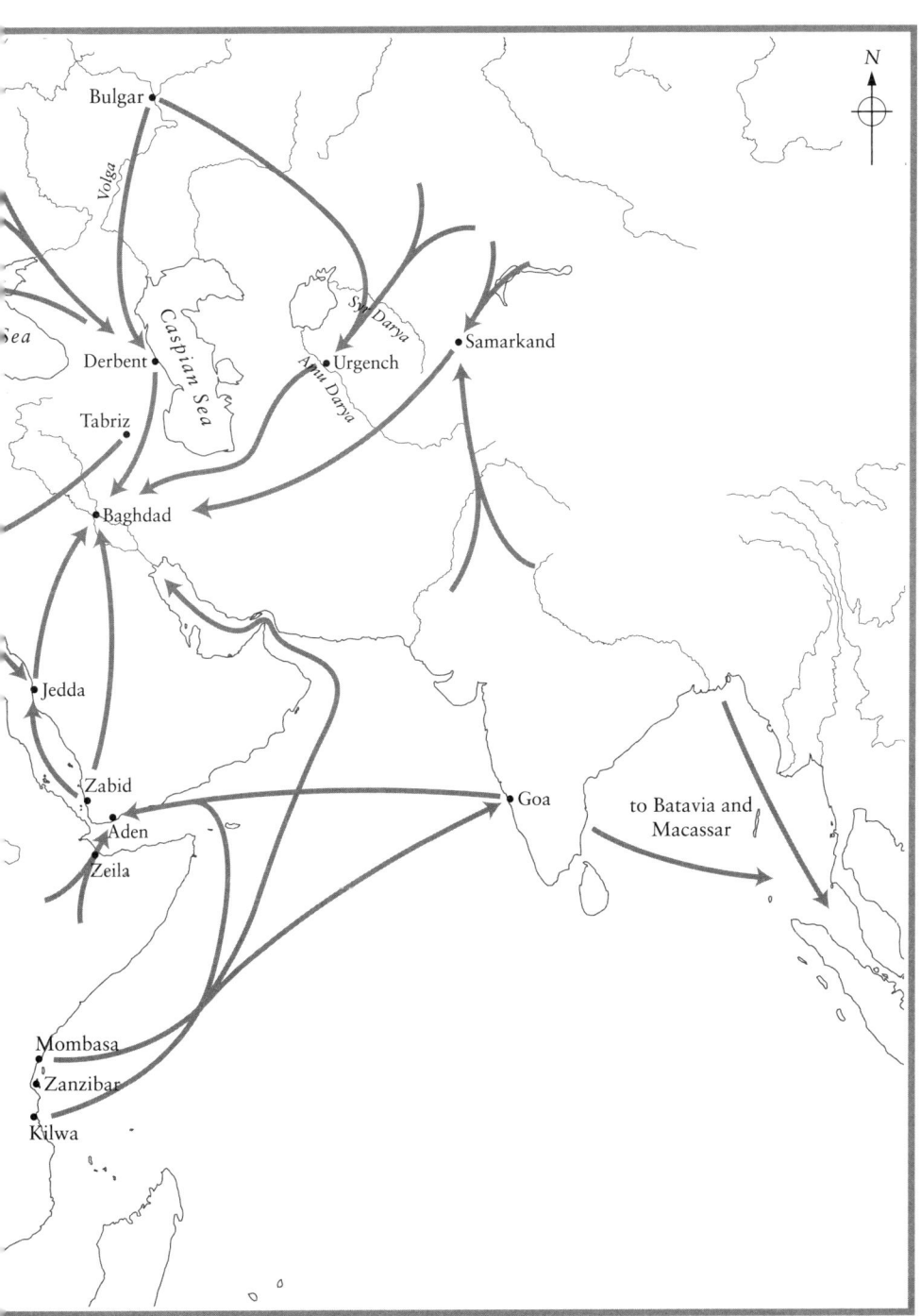

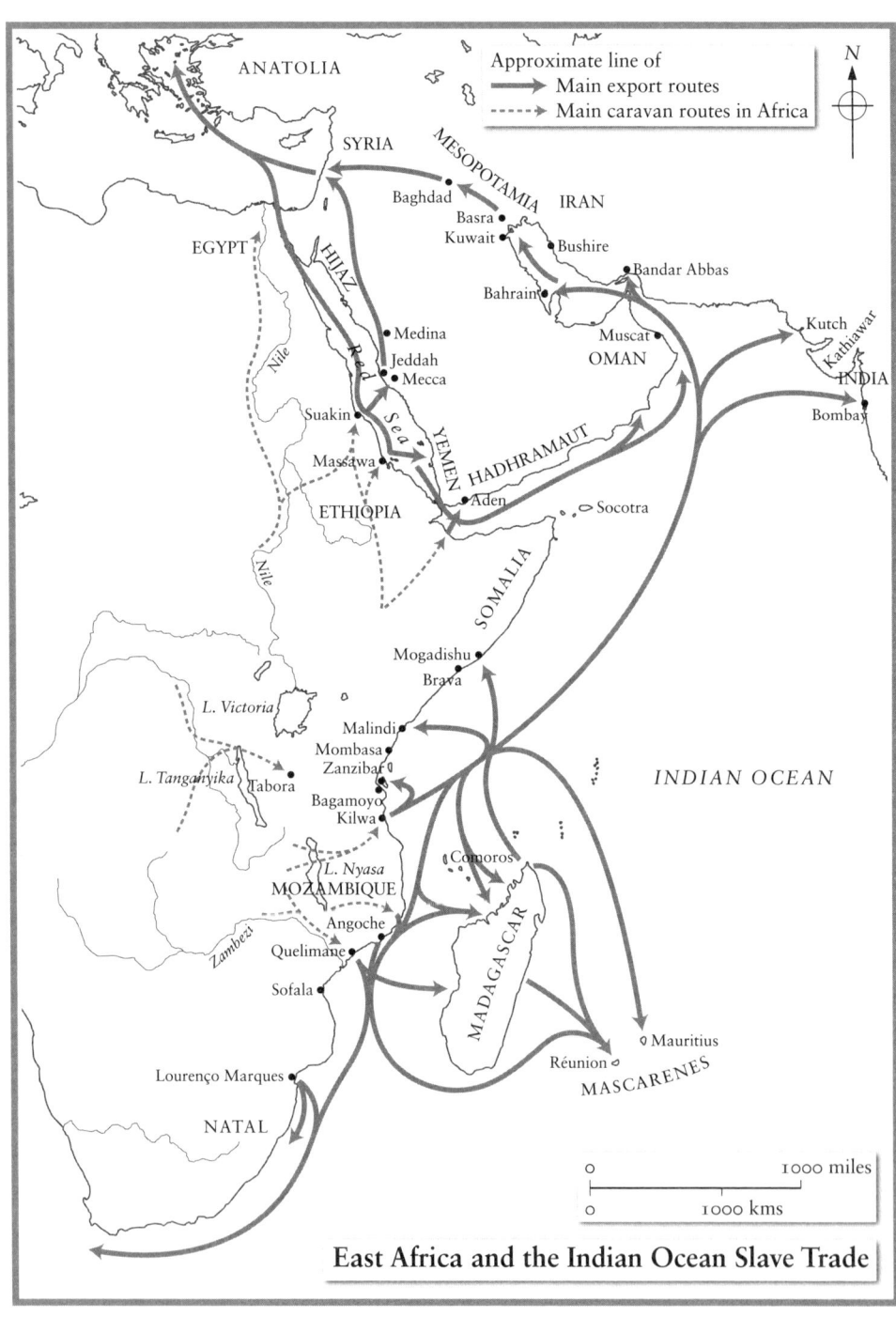

East Africa and the Indian Ocean Slave Trade

Prologue

It all started on the evening of 18 August 2018. At seventeen minutes past six, in a small village near the city of Kayes in western Mali, a group of young men armed with wooden batons and leather whips surrounded Hamey and attacked him.

'They ripped off my clothes and while I lay naked in the dirt, they whipped me and kicked me and beat me in public. Everyone was watching. The whole community. They were cheering and filming it all on their phones. It lasted for hours.'

Hamey – not his real name – is in tears as he relives the ordeal he suffered two years ago. It is an annihilating moment, suffocating with misery. He is in his late fifties, his ragged clothes are colandered with holes and he is ashamed to discuss his desperate plight.

We are sitting on the mud floor of a half-finished, fly-riddled, breeze-block shack on the outskirts of the Malian capital of Bamako, where he, his two wives and their twelve children have sought temporary refuge. He is hollowed out with emotion. There is pain in every word. 'Look at my situation,' he says, sobbing, 'look how we're living.'

Hamey was one of many slaves in a village which for hundreds of years has been – and, even in the twenty-first century, continues to be – brutally divided between slave-owners and slaves. Kayes is one of the most notorious regions in Mali to cling on to hereditary slavery. In this traditional rural community, generations of enslaved men and women have toiled in the fields for their masters, slaughtered and butchered animals for community rituals, cleaned houses, served families and performed all manner of menial and humiliating tasks. Women are routinely raped by the man of the house.

Precise figures for the number of enslaved men, women and children in Mali are especially difficult to reach, but Temedt, the country's oldest anti-slavery organization, which has arranged this meeting, estimates there are around a million people in this condition. Hereditary slavery has endured for close to a millennium here and its defenders continue to resist, often viciously, all attempts to put an end to it. These are our cultural traditions, they argue. Who are you to stop them? A few days before this interview, four anti-slavery activists were lynched in Djandjoumé, another village in Kayes.

> I had no choice in any of this. I didn't choose to be a slave. My father was a slave, my grandfather was a slave and many more generations before them were slaves.
>
> I was born into slavery, I considered myself a slave, and I was a slave until the day I refused to go on. I'd had enough of it. And that's when the violence began.

Hamey says he resisted all the attempts to subdue him – the constant threats and intimidation. Then, on the instructions of the village elders and without warning, the young men from the community's slave-owning families turned to violence:

> They took me to the village leader's compound and they asked me in front of everyone, 'So you don't want to be a slave any more?' And I said, no, I didn't. So they got out their clubs and whips and started beating and whipping me. The head of the village was determined to keep slavery going in his area. He said, 'We've had it here for hundreds of years, why should we stop now?'

Covered in blood, severely bruised and nursing broken bones, Hamey dragged himself home.

'Then the youths rushed to my house and drove me and my family out. They took my cows, my goats and my sheep. Suddenly I had nothing, but I still had everyone to feed.'

The family spent four months on the run, almost starving and plagued with thirst, reduced to scraps of food and dirty water whenever and wherever they could find them. Later, Hamey discovered that some among the mob which had attacked him had posted the film of his beating online.

'The mayor of the village was very angry with them. He said to them, "If you'd just killed him quietly, no one would have ever heard about this. Now everyone will know."'

Apart from the physical abuse he suffered, both during that ferocious attack and over the years that preceded it, Hamey is still scarred by one of the most sickening aspects of slavery in Mali, the equivalent of medieval Europe's *droit du seigneur*.

'They can take our wives and daughters whenever they like. I could never, ever accept that. It's rape. My master used to tell me, "She may be your wife but I can take her whenever I want her." He had the right to have sex with her.'

And he is traumatized, too, by what he says is the government's de facto acceptance of slavery and the violence it entails, as evidenced by the lack of action taken against the perpetrators. The mayor condoned the violence and supports slavery:

> Of all those men who beat me and humiliated me in public, no one was ever charged, no one was ever prosecuted. There is no justice here. The government basically encourages slavery. And the slave-masters think that slavery is a tradition which should necessarily continue until the end of time.

Hamey does not say so, but it is clear from his story that he has sacrificed his life for that of his children. He has no future. His life is over. As an illiterate runaway slave with virtually no education, with no possibility of ever returning home, he can only contemplate the sort of manual work for which, as a middle-aged man, crushed by his ordeal and still recovering from the assault, he is no longer physically capable.

'Deep down I'm free,' he says, though there is no joy in the words. 'Whatever my financial worries, I'm free. Live or die, I'll never be a slave again.'

Hamey is crippled with worry over his family's future. His wives are going door to door in the neighbourhood, taking in dirty laundry in their desperation to feed the children. The family is about to lose the roof over their heads, because the owner of this shack has just sold the building. He doesn't know where they will go next. Hamey will throw himself on the mercy of Temedt which, like so many charitable organizations in one of the world's poorest countries, is overstretched. He doesn't know what the future holds, but he is under no illusions.

'I have too much pain in my heart,' he tells me as we say goodbye. 'I'm closer to despair than hope.'

Bamako, 29 November 2020.

A Note on Sources

Any historian investigating slavery during the very first years of Islam is immediately confronted with a formidable challenge. It is the same difficulty facing anyone exploring social, political, economic and military life on the Arabian Peninsula in the seventh century and it is this: the earliest Muslim sources need to be treated with a significant degree of caution. In the absence of much archaeological evidence, without a wealth of inscriptions, coins or papyri to substantiate the official record, we have to depend on a number of Muslim scholars writing from around the mid-eighth century at the earliest, a minimum of 120 years or so after the death of the Prophet Mohammed in 632. Since these are the only substantial, book-length literary sources available, and notwithstanding their evident limitations, such as partiality, we must respect them and base our understandings upon them, while subjecting them to the usual critical historical inquiry and interpretation.

To take one important example, *Sirat Rasul Allah (Life of The Messenger of God)*, the earliest surviving biography of Mohammed, was written by Ibn Ishaq (*c.*704–*c.*67), who compiled it for the Abbasid caliph Al Mansur (r. 754–75), leader of the Islamic world, in the later eighth century. Ibn Ishaq was a collector of oral traditions about the Prophet, which formed the basis of his ground-breaking narrative biography. Then there was Mohammed ibn Saad (*c.*784–845), author of *Kitab al Tabaqat al Kabir (The Book of the Major Classes)*, an eight-volume collection of biographies of the most famous Muslim figures, above all the Prophet Mohammed and his Companions, Helpers and Followers. One of his volumes is dedicated to the Muslim victors of the Battle of Badr in 624, the first time in history a Muslim army had been put into the field, under Mohammed's leadership. Mohammed ibn Jarir al Tabari (839–923), the great Arab historian bar none, was putting the finishing touches to his magisterial thirty-nine-volume, 10,000-page *Tarikh al Rusul wa al Muluk (History of the Prophets and Kings)*, a key primary source including much material on the early Islamic era, only in 915.

All three scholars, writing from such distance, are critical sources for the lives and times of Islam's first slaves, as for much early Muslim history in general. The reliability of each can be questioned. Biography can tilt into hagiography.

Muddying the historical waters further, the principal source for the birth of Islam in and around Mecca in the early decades of the seventh century is Quranic exegesis, which brings its own problems of dating and interpretation. The earliest Muslim source on Mecca and its holy site of the Kaaba, to take another example, is Al Azraqi, the ninth-century editor of *Kitab Akhbar Makka (Book of Reports about Mecca)*, the first Arabic history of a single city. Azraqi claimed that the sacred stone dated back to the very beginning of time, before creation itself. 'The Kaaba was the froth on the water forty years before God Almighty created the heavens and the earth; from it the earth was spread out,' he wrote.[1]

For many Muslims these traditional accounts of the early years of Islam are accepted as completely authoritative sources and are beyond argument. In some quarters, challenges to them can be viewed as offensive or even as an attack on Islam. One person's legitimate historical inquiry is another's unpardonable offence to the Prophet. However, increasingly from the late twentieth century, a generation of more sceptical Western non-Muslim scholars have begun to question these earliest histories of Islam. They have directly challenged some of these sources, arguing that they should be regarded not so much as clear historical accounts as literary constructions, written long after the events they describe and with a clear agenda – to construct the edifice of Islam on strong, unimpeachable foundations.[2]

The potted biographies of some of the first Muslims, and the first Muslim slaves, pose as many questions as they provide answers. The lives of the three men and one woman which begin this book are recreated from close readings of some of these earliest, most important and partial Muslim sources. The life story of a leading figure like Salman al Farsi, the slave, soldier, diplomat and Companion to the Prophet, for instance, is vanishingly elusive. Read his entry in the *Encyclopaedia of Islam* and you could be forgiven for wondering whether he even existed – or at least whether the details of his life as recorded in the sources, such as a lifespan of 553, have been shaded into legend.

Moving from the earliest days of Islam towards the other end of our chronological spectrum, there is a sudden and dramatic expansion in the range of historical sources, especially from the nineteenth century. Valuable information can be gleaned from legal documents, including marriage contracts, wills, court cases, such as those between an enslaved person and a slave dealer or owner, manumission papers, tax papers, budgets and government directives.[3] They offer a welcome harvest of detail and information, especially statistics, which are otherwise frustratingly thin on the ground for the vast majority of the long period under review here, from the birth of Islam to today.

They also inevitably raise questions of bias and prejudice, particularly when it comes to Western observers – European and American diplomats, abolitionists, Christian missionaries, travellers and writers – passing judgement on slavery and the slave trade, often heavily influenced by Western perspectives on the Atlantic version, not to mention on Muslims and the Islamic faith, within the Ottoman Empire. The same could equally be said for medieval Arab Muslim attitudes towards Africans, which are also recorded here in some detail.

But what of the enslaved themselves? Where are their voices and why are they invariably crowded out by Western, mostly European, sources? The fact remains that, for all the strides made by historians in recent decades, the documentary evidence overwhelmingly privileges these external commentators. When they do appear, which is all too infrequently, the voices of enslaved men and women can emerge with extraordinary force and clarity, whether it is a full-length captivity narrative published in the USA, a one-paragraph manumission statement delivered to a British official in the Gulf, or testimony given to police investigators in Cairo. Yet a fundamental caveat remains: even when they do appear, such voices tend to make themselves heard indirectly, mediated by mostly European and American travellers, explorers, diplomats, officials, abolitionists, journalists, editors and publishers. Pioneering work by historians such as Ehud Toledano and Eve Troutt Powell has broken new ground in recovering and reconstructing these first-person stories, but the challenge remains.[4]

This book seeks to highlight, as much as possible, the voices of the enslaved and dwells on their first-person experiences and memories, whatever the limitations. There are, among other accounts, those of exceptional concubines in ninth-century Abbasid Baghdad; a fifteenth-century Andalusian poet writing from his captivity on the Iberian Peninsula; European and American men and women captured and enslaved by Mediterranean pirates and corsairs in the eighteenth and nineteenth centuries; a Circassian concubine detailing the abuse she suffered at the hands of an unscrupulous slave-dealer in Egypt in the mid-nineteenth century; a retired agricultural worker in Algeria reflecting in the 1940s on his childhood capture and enslavement; one of the last African eunuchs to serve in the Ottoman court, recalling in 1938 the agony of his castration as a young boy; pearl-divers appearing in the 1930s at the doors of the British Political Agencies along the Trucial Coast to record their manumission statements. It goes without saying that these sources can never be sufficient – they are too elusive, fragmentary and filtered – and the story of slavery in the Islamic world is necessarily incomplete and imbalanced. But that does not mean it should not be attempted.

Away from the partial and contentious documentary record, and in addition to several decades writing about and living and working in the Muslim world, long periods in Egypt, Sudan, Somalia, Morocco, Tunisia, Iraq, Syria, Jordan, Lebanon, Yemen, the United Arab Emirates, Pakistan, Afghanistan and Uzbekistan have all helped inform my understanding of this difficult subject. I have supplemented my studies with additional research and reporting in Libya, Turkey, Oman, Qatar, Mali and Mauritania to bring this neglected and compelling story into the twenty-first century.

A Note on Spelling

Is it to be Mohammed, Muhammad or Mahomet? Should it be the Quran, Koran or Qur'an? Transliterating Arabic is fraught with danger and can be a pedant's paradise. There are various systems for 'precise' Arabic transliteration, but they are generally very complicated and have little to recommend them aesthetically. My aim has been to make things as simple and comprehensible as possible for the general reader. I do not wish to throw diacritical marks all over the text like confetti, a dot beneath an 's' and an 'h' here, a line above an 'i' or an 'a' there, apostrophes and hyphens crowding in like unwelcome visitors. Asked to choose between *Tārīkh al-'Irāq bayna iḥtilālayn* (Abbas al Azzawi's *History of Iraq Between Two Occupations*) and *Tarikh al Iraq bayn al Ihtilayn*, I choose the latter without hesitation. Similarly, rather than *Kitāb al-Hayawān*, for Jahiz's famous *Book of Animals*, which is included among the illustrations, I prefer *Kitab al Hayawan*. Likewise for Turkish, generally I favour the simplicity of *Suleymanname*, the history of the great, sixteenth-century Ottoman sultan, over *Süleymannâme*. And yet we have Çandarlı Halil, not Candarli Halil, because that is how the fifteenth-century grand vizier's name is always spelt, and Beyoğlu, which not everyone will know is pronounced Bay-o-lu.

I have transliterated the guttural Arabic letter qaf or ق as 'q', rather than 'k' – unlike in some of my previous books, where I did the opposite, so am already guilty of inconsistency. When it comes to the problematic letter 'ayn or ع – virtually unpronounceable for those who do not know Arabic, I have (mostly) chosen to render it as 'aa', rather than either ''a', or even '3' – because what does an apostrophe, or for that matter '3', really mean to the reader who does not know

Arabic or the complexities of Arabic pronunciation? Arabic experts will surely know what is meant, and others will hardly notice its absence. Ma'mun becomes simply Maamun (in an earlier book he was Mamun), the Shafi'i school of Islamic jurisprudence becomes Shafi, but *sharı'ah* or *šarī'ah* becomes *sharia*, because that, rather than *shariaa*, will be most familiar to the general reader. And عبد, a slave, becomes *abd*, not aabd or 'abd.

I prefer not to hyphenate the definite article, so I have Al Mansur rather than Al-Mansur at the first mention, Mansur thereafter. Men and women all over the world spell their names differently and here I am happy to take my lead from the people themselves. So an Ahmed can be an Ahmad, if that is what he prefers, or perhaps even an Ahmet. And the late, great Turkish historian Halil İnalcik must rightfully retain that spelling of his name.

Eagle-eyed readers will surely find a number of other departures here from the most rigorous modern scholarly practice. 'There are some "scientific systems" of transliteration, helpful to people who know enough Arabic not to need helping, but a wash-out for the world,' T. E. Lawrence once wrote to the despairing editor of *Seven Pillars of Wisdom*, who was questioning the author's complete lack of consistency. 'I spell my names anyhow, to show what rot the systems are.' I would not dream of suggesting these systems are rot, but I would rather plead guilty to inconsistency than to confusing readers unnecessarily. And, to answer the question with which I began, the Prophet is Mohammed and the holy book revealed to him by Allah is the Quran.

Introduction

It is probably true to say that for every gallon of ink that has been spilt on the transatlantic slave trade and its consequences, only one very small drop has been spilt on the study of the forced migration of black Africans into the Mediterranean world of Islam and the broader question of slavery within Muslim societies.

John Hunwick, 'The Same but Different:
Africans in Slavery in the Mediterranean Muslim World.'[1]

A quarter of a century ago, my first book took me by camel across the largest hot desert on earth. The route followed some of the most historically significant slave-trading routes through the Sahara, along which, for more than a millennium, vast numbers of men, women and children had been trafficked north, typically in dreadful conditions, for onward sale across the Mediterranean and much of the Middle East.

My interest then was in mixing history with travelogue: it was in part an investigation, at the close of the twentieth century, of the nineteenth-century European, especially British, colonial penetration of Africa, also exploring the ancient desert slave trade and the experiences of the enslaved. The result was *South from Barbary: Along the Slave Routes of the Libyan Sahara*, published in 2001.

In the years since, I have continued to write about enslavement in the *Dar al Islam* – the Islamic world – generally in the margins of wider research. The subject featured, to a greater or lesser extent, in all my subsequent work, from studies of Tamerlane and Herodotus to histories of Baghdad, Islamic empires and the great Arab Conquests of the seventh and eighth centuries. But it had never been centre-stage.

Over time, I came to see this as reflecting the continued prominence within Western public discourse, especially within academic circles and the media, of enslavement in the American South and of the Atlantic slave trade over all other systems of slavery and the trade in human beings. Search the word 'slavery', for example, and Wikipedia's first entry is on the United States. Do the same for 'slave trade', and it is the Atlantic slave trade which comes up first. The literary focus is similar. *A Short History of Slavery*, published in 2007, typifies the heavy concentration on the US experience. Of the book's 235 pages, 201 focus on the Americas.[2] This is perhaps not surprising, as the exploration and recovery of the history of enslavement in the Americas and the Atlantic slave trade have been one of the great scholarly achievements of the past half-century and have brought about a huge change in public awareness.

Although there have been significant strides in recent years, particularly among a younger generation of non-Western scholars, there is still a comparative scarcity of general studies of enslavement and the slave trade in the Islamic world and a corresponding lack of awareness. This is something I thought worth addressing.

For these reasons, it is worth emphasizing at the outset, especially for American readers, that this is not a book about antebellum slavery in the American South. While there may be occasional and fleeting comparisons with plantation slavery, there is no detailed exploration in these pages of this extremely well-researched field. The focus throughout is on the geographical and historical heart of the Islamic world, including its sometimes fraught and bloody interaction with the West. To be clear, this history dwells on the core territories of North Africa, the eastern Mediterranean and the Middle East, with a close examination of sub-Saharan Africa, East Africa, Eastern Europe, the Balkans and the Caucasus. It does not include the populous Muslim nations and communities of South Asia and Southeast Asia, whose long histories of slavery could easily fill another book in their own right.

The combination of this already broad geographical scope with the widest chronological range – from the birth of Islam on the Arabian Peninsula in the seventh century to lingering examples of hereditary racialized slavery and disturbing campaigns of enslavement in the twenty-first – requires a careful balance between comprehensive detail and narrative thrust. This book, which is intended for the general reader, aims to provide the overarching information necessary to convey the complexities and nuances of many important themes – such as theological underpinnings, the use of concubines and eunuchs, manumission and abolition – without being overly exhaustive or detracting from the richness of individual stories which lie at the heart of the institution of slavery and from which we draw our own lessons and conclusions.

It goes without saying that slavery was never unique to the USA. On the contrary, it has been almost universal. It existed under the Shang dynasty of China (sixteenth to eleventh centuries BCE), in ancient Egypt, India, Africa, Europe and the Americas, and was an everyday reality in numerous societies. Writing in the fifth century BCE, the Ancient Greek historian Herodotus famously, and probably erroneously, recounted that the pyramids at Giza, which date to around 2,570 BCE, were built by slave labour.* Both Ancient Rome and Ancient Greece were slave-owning societies. The Vikings were slavers on a grand scale, too, so much so that the kidnapping, sale and forced exploitation of men, women and children was always a defining pillar of their culture. In 1841, to give a much later example, British colonial administrators estimated the slave population of India at 8 million to 9 million.[3]

Slavery in the Islamic world was not a constant and unchanging phenomenon. It evolved over time and was a dynamic institution which took on very different forms in different periods. It was shaped by changing circumstances, economic conditions, domestic and agricultural needs, international market forces and military requirements

---

* The etymology of the word 'slave' makes a fascinating, complicated and disputed history. From Slav as the commonly understood designation of origin follows Latin *sclavus*, Arabic *saqaliba*, Byzantine *sklavenos*, Italian *schiavo*, French and Occitan *esclave*. But it is not as straightforward as that. 'Saqaliba, Slav/slave may have started as an ethnic origin (a Slav) or an enslaved person of that origin or appearance, and later designates any unfree person with no indication of origin,' writes Anna Kłosowska. In Arabic, a number of words designating enslaved persons also refer specifically to their origin or appearance – thus *saqlabi/saqaliba* (Slav/s), *sudan* (African), *abd/abid* (black), *mamluk/mamalik* (thing/s or person/s possessed). See Anna Kłosowska, 'The Etymology of Slave' in *Disturbing Times: Medieval Pasts, Reimagined Futures*.

foremost among them. In the earliest days of Islam, for example, it proliferated as conquering Arab warriors enslaved defeated adversaries, together with their women and children. Captured women could become slave concubines, one of the longest-lasting forms of enslavement. Eunuchs, highly prized and extensively used by both the Byzantines and Persians, nearest neighbours and enemies of seventh-century Arab Muslims, were another early category whose last survivors lived on in twenty-first-century Saudi Arabia. Slave soldiers meanwhile endured for more than a millennium, from those who took up arms alongside the Prophet Mohammed in the seventh century to the last of the once-mighty Mamluks, who were gunned down in Cairo and Baghdad in the nineteenth.

Outside the domestic sphere, slavery also developed in response to specific economic demand as the requirement for free or cheap productive labour rose and fell over time. Wars, drought and famine, expanding empires, growing urban populations, the prevalence of manumission, low rates of reproduction among enslaved men and women, together with the surging demand in the later nineteenth century, and into the twentieth, for commodities such as cotton, cloves, copra, coconuts, dates, pearls and ivory, all affected the demand for slaves over different periods. Devastating African famines in the eighteenth century, for example, resulted in a short-term jump in slave exports as desperate parents sold their children into slavery. Some adults even chose – though, given their destitution, it seems more accurate to say they were forced – to exchange their freedom for slavery to escape starvation. During another severe famine in East Africa in the 1880s, large numbers of slaves entering the market depressed prices as people sold their families into slavery.[4]

In recent years there has been increasing attention from scholars on the trade in the late nineteenth and early twentieth centuries, when increasing numbers of enslaved Africans were exported to Egypt and the Gulf to work in those expanding agricultural sectors. Although it is surely right to emphasize the global economic, rather than the 'Islamic', nature of this trade, it is nevertheless worth noting that this short period was part of an unbroken history of slavery and the slave trade in the region which endured for more than 1,300 years.[5]

The institution expanded and contracted, in other words, within certain conditions and specific systems of production which provided the economic incentives for enslavement and slave labour. This was most manifest in agricultural slavery, especially during the nineteenth century, which is unfortunately by far the least documented, studied and understood category. With few exceptions, the glimpses in the sources are only brief and tantalizing.

We find, for example, large numbers of enslaved Africans scraping off nitrous topsoil to reclaim land in the southern marshes of Iraq in the ninth century; 'thirty thousand Zanzibari and Abyssinian slaves' working in the fields and orchards of the Al Hasa oasis of eastern Arabia in the eleventh;[6] unknown numbers cultivating Omani sugar-cane in the seventeenth; tens of thousands of Africans labouring in Egyptian cotton plantations, Omani and Yemeni date farms and Zanzibari clove plantations in the nineteenth; and a multinational cast of enslaved men from Africa, India, Iran and the Arabian Peninsula diving for pearls in the Gulf in the nineteenth and twentieth.

To these principal forms of agricultural work could be added a range of hard auxiliary labour, from masonry and quarrying to digging and maintaining wells and irrigation channels. It remains the case, however, that 'relatively little' is known today about agricultural slavery and further research in this area is needed. In the absence of more information, it is inevitable that there has been far greater focus on 'elite' forms of slavery, including royal concubines, eunuchs and slave soldiers.[7]

Slavery as an institution has demonstrated extraordinary longevity. It has continued into the modern era, declining, but never entirely disappearing, over the past several centuries. As late as the early 1950s, the first workers in the Qatari oil sector were enslaved men who were required to surrender as much as 90 per cent of their earnings to their owners.[8] Some of the last countries to formally abolish slavery came from the Muslim world, from Iran (1928), Yemen (1962) and Saudi Arabia (1962) to Turkey (1964), Oman (1970) and Mauritania (1981). Yet still it lingers. 'Saudi Arabia has the highest prevalence of modern slavery of all countries in the Arab States region,' states Walk Free, the international human rights group focused on the eradication of modern slavery, in its 2023 report on the country. It estimates that there were then 740,000 people 'living in modern slavery' there.[9] Here and in other parts of the Gulf, the highly restrictive conditions faced by some migrant workers under the controversial *kafala* system blur the lines between forced labour and slavery.* Despite its formal illegality, hereditary slavery persists today in both Mali and Mauritania.

Slavery in Africa long predated the Atlantic slave trade. For many centuries, the continent was – and, on a hugely diminished scale, still is – a source of enslaved men, women and children for a number of civilizations, ranging from India and the Islamic world to the Americas. From 1076 to 1600, an estimated one-third of the population of Muslim Ghana was enslaved, while from 1300 to 1900 around the same proportion of the Senegambia region (present-day Senegal, the Gambia and Guinea-Bissau, together with parts of Mauritania, Guinea and Mali) was in servitude. At times those figures rose considerably. Thus between 1750 and 1900, somewhere between one- and two-thirds of the Fulani jihad states of western and central Sudan consisted of slaves. By the time of the outbreak of the American Civil War in 1861, 'there were probably more slaves in the Muslim states of West Africa than in the Confederacy, or indeed in Cuba and Brazil'.[10]

The Atlantic slave trade lasted from the fifteenth to the nineteenth centuries. During that time between 11 million and 14 million Africans were enslaved. The slave trade practised within the geographical heart of the Muslim world, centred on North Africa and the Middle East, dates back to the seventh century, endured openly until the twentieth and, more covertly and in much smaller numbers, continues today. It sourced men, women and children overwhelmingly from sub-Saharan Africa, together with Eastern Europe, the Balkans and the Caucasus during the Ottoman period. The number of people captured and enslaved during these fourteen centuries, forcibly removed from their families to do service in foreign households, harems, armies and other occupations, approximates to the total captured and sold into slavery in the Atlantic slave trade – something in the order of 12 million to

---

* 'The *kafala* is a sponsorship system that applies to migrant workers in several Middle Eastern countries. It appeared with the discovery of oil and the regional development it stimulated. Simply put, the system ties the migrant worker to the *kafil* (sponsor).' See Asma Azhari, 'The *Kafala* "Sponsorship" System in Saudi Arabia: A Critical Analysis from the Perspective of International Human Rights and Islamic Law', *SOAS Journal of Postgraduate Research*, 2016–17.

15 million. That may be an underestimate. According to one study of human trafficking in North Africa, the Middle East and India, the Arab slave trade from 650 to 1905 enslaved an estimated 17 million.[11] It transformed societies and terrorized lives across huge tracts of the continent, especially in West, East, North and sub-Saharan Africa.

Studies of slavery and the slave trade within the Islamic world have consistently lagged behind those examining American planta-tion slavery and the Atlantic slave trade. As recently as the turn of the twenty-first century, Ehud Toledano, an expert on slavery in the Ottoman Empire, could observe that academic study of the history of slavery in Ottoman society and in the wider Muslim world was characterized by 'a deafening silence'. Around the same time, the Turkish historian Yusuf Hakan Erdem diagnosed a near-total 'collect-ive amnesia' about Ottoman slavery. So long in fact is the *longue durée* of slavery in the Ottoman Empire that its history really deserves an entire book, rather than the two chapters it receives here. Going back a little earlier, the late Anglo-American scholar Bernard Lewis reckoned it was 'professionally hazardous' for a young scholar to focus on slavery in Muslim societies. Such research was often consid-ered 'a sign of hostile intentions'. While a bibliography of slavery in Ancient Greece, Rome and the Americas ran into thousands of pages, he noted, the equivalent for the central Islamic lands could be printed on a single page.[12]

That was over thirty years ago. A new generation of scholars, including Moroccan, Tunisian, Algerian and especially Turkish researchers, has been making important inroads since then, debating slavery, slave-trading and abolition, although much of the Arab world continues to look the other way.[13] And while it is no longer true that the issue has been virtually ignored in the West, or that there is 'a con-spiracy of silence' on the subject, as Murray Gordon argued in *Slavery in the Arab World*, it nevertheless remains the case that this critically important branch of the history of international slavery is decidedly the poor relation by comparison with the richly mined history of American slavery and the Atlantic slave trade. A recent study of the life of Fezzeh Khanom, an enslaved African woman in nineteenth-century Iran, for example, begins with the words: 'The history of slavery in Iran has yet to be written.' In a study of the trans-Saharan slave trade,

John Wright detected 'a selective historical amnesia' about slavery among Arab scholars and a 'certain reluctance' to acknowledge it. More recently, Zeinab Badawi has argued in a history of Africa that there has been 'little, if any, meaningful discussion in Arab countries' on the subject. While Arab societies benefited enormously over many centuries from 'the blood, sweat and tears of African labour,' there has been no public debate on slavery reparations to mirror those in Europe and North America. 'The silence must be broken.'[14]

Why should any of this matter? Why is this apparently obscure history worthy of attention? These are questions a reasonable person might well ask. To which the answer must be that it is essential to understand this immense network of human trafficking for a number of reasons. First, its sheer scale shows that this was no fringe affair. In terms of the numbers of people enslaved it was on a par with the slave trade to the Americas. Second, it was not a short-lived business that fizzled out after a brief flourish long ago. It lasted almost 1,400 years, far longer than the Atlantic trade. And finally, it is necessary to examine it because it continues – and even flourishes – in parts of the Muslim world today, openly in some places, behind closed doors and through private messages on smartphone apps in others. This will be discussed in the final chapter on modern slavery.

Islam did not conceive slavery in the Middle East, any more than Christianity devised it on the shores of the Atlantic. It is just as wrong to call this phenomenon the Muslim slave trade as it would be to call its Atlantic version the Christian slave trade. Muslim Arabs, surrounded by the ancient slaving civilizations of the Byzantines and Persians, inherited the traditions of slavery from their pagan Arabian forebears and then adapted and refined the institution in an Islamic context.

One of the defining features of slavery as it evolved in the Islamic world, which contributes greatly to its extraordinarily rich and compelling history, was the sheer fluidity of slave status. This dynamic environment, in which manumission and the prospect of freedom so often hung within reach, enabled some men and women to shrug off their servitude and rise to the commanding heights of society – as political leaders and military commanders, as singers, poets and musicians, who could be the richest figures of their age. Unlike the plantation model of the American South, slavery here was also, in the words of one recent study, 'indescribably various and differentiated'.[15] It encapsulated the broadest, at times bewildering, range of occupations from crippling agricultural work, highly skilled artisan labour and domestic drudgery to elite concubinage, guardianship of sacred spaces, political leadership and military command.

The potential impermanence of slavery was also part of the pagan inheritance. There can be no more powerful or captivating example of this than Antara ibn Shaddad (525–608), who managed the transition from Arab-African slave to chivalric knight, ferocious warrior, paragon of manly virtue and romantic, hell-raising poet before his death on the cusp of Islam's arrival on the Arabian Peninsula.

Though much of his life is shrouded in mystery and supercharged by later literary legend, we know that he was born in Najd into the ancient Bedouin tribe of the Banu Abs; he was black, the outcast son of an Arab father, born into slavery to an Ethiopian slave mother called Zabiba ('black raisin'). 'Antara's father', writes the ninth-century poet and scholar Ibn Qutayba, 'did not recognize him as his son until he had reached manhood, because his mother was a black slave called Zabiba, and during the *Jahiliyya* [the pre-Islamic age of what Muslims considered ignorance or barbarism] the Arabs would consider the children of slaves to be slaves, no matter who their father was.'[16] His father promised him his freedom if he defended his tribe in battle, and Antara seized the opportunity with both hands, becoming one of the fiercest, most celebrated fighters of his time.

Antara's story serves as an early introduction to both the traditional Arab prejudice towards darker-skinned Africans and those of mixed Arab-African origin and to his powerful defiance of it, much of it expressed in verse.

> Fools may mock my blackness
> but without night there's no day!
> Black as night, so be it!
>   But what a night
> generous and bright!
> All the paltry Amrs and Zayds
> my name has eclipsed.
> I am the Lord of War![17]

Antara's battlefield heroics, together with his full-throttle poetry, revelling in bloodshed and the spoils of war, among them women, slaves and camels, have transfixed generations of Arabs. In one verse he writes of thrusting his spear into an adversary, whose severed jugular hisses like breath whistling through a harelip as the blood spurts out. One of his epic poems had the distinction of being included among the *Muaallaqat*, the seven 'suspended odes' said to have been hung in the Kaaba at Mecca, lodestar of Islam.

The lines between the real-life Antara and the Antara of legend are frustratingly unclear. This former slave has been called an Arab Hercules, likened to Homer, Virgil, Tasso, dragon-stalking Beowulf and Ezra Pound's Seafarer, the indomitable hero of Arab imagination.[18] Of Antara's enduring reputation as the quintessential Arab warrior-poet, a one-time slave who went on to take his world by storm, there can be no doubt. Yet the uncertainty over the historical facts of Antara's life is another reminder of the problems with these earliest, in this case pre-Islamic, sources.

This is a book for the general reader. It deliberately avoids the sort of complicated definitions of what constitutes a slave or slavery which may be favoured by specialist books.* The *Concise Oxford English Dictionary* defines a slave as 'a person who is the legal property of another and is forced to obey them'. Ehud Toledano, the Israeli scholar of Ottoman slavery, defines the institution as 'an involuntary relationship of mutual dependence between two quite unequal partners'. Both these definitions appear to be reasonable and comprehensible, and the rest of this book can be read with this understanding in mind.[19]

Language evolves continually. In recent years, the language of slavery studies, overwhelmingly focused on American slavery and the Atlantic slave trade, has moved away from the word 'slave' to 'enslaved person'. '"Slave" normalizes and reifies the condition of

---

* The Bonn Center for Dependency & Slavery Studies at the University of Bonn, for example, prefers 'asymmetrical dependencies' over 'slavery and freedom': 'Dependencies between actors are based on the ability of one actor to control the actions and the access to resources of another. This type of control over actions and access to resources is often reciprocal, and in this case, it is compatible with the autonomy of both actors. So the existence of strong asymmetries between actors is decisive for the loss of autonomy of one of them.'

slavery as a state of being, rather than an active process of dehumanization and bondage imposed on a person or people', says the National Archive Catalog of the USA. 'In contrast, "enslaved person" and its variants emphasize the condition in which kidnapped Africans and their descendants were kept while reinstating their personhood, and often their gender, age or profession.'[20] Mindful of readers tackling a book of this length, I use both terms throughout.

All of this is offered by way of signposting ahead of what can be challenging terrain. The history of slavery and the slave trade in the Islamic world is extremely long, rich, complicated and at times controversial.

And it begins in the Arabian Peninsula 1,400 years ago.

I

Four Slaves and the Birth of Islam

*And Allah has favoured some of you over others in provision.
But those who were favoured would not hand over their provision to those whom their right hands possess so they would be
equal to them therein. Then is it the favour of Allah they reject?*

Quran, 16:71

Let us begin with the story of Bilal.[1]

It was somewhere in the years after 610, in a wretched, rock-strewn corner of the Hijaz desert in the Arabian Peninsula.

Mecca was an inferno. The sun had arced up to its zenith in a blistering sky. The light was an eye-blinding blaze, the air stifling. The desert valley, crushed between two steep mountains, was lifeless apart from the flies, driven mad in this unventilated furnace. There were no trees here, no river to soften the desolation. It was a pitiless, rain-starved landscape, a suitable laboratory for persecution and torture.

On the ground, cruelly staked, was Bilal ibn Rabah, an Ethiopian slave, son of a slave father and mother. He had had his head turned by the upstart, self-declared Prophet Mohammed and had publicly rejected the community's age-old religion of many gods to become one of the preacher's very first Followers. This made Bilal one of the first Muslims, those who have made their submission – *Islam* – to God.*

---

* The precise chronological order of conversions to Islam is impossible to establish, with different sources making different claims, especially along sectarian Sunni/Shia lines. However, the identity of the earliest Muslims after Mohammed, including figures such as Ali, Abu Bakr, Bilal, Zayd and Mohammed's wife Khadija, is well attested.

Mohammed had been disturbing the peace. The turbulent preacher had been filling the minds of impressionable young men and women with dangerous nonsense – that everyone, rich or poor, no matter their creed, colour or class, was equal before God. This revolutionary idea, turning ominously into a movement, was dividing the community, setting neighbours and families against each other. It could not be allowed to continue, and punishment had to be meted out before things got any worse. While actions against the wealthier members of society had so far been limited to public insults and boycotting businesses, with threats of worse to follow, the poorest Meccans, who had responded most enthusiastically to Mohammed's preaching, had been attacked and beaten, thrown into prison without food or water, tortured and cast out into the desert.

So here lay Bilal, burning beneath the sky, outstretched limbs shackled to stakes driven into the sand. This alone would have been enough to kill him before too long, but his persecutors had other horrors in store.

Umayya ibn Khalaf, Bilal's owner, was one of the chiefs of the Quraysh, blue-blooded Meccan aristocrats from the same tribe as Mohammed. A haughty, well-fed man, he eyed the figure on the ground with contempt. Then he pulled out his long leather whip and started lashing the half-naked slave. Again and again he whipped him, cutting a lattice of welts across Bilal's face and chest. 'Renounce Islam,' he roared, 'or I'll kill you.'

'Ahad! Ahad!' Bilal screamed, eyes closed in a frenzy of pain. 'One! One!' What he meant, as Mohammed had been teaching his growing band of Followers, was that there was only one God, not the many idols worshipped by Meccans.

Incensed by this defiance, Umayya had a giant hot rock rolled on top of the spreadeagled slave to force him to renounce this new faith. 'Now, tell me your gods are Al Lat, Al Uzza and Manat,' he commanded. Bilal was fighting to breathe, lungs crushed by the dreadful weight. But still came the half-choked cries. 'Ahad! Ahad!' He was hanging on, but the end was near.

Word of these tortures reached Abu Bakr, a successful merchant and Mohammed's closest Companion. He rushed to the scene, saw what was happening and knew there was only one thing to do. Appealing to Umayya's basest instincts, he made an offer the grasping Meccan could not refuse: 400 dirhams for Bilal. From Umayya's point of view, it was a huge amount for a useless, recalcitrant slave. Kill him and he'd get nothing. A deal was struck on the spot and, in a life-changing moment of manumission as sudden as it was unexpected, Abu Bakr freed the half-dead man and Bilal was no longer a slave.

Freedom, though Bilal could not possibly have known it then, would bring him extraordinary, undreamt-of rewards. He would achieve great things and earn lasting renown in the annals of Islam. And for the next twenty-two years he would never leave Mohammed's side. Any event in the Prophet's life, whether sad or joyful, blood-stained or prayerful, was equally an important moment in the life of Bilal. He was Mohammed's constant attendant and one of his favourite *Sahabah*, the revered Companions of the Prophet, waking him in the morning with a breakfast of dates and camel milk, saddling his horses and camels, riding into battle alongside him against the Muslims' enemies, shoulder to shoulder with the man who would change the world forever. Bilal's name would live on gloriously for the next 1,400 years.

On a summer's night in 622, after the Prophet had learnt of a plot to assassinate him, the little band of Muslims quietly slipped out of Mecca in a life-or-death escape. Bilal joined Mohammed, Abu Bakr and 200 of the Prophet's most devoted Followers on the 200-mile *hijra* – or migration – across the desert to the town of Yathrib. It was a date of such importance that it became the beginning of the new Islamic calendar. From that moment, Muslim history took as its starting point the audacious *hijra* to Medina, just as the Christian calendar begins with the birth of Christ. The very footsteps of this former slave and his fellow travellers, in other words, reshaped time itself. As for Yathrib, the destination of the history-making *muhajirun* migrants from Mecca came to be known as Medinat al Nabi, City of the Prophet, in time simply Medina.

These were the earliest days of Islam and this was just the beginning for Bilal. In 624 he fought alongside Mohammed at the Battle of Badr, a warrior in the first Muslim army ever assembled. And it was a victorious force – of course, because it fought in Allah's name and with His blessing – defeating a larger contingent of Meccans and pointing to greater triumphs ahead. In the aftermath of the battle, Bilal had the long-awaited pleasure of coming face to face with his former tormentor Umayya, cowering before him. 'Ahad! Ahad!' he thundered and ran him through with his sword.

This was not the end of Bilal's story. More distinctions awaited him on the battlefield. He fought alongside the Prophet in the Battles of Uhud in 625 (indecisive) and in 627 Al Khandaq (the Trench) around Medina, a spirit-rousing victory, burnishing his credentials as a Muslim warrior.

Even greater honours were in store away from the battlefield. Mohammed appointed him the first *muaddin* (the caller to prayer) of Islam, so that when the Prophet invited his Followers to pray the new Muslim prayer, five times a day, all roads led to the former slave whose deep voice and soft words floated into the sky. Bilal had become the voice of Islam.

Allahu Akbar! Allahu Akbar! Allahu Akbar! Allahu Akbar!
Ashhadu an la ilaha illa Allah. Ashhadu an la ilaha illa Allah.
Ashhadu anna Mohammedan Rasul Allah. Ashhadu anna Mohammedan
   Rasul Allah.
Hayya aalas Salah. Hayya aalas Salah.
Hayya aalal Falah. Hayya aalal Falah.
Allahu Akbar! Allahu Akbar!
La ilaha illa Allah. *

This was the *adhan*, the Muslim call to prayer. These same words, first uttered by Bilal, would sound out across the massed ranks of hundreds, then thousands, later millions and in time – difficult to comprehend – billions of Muslims the world over.

---

* 'God is Greatest! God is Greatest! God is Greatest! God is Greatest!
I bear witness that there is no god except Allah.
I bear witness that there is no god except Allah.
I bear witness that Muhammad is the messenger of Allah.
I bear witness that Muhammad is the messenger of Allah.
Hurry to the prayer. Hurry to the prayer.
Hurry to salvation. Hurry to salvation.
God is Greatest! God is Greatest!
There is no god except Allah.'

Ever since his manumission, Bilal had a front-row seat in the early history of Islam. A new faith arose around him. But Bilal was far more than a mere member of the audience. He was one of the leading actors.

In 630, he rode alongside Mohammed again, this time with an army of 10,000 Muslims bearing down on Mecca in one of the defining moments in Islamic history. After years of bloody conflict with the city of his birth, beset by difficulties and desperation, the Prophet seized Mecca triumphantly with minimal casualties. It was the first Muslim conquest and it gave Mohammed and his Followers a totemic capital whose name would echo across the millennia.

Mohammed led his warriors directly to the Kaaba, the House of God built by Abraham and Ishmael, the sacred cube of black granite which worshipping Meccans had been revolving around for as long as anyone could remember. After he had ridden round it seven times on his camel, Mohammed entered it, smashed the idolatrous pictures inside (apart from two of Jesus and Mary), together with the 360 lead-strengthened idols, and then asked Bilal to call the *adhan*.

The sacred importance of the moment could hardly be overstated. Bilal hauled himself up the sheer side of the Kaaba, clinging on to the *kiswa*, the black hanging cloth draped across it. Up and up he clambered and eventually made it to the top, rolling on to the roof of the House of God exhausted, knowing that the eyes of the entire Muslim community were upon him. There had been some unpleasant, but not unexpected, remarks about the colour of his skin, sniping questions about why Mohammed should have bestowed such honours on this unremarkable African slave rather than a noble Qurayshi tribesman. Standing on top of the great Kaaba, he steadied himself, breathed in deeply and in a clear, ringing voice intoned the *adhan*, which echoed around the city. It was the greatest moment in his life. Bilal had called his way into history.

The conquest of Mecca was the symbolic preface to an era of unthinkable success: 120 years of lightning Muslim expansion across the Middle East, Asia, North Africa and Europe. Some of those men in Mecca and their sons, grandsons and great-grandsons would go on to ride across the furthest horizons to spread the glory of Islam and, in just a few generations, turn the world upside down.

All that, though, was yet to come. In 632, just two years after Mecca fell, so too did the Prophet, from an unknown illness. Bilal, his most loyal Companion, was distraught. From the moment Abu Bakr freed him and sent him to support Mohammed, the Prophet had been his strength and stay. Without Mohammed Bilal lost the will to call the Muslims to prayer and sought solace instead in jihad. With the permission of Abu Bakr (r. 632–4), who became the first Muslim caliph, the supreme leader of the Islamic world, on Mohammed's death and declared holy war in the Holy Land, Bilal left the Hijaz and rode north to fight in a series of all-conquering Muslim armies in Syria.

It was a great decade for the committed jihadist. Some of the most well-known Jewish and Christian cities of antiquity fell to Bilal and his fellow Muslim warriors. Damascus, where the blind Pharisee Saul, sight miraculously restored, had become the Christian Paul six centuries earlier, succumbed in 634. In 636, a Muslim army commanded by the Qurayshi general Khalid ibn Walid routed the Byzantines at the Battle of Yarmuk, east of the Sea of Galilee, bringing a millennium of Christian rule in Syria to a calamitous end. The emperor Heraclius, recently victorious over the Sasanian Empire of Persia, fled in disarray, his retreat a catalyst for a flurry of Muslim conquests. Next to fall in 637 was the fabulously rich entrepôt of Bostra, once the Roman emperor Trajan's capital of *Provincia Arabia*. Then the apocalypse. After months of soul-searching, aghast at the surrender to the 'slime of the godless Saracens', the white-bearded Patriarch Sophronius handed over the keys to Jerusalem, 'Zion, radiant Zion of the Universe', to the new caliph, Umar, mounted on his white camel. By the end of the 630s an alphabet of ancient cities from Antioch and Amman to Gaza, Homs and Hama had bowed to Muslim arms.

No book writes itself. Words had poured forth from Bilal in the many thousand *adhans* he had proclaimed to the faithful – at dawn and dusk, in Mecca, in Medina, in desert camps beneath the stars and on battlegrounds strewn with corpses. And in these *adhans*, and in his many years attending on the Prophet and in his great bravery on the battlefield, Bilal had written some of the first chapters in the history of Islam. Without ever realizing it, he had also left to posterity one of the earliest treatises on slavery in Islam.

Sometime around 640 – the precise details of a life lived more than a millennium ago remain indistinct – Bilal died in Damascus in his sixtieth year. There could be no more fitting place for his death. For Ibn Jubayr, the Andalusian poet and geographer of the twelfth century, Damascus was an earthly paradise. And it was the Prophet, after all, who in one of his most memorable *hadiths* – or sayings – all those years ago had told Bilal that 'I heard your footsteps ahead of me in Paradise.'[2]

Born a humble slave, tortured and almost killed for his refusal to renounce Islam, raised to glory on the battlefield and as the voice of Islam, Bilal died one of the most noble and distinguished Muslims in history.

One of Bilal's brother warriors at the Battle of the Trench in 627 was Zayd ibn Haritha.[3] Although he was not of African blood – he was born into the Kalb tribe, who came from the Najd desert in the heart of the Arabian Peninsula – he shared with Bilal a background of enslavement. Mohammed ibn Jarir al Tabari, the ninth-century doyen of Arab historians, described how while travelling with his mother as a young man in pre-Islamic times, Zayd had been seized from his tent by raiding horsemen from the rival Banu al Qayn tribe, taken to the market at Ukkaz and put up for sale. He was a fine figure of a man and was picked up for the healthy sum of 400 dirhams (another parallel with Bilal) by the nephew of Khadija bint Khuwaylid, a wealthy merchant, on behalf of his aunt. Later, when the Prophet married Khadija, she gave him Zayd as a wedding gift. Though the man was only ten years his junior, Mohammed adopted him as his son and Zayd was a slave no more.

Zayd's family meanwhile was bereft. It was the not knowing which was so painful. Years passed. The family's anguish was like a sore that cannot be healed. One day Zayd met fellow tribesmen visiting Mecca. He asked them to send a reassuring message to his family back home.

> Carry a message from me to my people, for I am far away,
> that close to the House* and the places of pilgrimage I stay.
> So let go of the grief that has deeply saddened you,

---

* The House of God, i.e. the Kaaba.

and do not hasten all your camels all over the earth.
I live with the best of families, may God be blessed;
from father to son, of Maad they are the noblest.

On receipt of this welcome news, his father and uncle hurried to Mecca in the hope of ransoming the young man. Father and son fell into each other's arms, overjoyed. Mohammed graciously told his visitors that Zayd was free to return to his original family – there was no need to pay any ransom – or, if he preferred, to stay with his new family in Mecca. Joy at this longed-for reunion quickly turned to devastation when Zayd announced that he would rather stay with Mohammed.

'Woe to you, O Zayd, would you prefer slavery to freedom, your father, your paternal uncle, and to your family?'

Zayd was unequivocal. 'Yes, for I have seen something in this man, and I am not the kind of person who would ever choose anyone in preference to him.'[4]

The matter was settled. To soften the blow Mohammed declared that Zayd would be his legally adopted son with full rights of inheritance.

Some say – though the point was hotly contested, and always will be – that Zayd was the first man to embrace Islam. He was certainly one of the Prophet's earliest and closest Companions. Along with Bilal he played a starring role in the *hijra* of 622, first accompanying Mohammed and his fellow migrants to Medina, then later risking his life for Mohammed on a return mission to Mecca to bring back the Prophet's third wife Aisha and his daughters.

Completely devoted to the Messenger of God, his life – like that of Bilal – was intertwined with that of the great man. No wonder he was known as Zayd al Hibb, the Beloved by the Prophet. In a sign of his affection for the younger man, his rejection of the pagan stigma attached to marrying former slaves and, if reports of Zayd's dark skin are to be believed, the Arabs' time-honoured sense of racial superiority, Mohammed gave his cousin Zaynab to Zayd in marriage. Zayd came to believe that Mohammed himself was in love with Zaynab and quickly divorced her, clearing the way for Mohammed to marry her. This was highly controversial. The prospect of the Prophet marrying the former wife of his adopted son threatened Mohammed's reputation and provided ammunition to his enemies. But a couple of helpful divine revelations arrived in good time and passed immediately into the Quran: 'Mohammed is not the father of any of your men, but he is the Messenger of Allah and the seal of the Prophets. Allah has full knowledge of everything.' (33:40); 'Call them by their father's names.' (33:5). From this moment, Zayd ibn Mohammed was no longer Mohammed's legal son and heir and reverted to his original name of Zayd ibn Haritha.

The affair caused such a furore among the conservative community of Mecca that Zayd even received a mention in the Quran, the only Companion to receive such a distinction in a holy book which contains few names of either people or places. In truth it was less about Zayd than it was a divine blessing of Mohammed's marriage to his adopted son's ex-wife. Still, no one could question the honour.*

However, this was all domestic business, not the adventures of a holy warrior. Zayd had his mind set on grander matters. Raised an Arab tribesman, warrior blood ran through him. Like Bilal in the years after the Prophet's death, his path was set. He would seek glory in holy war.

From 624 this former slave was rarely off the battlefield. Beginning at Al Qarada that year, he led a raid on a Meccan trade caravan heading north to Syria and plundered 100,000 silver dirhams, a vast treasure distributed among the warriors with a soon-to-be-traditional fifth share going to the Prophet, who gave it to the poor. Zayd went on to command another six military expeditions. Like all the best early Muslims, former slaves or otherwise, he was present at the Battles of Uhud and the Trench. Then, in the late summer of 629, disaster struck. During fierce hand to-hand fighting against the Byzantines at the Battle of Mutah, east of the River Jordan, he was fatally wounded by a savage spear-thrust and breathed his last alongside his fellow commanders.

Zayd died two years short of his half-century, the premature end of a life rich in incident and drama, a journey from free Arab tribesman to lowly slave, battle-seared holy warrior, beloved Companion of the Prophet and bloodied martyr.

---

* 'And when Zayd divorced his wife, We gave her to you in marriage, so that it should become legitimate for true believers to wed the wives of their adopted sons if they divorced them. God's will must needs be done.' Quran 33:37.

Leaders of the growing Muslim community came to pay their respects. The Prophet's third and youngest wife Aisha, *Umm al Muminin*, Mother of the Believers, provided a rousing epitaph, a tribute to his military leadership and prowess: 'The Messenger of Allah never sent Zayd ibn Haritha in an army without putting him in command of it, even if he stayed after he appointed him.'[5]

Heartbroken by the news of his Companion's martyrdom, the Prophet hurried to Zayd's family to offer his condolences. Surrounded by sobbing relatives, Mohammed was moved to tears. When asked why he was crying, he replied simply: 'This is the yearning of the lover for the beloved.'[6]

The Battle of the Trench in 627, fought around the perimeter of Medina, comes up again and again in the stories of these slaves-turned-warriors, bringing together some of the greatest Muslims in a roll call of the Prophet's most celebrated Followers. Fighting along-side Bilal and Zayd at this history-making battle was another legend called Salman al Farsi, Salman the Persian.[7] Although his early years remain a mystery, he became, according to one authority, 'a semi-legendary figure of early Islam', 'the national hero of Muslim Persia' and an exemplar of the country's conversion to Islam.[8] Salman was another who in the course of his three-score years rose phoenix-like from the immiserating depths of slavery to the summit of early Islamic society and scholarship.

In the account written by Mohammed's eighth-century biographer Ibn Ishaq, Salman was the son of the leading landowner in a Persian village called Jayy outside Isfahan. 'I was dearer to him than the whole world,' Salman recalled of his father. 'His love for me went to such lengths that he shut me in his house as though I were a slave girl.' Born a Zoroastrian, he studied for many years to become a fire-temple priest. Then one day he passed a church, heard prayers being offered up to God, looked in and liked what he saw. The Christian liturgy was attractive. He mentioned this to his scandalized father, who assured him that there was no good in that religion. Salman was having none of it. 'No,' he replied, 'it is better than our religion.' For this impertinence he was bound in fetters and imprisoned in the house.[9]

But Salman managed to escape, joining a caravan of Christian merchants bound for Syria. He attached himself first to a bishop then to a series of hermits, holy men and monks with whom he studied the sacred texts. In the years to come, famed for his knowledge of Zoroastrian, Jewish, Christian and Islamic texts, he would acquire the nickname *Abu al Kitabayn*, Father of the Two Books – the Bible and the Quran.

Long before he met the Prophet, in other words, his life had been a sustained spiritual quest. He was the living embodiment of one of Mohammed's most famous sayings: 'Seek knowledge even to China.' He conversed with priests and scholars, one of whom told him tales of great deeds about to be done by a charismatic prophet in a land of stony mountains and date palms, a man who was going to revive the religion of Abraham. Salman pressed on south along the ancient trade route linking Syria to the Arabian Peninsula – the same camel-trodden trails on which Zayd plundered the Meccan caravan in 624. He covered hundreds of miles in his search for the truth, his destination the Wadi al Qura, the Valley of Villages, a flourishing desert oasis.

Plans were all very well, but reality was rarely so straightforward: life in seventh-century Arabia brought with it the shattering prospect of capture and enslavement. And so one day Salman was betrayed by his Bedouin desert guide and seized and sold to a Jewish landowner in Medina. In a dramatic conversion – certainly not the one he had intended – the soul-searcher became a slave. But Medina, apart from being a melting-pot of Jews and Muslims, was also a place of mountains and date palms and here Salman met Mohammed. This was the prophet foretold by the Christian priest on his deathbed in Syria – complete, Mohammed's biographer Ibn Ishaq later reported, with 'the seal of prophecy' between his shoulders.[10]

Meeting the Prophet was one thing, escaping from slavery was another. Salman's journey to freedom would take time. The bargain he struck with his owner would test the ingenuity and application of even the most tenacious slave. He had first to acquire, and then plant, 300 date palms in addition to giving his owner forty ounces – a shade over a kilogram – of gold. Mohammed rallied his fellow Muslims to contribute date saplings and to plant them on the Jewish master's farm. Finally, when the Muslims were approaching their planting target but there was still no progress on the gold, the Prophet received a golden nugget, which he gave immediately to Salman. It weighed precisely forty ounces. Salman, a new Muslim, was free.

As far as manumission moments go, this one could hardly have been more splendid. According to a tenth-century account by the Persian scholar Abu al Shaykh al Isfahani, author of possibly the earliest biographical dictionary in Iran, Salman's release from servitude brought together the great and the good of early Islam. The Prophet himself dictated the document to one future caliph, his son-in-law and cousin Ali (r. 656–61), and had it witnessed by two more in Abu Bakr and Umar (r. 634–44), not to mention the former slave Bilal, among other Companions.

> Mohammed ibn Abd Allah, the Messenger of God, redeems Salman al Farsi by this ransom from Uthman ibn al Ashhal al Yahudi [the Jew] and the man from Qurayza, by planting three hundred date palms and [paying] forty ounces of gold. Therefore Mohammed ibn Abd Allah, the Messenger of God, has absolved the cost of Salman al Farsi. Mohammed ibn Abd Allah, the Messenger of God, and the *ahl al bayt** are his patrons and no one has any claim on Salman.[11]

These were the auspicious foundations of a glittering career. In 627, Salman took a decisive step into Muslim history books at the Battle of the Trench. The fate of the new faith hung perilously in the balance. Lose, and Islam was buried before it had truly been born, and with it its fledgling Prophet Mohammed. Win, and that was the end for pagan Mecca and Qurayshi prestige.

With a diminutive force of around 3,000, Mohammed and his Muslims were heavily outnumbered, yet Salman had a cunning plan. He advised Mohammed to dig a trench around Medina to nullify the Meccan cavalry. It was a simple but effective ruse. The Meccans were unable to pierce Medina's defences. The skies darkened, winds whipped up the sands and destroyed the besiegers' tents, rain hurled down from the heavens and the thirty-day siege collapsed in Qurayshi acrimony and bitter recriminations. Against all the odds, and thanks in no small part to Salman's inspired military preparations, the Prophet's

---

* Literally the People of the House, an expression designating the Prophet's extended family.

enemies had been seen off. Mohammed's star was in the ascendant, the Meccans were fading. From this point Salman, like Bilal, was one of the Prophet's most valued Companions. He had proved his mettle where it mattered most at this time – on the battlefield.

Unsurprisingly, Salman became a popular figure and people laid claim to him. While his fellow Muslims debated whether he was really one of the *Ansar* (the Helpers, Muslims from Medina) or *muhajirun* migrants from Mecca, the two pre-eminent groups in early Islam – they liked these arcane discussions, precursors of the torrents of Islamic jurisprudence which would come flooding in over the following centuries – Mohammed ruled that he was neither. Salman, he decided, was actually of the *ahl al bayt*, an honour which made him part of the Prophet's family. Salman, he said, was 'a sea which cannot be exhausted and a treasure which never comes to an end'.[12]

Some traditions reported that while Bilal was earning glory in Syria, the former slave Salman was winning his spurs as both soldier and diplomat in the world-changing Muslim conquest of Iran. After the Sasanian forces retreated in disarray from Al Madain (The Cities, as Arabs referred to the conurbation of Seleucia-Ctesiphon), their capital for the past 800 years, twenty miles south of the future site of Baghdad, Salman rode in with the victorious Muslims in the spring of 637. The holy warriors plundered fabulous quantities of royal treasure from this ancient capital on the Tigris.

Here in Al Madain was the royal crown of the Shahanshah, Persian King of Kings Yazdegerd III (r. 632–51), who had fled ignominiously and would spend the rest of his reign in flight from Muslim armies until his humiliating murder by a water-miller in 651. Here too were his robes of honour, brocaded with gold thread and adorned with gems, basketfuls of gold and silver, precious jewels, an arsenal of the most beautifully worked swords and jewel-studded coats of armour. In one looted chest there was a golden sculpture of a horse with a silver bridle and saddle decorated with rubies and emeralds. Another contained a silver figurine of a camel with a golden, ruby-covered halter and a rider of gem-encrusted gold. The Arab desert warriors, who had led lives as austere as they were punishing, had never seen anything like it.

The noble flames of the Sasanian Empire, for almost half a millennium a beacon of Persian civilization, were extinguished by the rough-and-ready Muslims. As one ancient dynasty gave way to the upstarts, and in a sign of his pre-eminence, Salman was appointed governor of this fabled capital.

After this personal triumph, Salman faded from sight. He lives on today in many-coloured splendour in Salman Pak – Salman the Pure – the Iraqi city named in his honour on the site of ancient Madain. His tomb, surrounded by intricate Islamic gilding, green and yellow holy texts and exquisite geometrical latticework, has remained the object of veneration for Shia Muslim pilgrims for at least the last 1,000 years.

In another sign both of the enthusiasm and questionable reliability of some of these early sources, Salman was credited with a superbly long life as a result of his conversion to Islam. Estimates of his age were put variously at 200, 300, 350 and even a bravura 553 years (hardly unique to Islam, we might note, recalling Noah's death at the millennium-challenging age of 950). Although the date of his death, like so much of his life, is uncertain, there is nothing vague about the position of this former slave in the history of early Islam.

Bilal, Zayd, Salman. Three stories, three slave warrior Muslims, three men.

One of the most remarkable women at this time without question was Hind bint Utba, the wife of Abu Sufyan ibn Harb, the Qurayshi chief. Though she was never a slave, we find her interacting with one at the Battle of Uhud in 625. Having lost her father, son, brother and uncle to Mohammed's Muslims at the Battle of Badr the previous year, Hind was determined on revenge. She fired up a slave called Wahshi ibn Harb, The Savage, Son of War, a javelin-throwing special-ist whose owner had already offered him freedom in return for killing the Prophet's uncle Hamza, spurring him on to do the deed in a series of racist remarks. 'Come on, you father of blackness!' she cried. 'Sat-isfy your vengeance and ours!'[13] The remark is telling in offering an early example – and there would be many more – of an Arab refer-ring pejoratively to an African's skin colour. Later she scoured the battlefield to mutilate Muslim corpses, making necklaces, anklets and pendants from their noses and ears. When she found Hamza's lifeless body, she cut out and chewed on his liver.

Hind appeared again in 630, still in ebullient form, berating her husband Abu Sufyan. Faced with Mohammed's Muslim army on its way to war with Mecca, he meekly converted to Islam – a swift matter of professing seven words, *la ilaha illa Allah, Mohammedan Rasul Allah*, there is no God but God, Mohammed is His Prophet – and surrendered the city to the Prophet. Hind was outraged. 'Kill this fat greasy bladder of lard!' she stormed, pulling on his moustache. 'What a rotten protector of the people!'[14]

But as magnificent as the raging, husband-bashing, liver-munching Hind unquestionably was, we must look elsewhere for a slave woman in the embryonic days of the new faith.

Unlike Bilal, Zayd and Salman, whose stories were traced in hagiographic detail by the early Muslim scholars, Sumayya bint Khabbat, despite her honoured status as the first Muslim martyr in history, struggled to get noticed.[15] For reasons best known to Ibn Ishaq, while the formidable Hind received several dozen mentions in his biography of the Prophet, Sumayya was not even mentioned by name once in the entire book. He dealt with her summarily in a single sentence of ten words and even then the reference was to the torture of her son Ammar ibn Yasir, a fellow Muslim convert: 'They killed his mother, for she refused to abandon Islam.' Ibn Saad did a little better, devoting eleven lines to a very brief character sketch in *The Women of Medina*, the 320-page final volume of his series on the early Muslims. He named her as Sumayya bint Khabbat, the daughter of Khabbat. Tabari gave Sumayya a couple of short paragraphs, though she appeared of more interest to our polymathic historian, as she did to both Ibn Ishaq and Ibn Saad, as the mother of Ammar.

We know only the barest details of Sumayya's life. She belonged to a man called Abu Hudhayfa and was given in marriage to Yasir ibn Amir, with whom she had a son called Ammar, who was freed by Abu Hudhayfa and would go on to blaze a successful, battle-filled career as one of the first Muslims and an honoured Companion of the Prophet. A veteran of the Battle of Badr, later a governor of the holy city of Kufa in Iraq, Ammar lived a long, distinguished life until his death, aged ninety, fighting for the Caliph Ali against the pretender and future caliph Muawiya Abu Sufyan (r. 661–80) at the Battle of Siffin in 657, during the First Fitna, the civil war between Muslims.

According to Ibn Saad, Sumayya and her son Ammar enjoyed the distinction of being two of the first seven Muslims in history.* Like Bilal and some of the earliest, lowliest Muslims in Mecca, she was tortured for her belief in Allah and the Prophet. Ibn Saad described how her persecutors put Sumayya and other Muslims in iron chain-mail coats and left them to burn under the desert sun until they renounced Islam.

But, although she might have looked like a frail, elderly woman, Sumayya was strong, and had seen enough in her long life as a slave to know what a bully looked like. Cooking painfully in her metal coat, she made up her mind to resist these rich merchants. Somehow, despite the temptation to give in, Sumayya held firm to her faith, a resolution for which she later paid the heaviest price.

One of Mohammed's sworn enemies in Mecca was Amr ibn Hisham, known to the Muslims as Abu Jahl, Father of Ignorance. He was the polytheist flag-bearer of the opposition to the Muslims and pursued a policy of torture and intimidation. In Ibn Ishaq's telling of the Prophet's life, Abu Jahl was an unintentionally entertaining leading villain. He regularly insulted, cursed and mocked the Prophet, threatened to split his skull with a huge rock. It sounded like a lot of bluster, but for the weakest members of Meccan society, especially foreigners like Sumayya without the protection of a tribe, Abu Jahl was a real danger. He heard about this defiant woman and her family and decided he would teach these wretched Muslims a lesson. One day in around 615 he found her and stabbed her with 'a spear in her private parts', killing her instantly. Sumayya went to her grave, Ibn Saad reports, the first martyr in Islam.

A decade after her martyrdom, Abu Jahl was fighting the Muslims at the Battle of Badr. There was fierce competition among the Prophet's warriors to kill the 'enemy of God'. One described how he struck Abu Jahl such a ferocious blow that it 'sent his foot and half his shank flying. I can only liken it to a date-stone flying from the pestle when it is beaten.'[16] Later the wounded but defiant Abu Jahl was finished off, his severed head thrown before the Prophet. Mohammed

---

* Ibn Saad's first seven Muslims are Mohammed, Abu Bakr, Bilal, Khabbab, Suhayb, Ammar and Sumayya.

consoled Sumayya's son Ammar with the news that Allah had killed his mother's killer. As with Bilal killing his former owner Umayya, so with Muslim warriors destroying their nemesis.

The stories of these four individuals – three men and one woman, all of them significant characters in the wider story of Islam in its infancy – are loaded with meaning and provide some of the earliest insights into slavery in the Muslim world – so early they bridge the transition from the pre-Islamic period to the era of Mohammed. However uncertain these sources may be, nonetheless they reveal a great deal about Muslim tradition and beliefs in the earliest days of the faith.

Bilal's story is burdened by the crushing weight of slavery. A foreigner without the protection conferred by tribal affiliation in a society in which tribe is paramount, he is an easy victim for a pagan master who treats him as he sees fit, before the Ethiopian is rescued and freed by the Muslim Abu Bakr. Bilal's personal narrative encompasses degrading slavery, torture and persecution and, in his very special case at least, freedom, honour and redemption. Neither Bilal's African blood nor his status as a former slave can prevent him from rising to the pinnacle of Muslim society and renown.

Zayd stands for something different. Born free, of Arab rather than African blood, he enjoys advantages unimaginable to Bilal, a slave at birth, not least in having that critical protection of his tribe. But he, like everyone else on the Arabian Peninsula, including his fellow tribesmen and women, runs the risk of enslavement. In the arbitrary, tough world of seventh-century Arabia, a free man or woman can become a slave in any place and at any time. Blood offers no protection. Zayd's story also confronts complex legal issues of adoption and inheritance to the point where the Prophet is forced to renounce his formal adoption of the younger man, remove Zayd's legal right to inherit and return his name to its original version. Zayd's situation is so complex and controversial it even requires divine revelations and Quranic verses to resolve it, but his sparkling career beyond his enslavement, liberation, adoption and un-adoption nevertheless testifies to the virtually boundless opportunities available for some former Muslim slaves. Although there were no guarantees, enslavement could be temporary and, as with Bilal, need not end a man or woman's hopes to achieve later freedom and distinction. And the colour of a man or woman's skin, as long as Muslims followed Mohammed's colour-blind example, must not matter either.

Salman, though less historically grounded in these ancient sources, offers a more spiritual perspective. He is the intellectual truth-seeker, the wandering scholar ambushed by harsh reality who, like Zayd, finds himself thrown into slavery. Salman can also be understood as a literary device, a one-man exemplar of the Prophet's approach towards slavery, above all in his apparent instinct to free slaves, a presumption towards humankind's freedom. It is only thanks to the personal, apparently miraculous, intervention of Mohammed that Salman finds his freedom, a liberty that he uses – as do Bilal and Zayd – to fight and conquer in the name of Islam. The story of Salman again makes clear that there can be life – crowned with achievement and accolades – after slavery.

And then Sumayya. Like almost all her sister Muslims, she is denied the opportunity to win laurels on the battlefield. Her story serves instead as an exemplar of faith-filled courage and steadfastness in the greatest possible adversity. She is the opposite of the Apostle Peter who, under pressure for his faith and to save his own skin, denies Christ three times. Unlike Peter, and in the teeth of full-blooded torture, Sumayya refuses to buckle.

Though she cannot compete alongside the men in the martial world of early Muslim warriors, Sumayya achieves something no less important and, in some respects, more impressive. Dying for the religion of Allah and his Prophet Mohammed, she establishes the tradition of martyrdom for the faith, a principle revered and adhered to by countless Muslims for the next 1,400 years. It is scarcely an exaggeration to say that a vein of martyrdom runs through Islamic history from the point of Sumayya's murder to the present day: it can be traced from the world-conquering Arabs of the seventh and eighth centuries, through to the dynasties of imperial Abbasids, Samanids, Seljuqs, North African Almoravids and Almohads, Andalusian Nasrids, Salahadin's Crusader-smashing Ayyubids, Iranian Ilkhanids and Safavids, Egyptian Fatimids, Tamerlane's rampaging Timurids, the Mamluks (slaves-turned-rulers) and mighty Mughals, the Sublime

Ottomans and right on to the twenty-first-century alphabet of self-declared jihadists operating around the world today, from Syria to Afghanistan, Cairo to Kabul, Bamako to Baghdad. Though they may not know it, this tradition begins a decade before the first Muslim army even went into battle, with the Muslim slave Sumayya.

Slavery, then, in this time of paleo-Islam, could be a temporary condition. It need not prove an insuperable barrier to achieving the greatest possible glory and winning lasting renown in Muslim history. A man or woman might subsist in domestic drudgery their entire lives – whether weighed down by grinding captivity, welcomed as a lowly member of the household or something in between – or be manumitted and lead a wholly different life. These things were in the hands of Allah.

As for how Muslims should think about slavery in the new world that had been revealed to Mohammed, how they should treat their slaves, what was permissible and what was not, there was (before the *hadiths*) only one place to look: the Quran.

2

Slavery 101:
Blueprints and Foundations

They invite you to the Fire while Allah invites you to Paradise . . .

Quran, 2:221

Divine in nature, the Quran can be prosaic in practice. Its 6,236 verses (6,666 in a different counting) represent the word of God as revealed to His Prophet Mohammed high in a cave above Mecca, later in Medina, in the years from 610. Yet though it is by definition a sacred text, appealing to humankind's highest nature, it is hardly shy of addressing deeply practical issues. This has its own internal logic. When you are seeking to remake a society, to return it to the true path (the religion of Abraham) from which it has supposedly strayed, it makes sense to include, among all the material on divinity, religious obedience, the delights of paradise and the terrors of hell, some sort of manual for everyday living.

This naturally included guidance on slavery. The institution vastly predated Islam in the Arabian Peninsula and much of the ancient world from Egypt to Greece and Rome, and was a ubiquitous fact of life in both the neighbouring Sasanian and Byzantine Empires. The Quran now had to provide Muslims with a clear direction. In this new-old religion, how were they to deal with slaves and slavery? How vital this question was to seventh-century Arabian society can be gauged from the frequency with which slaves appear in these holy pages.

Slaves are mentioned in at least twenty-nine Quranic verses, the uncertainty hinging on the often allusive and oblique language used to denote them. Most of these verses appear to originate in Medina, in other words dating to the time after Mohammed and his *muhajirun* migrants had fled to Mecca, and are legally expressed. They can be seen as the earliest building-blocks of a new Muslim society and address some elemental issues.

To begin with one of the Quran's most famous and fundamental pronouncements on slavery, Islam accepts the inequality between master and slave as divinely ordained:

> And Allah has favoured some of you over others in provision. But those who were favoured would not hand over their provision to those whom their right hands possess so they would be equal to them.
>
> (16:71)

The Quran acknowledges, then, that we are not all free. Slavery is real, it exists, it is part of the natural order, the Quran accepts it and is not proposing to abolish it. Some people are free, others are slaves. The fact that some have more possessions than others does *not* mean they have to give them away to their slaves in the interest of equality. For a society

Pages from an early Ottoman Quran from *Sura* 16, *Al Nahl* (The Bee). The chapter contains important references to slavery. The floral shapes here indicate verse endings.

accustomed to slavery from time immemorial, ruling it out at the outset would have done nothing to make Islam an attractive new alternative to tried-and-tested pagan polytheism for most people – apart, we might imagine, from the slaves. Prohibition would have spelt its failure.

This euphemistic expression in the Quran – 'those whom their right hands possess', in Arabic *ma malakat aymanukum* – is the most common of half a dozen terms used in the holy book to refer to slaves. It appears fifteen times, typically referring to concubines and what constitutes permissible behaviour towards them. Another critical word, which is used six times, is *raqaba*, meaning neck, generally used in the context of a slave being freed from his or her bondage. The traditional Arabic word for a slave – *abd* – tends to be used in the Quran in the much wider sense of humans as God's servants on earth, giving rise to later, specifically Muslim, theophoric names which remain common today: Abdullah, Slave of God, Abd al Rahman, Slave of the Most Gracious, Abd al Aziz, Slave of the Almighty, and so forth.

The Quran has much more to say on slavery. The tone is fairly stark in the following verse. There is no question of equality between a slave and a free man:

Allah sets forth a parable: a slave who lacks all means, compared to a free man to whom We granted a good provision, of which he donates freely, openly and secretly. Are they equal? Praise be to Allah. In fact, most of them do not know.

(16:75)

But in case that message was not clear enough:

He sets forth for you an example drawn from your own lives: would you allow some of those whom your right hands possess to be your equal partners in whatever wealth We have provided you, keeping them in mind as you are mindful of your peers? This is how We make the signs clear for people who understand.

(30:28)

So the legitimacy of slavery, as pronounced upon by the Quran, is not up for debate or challenge. That much is clear and will necessarily have a bearing on Muslim attitudes towards slavery – and, potentially, its abolition – for centuries to come.

The next question, moving from principle to practice: how to treat slaves? Here the emphasis in the Quran is on two intertwined features of the institution: slave-women-cum-concubines and manumission, a striking indication of the real-life prevalence of the former and the desirability of the latter in the brave new world of Islam.

In the chapter '*Al Muminun*', 'The Believers', the Quran specifically includes among 'successful' Muslims those who humble themselves in prayer, pay alms tax, avoid idle chat and guard their chastity 'except with their wives or those whom their right hands possess, for then they are free from blame' (23:6).

Divine permission for a man to have sex with his female slaves or concubines comes with these last three words in a verse that is repeated later on in the Quran for added emphasis. There is no blame attached here. This is lawful, permissible behaviour and does not detract from being a good Muslim.

The Quran is equally clear that for marriage there is an ideal hierarchy of female matches. A free Muslim woman is preferable to a Muslim slave, but if a man cannot afford the dowry required for a free woman, then an enslaved woman is next best. And, very importantly when choosing either a wife or a husband, a Muslim slave always trumps a free pagan – that is the road to hell:

> Do not marry polytheistic women until they believe; for a believing slave-woman is better than a free polytheist, even though she may look pleasant to you. And do not marry your women to polytheistic men until they believe, for a believing slave-man is better than a free polytheist, even though he may look pleasant to you. They invite you to the Fire while Allah invites you to Paradise and forgiveness by His grace. He makes His revelations clear to the people so perhaps they will be mindful.
>
> (2:221)

Striking a note of egalitarianism within an institution which depends fundamentally on inequality, the Quran makes no distinction between the Muslim faith of a free woman and that of a slave: 'Allah knows best the state of your faith and theirs,' it declares, a pronouncement echoed by Queen Elizabeth I of England 1,000 years later when she said she did not wish to open 'windows into men's souls'. In terms of punishment for 'indecent' behaviour after marriage, a slave woman was credited with lesser agency and greater leniency – fifty lashes rather than a back-shredding 100.

Sex is at the heart of much of the Quran's material on slavery. There are times when one wonders whether slaves even served other functions, such is the attention given to the sexual realm and the absence of detail on other types of work, domestic, agricultural or otherwise. In a sure sign that the practice prevailed in seventh-century Arabia at the time Islam was emerging, the Quran expressly forbids the prostitution of slave women and counsels mercy towards those who are bullied into it:

> Do not force your slave girls into prostitution for your own worldly gains while they wish to remain chaste. And if someone coerces them, then after such a coercion Allah is certainly All-Forgiving, Most Merciful to them.
>
> (24:33)

The holy book's preoccupation with sex shows no signs of diminishing in the afterlife. If anything, it remains a major consideration, perhaps a reflection of the need to galvanize and inspire male warriors at a time when the great Arab Conquests and the canonization process of the Quran were ongoing in parallel. That much is conjecture, but the Quran's version of paradise, unsurprisingly, is no nirvana of gender equality. The numerous references to beautiful, wide-eyed, full-bosomed virgin *houris* suggest there may be more in the Gardens of Bliss to look forward to for men with healthy sexual appetites than for female believers. The *houris* may not be slaves exactly, but few would doubt that Paradise in the Quran comes with women offering more than 'splendid' companionship. This is reinforced within the *hadiths*, several of which specify that each Muslim man can marry two luminescent *houris*.

We search the Quran in vain for any insights into the slave trade. Of Muslims trading slaves there is no mention. There is only a brief and solitary reference to the sale of the Prophet Yusuf – the Bible's Joseph – to a rich man from Egypt called Al Aziz. Yusuf is described as 'merchandise' and is sold for 'just a few silver coins', a transaction which receives no further comment. But presumably, by extension from the acceptance of slavery as an institution, the sale of slaves is also condoned.

The sacred text enjoins kindness and compassion towards slaves, ideally with a view to their emancipation. What is the challenging path for a good Muslim, it asks? 'It is to free a slave,' comes the answer (90:13). Again and again the Quran mentions the freeing of slaves as a worthy action and an inherent good, establishing the fundamental tension between ideal principle and real-world practice that would remain at the heart of slavery in the Islamic world for as long as the institution endured. On the one hand, owning slaves is wholly legitimate. On the other, emancipating them is one of the greatest actions a Muslim can perform.* Liberating slaves is urged as an act of expiation for sins committed in a variety of contexts: the penalty for the accidental killing of a Muslim, for unlawful divorce or for a broken oath – on a par with the virtue of feeding or clothing ten poor people. In the same verse outlawing the prostitution of slave girls, the Quran specifies what medieval Muslim scholars later interpreted as the contractual emancipation of a slave through the payment of instalments:

> And if any of those whom your right hands possess desires a document [deed of emancipation?], make it possible for them, if you find goodness in them. And give them some of Allah's wealth which He has granted you.
>
> (24:33)

So the Quran sketches out the broad outlines of the Muslim position on, and attitude towards, slavery. The picture which emerges, first of all, is complete acceptance of slavery as part and parcel of life on earth. There is no desire to eradicate it. It goes on to call for kindness towards slaves and, in a number of circumstances, urges their emancipation. In calling for slaves to be freed to expiate sins, in recommending the use of alms to emancipate them, and in insisting on humane behaviour towards them, the Quran was considerably more enlightened and friendly than any of the Christian, Jewish or Roman

---

* In *Slavery and Islam*, Jonathan Brown posits what he calls the 'Slavery Conundrum', consisting of three axioms which cannot be held coherently at the same time. First, slavery is an intrinsic moral evil. Second, slavery is slavery. Third, our past has moral authority over us. 'These axioms', he writes, 'form a conundrum because they cannot each be denied, but neither can they all be true.' See pp. 150–3.

systems. While Christians professed equality before God, Jews offered reduced penalties for adultery with slaves, and Romans prohibited slave prostitution, only the Quran did all three, resulting in perhaps 'the most progressive legislation on slavery in its time'. The advent of Islam 'enormously improved' the lot of the Arabian slave, conferring upon him or her quasi-legal rights, and represented a 'vast' enhancement on the slavery practised in antiquity, from Greece and Rome to the Byzantines and Sasanians.[1]

The Quran's clearly stated approval for a male slave-owner to have sex with his female slave would have consequences: as late as the dying days of the imperial Ottoman harem in Istanbul in the twentieth century and then in the depraved enslavement and rape of Yazidi women and girls in northern Iraq by so-called Islamic State fighters in the twenty-first. Note the Quran's clear distinction on gender – a man can have sex with his female slave. Allah does not disclose whether a woman can do the same with her male slave.

However, there was one way to find out. Shortly after the death of the Prophet in 632 a free-spirited woman in the Arabian Peninsula took one of her male slaves to bed as a sexual partner. It seems, since she later mentioned this to the then caliph, Umar, that she considered the action entirely legitimate. But Umar, a paragon of austerity, was scandalized. What could she possibly be thinking, the notoriously strict leader of the embryonic Islamic state asked? 'I thought that ownership by the right hand made lawful to me what it makes lawful to men,' she replied, unabashed.

This was decidedly not Umar's interpretation of the scriptures, and he summoned the Companions of the Prophet for their view. Their judgements, alongside those of Mohammed, would later emerge as important legal precedent for orthodox Sunni Muslims. The verdict was perhaps predictable: 'She has given the book of Exalted God an interpretation that is not its interpretation.' Having received the confirmation he required, Umar then forbade the woman from ever marrying a free man and ordered the slave to keep away from her. In effect, Umar was denying the woman the right ever to have sex again, a strict punishment for behaviour the woman evidently considered her right. For Umar's high-minded supporters, far from being a terrible injustice this was an act of commendable mercy since the caliph had refrained from imposing the classic penalty of *hadd* for illicit sex: stoning to death.[2]

If the Quran provided the divine architectural blueprint for slavery in the Islamic world, Muslim *fiqh*, or jurisprudence, built up from the seventh to the tenth century in a steady accretion of complex scholarly opinion, would lay its real-world foundations. *Fiqh* was based on the distillation and interpretation by the *ulema* clergy of *sharia*, the ideal of God's law. In this it was supported by the *Sunna*, the authoritative precedent of the Prophet, above all through the canonization of the *hadiths*, his reported sayings, as codified in the two most famous collections by the scholars Mohammed al Bukhari, who died in 870, and Imam Muslim, who died in 875 (although their authenticity was disputed for several centuries).

The triumvirate of Quran, *fiqh* and *Sunna* thereby established the overarching legal framework for the operation of slavery across the sprawling lands of the Dar al Islam, literally the House of Submission. This did not mean that slave-owners, slave-dealers, heads of state or plundering warriors universally followed the law – or what the Quran or the Prophet had counselled. Often there was a cruel chasm between theory and practice. For centuries to come, for example, African Muslims, though legally protected from enslavement as fellow Muslims, repeatedly bore the brunt of their co-religionists' devastating slaving raids, whose ruinous legacy can be felt to this day.

Nor did it mean that there was a single, universal code of law pertaining to slavery, or many other customs and practices, from one end of the Islamic world to the other. Different conditions, communities and regions could, and frequently did, require different approaches. Thus Muslim clerics and jurists regularly found themselves wondering 'what the Quran meant in the mountains of Iran surrounded by Zoroastrians and Buddhists while others did so among Christians in the deserts of North Africa'.[3]

Lawyers had their own differing interpretations, too. When we talk of Sunni Muslim law, properly speaking we are talking about the four separate orthodox *madhhabs*, or schools, of *fiqh*, which had emerged by the twelfth century: Hanbali, Hanafi, Shafi and Maliki. Each school dominated in different regions or was favoured by different dynasties.

Hanbali, for instance, was the preferred school in Iraq and Syria (and, much later, across the Arabian Peninsula), Hanafi for the Ottomans, Shafi in Southeast Asia and Maliki across North Africa and Muslim Spain. The heterodox Shia tradition later had two separate schools, the Jaafari and Zaydi, while the Ibadi school emerged from the break-away Kharijite* sect.[4]

The four orthodox schools shared broadly consistent views on slavery: its legitimacy within the rubric of Islamic law, the teachings of the Quran and Prophetic tradition; the permissibility of enslaving captives in war; the prohibition on enslaving free Muslims; the rights and protections afforded to slaves, including the possibility of manumission. There were, inevitably, certain nuances of legal interpretation and application between the schools. The Hanbali school was generally considered more conservative and literal, the Hanafi, which gave greater scope for personal opinion and reasoning, more liberal. The Maliki approach took account of community practices and local customs, while the Shafi school, combining elements of both Hanafi and Maliki approaches, aimed to strike a balance between textual interpretation and legal reasoning.

Early Maliki law, like the other schools, looked in mesmerizing detail at various aspects of slavery. It addressed with great sophistication the challenges of inheritance law, for instance in complex scenarios such as the case of the female slave who is pregnant at the time of her emancipation and whose husband is a slave at the same time; how to resolve the problem, to give another example, of a Christian owning a *mudabbar* (a slave who has been promised freedom on the master's death) who becomes a Muslim? The *mudabbar* must be separated from his master – no Christian can own a Muslim slave – but remains subject to certain requirements and a slave till the death of his master.[5]

---

* Kharijites, from the Arabic word for 'those who went out', were the earliest Islamic sect, separate from either Sunni or Shia Muslims. They rejected the doctrine of the caliph's infallibility and opposed the monopolization of power by one clan. They also rejected both Sunni claims to the caliphate by the Quraysh tribe and the Shia claims advanced by Ali's descendants, preferring a democratic election to the highest office. Removal of any leader who had sinned was obligatory for this puritanical movement, whose fanatical beliefs fuelled regular rebellions against established authority.

There were essentially two lawful means by which a person could become a slave. A man or woman could either be born into slavery or captured in war. While the first of these had always been important in ancient systems of slavery, for Muslims the second quickly became the dominant route during the early period of Islam. Enslavement during the small-scale raids across the Arabian Peninsula was soon dramatically surpassed by enslavement during the remarkable Arab Conquests from 632 to 750, one of the greatest feats of arms in history.

The Conquests fundamentally altered the concept of slavery. As several generations of marauding horsemen surged out of the Arabian Peninsula to subjugate the Levant, south-west and Central Asia, North Africa, the Iberian Peninsula and a swathe of the Indian Subcontinent, they utterly changed the world around them.

Baladhuri, the ninth-century author of *Kitab Futuh al Buldun (Book of the Conquests of Lands)*, the landmark account of the Conquests, described the caliph Abu Bakr calling on the Arabs to rise up in a 'holy war', which would win them great 'booty'. Those who took up arms, he wrote, were motivated both by straightforward 'greed' and 'the hope of divine remuneration', a rational ambition given the Quran's promise that 'Whoever fights in the path of God, whether he be killed or be victorious, on him shall We bestow a great reward'. (4:74). War meant treasure, treasure was divinely ordained and, among other things, it meant enormous quantities of slaves.[6]

Abu Bakr continued the Conquests where the Prophet had left off, heading north from Arabia. Mohammed had managed to subdue the Arabian Peninsula beneath the banner of the new faith, imposing peace on tribes accustomed to raiding and enslaving each other since antiquity. It was now time to let Islam explore beyond its first borders and plunder all manner of treasure, particularly slaves and slave women.

By the mid-630s, in the immediate aftermath of the Prophet's death and as Arab armies were ransacking the Holy Land, the diplomatic exchanges between rough-hewn Muslims and the sophisticated, courtly Sasanians of Iran pointed unmistakably to war. Before a sword had even been drawn or a spear thrown in anger, the Arab envoy Mughira ibn Shuba, a Companion of the Prophet, appeared before the Persian general Rustam, resplendent on an ornate throne.

Deliberately insulting his hosts, he mocked the Persians as excitable, decadent and lacking in restraint. 'We, the Arabs, are all equal to each other. We do not enslave each other,' he said (they enslaved others instead).[7]

Only a few years earlier, such a statement would have been wildly untrue. Tribal raiding and enslavement had been endemic on the Arabian Peninsula for generations. As it was, Mughira was merely informing his neighbours of the huge changes Mohammed had wrought. The internally raiding Arab tribesmen were a thing of the past. As newly minted Muslims, they now looked beyond the desert for their time-honoured marauding. Other nations and their peoples, rather than fellow Arab Muslims, were the fresh priorities for capture and enslavement.

Shortly after Mughira's provocations, a Muslim army routed the Persians at the Battle of Qadisiyya around 637, another historic Arab victory over the once world-illuminating empire of Iran which brought precious plunder – and more Persian slaves. One of the slaves taken by Mughira during the conquest of Iran, possibly at Qadisiyya, was a highly skilled blacksmith and joiner called Abu Lulua Firuz. Unusually for a non-Arab, and thanks to his particular talents, he was brought back to Medina to work for the caliph Umar. For the leader of the Islamic world it proved a fatal decision. Depressed by his servitude, disillusioned by the heavy taxes imposed on him by his master Mughira, and perhaps also vengeful after the Arab conquest of his country, Abu Lulua stabbed Umar to death while he was leading congregational prayers in 644.

Abu Bakr's brief, two-year caliphate launched what turned out to be less a military campaign than a 118-year period of intense warfare in which countless (because they cannot be counted) hordes of non-Muslims like Abu Lulua were captured and enslaved on several continents. The numbers of slaves owned by some individuals, especially the most wealthy, now rose spectacularly. In the earliest days of Islam, slaves were typically held in small numbers, with the richest individuals having several dozen as a maximum. It has been estimated, for example, that the Prophet owned a total of seventy slaves in his lifetime, typically of Coptic, Syrian, Persian (men like Salman) and Ethiopian (men like Bilal) origin.

Very soon, however, these numbers exploded. The third Muslim caliph, Uthman (r. 644–56), whose reign over the fast-expanding Islamic Empire began only a decade after Mohammed's death, was said to have had 1,000 Mamluk slave soldiers in his ranks – and once manumitted eighty in a single day. Owning slaves had become so common for Muslims by this time that even lowly privates fighting in the army of the fifth caliph, Muawiya (r. 661–80), founder of the world-conquering, Damascus-based Umayyad dynasty, which vastly expanded the Islamic realms until 750, could have up to ten each. The father of Abdullah ibn al Zubayr, the rebel who rose against the Umayyads in the Second Fitna Civil War (680–92) and took refuge in Mecca during a siege which smashed the holy Black Stone of the Kaaba to pieces, reportedly owned 1,000 male slaves and the same number of females. Umayyad princes, who became increasingly decadent during the first half of the eighth century, retreating from their lives in Damascus to relax in desert palaces abundantly stocked with wine and slave women, thought nothing of keeping this number of slaves.[8]

Slaves brought status. Just as eighteenth-century Englishmen and women plunged headlong into an emerging consumer society by flaunting everything from extravagant dresses and drinking mugs to periwigs and racehorses, late-seventh-century Muslims competed through the conspicuous acquisition of enslaved men and women. In 712, Qutayba ibn Muslim, governor of Khorasan, was facing a local difficulty from the ancient, previously subdued city of Samarkand in today's Uzbekistan. After a month-long siege and frenetic fighting, the city fell and punitive terms were agreed. Apart from a stupendous annual tribute of 2.2 million dirhams and a quarter of a ton of gold and silver bullion melted down from Zoroastrian idols and sculptures inside the fire temples, Qutayba demanded 30,000 healthy slaves of fighting age – no old men or young boys among them. An entire city sank into servitude.

While Qutayba was kept occupied in a series of slave-making campaigns in the deserts of southern Afghanistan, 4,000 miles to the west a fellow Muslim-in-arms was making a very different journey in the same cause – holy war, conquest and plunder – including unprecedented quantities of slaves. In the summer of 711, Tariq ibn Ziyad, a

Berber commander, led a Muslim army across the nine-mile Straits of Gibraltar on behalf of his chief, Musa ibn Nusayr, the newly appointed Arab governor of Ifriqiya (North Africa).

Nusayr's human plunder during his conquests on either side of the straits was shocking. Having kept the lion's share for himself and his men, he dutifully sent the caliphs in Damascus their rightful one-fifth share, despatching vast numbers of slaves back to successive Umayyad caliphs in the imperial capital of the Islamic world: 60,000 to Abd al Malik (r. 685–705), 30,000 to Al Walid (r. 705–15) and no fewer than 100,000 to Sulayman (r. 715–17).* Eighth-century statistics are extremely unreliable, but even allowing these figures as a general indication and remembering that commanders in the field retained the great majority of the treasure taken for themselves and their soldiers, the numbers are staggering. As a comparison, during the peak years of the Atlantic slave trade between 1750 and 1850, an average of 74,000 slaves were shipped annually from Africa to the Americas. During the entire period from 1501 to 1866, the annual number of slaves embarked is estimated to have exceeded 100,000 on twelve occasions.[9]

Slaves sometimes featured prominently in legal and diplomatic documents as part of the tribute demanded from newly defeated vassal states. When Sistan, the province encompassing modern eastern Iran and southern Afghanistan, surrendered to the Arabs in 650, the annual tribute agreed reportedly consisted of a million silver dirhams and 1,000 slave girls, each with a golden goblet.† Two years later, fresh from

---

* Between the late seventh century and the middle of the eighth, many North African Berbers, Ibadi Muslims who proclaimed their belief in man's equality before God, had successfully transformed their status 'from slaves to slavers', raiding to their south to enslave sub-Saharan Africans. See E. Savage, 'Berbers and Blacks: Ibadi Slave Traffic in Eighth-Century North Africa', *The Journal of African History*, Vol. 33, No. 3 (1992), p. 351.

† Almost 600 years later, slaves were still featuring prominently in the international trade to Afghanistan. Caravans from India, wrote the thirteenth-century author of *The Merits of Balkh*, arrived in the northern Afghan city of Balkh, bringing 'fine aromatic roots and fragrances such as aloe wood, camphor, and the like; delicious sweet things, such as sugar and sugar-candy; a multitude of precious goods of unlimited value; pretty slave girls and white slave boys from Turkistan; Tamghaji silver coins; Farghana silk . . .'. See Arezou Azad, 'Ecology, Economy, and The Conquest of Khurasan' in *The Umayyad World*, p. 342 (Oxford, 2020).

their lightning conquest of Egypt, the Arabs signed their first diplomatic treaty, the so-called *Baqt*, with the kingdom of Nubia. Although the circumstances are far from clear, and the text which has come down to us was written eight centuries after the event, Al Maqrizi, the fifteenth-century Egyptian historian, stated that among its stipulations was the requirement for the Christian state (as Nubia was by then) to supply the Muslims with annual cargoes of men and women, an obligation that appears to have lasted for between 500 and 700 years.

> Every year you shall deliver three hundred and sixty head of slaves to the Imam of the Muslims. They shall be slaves of good quality of your country, without defect, both male and female, neither extremely old nor children under age. Those you shall deliver to the governor of Aswan. If you harbour a runaway slave of a Muslim or kill a Muslim or a *dhimmi** or attempt to destroy the mosque which the Muslims have constructed in the centre of your city or withhold any of the three hundred and sixty slaves, then the truce and the security shall be abolished and we shall revert to hostility until God decides between us and He is the best judge.[10]

From the outset the Muslim world view was straightforwardly Manichean. Just as the Arabs divided the world into the Dar al Islam of fellow believers and the Dar al Harb, the House of War of the infidels, Islam made a clear distinction between Muslim and non-Muslim slaves.† Buoyed by their lengthening string of victories on the battlefield, a sure sign that these conquests were part of God's divine destiny, Muslims could be forgiven for thinking they carried the world before them. The new faith's superiority complex was clear in the stipulation that while a Muslim could be the slave of a Muslim master, non-Muslims were certainly not permitted to have Muslim slaves.

On one level a slave in the Islamic world *was* chattel, a commodity which could be purchased, sold, gifted, hired and inherited. But slaves

---

* *Dhimmi* were officially protected persons, non-Muslims who in return for their payment of the *jizya* tax and acknowledgement of Muslim authority were given legal protection and permitted freedom of religion.

† A third category, Dar al Sulh, House of Treaty, designated those lands which had a treaty of peace with Muslims, but was not universally recognized by Muslim jurists.

also possessed important religious and legal rights denied their counterparts in other slaving systems or countries. A mother must not be separated from her child, to give one important example. In the words of the Prophet, 'Whoever separates a mother from her child, God will separate from his dear ones on the Day of Resurrection.'[11]

The general principle which pertained in Muslim law was that a child inherited his or her mother's status, with one significant caveat. If the owner of a slave woman had a child with her, that child was considered to be born free – thereby avoiding the perversity of the man's child becoming his slave. There were other important consequences. The *surriyya* concubine who bore her master a child immediately acquired the higher status of *umm al walad*, mother of the child, a designation which meant she could not be sold, her child was free, and she herself became free on her master's death.

This struck at the highest levels of imperial Islamic politics for centuries to come. At first, and almost until the final, blood-soaked demise of the Umayyad dynasty in 750, virtually all the caliphs were the sons of free Arab mothers. Only the last three, who came and went with embarrassing haste in the death throes of the regime, were not. For the Umayyads, those princes who had been born to slave women were simply not considered for the highest offices. Maslama ibn Abd al Malik (d. 738), despite being the pre-eminent military commander of his generation, veteran of a courageous attempt to take Constantinople, was said to have been barred from becoming caliph because his mother was a slave.

All that changed – quickly. The Abbasids, masters of the Islamic world for half a millennium from 750 to 1258, proved remarkably more relaxed. While the caliphs Al Saffah (r. 750–54) and Al Amin (r. 809–13) both had free Arab mothers, the remaining thirty-five of the dynasty were the sons of concubines, a far cry from the persistent Christian disapproval of 'bastard' princes. The influence this conferred on caliph-making concubines was not to be trifled with. A number of women in Baghdad rose to the apex of political power and influence in what was otherwise a world dominated by men.

While the distinction between Muslim and non-Muslim was completely clear, the line between freedom and servitude frequently could be blurred. It was not a case of a man or woman being a slave one day and, once manumitted, free the next. When it came to manumission, a liberated slave was generally less likely to become a freeman than a *mawla* freedman, the addition of that single letter 'd' in English signifying a world of difference. The Arabic word *mawla* could, and can, mean many things. In the context of slavery, for the most part – but by no means always – it tended to refer to a person in a subordinate position, typically a non-Arab convert to Islam.*

Muslim society, and the language used to describe slavery, adapted swiftly to changing circumstances. From the time immediately after the Prophet's death, the seventh, eighth and ninth centuries were transformative. As well as the Arab Conquests, which generated huge numbers of slaves, they were marked by the formal canonization of the Quran and *hadith*, together with a growing body of Islamic law, and rising numbers of conversions to Islam.[12] How to assimilate all these conquered peoples, non-Muslims and otherwise, posed enormous challenges to the inexperienced masters of a growing empire.

In early Islam all *mawlas* were non-Arabian converts to the faith who came from outside the tribal network, a characteristic that relegated them at once to a low status in a society obsessed with tribe and the purity, both real and imagined, of bloodlines. In time, the *mawla* mentioned in the Quran as master, patron or guardian, came to refer – confusingly – to both the freedman *and* his or her patron in a contractual relationship called *walaa* that bound non-Arabs to Arab tribal society and the protection that conferred. *Mawlas* like Bilal, Zayd and Salman could transcend their status through heroism on and off the battlefield – 10 per cent of Mohammed's men at the Battle of Badr were *mawlas* – but it is not difficult to imagine that many more languished in impoverished obscurity and never troubled the chronicles.

---

* One of the main reasons for confusion is the impossibility of reaching a definitive, consistent understanding of the word *mawla* thanks to the complexity of Arabic. It can be used in many contexts, to denote a '"Lord, possessor, chief, benefactor, manumitter, protector, lover, follower, charge, cousin, ally, contractor, in-law, slave, freedman, client," as well as religious master, novice slave-owner, non-Arabian convert to Islam, and political agent.' See Daniel Pipes, 'Mawlas: Freed Slaves and Converts in Early Islam' in Robert Hoyland (ed.), *Muslims and Others in Early Islamic Society*, pp. 277–322.

It seems that manumission hardly changed the circumstances of a freed slave who could do little on his or her own. For financial support, legal protection and political patronage, the *mawla* freedman typically found himself in a position of continued dependence on the patron who had manumitted him. He depended so much on his patron, in fact, that he could even be considered 'unfree'.[13]

A slave *mawla* could join Arab society through manumission, a process whereby the manumitter – as seen earlier with Abu Bakr and Bilal – became his or her patron. And a free non-Arab *mawla* could also gain tribal affiliation through a contract. But, whether they were manumitted slaves or free persons, *mawlas* for the most part remained in a lowly position. In the words of Jahiz, the ninth-century polymath and writer: 'What proves that the profession of secretaries is low is that only subordinates or those in a servile condition practise it.'[14]

Nevertheless, there could be an enormous disparity between formal legal status and real-life outcomes. A *mawla* could transcend his position in society and upend the world. One of the most celebrated *mawlas* during the earliest days of the Abbasids in the mid-eighth century was Abu Muslim. A shadowy figure of Persian origin, he started out as a slave in the Iraqi holy city of Kufa on the banks of the Euphrates before rising steadily up the rungs of revolution to become the military chief of Abu al Abbas, great-great-grandson of Abbas, the Prophet's uncle. He established himself first as the essential linchpin between two centres of opposition to the Umayyads in Kufa and Khorasan, where the flames of revolution had been flickering from around 719. Then, as the Abbasid movement's outstanding military leader, he made himself master of Merv in 748 and sent his armies west, where he won fame on the battlefield in a series of victories over the Umayyads, having reputedly killed 60,000 people in cold blood.

In January 750, he led his outnumbered Abbasid forces against the Umayyad army of Caliph Marwan II on the banks of the Great Zab River, a tributary of the Tigris in northern Iraq. It was a rout, and a calamitous end for the Umayyads, a once-mighty dynasty which had pushed the frontiers of the Muslim Empire from the shores of the Atlantic in the west to the mountains of Afghanistan in the east. Marwan fled across Iraq into Syria, then Egypt, where he was hunted down and decapitated. His head was sent back to Abu al

Abbas, by now the first Abbasid caliph, already revelling in his throne title of Al Saffah, 'The Blood-Shedder'. 'Hold yourselves ready, for I am the pitiless blood-shedder and the destroying avenger,' he warned his followers on the steps of the mosque in Kufa after receiving his oaths of allegiance.[15]

The Blood-Shedder lived up to his name, hunting down and butchering the surviving male members of the Umayyad family with a devotion bordering on the obsessive. He was urged by his brother and successor as caliph, Al Mansur, founder of the imperial city of Baghdad, to deal with Abu Muslim, by now promoted to governor of Khorasan, who with his powerful military base was considered a growing threat to the new dynasty. After Saffah succumbed to smallpox in 754, Mansur wasted no time in attending to this powerful former slave. In 755, Abu Muslim was tricked into attending an audience with the caliph and was assassinated on the spot.

Thankfully, perhaps, as the scholars, lawyers and *hadith*-collectors toiled away in their libraries under the Abbasids in the ninth century, the term *mawla* disappeared and that distinction between free and slave sharpened. After several generations of Muslims had lived and fought and gone to their shallow desert graves, people no longer cared, or perhaps even knew, whether someone's great-great-grandfather had been a slave. The term quietly slipped out of use and Mawla Abdullah or Mawla Abd al Rahman became simply Abdullah, the Slave of God, or Abd al Rahman, Slave of the Most Gracious.

By the late eighth century the most common word used by the jurists for a slave was *abd* for men and *ama* for women – the Quranic euphemism 'those whom your right hands possess' was nowhere to be seen. With a meticulous attention to detail the scholars threw themselves into the minutiae of the institution, opining on, among other issues, emancipation (*itq*); the relation of the freed slave to the former master and client (*walaa*); cases in which the slave has been promised freedom on the master's death (*mudabbar*); the law concerning slaves in emancipation contracts (*mukatab*); the protection conferred upon the slave woman who bears her master a child (*umm al walad*).

One of the earliest Muslim slave manumission documents recorded appears in the monumental, 9,000-page, thirty-three-volume *Nihayat al Arab fi Funun al Adab (The Ultimate Ambition in the Arts of*

Erudition). This fourteenth-century encyclopaedia by the Egyptian Shihab al Din Ahmad al Nuwayri (1279–1333), who one day in 1316 left his dreary clerical job and 'mounted the stallion of reading', is as magnificent as its title suggests. It covers everything from Adam's first sneeze and the dimensions of the sky to the forgetfulness of the ostrich and the rise of Genghis Khan. Though it is a late source for early Islam, the cut-and-paste manumission contract included here accords completely with the description of such a document by the Egyptian jurist Ibn Abd al Hakam (772–829) in his *Al Mukhtasar al Kabir fi al Fiqh (Major Compendium of Jurisprudence)*, which perhaps was not quite as readable as Al Nuwayri's encyclopaedia, published five centuries later. It blends the legal with the Quranic – Allah naturally provides His blessing for the slave's manumission – cites a pertinent *hadith* about a slave in debt remaining a slave and stipulates, as we would put it today, that Terms & Conditions apply:

> _____ contracts with his slave, who is in his possession and ownership, confirmed as a slave and named _____ of _____ nationality, the Muslim, who is known to possess good qualities, piety, virtue and trustworthiness. This contract is according to His statement – He is Most High – 'Contract with them if you know some good in them.' It is made for a total of _____ money, to be apportioned in instalments and paid at the end of every month of _____ in the future. The master donates to the slave a portion of the instalment, a total of _____, of which the slave is absolved, according to God's statement – He is Mighty and Exalted – 'give them some of God's wealth that He has given you'. This is a valid and legal emancipation contract. His master grants him permission to earn money, buy and sell. When he fulfils this contract, he is considered one of the free Muslims: he possesses assets as they do and has the same responsibilities. No one has any claim on him beyond that of legal clientage. But if he defaults, even by a single dirham, he remains in the legal category of slavery, according to the Prophet's statement – God's peace and blessing be upon him – 'the slave is a slave as long as a dirham remains due'. Bearing witness to the contents of this contract on _____ date are _____.[16]

Lawyers then, as now, tended to make things look much clearer on the page than perhaps they were in real life. The formal triumvirate of Quran, *Sunna* and *fiqh* may have set the broad template of slavery within the Muslim realm but not everyone followed the law. Or, to put it another way, there was the law of the holy book, the Prophet and the earnest jurists on the one hand and then there was the often more compelling law of supply and demand – and desire – on the other.

As Muslim African states found to their cost and ruin for many centuries to come, their status as fellow Muslims, supposedly an inviolable legal protection against enslavement, all too frequently offered no defence against the rapacious greed of slavers with eager markets to satisfy. In 1391, for example, the Muslim king of Bornu, today's northern Nigeria, sent a desperate letter to the Egyptian Sultan Barquq (r. 1382–9; 1390–99), himself a former slave, beseeching him for urgent assistance against marauding Arab slave raiders who were ransacking his kingdom and enslaving his people, their co-religionists. 'These Arabs have devastated all our country, the whole of Bornu,' he wrote. 'They have seized our free men and our relatives, who are Muslims, and sold them to the slave dealers of Egypt and Syria and others; some they have kept for their own service.'[17]

Law as envisioned by Allah, His Prophet and the scholars was all very well while it counted, but sometimes it counted for nothing.

3

Race, Racism and Revolt

My verses serve me on the day of boasting
In place of birth and coin;
Though I am a slave, my soul is nobly free;
Though I am black of colour, my nature is white.

Suhaym (d. 660), a slave poet

We know that the Zanj are the least intelligent of men, the
least discerning, and the least concerned with their future.
Like the crow among mankind are the Zanj for they are the
worst of men and the most vicious of creatures in character
and temperament.

Jahiz (776–868)

'Hey, slave! Go and get me a coffee!'

My first reaction was uncertainty. Surely, I hadn't heard correctly. Tensions – like the temperature in Tripoli – were high and nerves were frayed. It was the summer of 2011 and I had returned to the Libyan capital to work with the rebels fighting the Gaddafi regime and to report on the revolution. After almost forty-three years in power, the government appeared to be on the verge of collapse, but it was proving a long verge and a slow collapse. The fighting was vicious and casualties on both sides were mounting. One of the young Libyan Arab *thuwar* (revolutionaries) I was having coffee with was talking to a black man in their group, who was much quieter and less ebullient than them. They were laughing among themselves and clearly thought that calling him a slave was amusing. It was equally clear that he did not.

Later, after I had established that I *had* heard correctly, I asked the fighter why he had called his friend a slave. He had used the very specific Arabic word *abd*. 'Oh, that's nothing,' he replied breezily. 'It's just a word. We all use it. It doesn't mean anything bad. He's a friend of ours. He knows we like him.'

Just a word – the familiar excuse or attempted justification. I already knew from decades working and travelling in the country that many Libyans were racist towards people with darker skin, but I hadn't realized that the brand of racism, and the language it used, was so directly shaped by Libya's history as a major centre of the desert slave trade. Thirty years ago, the British academic John Owen Hunwick, an expert on Islam in Africa, had argued that the old attitudes towards Africans, especially non-Muslims, which existed when slavery was practised, survived in the lands of Mediterranean Islam.[1] It seemed, in some quarters at least, that they still prevailed.

For many centuries sub-Saharan Africans had been raided, enslaved and trafficked north to this coast from what Arabs referred to as *Bilad al Sudan*, Land of the Blacks. Shackled in chains, brutally treated and cracked with thirst, many thousands stumbled across the desert beneath the lash of the slavers' whips, unknown numbers dying along the way. And now here we were in Tripoli, the city from which those slaves who had survived their journey had been despatched across the Mediterranean, and the young revolutionary was calling his friend a slave because the man was black.

It turned out that Libyans routinely refer to black Africans, both fellow Libyans and those from other countries, as *abid*, or slaves – and typically see nothing wrong with it: 'It's just a word.' For those who were not comfortable using such language, there was apparently a more polite Libyan term for black men and women: 'Africans', as though the paler-skinned Libyan Arabs and Berbers of the littoral were themselves not African but came from another continent of their own imagination.

If you looked carefully enough at the 2011 revolution, the racism was there to see. A rebel brigade in the commercial city of Misrata publicly celebrated its role in 'purging slaves, those with black skin'. Black men, Libyans and foreigners alike, were frequently accused of being mercenaries hired by Gaddafi to fight the rebels. With or without evidence, the accusation was sometimes enough to get many of them killed in acts of summary justice. On one weekend alone thirty bodies of mostly black men were discovered near Gaddafi's Bab al Aziziya compound in Tripoli. Many of them had been tortured before their mass execution.[2]

A militiaman in Tripoli spoke for many Libyans when he told a correspondent: 'Libyans don't like people with dark skin, but some are innocent.' Not that this type of racism was unique either to the revolution or to Libya. In 2000, anti-immigrant riots targeting workers in Libya from Ghana, Cameroon, Niger, Chad, Nigeria and Burkina Faso – the medieval Arabs' Land of the Blacks – broke out and dozens were killed. Human Rights Watch diagnosed 'a deep-seated racism and anti-African sentiment in Libyan society'. In the years after the Gaddafi regime's demise, refugees and migrants held in detention centres in Tripoli reported murders, rapes, beatings and forced labour. When one twenty-six-year-old refugee from South Sudan was waiting to go into a clinic for medical treatment, a guard held him back and allowed two lighter-skinned men to go before him. 'You're black. You're a slave,' he was told.[3]

In 2016, five years after the revolution, I was back in Libya as an adviser to the then prime minister, Faiez Serraj. The country was falling apart by then, beset by an intractable civil war pitting east against west. The challenges, predictably after the removal of a long-standing dictator who had eviscerated his state and its fragile institutions, were legion, but I had never anticipated modern slavery to feature among them. And then, in November 2017, I found myself, without warning, directly involved in an international uproar after a sensational story appeared in the media claiming that African migrants were being sold as slaves in secret auctions across Libya. The headline was as damning as it was difficult to comprehend: 'People for Sale: Where Lives Are Auctioned for $400'. A team of CNN journalists reported that they had personally witnessed a dozen men being auctioned off for 'as little as $400 each' and had been told that there were at least nine slave markets operating across the country, although the real figure was said to be much higher. The story was spreading around the world like wildfire. Complete transparency and the announcement of an immediate investigation seemed the most appropriate response, but the official reaction instead was outright denial and obfuscation. It couldn't be true. It had to be a conspiracy to keep Libya down. There was the familiar suggestion that this was the work of the famous 'hidden hands', all too often code for Israel or 'the Jews', blamed so conveniently by so many Arab dictators for so many things for so many years. The Libyan media, usually rumbustious and challenging to the government in this post-Gaddafi era, suddenly closed ranks and cast doubt on the story, suggesting there were 'hidden political objectives' at play. No one wanted to engage with the possibility that the story might have been accurate, a modern postscript to the country's history of trading in humans. The slave trade was supposed to have ended in the nineteenth century but, if CNN was to be believed, it had reappeared covertly in Libya in the twenty-first.[4]

Arab racism towards darker-skinned Africans goes back a long way, many centuries before the Libyan revolutionary in Tripoli called a black man a slave. When reading the ancient Arab literature on sub-Saharan Africans on the one hand and recalling many instances of contemporary racism on the other, it is difficult to avoid the conclusion that the prejudice is deeply ingrained.

The roll call of distinguished, even hugely venerated, Arab and Persian writers who spilt ink to express bigotry towards Africans during the first centuries of Islam is significant. These were not marginal voices in Arab culture. They were leading figures who bestrode the summit of Muslim intellectual and cultural life, famed across the Islamic world for their deep learning and scholarship. They were the medieval Dar al Islam's version of today's public intellectuals, philosophers, bestselling authors and 'thought leaders'.

The list includes men such as the great Jahiz, supreme Arabic prose stylist, a polymath and polemicist whose range, erudition and wit catapulted him to the peak of literary distinction in Abbasid Baghdad. The author of 231 works, Jahiz roved fearlessly and brilliantly across genres and subjects, from his seven-volume *Kitab al Hayawan (Book of Animals)*, which some have argued prefigured what came to be Darwin's theory of natural selection, to essays on pigeon-racing, Islamic theology, the Turk as horseman, miserliness, drunkenness, the Aristotelian view of fish and whether women should be allowed to make noises of pleasure during sex. Yet when it came to writing

about the Zanj, as Arabs routinely referred to the inhabitants of East
Africa and black Africans in general, this fiercely original and unruly
writer proclaimed an orthodoxy which was shared by his peers. He
disparaged their looks, intelligence and supposed viciousness in the
quotation included at the beginning of this chapter.[5]

There were similar sentiments from Ibn Qutayba (828–89), the
Islamic scholar and judge, an expert on Quranic exegesis, *hadith*, law,
grammar, philosophy, astronomy and history. 'Blacks are ugly and
misshapen, because they live in a hot country,' he wrote. 'The heat
overcooks them in the womb and curls their hair.'[6]

These were not dissenting voices, but followed a clear pattern of
Arab racial supremacy. Just as Muslims were by definition superior to
non-Muslims, so pale-skinned Arabs were inherently superior to dark-
skinned Africans, who were destined to be enslaved for the benefit
of Muslims. The tenth-century peripatetic historian Masudi (*c.* 896–
*c.*956), popularly known as the Herodotus of the Arabs, was the prolific
author of *Muruj al Dahab wa Maadin al Jawhar (The Meadows of
Gold and Mines of Gems)*, a vignette-filled history of the world from
Adam and Eve to the late Abbasid caliphate. Citing the Ancient Greek
physician Galen, he wrote that the Zanj had ten qualities: 'kinky hair,
thin eyebrows, broad noses, thick lips, sharp teeth, malodorous skin,
dark pupils, clefty hands and feet, elongated penises and excessive mer-
riment'. As if that was not enough, he added: 'his intellect is weak'.[7]

One man who did more than most to lend lustre to the Islamic golden
age was Ibn Sina, known in the West as Avicenna (980–1037), an outstanding, multi-talented physician, philosopher and father of modern
medicine, author of *Kitab al Shifaa (The Book of Healing)*, which
became a standard medical textbook across Europe for centuries. In
a passage urging the Muslim caliph's responsibility to wage jihad and
enslave the enemies of Islam, he argued that 'those who are far removed
from acquiring virtues are slaves by nature like the Turks and negroes'.
Echoing the language of the Quran, he insisted that this was simply the
natural order of things: 'For there must be masters and slaves.'[8]

These attitudes were by no means unique to Muslims. The Nestorian Christian Ibn Butlan (1001–64) was another golden age luminary,
a Baghdad-born physician whose major work, *Taqwim al Sihhah
(The Maintenance of Health)*, dealt with hygiene, diet and exercise

and was so influential it was still being published in Europe 500 years later. This scholarly Christian appeared no less enthusiastic than his Muslim counterparts in expressing attitudes which seemed to be as instinctive to Arabs of this time as breathing. When he wrote the following passage about Zanj women, he was not merely expressing his individual views. He was speaking for Arab society. Indeed, in his own mind, judging by the title of his buyers' guide to slaves – *Risala fi Shira al Raqiq wa Taqlib al Abid (A Treatise on the Purchase and Management of Slaves)* – he was performing a commendable public service. In it he advised his readers on what to look out for, gave some 'top tips' to avoid being taken in by unscrupulous slave-dealers ('How often has a scraggy girl been sold as plump, a dirty brown as a golden blonde, an ageing man as a full-bottomed boy, a bulging paunch as a trim, flat waist, a stinking mouth as perfumed breath') and guided his male readers on which women made the best sexual partners. He was drawn to Meccan women, who were, he thought, 'languorous, feminine, with supple wrists and of a white colour tinged with brown. Their figures are beautiful, their bodies lissom, their mouths clean and cool, their hair curly, their eyes sickly and languid.' Nevertheless, no matter where the slave came from, it was essential to examine the merchandise carefully and not buy on impulse, especially true when it came to buying slave girls for sex: 'a lecher should not shop for slave girls, for the tumescent has no judgement since he decides at first glance and there is magic in the first glance and charm in the new and strange'. Ibn Butlan's manual is a comprehensive guide to slaves and their different supposed qualities and characteristics. When it came to Zanj women, however, all the prejudices were distilled into one paragraph:

> The Zanj women have many bad qualities. The blacker they are, the uglier their faces, the more pointed their teeth, the less use they are and the more likely to do some harm. For the most part, they are of bad character, and they frequently run away. It is not in their nature to worry. Dancing and rhythm are innate and ingrained in them. Since their utterance is obscure, they have been compensated with music and dance. It is said that if a Zanj were to fall from heaven to earth, he would beat time as he fell ... They can endure hard work. If the Zanj

has had enough to eat, you can chastise him heavily and he will not complain. There is no pleasure to be got from their women because of their stench and the coarseness of their bodies.[9]

Arabs and Persian writers both contrasted what they considered the inherent virtues of the colour white – and pale skin – with the vices of black. Ferdowsi (940–c.1025) was the prince of Persian poets, preserver of the Persian language, literary guardian of his nation's soul, a man whose epic masterpiece *Shahnameh (Book of Kings)*, the world's longest poem by a single author, still dances across Persian lips 1,000 years after his death. In one of his verses, later echoed by his countryman Saadi (1210–c.92), another giant of classical Persian poetry, Ferdowsi voiced the typical view of white good, black bad:

> Do not hope for any good from the ignoble
> For the Zangi will not turn white from washing.[10]

Negative stereotypes occur repeatedly in Muslim writings about black Africans. One popular Persian anecdote expressed the common view that to be a black African was to be ugly, as well as intellectually deficient:

> A Zangi found a mirror and viewed his reflection in it. He saw a flat nose, an ugly face, a charcoal complexion, and inflamed eyes. Because the mirror did not hide his deficiencies, he tossed it to the ground quickly, saying, 'Whoever owned this ugly thing threw it away because of its ugliness.'

In Saadi's *Gulistan*, written in 1238 and destined to become one of the most popular works of Persian prose, we meet Khosaib, described as a 'stupid' black man who is appointed governor of Egypt by the charismatic, street-prowling Abbasid caliph Harun al Rashid (r. 786–809), star of *A Thousand and One Nights*: 'his intellect and discrimination were so limited that, when the tribe of Egyptian agriculturists complained and stated that they had sown cotton along the banks of the Nile and that an untimely rain had destroyed it, he replied: "You ought to have sown wool." '

Nasir al Din al Tusi (1201–74), the Persian philosopher, physician, mathematician, theologian and architect, has been described as one of the greatest scientists of medieval Islam, founder of trigonometry as a mathematical discipline in its own right. Here are his views on black Africans:

'If (various kinds of men) are taken . . . the Negro does not differ from an animal in anything except the fact that his hands have been lifted from the earth . . . Many have seen that the ape is more capable of being trained than the Negro, and more intelligent.'

Such views proved remarkably resilient within the Islamic world and endured long after the earliest days of Islam. Was there a greater intellectual of his time than Ibn Khaldun (1332–1406), doyen of Arab scholars, venerated master theorist on the rise and fall of civilizations and one of the greatest philosophers of the Middle Ages? Here was a pioneering historian, historiographer, father of sociology, political addict and author of a genre-breaking universal history. And yet, when it came to discussing African states, he proved even more chauvinistic than his fellow writers. 'Therefore,' he wrote in the *Muqaddimah*, his most famous work, an early foray into sociology, demography and cultural history, the African nations were 'submissive to slavery, because [black people] have little [that is essentially] human and have attributes that are quite similar to those of dumb animals.'[11] Ibn Khaldun was writing half a millennium after the great Jahiz, but there was little to differentiate the two men's description of the Zanj. Black Africans, in this view, were ugly, idolatrous and lacking in intelligence. Uncivilized, violent and even evil, they went about naked and ate human flesh.

No matter how far they rose within society – and pervasive racism notwithstanding, a number reached illustrious positions – Arab poets of African descent were subject to regular prejudice in the first centuries of Islam. They were known pejoratively as *Aghribat al Arab*, the Crows or Ravens of the Arabs. Their mothers were black and their fathers either did not recognize them or only did so unwillingly.

Why were they the objects of such abuse? For Professor Abduh Badawi of Khartoum, the answer was simple:

> The Arabs despised the black colour as much as they loved the white colour; they described everything that they admired, material or moral, as white. A theme in both eulogy and boasting was the whiteness of a man, just as one of the signs of beauty in a woman was also whiteness.

It was also a proof of her nobility. In the same way a man could be eulogized as 'the son of a white woman'. Similarly, they would boast that they had taken white women as captives.[12]

Some of these poets internalized the discrimination they faced and expressed it in their verse. The swashbuckling warrior-poet Antara ibn Shaddad, a freedman of mixed Arab and African race, wrote:

> Enemies revile me for the blackness of my skin
> But the whiteness of my character effaces the blackness.

One of the most talented was the slave poet Suhaym, whose nickname is a diminutive of blackness – 'little blackie' would be a direct translation. On a number of occasions, he referred to his colour with a mixture of regret (he said it damaged his romantic prospects – 'If I were of pink, these women would love me, but the Lord has shamed me with blackness') and defiance:

> My blackness does not harm my habit, for I am like musk; who tastes
>   it does not forget.
> I am covered with a black garment, but under it there is a lustrous
>   garment with white tails.

Nusayb ibn Rabah (d. 726) rose to become a court poet of the Umayyad caliph Abd al Malik, famous as the builder of Jerusalem's Dome of the Rock. His verses make repeated references to his colour, as in an instance when he has been racially abused by another poet, who wrote of him:

> I saw Nusayb astray among men
> his colour was that of cattle.
> You can tell him by shining blackness
> even if he be oppressed,
> he has the dark face of an oppressor.

Honour-bound to respond to this poetic mockery, Nusayb shoots back:

> Blackness does not diminish me, as long
> as I have this tongue and this stout heart.
> Some are raised up by means of their lineage;
> the verses of my poems are my lineage!

> How much better a keen-minded, clear-spoken
> black than a mute white!

He goes on to observe that musk, too, is black, something to be prized, but adds, 'there is no medicine for the blackness of my skin'.

One of the best known of these early Muslim poets from an African background was Abu Dulama (d. 777), a court poet and satirist under the caliphs Mansur and Mahdi (r. 775–85). Referring to his mother in this self-mocking couplet, he directly addresses what his colour means both to him and to wider Abbasid society:

> We are alike in colour; our faces are black and
> Ugly, our names are shameful.[13]

Probably the most common cultural trope used and adapted by Muslim writers to justify both their racist approaches towards the Zanj and to assert the inherent connection between blackness and slavery was the so-called 'Curse of Ham', a biblical interpretation first told in the Book of Genesis (9:20–27) suggesting that the descendants of Ham, son of Noah, were cursed to be slaves. Never mind that it was rejected by Arab jurists and that the story in the Bible only refers to servitude and makes no mention whatsoever of blackness, it nevertheless continued to serve as 'the single greatest justification for black slavery for more than a thousand years', from medieval Arabs to antebellum American plantation-owners. Blending Jewish and Christian versions of the story of Noah's curse on Ham's son Canaan – after Ham has seen his father, a wine-befuddled Noah, naked – Arabs came to see the tale, conveniently, as a curse of slavery meted out to black people. Masudi summarized this view in three lines: 'The traditionists say that Nuh [Noah], peace be upon him, cursed Ham, praying that his face should become ugly and black, and that his descendants should become slaves to the progeny of Sam.' Masudi's contemporary, Mohammed ibn Jarir al Tabari (839–923), the sober historian whose enormous *Tarikh al Rusul wa al Muluk (History of the Prophets and Kings)* was a fundamental source on the first centuries of Islam, agreed: 'Ham begat all those who are black and curly-haired ... Noah prayed that the hair of Ham's descendants would not grow beyond their ears, and that wherever his descendants met the children of Shem, the latter would enslave them.'[14]

The Curse of Ham was hardly unique to Muslims or Christians and could be found in Jewish tradition, such as the Babylonian Talmud, dating to around 500. Benjamin of Tudela, a Jewish adventurer who kept a diary of his travels in Europe, Asia and Africa between 1169 and 1171, wrote of the people of sub-Saharan Africa resembling 'beasts in every respect', eating herbs on the banks of the Nile and going naked. They were regularly captured by slavers from Aswan who lured them out by throwing figs, wheat and raisins as 'bait' then captured and sold them in Egypt as 'black slaves, being the descendants of Ham'.[15]

An apparent exception to the rule of Arab, Persian, Christian and Jewish bigotry came in a highly unusual essay by Jahiz, the same man who had dismissed the Zanj as 'the least intelligent of men' and whose own grandfather was reportedly black. The 'Superiority of the Blacks over the Whites' featured notional black speakers telling their Arab interlocutors about the 'noble' characteristics of black people, from their generosity, eloquence and singing to their 'bodily strength', 'physical toughness' and 'natural talent for dancing to the rhythm of the tambourine'. Jahiz listed those things where a dark colour was desirable and attractive, such as the Kaaba, lodestone of Islam, ebony, ambergris, night itself and Ethiopian and Sudanese women with dark eyes and lips. He noted, too, that both the Prophet's paternal grandfather, Abd al Muttalib, and his uncle, Abu Talib, were dark-skinned, suggesting Mohammed's mixed ancestry. And besides, he argued, the whole notion of blackness as some kind of divine punishment or defect was nonsense. Skin colour was simply down to the intensity of, and proximity to, the sun. Scholars have agonized over this famous essay, wondering if it can be taken at face value. Given that Jahiz was a professional satirist, it has been suggested that it was neither entirely serious nor did it necessarily reflect its author's real views. Others have argued that it was a polemic against Iraqi Arabs. If so, it must be a lone voice among so many – including Jahiz himself – who expressed the sort of opinions cited above.[16]

The one African nation and its people for which Muslim Arabs did have a distinct soft spot was Ethiopia, a kingdom well known to the tribesmen of the Arabian Peninsula, for whom it was a short sail from the Gulf of Aden. Affection for their Christian neighbour, an age-old trading partner besides, went back to the earliest days of Islam. Faced with mounting persecution from his adversaries in Mecca, the Prophet Mohammed sent some of his Followers to take refuge there in 615. Showing the Arabs' admiration for Ethiopians as a striking contrast to their disdain for other Africans, Ibn al Jawzi (1116–c.1201), the legal scholar, judge, preacher and historian, wrote *Tanwir al Ghabash fi Fadl al Sudan wa al Habash (The Illumination of the Darkness on the Merits of the Dark-Skinned Ones and the Ethiopians).*

Why did he write it? In his own words, and serving up an unconscious, backhanded compliment as he dedicated the book to them: 'I saw a group of the best Ethiopians broken-hearted and sad because of the darkness of their colour. So, I informed them that deference is based upon the doing of good, not upon physical beauty.' Jawzi's chapters 'On the Obviousness that there is no Preference for Light-Skinned Peoples over Dark-Skinned Peoples Based upon Colour' and 'On the Distinguished Dark-Skinned Males Among the Companions', together with numerous examples of distinguished black scholars, poets, jurists and leaders, look like a valiant, almost solitary, attempt to redress the balance.[17] Other Arab writers later joined the effort: Ibn Abd al Baqi, who wanted to examine 'the gems of their exalted virtues' in his book *Al Tiraz al Mankush fi Mahasin al Hubush (The Coloured Brocade Concerning the Good Qualities of the Ethiopians)*, written in 1583, and Al Suyuti (1445–1505), the prolific Egyptian historian, author of *Raf Shaan al Hubshan (On Raising the Status of the Ethiopians).*

The Arab admiration for Ethiopians was not always so high-minded and holy. Sometimes it was more straightforwardly physical. Although he praises the strength, bravery, generosity, good manners and cheerfulness of Ethiopians, Jawzi takes time to dwell on the attractive dark lips, eyelashes, pupils and hair of Ethiopian women, and the sweetness of their breath. Ibn Butlan, the expert guide on buying slaves, wrote approvingly of Ethiopian women's 'gracious, soft and weak bodies ... They are good, obliging, tractable and trustworthy and are distinguished by strength of character and weakness of body.' In other words, they made excellent concubines.

From the earliest days of Islam, then, with the partial exception of Ethiopians, black Africans – the Zanj of Arabic writings and imagination – had been the subject of a barrage of racist attacks. Their supposed negative characteristics and deficiencies had been laid bare again and again by mostly Muslim writers who, taken together, represented the *Who's Who* of Arabic and Persian literature. For Muslim societies during these centuries, it could hardly be clearer. Cursed from antiquity, the Zanj were fit for slavery and nothing else, a divine blessing from Allah graciously provided for the good of all Muslims. Do with them what you will, but don't expect too much.

The Zanj themselves had other ideas. And this time it would not be a question of words – in holy books, legal tracts, or medieval bestsellers. Instead, they would act. In 869 they struck back, leaping from their servitude in the marshy flatlands of southern Iraq into the annals of Islamic history by shaking the Abbasid caliphate to the core in one of the most spectacular, bloody and destructive slave revolts in history.

We must try to imagine what it was like. We do not stand a chance of understanding what happened, how it happened and why, until we can to some extent picture it, feel it and smell it. The horizontal desolation and blistering heat of the marshes. The stench of the overcrowded living quarters. The sting of the whip from the *wakil* overseers. Tens of thousands of enslaved men and women, suffering shoulder to shoulder. Every back-breaking day the same as the last: hours of scraping off the heavy layer of *sebakh* (natron topsoil), hauling it away on donkeys and piling it up in fetid mounds so that the nitrous land of rich landowners could be profitably reclaimed and cultivated to make their fortune.

Then one day in the summer of 869 a strange man appeared.* He looked like an Arab but sounded Persian, judging by his accent. He started speaking to some of the slaves, preaching to them that he received divine revelations and instructions from God. It didn't have to be like this, he told them. They didn't have to live as slaves. Why

---

* This retelling of the Zanj Revolt is closely based on the principal Arab source. The great historian Tabari, who was around thirty when the rebellion began, devoted almost two volumes, around 350 pages, to it – an indication of its importance. See *The History of al Tabari*, Vol. 36, *The Revolt of the Zanj* and Vol. 37, *The Abbasid Recovery*. Alexandre Popović, author of a 1999 monograph on the revolt, calls Tabari's account 'by far the best source from every point of view'.

shouldn't *they* be rich, like these landowners who were working them into an early grave?

The preacher said he had come to this place because Allah had sent him there to raise them out of this wretchedness and bring them great riches – many slaves and much property. Their masters wouldn't stand a chance if the slaves came together and revolted.

It was an auspicious time. For many observers, the old world seemed to be falling apart. Slave soldiers were becoming more powerful than the caliphs they ostensibly served. They had caused so much turbulence in Baghdad that in 835 the caliph Mutasim (r. 833–42) was forced to shift the capital of the Islamic world eighty miles north along the Tigris, founding a new city at Samarra. The once all-conquering empire was disintegrating, the caliphs were losing control. There had been five in the last ten years alone, each one more useless than the last, and most of them murdered in their palace. Civil war stalked the land, there was anarchy in Samarra, the Turk slave soldiers were running amok. The Saffarids and the Samanids, the Tulunids and Qarmatians, everyone appeared to be in open revolt. It was time to join them.

Who was this charismatic man who claimed to be a messenger from God? His name was Ali ibn Mohammed, born in an unremarkable village near Rayy, a few miles south-west of Tehran. He was not a Zanj, but his grandfather was a Sindian slave so he knew what slavery was.

Ali ibn Mohammed was an educated man, a former poet in the court of the caliph Al Muntasir (r. 861–2). He had been teaching children writing, grammar and astronomy. From 863 he had been moving around Bahrain and southern Iraq, roaming across the desert and rabble-rousing against the caliphate while claiming to have received supernatural revelations from the Quran. A prophet for some, for others he was a dangerous troublemaker. Some of his followers had already been killed. Then, in 868, God had ordered him to go to Basra, a turbulent city torn apart by tribal divisions. Here his supporters had been thrown into prison, along with his wife, daughter and oldest son. He talked strangely of divine powers and knowing what every one of his men was thinking.

So there he was in front of a band of fifty or so angry young men, having intercepted a group of slaves on their way to work and thrown their overseers into shackles with a handful of his followers. He raised a silk banner tied to a bargepole. It bore his name and that of his father, in addition to a message traced out prominently in red and green letters: 'Allah has indeed purchased from the believers their lives and wealth in exchange for Paradise. They fight in the cause of Allah and kill or are killed.' He was using the language of the Quran (9:111) and later he would use the egalitarian language of the Kharijites, rebels who taught that the most qualified man should lead, irrespective of the colour of his skin or whether he was a slave.

It was 7 September 869, another broiling day among the malarial marshes, and Ali ibn Mohammed had just proclaimed revolution. History would come to know it as *Thawrat al Zanj*, the Zanj Revolt.

Freedom was infectious. Within a couple of days, the fifty slaves had become 500. The numbers of the slave rebels grew with each skirmish. Their first haul was minimal – 250 dinars, 1,000 dirhams, three horses and assorted weapons – but it was a miracle and a fortune for the enslaved labourers. And success was no less contagious than freedom. These first fights generated momentum, inspiring more men to rise up against their masters.

Sometimes the revolt stuttered and swayed. On 22 October 869 the inexperienced Zanj army was defeated near Basra. Many were killed in battle, and many drowned in the steep-banked Al Kathir Canal. Ali himself was almost killed, fighting alone during a desperate retreat to his base on the Maymun Canal. Two days later, he called on his men to avenge this embarrassment. Three boats sailing out from Basra were ambushed. The Zanj women gave their men rocks with which to bombard the vessels. Overwhelmed, the Basrans, including some of the city's most distinguished men, fell in their droves. Prisoners were decapitated, their heads picketed on stakes as trophies. Those blood-encrusted heads which were not claimed later by their relatives were piled high on to a flat-bottomed Zanj boat which Ali ordered to be let loose to drift on the tide towards Basra, a warning that a new power was on the rise. The body count for Basrans was as apocalyptic as it was unexpected. It became known as *Youm al Shadha*, The Day of the Barges. Ali's fortunes were riding high. God was on their side.

One man who disagreed vehemently with this claim of divine support was Tabari, the main source for the Zanj Revolt, who was probably living in Baghdad as it tore Iraq apart. The high-minded historian, usually cool, clipped and non-judgemental in his prose, was so disgusted by the carnage of 24 October – perhaps incensed by black slaves brazenly throwing off their servitude – that from this moment on in his narrative, probably written around the beginning of the tenth century, he abruptly stopped calling Ali ibn Mohammed the Zanj leader and referred to him instead as 'the enemy of God', 'the cursed one' and, most frequently of all – 218 times across two volumes on the rebellion – *al khabith*, 'the abominable one'.[18]

Buoyed by their amphibious triumph, the Zanj marched and sailed and ambushed and pillaged and plundered their way to more victories over the winter. Basra appealed for urgent assistance from the caliph – there was yet another new one in Samarra, Muhtadi, Guided by God (r. 869–70), but he was beset by uprisings in the provinces and rivals plotting to seize his throne. By the summer of 870, the God-guided Muhtadi had been assassinated by his own military – Tabari described how, when he refused to abdicate, Turkish troops crushed his testicles until he died in excruciating pain. In the chaos the Zanj overran southern Iraq, taking the towns and cities of Al Ubulla, Abadan, Jubba and Ahwaz (in Iran), defeating a succession of rump caliphal armies and killing, torching and destroying everything in their path. The main trade route in and out of Basra was severed and suddenly the heartland of Iraq came under Zanj control. The villages around Basra which normally supplied it with provisions were destroyed and the city, still divided between two warring factions, its shrivelled defences reduced to fifty horsemen under a Turk commander, was put under siege. To make matters worse, an epidemic broke out within the city walls and Ali contracted an alliance with local Bedouin. His surging army was ready to overwhelm Basra.

In the late summer of 871, after a propitious lunar eclipse, Ali heard God's voice again: 'Basra will be a loaf of bread that you will eat from all sides; when the loaf is half eaten, Basra will be destroyed.'[19]

On 7 September 871, Basra fell. The Zanj army stormed the city and put the residents to the sword. Those panic-stricken Basrans who were not cut down in the first wave fled to the central mosque. After securing a promise of amnesty for the local population in return for the city's surrender a couple of days later, the local dignitary Ibrahim ibn Yahya al Muhallabi encouraged his fellow Basrans to assemble in front of his palace. Fearfully they arrived during the night. By sunrise their numbers had swelled to an enormous mass. Then they saw that they were surrounded by Zanj soldiers. A few members of the Muhallabi family were allowed to pass into their palace, the gates were shut behind them and then a signal was given. The Basrans had walked into a deadly trap and were slaughtered in cold blood. The rich were stripped, tortured to give up their gold and silver and killed. The poor were executed where they stood, roaring as they fell: *La ilaha illa Allah*, There is no God but Allah! – so loudly it could be heard miles away. The great mosque was burnt to the ground, the harbour was set on fire, killing more men, women, children and animals. Houses, shops, inns, markets, ships, cargoes, everything was consumed by the flames. The flower of Basran society fell with the city. Men like Al Abbas ibn al Faraj al Riyashi, a great grammarian, were hacked down at prayer, together with distinguished scholars, nobles, merchants and holy men.

Within the overflowing ranks of the Zanj were those who followed a proscribed Islamic sect and had been declared outlaws. Some were killed, others ran away. Many went underground and, in worsening conditions, were reduced to abominable depths. Masudi reported that many slaves hid in houses and down wells, only coming out at night to hunt dogs, rats and cats. They ate the corpses of their brother fighters and eyed each other greedily, waiting for the next man to die. Here is an eyewitness account of one hunger-crazed woman watching another dying:

> She had still not breathed her last when we fell upon her, cut her into pieces, and devoured her. Her sister was with us; while we were at the crossroads called Isa ben Abi Harb, she ran towards the river, with her sister's head in her hand, and began to cry. When asked the reason for her sorrow she replied: 'Those women gathered around my sister and, without letting her die a natural death, cut her into pieces. As for me, they robbed me, and all they left me of my sister's body was her head.' And she continued moaning over the portion that she received when her sister's body was distributed. There were many scenes of this nature and some more atrocious than the one just described.[20]

It was said that the Zanj only left Basra when there was no one left to kill, nothing left to rob. We may wonder at Masudi's report that 300,000 were killed in Basra – although, as a comparison, the population of Baghdad was about 800,000 at this time. Modern historians prefer 10,000–20,000 deaths.

Ali boasted that he had invoked Allah's judgement on Basra with His supporting angels wreaking havoc and bloodshed on the population. Aghast, Ibn al Rumi (836–96), the popular Baghdadi poet, composed a funeral ode for Basra, incandescent at the Zanj's sacrilegious treatment of the city's women:

> So many young virgins, God's seal intact
> exposed, unveiled by them in public!
> So many chaste young maidens enslaved,
> left with nothing to hide their faces.
> . . .
> Did any of you see how they were herded
> in captivity, bleeding head to toe?
> Did any of you see how the Zanj
> surrounded them and cast lots for them?
> Did any of you see them taken as slaves,
> those women accustomed to being waited on and served?
> . . .
> My heart burns at what the Zanj did!
> What a bitter insult. I am in so much pain
> at the thought of what the Zanj did! [21]

Basra the Brilliant had been violated, proud slave-owners had become tortured slaves, families had been slaughtered in their homes and the city's elegant palaces and sturdy mansions had been turned into heaps of ash. Ibn al Rumi ended with a call to arms, for vengeance against these 'vile slaves' who had shamed the entire caliphate. For Masudi, too, the world had been upended. The revolt offended his snobbish, quintessentially Arab obsession with bloodlines. So great was the 'insolence' of the Zanj, he wrote, that they

> auctioned off the women of the Hasan, the Husayn, and the Abbas
> families, descendants of Hashem, of Quraysh and of the most noble

Arab families. A young girl would be sold for two to three dirhams; the crier would announce her genealogy in these terms: 'Such-and-such, daughter of so-and-so, from such-and-such family!' Each black owned ten, twenty and even thirty of these women, who served them as concubines and performed humble tasks for their wives.[22]

Inconceivably, unacceptably, the natural order had been reversed. Pale-skinned aristocratic Arab women now grovelled before – and were being despoiled by – black African men. Masudi wrote of one enslaved Arab woman, a blue-blooded descendant of the caliph Ali, the Prophet's son-in-law, begging Ali ibn Mohammed to free her from her black owner. 'No,' he replied, 'he is your master and suits you better than any other.'[23]

You can sense the entire Arab and Persian world shudder in the rage-filled prose and apocalyptic poetry of Masudi, Tabari, Ibn al Rumi and others when they recounted the Zanj Revolt. But then these were the same men who subscribed to the Curse of Ham theory of black enslavement and who routinely denigrated black Africans in their writings.

September 871 was an unmitigated disaster for Basra, which now sank and shrank from a great port city and commercial metropolis to an obscure town on the Shatt al Arab, but let us not forget that this was also an epic victory for the Zanj, who sadly did not leave us their own chronicle. Here for once is a case of history being written by the losers. Ali's speeches, his actions and those of his army of slaves are not really his at all. They come down to us in the filtered words of very partial Arab and Persian writers; Ali of course hardly gets a fair hearing in any of these sources. Tabari's Ali, as we have seen, is 'the abominable one'. The Ali of Masudi's *Meadows of Gold*, meanwhile, is a man who 'massacred children and old people, men and women, and everywhere he sowed fire and destruction'.[24]

The capture and sacking of Basra was the high ground of the Zanj Revolt. But there was much more action to come. The 870s unfolded in an extended campaign of guerrilla warfare, frustrating the best efforts of the Abbasids to snuff out the revolt altogether. In 872, the caliph Mutamid, Dependent on God by title, but dependent on his slave soldiers and his brother and military commander-in-chief Muwaffaq in reality, sent a large army down from Samarra to crush the Zanj, but Muwaffaq's enemy eluded him again and again, stealing away along canals one minute, resurfacing to launch deadly counter-attacks from the marshes the next. Ali's Zanj were a maddening adversary, fierce in battle and impossible to pin down. Disease and fire ravaged Muwaffaq's camp and eventually, almost empty-handed, he limped back to Abbasid headquarters in Samarra in 873.

Ali ibn Mohammed grew into his role. He established the capital of his fledgling state on both sides of the Abu al Khasib Canal, a western tributary of the Tigris, and named it Al Mukhtara, The Chosen, stoutly defended by its encircling walls and a heavy iron chain and two enormous stone barriers to control access from the water. A ruler naturally should have his own grand palace, so Ali built himself one from bricks of baked clay, a few lesser ones for his chiefs, houses of sun-dried bricks and palm leaves for his people, a treasury and other government buildings for the tax-collectors, administrators and judges, a couple of bridges giving access to both sides of the city, a racecourse and a handful of markets and mosques to satisfy desires material and spiritual. Ali even minted his own money and styled himself the Mahdi, an eschatological messianic figure who was destined to eradicate evil and injustice – but apparently not slavery, for though Ali ibn Mohammed was leading a slave rebellion neither he, nor the liberated Zanj, desired to put an end to slavery. What they wanted was to have their own slaves.

At the height of their pomp and ambition the Zanj advanced on Baghdad, 'Fountainhead of Scholars', plundering poorly defended pilgrim caravans on their way. They were even spotted battling in Mecca, the holy heart of the Islamic world, almost 1,000 miles away. Tabari's volume on the Zanj Revolt ends with a gnomic sentence about 'a detachment of Zanj' attacking Mecca in 878–9, with what results he does not say. So great was Zanj power that sometime in the 870s, Hamdan Qarmat, founder of the Qarmatian Ismaili sect, a one-time ox-driver-turned-militant missionary, proposed an alliance with 'the Prince of the Blacks', saying he could bring along another 100,000 sword-bearing men.* He too had been profiting

---

* The Ismailis represent a minority branch of Shia Islam, who differ from the largest school, the Twelvers. While Twelvers believe in twelve divinely ordained imams, the last of whom is Mohammed al Mahdi, destined to reappear on earth one day from occultation, Ismailis instead recognize the succession of the imamate through the seventh imam, Ismail ibn Jaafar, from whom they take their name.

from the Abbasid loss of power in central and southern Iraq to extend his influence across the region. The two men discussed their options but after several hours they were unable to find common ground, so the proselytizer left Ali at prayer and quietly slipped away to Kufa.

In another intriguing what-might-have-been of history, the Arab historian Ibn al Athir (1160–1233) reported that in the spring of 876, Yaqub ibn Layth al Saffar, founder of the Saffarid dynasty of Sistan, who was leading his own uprising against the Abbasid caliphate, marched unsuccessfully against Baghdad. At Gundeshapur, intellectual nerve centre of the old Sasanian empire of Iran, Ali offered him an alliance and encouraged a second attempt on the Abbasid capital. This time it was Ali who was rudely rebuffed by a would-be partner with a stinging verse from the Quran. 'Say, O Infidels, I will not worship what you worship. You do not worship what I worship . . . To you, your religion, to me my religion.'[25]

Ali and the Zanj were forced to continue their rebellion alone. Perhaps they grew complacent, but towards the end of the decade the tide started to turn and the waters of the reinvigorated Abbasid military began to lap against the borders of the embryonic Zanj state. Unlike the short-lived puppet-caliphs who preceded him, the caliph Mutamid took a stronger line. With the help of his brother Muwaffaq he moved to stamp out the 'Anarchy at Samarra', crush Yaqub's Saffarid uprising in 876 and righten the Abbasid ship of state.

Something had to be done about the Zanj. In late 879 Muwaffaq gave his son Abu al Abbas command of an army of 10,000. The 880s opened with father and son at the helm of a combined army of 50,000 – mostly cavalry and infantry, supported by a fleet of 150 boats manned by experts in amphibious operations. They encircled Zanj-held towns, confiscated dwindling supplies of wheat, rice and barley and starved the population into submission. They razed walls, filled in ditches, burnt boats, retook and reoccupied the major centres in a ruthless, minutely prepared, brilliantly executed campaign which combined the carrot (Muwaffaq repeatedly offered a generous amnesty to those who surrendered, encouraging growing numbers of defections) with the stick (beheading those prisoners who did not).

Town by town, the Zanj forces were driven back steadily until they were holed up en masse in Al Mukhtara.

In February 881, Muwaffaq put the Zanj capital and stronghold – by now said to be a city of 300,000 – under siege, cutting off supplies of food and weapons. In an extravagant stroke of late-ninth-century psychological warfare he then built his own city – Al Muwaffaqiya – complete with its great mosque. Like his enemy he even started minting his own coins. Here in his new headquarters he received growing numbers of Zanj deserters, whom he pardoned and showered with gifts. They were then 'encouraged' to parade in their richly embroidered robes of honour in clear sight of Ali's increasingly beleaguered Zanj army, hemmed in and hungry behind their ramparts.

Muwaffaq's vice tightened. Supplies within the city walls dwindled, the numbers of deserters were said to run into the thousands. Boats sent out on furtive foraging missions along the canals were sunk and captured, their crew butchered one day, ostentatiously pardoned the next. From time to time, Muwaffaq catapulted the severed heads of Zanj soldiers into the heart of the city, which further sapped the defenders' morale. Then he launched a series of attacks against the capital to wear down his enemy. Both sides sustained heavy losses in some desperate fighting during which the Abbasid forces set fire to whole sections of the city. In one raid markets and houses were consumed in a wind-fanned inferno. In December, Muwaffaq launched a third major assault. After demolishing a section of the walls his men stormed into Al Mukhtara, burning offices and capturing the *minbar* pulpit of the great mosque as a war trophy. However, just as he was on the verge of victory, Muwaffaq was shot in the chest by a Byzantine slave archer. His wound was so serious that his commanders urged him to withdraw and recuperate in Baghdad, but the Abbasid commander demurred. The timing was not good. He had been informed of his brother and rival Mutamid's attempted escape from imprisonment by the powerful Turkish slave soldiers at Samarra to take refuge with Ahmad ibn Tulun, founder of the Tulunid dynasty governing Egypt and Syria. It was wiser, then, to stay in the field with his army. Muwaffaq ordered renewed assaults in February and March 883. Ali's palace and treasury were burnt, his secretary and vizier surrendered to the Abbasids, and many enslaved Arab women were rescued.

The blockade took its toll. There was no food left in the city. The markets no longer opened because there was nothing left to sell. Conditions deteriorated to the point where the Zanj were forced into grave-digging cannibalism, if we believe the ever-hostile Tabari. 'If one of them was isolated with a woman, child or man, he would slaughter that person and devour the victim. The stronger Zanj then assailed the weaker ones, and when they isolated a weak person, they killed him and ate his flesh. Then they ate the flesh of their children. Following that, they dug up corpses, sold the shrouds and ate the flesh.'[26]

The Abbasid forces bombarded the city section by section. After repeated attacks, the western part fell and was abandoned. The Zanj withdrew to the eastern half of Al Mukhtara to make their last stand. Those who sensed the end approaching continued to desert to Muwaffaq. A boat stuffed with reeds soaked in naphtha was launched to burn down one of the two bridges across the canal. Frantically the Zanj dived into the water and sank it before it reached its target, but soon the Abbasid boats were bumping against the bobbing heads of decapitated rebels. In May, Ali's harem and children, numbering more than 100, were seized and his residence burnt to the ground.

On 11 August, Muwaffaq offered up his prayers to the Almighty and launched the final assault. During more fierce fighting in the streets a messenger brought him news of Ali's death, but he carried no proof with him. Later, another herald rushed up and presented his commander with what he claimed was Ali's severed hand. The fighting continued. Then one of the Abbasid cavalryman galloped up to his commander, carrying a lance topped with a severed head. He lowered it in front of Muwaffaq. This time there could be no doubt. It was the head of the Zanj leader. Muwaffaq fell to his knees, pressed his head to the blood-stained earth and sent up a prayer of thanks to Allah. At last. It was over. The Zanj Revolt had been crushed.

The poets had their say. You didn't crush a slave revolt which had convulsed and humiliated the Abbasid caliphate for fourteen agonizing years, four months and six days and then say nothing about it. It called for florid, self-congratulatory verse.

Predictably, then, they sang the praises of Muwaffaq and damned Ali to the fires of hell. Here was Yahya ibn Mohammed al Aslami:

> Where are the stars of the heretic, the apostate,
> indeed he was not one of skill and shrewdness,
>
> Good fortune by the hand of a Prince, whose words are deeds,
> visited calamity upon him.
>
> The abominable one fell in battle and was left an easy prey
> to lions of the bush that swooped down on the field . . .

And then Yahya ibn Khalid:

> When the accursed rebel exceeded all bounds
> you swooped down upon him with the whirling sword and spear.
>
> And you cast him to the ground. Crows fly around him
> picking the joints and limbs from his body.
>
> He plunged into the depths of the scorching hell,
> under the weight of chains wearing him away.
>
> This he earned so justly by his numerous crimes
> and by the wicked deeds of his own hands.
>
> By saving it from the plotter you delighted all Islam,
> and rid it of infanticide.[27]

Though he was dead, Ali's journey was not yet over. His head was impaled on another lance and mounted on Muwaffaq's barge, which the Abbasid general ordered to sail slowly back to the city which bore his name. Then he commanded his son Abu al Abbas to continue sailing up and down the region's canals so that all could see for themselves that Ali was dead. Three months later, he instructed Abu al Abbas to take the by now unsavoury head to Baghdad. And so, on 30 November 883, Abu al Abbas and his men, immaculately dressed in their most gorgeous uniforms, entered the City of Peace and held a victory procession, triumphantly parading the head of the empire's most infamous enemy.

Without their cunning and charismatic leader, the Zanj Revolt petered out. There was a flash of opposition here and there, but it was quickly extinguished. A last grisly postscript came three years later, in the spring of 886, when Tabari tells us of the Zanj riot in the city of Wasit, south-east of Baghdad. Six Zanj prisoners in a guarded house in Baghdad were beheaded on the orders of Muwaffaq, their heads sent to him while their decapitated bodies were dumped in the sewer of the house. Sometime later, perhaps to concentrate minds during another time of unrest in Baghdad, caused by high food prices, Muwaffaq ordered these bodies to be hung up on display around the main bridge. With the passage of time and thanks to the heat, Tabari adds, 'they had already become swollen, foul-smelling, and parts of their skin had fallen off'.[28]

It is impossible to know the final death toll from the Zanj Revolt, but historians must always try. Their estimates range from the 500,000 suggested by Masudi and the widely quoted figure of 1,500,000 from Al Suli, the tenth-century Turkic scholar, to the less plausible 2.5 million claimed by the thirteenth-century historian Ibn al Taqtaqi. As the early Muslim chroniclers liked to put it: 'Allah knows best.'

Though they had been slaughtered in their many thousands, finally crushed by the weight of numbers against them, even in defeat the enslaved Africans had managed to achieve the unthinkable. Though they might not have put an end to plantation slavery in the Islamic world, as historians have previously suggested, they had risen up together, rocked the Abbasid Empire to its foundations and written themselves into history. It was the largest mass slave revolt in the Arab world, one of the most successful anywhere, in any period, and would never again be repeated.

4

Sex and Singing: The Concubines

They hid him from my eyes but his presence was
in the heart, enveloped but not concealed.

> The famous concubine and poet Arib al Maamuniyya
> (797–890), defiantly remembering her lover

[What] makes singing slave-girls fetch such extraordinary
prices is simply the desire they arouse ... three senses are
involved, not to mention the heart, which makes the fourth:
sight, in the contemplation of a beautiful and appetizing slave-
girl – for skill and beauty are only rarely found together for
the delectation of patrons taking their ease; hearing, as the
share of the man who simply enjoys the pleasure of listening
to a musical instrument; and touch, in lust and the urge for
sexual gratification ... Thus, time spent in the company of
singing slave-girls entails the most perilous enticement.

> Al Jahiz, 'Portrait of a Singing Slave-girl'

If black Africans, the Zanj of hostile Muslim writers, were the lowliest figures in the hierarchy of servitude, then the *qiyan*, elite singing slave girls or courtesans, the most accomplished of whom could become royal concubines, were surely the loveliest. Though few ever set eyes on them, they were, like the most famous poets – Abu Nuwas (756–814), Abu al Atahiya (748–828) and Bashar ibn Burd (d. *c.*784), to take three of the best known – the celebrities of their day. They occupied an exclusive segment of society and dominated a very specific, richly recorded period in history in the heart of the Islamic world from the time of the recklessly free-spending caliph Mahdi until the mid-ninth century, when such conspicuous consumption was no longer possible in a fracturing caliphate.

The lives of both concubines and poets were evidence of the social mobility possible in the Abbasid era, however capricious, arbitrary and exceptional it might have been. Glittering stars within the belletristic firmament, they also shared the rewarding and perilous space devoted exclusively to the caliph's enjoyment and pleasure. They could just as easily make life-changing fortunes from an amusing aperçu or bawdy joke as lose their heads from a slip of the tongue in front of a wine-addled caliph. As far as impromptu orders from the throne went, 'Cut off his head!' was almost as routine as Friday prayers, and much more entertaining. And being a woman was by no means a guarantee of keeping your head attached to your shoulders.

Poets and concubines equally could rise from the margins of society to its top tier. Abu al Atahiya, a permanently lovelorn poet, started out as a penniless pot-seller in Kufa, surviving on his wits. Despite falling violently in love with a beautiful slave girl called Utba, who belonged to one of the caliph Mahdi's wives and who moved him to pen some fairly impudent verse, he managed – just – to keep his head during the reign of half a dozen caliphs.

In one poem he offered an eighth-century version of the 'something in my eye' excuse when caught sobbing.

> How often I try, in shame, to hide my tears from some friend!
> When he looks at me closely, he scolds. Then I say: 'I am not crying,
> The cloak grazed my eye as I was putting it on.'[1]

The tempestuous story of Abu al Atahiya's unrequited love for Utba became a court scandal, and the dishonour brought the girl to tears in front of Mahdi, who had the poet publicly thrashed. Refusing to give up his romantic quest, Abu al Atahiya later sent the ruler of the Islamic world some verses pleading for Utba and, when that failed, announced he was giving up poetry. This was a big mistake. A poet who renounced poetry was as useful to the caliph as a concubine who withdrew her services. He was thrown into prison and then called before the caliph and made to watch as a man was beheaded in front of him. Mahdi turned to Abu al Atahiya. 'Choose either to make verses or to be sent after him,' he said. 'I shall make verses,' the poet wisely replied.[2]

There was one glaring difference between a poet and a concubine, however, notwithstanding that some of these *qiyan* were extremely talented poets in their own right. Unlike poets, concubines were not free, though some courtesans were. While their servitude was far removed from that of an agricultural or domestic slave, as slaves, or property, they could still be bought and sold, gifted and inherited, manumitted and freed. The market in the most beautiful women, underwritten by the caliph and his courtiers, men with the deepest pockets and largest egos in Baghdad, could be frantic, the sums involved colossal.

Mahdi, a byword for ostentation and extravagance, bought one woman called Maknuna, 'who took pride in her slender hips and high chest', for 100,000 silver dirhams. Basbas (Caress), who was in even greater demand, cost 17,000 gold dinars – a single gold dinar was worth around twenty silver dirhams and each dirham weighed around three grams. To put these kinds of sums in perspective, an untrained female slave typically cost twenty dinars during the tenth to thirteenth centuries, making Basbas 850 times more expensive.

Arab chronicles are full of scurrilous, sometimes hyperbolic tittle-tattle about concubines and the passions they aroused. Dananis, one of the most famous women of Harun al Rashid's harem, provoked his ageing wife Zubayda (Little Butterball), perhaps the greatest of the Abbasid queens, to extreme jealousy after the caliph showered the singing slave girl with lavish gifts, including a necklace worth 30,000 dirhams, supposedly in recognition of her artistic talents. The wily Zubayda later apologized to her husband after listening to the slave girl sing and excused her earlier fury by presenting him with another ten exceptionally beautiful slave girls, who duly produced more royal offspring. It is worth remembering that thirty-five of the thirty-seven Abbasid caliphs were the sons of concubines, a reproductive reality which maintained the dynasty for half a millennium and conferred considerable behind-the-throne influence and power.

Harun, like so many of his successors as caliph, was devoted to the sexual pleasures of his harem. Tabari wrote how, during the most scorching days of summer, when Harun would take an afternoon siesta in his pavilion, a silver urn was brought in to the caliph in which the royal perfume merchant had blended a fragrant mixture of scent, saffron, aromatic substances and rosewater. Seven tunics of fine Rashidi linen in a feminine cut were then dipped into the mixture. Every day, seven slave girls were brought into the caliph's chamber, where they observed a meticulous protocol. First, they removed their clothes and were dressed in the exquisitely scented linen shifts. Then they took their place on pierced seats above piles of burning incense, until their clothes were dry and their bodies were perfumed to the caliph's taste. Only once this elaborate process was complete could lovemaking begin.

The lives and careers of some of the most famous Abbasid concubines are well documented in at least half a dozen sources animated with the voices of these remarkable women. They sing magnificently across the ages.

There is a jaundiced, exaggerated and amusing treatise on singing slave girls from the incomparable Jahiz, who warns his readers of the clear and present dangers of these alluring sirens.[3] 'The singing slave-girl is unlikely to be true and loyal in love, for both by temperament and training she is disposed to set traps and spread nets to catch lovers in their toils,' he writes. Such a girl will begin by flirting with her admirer, shoot him exquisite longing looks, drink with him 'with gusto', feign grief when he leaves, send him snatches of poetry in *billets doux*, give him a lock of hair, present him with a belt and some sweets at Nowruz New Year or a ring and some apples at Mihrajan, the Persian festival of autumn. Sometimes this may be genuine, but, Jahiz continues, 'for most of the time she is not straightforward, but employs treachery and wiles to suck her victim dry and then abandons him'. She routinely plays rival lovers off against each other to her financial advantage. 'Had the devil no other fatal wiles, no other badge, and no other seductive charms, singing slave-girls would assuredly meet his purpose.' Jahiz freely acknowledged the intellectual range of the most accomplished *qiyan*, who typically had a repertoire of 4,000 songs, each of two to four lines, none of which mentioned God unless inadvertently, and mostly designed to separate a man from his money by stimulating his passion and libido. 'They are all on such subjects as adultery, procuring, love, youthful dalliance, yearning desire and amorous passion.'

Thrilling for some men, crushingly unattainable for many more, the large numbers of beautiful, elegant and fashionable slave girls introduced into Abbasid society were not to everyone's taste. Their racy behaviour appalled high-minded Muslims. The tenth-century philosopher Al Tawhidi complained that innocence had been lost and morals were sinking. 'They used to engage in courtship without suspicion,' he wrote. 'A man would openly call, converse with those in the house then take his leave. Now nothing will satisfy them except carnal intercourse.'[4]

Best known for his monumental *Kitab al Aghani (Book of Songs)*, a 10,000-page compendium of Arab and Persian music, the tenth-century Persian litterateur Abu al Faraj al Isfahani (897–967) was asked by Muizz al Dawla (r. 945–67), the Buyid ruler of Iraq, to compile a book of slave women poets. The result was *Al Imaa al Shawaair (The Slave Poetesses)*, a verse-and-anecdote-filled treasure trove. Then there was *Kitab al Muwashsha (The Brocaded Book)*, a handbook on court manners and good etiquette for grandees, by Abu Tayyib al Washsha (c.869–937), who echoed Jahiz's warnings to the young gentlemen of Baghdad. It was all the women's fault, of course. There was no greater disaster for a decent, educated young man than to fall in love with a slave girl, 'for their love is false, their passion adulterated and their desire tends to transience and inconsistency, whose object is greed and worldliness, so that their love is displayed before those who appear well-off and rich, soon to be transferred away at the sight of penury and hardship'. As soon as they saw you drowning in 'the sea of calamity', they would hit you with demands for fiendishly expensive presents: dresses from Aden, fabulously soft cloaks from Nishapur and turbans from Sus.[5]

And then there was Masudi, who provided a lively flow of stories about the *qiyan* in his wonderfully readable *Meadows of Gold*, and the much later *Al Mustazraf min Akhbar al Jawari (Choice Anecdotes from the Accounts of Concubines)* by the prolific Egyptian scholar and historian Al Suyuti, author of around 700 works. And last, but certainly not least, was *Nisaa al Khulafa (The Consorts of the Caliphs, Both Free and Slave)* by Ibn al Sa'i (d. 1276), an unmissable font of storytelling and a celebration of female virtuosity.

Sometimes the past can appear remote, impersonal and dry. Not here.

In these medieval sources it is immediate, highly personal and filled with spirit, passion and poetry. The women speak for themselves, in their own voices, an obvious rarity in the world of slavery which traditionally succumbs to the silence of those in servitude. Unrepresentative, certainly, for these were no domestic drudges, prostitutes or ordinary entertainers. They were elite women in a highly stratified society. Their lives were as far removed from an 'ordinary' household slave as the caliph was from a *judhaba* roast meat-seller on the streets of Baghdad. Yet their voices still talk to us compellingly across the great gulf of time. There is love, loss, learning, pain and hurt, grief, greed, bitterness, regret, rivalry and competition, wit, cunning, loyalty and betrayal, squabbles and quarrels, joy, friendship and camaraderie – all of it experienced 1,200 years ago, and reams of verse to commemorate it.

The stories also bear witness to the fragility of these women's positions. Whatever their beauty, however well trained and superbly skilled they might have been as singers, composers, poets and sexual companions, their lives remained completely dependent on the caliph's whim. Woe to the woman who ever forgot that. Take Farida, a favourite of the caliph Wathiq (r. 842–7) who, although besotted by her, once kicked her violently while she played the *oud* (a Middle Eastern lute) because he could not stomach the thought of his brother Mutawakkil (r. 847–61) succeeding him and taking possession of her. After Wathiq's death from dropsy, Mutawakkil duly succeeded to the throne, acquired Farida and ordered her to play the *oud* for him. When she refused and tore the strings off the instrument in fidelity to Wathiq, he had her whipped to death for her disobedience.

The lives of royal concubines were strictly policed and many women must have found their elegant captivity completely stultifying. Some experimented with lesbian affairs, though the price of discovery could be fatal. Tabari relates a chilling story in the words of Ali ibn Yaqtin, a courtier of Harun's brother and short-lived caliph Hadi (r. 785–6). Ali was dining one night with the caliph when a eunuch suddenly came up to him and whispered something in his ear. Hadi sprang up, told his guests not to leave, and only returned after a long while, out of breath. He was accompanied by the eunuch, now trembling, carrying a dish covered with a napkin. Hadi ordered him to reveal what was beneath it.

... behold, the dish held the heads of two slave-girls, with more beautiful faces and hair, by God, than I had ever seen before; there were
jewels on their heads, arranged in the hair, and a sweet perfume was
diffused from them. We found this a horrific sight. The Caliph said, 'Do
you know what these two were up to ... We received information that
they were in love with each other and had got together for an immoral
purpose. So I set this eunuch to watch over them and to report to me
what they were doing. In due course, he came to me and informed me
that they had got together, so I went along and found them under a
single coverlet committing an immoral act. I thereupon killed them.' ...
The Caliph then resumed his former conversation as if he had done
nothing unusual in the meantime.[6]

Fortunately, there are many more stories about these elite slave women
which do not involve such terrible violence. Apart from the flurry of
ripe expressions and sexually explicit material, their main focus tends
to be whimsical anecdotes and examples of wit, wordplay and verse-
capping competitions. These tales are what Herodotus, the man who
invented history 2,500 years ago, called the essence of history, the
'great and marvellous deeds' whose recording ensures that 'human
achievements may not become forgotten in time' nor 'without their
glory'.[7] The medieval Arab sources offer an extraordinarily vibrant
insight into a very specific form of female servitude and the lives of
the women who experienced it.

We will look now at three of them: Inan, Arib and Mahbuba.

'Inan was the first poet to become famous under the Abbasids and
the most gifted poet of her generation. The major male poets of the
time would seek her out in her master's house where they would recite
their verses to her and have her pass judgment.'[8]

This was the considered view of Ibn al Sa'i (d. 1276). Librarian
of the great Nizamiya and Munstansiriya law colleges, historian,
poet, Abbasid prodigy and prolific Iraqi scholar, Ibn al Sa'i compiled,
among many other works, his shimmering survey of thirty-nine
multi-ethnic royal concubines and wives from the golden age
of Baghdad to his own time 500 years later. *The Consorts of the
Caliphs* is his only work which survives intact. Here was a man who

at the age of sixty-three somehow dodged Hulagu Khan's caliphate-ending invasion and maniacal killing spree in the Abbasid capital in 1258, a date which lives on in infamy in Iraq to this day. Grandson of Genghis Khan, Hulagu admitted to killing 200,000 in Baghdad, while Muslim sources suggested a figure at least four times higher. Ibn al Sa'i was writing about the royal consorts shortly before 1258 and was self-consciously harking back to the halcyon days of the caliphate just as it and his beloved City of Peace stood on the brink of ruin. The stars of his book, exclusively female, are cultural icons, women who wrote verse, composed music, endowed law colleges and libraries, built bridges, waterways and mausolea, provisioned Mecca-bound *hajj* pilgrims and in some cases even had their funeral services conducted by caliphs – in addition to being their sexual companions.

And of these thirty-nine women, Ibn al Sa'i unhesitatingly ranked a woman called Inan at the pinnacle of poetic excellence. He was not alone in this verdict. Isfahani devoted the first and longest entry in his own book about slave women poets to Inan. He decided to begin with Inan because she was 'the most celebrated in her time and surpassed all others'. This was high praise from the author of the *Book of Songs*, a work which took him half a century to complete and a uniquely important source full of technical knowledge on music, melody, metre and verse. Inan received an entry in that, too.

Daughter of an Arab father and slave mother, Inan was brought up in the south-eastern part of the Najd in today's Saudi Arabia. Her education was essentially an Abbasid finishing school for musical courtesans and she was intensively trained in the arts of writing and reciting poetry, singing and musical theory. When she was considered ready, she was brought to Baghdad by her owner, Abu Khalid al Natifi – his name translates as seller of sweet nut brittle – who used her as the showy centrepiece of literary salons in his house. A blonde-haired woman, she was said to be so flawlessly beautiful that the nail of her little toe was deliberately nicked to ward off the evil eye by giving her a minor imperfection. But Inan's looks were just one facet of her. Her particular talent for the very public cut and thrust of poetic jousting, a good deal of it coarse and sexually explicit, ensured that the greatest poets and men of letters flocked to these soirées: the hell-raising Bacchic poet Abu Nuwas, the Lord Byron of Baghdad, with whom she had the most turbulent, society-shocking affair; Marwan ibn Abi Hafsa, the sordidly avaricious, Shia-bashing classical poet; Al Abbas ibn al Ahnaf, master of the courtly love genre and a favourite of the caliph Harun; Al Yazidi al Himyari, tutor to Harun's son and future caliph Maamun (r. 813–33), and many others besides.

One reason why Inan was so admired in her time, and is still celebrated today, is that she refused to be shackled by convention. In a world ruled by men she was, gloriously, her own woman. And though often mistreated and abused by those men who aspired to control her, Inan always managed to hold her own. She was fearless.

We hear from Isfahani of one occasion when, not feeling well, she refused to meet the poet Marwan, whom Natifi had invited to his house to see her. This defiance earned her a whipping from her master, who in another act of cruelty then asked his honoured guest to come and have a look at her. Seeing her weeping in pain and embarrassment, Marwan extemporized:

> Inan weeps tears that scatter
> like a broken string of pearls.

She replied with spirit:

> May the tyrant's right arm wither
> as his cruel whip unfurls!

Inevitably the brilliance of Inan's rapier-like repartee loses much of its élan in translation.* The sophistication of Arabic scansion, internal rhyming and competitive verse-capping disappears. What we are left with, though, is clear evidence of her intelligence, quickness of mind and readiness to use language which would land most people at the caliph's court in deep trouble.

In one public encounter with Abu Nuwas, she asked him if he knew much about scansion and, after he had boasted that he was

---

* 'Classical Arabic poetry remains undiscovered by English readers, mainly because there are so few readable translations,' writes Eric Ormsby in 'Questions for Stones: On Classical Arabic Poetry'. See *Parnassus: Poetry in Review*, Vol. 25, Nos 1 and 2 (2001), p. 18.

a master of it, lured him into making a fool of himself. Scan this, she said:

> *Akaltu al khardalah al shaami fi safhati khabbazi . . .*
> I ate Syrian mustard on a baker's platter . . .

He broke it down into metrical feet as follows:

> *Akaltu al khar . . . ti-tum ti-tum*
> I ate some shit . . . ti-tum ti-tum . . .

In an attempt to have his poetic revenge, as the courtiers chuckled away at his expense, he challenged Inan to scan the following contrived verse:

> *Hawwilu anna kanisatakum ya bani hammalati al hatabi . . .*
> Keep your church far from us, O sons of the wood-carrier . . .

She broke it down:

> *Hawwilu an tum-ti tum-ti nakani . . .*
> Keep away tum-ti-tum-ti he has fucked me . . .

Given the limitations of competitive poetry in translation, we must defer to Inan's contemporaries to get a better understanding of her brilliance and the high esteem in which they held her. Ibn al-Sa'i reports that when he heard Inan extemporizing verses after her whipping from Al Natifi, Marwan ibn Abi Hafsa exclaimed: 'If any man or *jinn* [spirit] alive is a greater poet than she, I'll free every single slave I own!'

A consistent feature in the stories about Inan is her sheer strength of character. Whether she is at the peak of her fortune or at a low ebb, she always looms large as an intensely vital force. The poet and writer Hasan ibn Wahb ibn Said described a visit to Inan during which they drank and feasted heartily together, sang and enjoyed themselves. She drank six goblets of wine and they made love five times, after which she was still unsatisfied. He asked her to sing him a famous song:

> O my two companions, lovers with no hearts
> and a beloved who does not sin
> O host of lovers how execrable is love
> if the beloved will not meet the lover

She tweaked it mischievously to give it a bawdier flavour:

> O my two companions, lovers have no cocks
> and there is no pleasure in a lover who is unattainable
> O host of lovers how execrable is love
> If there is flabbiness in the lover's prick

In time Abu Nuwas, who was just one of her many lovers, was completely smitten. The pair indulged in a series of romantic exchanges. Some of it was dangerously subversive, as when they turned holy verses from the Quran into smut and innuendo about the length of penises and lovemaking. Sometimes it was just heartfelt and lovestruck as in this declaration from Abu Nuwas:

> O Inan who resembles the wide-eyed oryxes
> You blame me for love of you
> Your beauty is like no other that I know
> It has left people besotted.

Then again it could be crude and confrontational:

Abu Nuwas:	What's your wish from an ardent lover
	Who wants a little drop from you?
Inan:	You are telling me that?
	Go wank yourself!
Abu Nuwas:	I'd like that but fear
	that you would be jealous of my hand.
Inan:	Perish you! And perish whosoever shall be jealous on
	your account
	Go fuck your mother, she is a hag!

Inan and Abu Nuwas were, for a while, *the* most famous couple in Baghdad – centre of the most sophisticated civilization on earth. But like so many public romances, it could not last. The break, when it came, was sensational. One day Inan sent a maid to his house with an invitation to dinner. The incorrigible Abu Nuwas promptly bedded the woman and then, to add poetic insult to romantic injury, crowed about his conquest in verse. The gloves were off. She responded in kind, mocking his homosexuality, which probably came as little surprise to those who knew, or knew of, this wine-drinking, boy-chasing libertine and show-off who celebrated his transgressive trysts in verse. This was a man who set the 'ripe, swelling buttocks' of 'beardless boys' to verse and boasted about his threesomes.

The cruelty of Abu Nuwas's rejoinder, the calculated act of literally devaluing her, can be felt all these centuries later:

> Inan of al Natif is a slave girl
> Whose cunt has become a public concourse for fucking
> None will buy her but if he be the son of a whore
> Or a pimp whosoever he may be.

The assault was deeply wounding on both a romantic and pragmatic level. Like so many men who set eyes on her, the caliph Harun, master of his age, unchallenged monarch of an all-powerful empire, was, Isfahani tells us, 'quite besotted and infatuated with her'. He was determined to have her. The problem was that Abu Nuwas's obscene, very public insult to Inan struck directly at his plan to purchase her. Scurrilous verse spread fast, so all of Baghdad knew what was going on. According to one version of the story, it was Harun's wife Zubayda who had 'persuaded' Abu Nuwas to pen this filthy verse about Inan precisely to discourage her husband from buying her. Whatever the truth of that, Al Natifi, asked what his price was for the most famous courtesan of her time, now proposed the colossal sum of 100,000 dinars – this at a time when an average married man and his wife required 300 dirhams a year for their living costs.[9] Harun accepted, but only on the basis that it was paid in dirhams at a ridiculously favourable (to the caliph) rate of exchange. Bravely, considering that Harun was perfectly happy to decapitate those who opposed him, Al Natifi demurred. Inan was then brought before Harun, who wished to inspect her at closer quarters. Perhaps as a straightforward negotiating ploy, Harun shook his head sadly. The price was too high.

Sensing that her value was in freefall and that she would be denied Harun's all-powerful patronage, protection and the riches they would bring, Inan reacted instinctively. She picked up her pen and pleaded with the enormously powerful Jaafar ibn Yahya, Harun's vizier, and his father Yahya to put in a good word for her with the caliph. She did this not in any ordinary letter or the sort of hastily knocked-out epigram which a less talented slave girl might have attempted, but in a full-length *qasida*, a classical and complicated form of poem, like an ode with its own set of rules honoured by custom. Still Harun dragged his feet, the fires of his passion for Inan cooled by the public accusations of sexual immorality and, just as bad for caliphal *amour-propre*, the brazenly targeted insult that only the 'son of a whore' or 'a pimp' would buy her. No. It was too bad. It couldn't be done.

Again, Inan picked up her pen. This time she wrote to Harun directly.

> I thrived in the shade of your love
> secure with you and fearing not your rejection
> Then the slanderers came between us and it pleased you
> to gladden the eyes of the slanderers at my expense
> By my life that was less fitting
> of you in justice – may I ever be your ransom.

Around this time, and probably just as well for all concerned, Al Natifi died. Harun, who was only flesh and blood, had been unable to put Inan out of his mind. Now he instructed his chief eunuch Masrur to set her on a bench at Baghdad's Bab al Karkh gate in the red-light district and auction her off to pay her master's debts. The mere act of doing this transformed one of the most brilliant and desirable *qiyan* into a low-class domestic slave. It was a scorching punishment. Masrur called out to the rapidly gathering crowd for their bids. It is not difficult to imagine their taunts and mockery. But Inan was made of stronger stuff. 'May Allah shame him who shamed me, and humiliate him who humiliated me,' she cried out in defiance.

Bidding, we are told, stopped at 200,000 dirhams, at which point a man acting discreetly for the caliph signalled that he was prepared to add another 25,000 to seal the deal and put an end to this unpleasant show. Harun had his woman and Inan had her caliph. She bore him two boys, both of whom died in their infancy. She accompanied him to the Persian province of Khurasan where he died, followed only a little afterwards by Inan.*

'I never saw a more beautiful or refined woman than Arib.'[10] If this verdict from Ibn al Sa'i sounds a little excessive, we might note, first, that he was quoting Ishaq al Mawsili (c.767–850), the pre-eminent musician of his generation, and second, that this very talented woman captured the hearts, and exercised the libidos, of no fewer than eight caliphs over at least seven decades: Amin (r. 809–13), Maamun (r. 813–33), Mutasim (r. 833–42), Wathiq (r. 842–7), Mutawakkil (r. 847–61), Mutazz (r. 866–9), Muhtadi (r. 869–70) and Mutamid (r. 870–92) all fell for her, and that is without counting their princely sons, a number of whom were equally enraptured.

Again, and as with Inan, her famous beauty was only part of the attraction. Having paid tribute to it, Ishaq went on to say that he had never seen someone who sang, played music, wrote poetry or played chess so well. 'She possessed every quality of elegance and skill one could wish for in a woman.' Matchless in her vivacity, conversation and presence of mind, she held her own easily among the greatest quartet of singers of her generation as well as being a celebrated poet in her own right. Writing several centuries later, Ibn Asakir, the twelfth-century historian, acknowledged the traditions which paid respect to Arib's poetry and song, one of which boldly stated: 'I never saw a woman with a more beautiful singing voice and knowledge of poetry.' For Isfahani, she was the greatest diva of her time.

Uncertainty surrounds her immediate origins. Born around 797, there were suggestions, never entirely discouraged, that she was the daughter of Jaafar al Barmaki, the second most powerful man in the empire after Harun, and one of his slave girls, a woman called Fatima whom he was said to love above all others. Jaafar's father Yahya, himself formerly the caliph's almighty vizier, was horrified by his son's infatuation with this lowly woman. 'Buy yourself a hundred

---

* Citing Isfahani, Ibn al Sa'i's version has Inan travelling to Egypt, where she died in 840/41.

slave-girls and get rid of her!' Jaafar supposedly ignored his father, married her secretly, only to lose her when she died giving birth to Arib. At least that was the story. In 803, the Barmakids were subject to one of history's bloodiest and most shocking reversals of fortunes, after simmering tensions between the caliph and the pre-eminent family of the empire suddenly boiled over. Overnight Jaafar went from the pinnacle of power in the Abbasid caliphate to a corpse hacked into three pieces and gibbeted for public display on three pontoon bridges across the Tigris. The picture is unclear, but if Arib were Jaafar's daughter, and therefore free at birth, she might easily have been sold into slavery on the collapse and destruction of the Barmakids.

Whatever the case, hers was a richly picaresque life which, with its unpredictable series of high-spirited, alternately ruinous and triumphant adventures, reminds us of Voltaire's *Candide* with brains. She next fell into the hands of a slave-dealer, who sold her to Abdallah ibn Ismail al Marakibi, an official in charge of Harun's docks. No doubt with an eye for making money out of her, as Natifi had done with Inan, he then had her educated in Basra, where she learnt reading, writing, poetry, singing and composition. At some point, we don't know when or at what age, Arib eloped with her master's guest, a handsome, fair-skinned and blue-eyed Khurasan army officer. This was the first suggestion of Arib's love of excitement and men in uniform. However, it didn't take her long to tire of him, at which point she headed north to Baghdad to find her fortune as a songster. Here she eloped again, this time with a man called Hatim ibn Adi, who soon bored her. The romantic interlude ended when Al Marakibi discovered her whereabouts and subjected her to a fierce whipping. 'O you, why do you beat me!' she cried. 'I am a free woman, but if I am a slave then sell me.' This reflected the ambiguity about her status. If she were the daughter of Jaafar, she was a freewoman. If she were not, or had not been acknowledged as his child, she was a slave, to be bought and sold at will.

News of this scandal – and doubtless of her beauty and many accomplishments – reached the ears of Amin, the last Abbasid caliph to be born of royal blood on both sides before the long line of his imperial successors born of slave mothers. He summoned Arib and her master to appear before him. Here he examined her skills as a singer with his uncle, Ibrahim ibn al Mahdi, the prince, poet and composer, who gave his unequivocal agreement. Having agreed to buy her, Amin was then sidetracked by his half-brother Maamun's attempt to seize his throne. Civil war quickly pulled the empire apart. Baghdad, the poets' 'paradise on earth', an 'abode of happiness' with its gleaming palaces and luxuriant gardens, descended into a war zone, a desolate, fire-scorched hell where widows ran screaming through streets prowled by dogs eating headless corpses. Amin was deposed as caliph and killed in 813 by Maamun's men – before he had paid for Arib. His death was a tragedy, of course, but debts were debts and a man had to make a living. In the swirling chaos Al Marakibi broke into Amin's half-destroyed palace and recovered his priceless slave girl.

Arib's adventures were only just beginning. Distraught by the bloody murder of her son Amin, who was stabbed multiple times, had his throat slashed and head cut off, Harun's wife Zubayda complained to her stepson Maamun, who is said to have purchased Arib for 50,000 dirhams. He was, we are told, so besotted by her that he kissed her feet. History knew her from this point as Arib al Maamuniyya, Maamun's Arib, a name which denoted both ownership and the caliph's patronage and protection that flowed from it. Whatever she felt about this new identity, which was simultaneously upgrading and degrading, she refused to alter her behaviour.

As one of Maamun's treasured *qiyan*, it went without saying that she owed her loyalty and sexual fidelity to the caliph alone. But that did not suit Arib. Unafraid to cuckold him in his own palace, she even risked sneaking in her own lover for late-night trysts in an exceptionally dangerous defiance of local custom. If discovered, this could have cost her her head.

The romances continued. She had an affair with another soldier, an officer called Mohammed ibn Hamid. During one of Maamun's campaigns waging jihad against the Byzantines, he sent one of his officers, Hamdun, to take a message to his half-brother (and successor as caliph) Mutasim's camp. The messenger rode hard through a dark and stormy night and stopped suddenly when he spotted another unknown rider heading in the opposite direction. It was Arib. Where have you been, he asked her? Visiting Mohamed ibn Hamid, she replied. What were you doing there, he asked?

> 'Are you serious?' the incredulous Arib shot back. 'There's Arib returning from Mohammed ibn Hamid back to the caliph's camp and you ask her what she has been up to? Prayed the *tarawih* [nightly Ramadan prayers]? Or recited some passages of the Quran to him? Or debated theology with him? O you imbecile! We moaned to each other, we talked, we made it up, we played, we drank, we sang, we fucked, then we parted.'

This sort of behaviour was going to reach the caliph's ears. When he discovered what she had been up to, Maamun locked her up in a dark cell with nothing but bread, salt and water for a month. As soon as she was released she broke into defiant song.

> They hid him from my eyes but his presence was
> in the heart, enveloped but not concealed.

According to one account, the caliph reluctantly accepted that Arib was incorrigible, manumitted her and allowed her to marry Mohammed ibn Hamid. Another source reports that when Maamun died in 833, it was Mutasim who bought her for 100,000 dirhams and manumitted her. Either way, it comes as little surprise to hear that her relationship with this army officer was no less turbulent than those which had preceded it. He visited her on one occasion and was complaining about this and that before she cut him off magnificently:

> You impotent! Do with us what we want to be done, and what we came for. Let my trousers be my halter and link my anklets to my earrings. And when it is the morrow, then send me your criticism written in one page and in return I shall send to you my apologies filling three.

Arib was irrepressible, big-hearted, generous and good-natured. She became the doyenne of high-society entertainers and thereby enjoyed ready access to a succession of caliphs and their courts, a sure sign of her many talents and that she was much more than the favourite companion of a single, oversexed monarch. An astute judge of character, Isfahani reckoned she stood out above all 'in the skill of her discourse and the speed of her retorts'. She was highly intelligent and wilful, did not suffer fools gladly, whoever they were, and delighted in speaking her mind. Her musical and literary skills meant that she was always in demand, a poet laureate who provided extra favours for the most fortunate of her many admirers. She wrote love poems on behalf of Mutawakkil to his favourite concubine Qabiha when she was ill, then composed Qabiha's gushingly grateful reply.

'Live happily ever after with Buran!' she began in a letter congratulating the caliph on his latest marriage in 826:

> A cherished pearl whose star
> follows the lofty course of Maamun!
> In a lap that's surely blessed –
> Buran's – kingship has come to rest.

It was one of the most sumptuous weddings of the age. The caliph's father-in-law, said Ibn al Sa'i, spent a staggering 50 million dirhams looking after the caliph and his entourage for seventeen days. Arib, when asked to write a poem to commemorate this wedding, mischievously added a couple of lines to remind the leader of the Muslim world that she was still there:

> O Sire, forget not what you promised me
> I ask for nothing other than what you know!

As the arena was for Roman gladiators, the *majlis* – literally translated an assembly of people sitting together – was for the *qiyan*. The royal *majlis* was the elite public gathering at which Arib and her singing slave girl sisters, together with other free male poets and musicians, performed for the caliph and his courtiers. It was a cross between a wine-lubricated literary salon, a poetry competition, musical recital and, depending on who was presiding, a den of iniquity where other, more sensual pleasures might be procured. Abu Ishaq al Husri, an eleventh-century scholar, put it thus:

> The majlis: its wine is the ruby, its blossom is the rose, its orange is gold
> and its narcissi are dinars and dirhams carried by the chrysolite ...
> a majlis in which the strings have begun to answer one another and
> the goblets to rotate; the flags of intimate friendship are fluttering and

the tongues of the musical instruments are speaking. We are seated between full moons while the wine cups are circulating.[11]

As a composer Arib was prolific, putting her name to more than 1,000 songs, even if they were not all of the highest quality – one critic acidly described her repertoire as 1,000 ballads in one. She was nicknamed the nightingale of the court for the sweetness of her voice and the range of her music.

Court life was ruthlessly competitive. There was a fierce rivalry, complete with its respective fan clubs, between Arib and Shariya, a woman twenty years her junior. Shariya was another strong character. Coming from a similar slave background, she was said to have been purchased and trained by no less an authority than Ibrahim ibn al Mahdi, son of one caliph (Mahdi), uncle of another (Amin) and a short-lived caliph himself (r. 817–19). More to the point, as well as being a princely poet he was considered one of the most talented musicians and singers of his day, a world apart from Al Natifi, the seller of sweet nut brittle. So Arib had competition. While she represented singing of the rich-in-tradition old school, as exemplified by Ishaq al Mawsili, Shariya was dismissive of the classical styles of composition and performance.

Al Isfahani tells the story of a singing competition hosted in Samarra by Abu Isa ibn al Mutawakkil, an Abbasid prince and sometime singer, pitting the two groups of *jawari* singing girls belonging to Arib and Shariya against each other. This was a rivalry, said Al Isfahani, which enthralled and divided elite Abbasid society. It was a tribal affiliation so intensely felt that 'The supporters of one party did not use to visit those of the other one, nor were they friends with each other.'

Just as it appears that Shariya has carried the day with a final song from Irfan, her favourite girl, Arib intervenes dramatically to ask where that song came from. Shariya says she composed it herself when a slave of Ibrahim ibn al Mahdi. Arib is suspicious. She asks for the singer Athaath to come forward, who confirms that the song in question had actually been composed by the eighth-century singer and teacher Zubayr ibn Dahman. Shariya is publicly humiliated. Relishing her triumph, Arib instructs her girls to carry on, delivering a final sting in the tail for her adversary: 'Take the way of truth and steer us clear of falsehood: sing in the ancient way!'

This was a woman who took no prisoners. Al Isfahani records another example of Arib at her provocative best in another court rivalry, this time with a performer called Abu Abdullah al Hishami, who was apparently determined to bring her down after she had publicly humiliated him. When he announced that he was stepping down from public performances, Arib remarked acidly that it was just as well for everyone because his singing was so bad. The court erupted into laughter. Another humiliation for Al Hashimi.

So confident was Arib in her own powers that provocatively she even took on the caliph and would-be composer Al Wathiq, according to *The Book of Songs*. 'Whenever Al Wathiq had written a melody, Arib would compose another melody on the same text, which surpassed his.' Some said she even tried to kill him.

In time success brought riches and riches brought her own retinue of slave girls. One of them was a woman called Tuhfa, who became famous in her own right and who described how, in an effort to ward off the colds which periodically afflicted her, Arib washed her hair every Friday with an astonishingly expensive pomade of sixty *mithqals*, or a little over 260 grams, of musk and amber.* Her slave girls eagerly kept the perfumed residue in jars and shared it among themselves, one of the many advantages of belonging to a rich mistress.

Arib appears in one of the most unusual and fantastically entertaining sources on Abbasid Baghdad. *Kitab Nishwar al Muhadara wa Akbar al Mudhakara (Table Talk of a Mesopotamian Judge)*, was the work of Al Muhassin ibn Ali al Tanukhi (c.939–c.994), a retired judge who lived in Baghdad. It is a strong-flavoured multi-volume memoir not for the faint of heart, teeming with purportedly true stories of clandestine incest, gay and lesbian affairs, enterprising pimps and forgers, wily ministers and ice-vendors, ingeniously cruel tortures and executions, extravagant caliphs and concubines, even an instance of cannibalism during a famine in Baghdad.

In this visceral compendium of anecdotes, she is remembered by Ibrahim ibn al Mudabbir, a senior courtier, drinking companion of

---

* 1 *mithqal* is 4.37 grams.

the caliph Mutawakkil, sometime poet and former lover of Arib, to whom he had dedicated a number of poems. At a time when both he and the elderly Arib had long since retired from public duties, her boat arrived unexpectedly one day in front of his residence on the Tigris.

'"Madam," I said, "how comes this?"

"I longed for you," she replied, "and wished to renew old times, and drink with you today."'

Another elegant boat containing her litter drew up and the old lady, apparently paralysed, was brought up to her former lover's mansion by her servants.

They chatted together about the old times, ate and drank wine. Arib instructed her slave girls, who included some very fine performers, to sing for them. Ibrahim enjoyed every minute of the performance. Among Arib's retinue were the singing slave girls Tuhfa and Bidaa, the latter of whom she later sold for the staggering sum of 100,000 dinars. As the wine went to his head, Ibrahim thought how nice it would be if Arib could set a recently composed verse of his to music and brushed away her protests that she had retired from this sort of thing long ago. The detail in the following reminiscence is so painterly in its scene-setting that you find yourself transported to the banks of the Tigris on a drowsy, wine-filled summer's afternoon, joining them sprawled out on Persian carpets while they feast and drink, sing and make music:

> She then thought for a little, striking her fan on the ground and humming to herself, and then told these girls to arrange a certain string in a particular style, to strike with a particular finger and to do various things until she had got the tune right, when she bade them sing the verses in a particular key, and put so and so in such and such a place. Then they proceeded to sing the lines as though they had heard them many times before. Ere the notes had issued from their lips I thought to myself: Here is Arib visiting me and setting my verses to music and acting as a professional singer; is she to go away without a present? Never, not though I were to die of want, hunger and poverty!

Ibrahim, flushed with wine and determined to give his old lover a suitable reward, asked his slave girls if they had anything to hand as a gift for their honoured guests. One gave him an anklet, another a bracelet, a third a necklace, a fourth an ornament. So far that was 1,000 dinars. In a grand gesture Ibrahim then got them to put the gifts in 'a basket of gold filigree' weighing 100 *mithqals* – almost half a kilogram – dismissed Arib's half-hearted refusal, and insisted that Tuhfa and Bidaa must keep them. The rest of the afternoon unfolded agreeably and Arib stayed until sunset. When she got up to leave her host saw her off to the river, at which point the crafty woman suddenly remembered she had a request to make. 'I bade her command me.' She told him that Ibrahim's wife had purchased an estate adjoining her own and that she, Arib, would like to pay his wife for it and add it to her own property. Whether this sobered Ibrahim up on the spot Al Tanukhi does not tell us, but Ibrahim, realizing that this was the sole reason for Arib's visit, went off to his wife, promised her that she would receive the purchase price, and returned to Arib with the happy news that it was all sorted. He would pay for it himself. She thanked him and left. 'Now the price of the property was a thousand dinars, so that her day's society and her setting my verses to music cost me two thousand one hundred dinars,' Ibrahim recalled, admiring her style. Reading this story more than 1,100 years after the event, we might remember those warnings from Jahiz and Washsha about the singing slave girls who could bring financial ruin upon young men. It is quite possible that Jahiz had Arib, among others, in mind when he wrote his sarcastic verses.

In later life, Arib looked back fondly and without rancour on an incident-filled life. Young men came to marvel at this remarkable old lady whose stories, when they were not sexually outrageous and astonishing, made them shake with laughter.

She admitted to having slept with eight caliphs, none of whom she had ever desired apart from Mutazz, who apparently reminded her of Abu Isa ibn al Rashid, the only royal she had ever really loved. 'Asked what she looked for in sex, Arib said that her two essential requirements were a hard prick and a sweet breath.' If the lover was good-looking, that was a bonus. As an old woman she was once visited by two impertinent young men who asked her whether she still wanted to have sex. 'Ah, my sons, the lust is present but the limbs are helpless,' she replied good-humouredly.

Her happiest day, she said, came at the palace of Ulayya bint al Mahdi, the famous princess, poetess and singer, her blue-blooded counterpart. With them were the princess's half-brothers Ibrahim and Yaqub. Ulayya had started to sing, followed by Ibrahim, with Arib singing and making music and Yaqub accompanying on the *mizmar*, an oboe-like reed pipe. It had been a heavenly moment of music, friendship and laughter.

Arib died in Samarra in around 891, several years after the Zanj Revolt had been suppressed and a few years short of her hundredth birthday. She had enthralled several generations of men. More important, and notwithstanding her earlier servitude, she had always been her own person.

Our musical trio comes to a climax with Mahbuba – 'The Beloved'. Like Inan and Arib, she stood head and shoulders above her *qiyan* sisters. 'Mahbuba,' says Ibn al Sa'i, 'was the foremost of her generation both as a poet and as a singer. She had a beautiful face and voice . . . as one of a group of four hundred slaves . . . she surpassed them all.'[12]

In *Meadows of Gold* Masudi devotes an entire chapter to her through the reminiscences of Ali ibn al Jahm (804–63), the noble poet and courtier famed for his biting epigrams. Her first master was a man from Taif, in today's Saudi Arabia, who had taken great care with her education. When Mutawakkil, the last great Abbasid caliph, acceded to the throne in 847, among his many gifts were '200 pages of both sexes', among them a young girl called Mahbuba, who would eventually become his favourite. Without mentioning her looks, Masudi writes that Mahbuba 'held a place in his heart unrivalled by anyone else'. Given that the caliph maintained a harem of 4,000 young women, each one of whom he was said to have slept with, this was quite the accolade.

Al Isfahani tells us that she was born in Basra and was presented as a beautiful virgin to Mutawakkil by her owner Ibn Tahir. At this early stage in her career in the imperial harem, however, her singing did not impress the caliph: 'he did not lust for her, and she also sang songs without eloquence or wit'. If true, she must have improved quickly.

Ibn al Sa'i and Masudi both describe how one day the celebrated poet Ali joined the caliph for a drinking session. Mutawakkil disappeared into one of his private chambers for a few moments and returned laughing. One of his slave girls – or the poet Qabiha, according to Ibn al Sa'i – had written his name, Jaafar, on her cheek in letters of musk. He had never seen anything so charming and wanted to celebrate the episode in a few lines of verse. He told Ali to start composing. Mahbuba overheard the conversation from behind a curtain and in the time it took for an inkwell and some paper to be brought and for Ali to start gathering his thoughts, she dashed down some verses. Masudi has her picking up her lute, playing around with the words and the music and then asking for the caliph's permission to sing:

> I swear by she who has written 'Jaafar' on her cheek with musk
> That I would give my soul for the place that she has written on.
> Just as she has marked her cheeks with letters of musk,
> So she has written a line of passion on my heart.
> See how the master obeys the slave, in public and in private!
> See those eyes which have looked upon a man like Jaafar!
> May God shower blessings upon him.

Mahbuba had managed to upstage both Ali, who had been asked to mark this unusual moment and was understandably 'dumbfounded', and the woman whose very original declaration of her devotion to the caliph looked like trumping all others. She had cleverly demonstrated her own love for Mutawakkil and thrust herself centre-stage. The caliph then asked Ali how he was getting on. He had come up with nothing. '"Pardon me, my Lord," I replied, "but by God my wits seem to have taken leave of me!" From then on until his death Mutawakkil was always reminding me of this occasion and teasing me about it.' Ali did not take his very public besting by Mahbuba well, Al Isfahani tells us. He 'remained surly and did not utter a word'.

Ali recalled another occasion when Mutawakkil and Mahbuba had had a lovers' tiff. Steaming with anger, the caliph told Ali that he had sent her to her rooms and had forbidden any of the servants to speak to her. He had then dismissed his drinking companions and had the wine taken away. The following day he told Ali he had dreamt he and

Mahbuba had been reconciled, prompting a slave girl called Shatir to say she had heard some murmurings coming from Mahbuba's rooms. Mutawakkil and Ali went off to see what it was:

> I wander through the palace and see no one
> To listen to my laments or speak to me.
> It is almost as if I had committed some act of rebellion
> For which even repentance could never atone.
> Who will intercede for me with a king
> Who came to me in a dream and pardoned me?
> Until morning brought back our separation
> And the fact that he has abandoned me.

Mutawakkil clapped his hands with joy, rushed in to see Mahbuba, who kissed his feet and streaked her cheeks with dust. The caliph and his favourite slave girl were joyously reunited.

In 861 Mutawakkil was assassinated in his palace by five of his own men. Tabari describes the violent confrontation in which the wine-addled caliph tried to fight off his sword-wielding assailants, lost an ear in the melée and managed to cut off the hand of one man before they all pounced on him and 'killed him and sliced him to pieces'. His bloody murder ushered in the decade-long 'Anarchy at Samarra', which allowed the Zanj Revolt, among other rebellions, to bring the Abbasid caliphate to its knees.

For the Mahbuba of Masudi's history, the murder of the caliph had equally ruinous consequences. As a slave girl, she was property to be disposed of as the victors saw fit. Mahbuba, together with the other women of the royal harem, found herself passed on to Bugha the Elder, one of the empire's leading military commanders. He had been acquired as a military slave by the future caliph Al Mutasim back in 820 and in the intervening decades had risen to the upper echelons of military power.

After Mutawakkil's murder, the poet Ali ibn al Jahm remained in demand and had retained his place at the top table as resident wit and drinking companion. One evening he watched as Bugha pulled back the curtains which separated the men from the women – an assault on their privacy and modesty – and ordered his slave girls to show themselves. All were dressed splendidly, gorgeously perfumed and 'glittering with ornaments and decorations'. All, that is, apart from Mahbuba, who wore no jewellery, no make-up and was dressed in white, the Muslim colour of mourning. Head hung low, she was ordered to sing but excused herself. Wasif, another of the military commanders, insisted and had a lute passed to her. Seeing that she had no option and unable or unwilling to hide her feelings for her dead lover Mutawakkil, she improvised a mournful song:

> What sweetness does life hold for me
> when I cannot see Jaafar?
> A king I saw with my own eyes
> murdered, rolled in the dust.
> The sick and the sorrowful,
> they can all heal;
> But not Mahbuba –
> if she saw death for sale,
> She would give everything she has to buy it
> and join him in the grave.
> For the bereaved,
> death is sweeter than life.

Incensed, Wasif ordered her to be thrown into prison. Masudi's chapter on Mahbuba ends with a dreadful air of finality. 'She was locked up and no one has heard her spoken of since.' Ibn al Sa'i offers an only marginally less desolate ending for Mahbuba. Just as Wasif is about to have her killed, Bugha steps in, acquires her from Wasif, manumits her and allows her to go where she likes. 'She left Samarra for Baghdad where she lived in obscurity and died of grief.'

Inan, Arib and Mahbuba were all exceptional women, which is why we know so much about them. Their lives have been passed down through writers, all of them men, paying tribute to this *fin d'une époque* golden age of Baghdad. Some of these top-table *qiyan* were immortalized as real-life legends. The passionate on-again-off-again romance of Mahbuba and Mutawakkil, to give a famous example, became one of the many wild tales of *The Arabian Nights*, which celebrated her as 'a girl of radiant beauty and grace, as well as wit and coquetry'.

The three women are as unrepresentative of the wider experience of female enslavement as the oversized life of a caliph was of the average man grinding out his existence in the Abbasid caliphate. For every prince, poet and concubine enjoying lavish banquets in palaces with wine served in crystal goblets and golden plates piled high with beef, lamb, meat, fish, fine pastries and exotic delicacies, there were countless thousands of ordinary men and women – artisans, traders, slaves, soldiers, singers, dancers, beggars and prostitutes, in a word the masses – who were forced to eke out sparse dinners of onions, beans and radishes, perhaps a vegetable or two and a crust of bread, in their tiny one-roomed mud hovels.

Yet however gilded their cage may have been, as unlike the servitude of their sisters in slavery at the time, Inan, Arib and Mahbuba, together with many more super-skilled women singled out by Ibn al Sa'i, Al Isfahani, Masudi and others, are important in conveying powerful examples of humanity in their own voices – the strength and defiance, courage and charisma, grief and joy of their lives.

They serve as a reminder, too, that there was no single institution of slavery but rather multiple forms of servitude encompassing both genders, all ages and many ethnicities. And even in this most elite sliver of slavery, however famously witty, glamorous and intelligent these women undoubtedly were, the whipping of Inan, the casual passing of Arib from one caliph to another and the persecution of Mahbuba clearly demonstrate the inherent fragility of their position and the dangerous reality of their captivity. No starker evidence of the fatal threats they faced can be imagined than the summary beheading of two slave girls caught in bed together by the caliph Hadi. If a verse or two went awry, if one of the *qiyan* failed to amuse or was lost for words, her position in Abbasid society and in the royal household could collapse.

If we are searching for a more 'ordinary', less high-society female slave, we run into a frustrating near-total silence. It is the lives of the great and good, not the ordinary man and woman on the street, which tend to be recorded in the sources, often in many-coloured detail.

Yet the silence is not complete. A white slab of limestone found in the Holy Land offers a tantalizing, poignant fragment of the life and death of a Muslim slave girl. Dating to between the last quarter of the ninth century and the first quarter of the tenth, it measures half a metre by half a metre. Eleven lines of Arabic script are crudely inscribed across it in an unsophisticated Kufic style, the letters squat and rectilinear. There is no floral decoration, no other ornamentation. It is just script. The simple stone, broken in its lower-right corner, marks the final resting-place of an unnamed slave girl who belonged to the caliph Maamun's grandson:

> In the Name of God the Merciful and Compassionate
> This is the grave of the slave girl and the mother of children of Musa ibn
> Yaqub ibn al Maamun surnamed Umm Mohammed
> She died leaving behind 20 of her children and
> Grandchildren; all of them and she herself were afraid of her
> death in a distant foreign land, anxious about it
> And indeed she died while travelling to Jerusalem
> In this place and none of them was present with her
> Except one person. May God have mercy on
> Whoever prayed for her and took warning
> By her death and may she be helped and strengthened by God's mercy.[13]

Her life, with all its hardship and suffering, is distilled into eleven lines, centred around her fear. Even here, in death, her identity is subsumed by the men around her, both her owner Musa and her son Mohammed. She is simply *Umm Mohammed*, literally the Mother of Mohammed. What her own name is we will never know. She might have been Fatima, Buran or Qabiha or any other name, but whoever decided the inscription omitted that detail. There are no flashing epigrams here, no jibes or teasing *billets doux* to jealous caliphs. All we know about this unnamed woman, bought as property for the pleasure of a wealthy young man, is that she bore him a number of children as a slave and had twenty children and grandchildren, every one of whom shared her fears about her dying in a faraway foreign land. We know nothing about any hopes or dreams she may have cherished during her life. In this fragmented, fragmentary biography there is just the reference to her fear. And that one fear which these thin lines in limestone describe, that dread she may have harboured for many years, tragically came to pass. She died virtually alone, far away from her loved ones, perhaps as she made her pilgrimage along a dusty, sun-burnt road to Jerusalem. We don't know when she was born, when she died or where she lived. Apart from this solitary epitaph she left no other trace. There is no Masudi, Ibn al Sa'i or Al Isfahani to bring her to life. She was, like so many other nameless women, just the Mother of Mohammed. Everything else about her is our imagination.

We are drawn like moths to the candlelight to women like Inan, Arib and Mahbuba because we love their stories. We admire their beauty and high spirits, are dazzled by their *bons mots* and poetic jousts and can relate across the centuries which separate us to their struggles and suffering. They are the cultural heroines of their age. The chroniclers chart the trajectories of their careers through carefully preserved anecdotes, piling layer upon layer of life on to the page, like a sculptor building up a three-dimensional figure. Through the force of their writing and the vitality, intelligence and personalities of the *qiyan* they describe, they manage to bring these women alive to the point where we may even convince ourselves that somehow we know them, or can at least understand them.

But perhaps the more convincing version of women's servitude in these first centuries of the Islamic Empire is that suggested by the scant words roughly traced across the limestone slab, far away from the rarefied, brightly sparkling, wine-quaffing world of Abbasid high society. Just as the Tomb of the Unknown Soldier tells a universal story of war and loss, more compelling than the pomp and circumstance of a general's marble sarcophagus, so this skeletal life set in stone speaks to us sorrowfully and takes us down to earth with a jolt. The noisy, brilliant and beautiful singing slave girls are no less real for their rarity, but the great numbers of women, silenced into anonymity by the absence of historical records, whose lives were not even marked by a few chiselled lines on a gravestone, tell their own story of slavery and the suffering it entailed.

5

Slave Soldiers

I have seen slaves on horseback, while princes go on foot like
slaves.

Book of Ecclesiastes, 10:7

There were many advantages to Muslim rulers in having slave soldiers. Amid the shifting sands of tribal allegiances, they were generally
considered a bedrock of loyalty to their leader. With the right quantity
of gold and silver, they could be sourced from tried-and-tested warrior stock, above all the hardy Turks of Central Asia. And, even better
for the leader looking to the long term, they could be bred, educated,
trained and moulded into the perfect corps. That was all to the good.
Yet they brought with them an obvious and inherent danger.

It was manifest most spectacularly in 861, when rebellious slave
soldiers turned on their master in the new capital of Samarra. According to Tabari, the caliph Mutawakkil, he of the 4,000 concubines, had
had an unusually happy day on 10 December, enjoying himself in the
company of his boon companions and singers. He had been given
a beautifully embroidered green silk gown by his favourite concubine Qabiha, mother of the future caliph Mutazz, had played with his
son Muntasir, and had been drinking, feasting and generally making
merry. Much later that night, at around 1 a.m. on the morning of 11
December, a group of elite Turkish slave soldiers burst into Mutawakkil's private chambers, found the leader of the Islamic world in
his cups, hacked at him with their swords and chopped off an ear
before slitting his throat and slicing him to pieces. The slaves had
killed their master.

It happened again, only six months later in 862, this time to Muntasir, the man the Turks had raised to the throne to replace Mutawakkil and then pulled down and killed, bled to death by a poisoned lancet. And again in 866 to Mustain (r. 862–6), Mutawakkil's successor, a caliph widely mocked for being a puppet of his Turkish masters.*

Mustain was forced to abdicate in return for his life, an agreement which the Turks swiftly reneged upon. His head was sent to Mutazz, his cousin and successor, who calmly ordered it to be put to one side before he completed his game of chess. What goes around often comes around. In 869, Mutazz was tricked into letting his coup-plotting Turk assailants into his palace, then kicked and beaten with clubs. Having been forced to abdicate formally in favour of Muhtadi, he was dragged in his torn robes into a prison cell where, shut up in the midsummer heat and left without food or water, he died within three days. Masudi suggested he might have been dealt an excruciating death: 'an enema of boiling water'.

His cousin and successor Muhtadi, son of a Greek slave girl, was the last of the caliphs to rule nominally during this tortured, decade-long 'Anarchy at Samarra'. A more pious sort of Muslim than his predecessors, he disposed of the singing slave girls, banned music at court, killed the palace lions traditionally kept for animal fights, fasted regularly and presided in person over the courts of grievances. None of which managed to stop the rot – or indeed the roll call of murder at the hands of these slaves-turned-masters. After eleven months as the puppet caliph, valiantly trying to set the ship of state on a more even course, he too fell victim to his Turkish slave soldiers in the summer of 870.

During yet another uprising, he was first struck by an arrow and

---

* Masudi includes the following verse about Mustain in *Meadows of Gold*, his history of the Abbasids:

> A Caliph in a cage,
> Between Wasif and Bugha.
> He repeats whatever they say,
> Just like a parrot.

Wasif and Bugha the Younger were two of the leading Turks in ninth-century Samarra and were instrumental in stripping Abbasid caliphs of their power. Both men had royal blood on their hands.

then wounded by a sword. Knocked about and spat at in the face, he was handed over to a man who delivered the most agonizing death, Tabari reported, 'kicking him in the testicles until he died'. In *The Crisis of the Abbasid Caliphate*, the thirty-fifth volume of his sprawling history, he wrote that people were 'appalled' by how the Turks had 'assumed control over the affairs of the Muslims' and offered a bleak summary of the Samara period: 'The Turks killed any caliph they desired to kill and appointed in his stead whomever they wished, without reference to the religious authority and without eliciting the opinions of the Muslims.'[1]

The story of the Muslim slaves who killed their Muslim makers and who in turn became the de facto masters not of a handful of other slaves, not of a household or even a country, but of the entire Islamic Empire – disintegrating as it might have been – is one of the most remarkable episodes in any history of slavery anywhere in the world. It turns the institution of slavery completely on its head in a real-world enactment of the verse from Ecclesiastes at the beginning of this chapter about slaves on horseback and slave-like princes on foot. To suggest that it represents one of the most gravity-defying instances of social mobility ever witnessed seems somehow a pitiful under-statement. In this genre-bending model of slavery, the slave soldiers anticipated the *kul* household slaves who belonged to much later generations of Ottoman sultans. Their official slave status, as will be explored in Chapter 10, neither prevented them from owning their own slaves or from amassing fabulous riches and political power.

In some cases, in Egypt, Syria and Baghdad, former slaves even founded and maintained ruling dynasties over several centuries. And even when they did not rule directly, for the next 1,000 years they remained a formidable force behind the throne to be reckoned with, on and off the battlefield. Going further, the building of Samarra, according to one historian, was 'one of the greatest events in Islamic history' because it laid the foundations of what would become a mil-lennial institution: the 'one-generation nobility' slave soldiers, whom we will encounter shortly.[2]

The rebellion of the Zanj was one of history's most tumultuous slave revolts, but it was eclipsed in scale and significance by these

Cavalrymen armed with lances in an illustration from Nihayat al-Su'l, dated 1371 from Mamluk Egypt or Syria. The Mamluks were the ultimate slave-soldiers of the Islamic world.

pale-skinned opportunists. The Turkish slave soldiers of Samarra, followed several centuries later by the Mamluk dynasty of Egypt and Syria, which ruled from 1250 to 1517, and the final gasp of Mamluk power in Iraq from 1704 to 1831, represented altogether more startling and far more enduring examples of formerly enslaved soldiers who went on to occupy the very heights of military and political power.

This was not so much a case of the revolution devouring its children, as Jacques Mallet du Pan (1749–1800), the Genevan student of the French Revolution, famously put it, but of the revolutionary Turks in Iraq, followed by their Mamluk successors in Egypt and Syria, devouring their fathers and creators. They managed to destroy not only caliphs and sultans at an individual level but the wider Abbasid caliphate, which collapsed during the Samarra anarchy and never regained the zenith of its imperial power, and the Ayyubid sultanate, established by the Crusader-routing Saladin in 1171, which they annihilated completely.

While the first seeds were sown in Baghdad, it was in Samarra that the new system of slave soldiers was first instituted on a history-changing scale. It began innocently enough during the caliph Maamun's reign when, according to the ninth-century scholar Ibn Qutayba, he ordered the Abbasid prince Abu Ishaq, a younger son of Harun, soon to become the future caliph Mutasim, to purchase Turks – known as *ghilman*, boys or servants – to boost his military strength.

After the cataclysm of the civil war between Maamun and Amin, which ended with the former killing the latter in 813, above all the new caliph needed an army which would remain loyal to him. The existing forces from Khorasan, together with the old *Abna* elite military class, were both broken and of dubious loyalty to the new Maamun regime. It went without saying, too, that the Abbasid caliphate was in poor health. It had lost swathes of territory from Syria and Palestine to Egypt and northern Iran. New blood was needed. And for Abu Ishaq the private force of prize Turk warriors proved a keen-bladed weapon in his accession to the throne. All that military power in one man's hands concentrated minds.

Some Turks he bought in Baghdad, others were sourced at origin in Central Asia. In his *Kitab al Buldan (Book of Countries)*, the ninth-century Arab geographer Yaaqubi quotes a man called Jaafar al Khushshaki, presumably a slave-dealer, saying: 'During al Maamun's reign, al Mutasim would send me to Nuh ibn Asad in Samarkand to purchase Turks. Each year I would bring him a certain number such that, during the reign of al Maamun, he had accumulated some three thousand of the slave recruits.'[3]

Why the fascination with the Turks as soldiers? The answer was simple. If you wanted the finest, most exquisite dresses and robes, like the gifts-seeking singing slave girls Jahiz warned his readers about, you got them from Aden on the southern tip of the Arabian Peninsula. If it was the warmest, fluffiest cloaks you were after, all roads led to Nishapur, one of the great commercial and cultural capitals of Khorasan. But if it was soldiers you needed and you had money to burn, you looked to the Turks and no further. These were not Turks from today's Turkey, but their ancestors from further east. Some of the imported slave soldiers appear to have been khazars from the steppe north of the Caucasus. The majority, however, were either Ghuzz or Tughuz-ghuzz tribesmen from the lower reaches of the Syr Darya River or Qarluqs from the Kazakh steppes. Many may have come from what is now Uzbekistan. This was recruitment based on what today would be called racial and ethnic profiling. Ninth-century Arabs would have considered it common sense.

Never mind that it had been massively diluted by the Abbasid caliphs' tendency to breed with their cosmopolitan concubines over five centuries, the Arabs bowed to no one in their fixation on blood and the supposed purity of the Arab tribesman. But when it came to martial, especially cavalry, skills they recognized the most accomplished when they saw it.

In a typically penetrating essay on 'The Merits of the Turks', Jahiz devoted a long passage to their many sterling qualities. If 1,000 Turkish cavalrymen were up against it in battle, he wrote, 'they will lose all their arrows in a single volley and bring down a thousand enemy horsemen. No body of men can stand up against such a test.' The Turk was a superbly accurate mounted archer with two pairs of eyes, 'one at the front and the other at the back of his head'. Armed with two or three bows and always carrying spare bowstrings, he would 'hit from his saddle an animal, a bird, a target, a man, a crouching animal, a marker post or a bird of prey stooping on its quarry'. His mounts were hardy in the extreme, and the Turkish cavalryman was entirely self-sufficient and multi-skilled. 'The Turk is at one and the same time herdsman, groom, trainer, horse-dealer, farrier and rider: in short, a one-man team.' He was invariably tougher than his enemies, a man for whom the expression 'soldier on' might have been invented. Jahiz writes:

> When the Turk travels with horsemen of other races, he covers twenty miles to their ten, leaving them and circling around to right and left, up on to the high ground and down to the bottom of the gullies, and shooting all the while at anything that runs, crawls, flies or stands still. The Turk never travels like the rest of the band, and never rides straight ahead. On a long, hard ride, when it is noon and the halting-place is still far off, all are silent, oppressed with fatigue and overwhelmed with weariness ... When at last they reach it, the horsemen all drop from the saddle and stagger about bandy-legged like children who have been given an enema, groaning like sick men, yawning to refresh themselves and stretching luxuriously to overcome their stiffness. But your Turk, though he has covered twice the distance and dislocated his shoulders with shooting, has only to catch sight of a gazelle or an onager near the halting-place, or put up a fox or a hare, and he is off again at a gallop as though he had only just mounted. It might have been someone else who had done that long ride and endured all that weariness.

In short, these superhuman Turks were the perfect material to become the linchpins and beating heart of the military:

Theirs are the glorious days, the famous battles, the vast conquests . . .
They it is who carry the standards and banners, the kettledrums, bells
and trappings. Theirs are the neighing, the dust flying, the spurring
on, the cloaks and weapons flapping in the wind, and the thunder of
hooves; they are the unerring in pursuit, the unattainable when pursued.

As the Greeks were to philosophy, the Chinese to craftsmanship and
the Arabs to science, poetry and the arts of civilization, Jahiz concluded, the Turks were to war. And he was hardly alone in his glowing
verdict. 'The most precious slaves are those arriving from the land of
the Turks,' wrote Ibn Hawqal, the tenth-century Iraqi scholar and
geographer. 'There is no equal to the Turkish slaves among all the
slaves of the earth.'[4]

Once installed as caliph in 833, Mutasim wasted no time sourcing
increasing numbers of Turkish slave soldiers, according to Yaaqubi.
The unintended consequences started to arise almost immediately.
Within just a couple of years, the bullying behaviour of these warriors
had become so poisonous and destabilizing for the hard-pressed population of Baghdad that in 835 Mutasim had to relocate his imperial
capital, the peerless 'City of Peace', to the new, purpose-built garrison
city of Samarra. It was from here that he and the next seven caliphs
ruled – or perhaps we should say purported to rule, or even were ruled
by slave soldiers – until normal service was resumed back in Baghdad
in 892. This dramatic move to Samarra was partly a reaction to the
growing tensions in Baghdad between the local population, especially
the *Abna*, and the thousands of Turkish *ghilman* that Mutasim had
recruited from the Caucasian and Central Asian steppes and resettled in the city. Baghdadis grew resentful of these hordes of Asiatic
interlopers, charging through the streets of the capital on horseback,
knocking down anyone in their way, including women and children.
The sharp-elbowed *ghilman* made a mockery of the established order
and grabbed lucrative court positions, despite being only recent, often
only nominal, Muslim converts and unable to speak Arabic. Clashes
broke out on the streets and in the barracks, and there were a number
of murders. And there were also additional reasons for local jeal-
ousies. The talents of the youthful *ghilman* frequently extended from
the battlefield to the bedroom, where they gave forbidden pleasure to

some Abbasid courtiers. 'The same boy could be at once slave, guard, muse and bedfellow to his master.'[5]

While the sources are not clear on the precise provenance of the Turks, some of the earliest, and in time the most famous and infamous, are mentioned by name. We hear, for example, of Wasif, who started out as an armourer and whom we last saw humiliating the singing slave girl Mahbuba, and Ashinas, a soldier receiving the first grants of land in Samarra. Then there was Itakh, a kitchen cook-turned-military man, procured, like Wasif and Ashinas, in Baghdad. These three rose to become effectively Mutasim's *capi di tutti capi*, their influence felt at the highest reaches of government and the military long after he had died. Ashinas was promoted governor of Egypt, a position he held until around 845. Wasif was instrumental in the plot to kill Mutawakkil in 861 and played a leading role in appointing and disposing of – sometimes literally – a series of Samarra-based puppet caliphs. Rivals were despatched as a matter of course over several decades.

Mutasim's Turks and the tribesmen from the Ferghana Valley (Uzbekistan) were kept in new barracks strictly separated from the civilian population in Samarra. Slave girls were purchased as wives for them and they received allowances for any children they produced. It soon proved best not to breed a slave army, however, because the offspring of the *ghilman* (slave soldiers) tended to be softer, more integrated and more family-focused than the roughly hewn young warriors of the steppe. In practice this meant an increasing reliance on the slave trade and continuing imports of fresh blood, be it young men captured and imprisoned by local raiding parties in Central Asia or even families selling their sons into slave soldiery, well aware of the attractive career prospects this recruitment could bring. Sons produced locally were likely assimilated into a variety of positions from religious scholars to administrative officials. In exceptional cases, such as that of the dynasty-founding Ahmad ibn Tulun, they could rise to the summit of Abbasid government and society.

The regimen for an acceptable slave soldier was based on education, military training and conversion to Islam, a process forcefully inculcating both 'cultural dissociation and personal dependence'.[6] A great hippodrome was built in Samarra specifically for the *ghilman* to hone their skills on horseback. We know that eunuchs, an entirely separate category of slaves operating in the Islamic world, played an important role in educating the officers. Precisely when the *ghilman*, the prototypes for the later Mamluk slave soldiers of Egypt, Syria and Iraq, were freed during their careers remains unclear. It is thought their manumission may have occurred on completion of their education and training, at which point they became *mawali* freedmen, bound to their masters and employers by the *walaa* contractual obligation described earlier. They were free but not free, in other words. Raised within an extreme cult of loyalty, they were bound to serve their masters.

While it is difficult to reach a precise figure for the size of the Turkish force at Samarra, by the time of Maamun's death in 833 it probably numbered 3,000 to 4,000 and may never have exceeded 15,000.[7] Much less debatable is that this relatively modest force played a commanding role in the life and fortunes of the Abbasid caliphate out of all proportion to its size. And it provided the theoretical and practical foundation for the later slave soldiers – the Mamluks – who would transform not just Egypt, Syria and Iraq on a far grander scale than the Samarra Turks had reshaped the Abbasid caliphate, but who would also put both invading Mongols and Crusaders to the sword.

The Prophet Mohammed had first established the concept within a Muslim framework by including modest numbers of slave soldiers among his earliest armies of Islam. In instituting slave soldiery along the lines of the Samarra Turks, a system which encompassed the recruitment, trade, education, training, religious conversion, manumission and deployment on the battlefield of former slaves, Mutasim and his Abbasid successors had ushered in their own destruction on the one hand and established on the other a hugely important phenomenon that would last 1,000 years and remain unparalleled outside the Muslim world. More often than not, from Iran to India, Turkey to Morocco, slave soldiers were pre-eminent within the armies they served. And every once in a while, the most accomplished, ruthless and cunning of them could transcend their military role, seize the highest office in the land and found a dynasty.

If you were to climb Cairo's Citadel of Saladin, planted on a 200-metre spur of the Muqattam Hills, you would have one of the world's greatest city views, the perfect spot from which to find your bearings in space and time. Here is the Egyptian capital in all its sprawling, steaming, stinking, minaret-studded magnificence. Brainchild of an Iraqi Kurd, built by thousands of captive European slaves, home to generations of caliphs and concubines, sultans and slaves, warlords, pashas (governors) and assorted ruffians, this vast fortress-city is one of the defining symbols of the great capital Egyptians know and love as Al Qahira, The Victorious.

The choice of what to look at from up here is mesmerizing. Put to one side the distraction of the Great Pyramid of Cheops at Giza, barely perceptible through the smog and skyscrapers beyond the glimmering Nile. No need to reflect on the ruins of impenetrably distant Memphis, enclosed by date palms further south.

What we are interested in is much closer to hand beneath the Citadel: one of the Egyptian capital's greatest monuments, which stands like a guard on the south-eastern fringes of the maze of medieval Cairo. First there is the mighty Mosque and Madrassa of Sultan Hasan with its quartet of staggered minarets and then, a little to the left, the ninth-century Ibn Tulun Mosque, its squat, corkscrew minaret rising over an immense, sun-fired courtyard within four *riwaq* arcaded halls. In one of the world's most densely packed urban settings, it is a pause for breath and a giant, spirit-lifting celebration of space. Completed in 879, it is also the oldest mosque in Egypt surviving in its original form.

This boast in stone – or, strictly speaking, well-fired red brick faced with carved stucco – is important because of the man whose name it bears: Ahmad ibn Tulun. Born in 835, he was the son of Tulun, a Turk who was part of a corps of slave soldiers sent as tribute, together with money and horses, to the caliph Maamun by the governor of Bukhara around 815. Tulun soon rose to become the captain of the caliph's elite guard and probably served in Egypt as part of Mutasim's force of Turkish slave soldiers sent to put down a rebellion in 829–30.

By all accounts Ibn Tulun was an exceptional individual who received his military training in Samarra – he was apparently a superb archer – and his religious instruction in Tarsus in Cilicia, today's southern Turkey. He came to the caliph Mustain's notice by distinguishing himself as a military leader, organizing the defence of a trade caravan which had been attacked by Bedouin tribesmen near Edessa while his fellow officers stood by and did nothing. It helped, first of all, that this caravan was carrying a precious supply of luxury Byzantine goods intended for the caliph, and second, that Ibn Tulun managed to retrieve all the stolen property and deliver it to the caliph. His royal reward, his biographers tell us, was a female slave who later bore him a son, Khumarawayh, an indication that by this time, if not before, Ibn Tulun was either a free man or a *mawla* freedman since slaves could not own property, including other slaves, under Islamic law.

Ibn Tulun's career took a decisive turn in the summer of 868, when he left Iraq for good and arrived in the Egyptian capital of Misr al Fustat, the City of the Tents, founded by the victorious Arab general Amr ibn al As on the site of the future Cairo after routing the Byzantines here in 641. Selected as a pious Muslim who had already demonstrated his ability to lead, he had been promoted to the position of *khalifa* or resident governor of Egypt on behalf of the Turkish commander Bayakbak, whom the caliph Mutazz had appointed. Over the next decade this intelligent and ambitious man deftly consolidated his hold over Egypt, taking control of the entire security, intelligence and financial apparatus by outmanoeuvring the senior officials charged with these responsibilities. He was cool, calm and collected, a charismatic and self-confident leader who enjoyed the company of poets, writers, architects, physicians and the *ulema* clergy.

Slavery remained a daily feature of life in ninth-century Egypt. There were military slaves, domestic slaves, concubines for the wealthiest members of society and markets in which to buy them, just as there were a couple of centuries later, when Ibn Butlan was writing his guide to buying slaves. Interestingly, one of the first things Ibn Tulun did on his arrival in Egypt was to turn a square into a slave market in one of Fustat's busiest residential districts, just east of the Mosque of Amr ibn al As, the first mosque in Egypt and Africa, named after the man who brought Islam to Egypt in 639.

Here was a man of soaring ambition. In 870 he founded his own capital, Al Qatai, consisting of 1,000 plots within a settlement of one square mile. The move was driven in part by the discovery that Fustat was simply not big enough to accommodate his large and expanding garrisons. A leader who wished to reshape his world required military mettle to do it. Each unit of his extraordinarily multinational, polyglot army received its own concession inside the city: Bedouin warriors, regular Arab forces, Byzantine mercenaries, Berbers, steppe fighters from Ferghana, Nubian infantry, black slaves and Turkish *ghilman*. To this military might his Dar al Imara, the amir's palace, added a powerful political presence. Commercial life centred on the Suq al Ayyarin market of money-weighers, complete with drug-sellers and grain-dealers, the Suq al Famiyyin peas' market with butchers, fruit- and vegetable-sellers, roasters and spice merchants, and the Suq al Tabbakhin cooks' market with the hustling moneychangers, bakers and sticky-fingered confectioners. There was a parade ground and park, aqueduct-watered gardens, a hippodrome and a public hospital, Egypt's first – funded by turning the Fustat slave market into an endowment.

And finally, there was the crowning glory and spiritual centrepiece of the new Egyptian capital, Ibn Tulun's mosque, commissioned in 876. It was as though this Turkish outsider, a newcomer to Islam, was overcompensating for his foreignness and lack of Muslim heritage by proclaiming his belonging and faith on an extravagant scale. Twelve *muaddins* were installed in three groups of four in a room near the minaret to continuously recite the Quran, day and night, and sing praises to the Prophet. Egyptian in its plan and structure, with its bell-shaped capitals inspired by the Amr ibn al As Mosque just a couple of miles to the south-west in Fustat, it had more than a whiff of Iraqi influence about it. The fired bricks, the decoration of the carved and moulded stucco, the trio of *ziyada* external courtyards, above all the evocative corkscrew minaret, brought overpowering shades of Samarra to Egypt. Legend has it that the design of the minaret, rectangular at its base, circular at its summit, was inadvertently that of Ibn Tulun. During a meeting with his officials he was supposed to have been seen absent-mindedly wrapping a piece of parchment round his finger. Asked what he was doing, the embarrassed ruler said he was planning the design of his new mosque's minaret – a recreation of the famous spiral minaret of Samarra which had towered over his childhood. Either way, Al Qatai and this huge mosque was all a big step up from Fustat. Anyone would think Ibn Tulun had his mind set on greater things than provincial governorship.[8]

His growing influence and autonomy started to worry Muwaffaq, the military chief and, as we have seen, power behind his caliph brother Mutamid's throne. Ibn Tulun opportunistically stoked the rivalry between the brothers, deliberately submitting far larger revenues to Mutamid than to Muwaffaq, whose ongoing campaign against the Zanj rebels in southern Iraq required steady flows of financial support. In 876, to cite one example, he collected 4.3 million dinars in revenues, of which he sent 2.2 million dinars to Mutamid and 1.2 million dinars to Muwaffaq. Relations between Ibn Tulun and Muwaffaq soured to the point where, in the same year, the infuriated Abbasid regent sent a Turkish-led force to bring the upstart governor, son of a slave, to heel. The expedition did not get very far, ending before it had even reached Egypt amid a chorus of protests from the soldiers about unpaid salaries. They refused to move.

By 878, a resurgent Ibn Tulun, now styling himself Mawla Amir al Muminin, Servant of the Commander of the Faithful, had been appointed to command over Syria and the Cilician frontier. He captured Damascus, Aleppo, Homs and Hama for his expanding kingdom, installing his *ghulam* (slave soldier) Lulu in charge of an army, and established the borders of the territory which Saladin and the later slave dynasty of the Mamluks would govern centuries later.

There was nothing squeamish about Ibn Tulun. Ruthlessness was put to effective use whenever required. His son Abbas ventured into open rebellion against him at the head of an army of 10,000 infantry and 800 cavalry, running amok in Alexandria and further west into today's Libya. When he was eventually captured and paraded humiliatingly on the back of a mule, Ibn Tulun ordered his miscreant son to gouge out the eyes and amputate the hands of his fellow conspirators. To his father's consternation – he was apparently hoping the younger man would refuse to commit such a dishonourable act – Abbas complied, at which point Ibn Tulun had him publicly whipped, imprisoned and disinherited.

In the autumn of 882, Ibn Tulun received an urgent letter which offered the tantalizing prospect of redirecting the course of Islamic history. The prisoner-puppet Mutamid wrote to inform his governor that he was planning to escape his captivity in Samarra and set out for Syria under the pretext of going on a hunting expedition. Ibn Tulun hastened to make plans to rescue Mutamid. Having the pliant leader of the Islamic world at his side in Egypt would have been a stunning coup, but it was not to be. The wily Muwaffaq learnt of the plan through his spies and recaptured his brother in early 883.

A year later Ibn Tulun died. In a short space of time he had restored security, reformed the administration of Egypt, introduced a number of effective agricultural irrigation projects and accumulated reserves of 10 million dinars. That was the least of his legacy. More important was that this son of a Turkish slave had risen to become the first independent ruler of Muslim Egypt. So entrenched was his personal power by the time of his death that his son Khumarawayh (r. 884–96) was able to succeed him like an heir on what was now effectively the breakaway Egyptian throne, autonomous from, but loyal to, the Abbasids. Ibn Tulun had surpassed the slave soldiers of Samarra who had exercised power behind the caliph's throne. He had inaugurated a new dynasty that, like his mosque, bore his name: the Tulunids.

Khumarawayh inherited from his father an army which was by now a far cry from the modest Turkish force the Abbasid caliphs had installed at Samarra. It had swelled to 24,000 Turkish *ghilman* in addition to a separate force of 42,000 black slaves and free men. With their black turbans, black cloaks and black skin, wrote the fifteenth-century Egyptian historian Ibn Taghribirdi, Khumarawayh's personal guard of 1,000 resembled 'a black sea spreading over the face of the earth, because of the blackness of their colour and of their garments. With the glitter of their shields, of the chasing on their swords, and of the helmets under their turbans, they made a really splendid sight.'[9]

The Tulunids were one of Egypt's shorter-lived dynasties. Khumarawayh's fourteen-year-old son Abul Asakir Jaysh managed to rule only for a few months before being deposed and killed, leaving his even younger brother Harun to hold sway briefly from 896 to 904. At this point the resurgent Abbasid caliphate, newly reinstalled in Baghdad and reinvigorated after putting down the Zanj Revolt and the Kharijite Rebellion, decided enough was enough and invaded Syria. In Harun they faced an opponent as indolent as his grandfather had been irresistible. He was proof of the old adage that to go from glory to ruin within three generations was the easiest thing in the world. He revelled in dissolute luxury and carnal pleasures, leaving his vizier to run the affairs of state under the suspicious watch of the military. Harun's army mutinied and killed him in 904, leaving his uncle Shayban, another of Ibn Tulun's sons, to resist.

The following year, the Tulunid dynasty and interregnum was brought to a blood-filled halt as the Abbasid caliphate marked its reassertion of imperial control by plundering and razing to the ground Ibn Tulun's magnificent city of Al Qatai. Only his mosque was left standing. If the toll to the built environment was appalling, the cost in human lives was even worse. Ibn Taghribirdi reported the new governor issuing a vengeful command against the fiercely loyal black troops, backbone of the Tulunid army. They were rounded up and taken to Mohammed ibn Sulayman, the new governor sent by the caliph. 'He gave orders to slaughter them, and they were slaughtered in his presence like sheep.'[10]

Ibn Tulun had done all the hard work for this short-lived dynasty. His bloodline successors were ineffective, a reminder of why the sons of slave soldiers tended to be excluded from becoming military men themselves.

The turbulent story of the Tulunids was in fact a microcosm of the philosopher and historian Ibn Khaldun's grand theory on the rise and fall of civilizations. He argued that *asabiyya* or group solidarity was a mainstay of political power and an essential ingredient in the rise of a new civilization. That solidarity inevitably declined in the more civilized, more luxurious, less austere setting of the city. While a strong leader, like Ibn Tulun, could delay the inevitable decline, within five generations it was all over. Every civilization and every dynasty contained within it the seeds of its own destruction. And so it proved with the Tulunids, who imploded with a whimper long before five generations had elapsed.

And yet we might still pause for a moment and consider that, however useless his descendants proved, this was the humble son of a slave who, by deploying his exceptional talents on two continents, rose to the very top of political and military power, built his own capital, governed with great aplomb, powerfully asserted his autonomy from the Islamic Empire and even gave his name to a dynasty as well as a short but highly significant era in Egypt's tumult-filled history. Neither the Zanj nor the Turkish slave soldiers of Samarra ever managed anything quite as effective as that.

Mamluk (مَمْلُوك). Noun. Arabic. Singular (plural *mamalik*) (مماليك). A thing or person possessed. From the passive participle of the verb *malaka*, to take possession of.

In the history of slavery in the Islamic world, the Mamluks had no equal. They were the ultimate military slaves-turned-rulers, the perfect enforcers. While the Zanj in southern Iraq, the Turkish *ghilman* in Samarra and the Tulunids in Egypt had upended history with their challenges to authority, none could compare with the Mamluks, who stormed to power in Egypt and Syria in the thirteenth century, maintained their outright ascendancy for more than 250 years, and then obstinately clung to power as Ottoman vassals for several hundred more years until Mohammed Ali, founder of modern Egypt, brought the curtain crashing down there in 1811.

Long-term Mamluk dominance in Egypt was facilitated by the Battle of the Blacks, also known as the Battle of the Slaves, a savage two-day conflict which tore Cairo apart and completely changed the seat of power during two stifling days in August 1169. The context was Saladin's appointment as vizier that year, his sidelining of his boss, the Fatimid caliph Al Adid (r. 1160–71), and his preference for his Mamluk cavalry units from Syria over the Fatimid military, which relied heavily on regiments of black African slave troops known as *Abid al Shiraa*, or bought slaves. According to later pro-Saladin chroniclers, Saladin discovered a plot by the caliph's chief black eunuch Mutamin al Khilafa to remove him in tandem with the Crusaders. Saladin had the man beheaded, replaced him with a white eunuch and dismissed the remaining black palace eunuchs. Fifty thousand African troops rose in fury and attacked the Dar al Wizara, Saladin's palace of the vizier. For a time they pushed the Syrian forces back until a messenger from Al Adid appeared, calling on Saladin's men to eliminate them. 'Beware of the slave dogs! Drive them out of the country!' Having believed they were fighting for the caliph, this abrupt betrayal, together with Saladin's brutal attack against Al Mansura, the quarter where the black troops lived with their wives and children west of the Citadel, hastened their surrender. Though Saladin granted them safe passage to Giza across the Nile, they were hacked down in cold blood. 'God destroyed them for their sins,' wrote Al Maqrizi, the fifteenth-century Egyptian historian, accusing the black Africans of overreaching themselves. As far as slave soldiers were concerned, the lasting legacy of the Battle of the Blacks was crystal-clear. No black soldier would bear arms again in Egypt for centuries. Henceforth, black slaves were relegated to menial roles within the military. Within a couple of years Saladin had destroyed the Fatimid dynasty, seized power and founded the Ayyubid line. By removing the black slave troops as Egypt's military muscle, he had also cleared the way for the Mamluks.[11]

Mamluk power reached its pomp in Egypt from the second half of the thirteenth century. The historian Maqrizi, who reckoned 50,000 of Saladin's slave prisoners had toiled away to build his Citadel on the Muqattam, pinpointed the precise moment at which the mighty Mamluks of Egypt were born:

> The Ayyubid sultan Al Malik al Salih [r. 1240–49] was the ruler who created the *Mamluk* battalion of the Al Bahriyya in Egypt. The confrontations that he experienced on the night in which he had been deposed were the reason for this. During this event his Kurdish soldiers and others deserted him and only his *mamalik* slave soldiers remained with him. He felt a sense of gratitude to their fidelity.

He continued purchasing slave soldiers until they became the backbone of his army, replacing his father's and brother's commanders. 'They were his loyal entourage and faithful guards. Since their barracks were near his pavilion on the island of Al Rawda in the Nile, they were named Al Bahriyya [of the river].'[12]

Al Malik al Salih was effectively the last of the Ayyubid line. There was a final gasp from his son Turanshah, who managed to hang on for a few months until the spring of 1250. But within a short space of time, and having completely ignored his father's wise advice, he had managed to alienate the powerful Bahri Mamluks by appointing his own Mamluks to important positions. More controversially still, he promoted a number of black slaves to prominent roles including those of *ustadar* (master of the royal household) and *amir jandar* (master of the royal guard).* A reportedly unintelligent young man with a nervous twitch, he once went about chopping off the tops of candles while shouting, 'This is how I will deal with the Bahris!' – a boast which did little to endear him to those with the sharpest swords. More to the point, it proved an empty threat since the Bahris struck first.

Turanshah was assassinated by the Mamluk commander Faris al din Aqtay, who cut out his heart and reportedly took it to cheer up the defeated French king Louis IX, taken captive at the Battle of Mansura during the 1250 Seventh Crusade to destroy the Ayyubid dynasty in Egypt and recapture Jerusalem. Turanshah's murder opened the way for Al Salih's widow Shajar al Durr (Tree of Pearls), a former child slave and concubine, possibly Turkic or Armenian in origin, to become the first and to this day only female Muslim ruler in Egyptian history, her short reign blighted by the refusal of the last Abbasid caliph Mustasim (r. 1242–58) to recognize her. After only four months on the throne during the winter of 1249–50, a pragmatic solution was found with the installation of Izz al din Aybak as sultan. He married Shajar al Durr, she abdicated, and the Mamluk dynasty was born out of a bloodless coup.

Though all too brief, her reign as queen of Egypt was a critical time with a lasting legacy. It witnessed the end of the Crusaders' efforts to conquer the southern Mediterranean, the demise of the Ayyubid dynasty and the birth of the epoch-making Mamluk sultanate. 'Things were near to a total defeat involving the complete destruction of Islam,' wrote the Egyptian historian Ibn al Furat (1334–1405), 'but Almighty God sent salvation.' Just as 'the damned king of France' Louis IX was close to victory, the Bahri Mamluks launched their attack on the Crusaders and demolished their battalions. 'This was the first encounter in which the polytheist dogs were defeated by means of the Turkish lions.'[13]

---

* Structures of Mamluk power, and integration more widely, could at times be colourblind in a way that would have been unthinkable in either Europe or North America even centuries later. Al Malik al Salih had a black mother but acceded to the Ayyubid throne without incident. He was idolized by his Bahri Mamluks, with whom he laid the foundations of the Mamluk sultanate that would endure until 1517.

As glorious as it undoubtedly was, as successful as it proved as the scourge of both Mongols and Crusaders, we should be clear at the outset that this new state depended absolutely and entirely on slavery, on the provision of continual supplies of fresh blood by land and by sea for several centuries. The Mediterranean provided the great slave-trading sea for this slave warrior-ruler caste system, as it did for all other categories of slaves, satisfying demand around the basin, from Muslim North Africa to the slave-filled cities of Venice, Genoa, Marseilles, Barcelona and Valencia. From the perspective of human oppression, this sea, lovingly celebrated as the font of civilization in both European and American literature, was, in the words of one history of slavery, 'a veritable vortex of horror for all mankind, especially for the Slavic and African peoples'.[14]

So successful was the Mamluk model that it extended far beyond the Arab world into the Indian Subcontinent. Founded in 1206 by the Turkic general Qutb al Din Aibak, who had been sold into slavery as a child, the Mamluk dynasty ruled over northern India until 1290. Among the eleven sultans of Delhi it counted the remarkable Razia Sultan (r. 1236–40), an almost contemporary of Shajar al Durr in Egypt, the first and only Muslim woman to have sat on the Delhi throne. She challenged and, for a time, overcame the prevailing prejudices against her gender, refusing to be addressed as Sultana, which she argued was the title of a sultan's wife rather than the supreme ruler that she was. She gave up her purdah to dress in traditional male clothes, riding through Delhi on the back of an elephant and minting coins in her own name – Pillar of Women, Queen of the Times.

In *Futuh al Salatin (Gifts of the Sultans)*, his history of the Muslim conquest of India, the fourteenth-century Delhi scholar Abdul Malik Isami expressed the prevailing brand of chauvinism she was up against:

> All women are in the snare of the devil; in privacy, all of them do Satan's work. Confidence should not be placed in women; devils should not be relied upon ... In public women look better than a flower garden, but in privacy they are worse than a fireplace. When the passions of a pious woman are inflamed, she concedes to an intimacy even with a dog ... To wear the crown and fill the throne of kings does not benefit

a woman; this is the role exclusively meant for the experienced type of man. A woman cannot acquit herself well as a ruler, for she is essentially deficient in intellect.[15]

In 1240, disgruntled Turkic officers conspired to depose her. She and her husband were killed by robbers while attempting to regain her throne.

Hard-nosed meritocracy, frequently ruthless to the point of death, was a defining feature of the Mamluk system. While any stupid, idle and dissolute young man could and often did inherit the caliph's throne from his father, this was effectively inconceivable under the Mamluk sultanate. From 1250 any man who aspired to be sultan of Egypt had to plot, manoeuvre or fight his way to the top, demonstrating outstanding leadership – often accompanied by supreme ruthlessness – following a meticulously focused elite education and training programme lasting several years which was reserved exclusively for the Mamluk class. The system was expressly designed to raise to power the most exceptional individuals.

Perhaps no one personified this inbuilt quality control better than Baybars (r. 1260–77), who came to define the heroic period of the Mamluks. The sources describe how as a young boy he was brought from Sivas to southern Anatolia and then despatched to a slave market in Syria, together with other Qipchaq prisoners. Put up for sale on a bench, he was offered to a high-ranking officer as a scribe. To demonstrate his ability, Baybars improvised a verse which so impressed the man that he bought him on the spot. He never looked back.

Although he had already earned distinction in decisive battles that shattered King Louis's Seventh Crusade in 1250, it was a decade later that he took part in one of history's most epochal encounters. In 1257, Genghis Khan's grandson Hulagu wrote a letter to the Abbasid caliph Mustasim in Baghdad, threatening to 'turn your city, lands and empire into flames'. This was no bravado. Mustasim, yet another example of the perils of hereditary monarchy, was a weak leader more inclined to enjoying the twin pleasures of the hunt and his harem than defending the Dar al Islam. In 1258 Hulagu's troops fell upon Baghdad. The great Abbasid palaces were consumed in the blaze he had promised, alongside mosques and law colleges, the tombs of the caliphs, markets, libraries and street after street of homes. The great Muslim metropolis, heart of what had once been the most sophisticated civilization in the world, went up in smoke. Several hundred thousand Baghdadis were butchered in a terrible slaughter.

Two years later, Baybars was one of the two Egyptian commanders alongside his sultan Qutuz facing Hulagu's all-conquering Mongol army under its general Kitbuqa at Ain Jalut, the Spring of Goliath, in south-eastern Galilee. Battle was joined on 3 September 1260. Baybars, who commanded the vanguard, put the Mongols to the sword in an encounter that hastened the end of the Mongol presence in the Middle East. Psychologically its legacy went far beyond this battlefield. Just as Herodotus understood that the Greek victory over the Persians at the Battle of Marathon in 490 BCE was critical because 'until that day came, no Greek could hear even the word Persian without terror', so the Mamluk triumph at Ain Jalut ended the persistent myth of Mongol invincibility and burnished the credentials of the Bahri Mamluks. It also led to the rise of Baybars himself. Disappointed not to receive the governorship of Aleppo or an appointment of equal distinction after his battlefield heroics, Baybars conspired with his fellow Mamluk officers to assassinate Qutuz in late October. With his murder, and after heated negotiations among his would-be successors, Baybars was raised to the throne.

Under his rule the military forces of Egypt and Syria doubled in size, while his elite corps of royal Mamluks quadrupled in strength to 4,000. The first Mamluk sultan to build barracks for his Mamluks, he systematized the supply, recruitment, military training and religious education of slave boys. During this first Mamluk period, also known as the Turkish or Bahri period, which lasted from 1250 to 1382, Mamluks were overwhelmingly recruited from the Turkish Qipchaq tribes of the Golden Horde in what is today southern Russia and Ukraine. They came either by sea through the Bosphorus and Dardanelles, or by land across eastern Anatolia, the Caucasus and Azerbaijan and south-west across the Levant.

Under the rigorous system instituted by Baybars, the education and training culminated in the boys' manumission in early adolescence, at which point they were given a horse, equipment and a military position in the royal Mamluks under the command of the head of the household, to whom they were bound by the *walaa* contractual relationship. How far they then rose up the career ladder as freedmen depended on their ambition, talents, strength, cunning, ruthlessness and good fortune. They also received revenue-producing land grants which resulted, over time, in a landed gentry ruling class so far removed from the classical notion of slavery that even the most elastic understanding of the word fails to encapsulate it.[16] For Mamluk boys, then, slavery was a distinctly time-limited and paradoxical phenomenon based on an elitist education which launched them to the very top of the social, political, military and economic pyramid.

In terms of power projection, the Mamluk system worked. Mamluk might stretched from Egypt into Greater Syria and Nubia, while heavily influencing the Hijaz, the Red Sea littoral and eastern Libya. One measure of its success, of course, was its long duration of several centuries. But it was more than that. Under this quintessentially meritocratic system, the most competent senior officers and sultans were able to rise to the top. Baybars's record both as warrior and then sultan is second to none. He played a leading role in routing the Mongols at Ain Jalut in 1260, defeated the Crusaders in three campaigns, captured the famous Krak des Chevaliers fortress in 1271, conquered Nubia in 1276 and defeated another Mongol army in southern Turkey in 1277, the year of his death. A bronze bust of Baybars, nicknamed Abu al Futuh, the Father of Conquests, today stands proudly within the Egyptian National Military Museum.

Twenty years later, Baybars was followed by Al Nasir Mohammed, who reigned three times (1293–4; 1299–1309; 1310–41) and dominated the first half of the fourteenth century. His sultanate, a time of peace and prosperity, witnessed the end of the long-running Mamluk–Mongol wars, represented the zenith of Mamluk power and a high-water mark for Islamic Egyptian culture. A frenetic builder, he presided over countless public works from mosques and madrassas to aqueducts, baths and canals. In Cairo, his Great Iwan, a monumental throne hall, dominated the Citadel inside which it was constructed.

The purchase of Mamluks, together with slave girls, is thought to have reached its apogee during Al Nasir's long reign. He despatched slave-traders to the Mongol Golden Horde, to Tabriz, Anatolia, Baghdad and beyond. On arrival the youths were showered with 'splendid clothes, golden belts, horses and gifts in order to impress them', Maqrizi reported.[17] In an inflationary splurge, the historian continued, Nasir increased their pay from three dinars to five to seven to ten. It was a highly revealing sign of the times that the man he chose to broker the landmark peace treaty between the Mamluks and the Mongols in 1323 was Majd al Din al Sallami, a well-known and highly respected international slave-trader from northern Iraq. He travelled on business regularly between Cairo and Tabriz, the seat of the Ilkhanid Empire in Iran, trading slave boys and girls on the one hand and managing his bulging diplomatic brief on the other. In this case slave-trading and diplomacy were no more than two sides of the same coin.

The Mamluk sultanate endured over two distinct phases. The Bahri period was peak Mamluk power. These sultans, Maqrizi wrote, were mighty 'rulers who ruled kingdoms and commanders who fought the Holy War', conquerors of both Mongols and Crusaders, the enemies of Islam. The second Mamluk era, known as the Circassian period from 1382 to 1517, when the Qipchaq Turks were displaced by a new line of Circassian Mamluks from the Caucasus, was a different matter. These later sultans, Maqrizi tells us, were 'the most contemptible, indolent and despised among men, most deprived spiritually, utterly ignorant of the ways of the world, and deviating from the true faith'.[18] It is worth noting that it was one of Al Nasir's posthumous triumphs, as well as an indicator of dynastic decline, that eight of his sons and four of his grandsons became Mamluk sultans of Egypt. A system expressly designed to be meritocratic had succumbed to the temptations of personal interests and hereditary authority. Perhaps it was no surprise that eight of his sons ruled for just twenty years between them and his four grandsons another twenty, the last of whom was toppled by Barquq, founder of the new Circassian Mamluk dynasty.

Ibn Khaldun, the philosopher who likened black Africans to 'dumb animals', spent a quarter of a century living and working in Egypt from the 1380s, teaching jurisprudence and *hadith* at Al Azhar and serving as the grand *qadi*, the most senior judge of the Maliki school, under Barquq among other Mamluk sultans. Looking back on the Abbasid caliphs' recourse to slave soldiers to prop up their crumbling empire and the later Mamluk version in Egypt, which he was observing as an eyewitness, he offered his unqualified approval of the system. After the Mongols had routed the Abbasids, he wrote, Allah had intervened to restore Muslim unity and defend the faith, sending in Turkish rulers and 'helpers' brought in under the rule of slavery which contained 'a divine blessing':

> cured by slavery, they enter the Muslim religion with the firm resolve of true believers and yet with nomadic virtues unsullied by debased nature, unadulterated by the filth of pleasure, undefiled by the ways of civilized living, and with their ardour unbroken by the profusion of luxury. The slave merchants bring them to Egypt in batches, like sand-grouse to the watering places, and government buyers have them displayed for inspection and bid for them ... Islam rejoices in the benefit which it gains through them, and the branches of the kingdom flourish with the freshness of youth.[19]

Though he did not declare an interest, as a modern writer in the pay of a patron whose work he was evaluating might, Ibn Khaldun knew where he stood. Perhaps it is unfair to wonder if he would have been such an enthusiast had he not been on the state books.*

Ibn Khaldun knew, better than most, that dynasties have their time in the sun before they come crashing down to earth. The cracks started appearing in the later fifteenth century and a series of wars with the Ottomans, beginning in 1485 and ending inconclusively in 1491, suggested a new power was on the rise. Among the internal tensions besetting the Mamluk state around this time, the repeated struggles for the throne by rival amirs foremost among them, was the controversial decision by the teenage Sultan al Nasir Mohammed ibn Qaitbay (r. 1496–8) to create a corps of black African slave arquebusiers. This challenged Mamluk practice and thinking on two fronts. First there was the inevitable racial dynamic. Just as Arabs looked down upon Turks, Circassians and black Africans, the Mamluks

---

* 'In his failure,' Patricia Crone wrote of Ibn Khaldun, 'the political evolution of Islam has come full circle. It was because the Arab fixation on the tribal past had been religiously fixed that the Muslims handed over power to slaves and tribes; and it was because power had thus been handed over to slaves and tribes that a medieval Muslim became a statesman *manqué* who could do no better than to sublimate his disappointment into a theory of the circulation of tribal elites.' *Slaves on Horses*, p. 91.

looked down upon African slaves. Second, while modern readers can understand the technological advances brought by gunpowder, many Mamluks, steeped in their traditional martial culture – a tried and tested world of clashing swords, hurling lances and charging cavalry – considered it an intolerable affront. An arquebus, according to this way of thinking, was a base weapon 'with which even a woman could stop a number of men'. Never mind that it was brutally effective.

The Mamluk chronicler Ibn Iyas (1447–c.1522), eyewitness of the Ottoman invasion of Egypt in 1516–17, also criticized Nasir for parading through the streets in loud and lavish processions to the sound of horns and drums and his black slaves firing off their handguns. 'He has disgraced the honour of the kingdom,' he fumed. In another version of the story, Ibn al Himsi al Ansari (1437–1522) wrote that Nasir honoured Faraj Allah, chief of his black arquebusiers, by presenting him with a kind of Mamluk uniform and, pouring salt into the wound, then married him to a white Circassian concubine. This triggered a battle between the royal Mamluks and 500 black slaves in which fifty of the latter were killed.[20]

Nemesis came on 24 August 1516. Strictly speaking it occurred in two stages. First, at the Battle of Marj Dabiq, twenty-five miles north-east of Aleppo, when Ottoman forces under Sultan Selim I (r. 1512–20) defeated a Mamluk army led by the aged Mamluk Sultan Al Ashraf Qansuh al Ghuri (r. 1501–16), who was decapitated on the battlefield. Ottoman cannon turned the desert plain into a slaughterhouse, wrote Ibn Zunbul (d. c.1574), the Mamluk historian and eyewitness to the Ottoman conquest. 'The plain was littered with mutilated remnants of this confrontation. Corpses lay in heaps, many without heads. Faces of the fallen were smeared with blood and grime, disfiguring their features. Slain horses lay scattered about, their saddles thrown from their backs.'[21]

Then, on 22 January 1517, Selim delivered the *coup de grâce* at the Battle of Ridaniya at the gates of Cairo, routing the Mamluk forces of Sultan Al Ashraf Tuman Bay, whose six-month reign ended with his hanging on the walls of the Egyptian capital. On Selim's orders there followed a wholesale massacre of the Mamluks.

For the Islamic world the Ottoman conquest of the Mamluk state was a seismic event, an earthquake that shattered the reigning order.

It transferred a swathe of Muslim lands stretching from Egypt, Syria and Palestine to the Arabian Peninsula from an ailing Islamic power to an altogether more vigorous Muslim successor. Greater numbers, technological superiority and brilliant leadership had enabled the Ottomans to triumph over a once-mighty military caste which had proved resistant to change and whose state was mired in economic decline. Outgunned and outnumbered, unable and unwilling to embrace new battlefield technologies, the Mamluks exited stage left. From this point they were demoted to vassal rulers and would never again be sultans. In fact, no Egyptian ruler would bear the title of Sultan again until 1914.

It would be a mistake, though, to think that that was the end of the Mamluks. For several centuries a well-oiled machine had produced a highly robust class of ruling soldiers and administrators first from the Golden Horde steppe, latterly from the Caucasus, and no one was about to bring that to an end.

In practice this meant that there were long Mamlukian postscripts in both Egypt and Iraq. Mamluks continued to hold considerable power and influence in Egypt, albeit now their wings were clipped by their Ottoman overlords. The steady flow of slave boys and girls to Cairo continued unchecked, binding Muslim and European merchants across the eastern Mediterranean, Black Sea, Crimea and the Caucasus in the enduring trade in humans. The Mamluk system evolved in Egypt so that sons of Mamluks, who had traditionally been prohibited from serving in the elite Mamluk regiments and highest state offices, were now able to serve in those roles, a reform which introduced family loyalties and hereditary competition between rival Mamluk houses, thereby undermining a core principle of Mamluk solidarity. It was only in 1811 that the Mamluk story in Egypt came to its apocalyptic end.

As so often, mass killing came with exquisite courtesy and a smile. Mohammed Ali, the Ottoman's *wali* (governor or viceroy) in Egypt, invited 500 of the Mamluk great and good to a magnificent ceremonial in the Citadel to celebrate the investiture of his son Tusun with the command of the army. The ritual of coffee and sweetmeats was the prelude to a cold-blooded massacre. Gates were locked shut, allowing the *wali*'s men to rain down musket fire and shoot the hapless

Mamluks, confined in close quarters, like fish in a barrel. Almost all 500 were killed in the Citadel, the cue for a wider slaughter of Mamluks across Egypt. It was a shabby end to a once-great dynasty.

In Iraq there was a final burst of Mamluk glory and defiance in the eighteenth and nineteenth centuries. It followed a period of violence and bloodshed on a scale that was unusual even for Baghdad, so often a cauldron of killing. From the Ottoman Sultan Murad's savage conquest of Baghdad in 1638 until 1704, thirty-seven pashas of Baghdad came and went in a pain-filled succession of poisonings, strangulations, stabbings and beheadings, interspersed with death from disease and the occasional eccentrically bloodless retirement, each man averaging a mere twenty-one months in office. The Mamluk dynasty of Iraq put an end to this. A total of ten Mamluk pashas ruled from 1704 to 1831, each ruler averaging a little less than thirteen years at the helm.

It started with Hassan Pasha, Georgian by birth and raised in Istanbul as the son of one of Sultan Murad's *sipahis*, or Ottoman cavalry officers. He was appointed governor of Baghdad in 1704, from which time Ottoman sultans suddenly found themselves completely powerless to appoint their successors and were reduced to the indignity of merely confirming these appointments. Hassan Pasha took a leaf from the Ottoman book of importing child slaves from Circassia, Georgia, Daghestan and the Caucasus, schooling them in special colleges, converting them to Islam and training them to form an elite, paleskinned cadre of civil servants and military officers – the Janissaries. Istanbul approved the policy at the time, in order to allow Hassan to suppress the unruly tribes and continue sending taxes to the imperial treasury and not, as actually happened, to establish a force that would underpin almost total Mamluk autonomy in Iraq. A new Office of the Incomers was established and commissioned to buy and train the regular cargo of fresh-faced boys.* The steady stream of Mamluks

---

* One consequence of this mass importation of young boys was pederasty, which was forever associated with the Mamluk era. Homosexuality was said to thrive in the dormitories where they slept, supervised by tutors, while unscrupulous Baghdadis reportedly enticed the boys to commit 'unthinkable' acts. The stigma of these youthful indiscretions could be long-lasting. A Mamluk who was known to have indulged in homosexual practices in his past was routinely referred to as 'that broken-eyed fellow', a reference to his supposedly shame-faced inability to look people in the eye.

that flowed unchecked from Georgia to Baghdad formed the basis for a new dynasty that wielded power entirely at its own pleasure, not at that of the Ottoman sultan. Successive sultans and their silk-robed, high-turbaned grandees pacing the corridors of the Topkapi Palace might have bridled at this defiance of the imperial writ, but they were unable to do anything about it. While some did their worst to bring upstarts to heel, a policy that included numerous assassination missions, wily Mamluk pashas did what they could to stay alive.

Lieutenant William Heude, a young British officer in the East India Company in Madras, who passed through Baghdad in 1817, described one of several attempts on the life of Ahmed Pasha (r. 1723–47). The sultan once sent an envoy with a *firman*, or imperial decree, for Ahmed's head. With a prodigious network of agents, the pasha typically learnt of such plots before the messenger reached Baghdad and was able either to intercept the *firman* or assassinate its bearer. This time, however, Ahmed Pasha discovered the plot with only hours to spare. At the gates of Baghdad he met the official, greeted him with enormous courtesy and invited him to play *jareed*, 'a warlike game in practice amongst the Turks', in which cavalry officers raced at high speed on their mounts and threw blunted lances at each other. Unable to refuse, the man found himself pitted against the highly skilled pasha, who armed himself with 'a steel-pointed javelin, hurled it at his insidious but unsuspecting adversary with all his force, and killed him on the spot'. The messenger's papers were opened, sealed up again and sent back to Istanbul with a letter expressing the most profound condolences for the 'unfortunate accident' that had befallen him.[22]

In 1750, after four sultan-appointed pashas had failed to hold Baghdad in the teeth of local opposition, the former Mamluk slave Suleyman the Lion took power in Baghdad, initiating a fully-fledged Mamluk family dynasty that would last for almost a century. He delighted in sending no revenues to the Ottoman sultan while making false claims for fictitious repairs to the city's fortifications. The sultan had tried to have him assassinated several times, sending three or four messengers with a secret mandate for his head, but Suleyman's 40,000 Janissaries would not countenance it. He had 'always made it a rule to send the heads of those very messengers to Constantinople instead of his own'.[23]

Like their counterparts in Egypt, the Mamluks bowed to no one in their exercise of arbitrary power. Yet for once in this thoroughly patriarchal society in which political power was reserved exclusively for men, royal women now moved to the centre-stage of political life in Baghdad. Suleyman's indomitable wife Adila Khatoun, the wealthy and ambitious daughter of a pasha, did not forget her husband had once been her father's slave, and refused to leave the politics to men.[24] She promoted favourites, eliminated rivals and was implicated in several political assassinations.

Baghdad's Mamluks bestrode Iraqi society and revelled in their finery. Dr Edward Ives, a former naval surgeon who passed through Baghdad in 1758, was particularly struck by the sartorial elegance of the *aghas* (an honorific Ottoman title denoting a chief, master, lord or commander, in both military and civilian settings). A senior Mamluk official might wear a green or white turban, made of linen or camel's wool shawl-cloth. Alternative headgear was a stiff cloth bonnet, black and quilted and at least twelve inches high, round which white or green linen cloth was twisted. A long shirt was tucked into linen drawers beneath another pair of loose camel-wool trousers. Sewn to the ankle of these trousers was a pair of thin yellow slippers without heels, worn within another pair, the outer set left by the door when entering a house. The dapper gentleman would wear a close-fitting, calf-length buttoned tunic over the linen shirt, and over this another tunic of similar length, with fine linen lapels, buttons at the wrist and 'an open petticoat-like tail'. The addition of a handsome sash, trimmed with gold or silver embroidery, gave the ensemble added panache; and an embroidered handkerchief accompanied a timepiece in a pocket under the lapel. Finally, a third tunic, silk-lined and made of delicate cloth or shawl-cloth, was worn loosely over the other layers, either buttoned or open, and usually thrown off at home. The above was considered summer wear, winter dress differing only in the material worn rather than in the number of layers. Ives marvelled at the numerous styles of headwear, the most impressive being three feet high with huge circumferences, covered with fur.[25]

These gorgeously dressed, dandified officials were part of a highly stratified order of Mamluks, which by now dominated public life to such an extent that being an indigenous Baghdadi severely restricted one's career opportunities.

The training of the Mamluks' apparently limitless pool of Caucasian boys consisted of reading, writing, swimming, horse-riding and martial skills. Some were destined for the upper echelons of the pashalik, where they would rub shoulders with the leaders of the great families; others would serve in the pasha's bodyguard, at court or in the civil administration. Once their training was complete, most Mamluks joined the pasha's inner circle, where they could take up positions such as agha of the wardrobe, agha of the coffee, agha of the carpets, warden of the private apartments or commander of the Georgian Guard, the last consisting of three regiments, each 1,000-strong. Mamluks in the pasha's outer circle were assigned to public-administration duties, and could find themselves working as scribes, tax-collectors or, in some cases, extremely senior government officials.

The closing decades of the eighteenth century were the golden era of the Mamluk dynasty in Baghdad. The Georgian-born Suleyman the Great, the only pasha to enjoy such a moniker in four centuries, ruled energetically from 1780–1802, after which things started to fall apart. Said Pasha (r. 1813–16) was an extravagant, pleasure-seeking youth who lacked the iron personality required to keep a grip on power in Baghdad. He was deposed and killed by his brother-in-law Daud Pasha (r. 1816–31), who presided over the golden sunset of the Mamluk dynasty and a court whose splendour was said to rival that of the imperial capital. Daud was considered cowardly and irresolute as well as capable of extreme bravery, a modernizer who reformed the army, developed textile and munitions industries, cleared canals, built bazaars and founded a printing press, yet was equally opposed to the march of progress, especially when it threatened the survival of the Mamluks. In the post-Enlightenment age of revolution, the dynasty of slaves looked more anachronistic by the day.

Istanbul took the lead in 1826, when the modernizing young Sultan Mahmud II (r. 1808–39) moved decisively against his Janissaries, whom he considered a reactionary and corrupt force standing in the way of his reforms, especially those that involved the adoption of modern military methods of training, gunnery and other innovations. Mutinies and defeats on the battlefield had strengthened Mahmud's determination to push through the reorganizations that up to that point had been vigorously resisted. This time the inevitable mutinies that followed the order for the Janissaries to submit to new training were directly confronted. Cannon rumbled into action against the Janissaries' barracks, which within minutes were reduced to an inferno. Eyewitnesses put the number killed at 6,000, with thousands more hunted down and killed across the empire in what became known as the Auspicious Incident. Mahmud had struck at the heart of traditional military power, the Janissaries were abolished at a stroke, and all eyes turned next to Iraq.[26]

In Baghdad, Daud Pasha ordered a meticulously choreographed parade in which eighteen companies of Janissaries were strategically stationed in the centre of the great Ottoman palace of the Saray. While the sultan's decree announcing their abolition and the formation of a new force was bellowed out, the raging thoughts of mutiny that followed the immediate reaction of astonishment were cooled by the rectangle of field guns trained upon them and the rows of Mamluk soldiers ready to cut them down at a moment's notice. After a tense silence, the Janissaries threw down their fur *kalpaks* and replaced them with the headgear of the new Nidham Jadid army that had been announced. To the gunners' great relief and no doubt that of Daud, the artillery pounded away in celebratory volleys rather than initiating the mass execution that had been feared. The transition from the Janissaries, so violent in Istanbul and throughout Ottoman lands was, for once, entirely peaceful in Baghdad.

Then, in 1830, Sultan Mahmud moved decisively against the Mamluks. He sent an envoy to Baghdad to enforce Daud's retirement. The pasha resorted to the usual measures, sending in his henchmen to the envoy's lodgings and strangling him to death before sending a florid letter of condolence and lavish presents to the sultan, expressing Daud's heartfelt regrets that the distinguished ambassador had succumbed to cholera. Mahmud responded by sacking Daud and appointed as pasha Ali Ridha, a junior army officer from outside the Mamluk ranks. After a devastating plague, ruinous flooding and a ten-week siege, Ali Ridha took Baghdad on 14 September 1831.

In the bloody annals of Baghdad's history, ousted rulers were invariably executed. Fortunately for Daud, Ali Ridha pardoned him and the last Mamluk pasha spent the remainder of his days in the service of an imperial authority he and his slave-pasha ancestors had so artfully resisted. He was appointed *wali* of Bosnia, then promoted to the high office of president of the Council of State before receiving the governorship of Ankara. In 1845 he became the highly respected guardian of the shrine at Medina, home to a large retinue of Abyssinian slave eunuchs. He died in 1851, after an extraordinary life that saw him go from free-born Christian boy to Muslim slave and then, successively, to grandee, all-powerful pasha, penniless prisoner and fugitive on the brink of execution, before an unexpected pardon allowed him to spend his last twenty years in the highest offices of the Ottoman Empire, enjoying the hard-earned respect of a venerable old man.

It was a fate that would have been envied by his former Mamluk friends and colleagues. On the third day of taking office, Ali Ridha called a general *diwan*, a council of notables, in Baghdad, where the imperial decree was read confirming his appointment as governor of Baghdad, Aleppo, Diyarbakir and Mosul; it was the first time a pasha had been granted command over all these provinces. The old title of caliph, abandoned in 1517 and less relevant than ever, was reintroduced. In practice, however, the new pasha held sway only in Iraq. All the Mamluk structures and positions were summarily abolished. In front of him, surrounded by his Albanian troops, stood the orderly lines of proud Mamluks, now officially an anachronism. Ali Ridha's retirement to a private room was the cue for his forces to slaughter them where they stood. Those who survived the initial volley from his musketeers were cut down by sabres. Others in the city were hunted down and killed.

The dynasty of slave-pashas that had ruled Baghdad for 130 years with so little interference from Istanbul that it had become virtually independent, that had restored power, style and grandeur to a city that had sunk into provincial obscurity, had been completely extinguished. A thousand years after Maamun and Mutasim had first introduced slave soldiers into the Muslim world on a large scale, their nineteenth-century brothers-in-arms bowed their last in a hail of musket shot.

6

Guardians of Sacred Spaces:
The Eunuchs

*What harm had I, or anyone connected with me, ever done to
you or yours, that you should have made me a nothing instead
of a man?*

Herodotus, *Histories*, 8:106

They are the last of their line. The last men standing. Last of an
800-year-old tradition of eunuch guardians (*aghawat*) serving in the
holiest sanctuary of Al Masjid al Nabawi, the Prophet's Mosque, in
the Saudi Arabian city of Medina. These eight old men, some in their
eighties, one said to be 110, stare at us with a range of expressions
that challenge what little we might know or think about a word that
is passing – mercifully – into history.

Saeed Adam Omar, the green-sashed Sheikh of the Guardians who
died shortly after his portrait was taken in 2013, confronts us with
a look of melancholy. Loss and longing pierce us disconcertingly, a
feeling accentuated by the life-size picture almost two metres high.
In the darkness of London's Leighton House Museum, the whiteness
of these men's *abaya* robes and *amama* turbans dazzles with its radiance. Ahmed Masibo Saleh, shoulders rounded with age, is dignified
in his frailty. He does not look well. Yet the atmosphere is not all
freighted with gloom. Far from it. Ahmed Ali Yaseen, dressed in white
with a gold-embroidered brown *abaya*, has an air of winking benevolence and amusement about him. A hint of a smile twitches on
his lips. He might even be flirting with the camera. Then there is the
bespectacled Nouri Mohammed Ahmed Ali, Saeed Adam's successor

as Sheikh of the Guardians, who looks at us square-on, his right hand dangling prayer beads beneath a turquoise and silver ring. He considers us impassively, exuding an aura of authority. He might be a successful and well-fed accountant nearing retirement. With a face like a well-loved, saggy sofa, Ali Bodaya Ibrahim looks like any child's favourite grandfather, grumpy old man one minute, trick-playing joker the next. Abdallah Adam, wispy-bearded and lightly wrinkled, is a vision of white, wearing a simple white *saya* robe-cum-jacket over a buttoned-up white *sediery* shirt. He gazes at us with intensity, perhaps an accusation in his eyes, or is this just our imagination? Either way, it is a troubling image. Imam Hussein Zaino, smooth-faced and dark-robed, is so immaculately presented he could almost be a dandy. He interrogates us with a quizzical expression. Resplendent in his gold-fringed white *abaya*, Abdallah Ali Sheikh is the only man here who refuses to meet our eye. He looks away from us regally as though he cannot be doing with such nonsense as sitting for a portrait.

For decades these men, castrated and sold when they were young Abyssinian (Ethiopian or Eritrean) slave boys as recently as the 1940s, have been guardians of the Prophet's Mosque, which houses the tomb of Mohammed and his first two successors, Abu Bakr and Umar. The eunuch society of Medina dates back to the twelfth century and was established either by Sultan Nur al Din (r. 1146–74) or Saladin (r. 1174–93). Certainly, Slavic and Abyssinian eunuchs were already in attendance and on duty when Ibn Jubayr, the Andalusian poet and footloose geographer, visited Medina in 1184. In Mecca the tradition of appointing eunuchs to look after the Kaaba in the Masjid al Haram or Sacred Mosque goes back much further, reportedly to the time of the caliph Yazid I (r. 680–83).

For centuries emasculated men like Saeed Adam Omar and his eunuch colleagues, together with untold thousands of their predecessors, have been the custodians of the keys to the burial chamber of the Prophet, a place of enormous sanctity. It is the holy of holies. While once they numbered in their hundreds, today they have dwindled to the final few. Too old now to perform most of their duties, such as patrolling the hordes of Muslim visitors thronging to the mosque to catch a fleeting glimpse of the Prophet's tomb, they exist in exalted semi-retirement. Creaking backs mean they are no longer required to separate the male pilgrims from female, wash down the floors of the burial chamber with rosewater, clean the tomb with reverence and devotion, present holy Zamzam water to the king and other visiting dignitaries, or undertake the most menial tasks. In their dotage they are free to pray with pilgrims and live out their unobtrusive lives silently behind the scenes.

We will never know what these dignified and pious old men were thinking as they sat for these rare portraits that throw a partial light on to their very secret and hidden world. They were not interviewed at the time, nor since, and most, if not all, have subsequently died. In 2022, a Saudi newspaper reported that there was only one eunuch guardian left alive in Medina, and none in Mecca. Adel Quraishi, the Saudi photographer chosen by Prince Faisal bin Salman Al Saud, governor of Medina, to capture these luminous images, said the men made him feel at ease. 'There was light in the room – not my own lighting, but there was something beyond that,' he said. 'A beautiful energy.'[1]

It is only fitting that these large images celebrate the humanity of these men. They are first of all a tribute to their sheer survival – dizzying numbers of boys died under the knife and razor blade – and an acknowledgement of the honour they have earned after long lives of servitude and service. There will be no more eunuchs to replace them since the fatwa or religious edict to stop the practice of appointing them issued by Sheikh Abdul Aziz Bin Baz, the late Grand Mufti of Saudi Arabia, in the late 1970s – the country abolished slavery in 1962. That we are even discussing the final fading away of slave boys-turned-eunuchs in the third decade of the twenty-first century seems extraordinary.

There is no mention of pain here. No reference in the exhibition, the photograph captions or the Saudi newspaper to the terrifying ordeal of castration as an unsuspecting, violently enslaved young boy in East Africa, or of the physical and psychological scars it left. And, of course, there is no reference to the wounding irony of a situation whereby these eunuchs and countless others over many centuries before them devoted their lives to guarding the tomb of a man who was expressly opposed to castration, a mutilation of God's creatures which was specifically prohibited by Islamic law.

Muslims did not invent eunuchs. They are as universal, almost, as slavery itself. Mutilated men served in China 2,000 years ago, at least from the time of the Han Emperor Huan (r. 146–68), who appointed eunuchs to powerful positions at court. Men sentenced to castration were also used as slave labour there. In the ancient world they go back much further. Ancient Egyptians at times castrated prisoners of war and rapists. Judging by their stone friezes, the Assyrians, who ruled today's Syria and Iraq from the tenth to the seventh centuries BCE, appear to have maintained beardless eunuchs at court. Ancient Persians may have adopted the practice of castration from the Babylonians and Assyrians. Eunuchs first appeared in Persia under the world-conquering Cyrus the Great (r. 559–530 BCE), king of kings, scourge of Central Asia and founder of the earth-shaking Persian Empire. He employed eunuchs as slaves in many roles, from doorkeepers to messengers and, most importantly, guardians of the royal harem.

There were compelling reasons for this, according to the Greek historian and commander Xenophon (430–354 BCE), who wrote an important passage about eunuchs prefiguring their use in the Muslim world in a variety of roles, including as guardians of women and military leaders. Cyrus, he wrote, reckoned that since they had no family of their own, they would stand by those who enriched them. He justified his use of eunuchs by likening them favourably to castrated animals. High-spirited horses, when gelded, stop biting but are still fit for the battlefield. Likewise, dogs, when castrated, stop running away from their masters but remain useful for guarding and hunting. So too, castrated men become 'gentler' but no less diligent: 'they are not made any less efficient horsemen, or any less skilful lancers, or less ambitious men ... no one ever performed acts of greater fidelity in his master's misfortunes than eunuchs do'.[2]

Writing in the fifth century BCE, the Greek historian Herodotus, who loved tall tales, told the shocking story of a man called Hermotimus, the most honoured eunuch of Great King Xerxes (r. 486–465 BCE).* Among

---

* In Herodotus' *Histories*, the embittered eunuch Hermotimus years later runs into Panionius, the slave-trader who had him castrated. Telling his tormentor how happy he is now, Hermotimus encourages his former master and family to settle in his home town of Sardis. No sooner has Panionius arrived with his four sons than Hermotimus vows vengeance on the man who has made a living from 'the wickedest trade on earth' and who has turned him into 'a nothing instead of a man'. He forces Panionius to castrate all four sons, with his own hands, and then compels them to castrate their father. Revenge is a dish best served with the sharpest knife. *Histories* 8:104–6.

the barbarians, he wrote, eunuchs fetched higher prices than intact men because 'they are trustworthy in every respect'. Much later Muslim caliphs, kings and sultans across the Islamic world, from Morocco to Medina, India to Istanbul, would employ them for the same reason.

Eunuchs continued to be used by Ancient Greeks and Romans and the Persians and Byzantines after them. They entered the Muslim realm for the first time in 627, when the Prophet Mohammed was given a eunuch, Mabur, together with two slave girls, by the Byzantine ruler of Egypt. He gave away one girl and kept the other, Mariyya, as a concubine (he later married her after she converted to Islam), retaining Mabur to serve her. The same year, Mohammed had been given a beautiful Jewish captive, Rayhana bint Zayd, as a concubine. While the Prophetic example conferred the ultimate legitimacy in the minds of many future Muslims, Mohammed actually countered this with a clear-cut condemnation and prohibition of castration. 'Whoever kills a slave, him will we kill,' ran a famous *hadith*. 'Whoever cuts off the nose of a slave, his nose will we cut off; and whoever castrates a slave, him also shall we castrate.' In another *hadith*, responding to a man asking to be castrated to control his sexual desire, the Prophet had replied: 'Fasting is the castration of my *umma*.* It is better for the body.' To add even greater scriptural authority, two verses in the Quran which warn against altering God's creation are widely interpreted as a prohibition on castration.[3]

And yet, despite these injunctions, the rulers of the Muslim world still made free and increasingly extensive use of eunuchs from the time of the Prophet in the seventh century to the wrinkled guardians of his mosque in Medina in the twenty-first. That this indicated an obvious tension between Islamic law and Muslim practice was only self-evident. What some might call hypocrisy or looking the other way others could justify as a pragmatic solution to an otherwise irresolvable problem. The facts of the matter were thus. Firmly in the background during Mohammed's life, marginal under the Umayyads, eunuchs then came into the Muslim world in considerable numbers under the Abbasids, when the importation of concubines on an industrial scale required suitable – meaning emasculated – men to guard them from impious

---

* The *umma* refers to the entire community of Muslims.

eyes and forbidden touch. Eunuchs were needed in order for successive rulers of the Islamic world to maintain harems that sometimes accommodated several thousand women. If Islamic law prohibited castration, so be it. Have the slave boys castrated by infidels outside the Dar al Islam and exported to Baghdad and beyond. There is 'no evidence in any source of a Muslim ruler or jurist who clearly condemned the ownership of eunuchs and refrained from purchasing them'.[4]

Before we go any further, in order to understand exactly how a boy becomes a eunuch, we should dwell for a moment on the procedure countless thousands of young slave boys, black and white, were forced to undergo before – for those who survived – being sent off to serve in a Muslim ruler or plutocrat's court, household, harem or army. Readers of a sensitive disposition, look away now.

In a passage describing the variety of eunuchs who entered the Muslim world, the tenth-century Arab geographer Muqaddasi wrote of the Saqaliba (Slavs), who were castrated in Al Andalus and in Pechina (Sicily) by Jews and sent on to Egypt, the Rum (Byzantines), who performed the castrations themselves and assigned the boys to work in churches and monasteries, and the Habash (Africans), about whom he gave no other information. Looking at the *longue durée* of the making and sourcing of eunuchs, Muqaddasi might have added the steppes of Central Asia – the *Bilad al Atrak*, Land of the Turks. But of these main slave-producing areas, in which eunuchs constituted a very small minority of the overall human cargo, it was sub-Saharan Africa, *Bilad al Sudan*, the Land of the Blacks, which would come to predominate from the eleventh century.

Muqaddasi can be forgiven for his confusion about the exact nature of the procedure, which reflects the different versions practised: there was, first of all, partial castration, the removal of either penis or more usually the testicles, and then there was total castration, the removal of both. 'Some say that the male organ and the scrotum are completely removed with one stroke. Others say that the scrotum is cut open and the testicles are taken out of it.' Either way, he continues, 'After the castration a rod made of lead is put in the urinary opening, so that the opening would not cicatrize before being healed.'[5] The main distinction between eunuchs was that between a *khasi*, who had his testicles removed, and a *majbub*, who had both penis and testicles cut off. The former, who typically retained a strong sexual appetite, were mostly used in the military and police, as messengers, intelligence agents and guards. The *majbub* were mainly used in royal and noble palaces, routinely employed in and around the harem.

The most detailed accounts of castration come relatively late in the day, in the later nineteenth century when, buoyed in some regions by global economic demand, slavery within the Muslim world and the abolition movement largely outside it were both at their peak. The following passage, to give a graphic example, is based on the studies of Count Raoul du Bisson, the French aristocrat and explorer who travelled in Abyssinia in 1863, observed the operations by Christian monks first-hand and published his findings in *Les Femmes, les eunuques, et les guerriers du Soudan* five years later:

> The manner of performing the operation is as barbarous and revolting as the nature of the operation itself, and the cruel and ignorant after-treatment is as fully in keeping with the whole. The little, helpless, and unfortunate prisoner or slave is stretched out on an operating table; his neck is made fast in a collar fastened to the table, and his legs spread apart and the ankles made fast to iron rings; his arms are each held by an assistant. The operator then seizes the little penis and scrotum and with one sweep of a sharp razor removes all the appendages. The resulting wound necessarily bares the pubic bones and leaves a large, gaping sore that does not heal kindly. A short bamboo cannula or catheter is then introduced into the urethra, from which it is allowed to project for about two inches, and no attention is paid to any arterial haemorrhage; the whole wound is simply plastered up with some haemostatic compound and the little victim is then buried in warm sand up to his neck, being exposed to the scorching rays of the sun; the sand and soil is tightly packed about his little body so as to prevent any movement on the part of the child, perfect immobility being considered by the monks as the main element required to promote a successful result.[6]

What were the chances of surviving such an ordeal? The answers vary considerably according to the period and place in which the castration occurred, the type of procedure performed and what the practitioner told the person writing about it. Du Bisson, to begin with, estimated the mortality rate at 90 per cent for total castration, meaning the complete removal of penis and testicles rather than one or the other. This was by far the most dangerous option. The Frenchman reckoned that an astonishing 35,000 little African boys were sacrificed to produce Sudan's average annual production of 3,800 eunuchs.

Some environments, such as tropical Africa, brought heightened risks of fatal infection. Recent studies based on the price differential between castrated and uncastrated slave boys – the former typically cost three to four times as much as the latter – suggest a mortality rate of 66–75 per cent, rising to 90 per cent in sub-Saharan West Africa and Central Africa. Johann Ludwig Burckhardt, the Swiss explorer and Arabist, visited a major castration centre near Asyut in today's Upper Egypt in 1813–14. It was a monastery run by Coptic monks who doubled up as 'surgeons' and who told him that the mortality rate was a scarcely credible 2 to 3 per cent. More recent work indicates that the true figure was closer to 33 per cent.[7]

The first three days after castration, during which the boys were unable to urinate, were both agonizing and critical to survival. If the wound healed around an open, functional urethra, the chances were good. If the passageway remained blocked or infected, a hideously painful death was all too common. Other styptic substances used for cauterization in this death-courting procedure included hot oil, dust or tar – and honey, butter and mule dung, not to mention charms and incantations. The age of the boys castrated typically ranged from six to twelve.

There were numerous castration centres in Europe (including Prague, Pechina, Verdun and Al Andalus), in Central Asia (Khwarizm, Bukhara and Samarkand), the Caucasus (Armenia) and in Africa (Washlu in Abyssinia, Aswan, Asyut, 'the metropolis of the mutilators', Hayda and across Upper Egypt and today's Burkina Faso, Niger, Nigeria, Libya and Chad), and even, despite the clear prohibition in Islamic law, in the Hijaz, as well as in the very heart of the Ottoman Empire in the sultan's Topkapi Palace in Istanbul. Starting in the fifteenth century, eunuchs were imported by the Ottomans for half a millennium. If you wanted a eunuch, or indeed thousands of them, supply was not a problem. A gargantuan trading network facilitated the transport of immense numbers of castrated slave boys across Africa to their new places of work.

Ethiopians and Nubians came north along the Nile or through Red

Sea ports such as Massawa and Suakin. Other Africans from the east coast were trafficked through Somalia and Yemen (where they served the royal courts of the Rasulid dynasty (r. 1229–1454) in a wide range of political and military roles). Some African boys were forced across the Sahara from Bagirmi, Dongola, Darfur, Kordofan and Sennar (today's Sudan, north-western Eritrea and western Ethiopia) before hitting the Nile. Many others, from today's Mali, Niger, Nigeria and Algeria, attempted the deadly northward trek across the Sahara to Tunis, Tripoli and Morocco. From the coast a voyage across the Mediterranean awaited.[8]

For those young boys who survived their gelding, the physical consequences, to say nothing of the psychological damage, were severe and lifelong. They ranged from persistent urinary tract infections and incontinence to chronic pain and osteoporosis. Eunuchs serving in the Ottoman sultan's Topkapi Palace in Istanbul routinely carried silver quills in their turbans which doubled as catheters. The Chinese saying 'as stinky as a eunuch' gives an indication of the lingering smell of urine that eunuchs might bring with them. Longer than average limbs – fingers could almost touch the knees – were another common side-effect of the castration, together with a high-pitched voice that never broke, and beardless, prematurely wrinkled faces. The hormonal changes brought on by the operation often led to eunuchs being either obese or unusually slim. Eunuchs could also live long lives. There are a number of them recorded living well into their eighties and even nineties. Beshir Agha (c.1655–1746), for instance, was an Abyssinian slave who served as the chief eunuch of the Ottoman imperial harem for thirty years, dying at the beginning of his tenth decade. The last eunuchs in Medina included men well into their nineties.

Writing in the ninth century, the God-fearing Muslim Jahiz blamed the Christian Byzantines for the merciless act of castration, swerving his gaze conveniently from the unstoppable demand for vast numbers of eunuchs at the heart of the Islamic Empire he served and whose royal patronage he enjoyed. The results of this criminal human mutilation were, he wrote:

> Larger bones and larger feet. Strong sexual desire. Great appetite. Eunuchs will grow no beard if the operation was performed before adolescence.

They will not go bald. Eunuchs suffer quick changes of mood due to hormone imbalance. They can endure longer riding distances than the ordinary person and can run longer distances than an ordinary person. If the eunuch has had his organ removed, he has a change of voice, and will sound like a child. Eunuchs will have a distinctly different walk from a normal person, due to the damage of castration to some of the body's nerves and cords in the lower body. A *majbub* will suffer later in life from significant flatulence of their stomach and deformation of their eyes. Both categories share a bad odour, and later in life they suffer from bending limbs.[9]

Jahiz did not examine the contradiction between Islamic law and real-world practice within the Muslim world. This was neatly and tragically expressed by the short-lived Ottoman grand vizier, Mesih Pasha (d. 1589), a Bosnian-born, originally Christian eunuch who had been castrated within the Ottoman Empire. When he received a complaint about an apparent legal injustice which had occurred under his watch, he replied: 'Did they first ask the Divine Law before they removed my testicles so that I therefore too should handle such matters according to the Divine Law?'[10]

In 2022, a Saudi newspaper echoed Jahiz's note of denial, branding 'a false anecdote' the suggestion that the eunuch guardians were slaves purchased by rulers and wealthy individuals to be servants of the shrines in Mecca and Medina. In the tenth century, Jahiz had blamed the Byzantines. In the twenty-first, it was the Italians' fault. According to Saeed Adam Omar, the then Sheikh of the Guardians, it was the Italian invasion of Abyssinia in 1935 that was responsible for the castration of young boys 'in order to stop our breeding'. Given that the tradition of importing huge numbers of eunuchs to Medina and Mecca went back more than 1,200 and 800 years respectively, this explanation need not be taken seriously.[11]

First to embark upon the mass purchase of concubine slave girls, the Abbasids were also the first Muslim dynasty to import eunuchs on a grand scale in parallel – both to guard the royal women and to fill other important positions. The caliph Harun al Rashid appointed a eunuch called Masrur to run the office of *barid*, his intelligence network in

Baghdad, one of the most important and powerful state positions. When it came to eliminating the mighty Barmakid clan, who had served the Abbasids loyally and lucratively for several decades, Harun chose Masrur, rather than his sons or other officers, for this task.

Tabari tells the story of how in the winter of 803 Harun sent Masrur to the vizier Jaafar ibn Yahya al Barmaki's palace with orders to bring back his head. The bewildered executioner, old friend and boon companion of Jaafar, returned to the caliph, after the terrified vizier had implored him to make sure Harun was not in his cups and that the instruction was genuine. 'Bring me Jaafar's head, motherfucker!' the caliph roared. Three times Masrur queried the order, until eventually Harun could take no more. 'If you come back to me again and don't bring Jaafar's head, then I shall find someone who will first of all bring me your head and secondly Jaafar's,' he barked.[12] Masrur was left with no option but to carry out the order. Peerless Jaafar, whose Barmakid family was celebrated in *The Arabian Nights* as 'bright stars, vast oceans of generosity, impetuous torrents of kindness, beneficent rains . . . the refuge of the afflicted, the final resort of the comfortless', was summarily executed.

Eunuchs surfaced in some of the defining moments in the life of the Islamic Empire. They were especially prominent during transfers of power, a difficult, dangerous and sometimes fatal time. An Umayyad eunuch transferred the caliphal insignia, which descended from the Prophet Mohammed according to Muslim tradition, to the Abbasids in 750, a pivotal moment. Sabiq al Khwarizmi, a eunuch belonging to the future caliph Saffah, founder of the Abbasid dynasty, was the only man trusted with the knowledge of his master's whereabouts when the future caliph was in mortal danger, hiding from his enemies. Al Khwarizmi rallied Saffah's supporters, playing an instrumental role in raising him to the throne. Saffah used him again to test the loyalty of his brother Abu Jaafar, the future caliph Mansur, whom he had ordered to execute the Muslim general Abu Muslim. When Mansur died in Mecca in 775, his eunuchs were there to help prepare his body for burial and his black eunuch Abu al Anbar announced the news to the public. On Harun's death in 809, eunuchs again played a crucial role behind the scenes to ensure his son Amin acceded to the throne.

Amin scandalized Muslim society with the unbridled lust he demonstrated for his eunuchs. Tabari reported how he formed two 'regiments' of them, one for whites, whom he nicknamed locusts, the other for blacks, whom he called ravens. He fell in love with a eunuch called Kawthar to whom he wrote some gushing, lovelorn poetry. Regrettably for his subjects, but enjoyably for history, some of it became public:

> The full moon describes the beauty of your face.
> I become confused: am I looking at the moon or at you?
> If the soft narcissus flower breathes
> I imagine it as the scent of your mouth
> Kawthar is my religion and my world
> My illness and cure
> The most failing people are
> Those who blame a lover for his beloved.

This was no way for the Amir al Muminin, the Supreme Commander of the Faithful, to behave. Amin's love affair with Kawthar became the stuff of mocking verse, as recorded by Tabari:

> The caliph's active homosexuality is a marvel,
> even more marvellous than is the vizier's passive homosexuality.
> One of them buggers, the other gets buggered . . .
> But one of them plunged into Kawthar,
> and being covered by donkeys did not satiate the other.

Kawthar was hardly alone in enjoying, or perhaps merely enduring, Amin's sexual attention. The caliph was said to be enthralled by two more eunuchs called Nawfal and Badr, prompting another scything riposte from a poet:

> Half of your life is dedicated to them
> The other half is dedicated to drinking
> Even harlots have no luck with you.

Abu Nuwas, the voraciously sexual poet who enjoyed a tumultuous liaison with the concubine Inan and was no stranger to scandal, scoffed at these very public transgressions. 'He has promoted eunuchs until he has made impotence a religion,' he snarled.

Where Amin led, others followed. For a time, it became fashionable for well-born men to have affairs with eunuchs. Mortified by her son's transgressive behaviour, the royal queen Zubayda, illustrious granddaughter of the caliph Mansur, resorted to dressing up the most beautiful concubines in close-fitting boy's clothes, cropping their hair short and sending them to him to divert him from this sinful practice. Her ruse apparently worked. Amin, said the chronicles, was completely captivated.[13]

There can be little doubt that the peak of Abbasid consumption of eunuchs came with the caliph Muqtadir (r. 908–32), who numbered a staggering 11,000 eunuchs in his imperial household, 7,000 of them black, 4,000 white, all under the watchful eye of the chief eunuch Safi al Hurami, Safi of the Harem. Many, if not most, would have guarded the 4,000 women, both free and enslaved, the caliph kept in his harem. Muqtadir had stiff competition within the Muslim world. The Fatimid caliph of Cairo, Al Aziz (r. 975–96), was said to have kept 10,000 concubines and eunuchs. According to Ibn Abd al Zahir, the thirteenth-century Egyptian chancery scribe and historian, on the eve of the Ayyubid takeover from the Fatimid dynasty in Cairo in 1171 the court numbered 12,000 souls, of whom the only uncastrated men were the caliph and the male members of his household. The Mamluk court of Delhi reportedly boasted 12,000 eunuchs and an equal number of Mamluks.[14]

Eunuchs, like the elite singing slave girls and the military Mamluks, could transcend their slave origins and rise to the very top of society. Among the eunuchs who made their way to the summit of the military and political pyramid, first must surely be Munis al Khadim, whose origins are uncertain – he was either a Byzantine Greek or a Turk from Central Asia. Either way, Munis was chief of military police towards the end of the reign of the caliph Mutadid (r. 892–902) before his promotion to become commander of the entire Abbasid army under the eunuch-collecting boy caliph Muqtadir. Munis saved the caliphate by putting down a coup against his infant caliph in 909, while his colleague Safi followed up by putting the rebel Al Murtada to death by crushing his testicles, a pointed choice of execution from a man who had lost his own. Safi had earlier helped secure the throne for Muqtadir, ensuring he received the traditional *bayaa* oath of allegiance by secretly escorting him to the palace where the caliph Muktafi (r. 902–8) lay dying. Safi, like so many of these high-ranking eunuchs, was generously rewarded. After he had seen Safi's house, full of priceless jewels, gold, silver, weapons, robes, silks and the finest furniture, Al Suli, the tenth-century poet, scholar and boon companion of three caliphs, including Muqtadir, said he had never seen riches like it.

Munis went on to have a long and valiant military career in the service of the caliph. He was victorious in twelve separate campaigns – against the Byzantines, Fatimids and the Qaramita, as well as putting down a rebellion in Iran – fully deserving his nickname of Al Muzaffar, Always Victorious. Over time, however, Munis found himself in a battle of wills with the caliph's mother Shaghab, whose extravagant expenditure and considerable influence made her a rival centre of power. Matters came to a head in 929, when Munis wrote to Muqtadir asking him to expel the queen and her courtiers, a request given added force by a show of strength from his men at the palace.

'You are my mentor, my respected elder, without whom I would never dream of ignoring or conducting the affairs of the state,' the caliph wrote back in an astonishing display of deference from the imperial monarch to a eunuch, while refusing the request. In an unprecedented overreaching of his authority, Munis then proceeded to sack the royal palace and instal Muqtadir's brother Mohammed al Qahir as caliph. A briefly successful counter-attack from Shaghab preserved the throne for her son but it was only delaying the final fall, Muqtadir's ruin and death coming on the battlefield in 932 at the hands of an army led by Munis, the man who had served him faithfully for thirty years. There were lasting, negative consequences of this fatal breach of trust. 'Munis's actions were the cause and origin of many provincial governors rebelling against the caliphs in future times, and of being too ambitious,' wrote the historian Ibn al Athir. 'They could never have imagined what Munis did to the caliph. After that, the caliphal prestige and dignity were torn apart.' It was the end, too, of a united Abbasid army.

Kings and caliphs could be famously ungrateful. A year after despatching Muqtadir, Qahir returned the favour after learning that Munis was plotting another coup. For a man who had spent decades operating at the very highest level of the caliphate, the once all-powerful eunuch met an ignominious end: 'he was dragged by the foot to the gutter and there slaughtered like a sheep while Al Qahir looked on', wrote Ibn Miskawayh, the tenth-century Persian historian and philosopher. Munis's head was taken to the palace to be stored in the 'treasury of heads, as was the custom'.[15]

In the most exceptional cases, a eunuch could even seize outright power, as his Mamluk counterparts did with such impunity, though this was a rarity. The eunuch Yazman earned the distinction of being the first eunuch on record to rebel, when he seized power in Tarsus, which he ruled from 882 in defiance of his master Ibn Tulun. In 896, twenty eunuchs belonging to Ibn Tulun's son and then ruler Khumarawayh took a big step beyond rebellion when they killed him in Damascus – apparently to prevent the scandal of their illicit relations with the royal concubines reaching his ears. The murder of the ruler set a tantalizing precedent for rebellious eunuchs for centuries to come.

Sharaf al Din Kurdbadhu, a leading eunuch under the Seljuq Sultan Sulayman Shah (r. 1159–61), ruler of Iraq and Kurdistan, sometimes struggled to manage his wayward master. During one argument between the two men, the sultan called on his court jesters to lift up Kurdbadhu's robes to reveal the absence of his genitals. This was an unacceptable humiliation. The eunuch consulted the military commanders, already wearied by the sultan's erratic behaviour, and then arrested Sulayman Shah and had him killed, together with his vizier and retainers. Kurdbadhu then neatly helped the sultan's nephew Arslan Shah (r. 1161–77) replace his uncle on the throne.[16]

The story of Abu al Misk Kafur (905–68), a Nubian eunuch whose name translates as Musky Camphor, is perhaps the most compelling instance of a eunuch who rose to the top. Sold as a ten-year-old boy to Mohammed ibn Tughj al Ikhshid, founder of the Ikhshid dynasty that ruled over Egypt and southern Syria from 935 to 969, Kafur won his master's trust initially as tutor to the ruler's two sons, later as one of his military commanders. On Al Ikhshid's death in 946, Kafur, guardian of the young heirs, became the de facto ruler, a position he successfully maintained until his death in 968.

Apart from demonstrating how one exceptional eunuch could make himself master of a kingdom, the career of Kafur also offers an amusing insight into the soaring ambitions of Mutanabbi (d. 965), one of the greatest poets in the Arabic language, as well as the sort of racist, public abuse a castrated man – even a ruler – could face. From 948 Mutanabbi attached himself first to the Hamdanid court of the independent emirate of Aleppo until, realizing that he was not going to be appointed a governor there, in 957 he headed west to Egypt where he intended to make his fortune. It started promisingly enough with a barrage of panegyrics lauding Kafur's statesmanlike qualities. His brilliance as a ruler, Mutanabbi wrote, knew no bounds:

> He has surpassed the scope of panegyric, as if,
> with the best of praise, he is being censured.

Obsessed with promotion, Mutanabbi continued to praise him in verse, hinting in increasingly unsubtle terms of his desires for high political office. By 959, however, when it became clear that the long-wished-for governorship was not going to happen, Mutanabbi sharpened his pencil and switched abruptly from panegyric to biting, racist satire:

> More stupid than a slave and his woman
> is one who makes a slave his ruler

> The slave's nature is concerned with nothing
> but his fetid genitals or his molars
> He does not make good on his promise on the appointed day
> and does not remember what he said yesterday

> Do not expect good from a man
> over whose head the slave trader's hand has passed
> If you have doubt about the way he is
> just take a look at his race

Mutanabbi was sore. On escaping the Egyptian capital of Fustat in 962, he published this blast against the eunuch king:

> He is one of the soft-bellied, bloated ones
> that cannot be counted either a man or a woman

> The eunuch has become the lord of runaway slaves there
> with the freeborn subjugated and the slave worshipped

> Do not buy a slave unless he comes with a stick,
> for slaves are surely filthy nuisances
> I never thought I would live to a time
> when a dog would ill-treat me, while being praised.

His parting shot included a last vicious dig at Kafur's mutilation:

> Before knowing the eunuch, I thought
> That the head was the seat of understanding
> But when I saw his mind at work
> I realised that brains are in the testicles.[17]

The truth for the next 1,000 years, for Abbasids, Seljuqs, Zengids, Fatimids, Ayyubids, Mamluks, Ottomans and the Qajars of Iran, among other dynasties, was that reliable eunuchs made far better officials than temperamental poets. Abbasid caliphs regularly appointed eunuchs as provincial governors. Men like Takin al Khadim, assigned to govern Egypt in 910, Qinbaj al Khadim (Iran, 910), Bishr al Khadim (Tarsus, 914) Subuk (Basra, 923), Nujh (Isfahan, 924) and Thumal (frontiers of the Byzantine Empire, 917–31). Jahiz reported, erroneously, that eunuchs were chosen for senior political and military positions on the frontier because they were so enraged at their earlier castration in the Byzantine realm that they would make the finest servants of the Islamic Empire, fighting the infidels with fire in their bellies.

Again and again eunuchs showed their mettle in public service, overcoming or rather mitigating the tragedy of their early mutilation to play leading roles in the dynasties they served. Abu Talib Mohammed Tughrul (r. 1037–63), founder of the Seljuq Empire, fell in love with a youth called Khumartakin al Tughrai. He loved him so much he had the poor fellow castrated so that he could remain with him in the presence of his chief wife. Over time Khumartakin grew so powerful at court that at audiences with him chamberlains and commanders stood in deference before him.

Eunuchs may have become powerful figures but they were not spared the dangers of court intrigues, which were frequent and not uncommonly fatal. The Persian bureaucrat Amid al Mulk al Kunduri was castrated as a mature man, punishment for secretly marrying the woman Tughrul had sent him to meet to request her hand in marriage. Notwithstanding this awkwardness, he still rose to become a dominant figure as Tughrul's vizier. Having vigorously opposed the succession of Alp Arslan (r. 1063–72), however, he was doomed and duly beheaded in 1064. Ibn al Athir took grim pleasure in describing how the eunuch's penis was buried in Khwarizm, his body in Kundur, his blood in Merv and his head (minus the skull, which was sent to Kirman) in Nishapur.

Another prominent eunuch at this time was Saad al Dawla Goharain (d. 1100), who faithfully served Sultan Alp Arslan and his son Malik-shah in a number of important positions before his death in battle. No eunuch before him had ever enjoyed such influence and freedom of action, Ibn al Athir wrote. 'He was judicious, generous and of upright conduct. He did not extract money from those under his authority. His good qualities were many.'[18]

This wholly positive verdict can be contrasted with the disdain expressed by a number of much later, mostly European, travellers who emphasized the supposed greed, corruption, cruelty and physical repellence of eunuchs, especially those serving in the Ottoman court and at the Prophet's Mosque in Medina. Their accounts perhaps speak to their own character, beliefs and attitudes as much as those of the eunuchs they were observing. For a number of foreign, Christian writers, eunuchs were strange and exotic. They were also a blank canvas on to which they could project their feelings and fantasies. In his *Lettres persanes*, an early Orientalist foray published in 1721, Montesquieu introduces a fictitious chief eunuch who laments his lot in life. Looking back on his earlier years, sexual frustration is one of his chief miseries. 'I never led a woman to my master's bed without feeling wild rage in my heart, and despair unutterable in my soul,' he confesses.[19] The many instances of eunuchs managing to have sexual relationships with women, as well as marrying them in later life or retirement, indicate that these desires certainly did not die with castration, particularly when it was not complete.

The most accomplished eunuchs could make the political weather, bending history to their whim and leaving lasting legacies. The white eunuch Baha al Din Qaraqush (d. 1201) rose to become a military commander under Shirkuh, a Kurdish vizier during the Fatimid caliphate. Qaraqush emerged from the tumultuous Battle of the Blacks in Cairo in 1169 in a strengthened position and played a key role in propelling Shirkuh's nephew Saladin to the throne. Qaraqush was initially entrusted with keeping the deposed Fatimid caliph Al Adid under palace arrest. After the caliph's death in 1171, followed by Saladin's abolition of the Fatimid caliphate, Qaraqush enforced a strict separation of the 250 remaining men and women of the Fatimid royal family, ensuring that the dynasty could not reproduce itself. As if all that were not enough on his remarkable curriculum vitae, Qaraqush then led the construction of the Citadel of Cairo, which Ibn Jubayr, passing through in 1183, reckoned 'a wonder amongst wonders'.[20] The devout Muslim took particular delight in seeing Saladin's latest batch of Christian slaves, bound behind camels, being marched from Alexandria to the Egyptian capital, where they were put to work on the Citadel, one of the medieval world's greatest forced-labour projects. Al Maqrizi estimated there were 50,000 prisoners slaving away on it. Qaraqush went on to fortify and lead the ultimately unsuccessful defence of Acre against Richard the Lionheart from 1189 to 1191.

Under the Mamluks there was a burst of eunuch one-upmanship as a series of high-spending sultans and grandees scrambled to outdo each other in flamboyant funerary architecture presided over by pious eunuchs. In the heart of Cairo's sprawling Qalawun complex, which housed a hospital and college, eunuch guardians maintained their vigil over the mausoleum of Sultan Qalawun (r. 1279–90). Not to be outshone by his father, Sultan al Nasir Mohammed, who ruled Egypt and Syria three times between 1293 and 1341, completed his eponymous Nasiriyya College in 1304, attached to which he added royal tombs for his mother and his late son, guarded by a retinue of eunuchs and Quran readers. In 1359, Sultan Hasan stipulated a retinue of ten eunuchs to maintain his great mausoleum-madrassa complex beneath the Citadel. Mamluk sultans were still building mausolea on the cusp of the fifteenth century. In the 1390s, the Circassian Mamluk Sultan Barquq built his mausoleum, madrassa and Sufi *khanqah* convent in Bayn al Qasrayn (Royal Way) in old Fatimid Cairo, specifying in his deed of pious foundation residences for three eunuchs close to his tomb.

The trend of employing eunuchs to add posthumous lustre to one's legacy proved irresistible to the most ambitious eunuchs themselves. Shahin al Hasani, chief of the royal corps of Masters of the Robe under Barquq's son Sultan Faraj (r. 1399–1412), left a provision for the employment of 'a man who is one of the people of probity and piety, of morality, chastity and fidelity, a eunuch from among the free people of the founder of the endowment'. The eunuch was granted the right of permanent residence in Faraj's yet to be built tomb.[21]

In 1574, the Ottoman Sultan Murad III (r. 1574–95) appointed Mehmed Agha, an Abyssinian eunuch, to an entirely new position: Kizlar Agha, literally agha of the girls, or chief harem eunuch. Though it might not have sounded impressive, the office would become one of the most powerful within the empire, especially when the management of the holy cities of Mecca and Medina, together with the stewardship of all the charitable foundations within the Ottoman realm, fell under its remit. This was a position which brought with it virtually unprecedented, round-the-clock access to the sultan and riches far beyond the most avaricious dreams of most men and women in the empire. Officially the chief eunuch ranked after the sultan and grand vizier in precedence. In practice, he could become even more powerful than that.

Access to the House of Felicity, or the imperial apartments, was guarded zealously. The price of penetrating this inner sanctum without permission, or setting eyes upon the sultan's wives or concubines, was death. In 1599, an Englishman discovered for himself the absolute power wielded by the harem eunuchs. As part of a diplomatic approach to Sultan Mehmed III (r. 1595–1603), with whom she wished to cement an alliance in the face of a mounting Spanish threat, Queen Elizabeth I sent the Ottoman sultan a complex clockwork organ, lavishly studded with jewels. Accompanying it with orders to assemble it for its royal recipient was Thomas Dallam, an organ-builder.

One day, sitting in the imperial apartments surrounded by the scattered innards of the organ, Dallam noticed panic-stricken people rushing away from the area. He asked his dragoman what was happening and was told the sultan was approaching with his concubines. If Dallam or anyone else was discovered there, they would be killed instantly. Within a flash his companions had disappeared, leaving Dallam to face the black harem eunuchs alone. 'I runn as faste as my leggs would carric me aftere, and four neageres or blackamoors cam running towards me with their semetaries [scimitars] drawne,' he wrote; 'yf they could have catchte me theye would have hewed me all in peecis with their semeteris.'

Dallam was fortunate to escape the sword-bearing eunuchs, or

1. Born into slavery on the Arabian Peninsula, Antara ibn Shaddad (525–608) was later freed by his Arab father after fighting for his tribe. He became a celebrated warrior and a poet whose romantic, hellraising verse is still revered by Arabs.

2. *Above left:* Bilal ibn Rabah was born an Ethiopian slave in 580 and later became one of the Prophet Mohammed's dearest Companions and Islam's first *muaddin* (caller to prayer). Here he leads prayers on top of the sacred Kaaba in Mecca.

3. *Above right:* Salman al Farsi – the Persian (*c.*568–*c.*653). Originally a Zoroastrian, subsequently a Christian, he was later enslaved. He became one of the earliest Muslims and another devoted Companion. This miniature from *Siyer-i Nabi*, the fourteenth-century epic on the life of the Prophet shows him, *centre*, being ransomed by Mohammed.

4. A slave market in Zabid, Yemen, thirteenth century. Yemen was one of the last countries in the world to outlaw slavery in 1962.

5. A page from the illuminated *Book of Animals* by the Iraqi polymath Al Jahiz (776–868). Like many medieval Arab and Persian writers, he expressed considerable prejudice towards black Africans.

6. *The Kapi Agha*, chief of the white eunuchs of the Ottoman Sultan Ahmed III (r. 1703–30). Eunuchs were one of the longest-lasting categories of slaves in the Islamic world, enduring from the seventh century to the twenty-first.

7. *The Kizlar Agha*, chief of the black eunuchs of the imperial harem during the sultanate of Ahmed III. This position had become one of the most powerful and lucrative within the Ottoman Empire.

8. Saeed Adam Omar in Medina, 2013. Omar was one of the last survivors of an 800-year tradition of eunuchs guarding the Prophet's Mosque in the city.

9. Interior of the Ottoman sultan's imperial harem engraved by François Denis Née (1732–1817) after Antoine Ignace Melling. Melling served as imperial architect to Sultan III (r. 1762–1808) for eighteen years, giving him greater access to the Ottoman court and palace than any Western artist since Gentile Bellini.

10. A feast for the Valide Sultan, mother of the ruling sultan, with Madame Girardin, wife of Pierre de Girardin, the French ambassador to the Ottoman Empire from 1686 to 1689. *Bottom left*, the black eunuch is keeping vigil.

Clockwise from right:

11. A concubine in Iran, nineteenth century. Concubinage was one of the longest-lived forms of slavery in the Islamic world.

12. Concubines in a bathhouse in the Topkapi Palace harem. An eighteenth-century miniature from the Ottoman poet Fazil Enderuni's scandalous *Zenanname (Book of Ladies)*, which was banned in the Ottoman Empire.

13. Eunuchs in the Islamic world could rise to the commanding heights of society in a wide range of military, political, court and financial positions. One such eunuch was Agha Mohammed Khan, who who founded the Qajar dynasty in 1795 and is shown here leading his army to capture Tbilisi.

14. An eighteenth-century painting of Sultan Selim III (r. 1789–1807) receiving high officials at a religious festival in the Topkapi Palace. With the exception of the clerics approaching the throne (*centre*), everyone pictured here was a slave of the sultan.

15. *Above left:* A sixteenth-century Turkish Janissary going to war. The slave soldier Janissaries played a decisive role in Sultan Mehmed II's conquest of Constantinople in 1453.

16. *Above right:* Christian boys being enslaved as part of the Ottoman *devshirme*, a child levy, to become soldiers and bureaucrats. Most were forcibly taken, others were volunteered by impoverished parents.

17. *Above:* Roxelana (1506–58) was one of the most famous and powerful women of her age. She broke the bonds of her slave concubinage to become Haseki Hurrem Sultan, the wife of Suleiman the Magnificent.

18. *Right:* Hayreddin (*c.*1478–1546), better known in the West as Barbarossa, meets his master, Suleiman the Magnificent (r. 1520–66), in Istanbul in this illustration from the *Suleymanname*.

19. Hayreddin, 'Best of the Faith', was the ultimate Ottoman slave-trafficker. He was, to Europeans, 'the personification of Muslim privateering and human trafficking in the Mediterranean'.

20. Sultan Baybars, the Mamluk sultan of Egypt (r. 1260–77), was one of the greatest examples of upward mobility by a former slave. Enslaved as a young boy, he rose through the military ranks, commanded at the Battle of Ain Jalut in 1260 and then seized power.

what he called the 'runninge wolves'. Despite his terror as he ran for his life, he managed to catch a glimpse, or so he claimed, of the 'Grand Signior' on horseback, accompanied by his concubines, some riding, others on foot. He also left us an arresting description of the eunuchs, 'brave fellowes in their kinde, that weare gelded men, and keepers of the conquebines; neagers that weare as blacke as geate [jet], but verrie brave; by their sides great semeteris; the scabertes semed to be all goulde'.[22]

In rare instances castration could be voluntary. In 1559, a year after Elizabeth had come to the English throne, a Venetian family including two brothers called Gazanfer and Cafer was captured at sea by pirates. While their mother and sisters were freed, the two boys were enslaved and sent to Hungary, where they became favourites of the future Ottoman Sultan Selim I. The prince was so attached to them that one day, lavishing presents on them, he requested both youths join his corps of eunuchs. They agreed to be castrated, how reluctantly the sources do not reveal. Gazanfer Agha, as he became known, rose to become chief white eunuch, serving Sultans Selim II, Murad III and Mehmed III as one of the most powerful officials in the empire for thirty years. Implicated in a court intrigue to depose the famous vizier Sinan Pasha, Gazanfer Agha and Osman Agha, the first chief black eunuch, were both executed in 1603. Gazanfer's brother Cafer, once thought by historians not to have survived the castration, appears to have been appointed head of the privy chamber, a senior office he retained until his death in 1582.[23]

Ottavio Bon, the Venetian *bailo* or ambassador in Istanbul between 1604 and 1607, wrote of 200 eunuchs in the palace who had all undergone total castration – 'they are all of them not only gelt, but have their yards also clean cut off'. Chosen from among renegades, meaning European converts to Islam, they had all agreed to be castrated for career reasons, seduced by the prospect of becoming great men: 'few, or none of them, are gelt and cut against their will'.[24]

Such ambitions were not to be sniffed at. Writing in the late seventeenth century, the inveterate Ottoman traveller and diarist Evliya Çelebi (1611–82) included the chief black and white eunuchs, together with their more junior colleagues, in the lucrative web of corruption which was entangled over important government appointments. 'They say the fish stinks from the head,' he wrote. In the time of Sultan Selim II (r. 1566–74), viziers appointed to govern Egypt dutifully did their job, sending back the gift of 12,000 gold pieces to the sultan each year. Now, said Çelebi, just to secure the appointment, the viziers had to pay 1,500 purses in bribes to the sultan, his favourite concubines, the sultan's mother, the grand vizier, the princes and their lieutenants, the chief black eunuch, the chief white eunuch, more junior eunuchs, the chief judge, the viziers of the sultan's council, the financial officers, and more than 100 others.[25] Eunuchs, especially the most senior ones, routinely enriched themselves through these bribes and payments for favours.

From the sixteenth century, according to the French jeweller and traveller Jean Chardin (1643–1713), author of a study of Iran and the Middle East, the Georgians and Circassians were the favourite choice as eunuchs in Iran. By the time of the Qajar dynasty (r. 1789–1925), for whom they played a critical role in the state bureaucracy, eunuchs took their place among a highly cosmopolitan – racially, religiously and ethnically mixed – population of the enslaved. It included unspecified Africans, Kurds, Turkmen, Azeris, Armenians, Shirazis, Qazvinis, Isfahanis, Georgians and Circassians. Fath Ali Shah Qajar (r. 1797–1834), for example, had a multinational palace entourage of 300–1,000 Africans, Georgians, Turkmen, Armenians, Jews and Iranians. Among their other responsibilities, the eunuchs devoted much of their time to supervising the lives of the 700 women and 600 children the shah reportedly maintained in his harem. The royal predilection for palace eunuchs showed no sign of abating as the nineteenth century wore on. Indeed, towards the end of the long reign of Naser al Din Shah Qajar, 'Pivot of the Universe' (r. 1848–96), there was a sharp increase in their numbers. Between 1889 and 1895, according to Jean-Baptiste Feuvrier, the shah's personal physician, the harem grew from forty black and white eunuchs to 100. His first-ranking wives each had three or four.[26]

Eunuchs in Iran, as elsewhere, were greatly valued. Their official dress and their title of *agha* signalled their authority and the respect in which they were held. For those at the highest level the rewards were enormous. Bashir Khan, Naser al Din Shah Qajar's chief eunuch, could earn as much as 2,000 *tomans* (10,000 Maria Theresa thalers, or Spanish dollars) annually, compared with the twenty to thirty *tomans* received by a simple bodyguard in the *ghulam-i shahi*, the shah's enslaved people.[27]

There can have been no more infamous Iranian eunuch around this time than Agha Mohammad Khan Qajar (r. 1789–97), who was feared for his legendary brutality. However, his greatest distinction, surely unique for a eunuch, was to found a dynasty – the Qajars. Through a combination of military prowess, political manoeuvring and strategic alliances he rose from opportunist soldier serving the Zand dynasty to prowling independent warlord, expanding his control over various regions of Iran until he had established himself as the dominant ruler. During his campaign in 1794 that toppled Lotf Ali Khan, the last Zand ruler of Iran, he sold all the women and children of Kerman into slavery and killed or blinded all its male inhabitants – 20,000 eyeballs were piled up in front of him. Later that year he declared himself shah of Iran, marking the beginning of the Qajar dynasty. His bloody rise to power laid the foundation for the dynasty's ascendancy.

For centuries Abyssinia retained its position as the chief source of black eunuchs for the Ottoman court. They were the most desirable and most expensive, more valuable than their Caucasian counterparts. Conquered by the Ottomans in the 1550s, Abyssinia extended across what is today southern Egypt, Sudan, Djibouti and the Ethiopian littoral. Together with masses of other young men, women and girls, young boys were seized and enslaved here in their droves, before being castrated in Upper Egypt then forced to trudge north on brutal marches across the desert to Cairo – though many never made it that far. There they were sold by slave-traders and transported to Istanbul for service in the sultan's Topkapi Palace. Such was their visibility and influence at the Ottoman court in the early seventeenth century that the period has been dubbed the 'Sultanate of the African Eunuchs', which overlapped with the 'Sultanate of Women'.[28]

It was in Abyssinia in around 1655 that Beshir Agha was born. He was an African slave who was destined to become one of the richest, most famous and longest-serving eunuchs in Ottoman history, the most powerful individual in the entire empire.[29] Sold into slavery as a young boy, Beshir appears to have been owned initially by either the Ottoman governor of Egypt or another provincial notable. There he would have received an Islamic education, supplemented later by lessons in court protocol in the Topkapi Palace. Beshir was exceptionally gifted. By 1707 he was appointed chief harem treasurer, a position which typically led to the ultimate promotion to chief harem eunuch. Sometime before 1716, having been exiled in Cyprus after falling victim to the politics of court factions, he was made master of the Prophetic Sanctuary, chief of the tomb eunuchs in Medina – whose frail successors maintained their vigil into the twenty-first century.

The tomb eunuchs or guardians in Medina were the servants of the Prophet's threshold, entering the sacred enclosure in a solemn procession every day at dusk to light the great oil lamps in a time-honoured ritual, check there were no pilgrims overstaying their welcome and then lock the gates. The most junior eunuchs were responsible for clearing away dirt and rubbish from the mosque and tomb enclosure. More senior eunuchs served as doormen, controlling access to the sanctuary containing the graves of Mohammed, Abu Bakr and Umar. When they finished their work they returned to their homes in Harat al Aghawat, the eunuchs' quarter of Medina, a clear indication that there were sufficient numbers of them to have their own neighbourhood.

Muslim accounts of the eunuch guardians tend to be respectful, emphasizing their piety, dignity and generosity as benefactors of the poor. Visiting Medina in 1184, Ibn Jubayr praised the dignified appearance of the Abyssinian and Slavic eunuchs. 'They present an elegant appearance and are meticulous in their clothing and bearing,' he wrote. Arriving in Medina in 1326, at the outset of his 75,000-mile, twenty-nine-year journey across the world, the Moroccan traveller Ibn Battuta (1304–69) similarly drew attention to their 'handsome appearance' elegant clothes and 'clean, meticulous look'. He also remarked on the stipends they received from Egypt and Syria, which contributed to their considerable prosperity.

Centuries later, Princess Musbah Haidar, daughter of the grand sharif of Mecca, wrote affectionately in her memoirs of the palace eunuchs of the Ottoman royal household in the years before the First World War. 'The fun was contagious for there were no [other] children in all that gloomy palace; and these gentle creatures [eunuchs] always nourished a great love and adoration for them, especially for these two little Sherifas whom they would call *bizim kilar* (one belonging to us!).' Around the same time, another account of life in the imperial harem argued that it was a mistake often made by foreigners, and sometimes Turks, to see the palace eunuchs as 'ferocious, full of hatred and of contempt towards men'. On the contrary, there was nothing wicked or ferocious about them. 'These unfortunate beings were only sought out and taken from their countries to be employed as barriers between the *harem* and the *selamlik* [men's quarters], between women and men.'[30]

Foreigners tended to be more repulsed by the eunuchs. Some allowed contempt to colour their prose. In 1811, Burckhardt likened eunuchs' hands to those of a 'skeleton' and reckoned their whole appearance 'extremely disgusting'. Attending a banquet in Mecca in 1853, Sir Richard Burton, the English scholar and explorer, was required to defer to an honoured eunuch. As a man, he wrote, it taught him a lot about humility to kowtow to 'this high-shouldered, spindle-shanked, beardless bit of neutrality'. The tomb eunuchs tended to be married, Burton noted, some of them having three or four wives, 'which would have aroused Juvenal's bile'.* Caricatures and stereotypes were the order of the day. Thus, for Burton, the eunuch was 'disconnected with humanity . . . cruel, fierce, brave and capable of any villainy'. In 1936, the British writer Norman Mosley Penzer pronounced Cevher Agha, one of the last chief black eunuchs, 'cruel and vile', a 'huge, swollen, balloon-like creature', representative of a system that was 'rotten to the core'.[31] Perhaps the eunuchs thought just as little of these prurient infidels.

It is doubtful that such literary criticism would have hurt Beshir Agha. He had bigger things on his mind. In 1716 he was appointed chief harem eunuch, a position he held for the next thirty years until

---

* In his *Satires*, Juvenal attacks the behaviour of those Roman wives who sleep with eunuchs:

> There are girls who adore unmanly eunuchs – so smooth,
> so beardless to kiss, and no worry about abortions!
> But the biggest thrill is one who was fully-grown,
> a lusty black-quilled male, before the surgeons
> went to work on his groin. *Satires*, 6.366–70.

his death. Ironically his appointment came just a year after an imperial edict from Istanbul to the governor and chief justice of Egypt forbidding castration, a practice which it said had turned parts of Fayyum, Jirja and Cairo itself into 'terrible places resembling slaughterhouses'. Yet this was just one of many reminders of the yawning chasm between official pronouncements and real-world practice, a jarring juxtaposition to the edicts specifically requesting more eunuchs which were issued in 1722 and 1737.[32]

Among Beshir's many responsibilities was providing entertainment for the court. He played a pivotal role in putting on the *Ciragan Eglenceri*, or Lantern Entertainments, an annual, ostensibly private, spring festival in Istanbul for the imperial household, especially the royal women, to celebrate the blooming of the tulips. Under his vigilant eye, pavilions sprang up along the Golden Horn and the western shores of the Bosphorus. It was a welcome opportunity for the women to exchange their gilded confinement within the Topkapi Palace for al fresco amusement and feasting on the waterside. 'During daylight hours they passed the time in delightful music and conversation, jokes and games; and at night, they enjoyed the lanterns and the tulip beds,' wrote the court historian Mehmed Rasid Efendi. The festival came to an extravagant climax with Beshir's presentation of gifts to the women in strict order of precedence and extravagance.[33]

At a time when the grand vizier had virtually supplanted the Ottoman sultan as the empire's chief authority, Beshir Agha proved a ruthlessly effective maker and unmaker of viziers, raising one to high office one moment, deposing and exiling him the next. In 1739 he negotiated the Treaty of Belgrade with Russia and the Habsburg Empire in which Serbia, Bosnia and Wallachia were returned to the Ottomans, ushering in a welcome peace after the Austro-Russian-Turkish War of 1735–9.

Beshir also exercised immense cultural influence through his lavish sponsorship and commissioning of numerous mosques, Quranic schools, theological colleges, libraries, Sufi orders and even public drinking fountains. His library of 1,007 volumes alone provides a fascinating window into his mind. It contained, among other works, 105 volumes of *hadiths*, 105 studies of Islamic law, seventy-five books of Quranic exegesis, fifty-eight volumes on history, forty-eight titles on Sufi mysticism, thirty-five texts of literature and poetry, thirty-two grammar books, nineteen volumes on astronomy and astrology and seven on morphology.[34]

Beshir died of natural causes on 3 June 1746, having served two sultans as chief harem eunuch. He was buried within the Eyüp Sultan Mosque complex on the Golden Horn, a sign of the great esteem in which he was held and the enormous authority he maintained until his death. The shrine and wider district are named after Abu Ayub al Ansari (d. 674), one of the Prophet Mohammed's closest brothers-in-arms, whose tomb is among Istanbul's most sacred places of pilgrimage. Centuries later, Muslim pilgrims flock here in their thousands to venerate these ancient heroes of the faith. An inscription above Beshir's tomb pays tribute to the slave who became one of the empire's most remarkable eunuchs:

> The former support of the Abode of Felicity,
> Beshir Agha, possessor of virtue, commander of nobility,
> Lies here. For many years, with his acts of generosity, which were
> the most brilliant adornment of the seat of power,
> He behaved as a slave to the summons of prayer ...
> May God forgive his sins.
> May his place be in the paradise of his boon-companions, the men of
> learning.[35]

Purchased for thirty piastres, Beshir left a fortune of 30 million piastres, 160 horses and 800 jewel-studded watches on his death. He also bequeathed a strengthened Ottoman bureaucracy staffed with decent lawyers and efficient administrators. Born in Abyssinia, seized and enslaved by slave-traders, castrated as a young boy in Egypt, he had risen to the summit of statesmanship during his long and turbulent life, navigating imperial politics with the greatest aplomb and arguably wielding more influence over Ottoman affairs, from court culture and regional political life to foreign policy and the Islamic religion, than any other man alive.

The eunuchs who worked in the Muslim world, serving every whim of caliphs, kings and sultans for many centuries, have little voice. They are written about and described by other writers and travellers, mostly uncastrated men, be they fellow, mostly sympathetic Muslims or generally more antagonistic foreigners. It is only in the twentieth century, during the last gasp of eunuchism in the Ottoman Empire, that we start to hear from these most elusive of individuals directly. For once we can listen to their stories, however fragmentary, in their own voices.

Born in the closing years of the nineteenth century, Tahsin Agha was one of the last black eunuchs of Istanbul. Among his earliest memories as a young village boy in Abyssinia was the horror of seeing his mother killed in front of him by slave-traders. The same men left his little brother in the jungle to be killed and eaten by wild animals. His next memory, as violent and merciless as his first, had been seared into his life forever:

> Slave-traders took me to an open space where they tightly tied my legs to a pole. They tightly gagged my mouth with cloth. I had the most horrible pain of my life, but did not scream. Then they poured hot oil on me as soon as they emasculated me to prevent gangrene. I am still astonished that I did not die or lose my mind because of the pain.

Sold initially to a senior Ottoman official for the equivalent price of three dozen cups, three dozen plates and a dozen glass jugs, on his master's death he was sent to finish his education and begin work in the sultan's palace, by now Dolmabahçe on the European side of the Bosphorus. When interviewed in 1938, he was teaching literature at Erenköy Girls High School in Istanbul's Kadikoy district. 'If you wrote a novel about your life, what would you name it?' the Turkish journalist asked Tahsin. '*Scream*,' he answered immediately, 'because I still remember my mother and brother screaming whenever I see a young woman or children screaming.'[36]

As important figures of power, the very last eunuchs of the Ottoman Empire found themselves directly caught up in the turmoil of its demise. By 1903, there were still 194 African eunuchs registered in the service of the Ottoman family.[37] As *primi inter pares*, the chief black eunuchs were particularly vulnerable. Cevher Agha, chief black eunuch-turned-spy chief of Sultan Abdul Hamid II (r. 1876–1909), compiled a list of those opponents of the regime who were plotting his master's removal and replacement with a democratic government.

Then, in 1908, came the bombshell of the Young Turk Revolution, when discontent within the army, piled on to political dissent led by a combustible mix of secularists, nationalists and liberals, ignited into military rebellion. Under mounting pressure, Abdul Hamid was forced to restore parliament and the short-lived inaugural constitution of 1876 that he had suspended thirty years earlier. The orthodoxies of the Ottoman Empire were turned on their head. Power leached away from the sultan and now flowed towards the new nexus of authority, the Young Turks' Committee of Union and Progress (CUP). The talk in Istanbul was of liberty and reform. Cevher was a marked man. On 27 March 1909 he was executed and hanged from a lamp-post on Galata Bridge.

Succeeding him as chief harem eunuch in this febrile atmosphere was Nadir Agha, another Abyssinian, born in around 1874. When he was just six or seven, he saw his father and many men and women slaughtered during a savage raid by slavers on his village. He was stabbed in the head and chest and left for dead.

'Twice slave-traders kidnapped me,' he recalled in a rare surviving interview with a chief black eunuch. 'I escaped at midnight and returned to my village passing through the jungle among lions and elephants. However, slave-traders kidnapped me again, and then they took me to Saudi Arabia,' first to Mecca, thence to Medina, 'the biggest market for the slave-traders', especially for African slaves. He was one of 200 enslaved men, women and children.

He was purchased by Seyyare Hanim, wife of Emir Abdullah, brother of the sharif of Mecca, and renamed Nadir. After three years in Mecca and Taif, in around 1889 he was given, along with twenty-one other Abyssinian eunuchs, to Sultan Abdul Hamid and was employed in the newly built Yildiz Palace. In that same year, during the five-day state visit to Istanbul of the German Emperor Kaiser Wilhelm and his wife Empress Augusta Victoria, a blur of banquets with solid gold, jewel-encrusted plates and goblets, there was a moment of inadvertent royal humour. The empress visited the harem and met the Kizlar Agha at the Gate of Felicity. When it was explained to her that he was an extremely important official, 'the Empress, trying to make conversation – and knowing nothing of eunuchs – brightly asked the Kizlar Agha through the interpreter whether his father had also been a eunuch'.[38]

Nadir soon became a firm favourite, recognized for his loyalty, honesty and intelligence. In a reminder of the shattering loss of family that all eunuchs suffered, Nadir told the sultan of his burning desire to be reunited with his surviving sisters. Through a special envoy the sultan contacted Menelik II (r. 1889–1913), emperor of Ethiopia, asking him to make inquiries. Eventually a letter arrived with news. 'I listened to its translation with great excitement. It said that they had searched for my family and after investigating, they discovered that they had emigrated to Kenya. They apologised because they could not present me with positive news.' The gift of a gold coin, two elephant tusks and the award of two Orders of the Lion can have been little comfort. He never saw his sisters again.

Nadir was sufficiently trusted by the sultan to play a critical role in the attempted counter-coup against the Young Turks government in 1909, which resulted instead in Abdul Hamid's removal as sultan after fierce fighting in the capital. Nadir was described by General Ali Galip Pasiner, the man who arrested him and everyone else in Yildiz Palace, as 'a clever, self-confident, well-behaved, graceful black man', a verdict shared by the *New York Times* correspondent, who thought him 'a man of extraordinary diplomatic and political talent', the most intellectually brilliant among the Association of Mohammedan Union, the conservative and religious opposition to the CUP.

For his key part defending the old order, however, Nadir was sentenced to death. He was only spared execution by turning state

Nadir Agha, an Abyssinian eunuch, one of the last to serve the Ottoman Empire. Captured and enslaved in Africa as a boy, he spent years working for Sultan Abdul Hamid II before his court career ended abruptly in 1909.

evidence and revealing the sultan's many hiding places for his valuables, including a subterranean chamber, protected by an armoured-plated door, which contained bags and valises stuffed with 700,000 Turkish *lira*, gold, diamonds, rubies and sapphires worth many millions, stocks and shares certificates and records of foreign bank accounts – Reichsbank, Deutsche Bank and Crédit Lyonnais – containing another 25 million *lira*. From his exile in Salonika the deposed sultan, now reduced to a household of three wives, two sons, six eunuchs, twenty-four concubines and female servants and nine male servants, expressed regret that Nadir's name had not appeared in the list of those executed in Istanbul. 'Abdul Hamid had a stone in the place where his heart ought to be, and innocent blood flowing in floods had no effect on him whatsoever,' Nadir told a court martial.

In return for his evidence and assistance in locating the sultan's hidden treasures, Nadir was spared the hangman's noose and freed. Life after all the years of imperial service was quiet and far removed from the dangerous cut and thrust of powerplays at court. An enterprising man, he moved across the Bosphorus to the Asian side of Istanbul, purchasing a house and some land in the Göztepe district on the shores of the Sea of Marmara. Although he had very little money – in an interview in 1934 he said he was then down to his last 700 *lira*, borrowed from a friend – he managed to buy a herd of forty Crimean dairy cows at auction and opened a dairy, which he claimed was the first in Istanbul to deliver milk in closed-top bottles. He also helped organize a retirement association to assist former court eunuchs in need. He died in 1962 and today is remembered by a street in Göztepe that bears his name.

After half a millennium of service to the Ottoman sultans, the final chief black eunuch was Fahreddin Agha. His tenure lasted little more than a month between April and May 1909, the swansong of an institution being consigned to history by the Young Turks. On 20 May that year, dressed in the splendour of his official regalia, he joined fellow grandees, glittering with medals and festooned with frogging, for a Muslim religious festival in the Hall of Ceremonies, only to be curtly instructed – twice – by the lord chamberlain to leave the chamber since the Ottoman Empire which he served no longer existed. He was stripped of his title of Devletlü (His Highness), barred from attending state ceremonies and sent packing. It must have been a deeply wounding experience.

In 1976, a year before his death, Fahreddin told the story of his life to a friend in Istanbul. He remembered his childhood as if it was yesterday, he said, describing how, when he was just seven or eight, he was playing chase with his village friends one day when armed Arab horsemen suddenly burst in on the scene:

> They caught us. One of them closed my mouth and I almost suffocated. My eyes went out of their sockets. They took all my friends and me away. I didn't understand their language. I later understood they were talking Arabic. We arrived in a village and were put in a yard. There were other children like us. They talked the same language as us. They were sobbing. We didn't understand why they had kidnapped us. We shared the same sorrow. We stayed three days without drinking and eating. We were afraid. A few days later, we were castrated [in Massawa, today's Eritrea]. During numerous years, I never forgot the pain and the tortures endured.

Later they were put on a boat. Relieved to have escaped 'the monsters', they still had no idea where they were going. 'We thought they were going to throw us in the ocean.' Seized from their families, the young children were terrified:

> Our villages, our brothers, our sisters, our mothers were far behind. Will it be possible to see them again one day? Some of us cried all the time. We were afraid to be drowned. We were seeing the sea for the first time and we were afraid. We were all gathered on the boat. We looked at the waves. Which other misfortune was waiting for us?

There was a tantalizing moment of hope when a British patrol intercepted the boat, arrested the Arab slave-traders and escorted the group to Aden. Thinking they would be reunited with their families, the children shouted with joy. But the British commander, speaking through a translator, told them that since the slave trade was illegal the children would be given to trusted officials instead. Fahreddin was given to an Ottoman officer who took him to Istanbul, where he was presented to a Circassian pasha, the first step on his route to becoming a palace eunuch. As Fahreddin remarked sadly: 'Can somebody offer a human as a gift?'[39]

For the Young Turks, maintaining palace eunuchs in this new age of progress was complete anathema. Lutfi Simavi, the newly appointed lord chamberlain who had humiliated Fahreddin in the Hall of Ceremonies, confided in his diary that their continued existence was incompatible with modern civilization. It was backward, uncivilized and un-European. Besides, 'the barbaric operation to which the wretched blacks had been exposed is an assault on humanity'.[40]

With the collapse of the Ottoman Empire the last of their line were left to live out their lives in quiet and seclusion. However, in the holiest places of Islam, in Mecca and Medina, the tradition of appointing eunuch guardians lived on deep into the twentieth century. The last eunuch was recruited in 1984, in defiance of the earlier fatwa. One by one, the old men have since died, leaving scattered memories of an unobtrusive life of service.

One of the earliest memories of these men, judging by the elusive first-person accounts, remains as scar tissue, a psychological wound to accompany the lifelong physical disfigurement. It is of Arab slavers riding into peaceful African villages like the horsemen of the apocalypse. For centuries the profit-seeking predators brought terror and bloodshed to these poorly defended communities. Children saw their mothers and fathers slaughtered in front of them. In the flash of a few moments their freedom and innocence ended: lives were shattered. Girls were forced into slavery, boys were hauled off to be mutilated in crude operations that killed untold numbers.

Islam prohibited this mutilation, yet for many centuries those who had survived it were pressed into service in its holiest sites and at the heart of its many empires.

7

Rogues and Renegades:
Slavery in the Mediterranean

So, let us excoriate past Mediterranean evil, and let us remember the infinite sufferers. But nobody should cast the first stone.
Nabil Matar, *Mediterranean Captivity
Through Arab Eyes, 1517–1798*

There has long been a tendency in the West to consider piracy and enslavement in the early modern Mediterranean as a uniquely Muslim-led phenomenon against first European and later American Christians. One reason such views have erroneously prevailed is the heavy concentration on 'Barbary corsairs' by almost exclusively Western writers.[*] European historians have long seen Christians as the main victims of Muslim pirates or corsairs while largely 'forgetting' that the enslavement of Muslim prisoners in Christian lands was a common phenomenon. So much so, it has been argued, that the number of Muslim slaves held in European prisons and plantations was in reality far higher than that

[*] While Europeans and Americans referred with dread to both the 'Barbary corsairs' and the 'Barbary coast', few if any of the indigenous inhabitants of North Africa would have used the word 'Barbary'. It was derived from the Greek *barbaros* for babbler, a pejorative term used for all non-Greek-speakers, in other words foreigners, whose unintelligible languages supposedly sounded to Greek ears like '*bar*'. From there it was a short step via the Roman world to *barbarus* for a foreigner, savage or barbarian, a negative perspective which, centuries later, Arabs, and afterwards Europeans and Americans would adopt towards the inhabitants of North Africa. The word Berber, for the original tribes of north-west Africa, is thought to share the same etymology. The indigenous, as opposed to Arab, inhabitants of the region refer to themselves as *Amazigh* (plural *Imazighen*), the free people.

of Mediterranean Europeans languishing in North African or Ottoman captivity.[1] The Mediterranean was in fact a hybrid, free-for-all, deeply entangled, multi-faith world in which all too often Muslims found themselves captured and enslaved by Christian pirates, the Knights of Malta, the Knights of St John and the Knights of St Stephen foremost among them.

It all depended on where you were standing. The perspective from either side of the Straits of Gibraltar could hardly have been more starkly opposed. One European's 'barbarian' Barbary corsairs were another North African's *ghuzat al mumineen*, or warriors of the faith, celebrated seaborne fighters winning holy distinction against the infidels. As the Algerian historian Ahmed ibn Mohammed al Maqqari wrote in the 1620s, 'there were some who went on the sea jihad and found fame'.[2]

During the seventeenth, eighteenth and nineteenth centuries, European and later American consuls and North African corsairs were adversaries locked in a deadly, slave-taking, blood-letting conflict that pitted Christian West against Muslim East and struck terror across the Mediterranean. Such hostile sentiments tended to be passionately reciprocated. For many Muslims on the North African littoral, especially those who had been forcibly ejected from the Iberian Peninsula during the centuries-long Reconquista which had culminated in 1492, the Christian states to their north, Spain in particular, were legitimate enemies. It followed that European shipping, including its human cargo, were their rightful prizes. War meant prisoners, prisoners meant slaves and slaves meant money.

In reality, divisions were not always so clear-cut. In the turbulent seas of the Mediterranean, fine distinctions could prove as slippery as a ship's deck drenched with rain, blood and human entrails. When, for instance, did a corsair, strictly speaking a state-supported privateer with letters of marque authorizing attacks on certain countries' shipping, become a rogue pirate operating outside the law? A lawyer scrutinizing the carefully worded text of a treaty between a European power and the regency of Algiers, Tunis or Tripoli, in which the former paid the latter a fee in return for not having its ships attacked and captured, might easily draw a neat line between the two. Your average European or North African was just as likely to see them as synonymous. Was a ship flying the flag of a European country which had agreed a tribute-for-protection treaty but carried on board a sailor who may have come from a country without such a treaty fair game? For the booty-hunting corsairs, unequivocally yes. For the European nations, certainly not. And was a renegade, a European Christian who had perhaps only notionally converted to Islam ('turned Turk' in the parlance of the time) really a religious warrior fighting jihad against the Christians, or was he merely a ruthless chancer prepared to kill and enslave, irrespective of religion, in his quest for treasure? Is it right to see the corsairs as a uniquely Muslim phenomenon when so many of the most famous among them were European renegades, often converts of convenience? These are just some of the nuances at play.

Bias against Muslims, then as now, could be instinctive. As Jacques Philippe Laugier de Tassy, a career diplomat who served as chancellor in the French consulate in Algiers from 1717, wrote in *Histoire du royaume d'Alger*, prejudice against the Turks and all Muslims was firmly rooted in most Christians. He pointed the finger at 'Spanish Monks, who spread a thousand Falsities in order to inhance the Merit of their Voyages into Barbary for the Redemption of Slaves' as well as 'the false Relations of pretended Slaves, who beg round the Country, with Chains about them which they never wore in Africa'. His was an unusually enlightened view at a time when Algiers was a hate word for most Europeans. Laugier de Tassy wrote his history, he explained, deliberately to counter the prevailing anti-Muslim prejudices of his age.[3]

Certainly, it was a rare Christian voice to draw uncomfortable parallels between European and American slave-trading on the one hand and that version practised along the North African coast on the other. Charles Sumner, the abolitionist American senator from Massachusetts between 1851 and 1874, was one such man. When it came to buying and selling slaves, he wrote in *White Slavery in the Barbary States* (1847), 'we are not entitled to charge the Algerines with any exclusive degree of barbarity. The Christians of Europe and America carry on this commerce one hundred times more extensively than the Algerines.'[4]

For centuries untold hundreds of thousands of Muslims found

themselves shipped off to slave markets in Malta and Marseilles, Malaga and Livorno, the mirror image of the misery-filled markets in Algiers, Tunis, Tripoli and Salé, the nest of corsairs on Morocco's Atlantic coast, known to generations of English men and women with fear and loathing as the 'Sallee Rovers'.

In Naples there were an estimated 20,000 Muslim slaves in the early sixteenth century, 12,000 in Sicily in the later sixteenth and 100,000 in Spain at the end of that century. On Malta, long a centre for harrying the fleets of Tunis and Tripoli, estimates range from 1,500–5,500 Muslim slaves in the early seventeenth century, rising to 10,000 by 1720.[5] Sixteenth-century Italian states, especially Sicily, teemed with tens of thousands of Muslim or former Muslim slaves and such enslavement continued, albeit at a lower level, across the eighteenth century. Although the French and Ottomans maintained an alliance that lasted from 1536 until the cusp of the nineteenth century, for King Louis XIV (r. 1643–1715), the 2,000 or so *esclaves Turcs* who powered his showboating galleys in abominable conditions were proof positive of royal glory, Christian, specifically Catholic, ascendancy, and Muslim servitude.* Right across Europe, from Paris to Palermo, Vienna to Valletta, Berlin to Budapest, Salzburg to Santiago de Compostela, Rome to Livorno, this attitude was given tangible expression. Muslim slaves found themselves sculpted in bronze, stone and marble – in churches, chapels, mausolea, palaces and public squares, always 'chained, crouching and crushed under Euro-Christian victory'.[6]

To be enslaved as a galley rower was a brutal, dragged-out death sentence. They were shackled hand and foot, excreting where they sat, barely fed and so thirsty they sometimes drank sea water. Virtually naked apart from linen breeches, they were burnt raw by the sun; 'sleep deprivation on the narrow bench propelled them towards lunacy; the stroke keeper's drum and the overseer's lash – a tarred rope or a dried bull's penis – whipped them beyond the point of exhaustion'.[7]

The Sun King's Muslim galley slaves were so highly prized that they fell outside the traditional system of ransom and exchange. Death,

---

* The *esclaves Turcs* in France were Turks and Ottoman subjects more widely, especially North African Arabs and Berbers such as Algerians, Moroccans, Tunisians and Tripolitans.

escape or, at a push, incapacity – as long as the infirm slave could find a healthy replacement – were their only way out. Enslaved Muslim Arabs, Turks, *Amazigh* Berbers and 'Moors' across the continent counted among their number papal galley rowers and gravediggers, heavy labourers, builders, porters, miners, tavernkeepers and domestic servants. These men were the Muslim counterparts of the European Christian architects, builders, marble-cutters, stonemasons, carpenters, decorators, ironsmiths, doctors, astrologers and dogsbodies who toiled away for the mass slave-importer and palace-building Moroccan sultan Moulay Ismail (r. 1672–1727). At any one time he was said to have over 25,000 European slaves in his possession, one of whom we will meet shortly. His imperial capital of Meknes contained so many they even had their own quarter in the heart of the city, with separate residences reserved for the British, French, Portuguese and Spanish captives.

How many such enslaved Muslims and Christians are we talking about here? Unsurprisingly, it is difficult to reach a precise figure and this is fraught, vigorously contested territory. Looking first at Muslim slaves in Europe, the Italian historian Salvatore Bono has estimated there were between 400,000 and 500,000 on the Italian Peninsula alone between 1500 and 1800. By his calculations, 'at least two million slaves' from the Muslim Mediterranean entered Europe from the sixteenth to the nineteenth century. Turning to Christian slaves in North Africa, the American historian Robert C. Davis proposed that 1,000,000–1,250,000 'white, European Christians were enslaved by the Muslims of the Barbary Coast' in the 250 years from 1530 to 1780.* The lower figure agrees with the estimate of Bono, who uses it to suggest an overall total of 5,000,000 enslaved during this period, including at least 2,000,000 'black slaves' taken into the Islamic world.[8]

All such estimates should necessarily be taken with great caution.

---

* The Lebanese-American scholar Nabil Matar, among others, has challenged Davis's estimate, noting, to cite just one example, that the 1,250,000 figure relied in part on an eighteenth-century list of 160 British ships captured by Algerians between 1677 and 1680. This was assumed to have resulted in the enslavement of 7,000–9,000 men and women. In fact, the true figure was ninety-one ships taken containing a total of 918 seamen, or one-tenth of the higher estimate: 'the Algerians would have had to capture 1,000 ships' to justify the figure.

Starting in the fifteenth century, as they spread proto-colonially along North Africa's Mediterranean and Atlantic coastlines, the Portuguese and Spanish filled their prisons and presidios with thousands of Muslim captives, while thousands of other Muslim slaves toiled in Maltese, French and Italian galleys. In the first decade of the seventeenth century, according to Ahmad ibn Qasim al Hajjari (c.1570–c.1640), the Moroccan writer and envoy to France and the Netherlands, there were 5,500 Muslim prisoners in Venice and Malta alone. When, in 1624, the ruler of Algiers wrote to King James I of England, he noted that English sailors had captured some 'Moors and Turks' and that Algiers sailors in response had taken and sold some Englishmen. He considered this tit-for-tat and proposed a practical solution: 'if your Majesty shall be pleased to send us the Moors and Turks, We shall suddenly and out of hand put the Christians at Liberty'.[9]

The border between freedom and slavery in the Mediterranean could be crossed and recrossed within moments. In 1748, Maltese, Hungarian and Georgian slaves on board the Ottoman ship *Lupa* rose up, seized control of the vessel, enslaved its crew, which included Mustafa Pasha, governor of Rhodes, and sailed into Malta. Under Mustafa's leadership the newly enslaved Muslims planned to revolt in the summer of 1749, by poisoning food at a feast day, assassinating the grand master in his sleep, freeing their fellow Muslims and sending a signal for relief to a combined fleet from Tunis, Tripoli and Algiers. However, the plot was discovered and its leaders – barring Mustafa, who was spared after French intercession – were tortured and executed. Eight were branded and condemned to the galleys for life, some had their flesh torn off with red-hot pincers, others had their arms and legs smashed with sledgehammers, and 125 were hanged in Valletta's Palace Square.[10]

Slave status need not be fixed for life. Often it could be fluid and fleeting. History provides one astonishing example of how a man could rise from pirate victim and slave to one of the most famous, feared and celebrated pirate corsairs of all time. When still a young man, Oruç Reis (c.1474–1518), one of the two Barbarossa Brothers whose very name would terrorize a couple of generations of Europeans, was captured and enslaved by the Knights of St John – another brother, Ilyas, was killed in the same encounter. Headquartered in Rhodes after the destruction of the Latin kingdom of Jerusalem in 1291 and notwithstanding their agreement in 1480 not to attack Ottoman shipping, the Knights Hospitallers continued to prey on merchant vessels travelling between Egypt and Ottoman lands. Forced to work as a galley slave in the most agonizing form of servitude, Oruç Reis was later ransomed and became a privateer himself, storming to power in Algiers in 1516 and establishing an Ottoman stronghold in North Africa which would last for more than 300 years, significantly changing life in the Mediterranean.

Oruç's younger brother and partner in piracy was Hizir Reis (c.1478–1546), also known as Hayreddin, 'Best of the Faith', whose maritime career was longer-lived and even more blood-spattered and illustrious than that of his sibling. In 1533, Sultan Suleiman the Magnificent appointed him Kapudan Pasha, grand admiral of the Ottoman navy, a promotion he celebrated with the conquest of Tunis a year later. The brothers-in-arms played a pivotal role in the rise of North African corsairing, Hayreddin especially becoming, in European minds, 'the personification of Muslim privateering and human trafficking in the Mediterranean'.[11] For the Ottomans and many of their Muslim subjects across the Mediterranean, on the other hand, the brothers were war heroes and faithful servants of the expanding Islamic Empire.

Faith was little or no protection when it came to piracy and enslavement. Innocent men and women from both the Muslim and Christian worlds, including those destined to become some of the most famous writers of their age, found themselves caught up in this vicious conflict on the water. In 1520, Hassan al Wazzan, a Granada-born Muslim diplomat and traveller, was captured by Spanish corsairs near the island of Jerba off the Tunisian coast. Too valuable to be despatched into the back-breaking life of a galley slave, he was instead given to Pope Leo X as an educated, highly travelled ornament for the papal court. Al Wazzan's probably tactical conversion to Christianity persuaded the pope to free him from slavery, allowing the rechristened Johannes Leo de Medicis freedom to continue his studies and write his groundbreaking *Cosmographia et geographia de Affrica* (1526), later published as *Description of Africa*, the most authoritative study of the continent prior to the great age of exploration in the nineteenth century. Having been exiled with his family to Fez in the final years of Ferdinand and Isabella's Reconquista (1479–92), Leo

Africanus, as he is better known in the West, is thought to have returned to Morocco where he died sometime after 1550.

A generation later it was the turn of Miguel de Cervantes, the greatest writer in the Spanish language and author of the first modern novel, to fall foul of the corsairs. Proud veteran of the Battle of Lepanto against the Ottomans in 1571, where he had been so badly wounded that he lost the use of his left arm, Cervantes was captured by Algerian corsairs while sailing with his brother Rodrigo from Naples to Barcelona in 1575. This was around the time, in the words of a memorandum from Marseilles in 1564, when it was 'raining Christians in Algiers'.[12] Cervantes languished in chains in the filthy, steaming bagnios or prison-houses of Algiers for almost five years, writing poetry, letters and various studies, and making four daring but unsuccessful attempts to escape. He was finally released in 1580 by the Trinitarians, a religious charity devoted to ransoming Christian captives, though only after his family had managed to raise the crippling sum of 500 escudos for his freedom.

Cervantes's life-changing captivity in Algiers bore exceptional literary fruit, from his two plays *Los tratos de Argel (The Treatments*

Europeans ransomed from slavery in a public fundraising ceremony. An image from Pierre Dan's *Historie van Barbaryen, en des zelfs Zee-Roovers*, 1684. Dan was a French Trinitarian friar who travelled to Algiers in 1634 on an unsuccessful mission to ransom French captives. The redemptionist orders staged public ceremonies showcasing recently freed captives to raise money for their expensive work.

of Algiers) and *Los baños de Argel (The Prisons of Algiers)* to *Don Quixote* (1605), which includes a long, apparently autobiographical section known as 'The Captive's Tale' in which a Spanish sailor tells the story of his enslavement in Algiers.* Judging by this account, which abounds in descriptions of the slave master's cruelty, Cervantes understandably did not feel well disposed towards Algerian corsairs.

Yet North African pirates and corsairs did not sail out of a vacuum, launching themselves against the commercial shipping and sailors of a blameless Christendom. They arose in a specific context of European invasion, occupation and fledgling colonialism in North Africa. Through much of the fifteenth, sixteenth and into the early seventeenth centuries, many generations of coast-dwelling North Africans cringed when they spotted heavily armed, southwards-heading European ships on the horizon. They understood what they meant.

The Portuguese began with a lightning conquest of the port city of Ceuta in Morocco in 1415, a major step on their way to empire. (More than 600 years later, Ceuta remains a Spanish autonomous city, the subject with the sister Spanish enclave of Melilla of a long-running dispute with Morocco, which considers them foreign colonies.) By 1471, the Portuguese had stormed Asilah on the north-western tip of Morocco's Atlantic coast, occupying neighbouring Tangier, gateway to Africa, on the southern side of the Straits of Gibraltar later that year. The Portuguese procession of invasion and occupation continued into the sixteenth century with the seizure of Mazagan (Al Jadida) in 1502, Mogador (Essaouira) in 1506, the founding of Casablanca in 1515 and the capture of Mehdia, a little further north on the Atlantic coast, at the same time.

In the race to seize possessions in North Africa, the Spanish would not be left behind by their smaller Iberian neighbour. They took

---

* 'I was one of those held for,' the captive recalls. 'They put a chain on me, and so I passed my life in that bagnio . . . Though at times, or rather almost always, we suffered from hunger and scanty clothing, nothing distressed us so much as hearing and seeing at every turn the unexampled and unheard-of cruelties my master inflicted upon the Christians. Every day he hanged a man, impaled one, cut off the ears of another; and all with so little provocation, or so entirely without any, that the Turks acknowledged he did it merely for the sake of doing it, and because he was by nature murderously disposed towards the whole human race.'

Melilla in 1497 and Oran, the port city in north-western Algeria, in a bloody assault led by the Navarrese general Pedro Navarro in 1509. A year later, Navarro, a veteran of conflicts with North African pirates in Italy, took Béjaïa, or Bougie, in Algeria. Then, in the summer of 1510, Tripoli experienced first-hand another Navarro-led conquest in a savage assault in which up to 5,000 Libyans were killed and up to 6,000 enslaved from a population estimated at between 15,000 and 20,000. In 1535, just a year after Hayreddin Barbarossa had conquered Tunis, the city fell to a huge fleet assembled by the Habsburg Emperor Charles V and his allies. Again, the human toll was enormous, with an estimated 30,000 left dead in a city that stank so badly of putrefying corpses that the emperor was forced to withdraw his camp several miles to the south-east to avoid contamination. Later that summer, Hayreddin responded with a punitive strike against the garrison town of Mahon on Minorca, taking 5,700 Spanish captives back to Algiers for sale in the city's slave markets. In 1610, the Spanish went on to acquire Larache, south of Asilah. The English, surprisingly absent from this scramble for coastal possessions in North Africa, finally got in on the act in 1661, when the newly enthroned Charles II (r. 1660–85) acquired Tangier as part of the dowry of his Portuguese wife, the Infanta Catherine of Braganza.

The North African trade in Christian slaves was making enough impact in England by this time for Samuel Pepys to refer to it in an entry from 8 February 1661, revealing a number of details, not least the slaves' requirement to earn, beg, borrow or steal money for their masters every day, that would become common to captivity narratives:

> ... went to the Fleece Tavern to drink; and there we spent till four o'clock, telling stories of Algiers, and the manner of the life of slaves there! And truly Captn. Mootham and Mr. Dawes (who have been both slaves there) did make me fully acquainted with their condition there: as, how they eat nothing but bread and water ... How they are beat upon the soles of their feet and bellies at the liberty of their padron. How they are all, at night, called into their master's Bagnard; and there they lie. How the poorest men do use their slaves best. How some rogues do live well, if they do invent to bring their masters in so

much a week by their industry or theft; and then they are put to no other work at all. And theft there is counted no great crime at all . . .[13]

A decade later, in 1671, the Irish-born English Admiral Edward Spragg launched a punitive raid on Algiers killing more than 3,000, destroying ten corsair ships and toppling the Janissary-led regime, replacing it with a dey* whose descendants would rule until 1830. The French were not to be left out, either. In 1683 a French fleet launched a devastating attack on Algiers which was so severe that whole streets and neighbourhoods were unrecognizable after the bombardment and resulting inferno. Little wonder, then, that for many if not most North African Muslims, the pirates and corsairs were heroic defenders of the faith against the regularly encroaching infidels.

External powers with predatory eyes on the North African littoral were by no means limited to Christian Europe. A resurgent Istanbul turned much of the Mediterranean, especially the east, into Ottoman waters in the sixteenth century, thanks in great part to its active backing of corsairs, not least the history-changing promotion of Hayreddin from freelance corsair to Ottoman admiral and chief naval strategist. In 1551 the Ottomans took Tripoli, followed by the holy Islamic city of Qairouan in 1557, Djerba in 1558 and Tunis in 1569. Then came the briefly ruinous Battle of Lepanto in 1571, when the allied forces of Spain, Genoa, Venice and the Papal States sailed a combined fleet against the Ottomans in the largest galley battle fought since antiquity. It 'was so bloody and horrendous that the sea and the fire seemed as one', an anonymous memoirist noted at the time.[14] The Ottomans lost 230 warships in an encounter in which more than 40,000 were killed and 10,000 wounded, the second-largest body count in a single-day European battle after the carnage of Cannae in 216 BCE, when 58,000 lost their lives in Hannibal's rout of the Romans. And yet even this defeat did not prevent the Ottomans from bouncing back in breathtakingly short order, building 150 fully equipped ships within five months and retaking Tunis – yet again – in 1574. Ottoman power, tipping into domination, endured across much of North Africa well

---

* Dey was an honorific title given by the Ottomans to the rulers of Algiers, Tunis and Tripoli from this time.

into the nineteenth century and in some places, such as Tripoli, as late as the twentieth.

Much of the maritime violence in the Mediterranean and beyond, it must also be said, was European on European, as with English and Flemish pirates marauding along Ireland's Atlantic coast in the early 1600s – in 1606 alone they took more than 100 ships here – Dutch, French and Spanish pirates attacking English sailors in the Mediterranean, and English pirates returning the favour in the late 1620s against French, Venetian and Spanish shipping.

The Barbary corsairs often turned out not to be the North African Muslims of popular Western imagination. To give one striking example, of the fifty-two captured by the Dutch in November 1614, just four were actually North African Muslims (three from Salé and one from Oran), while forty-eight were fortune-seeking sailors from England and the Netherlands.[15]

Tunis, to take just one of the four major corsair port cities, was an extraordinarily cosmopolitan place at this time. Apart from the indigenous Tunisians and ruling Turks on the Muslim side, Spanish sailors rubbed shoulders with Frenchmen, Dutchmen, Portuguese, Irish, Greek merchants and Armenian brokers.

Algiers was even more mixed. Of the thirty-five corsair captains and galley-owners listed in the 1580s, only ten were Turks. The rest were a polyglot mix of six Genoese, three Greeks, two Venetians, two Spaniards, two Albanians, one each from France, Hungary, Sicily, Naples, Calabria and Corsica, one Jew and three sons of renegades. The then admiral of the Algerian fleet was himself an Italian renegade.[16] The Genoese were rarely absent from the Mediterranean fray. One of the republic's most famous figures in the sixteenth century was Andrea Doria (1466–1560), whose splendid career as *condottiero*, admiral and ultimately ruler of Genoa offered a Christian counterpart to the rise of the Barbarossa brothers.

The Algerian fleet grew steadily so that by 1623, according to Sir Thomas Roe, the English ambassador to the Sublime Porte in Istanbul, who concluded a treaty with Algiers a year later, it counted seventy-five sail and several hundred smaller boats. No longer did sailors leaving Italy hear the farewell words of warning, 'May God preserve you from the galleys of Tripoli', as they had in the 1580s, because when it came to piracy Algiers was now the greatest threat. Flexing their muscles, the Algerine corsairs launched into a series of predatory, plundering raids against Madeira (1617), Alexandretta (1624), Iceland (1627), England (1631) and boldly on into the Atlantic in the 1630s.

The European prisoners enslaved in these attacks returned in chains to fill the stinking, rat-filled, lice-infested bagnios of Algiers. Although we must take contemporaries' estimates with caution, a Portuguese captive in the city reported that between 1621 and 1627 there were 20,000 prisoners languishing in the city, half of whom were European Christians, a cosmopolitan collection of Portuguese, Flemish, French, Spanish, Scottish, Irish, Dutch, Danish, Slav and Hungarian, the other half a geographically bewildering mix of Syrian, Egyptian, Ethiopian, residents of New Spain and apparently even some Chinese and Japanese. The Flemish aristocrat Emanuel d'Aranda was captured and enslaved in Algiers between 1640 and 1642. In his 1656 memoir, *Relation de la captivité, et liberté du Sieur Emanuel de Aranda mené esclave à Alger en l'an 1640 et mis en liberte l'an 1642*, recently translated as *Short Story of My Unfortunate Journey, during Which I Was Captured by the Turks, of My Experiences during Slavery, and of How I Regained My Freedom*, the most popular Barbary captivity narrative of the seventeenth century, he wrote of 'six hundred thousand Christians' enslaved in Algiers from 1536 to the 1640s.[17]

The picture in the Mediterranean, in other words, was complicated. To make things even more confusing, regularly shifting alliances across Europe further blurred the many dividing lines that were observed, straddled, crossed and simply ignored by pirates and privateers from the fifteenth to the nineteenth century. Any assessment of North African corsairing and piracy must recognize this wider context.

Though piracy, like slavery itself, has been virtually ageless and universal across all the world's seas and oceans, it reached its apogee in the Mediterranean between the late sixteenth and mid-seventeenth centuries. Joseph Morgan, who served in the British consulate in Algiers and was the author of *A Complete History of Algiers* (1728), was more specific than that. He pinpointed the year 1641 as the high point of corsair activity. That year the Ottoman regency of Algiers had at least sixty-five pirate ships cruising for prizes, in an addition to an unknown number of galleys or galliots plus other vessels in port, without counting the corsair fleet of Tunis, Tripoli, Salé and the smaller ports such as Tetouan in Morocco. 'And this', he wrote, 'I take to be the Time when those Corsairs were in their Zenith.'[18] The English government appeared to agree. In December 1640, the same month in which Archbishop Laud was impeached, the new Long Parliament established a Committee for Algiers to manage the ransoming of English captives at a time when the number of English prisoners held in that city was estimated at between 3,000 and 5,000. Precise statistics are impossible to arrive at before the nineteenth century, but those figures which are available suggest Morgan was on the right lines.

For British sailors alone, the first half of the seventeenth century was terrifying on the high seas. Between 1609 and 1616, the British lost an astonishing 466 ships to North African corsairs. In a whirlwind of corsairing between 1613 and 1621, the Algerians took 936 ships and smaller boats, enslaving thousands of Europeans who were transported back to Algiers for sale or, if they were more fortunate, ransom. Even if that was successful, though, it might still take years to arrange.

When we think of piracy and corsairing we tend to think of ships attacking, boarding, capturing, perhaps even sinking, other ships. That was certainly the norm, but there was another important and less well-known aspect of the North African corsairing, no less terrifying for those who found themselves on the wrong end of it.

From at least the early sixteenth until the early eighteenth century, corsairs regularly tried their hand at slaving raids on European coastlines, targeting in particular Spain, Italy, Greece and the Mediterranean islands, but also chancing their luck further afield in Ireland, Scotland and the southern and western coasts of England. In the 1620s, the Devon and Cornish coasts were attacked again and again by corsairs from North Africa, so much so that Sir John Eliot, vice-admiral of Devon, wrote that the seas around England 'seemed theirs'. In some parts of the Mediterranean these ransacking attacks became virtually annual phenomena, driving terrified and poorly protected coastal populations inland for safety, so that writing about the corsairs in the

1580s, Diego de Haëdo, the Spanish Benedictine abbot and historian who was enslaved in Algiers at the same time as Cervantes, could note that 'they have ravaged and ruined Sardinia, Corsica, Sicily, Calabria, the coasts of Naples, Rome and Genoa, the Balearics, and all the coasts of Spain'.[19] Stone watchtowers sprang up along the European littoral, providing an early warning system from the Iberian Peninsula to Liguria, Sicily and far beyond.

One of the most remarkable instances of long-distance corsairing, and a cold-blooded demonstration of power and ambition, came around this time of peak piracy in 1627, when two groups of cooperating corsairs from Algiers and Salé launched savage, back-to-back raids on Iceland for the first time – it was *terra incognita* for them up to this point – killing dozens and capturing and enslaving more than 400 men, women and children, who were then taken back for sale or ransom in the two port cities. The leader of the attack was not a North African at all. He was a rich, intelligent and opportunist Dutch renegade called Jan Janszoon, also known as Murad Reis, grand admiral of the Salé Rovers.

It is thanks in great part to Reverend Ólafur Egilsson, a Lutheran minister in his sixties who was one of the first to be captured with his wife and two young sons, that we know about this audacious land attack, a 6,000-mile round trip from the southern Mediterranean coast. His account, written at the behest of his local bishop, is extremely valuable as the only captivity narrative with a detailed, eyewitness description of a slaving land attack by North Africa-based corsairs.

Egilsson was brought in front of the captain and beaten and kicked in his back while being interrogated about possible hidden money 'until I was too hoarse to scream any longer' and he could barely stand let alone walk. He was then ordered to travel to Denmark to seek ransom money from King Christian IV (r. 1588–1648) who, short of money while fighting the Thirty Years' War, was in no position to help. After that six-month effort proved futile, Egilsson spent a decade in Iceland trying to raise the funds required. In the end, just thirty-four enslaved Icelanders of the hundreds taken captive were ransomed in 1637. These included Egilsson's wife, with whom he was briefly reunited before his death in 1639, but tragically not his children, who he never saw again after his departure from Algiers.

The Tyrkjarànio – Turkish Raid – as the notorious attack became known to Icelanders was such a shock that Egilsson's story, first written in 1628 and only translated into English for the first time in 2016, lives on in the national memory to this day. When Turkey and Iceland played a football match in 1995, the headline in Iceland's most popular newspaper proclaimed: 'Don't let the Turks ravish us again!' Never mind that 'the Turks' had had nothing to do with it in the first place.[20]

Egilsson was not alone in recording the agonizing details of the attack. An official report compiled by the lawyer Klaus Eyjólfsson included much eyewitness testimony, such as the story of Bjarni Valdason, a local man who tried to escape the pirates:

> They struck him across the head above the eyes and killed him. When his wife, who had been fleeing with him, saw this, she at once fell across his body, screaming. The Turkish took her by her feet and dragged her away, so that the cloth of her dress came up over the head. Her dead husband they cut into small pieces, as if he were a sheep. They took the woman to the Danish houses and threw her in with the other prisoners.

Worse was to follow. Houses were set on fire, a woman who was unable to walk was thrown into the flames with her two-year-old baby. 'When she and the poor child screamed and called to God for help, the wicked Turks bellowed with laughter. They struck both child and mother with the sharp points of their spears, forcing them into the fire, and even stabbed fiercely at the poor, burning bodies.'[21]

It is instructive, too, to note that both of the two linked corsair attacks on Iceland were commanded by European renegades: the raiders from Salé by Jan Janszoon, those from Algiers led by 'that soul ripper named Móraõ Flaming [Murad Fleming]', a fellow Dutchman. That was by no means the full extent of European involvement in this well-organized military attack. 'I think most of those attacking us were English,' Egilsson wrote.

The attack on Iceland may have been exceptional, but routine corsairing and piracy continued unabated. Between 1641 and 1644, Algerian corsairs captured another 1,700 'Christian' ships. Nor was this merely an isolated explosion of piratical slave-taking. Algerian corsairs alone took another 353 English ships in the decade from 1672 to 1682.

How many people were enslaved when these ships were taken is, like the overall figure for those taken into slavery, disputed. Concentrating on Christian captives – an omission which immediately neglects the Muslim victims of corsairs and pirates – Robert C. Davis has estimated that in the 1609–16 and 1672–82 incidents above, for example, the 466 and 353 ships captured equated to the enslavement of 5,600–9,300 and 4,200–7,000 prisoners respectively. As noted earlier, these calculations have been dissected and challenged and therefore come with significant caveats. It must also be emphasized that contemporaries reporting facts and figures were not always disinterested witnesses either. They frequently had their own agendas. When, for example, the Trinitarians claimed to have ransomed a spectacular 900,000 captives between 1198 and 1787, it was later revealed that one ransoming of forty captives had been documented in the records as 40,000. We have already heard what the Frenchman Laugier de Tassy thought of the Spanish monks and the 'thousand Falsities' they told.[22] It is worth bearing this in mind when we come to look at the first-hand accounts of white slaves who survived their ordeals in North Africa and lived to tell their luridly compelling tales.

Scholarly debates aside, we have to accept that this was a world of shipwrecks, drownings, desertions and accidents, of honest mistakes, clerical errors and calculated exaggerations, of literary excess and uncertainty about the numbers of those transported for onward sale in the African interior or the wider Muslim world. We may never know the precise figure for the number of people captured and enslaved by the Barbary pirates and corsairs on the one hand and those Muslims taken by European corsairs and pirates on the other. We can nevertheless recognize that the numbers were enormous to the point of unfathomable – quite possibly up to 3 million – and that the toll on human lives was nothing less than devastating.

The Dutchwoman Maria ter Meetelen was one in a million. Born into an impoverished Catholic family in 1704, she survived a tough slum childhood in Amsterdam and was already fending for herself from the age of thirteen, all the while dreaming of something better than the life of a maid. At the age of twenty-one she cropped her hair, donned a man's coat and trousers and launched into a cross-dressing expedition across Europe. She travelled through Holland, France and Spain, where she was press-ganged into a regiment of Frisian dragoons. Her adventures were only just beginning. Betrayed as a woman before she saw any military action, she pretended to be a nun in Madrid before tiring of enforced celibacy and marrying a Dutch ship's captain in 1728. Sailing with him from Cadiz to Holland in 1731, she was captured by Moroccan corsairs, the enslaved crew and passengers taken first to Salé, thence to the imperial city of Meknes, seat of the Moroccan Sultan Moulay Abdullah (r. with interruptions 1729–57), whose property they became. Ter Meetelen's husband died within six months of arrival in Morocco, making her position extremely precarious.

Desperate to avoid becoming a concubine of the sultan, who had taken a close interest in her, she refused to convert to Islam despite threats that 'the king would have me burnt and my flesh would be ripped from my body and I would be put to death with all manner of tortures'. Using all her powers of persuasion, she managed to secure his permission to marry a fellow Dutch slave instead. For the next dozen years she ran a series of taverns selling wine, brandy and the local firewater to Christian slaves, while her husband was often sent away on hard slave labour. She navigated the numerous, life-threatening changes of power with acumen. In 1743, after a decade-long effort by the Dutch state, Ter Meetelen was at last ransomed. She took leave of the sultan with a few 'exceptionally charming' compliments, prompting the delighted monarch to exclaim: 'As true as I live, this Christian woman is worthy of being a princess!' All that remained was the obligatory memoir, which caused a sensation when it appeared in 1748 – it was published recently as *The Curious and Amazing Adventures of Maria ter Meetelen; Twelve Years a Slave (1731–43)*. Her second husband and two remaining children had all died by 1750, at which point this enterprising Dutchwoman disappeared from the historical record with the suggestion that she was heading for new adventures in South Africa. In the words with which she began her rollercoaster story: 'The course of life is curious.'[23]

Maria ter Meetelen's is one of the most remarkable captivity narratives because it is written by a woman. Virtually all of the other stories are told by men. But it shares a number of the characteristics of this unusual body of writing. It is by its very nature self-dramatizing. The attention-grabbing titles of these books, often written by an escaped or ransomed slave who now needed to raise money urgently, set the stage for the drama which would surely unfold – how much of it was genuine, how much exaggerated or even falsified remains a bone of controversy to this day. Thus we have *A Curious, Historical and Entertaining Narrative of the Captivity and almost unheard of Sufferings and Cruel treatment of Mr Robert White, Mariner*, which appeared in 1791; another from the rare female perspective, the *History of the Captivity and Sufferings of Mrs Maria Martin who was six years a slave in Algiers; two of which she was confined in a dismal dungeon, loaded with irons for refusing to comply with the brutal request of a Turkish officer*, was published in 1807.

A recent survey of captivity narratives – a starting point rather than a comprehensive tally – lists 120 titles in this peculiar literary genre, of which thirty-three were French, twenty-nine British, seventeen American, fourteen German, seven Italian, seven Spanish, six Dutch, three Danish and Norwegian, two Portuguese, one Icelandic and one Swedish. Another recent work notes that more than 100 American Barbary captivity narratives alone were published between John Foss's 1798 book *A Journal, of the Captivity and Sufferings of John Foss, Several Years a Prisoner at Algiers: together With Some Account of the Treatment of Christian Slaves When Sick, and Observations on the Manners and Customs of the Algerines* and the many editions

Dutch engraving by Jan Luyken of the slave market at Algiers, 1684.

of Captain James Riley's bestseller of 1817, which will be discussed below.[24]

The titles of some of these books are manna for historians. One of the most hair-raising and compelling tales comes in *The History of the long captivity and adventures of Thomas Pellow, in South-Barbary. Giving an account of his being taken by two Sallee Rovers, and carry'd a slave to Mequinez, at eleven years of age: his various adventures in that country for the space of twenty-three years: escape and return home. In which is introduced, a particular account of the manners and customs of the Moors; the astonishing tyranny and cruelty of their Emperors, and a relation of all those great revolutions and bloody wars which happen'd in the kingdoms of Fez and Morocco, between the years 1720 and 1736. Together with a description of the cities, towns, and publick buildings in those kingdoms; miseries of the Christian slaves; and many other curious particulars.* The book's title, more a rambling paragraph, expresses the negative European views of 'the Moors' which, with some honourable exceptions, were entirely typical of their time.

Pellow was an eleven-year-old Cornish lad dreaming, like Maria ter Meetelen, of a life of adventure. In the summer of 1715, having successfully brushed aside his parents' strenuous objections, he set sail from Falmouth on a ship skippered by his uncle. If only he had listened to them. Intercepted by heavily armed Moroccan corsairs on the return voyage off Cape Finisterre, Pellow almost drowned in a sea battle before being rescued, enslaved and despatched to the imperial court of Sultan Moulay Ismail at Meknes, then home to many thousands of European slaves. Separated from his uncle, the youngster was then given to the sultan's son, Moulay Spha, who put him under extreme pressure to convert to Islam. For months Pellow endured beatings and bastinadings – in which captives were suspended upside down with bound ankles to have the souls of their feet thrashed – but still would not renounce his faith. 'My tortures were now exceedingly increased, burning my flesh off my bones by fire, which the tyrant did, by frequent repetitions, after a most cruel manner,' he later recalled. It was enough to make him 'turn Turk', though he claimed this was only a superficial conversion and that 'I always abominated them and their accursed principle of Mahometism'.[25]

Pellow's life in North Africa has all the elements of a real-life *Candide*. Adventures pile up, whisking our narrator hero into a procession of dangerous escapades, human misery, torture, promotion through the hierarchies of slavery, daring escape and ultimate redemption. Guardian of the sultan's 4,000-strong harem of concubines one year, commander of slave soldiers the next, Pellow's career in the service of the self-styled Prince of the Faithful and Overcoming in God became the stuff of legend. In 1731 he even found himself at the head of a huge caravan of 30,000 soldiers and 60,000 camels joining a slave-hunting expedition to Guinea on the west coast of Africa, 'stripping the poor negroes of all they had, killing many of them, and bringing off their children into the bargain'.

In European accounts Moulay Ismail was a powerful, capricious monarch who revelled in his life-and-death dominion over his fellow creatures. 'It is one of his common diversions, at one motion, to mount his horse, draw his scimitar, and cut off the head of the slave who holds his stirrup,' the French padre Dominique Busnot reported in his history of Moulay Ismail's reign in Morocco.[26]

The Moroccan ruler enjoyed marrying his slaves off to each other in mass wedding ceremonies, the aim being to breed a new generation of slaves to serve him and his monumental palace-building project in Meknes. He regularly ordered 'great numbers of people before him, whom he marries without any more ceremony than pointing to the man and woman and saying, "*Hadi yi houd Hadi*," that is to say, "That take that," upon which the loving pair join together, and march off as firmly noosed as if they had been married by a Pope,' Pellow wrote. 'He always yokes his best complexioned subjects to a black helpmate, and the fair lady must take up with a negro.'

Pellow himself took part in one of these enforced weddings, joining a group of 800 men and 800 women. He was shown eight black women, but pleaded with the emperor not to make him marry any one of them, 'not at all liking their colour'. There followed seven 'mulattoes', which Pellow again rejected, risking death at Moulay Ismail's hands by requesting a bride 'of my own colour'. He was finally married off to a pale-skinned woman.

Spectacular promotion as a slave was all very well, but Pellow never stopped dreaming of returning home to resume life as a free man. In

1737, after years of political turmoil following Moulay Ismail's death in 1727, he escaped in a dangerous journey across the Atlas Mountains. In Gibraltar, where he was mistaken for a 'Moor', he was initially refused permission to disembark, but eventually found his way back to England. Visiting the Moroccan ambassador in London, he was invited to dine with the envoy. There is something touching about the discombobulated Cornishman's relief when the ambassador offered him that much-loved Moroccan staple, 'my favourite dish, cuscassoe', the famous couscous. Finally, on 15 October 1738, he was reunited with his parents at the family home in Cornwall after his 'long straying and grievous hardships amongst those monsters and ravenous wolves of infidelity'. After twenty-three years of captivity and slavery in Morocco, Pellow struggled to fit in in a country he had left as a child. The years ahead would doubtless be difficult – and it is unlikely his parents would be offering him much couscous – but his 'frightful and amazing' adventure was over.

'Heroic Captain Ward, lord of the ocean, terror of kings . . . conqueror of the Western world . . .'.[27] Captain Ward was the devil-take-the-hindmost antihero of *A Christian Turn'd Turk*, a scandalously piratical play by the English dramatist Robert Daborne, first published in 1612. Daborne's pirate chief is a brash, brave character who glories in his rags-to-riches transformation:

> . . . This maxim I hold:
> He lives a slave, that lives to be controlled.

Although he converts to Islam in a move which would have appalled Jacobean audiences, it is a conversion born of love for a beautiful Turkish woman. Ward even compares religion to slavery, while not dwelling on how his piracy enslaves others:

> The slavery of man, how this religion rides us!
> Deprives us of our freedom from our cradles,
> Ties us in superstitious bondage.

The play ends with a flourish of bloodletting. The Turkish governor of Tunis has Ward's corpse torn in pieces and pronounces the damning epitaph: 'Ward sold his country, turned Turk, and died a slave.'

For every European 'I-survived-my-cruel-captivity-and-slavery' writer there was a European renegade who specialized in slaving, none more famous than the real-life Captain John – or Jack – Ward.

Born into an impoverished fishing family in Faversham, Kent, around 1553, he became a privateer and plundered Spanish ships under licence from Elizabeth I. Around 1603, he deserted from the new king's navy with thirty of his fellow sailors, stole a barque from Portsmouth harbour and was elected captain. By 1605 the man who only recently had been a poor, drunken sailor in his fifties had become the handsomely rich captain of the *Gift*, a 200-ton, 32-gun warship crewed by around 100 mostly English ruffians. That year, Ward made Tunis his base in a deal with Kara Osman Dey, the commander of the Turkish Janissaries and de facto military ruler. Here he converted to Islam and became Yusuf Reis.

In 1607 he took the spectacular prize of *Reniera e Soderina*, a 1,500-ton Venetian argosy crammed with silks, velvet, cotton, indigo, cinnamon, spices and other treasures worth between £500,000 and £2 million – or £103 million and £412 million today. The lower estimate was that of the English government, keen to downplay the attack and avoid war with Venice. Ward was no longer just the talk of drunken sailors in English ports. He wasn't merely among 'the most notorious figures in English Renaissance writings', the subject of violent plays and shock-horror pamphlets.[28] He was an international phenomenon.

In November 1607, Sir Henry Wotton, England's ambassador to Venice, appeared before the doge and his cabinet. Much of the meeting was spent discussing Ward, who was, the tight-lipped envoy told the Venetians, 'Beyond a doubt the greatest scoundrel that ever sailed from England.' Ward proved a constant irritant for Wotton, who, in 1608, found himself presenting an intelligence report on him to the doge: 'John Ward, commonly called Captain Ward, is about 55 years of age ... Speaks little, and almost always swearing. Drunk from morn till night. Most prodigal and plucky. Sleeps a great deal, and often on board when in port. The habits of a thorough "salt." A fool and an idiot out of his trade.'[29] That was a grave underestimation of Ward, who was nobody's fool. Everything and everyone was fair game. 'If I met my own father at sea, I would rob him and sell him when I was done,' he boasted.

Was Ward a Muslim pirate? Notionally, yes. Was he a North African? Hardly, and only insofar as he chose to make Tunis his base. He was an Englishman on the make, one of countless European Christian renegades whose very notoriety – *as* Europeans – has, over the centuries, made the Barbary corsairs the stuff of legend while simultaneously eclipsing the once-forgotten, now merely neglected story of Christian corsairs and pirates enslaving Muslims the length and breadth of the Mediterranean.

European renegades were not the exotic fringe of North African corsairing. They were its heart and soul – more than half of the corsair captains of Algiers between 1580 and 1680 were originally European – and frequently rose to the highest positions as 'admirals' of the regencies' fleets. What more spectacular example than Giovanni Dionigi Galeni, an Italian farmer-turned-galley-slave-turned-corsair? Captured in 1536 by one of Hayreddin's corsairs, he converted to Islam and became Kılıç Ali Pasha, exchanging the skin-splitting manacles and oars of a galley wretch for the command and ownership of his own galley. He rose through a series of positions until, after his valiant performance at the Battle of Lepanto, he was appointed to the highest of all, Kapudan Pasha, grand admiral of the Ottoman fleet.

No survey of European renegades could be complete without reference to Ward's contemporaries, the Dutchmen Simon Danseker and Jan Janszoon. In 1607, Danseker left his wife, family and home in Marseilles, stole a ship and arrived at Algiers, where as an enemy of the hated Spanish he was made welcome. He assumed command of a corsair squadron and earned the nickname of Captain Devil for his bold and hugely successful style, taking at least forty ships and growing fabulously rich. As the chief naval architect of Algiers, he played a critical role introducing the European-style 'round' ships rigged fore and aft, thereby extending the corsairs' range to Iceland and beyond. Before his capture and beheading in Tunis in 1615 he was one of the two most famous 'Barbary' pirates of his time. *Newes from Sea, of Two Notorious Pirates, Ward the Englishman and Danseker the Dutchman, with a True Relation of All or the Most Piracies by Them Committed unto the 6th of April 1609*, a pamphlet published in London, was hugely successful, outselling another of the publisher's less exciting titles: Shakespeare's *King Lear*.

Ward and Danseker earned a rare and honourable mention in an Arabic text by the seventeenth-century historian Ibn Abi Dinar. 'Of the greatest corsair captains in his time', he wrote of Yusuf Dey (r. 1610–37), Dey of Tunis, 'were Captain Samsom and Captain Wardiyya: they were Christians, and sailed in his time while still Christians, but they turned Muslim later. They were famous at sea.'[30]

Jan Janszoon earnt lasting fame and infamy as the mastermind of that 1627 Iceland attack, one of the corsairs' most far-flung expeditions ever. He turned his hand to corsairing first in Algiers, latterly in Salé, where he became the all-powerful Murad Reis, member of the port's ruling council, admiral of the fleet, harbour master, tax-collector and customs supremo. In 1631 he sacked Baltimore, the southernmost town in Ireland, and took 154 prisoners, mostly women and children. It was the only recorded instance of a Barbary corsair slaving raid in Ireland.

His contemporary, the Englishman Peter Easton, exemplified the social mobility that could be enjoyed by the most successful renegades, pirates and corsairs, rising from impoverished farm labourer in Somerset to state-backed privateer protecting the Newfoundland fishing fleet to the commander of 2,000 pirates. Easton later relocated to North Africa, attacking Spanish ships before accepting the offer of asylum and well-heeled retirement from the Duke of Savoy. In an unlikely fairy-tale ending, the seriously rich Easton purchased a marquisate of the Duchy of Savoy, married a noblewoman and basked in the fame and wealth he had earned as *il Corsaro Inglese*.

The most blue-blooded renegade was surely Sir Francis Verney, who left England in 1608, having lost a court case over his inheritance, sold his estates and broken with his family. Within a year he had taken a handful of French and English ships and was roaming the Mediterranean alongside Ward, 'turning Turk' before falling foul of Sicilian corsairs and descending from slaver to slave, spending two years in captivity as a galley oarsman. Ransomed to a Jesuit, he won his freedom in exchange for converting to Catholicism and, now penniless, was forced to enlist as a common soldier in the service of the Spanish viceroy of Palermo. William Lithgow, the Scottish traveller and writer, discovered the English adventurer 'in the extremest calamity of extreme miseries' in the paupers' hospital in Messina, where he died in 1615, aged thirty-one.[31] There was no marquisate, beautiful noblewoman or fairy-tale ending for Verney.

The obvious temptation, after reading all these full-blooded stories of renegades and slave survivors, is to conclude that all the piracy and enslavement traffic was one-way. Yet this would be in defiance of all evidence to the contrary. We have seen that corsairing and piracy was a free-for-all which paid little respect to faith or nationality. Europeans preyed on Europeans, Muslims on Christians and Jews, Christians and Jews on Muslims, ships crewed by both Christians and Muslims on ships crewed by both Christians and Muslims.

The difficulty for historians trying to assess the balance of activity is not helped by the overwhelming dominance of European Christian, and later American, captivity narratives. Of Muslim literary reminiscences there is sadly little sign. That is because, unlike their Christian counterparts, Muslim captives who lived to tell their tale generally did not try to sensationalize or monetize it. It was far more a case of internalizing their experience at the hands of the infidels and sharing their stories orally. They did not go for the more egotistical, author-as-narrative-hero accounts which became so popular in Europe and the United States. 'Captivity was God's will, and every Muslim had to accept it and not make too much of it.'[32] Thus the silence, perhaps extraordinary to Western readers, of Hassan al Wazzan (Johannes Leo de Medicis), whose groundbreaking *Description of Africa* did not contain a single word about its famous author's earlier capture by Spanish corsairs. It simply was not part of his story. Writing in around 1632, Ahmad ibn Ghanim, the Andalusian author of a study of heavy artillery and siege engines, dealt with his seven-year captivity in a few brief and ruthlessly matter-of-fact lines.

There were exceptions. A pioneering new study of Mediterranean captivity through Arab eyes has excavated some of the most prominent.[33] Take the Andalusian poet Abd al Karim al Qaysi, who wrote from his captivity in Úbeda in southern Spain in around 1485. He described mournfully to a friend how he had been 'humiliated and chained' among infidels whose hearts were 'as hard as rock' and who kept him slaving from sunrise to sunset:

My body has grown weak, and my complexion has changed,
My eyes are swollen with tears and my bowels burn:
You cannot think that someone in my condition is alive.

Life as a galley slave was a living hell for Muslims and Christians alike. On 23 April 1682, Abd al Nabi Suleyman wrote a letter from Marseilles to Moulay Ismail, the Moroccan ruler who had tormented Joseph Pellow, on behalf of 'all the captives enslaved on the French king's ships'. Appealing for help, he described how the 'French dogs' tortured and humiliated their Muslim slave captives, keeping them naked, hungry and in heavy chains, beating them, insulting the Prophet and ridiculing both their religion and the Moroccan sultan.

Born in Morocco's imperial city of Meknes, Ahmad al Ghazzal (d. 1777) was the secretary to Sultan Mohammed ibn Abdullah (r. 1757–90). Sent by the Moroccan ruler to ransom Muslim captives in Spain in 1766, he left a detailed account of his mission. Many of the enslaved prisoners were 'heavily shackled' after repeated escape attempts. Most of the 204 he saw in one location, the vast majority from Algiers, were being used as forced labour to build the road from Madrid to the royal seat of El Escorial. They had originally numbered 300, but many had died, fallen sick or escaped. Among the numerous complaints he heard from the captives were those relating to cruelty at the hands of Muslim supervisors who had converted to Christianity, hunger, unjust treatment in hospital and crushing physical work. However, it was not all doom and gloom. In a hospital in Madrid, Al Ghazzal reported the 'kindly' and generous treatment of a friar who provided the captives with food and drink and ensured their clothes and beds were kept clean. In the port city of Cartagena in south-east Spain the envoy encountered a staggering 'five ships full of Muslim captives', who were eventually ransomed and sailed to Cádiz. In total, Al Ghazzal managed to ransom 1,600 Muslim captives. This did not indicate any end to Christians taking Muslim captives. A dozen years later in 1779, Mohammed ibn Abdullah sent another ambassador to Spain to ransom prisoners and then again in 1781–3, this time to Naples, where he ransomed 610.

Writing in 1725, the British diplomat and author Joseph Morgan related the story of a 'Moor' from Tripoli who was enslaved in Cádiz.

In punishment for attempting to escape he had his 'Ears cut off according to Custom' and was eventually ransomed, only to be enslaved a second time, this time in Lisbon. Agonizingly for him, he fell into the hands of the Spanish Inquisition, which by the early seventeenth century had largely purged the country of Jews and Muslims. After torture failed to elicit his conversion to Christianity, he was sent as a slave to Terceira in the Azores.[34]

Reading through these documents by Muslim captives under Christian control, rare mirror images in miniature of the white slavery narratives, it is not difficult to understand why so many writers include the expressions 'may God destroy them' after every reference to the Europeans and 'may God mutilate him' after mentions of Christian kings and emperors.

Cruelty – and mercy – towards captive slaves resided on both sides of the principal religious divide between Christians and Muslims. It is easy to forget this in the maelstrom of accounts from men and women like Maria ter Meetelen, Joseph Pellow, Ólafur Egilsson and so many others.

Captivity narratives were by no means a European monopoly. Americans had their share of similarly sensational, often sensationalist, accounts. Within a few years their outraged, grief-stricken, heartstring-pulling books contributed to the growing conviction that 'Something must be done'.

8

The United States Goes to War

Indeed, truth and justice demand from me the confession that the Christian slaves among the barbarians of Africa are treated with more humanity than the American slaves among the professing Christians of civilized America.[1]

Charles Sumner, *White Slavery in the Barbary States*, 1847

In 1798, as North African corsairs continued to prey upon American and European shipping, American readers were treated to a new offering: *A Journal, of the Captivity and Sufferings of John Foss, Several Years a Prisoner at Algiers: together With Some Account of the Treatment of Christian Slaves When Sick, and Observations on the Manners and Customs of the Algerines.*

On 25 October 1793, two days out from Cádiz, pirates in a vessel rigged up to look like a British privateer attacked the Baltimore brig *Polly*. Armed with pistols, scimitars, pikes, spears, lances, knives and any other weapons they could lay their hands on, they boarded the American ship and ordered everyone forward on pain of a general massacre. Taken back to Algiers, Foss and his fellow prisoners were brought before Sidi Hassan, Dey of Algiers (r. 1791–8), who told them that he had already made several unsuccessful efforts to negotiate a peace treaty with Washington. None of his diplomatic approaches had received a satisfactory answer. As a result, 'he was determined never to make a peace with the United States', adding the memorable threat: 'Now I have got you, you Christian dogs, you shall eat stones!'[2]

Foss's story contains many of the stereotypes Europeans and Americans routinely employed when describing the 'Turks', 'Moors',

'Mahometans' and 'barbarians', terms they tended to use synonymously. Thus Foss's captors are 'more like monsters than human beings', in thrall to 'the imposter Mahomet', and naturally cruel: 'these merciless Barbarians are taught by their religion to treat the Christian Captives with unexampled cruelty, and that in so doing they do God service!'. Well aware that gore sells, he includes a chapter describing, in grisly detail, the punishments inflicted on 'Christian slaves, Mahometans, Jews and Renegadoes'.

Foss's story had a wider significance which went beyond the literary depictions of barbarously cruel Moors. It formed part of the steadily evolving and broadly deteriorating diplomatic relations between America and the North African regencies which would, within less than a decade, result in a total change of behaviour by Washington.

America had found itself in a unique position following independence in 1776. British protection was no longer forthcoming for American vessels, leaving the new nation, which did not yet have its own navy, to rely first on the French and then, when that policy was found wanting, to take measures into its own hands. American trade with Spain, Portugal and the wider Mediterranean would be 'annihilated unless we do something decisive', the future president Thomas Jefferson wrote in a letter of 1784 outlining a new, more aggressive policy. 'Why not begin a navy then and decide on war?'[3]

But first diplomacy. Talks were held in 1786 between the regency of Tripoli, represented by Sidi Haji Abdul Rahman Adja, its ambassador in London, and the United States, represented by John Adams, then America's first ambassador to Great Britain, and Jefferson, America's most senior diplomat in France. Though they were remarkable on one level – they were the future superpower's first diplomatic exchanges with the Muslim world – they yielded nothing. When it came to attitudes towards Muslims, there was little difference between early Americans and their European counterparts.

Writing to Jefferson, Adams claimed to have found the meeting entirely beneath him: 'very inconsistent with the Dignity of your Character and mine, but the Ridicule of it was real and the Drollery inevitable. How can We preserve our Dignity in negotiating with Such Nations? And who but a Petit Maitre [a fop or fool] would think of Gravity upon such an occasion.'[4] As for the ambassador, when asked why Tripoli would make war on a country that had done it no harm, he reportedly replied in words that must have given both Americans pause for thought:

> It was written in their Quran, that all nations which had not acknow-
> ledged the Prophet were sinners, whom it was the right and duty of the
> faithful to plunder and enslave; and that every Mussulman who was
> slain in this warfare was sure to go to paradise.

The ambassador added, 'That it was a law, that the first who boarded an enemy's vessel should have one slave more than his share with the rest, which operated as an incentive to the most desperate valour and enterprise ... which so terrified their enemies, that very few ever stood against them.'[5]

It was, in other words, just as the Algerian historian Al Maqqari had written in the 1620s, jihad on the high seas. Yet whatever the Quran and Tripoli's ambassador had to say on the subject, a treaty *was* eventually concluded between the USA and Tripoli a decade later in 1796 – following similar tribute-for-peace treaties agreed with Morocco, the first country in the world to recognize the independent United States, in 1786, Algiers in 1795 and finally Tunis in 1797 – and an American consulate in the city was opened the following year. It was an encouraging start.*

Treaties were fine, but not everyone respected them. Marauding North African corsairs refused to comply, preferring instead to sail and plunder. Foss's brig *Polly* was one of eleven American ships captured by corsairs from Algiers around this time, starting from their first seizure of an American ship in 1785, bringing the total number of Americans enslaved to 119 and resulting in a demand from the dey for a ransom of $2,435,000, an eye-watering figure. The cost of the landmark tribute-for-payment treaty of 1795, together with annual tribute, a 36-gun American warship thrown into the package to compensate for late payments by Washington, and assorted presents to sweeten the dey, bal-looned to almost $1 million – or, to put it another way, around one-sixth of the annual federal budget of $5.7 million. Something had to give.[6]

The painful truth was that piracy, corsairing and the mass enslavement

---

* Remarkably, the Moroccan–American Treaty of Friendship, which has endured to this day, is the longest uninterrupted treaty in US history.

of American sailors by the regencies of Algiers, Tunis and Tripoli and the corsair republic of Salé were becoming, year after mortifying year, intolerable for Washington. Although the threat was spread right across the North African littoral and tended to be dominated by the most powerful regency of Algiers, one leader stood out with his increasingly barefaced demands. His pugnacious family had carved out de facto independence from Ottoman rule since appearing on the scene in a flurry of bloodletting in 1711. By the dawn of the nineteenth century, when Tripoli harbour was teeming with American and European slaves clanking wretchedly in their chains, many in Washington believed that the truculent, treaty-breaking Pasha of Tripoli had pushed his luck too far.

On Friday, 15 May 1801, James L. Cathcart, the hard-pressed US consul in Tripoli, issued an urgent circular to his fellow American agents and consuls in France, Spain, Portugal, Italy, 'the Barbary States' and British garrisons in the Mediterranean. It contained news which was destined to shatter the fragile status quo in the Mediterranean, announce an increasingly formidable new power on the world stage and put the slave-taking North African regencies under notice that their time of preying upon foreign vessels with impunity was going to be challenged like never before. 'I am sorry to inform you', Cathcart wrote, 'that our Flagstaff was chop'd down upon Thursday the 14th instant and War was declared in form by the Bashaw of Tripoli against the United States of America.'[7]

The bashaw, or pasha, was Yusuf Karamanli (r. 1795–1832), whose forces had surrounded the American consulate, forced a way in and cut down the flagpole in a bold declaration of war. Yusuf had been infuriated by Washington's refusal to pay a sudden demand for $25,000 and agree to a revised treaty yielding an annual tribute of $250,000, the equivalent of about $630,000 and $6.5 million today.[8]

A year earlier almost to the day, Yusuf had written to John Adams, now the American president, noting that the United States, despite its agreement to put Tripoli on 'the same footing of friendship and importance' as 'the other regencies of Barbary' – meaning pay the same high protection fees as those being demanded by his neighbours – was not honouring its commitments. Yusuf now wanted to see 'deeds' not 'empty words ... But if only flattering words are meant, without performance, everyone will act as he finds convenient.' He had requested 'a speedy answer', hinting none too subtly that a delay would be 'prejudicial to your interests'.⁹

For Washington, this was extortion plain and simple. For Yusuf, extracting protection fees was Tripoli's rightful modus operandi. America to his mind was treating Tripoli as a junior dependency of Algiers, yet he was a sovereign power. How else was he to behave?

The piratical pasha had form when it came to unleashing violence against anyone who might oppose him. In 1790 he had lured his brother, the bey Hassan, into a carefully prepared trap within Tripoli Castle and killed him in their mother's arms, shooting him at close range before his black slaves finished him off with their knives. A year later, he turned against his ailing father Ali Karamanli (r. 1754–93) and launched an attack on Tripoli. In the ensuing chaos an Ottoman-sponsored corsair and Georgian renegade called Ali Burghul, recently expelled by the Dey of Algiers, sailed into Tripoli at the head of a Turkish fleet in the summer of 1793 and, armed with a *firman* from the Porte reasserting Ottoman rule, deposed Ali and seized power. He did not last long. Whatever their familial disputes, blood was thicker than water. In 1795, Yusuf and a brother successfully led an army of 30,000 against the usurper before Yusuf ruthlessly brushed his sibling aside and declared himself pasha. He celebrated his accession to the throne with a ferocious crackdown on security, making liberal use of the death penalty to concentrate minds.

Tripoli's king of the corsairs wasted little time increasing his pirate forces. Spanish shipwrights from Cartagena built him a new fleet of fast corsair vessels under the command of Murad Reis, a Scottish renegade who as Peter Lyle had escaped from an English ship, converted to Islam and thrown in his lot with the ebullient pasha to become his admiral of the fleet or pirate-in-chief. In 1800, the Tripoli fleet consisted of eleven ships. By 1805, that number had more than doubled to twenty-four, in addition to a throng of smaller skiffs. From Yusuf's point of view, taking on the United States, a newly independent nation with an undistinguished navy whose entire history barely predated his rule as pasha, was nothing to be alarmed about. 'I do not fear war, it is my trade,' he boasted.¹⁰

Besides, his star was dazzlingly in the ascendant. From 1795 to

1805, Tripoli's increased maritime power had resulted in lucrative (for Yusuf) treaties with Spain, France and Venice. Those countries who had failed to reach agreement with the pasha, such as Denmark, Holland and Sweden, who may have baulked at both the price and principle of this protection racket, soon discovered that the alternative cost of running the gauntlet and risking captured shipping and the enslavement of their crews was hardly more palatable.

Yusuf started to feel, correctly, that his protection had been purchased too cheaply by comparison with what Mustafa Baba, his more powerful neighbour the Dey of Algiers, had managed to extract. He began to request more money from Washington but was consistently rebuffed.* A year after his unheeded warning, Yusuf found it convenient to act. So down came the US flagpole in the American consulate.

In fact, Yusuf had seriously underestimated his newest adversary. In direct response to the challenges of North African piracy against American shipping, the Naval Act of 1794 had laid the foundation of a permanent navy and allocated the staggering sum of $688,888.82 (the equivalent of almost $20 million in 2025) for its first six frigates, each vessel mounting at least 32 guns.[11]

Confident in America's growing sea power, the newly elected President Jefferson decided on a harder line with Tripoli, traditionally the weakest of the Barbary powers, and despatched a squadron of three frigates to the Mediterranean to make his point. In the first military encounter on 1 August 1801, after a three-hour battle of raking broadsides west of Malta, American sailors from the schooner *Enterprise* captured *Tripoli*, one of the pasha's cruisers and, to Yusuf's intense fury, threw her guns and equipment overboard. To punish the captain for this humiliating loss, the pasha had his defeated captain ignominiously paraded through Tripoli on a donkey, long an object of ridicule in the Arab world, with a putrid garland of sheep's entrails hanging round his neck.

There was more to come. In 1802, Jefferson ordered a new, larger

---

* On 17 October 1802, Mustafa Baba wrote to Jefferson warning the American president not to appoint Cathcart consul in Algiers. 'We have been much dissatisfied to hear that you would think of sending near us the consul that you had at Tripoli,' he wrote. 'Whenever he comes, we will not receive him. His character does not suit us, as we know wherever he has remained that he has created difficulties and brought on a *war*. And as I will not receive him, I am sure it will be well for both nations.'

squadron of six ships to blockade Tripoli, burn enemy shipping and take prizes. Then, in 1803, the 1,240-ton, 36-gun frigate *Philadelphia*, pride of the American fleet, disastrously ran aground on an uncharted reef two miles outside Tripoli harbour while giving chase to a ship. Unable to refloat the stricken vessel and coming under heavy fire from enemy gunboats, William Bainbridge, her captain, was forced to strike his colours. The Scottish renegade Murad Reis led the boarding party that seized control of the ship and immediately enslaved its American crew. Mockingly, he asked the sailors whether Bainbridge was a coward or a traitor. 'Who with a frigate of 44 guns and 300 men would strike his colours to one solitary gunboat must surely be one or the other.'[12]

More than 300 officers and crew were imprisoned and the frigate was seized and plundered. While the officers were well treated, the crew, according to Seaman William Ray, were spat on by the Janissaries, armed with sabres, muskets and pistols, as they were shoved into 'the dreadful presence of his exalted majesty, the puissant Bashaw of Tripoli', sitting on a dais on a throne inlaid with fine mosaics and covered with a rich, gold-fringed velvet cushion 'bespangled with brilliants'. Neapolitan slaves swiftly stole the sailors' clothes before the Americans had their arms and legs clapped in heavy irons and were then put on meagre rations for two weeks. Next they were forced into the slave-labour construction of Tripoli's city walls, hauling sacks of sand and heavy rocks of up to four tons. In a later account, Seaman Elijah Shaw wrote how he and his famished comrades, bareheaded, barefooted and 'burnt to a perfect blister' by the sun, were regularly whipped with heavy knotted rawhide whips while toiling at their back-breaking work in chain gangs. Shaw took a macabre interest in the whips, which were 'the size of heavy raw-hides, the tip being split about eight inches, and three half-hitch knots taken in each strand. The Turkish drivers seemed to take great pleasure in severe treatment and when they thought we did not draw hard enough they applied their whips with an unsparing hand.'[13]

Emboldened by the unexpected capture of this prize American warship, Yusuf pressed home his advantage, demanding a total ransom and tribute of $450,000, nearly double the sum he had insisted upon at the time he had first declared war against the United States in 1801.

There was far more at stake here than money. From the American perspective there was unfinished business in Tripoli harbour. Determined that the *Philadelphia* should not remain in enemy hands to become the pasha's most powerful pirate ship – or be sold to Algiers for continued piracy against American vessels – Commodore Edward Preble hatched a daring plan to retake or destroy her. On the night of 16 February 1804, the dashing twenty-five-year-old Lieutenant Stephen Decatur led a disguised boarding party of sailors and marines into the harbour on *Intrepid*, a captured Tripolitan ketch. After boarding *Philadelphia* and killing twenty of the corsair crew silently with their cutlasses, the Americans discovered that the ship was in no condition to be sailed away and instead set it on fire with explosives with the loss of no men. This was considerably more than a shot across the bow. Nelson himself was in no doubt about the audacity and significance of the raid. It was, he reportedly declared, 'the most bold and daring act of the age'. Decatur's derring-do caused ripples across North Africa. It 'made much noise' in Tunis, George Davis, the American consul there, wrote, 'the only occasion on which I have heard our countrymen spoken of with due respect'.[14]

Buoyed by its success, the USA then went one step further and launched a military expedition to topple Yusuf and install his brother Ahmed on the throne. It was the first ever American attempt at enforcing regime change overseas. Like a number of subsequent US interventions, this one did not entirely achieve the desired result. Yusuf was not overthrown and lived instead to fight another day, but there were two other important developments: first, the capture of the eastern Libyan city of Derna, America's first land battle on foreign soil after a stirring, 600-mile march from Alexandria led by William Eaton, former consul in Tunis; second, a peace treaty on highly favourable terms for the Americans, swiftly agreed by the pragmatic Yusuf in 1805. Two centuries later, US Marines the world over celebrate their victory in the First Barbary War of 1801–5 every time they sing the opening lines of their hymn:

> From the Halls of Montezuma
> To the Shores of Tripoli;
> We fight our country's battles
> In the air, on land, and sea . . .

The Americans had emerged victorious in a breakthrough war – the longest conflict fought by the United States between the American Revolution and the Vietnam War – that with great fanfare introduced a new military power to the international scene. As Pope Pius VII remarked: 'The United States, though in their infancy, have done more to humble the anti-Christian barbarians on the African coast than all the European states had done for a long period of time.'[15]

Yusuf may have been momentarily humbled, but he was by no means finished. Having survived American efforts to oust him by land, he manoeuvred cunningly through the Napoleonic Wars, a period of chaos that admirably suited the state of Tripoli. Yet the balance of power between the corsairs on the one side and the Americans and Europeans on the other was unquestionably shifting.

Fresh from making peace with Britain on 17 February 1815, America declared war against Algiers a fortnight later on 2 March. Washington's most recent attempts to free enslaved American sailors, whose numbers there had been increased by renewed corsairing, had come to naught. As Haji Ali, Dey of Algiers (r. 1809–15), had told Mordecai Manuel Noah,* the American consul in Tunis, in 1813: 'My policy and my views are to increase, not to diminish, the number of my American slaves, and not for a million dollars would I release them.'[16] Corsairing capitalism, after all, was the tried-and-tested business model of the North African regencies.

Captain James Riley, from Connecticut, who had been at sea from the age of fifteen, was one of the many unfortunate Americans enslaved at this time. Captured in 1815, his adventure was mercifully short-lived, allowing him in 1817 to publish the most wildly successful American captivity story of all time: *An Authentic Narrative of the Loss of the American Brig 'Commerce', Wrecked on the Western Coast of Africa, in the Month of August, 1815, with an Account of the Sufferings of the Surviving Officers and Crew, who were Enslaved by the Wandering Arabs of the Great African Desert or Zahahrah*. The book was

---

* Mordecai Manuel Noah was a diplomat, playwright and editor who was considered the most prominent Jew in America. Opposed to the enslavement of Americans in North Africa, he was an outspoken advocate of the enslavement of Africans in America. 'To emancipate the slaves,' he once wrote, 'would be to jeopardize the safety of the whole country.' He was, according to the *Freedom's Journal*, the first black newspaper in the USA, the black man's 'bitterest enemy'.

an immediate sensation, running into twenty-eight editions and selling almost a million copies. British, French and German editions soon followed and there were celebrity endorsements from, among others, Henry Thoreau and James Fenimore Cooper. In 1860, Abraham Lincoln cited it as one of the three most influential books in his life – the other two were the Bible and *The Pilgrim's Progress* – which had shaped his views on slavery. Riley's wrenching story, which remains in print to this day, described how the American slave-sailors died off one by one, beaten, starved, sunburnt, forced to drink camel urine and worked to death. It was published in the immediate aftermath of renewed heroics from the decorated *Philadelphia* veteran Stephen Decatur.

By May 1815 Decatur was a commodore, an established American hero and seasoned naval commander with victories against Britain, France and the North African regencies under his belt. On 15 May he sailed out of New York at the head of a squadron of ten ships, at that time the largest American fleet ever assembled. His orders were clear: destroy Algerine ships and bring the dey to terms imposed by the United States. On 17 June, high up on the main mast of the *Constellation*, a 38-gun frigate and one of the six original US Navy warships, a lookout spotted a suspicious-looking frigate off the Spanish coast at Cape Gata, east of Almeria. It turned out to be *Mashuda*, the flagship of the Algerian fleet under the command of the veteran Hamidou Reis, doyen of corsairs, holy war hero and scourge of American and European shipping over many years. Reis was reputed to have captured 200 ships in a long and illustrious – if you happened to be a North African Muslim – career of piracy.

After a courageous attempt to defend herself, *Mashuda* was overpowered by the American squadron. Pounded by repeated close-range broadsides from *Constellation* and *Guerrière*, Decatur's 74-gun flagship, she soon surrendered. When the American sailors boarded her and stepped on to her bloody decks, they found themselves with 406 prisoners on their hands. More to the point, they had also killed the last of the great corsairs.

On 28 June, Decatur and his squadron appeared menacingly off Algiers, determined to dictate terms. Two days later a treaty was signed with Omar Agha (r. 1815–17), the new dey, dramatically ending American tribute and ransom payments. Decatur then sailed east and signed similar treaties with Tunis and Tripoli in July and August respectively. Algiers proved reluctant to rein in the plundering, however, and in 1816 Omar Agha tried to renegotiate the treaty along the lines of the tribute-for-peace agreement of 1795, threatening to expel the American consul if Washington refused. The dey had failed to notice that the weather had changed. President Madison was unmoved by the threat 'because the United States, whilst they wish for War with no nation, will buy peace of none,' he wrote to the dey. 'It is a principle incorporated into the settled policy of America, that as peace is better than War, War is better than tribute.'[17]

Britain agreed. On 27 August 1816, a combined Anglo-Dutch fleet under the command of Admiral Edward Pellew, consisting of five line-of-battle ships, ten heavy frigates, four bomb vessels and a corvette, anchored before the fortified defences of Algiers. It proceeded to unleash a ferocious day-long barrage consisting of 118 tons of powder and more than 500 tons of shot, in addition to the remorseless volleys of rockets and shells. The dey's losses were devastating: the citadel, mole, batteries and naval and military storehouses of Algiers were all shattered, the corsair fleet of four frigates, five corvettes and twenty-five gunboats destroyed. The dey agreed to put an end to Christian (certainly not Muslim or African) slavery, free 1,200 Christian slaves, repay the ransoms he had received from Sicily and Naples in 1816 totalling $382,500 and pay the British consul $30,000 as compensation for the loss of his property.[18] Pellew was elevated to the peerage later that year, becoming the 1st Viscount Exmouth, his coat of arms including the remarkable image of a Christian slave holding a crucifix aloft as his fetters fall to the ground.

The British bombardment of Algiers was an operation against both piracy and the slave trade. It also demonstrated the use of the Royal Navy as 'the armed wing of anti-slavery diplomacy', a role it would pursue with vigour and fearsome weaponry for decades to come.[19]

Faced with increasingly powerful Western navies, the state-supported corsairs were fast losing their ability to terrify Mediterranean shipping. In Tripoli Yusuf Karamanli found himself under mounting pressure from the resurgent European powers, his revenues and authority declining in tandem to the point where the British consul, Hanmer Warrington, who served in Tripoli from 1814 to 1846, was considered, in the words of his French counterpart, 'more master of

An Anglo-Dutch fleet bombarding Algiers on 27 August 1816. The annihilating, nine-hour attack brought the Dey of Algiers to the negotiating table, resulting in a treaty in which he agreed to end Christian slavery. A painting by Nicolaas Baur, 1818.

the country than the Pasha himself'.[20] Dramatic evidence of this came in 1816, when Warrington controversially insisted on the hanging of a corsair captain who had seized a Hanoverian ship sailing under British protection. The consul successfully demanded that his Christian sailors, and not the pasha's Muslim officials, carry out the public execution from the ship's yardarm. Further humiliations followed. In 1819, an Anglo-French fleet forced Yusuf to release Christian slaves and prisoners held in Tripoli and, still worse, to accept peace treaties equating to the virtual suppression of piracy and protection payments.

In 1827, following orders from the Ottoman Sultan Mahmud II for naval support during the Greek War of Independence, Yusuf despatched the feeble remnants of his corsair fleet – a few poorly armed fishing boats, in the derisive verdict of the Turkish admiral – only to see them swiftly destroyed at the Battle of Navarino, prelude to Ottoman recognition of Greece in 1832. It was one of the first cracks to appear in the Ottoman Empire.

In a brazen turning of the tables Britain and France now started demanding punitive compensation payments from Yusuf for insults towards its consuls. France demanded 800,000 francs for this reason in 1830, Britain 200,000 piastres for another diplomatic offence around the same time.[21]

Framing piracy as the unique preserve of barbaric North Africans preying upon white European Christians, as opposed to the cosmopolitan free-for-all which it was in reality, became standard Western policy. Depicting Algiers as a violent pirates' lair that needed pacifying followed the same narrative. Whether this really was 'one of the earliest and most tenacious modern images of the alterity of violence', it undoubtedly played a powerful role in justifying imperial intervention.[22] Certainly, Algeria was a turbulent place, but the brutality of daily life there was as nothing compared to what was about to befall the country at European hands.

In 1830, the French occupied Algiers at the launch of an exceptionally bloody colonial incursion into Africa. It was a hammer blow for the Ottomans and the *coup de grâce* for the North African corsairs. By the 1830s the combination of British, French and American naval power had purged the Mediterranean of corsairs for perhaps the first time since the Roman era, a devastating shock to Tripoli's vulnerable economy. Shorn of tribute payments, unable to increase revenues from the desert slave trade, now under attack, and heavily indebted to foreign creditors, Yusuf's extravagantly maintained regency of Tripoli resembled a bankruptcy waiting to happen. In 1832 a revolt and attempted coup brought on by his desperate attempt to raise taxes to pay debts totalling $500,000 to Britain and France led to his public, tearful abdication in favour of his son Ali.

On 26 May 1835, responding to the new pasha's request for military assistance during a civil war, a Turkish fleet of twenty-two ships carrying artillery pieces and a force of 5,000 sailed into Tripoli. Ali Pasha Karamanli was detained and deposed, Istanbul resumed direct control and the once-grand regency of Tripoli was demoted within a few hours to a humble Ottoman *vilayet*, or province. Frail to the point of senility and cruelly impoverished after his son Ali had plundered his personal property and estates, Yusuf was allowed to live out his last pitiful days in the city from which the once-resplendent king of the corsairs had lorded it so triumphantly.

The thread of anti-Muslim prejudice which runs through the European and American captivity narratives was heartily reciprocated by many, if not most, Muslims and was evident in their 'May God destroy them' references to their northern neighbours. Bigotry worked both ways. Captivity and enslavement were practised by 'Christians and Muslims and Jews, Europeans and North Africans and Levantines, kings and sultans, scholars and investors, merchants and sailors, even Sufis and priests and nuns. Everyone was complicit ...'. For several centuries, millions of men, women and children all around the Mediterranean suffered the torments of slavery after being captured in land and sea attacks by corsairs and pirates, untold numbers of them labouring in appalling conditions and dying far away from the families they had not seen in decades. However charismatic and celebrated they may have been in some quarters, few if any of the seafaring slavers, be they Muslim, Christian or Jewish, come out of this with their reputations glowing. As the historian Nabil Matar concludes, 'nobody should cast the first stone'.[23]

By 1830, then, the long and turbulent period of corsairing from North Africa was over. On the one hand, North African Muslims, and their European renegade colleagues, had lost a lucrative, occasionally glorious and exceptionally violent way of living. On the other hand, their lives on the high seas had also become safer with the demise of Christian piracy.* While corsairing had been decisively suppressed, ending the centuries-old trauma of enslavement and captivity, for one ancient channel of the slave trade with its terminus on the shores of North Africa it remained lucrative business as usual.

---

* The year 1830 cast a wider, darker shadow across the North African littoral, introducing the agonies of French-led colonialism which would last well into the twentieth century. Libya only achieved independence in 1951, Morocco and Tunisia in 1956. And Algeria, whose capital had once harboured the most powerful corsair fleet, first had to fight a brutal, eight-year war with France from 1954 to 1962 to win its independence, only achieving it after suffering systematic atrocities and a death toll estimated at 1,500,000 by Algerian historians and 400,000 by the French.

9

The Saharan Slave Trade

... the endless misery into which the finest and most popu-
lous regions of this continent are plunged by the slave-hunting
expeditions of their merciless Mohammedan neighbours.
Heinrich Barth, *Travels and Discoveries in*
North and Central Africa, 1857

More than a quarter of a century ago, on New Year's Eve 1998, I rode my favourite camel Asfar, a sweet-natured animal, into the Libyan oasis town of Murzuq. Our caravan consisted of two British travellers, a Tuareg guide and five camels. It was a diminutive version of the slave-trafficking caravans which had plied the many routes across the Sahara for fourteen centuries, transporting captive men, women and children – or at least those who survived the exceptionally dangerous, frequently fatal journey – to the North African coast. This was the desert counterpart to the lethal Middle Passage of the Atlantic trade. Huge numbers of enslaved Africans had passed through Murzuq, one of the most important centres of the Saharan slave trade.

Starting from the ancient town of Ghadames, another once well-trodden slaving oasis, we had been travelling south-east for several weeks and almost 500 miles. We had traversed the vastness of the Hamada al Hamra (Red Plain), horizon after desolate horizon unfurling before us. Days of desert winds fizzing into our faces, penetratingly cold in the morning, scouringly hot as the sun swung up into the sky. Days of soft Saharan silence, disturbed only by the soporific pad-padding of the camels, mile after mile. And then, just as we were tiring of this monotony, we had had our first sight of the Awbari Sand Sea: golden dunes, piled high, row after row of them massed together in gentle curves, each one sculpted by an invisible wind. As you looked further into the distance their contours steadily faded in the white fulgor, merging into each other until all that remained was a mass of shapeless, eye-dazzling sand.

Crossing the vertiginous dunes had been hard going. Camels had slipped and stumbled, loads had been shed and tempers had frayed. Burning days gave way to shivering nights beneath the stars. Tuna fish pasta was becoming the dread that dare not speak its name. But here we were, riding into Murzuq, morale high, beards full and waistlines diminished.

A cohort of European, mostly British and German, explorers and campaigners against the slave trade had ridden into Murzuq in the eighteenth and nineteenth centuries: the German explorer Friedrich Hornemann in 1798; the English explorers Joseph Ritchie and George Francis Lyon in 1819; the outspoken evangelical Christian James Richardson, North African representative of the British and Foreign Anti-Slavery Society, in 1846; and, in 1869, Gustav Nachtigal, the German doctor and explorer.

Most had been greeted with great pomp and circumstance on their arrival – a welcoming, feast-giving bey or sultan of Fezzan (south-western Libya), surrounded by his body of horse, a retinue of slaves, dancers, drummers, pipers and courtiers. Hornemann had been welcomed by Mohammed ibn Sultan Mansur, the sultan of Fezzan, resplendent on a throne flanked by white Mamluk slave soldiers, black African slaves with drawn sabres, lances and halberds, and his numerous court. After the elaborate greeting, the sultan had ridden back into town preceded by kettle-drummers and waving banners, his courtiers prancing and curvetting their horses on either side of their monarch.

Our late-twentieth-century entrance was more modest, though all activity seemed to come to a standstill as we rode into town. Drivers stopped their vehicles in the road to look at the unlikely sight. Shopkeepers hurried to the front of their stores, shouting out greetings – '*Alhamdulillah aala al salama*!', 'Thank God for your safety!'. Children cheered and shouted, trotting along behind us in excitement.

Like so many journeys, this one had started with a book. As a teenager a decade earlier I had visited Tripoli with my father and together we had made the bibliophiles' pilgrimage to Dar Fergiani, the Libyan capital's most celebrated bookshop. Here I picked up the book which now, all these years later, I can say changed my life. *A Narrative of Travels in Northern Africa in the Years 1818–20* by Captain G. F. Lyon, which sits beside me as I write, thrust the desert before me for the first time. Here was the romance and glory of the Sahara, loyalty and companionship, adventure, betrayal, tragedy and death – with a compelling cast, entirely of its time, and as depicted by a very English writer, of intrepid explorers, treacherous sheikhs, murderous slave-hunters and beleaguered slaves.

It was an account of the expedition into the Libyan Sahara led by Dr Joseph Ritchie, 'a gentleman of great science and ability', directed by the British government to reach and chart the River Niger from the north, one of the last remaining puzzles of African exploration. Unfortunately, the enormity of his mission was not matched by corresponding resources and, eight months after leaving Tripoli disguised as a Muslim convert, the penniless Ritchie died an agonizing death from bilious fever in Murzuq, leaving his ebullient companion and then Lieutenant George Francis Lyon to record their adventures, alongside his watercolours of the desert and its peoples.* I read his highly charged tale with its detailed maps, sketches, observations and meteorological register, poring over his many pictures – a 'Tuarick on his Maherry', the stout Murzuq Castle, a slaving caravan struggling through a sandstorm – and felt the irresistible pull of the desert. I started to dream of a similar journey by camel.

Looking back at the ancient and extraordinarily resilient Saharan slave trade, which started in the seventh century and endured as late as the twentieth, it is clear that Lyon – and Ritchie briefly before he died – proved an important source of information at a critical time. Until they began corresponding from Murzuq with Colonel Hanmer Warrington,

* In the nineteenth century, according to Richardson, Murzuq was known as Bilad al Hemah, Fever Country.

British consul in Tripoli, in May 1819, sending him heart-rending descriptions of the trans-Saharan trade in men, women and children, he appears not to have been aware of the reality on the ground.

One day in late August, Lyon rode out to witness the 'piteous spectacle' of a northbound caravan of 1,400 slaves led by 'Arabs, Tripolines and Tibboo' arriving in Murzuq. The enslaved Africans were in an appalling condition after the vast distances they had covered from the place of their violent capture, as much as 1,000 miles to the south in a belt of territory stretching across the Sahel in what is today Niger, Chad, Cameroon and northern Nigeria – the Arabs' *Bilad al Sudan*, extending from the Nile to the Atlantic. He recorded:

> These poor oppressed beings were, many of them, so exhausted as to be scarcely able to walk. Their legs and feet were much swelled, and by their enormous size, formed a striking contrast with their emaciated bodies. They were all borne down with loads of fire-wood, and even poor little children, worn to skeletons by fatigue and hardships, were obliged to bear their burden, while many of their inhuman masters rode on camels, with the dreaded whip suspended from their wrists, with which they, from time to time, enforced obedience from these wretched captives.

Lyon painted a dismal picture of the human trade, those who profited from it and those who suffered under it. 'All the traders speak of slaves as farmers do of cattle,' he wrote. 'Those recently brought from the interior were fattening, in order that they might be able to go on to Tripoli, Benghazi or Egypt: thus, a distance of 1,600 or 1,800 miles is to be traversed, from the time these poor creatures are taken from their homes, before they can be settled.' They may have passed through the hands of up to ten masters, he continued, each time hoping their latest purchaser was the last, before continuing their long journeys 'under a burning sun, with new companions, but with the same miseries'.

Unable to complete his improbable riverine mission, Lyon nevertheless diligently compiled his findings on the desert slave trade. He closely observed the manner in which slaves were marched across the desert, tried and failed to save a dying fourteen-year-old slave girl and was eyewitness to a number of other deaths which were a grim reality of the Saharan slave trade. One day he went to watch a slave auction in the Murzuq market, noting how the sultan received 25 per cent of the sale price of each slave – as good an example as any of how the authorities right across the desert and beyond were economically enmeshed in, and directly incentivized by, the trade. Around the same time he observed several more caravans arriving with another 1,000 or so slaves.

Lyon also bore witness to the humanity of the slaves he was travelling with, admiring their patience, resilience, endurance of thirst – they were only allowed to drink once in twenty-four hours – and their lack of 'despondency' in the greatest possible adversity. A compassionate man, he paid tribute to their 'good-humoured gaiety' and songs – which relieved his own exhaustion. He routinely repaired the slaves' worn-out sandals.

By the time he made it back to Tripoli, Lyon's experience travelling among slaves and slave-drivers had affected him keenly. One of his last reflections was on the cruelty the slaves suffered at the hands of their masters:

> None of the owners ever moved without their whips, which were in constant use; that of Hadje Mohammed more so than the rest: in fact, he was so perpetually flogging his poor slaves, that I was frequently obliged to disarm him. Drinking too much water, bringing too little wood, or falling asleep before the cooking was finished, were considered nearly capital crimes and it was in vain for these poor creatures to plead the excuse of being tired; nothing could at all avert the application of the whip.[1]

Though the Ritchie and Lyon mission to chart the Niger was an abject failure, Lyon's more important legacy was to place abolition of the slave trade higher up London's agenda. If Warrington knew little about the horrors of the trans-Saharan slave trade in May, by June, moved by the correspondence he had received from the explorers, he was writing to London to discuss prospects for 'the suppression of the Black Traffic'.[2] Neither Warrington nor Lyon were to know that the British plan to replace it with the 'legitimate' commerce from which Britain would materially benefit would never materialize, leaving much of the region in dire economic straits.

Lyon's first book led, exactly 180 years later, to my own: *South from Barbary: Along the Slave Routes of the Libyan Sahara*. No charting the course of a famous river in the age of GPS, no reporting back to the British government with impassioned narratives (that would come much later, in 2017, when reports of African migrants in Libya being sold as slaves horrified the world). It was a desert expedition by camel and a travel history of the ancient Saharan slave trade, connecting some of its most important centres and routes and travelling with a number of Tuareg and Tubu tribesmen, descendants of their slave-driving ancestors.

In Tripoli, a major terminus of that trade, I visited the old British consulate on Sharaa al Kuwash (Baker Street), which had once been a hive of diplomatic activity directed towards its abolition. A plaque put up by the Mummar al Gaddafi regime (r. 1969–2011) referred to 'the so-called European geographical and explorative scientific expeditions to Africa' which had set off from this building but which were, the Libyan government maintained, 'colonial ones to occupy and colonize vital strategic parts of Africa'. In the quarter-century since our expedition, that aspect of the Gaddafi narrative has found increasing favour. In the labyrinthine *medina*, or old city, of Ghadames we visited the cramped quadrangle of Mulberry Square, once the market for male slaves and the sole reminder of the town's former role in the trade.

After a journey of more than 1,500 miles, most of it bumping along by camel or walking alongside our five ships of the desert, we reached the remote oasis of Kufra, the one-time headquarters of the Sanusi Order, an orthodox, revivalist Sufi brotherhood which preached pure devotion to Islam. On a less spiritual plane, it also profited mightily from the northbound trade in African slaves that passed through the settlement. Here we were also travelling in the footsteps of the Egyptian explorer, diplomat, royal tutor and Olympic fencer Ahmed Hassanein Bey. *The Lost Oases*, his elegant account of the expedition, which won him the Royal Geographical Society's Founder's Medal in 1924, is peppered with references (twenty-eight) to the numerous slaves he met – and in one instance employed – during his journey the year before: slave cooks, camel boys, messengers, retainers, favourite slaves and general dogsbodies. Though the slave trade by this time had been forced underground, slavery itself was still going strong in the second decade of the twentieth century. The last recorded caravan of slaves arrived in Murzuq in 1929.

Hassanein Bey also expressed the ambivalence of slavery in the Muslim world, which can surprise Western readers less familiar with the institution outside the far better known North American, Caribbean and Brazilian plantation version. He writes of how the 'favourite male slave' tended to be 'very well treated' as part of the family. That of Sayed Idris, the then head of the Sanusi Order, for example, was 'not only the most trusted man' and treated as a confidant, but also enjoyed 'more power and authority among the Beduins themselves than many a free man'. The Egyptian also noted that whereas favourite slaves tended to be well dressed, reflecting the prestige of their master, 'The shabbiest slave that you see in an oasis is generally the freed slave, who curiously enough is looked down upon by the other owned slaves, and himself feels ashamed that he is a freed slave and belongs to no one!'[3]

We cannot tell all the stories of the slaves who travelled across the Sahara for more than a millennium. They are like ghosts from another era who have left imperceptible traces of their passing through some of the most inhospitable territory on earth. We want to hear their voices, to know what they experienced, how they lived and what they thought, what sort of lives they went on to lead and where, but there is no crop of memoirs to guide us. We do not have the many first-person accounts which emerged from both the Atlantic slave trade and from those corsair-captured men and women who lived to tell the tale of their enslavement on the North African coast. We hear them instead in the stories told by other people, invariably men, generally foreign and especially Western: men like Lyon, Richardson and Nachtigal, surveying the world around them with mostly European eyes and the prejudices and agendas – often abolitionist – of their time.* And we hear them, *en passant*, from Arabs, from the globetrot-

---

* A new generation of scholars is increasingly looking to non-Western sources, wherever available, to counter this imbalance. Amal Altaleb's 2015 study *The Social and Economic History of Slavery in Libya (1800–1950)*, to take one example, uses legal records from the Islamic courts of Tripoli and Ghadames to investigate her subject.

ting, slave-collecting Ibn Battuta, who made sure he always had one or two slave girls in his entourage during his long travels in Africa in the fourteenth century, to the slave-employing Hassanein Bey in the twentieth. The great Moroccan traveller was a serial user and purchaser of slave concubines. In one of the more extreme scholarly estimates, it has been suggested that the Moroccan married and divorced more than twenty women during his three decades on the road, fathering and abandoning seventy children along the way.[4]

These were men for whom slaves and slavery were a normal part of daily life. Lyon met a young Arab boy on the road between Tripoli and the Fezzan, who reacted contemptuously to the Englishman's remark that slavery was looked upon with horror in England. 'Damn their fathers, the asses!' the boy said of black Africans. 'What are they made for but to serve us? Go then and take them for they are Kaffirs and we cannot do without them.'[5]

In Mali half a millennium earlier, Ibn Battuta was scandalized by the nudity of slave women and the sultan's daughters, who appeared in public exposing their 'private parts'. 'I saw about a hundred slave girls coming out of his palace with food, with them were two of his daughters, they had full breasts and no clothes on,' he noted indignantly.[6] It almost goes without saying that the Moroccan was not scandalized by slavery itself. That would have been as inconceivable a reaction for an Arab Muslim in the fourteenth century and for much, if not most, of the period from the seventh to the nineteenth century. In 1353, Ibn Battuta received a message from the Moroccan Sultan Abu Inan commanding him to return home. During that westward journey he reached the desert oasis town of Takedda in Niger, where he offered another glimpse of slavery in Muslim Africa. 'The people of Takedda have no occupation but trade,' he wrote. 'They travel each year to Egypt and import some of everything which is there in the way of fine cloth and other things. Its people are comfortable and well off and are proud of the number of male and female slaves which they have.'[7]

And within the particular environment of the Sahara, slaving was so routine that it was an inherent part of long-distance travel. When Ibn Battuta set off on his final leg home from northern Mali on 11 September 1353, after just under thirty years on the road, he was travelling with a caravan of 600 female slaves, destined largely for roles as domestics or concubines. His journey took him almost 1,000 miles on the westernmost of the Saharan slave routes to Sijilmasa, on the northern fringes of the Moroccan desert, thence across the snow-shrouded Atlas Mountains to Fez.

In recent years there have been renewed and welcome efforts to unearth the voices of the voiceless, to bring the enslaved men and women into the narrative to tell their own stories in their own words, however elusive the evidence. Some brief, partial but extraordinary glimpses and insights into their lives have been made available as will be seen, especially those from the nineteenth century, through letters, court records trade registers and face-to-face interviews with former slaves and their descendants. These have helped restore some human-ity to a field which can occasionally lose itself in arcane debates about statistics.

But for all the gains which have been made, we must acknowledge that huge questions remain unanswered. The sources of reliable information before the nineteenth century, when European officials began recording the numbers of slaves passing through certain centres of the trade, such as Murzuq and Ghadames, are vanishingly rare. We don't know, to begin with, precisely how many slaves crossed the Sahara throughout the *longue durée* of this trade. One of the most widely used estimates of 4,820,000 for the period 650–1600 not only excludes more than three centuries but is caveated with enormous uncertainty. That figure 'could be twice as many slaves as the number actually transported or consid-erably less than the total volume'. Broadening the category to include the Red Sea and East African trade between 800 and 1600, a total of 7,220,000 is offered as the roughest of approximations: 'a range of 3.5 to 10 million is more accurate'. We can be sure, though, that whatever the true figure, the men, women and children seized from their sub-Saharan homes by Arabs and Africans in slave-taking *razzias* (raids) of terrifying violence and brutality were part of a 'vast exodus of enslaved human beings' to the Mediterranean and beyond.[8]

Our ignorance extends to not knowing how many of these slaves were men and how many women, a key factor in determining starkly different life stories. We do not know, either, how many men, women and children succumbed to the numerous perils of this journey.

Disease, infection, starvation, thirst, cold, exhaustion and murder stalked them constantly, leaving huge but unknown numbers dead, dying and unburied where they fell. From time to time the sources abruptly lift the veil on this life-and-death forced march across the desert, revealing details that make desperate reading.

One of the most dreadful examples is the large caravan travelling from Lake Chad to Murzuq in the midsummer heat of 1849. In that instance, 1,600 slaves suffered horrifying deaths by thirst on a caravan woefully organized by the five Tubu and Arab slave-drivers, who died alongside their charges, together with 400 camels and forty horses. It was, in the words of the British consul in Tripoli, 'one of the most appalling disasters that ever took place in this quarter of the Globe connected with the Slave Traffic'.[9] That was surely an extreme case, but it is clear from this period of the nineteenth century alone that a high death count was hardly a rarity. It was almost certainly 'priced in' by the merchants. Another 195 slaves, a quarter of the caravan, died on the same route later in the same year. And in 1850, a caravan travelling from Wadai to Benghazi in eastern Libya lost a quarter of its 1,600 slaves due to cold and exhaustion. More than 2,000 deaths on just three caravans. We can only imagine the faceless, nameless, unknown numbers of other recently enslaved Africans who never made it to the North African coast.

For those who did survive the journey across the Sahara, in which women appeared to have outnumbered men (some studies reckon by up to two to one), we can make educated guesses at the roles they went on to take – concubines, cooks, maids, agricultural workers, livestock managers, secretaries, commercial agents. And there is uncertainty, too, about the numbers of those who were never intended to reach the littoral but were put to work instead within the Sahara – salt-miners, gum-collectors, date palm-workers, well-diggers and other agricultural labourers. We are dealing, to a great extent, then, with the lives of the very real but invisible, intangible and, in the historical record, almost completely inaudible.

We are on much surer footing when it comes to understanding the routes across which these millions of slaves were roughly driven across the desert. While maps typically show a series of neat solid lines running from sub-Saharan Africa to the coast along a north–south axis, the reality was much messier. It is more accurate to consider them as 'capillaries rather than arteries', part of an evolving network of communications which changed according to time, supply and demand and, by the time of the nineteenth century, the competing forces of abolitionism on the one hand and global markets catering to regional and international consumers on the other.[10]

Moving from west to east, one route connected western Sudan, broadly today's Mauritania, Senegal, Gambia, Guinea, Guinea-Bissau, Mali and Burkina Faso, to Morocco and Algiers – Ibn Battuta would have travelled part of this route on his way home to Fez. Next came a route stretching from the central Sudan – the Kanem, Bornu and Hausa states which today include Ghana, Mali, Niger, Cameroon, the Central African Republic, Chad and Nigeria – to Tunis and Tripoli. An additional route to the east of this rose up in the nineteenth century, running across the eastern Sahara from the sultanate of Wadai (eastern Chad) via Kufra to Benghazi. And the easternmost route, the *Darb al Arbaain* (Forty Days' Road), rose along the Greater Nile Valley, linking Nilotic Sudan, particularly Sennar and Darfur, to Egypt. Of these various slave-trading routes, the most enduring ran more than 1,300 miles almost directly south–north from Lake Chad to Tripoli through Chad and Niger. It dated back at least a couple of millennia to the Garamantes, an ancient civilization of warrior-traders ruling a swathe of the Sahara from their Libyan homeland. The reasons for its longevity were straightforward. It was shorter than most of the others and provided swifter access to the Mediterranean via a road well provided with resting-stop oases and regular wells.

It was the fatal misfortune of sub-Saharan Africans to become, with gold, the staple northbound 'commodity' of the desert trade for many centuries. While other products included silver, tin, ivory, ostrich feathers, hides, honey, gooroo nuts, red peppers, dates and civet (an essential ingredient for making perfume; Lyon reported 'a savage old [civet] cat' could be sold for three or four slaves), slaves and gold were the most lucrative prizes.

Starting as early as the mid-seventh century, when Egypt's Arab conquerors imposed the *Baqt* treaty on their Nubian neighbours to the south, requiring an annual tribute of 360 'slaves of good quality', Arabs and later the Ottomans looked upon the Africans of the interior as a bottomless reservoir of slave labour: 'slavery and unbelief were increasingly read onto the bodies of dark-skinned Africans'.[11]

Arab slavers launched slave-taking raids right across sub-Saharan Africa. They operated especially along the East African coast in a region which today includes Kenya, Tanzania and Mozambique, and also travelled further west into the Central African interior around the Congo River Basin. Some captured slaves in West Africa, in a vast region encompassing Mali, Niger and Nigeria among others, which otherwise tended to be dominated by North African traders.

Slave-taking raids were highly organized, often state-sanctioned military expeditions which could last several days and involve up to 2,000 warrior horsemen. One might begin with a surprise, encircling attack at dawn or even the siege of an entire town or village. Raiders sometimes seized control of the water supply and forced the community into slavery that way. For the Muslim rulers of the Kanem-Bornu Empire, which ranged across Libya, Chad and Nigeria from the eighth to the fourteenth centuries, virtually everyone and everything was fair game: rival Muslim states, ungoverned Muslim territories like Tuareg Air and Bilma, and, of course, pagan communities. Men who dared to resist were slaughtered on the spot, often with the commercially worthless elderly and infirm. A settled community living in peace could be wiped out and thrust into slavery in a stroke. Children were often separated from their parents, irrespective of their age and needs, and family huts were set on fire as armed raiders cut a swathe through an unsuspecting village. These were scenes from the apocalypse.[12]

The *Baqt* treaty lasted between 500 and 700 years. The raiding and enslavement of sub-Saharan communities persisted for much longer. African slaves taken through the Sahara were still being covertly shipped across the Mediterranean from Benghazi as late as 1910.

It is a broiling day in Bamako. Late summer, 2020, 38 degrees and counting. Though much of his face is hidden behind a face mask, it is not difficult to notice that Dr Abdel Kaider Haidara, a large man in an immaculate white *boubou* and neat brown cap, is grinning broadly beneath it.

He says:

> During its Golden Age in the fifteenth and sixteenth centuries, Timbuktu drew in all the world. We had one of the world's greatest libraries here, as many as half a million manuscripts, the oldest going back a thousand years. Huge numbers of these manuscripts were produced in the city, and many were collected over the centuries by private families living here. The authors of these texts were Malian, Asian, Andalusian, Maghrebi, Egyptian, Syrian, Iraqi, Yemeni. They came from everywhere in the trans-Saharan caravans and they wrote about everything under the sun: sex tips and science, poetry, philosophy, black magic and astronomy, mathematics, medicine, religion, history, geography, peace-keeping, good governance, human rights and, yes, of course, slavery.

Haidara is a hero. He is the living embodiment of the death-defying efforts to preserve Mali's Islamic heritage from the destructive forces of fanaticism. In 2012, the jihadists of Al Qaeda and Ansar Dine stormed across northern Mali and imposed their brutal form of sharia law on Timbuktu, destroying ancient Sufi shrines, carrying out public whippings and amputations and terrorizing the population. By that time, after years of travelling around Mali collecting lost manuscripts on behalf of the national library in Timbuktu, Haidara, a fluent Arabic speaker, had assembled a collection of 377,000 texts, some dating back to the eleventh century. They were now in extreme danger. Haidara then masterminded the covert operation to smuggle tens of thousands of the city's ancient manuscripts more than 600 miles south to the safety of Bamako, the Malian capital, right under the noses of the jihadists. He used every which way he could, from donkey carts and taxis to boats and teenage couriers, to save these Arabic-language texts from the book-burning that was destined to be their fate at the hands of the iconoclasts. His courageous story reverberated across the world, so that the man who saved all these books has himself become the subject of books.[13]

'These Arabic language manuscripts from Timbuktu are much more than our Malian cultural patrimony. They are Africa's collective memory, a living, breathing part of our world heritage. Our mission is to preserve them for humanity forever.' He takes me around the rambling offices where, sitting at desks beneath bright lights, his team of men and women in blue tunics are cleaning, restoring and digitizing this priceless treasure trove. Many of the manuscripts here date to Timbuktu's golden age, when the city's command of many of the trans-Saharan trading routes made it rich both in terms of its gold, silver, salt and slaves but, more important, as a world-famous intellectual capital. Timbuktu was a sanctuary for scholars, a cosmopolitan city of knowledge, learning and tolerance. In the account of his visit to Timbuktu at this time, summarized in *Description of Africa*, Hassan al Wazzan, the Muslim diplomat and traveller, highlighted the importance of the thriving book trade: 'There are in Timbuktu numerous judges, teachers and priests, all properly appointed by the king. He greatly honours learning. Many hand-written books imported from Barbary are also sold. There is more profit made from this commerce than from all other merchandise.'[14]

Perhaps there is no greater representative of Timbuktu's golden age of scholarship than Ahmad Baba (1556–1627), a Berber writer who had been deported to Morocco for sedition in the wake of the Moroccan invasion of the Songhay Empire in 1591. During his exile from Timbuktu he witnessed the North African prejudice towards black-skinned people in which blackness was directly associated with slavery, irrespective of whether or not the individual was a Muslim – and therefore protected from enslavement. He saw, too, how one Muslim state (Morocco) had invaded another (Songhay), illegally enslaving whole swathes of its Muslim population. In 1615, by which time he was back in Timbuktu, he sat down to write an answer to a series of detailed questions he had received on this subject several years before from traders in the oasis complex of Tuat, a key resting-place for trans-Saharan caravans, where slaves were brought and processed for onward transport to North Africa. It is clear from the questions they asked that there was a great deal of confusion and uncertainty regarding the permissibility of enslaving people who claimed they were Muslims.

In a charmingly honest passage which resonates across the centuries, Ahmad Baba confesses that he had been meaning to get round to this task immediately, 'but something prevented me from so doing until it passed into the category of things forgotten'. His correspondent had chased him up, so it was now time to share his thoughts. The result was *Miraj al Suud*, or *Ahmad Baba's Replies on Slavery*.

The Timbuktu scholar first of all gave short shrift to the so-called Curse of Ham story, which many generations of Arab Muslims had interpreted as a curse of slavery meted out to black people after Ham supposedly saw his drunken father Noah naked. Ahmad Baba cited both Ibn al Jawzi and Ibn Khaldun to destroy this claim, which had been used to justify black African slavery. Having dismissed the racial basis for slavery, he went on to make a definitive pronouncement on religious-based slavery, arguing that:

> the cause of enslavement is unbelief, and the unbelievers of the Sudan are like any other unbelievers in this regard – Jews, Christians, Persians, Berbers or others ... there is no difference between any unbelievers in this regard. Whoever is enslaved in a state of unbelief may rightly be owned, whoever he is ...

Infidels, in other words, were fair game. By contrast, Ahmad Baba continued, were those 'who converted to Islam of their own free will, such as the people of Bornu, Kano, Songhay, Katsina, Gobir and Mali and some of [the people of] Zakzak. They are free Muslims who may not be enslaved under any circumstance.'[15]

So there was no question of abolishing slavery. Ahmad Baba was certainly not advocating that. He was rejecting the racial equation of blackness with slavery, reaffirming the prohibition on enslaving Muslims – which he knew was regularly happening in Muslim lands between the Senegal River and Lake Chad – and advocating the continued enslavement of non-Muslims.

Saharan slave-raiding was not exclusively Arab-on-African but frequently also African-on-African. Here as elsewhere, old habits died hard. In 1665, fifty years after Ahmad Baba's famous treatise and a year before the Great Fire of London, a Tuareg ruler called Khadakhada celebrated his victory over a rival Tuareg clan by enslaving the free men. Hearing this news, the ruler of Agades wrote to him, requesting that Khadakhada liberate them, even if they were black. 'The other replied to him that he made no prisoners of free men. All the prisoners were black, therefore slaves, for a Black, when he has been raided becomes a slave.'[16]

Further south in the central Sahel and savannah, some of the most notorious enslavement of African Muslims by fellow African Muslims occurred in the run-up to, during and in the immediate aftermath of the jihad led by the Islamic scholar Usman dan Fodio against the slave-taking Hausa states in today's northern Nigeria from 1804 to 1808. Rebelling against the illegal enslavement of Muslims, dan Fodio marshalled his forces to a victory resulting in the creation of the Islamic revivalist Sokoto caliphate (1808–1903), also known as the Fulani Empire. It became Africa's pre-eminent slave state, enslaving both non-Muslims and Muslims to the extent that at times more than 50 per cent of its population was enslaved. By 1900, the number of slaves was estimated at 1 million to 2.5 million. Just as the Mediterranean could be a slaving free-for-all, so regular regional conflicts here created the conditions for taking slaves as the spoils of war.[17]

Ali Eisami, a Muslim Kanuri captured and enslaved in his homeland of Bornu during jihad, bore witness to these devastating upheavals. He was bought and sold, taken west to the coast and eventually embarked on a European slave ship bound for the Americas in 1818, only to be intercepted by the Royal Navy. He was liberated and taken to Sierra Leone, Britain's colony for freed slaves, where he became William Harding and later worked on his memoirs with a German missionary. 'The Phulas caught me. They sold me,' he recalled of his enslavement. 'The Popos took us. To a white man they sold us. The white man took us. We had no shirts. We had no trousers. We were naked. Into the midst of water, into the midst of a ship they put us. Thirst killed somebody. Hunger killed somebody . . .'.

The many thousands of enslaved Hausa prisoners of war who were less fortunate than Eisami were swept up in this turbulence in today's Yorubaland (encompassing Nigeria, Togo and Benin) and trafficked across the Atlantic to the Americas. In fact, Hausa Muslims were regularly found on both sides of the divide – as slaver and enslaved. Among the enslaved men, those in their adult prime were exported across the Atlantic, while women predominated among the groups trafficked across the Sahel and Sahara to North Africa and the Ottoman Empire. During their eighteenth-century wars of expansion in West Africa, Asante rulers, who used slaves in agricultural production, weaving, mining and domestic service in royal palaces, enslaved their prisoners and sold them to both Europeans, for the Atlantic slave trade, and North Africans, for the Saharan. For the kingdom of Dahomey (Benin), with its economy built on conquest and slave labour, the Atlantic slave trade was paramount, 'one of the mainstays of the ruling house'.[18]

It is worth emphasizing, as we brush the shores of the Atlantic, that the slave trade across that ocean cannot be neatly separated from the trade to the east. For hundreds of years and well into the nineteenth century there were Europeans enslaved in North Africa, Turks in West Africa, Yoruba Muslims teaching the Quran in Brazil, together with Hausa, Wolof, Mandingo, Fulani, Vai and Tukolor Africans – many of them Muslim – captured, enslaved and shipped across the Atlantic to labour on plantations, in mines and in houses in the American South, Brazil and beyond. 'This was a true *histoire croisée*, and nowhere was the web more tangled than in Islamic Africa.'[19] Demand fuelled supply, and the insatiable demand from the New World for African slaves, Muslim and otherwise, provided a powerful incentive for both raids and internecine war, resulting in the profitable capture, enslavement, sale and export of this vast human capital.[*]

Enslavement had no respect for religious, social, ethnic or educational distinctions and took in the high-born as well as the low. Thus Abd al Rahman Ibrahima (1762–1829), a blue-blooded Fulani Muslim prince from Guinea, highly educated in Timbuktu, was shot, captured in battle and then enslaved by Mandinka merchants during a regional conflict in 1788. He was sold, shipped across the Atlantic and put to work on a plantation in Mississippi for the next forty years. He was only released in 1828 and died just a year later on his return to Africa, not living to see his five sons and eight grandchildren emancipated.[20]

Omar ibn Said (1770–1864), a Fulani Muslim scholar and merchant, an expert in mathematics, astronomy and theology from today's Senegal, was captured during another conflict in 1807 and trafficked

---

[*] The first enslaved African Muslims in the Americas came from Spain to Hispaniola in 1502. They were followed by enslaved Moroccans, who were used to explore what is now Arizona and New Mexico in the 1520s and 1530s. Estimates for the number of enslaved Muslims in the Americas vary substantially, from 40,000 out of a slave population in the United States of 4.5 million in 1860 to 2.25 million to 3 million to cover the Caribbean and both North and South America. See Richard Brent Turner, 'African Muslim Slaves and Islam in Antebellum America'.

to a savage slave-owner in South Carolina. He later escaped to North Carolina and remained enslaved there until his death in 1864. He was thought by white Americans to have converted to Christianity but maintained a studied ambivalence in *The Life of Omar Ibn Said Written by Himself* (1831) – the only autobiography of an enslaved individual in the United States written in Arabic – which suggests that he may have been merely hiding his Muslim faith during his long persecution.[21]

The divergence between pious proscriptions against enslaving Muslims and real-life practice was nothing new, either in Timbuktu or wider Muslim Africa. Hassan al Wazzan, or Leo Africanus, had hinted at it during his description of the fabled city in the sixteenth century. The prodigiously rich king then had huge numbers of soldiers and slaves, many of them Muslim, among his retinue. 'This king makes war only upon neighbouring [therefore Muslim] enemies and upon those who do not want to pay him tribute,' the Granadan traveller wrote. 'When he has gained a victory, he has all of them, even the children, sold in the market at Timbuktu.' Al Wazzan referred to slaves elsewhere during his Timbuktu visit, noting that the slave women selling produce in the market were unveiled, unlike free women, and that 'the citizens have at their service many slaves, both men and women'.[22]

The fact was that Timbuktu was one of the great southern centres of the Saharan slave trade. A slave even features in one version of how the city got its name. When nomads first settled here in the early twelfth century, the story goes, they camped a few miles away from the River Niger to avoid diseases and the humidity. One of their slaves looking after the nomads' belongings while they were away was called Buktu, from where the name Tim Buktu, the well of Buktu, is said to have arisen.[23]

Some remarkable documents from Timbuktu continue to emerge in recent years, revealing the extraordinary scope of slavery within the Sahara and the enormous variety of roles slaves could fulfil. Some of these sources challenge traditional understanding of the nature of the relationship between master and slave. Take the fascinating series of letters to and from a couple of high-status, highly literate slaves from

Ghadames living and working as commercial agents in Timbuktu in the latter part of the nineteenth century.[24]

Sanbu Isa and Anjay Isa, who both bore their master's name, worked for Isa ibn Hamida, whose trading network connected the Sahara with the Sudanic region of Mali to the south. Goods destined for the north included gold, textiles, foodstuffs, kola nuts, ostrich feathers and slaves, while Saharan merchants sold salt, tobacco and textiles. When Anjay died in the early twentieth century thirteen books in Arabic were found in his home, indicating a striking level of familiarity with Islamic law, Arabic grammar and religious literature. This certainly defies the common assumption that slaves were all poorly educated. So too the friendly, respectful and sometimes familial greetings exchanged between master and his slaves in their correspondence – the letters routinely begin with 'full and generous greetings', 'full greetings and general respects' and other similar phrases.

Clearly there was a considerable degree of latitude afforded to these sophisticated slaves who appear to have been treated as part of the family. In one letter to Isa, Anjay comes close to rebuking his master for the criticism of various transactions the slave has completed. 'Salt is not sold quickly and gold is not found easily,' he writes firmly. 'But you are absent and I am present here. It is those who are here on the ground who can see and know what those who are not here cannot see and cannot possibly know. This is the difference between you and me.' It is quite the retort. Later he resumes a more deferential style, assuring Isa of his loyalty and good service:

> To you I am like the mouse that is in the house of the people. He does not abandon these people of the house. You and I are like that. So rest your heart in peace about me. From me you will only see things that please you, God willing. I swore an oath to God Almighty never to betray you. Even if people tell you that I am stealing your money, I will walk to you on my two feet, God willing, I will walk to you myself and you will do with me what you want.

We cannot know exactly what kind of man Isa was, how cruel, enlightened or otherwise he may have been. But we do have some clues. We know that his concubine, a woman called Yajida, may also have been involved in his trading enterprise. A letter from Yajida to Anjay, an extraordinarily rare instance of a female slave writing in this vein, finds her acting possibly as a business partner or even trading on her own account, firing off a series of instructions to her brother slave. Here she is discussing hulled rice, tobacco, cotton strips, turbans and a woollen blanket. Poised and perfectly in control, she ends her letter with a no-nonsense, get-on-with-it directive. 'As for the blanket that I mentioned to you already in the letter, do not ask where it is,' she writes. 'Just send me its price with the writer of the letter.'

First-person accounts from those who survived the bloody slaving raids in Africa are rare. One of the most remarkable sources is an interview from the 1940s with Griga, an elderly former slave then in his late nineties, first published in French in 1971. It takes us to the heart of the Algerian Sahara in the late nineteenth century.[25]

Sunlight clattered through the date palms. The shade of the trees gave some respite from the skin-pricking heat, but it was a ferociously hot day. A group of already sweating black African slaves were getting ready for a dangerous and unpleasant underground mission in Timimoun, a sun-beaten oasis in the Western Sand Sea of Algeria. Spreading for four miles around the many slaves, handful of masters and overseers and a gaggle of curious village children was the bristling forest of date palms and the Amraïer foggara which irrigated it – an ancient hydraulic system bringing water from the 300 wells here to the surface.

One of the slaves in this throng was a man called Griga, son of a Fulani slave woman, who was himself captured and enslaved at the age of fourteen. He would never be able to forget that evening in 1862, when roaring, sword-wielding Tuareg raiders burst out of a sandstorm and encircled and set fire to Matankari, his village in Hausaland, southern Niger. 'My friend Makoko tried to escape by slipping in between two Tuaregs,' he later recalled, 'but one of them saw him and nailed him to the ground with a spear and Makoko shrieked in pain.' Four old women, useless from a commercial point of view, had their throats slit, a eunuch had his arm cut off before being stabbed to death, and seventy-eight terrified villagers, Griga among them, were marched off into the desert under a barrage of whips, their hands tied together with ropes of goat hair. Griga was an eyewitness to many horrors. He saw two boys from his village roughly castrated, writhing, struggling and screaming in pain and terror. One bled for hours, the crude 'dressing' of wood tar powdered with ground camel dung proving incapable of stemming the flow. As a last resort his savage wound was cauterized with a red-hot iron – 'Hideous new screams! The smell of burnt flesh!' – but to no avail. He died that night. 'Do you think anyone could ever forget that?' Griga asked. 'Even in my tomb I shall see once again the frightful spectacle of those tortured children.'

Soon after this Griga's party was ambushed by a different branch of Tuareg in renewed scenes of slaughter and bloodshed and the enslaved villagers fell into new ownership. Griga was eventually purchased for 200 francs by Si Abdelkader ben Kouider of Timimoun, who was then looking for some black male slaves to tend his garden and some female slaves, including concubines, for his house. In addition, the elders of Timimoun had asked him to select and procure twenty beautiful female slaves for Mohammed IV, sultan of Morocco – 'young women, well formed, with firm and ample breasts, plump and rounded buttocks, light complexions, and attractive faces'. The gift was to encourage the Moroccan ruler to protect them from the steadily advancing French. Si Abdelkader duly found the required women, who cost up to 600 francs, and, according to Griga, bought and sold a few other slaves. Eunuchs were sold for 500 francs.

Griga worked in his master Si Abdelkader's date gardens, a skin-tormenting job which required him, among other things, to pollinate female date palms, climbing up the trunk to powder pollen on to the clusters of flowers, taking the greatest possible care to avoid the thousands of sword-like spikes raised like a battalion beneath the leaves, before descending with bleeding arms, legs and chest to repeat the process on the next tree.

On this occasion, though, Griga and his fellow slaves had a different, far more life-threatening job to do. The flow of water passing along the underground tunnel linking the 300 wells had dwindled to a feeble trickle due to obstructions caused by collapses. Its urgent refurbishment was such a big job that it required a general levy of slaves from right across the community to work in the tunnels. At dawn the drums sounded up and down the oasis streets summoning the slaves. Teams of ten African slaves were detailed to clean out and rehabilitate the vertical wells and sections of the horizontal tunnel. Griga was under no illusion as to the perils of this 'mole-like work' in which a blockage frequently 'entombed or crushed' the subterranean slaves. It demanded an 'incredible, superhuman effort, in a narrow, dark and humid tunnel, to create a passage through this stopper of sticky, clayey paste', behind which the water was rising inexorably.

Griga descended one of the deepest shafts, around thirty-seven metres below ground, without a rope. It was painful going, thrusting hands and feet into the roughly chiselled crevices down the shaft. Regularly falling stones smashed into his head. A second slave joined him at the bottom of the well, sending another shower of stones on to Griga. Cramped uncomfortably in the tiny tunnel, the two men cleaned out the surplus soil, clay and gravel by lamplight, piled the damp spoil into a basket, had it hauled to the surface on a rope and, by now completely spent and panting with exhaustion, made their way gingerly back to the surface, allowing two new slaves to take their place underground.

Griga takes up the story again:

> Suddenly, farther down around the one hundredth well, we hear cries. Everyone runs, gathers together, and discusses. It seems to me that someone is calling for help. We run there. The slaves explain that while descending the well, Moumen, the slave of Abdelali, had slipped and fallen forty cubits [eighteen metres]. Two men had just gone down to try and bring him up. Si Abdelkader and Abdelali, having been immediately informed, show up.

Two ropes were lowered down the well and placed under Moumen's armpits. After a monumental effort he was eventually hauled up to the surface, where he was laid out on the ground, clearly in great pain and breathing with difficulty.

> Si Abdelkader bends over him, prods him, then slowly straightens up, shaking his head.
>
> 'He will die,' he said. 'His thighs and his ribs are broken. Take him to the village, and the rest of you, instead of looking and doing nothing, get back to work!'

'It's a loss for me,' said Abdelali, by way of funeral oration. 'I bought him last year for two hundred francs!'

Moumen died the next day at daybreak, just as the drum was calling his brothers to work.

This single tragedy in the desert, remembered in vivid detail by Griga and retold decades later, when he was in his late nineties, to Fernand Mercadier, the French commandant of Timimoun from 1944 to 1947, shines a narrow but piercing light into the lost world of Saharan slave agriculture. To a very great extent it remains *terra incognita*, in which unknown numbers of African men, women and children toiled away for centuries. It is unlikely that Abdelali was unique in his reaction to losing Moumen. For all too many masters, a slave was not really a man or a woman but a piece of property. For others, such as Isa, he or she was a valued member of the household.

Griga's testimony is a powerful reminder, too, of the enormous variety of roles which slaves fulfilled within and around the great African desert for numerous generations. There was no single overarching form of servitude, as with plantation slavery in North America and the Caribbean, but rather numerous types, notwithstanding the heavy predominance of enslaved females bought and sold within the Saharan trade for more specific roles within the house.

There were commercial agents and concubines, salt-miners in Bilmar and Kawar (north-east Niger), slave soldiers of eastern Sudan and their western counterparts, the Abid al Bukhari, an all-black slave army that numbered 150,000 at its peak established by the Moroccan Sultan Moulay Ismail, that inveterate collector of slaves, in the dying years of the seventeenth century. Then there were all the unsung domestic and agricultural workers, those like Griga who cultivated date palms and laboured underground when the need arose, slaves who tended livestock and those who, reduced to the status of a donkey, joined these beasts of burden to ensure the draw-wells kept working.

One of the toughest forms of slavery in the Sahara, with an ancient heritage, was salt-mining. Such were the conditions that it was said that no slave lasted longer than five years in the salt mines. The Iraqi geographer Ibn Hawqal in the tenth century and the Andalusian Arab historian Al Bakri in the eleventh referred respectively to a salt/gold exchange between Mauritania and Morocco and the salt trade in the Ghana Empire. One of the first sources to describe salt-mining in any detail, and the slaves who laboured in it, was the Moroccan traveller Ibn Battuta. After a twenty-five-day journey from Sijilmasa, the great entrepot linking the medieval Maghreb with the Sudanic region, he arrived at the salt-mining settlement of Taghaza (northern Mali) in March 1352. Ibn Battuta took an immediate dislike to it, complaining about the flies and brackish water, but left a precious picture of one of the most important products in the trans-Saharan trade:

> It is a village with no attractions. A strange thing about it is that its houses and mosques are built of blocks of salt and roofed with camel skins. There are no trees, only sand in which there is a salt mine. They dig the ground and thick slabs are found in it, lying on each other as if they had been cut and stacked under the ground. A camel carries two slabs. The only people living there are the slaves of the Massufa, who dig for the salt. The Blacks come from their country to Taghaza and take away the salt ... The Blacks trade with salt as others trade with gold and silver; they cut it in pieces and buy and sell with these. For all its squalor, *qintars* of *qintars* of gold dust are traded in Taghaza.

For many centuries salt and slaves were inextricably intertwined in the nexus of Saharan trade. You could not have one without the other. Travelling in Upper Senegal in 1689–90, Cornelius Hodges of the English Royal African Company reported that the 'salt of ye Moors' was being transported more than 1,000 miles by camel and traded for gold, slaves and clothes. Some of the caravans were vast, stretching into several thousand camels, each animal plodding gamely along beneath two slabs of salt weighing a total of 180 kilograms. In around 1810, the merchant Al Haj Shabeeny reported that a merchant could turn a profit of 50 per cent on salt when trading it in Timbuktu for slaves, gold dust, ivory and pepper. In the 1840s, the French explorer Anne Raffenel said he was unable to purchase even a grain of salt unless he had a slave to sell. Even allowing for the exaggeration of a nineteenth-century European explorer writing about the slave trade, it remains a revealing comment.[26]

Ahmed Lamine ech Chenguiti was a writer from the Adrar Plateau, the northern Mauritanian region of the Sahara. The author of a 1911 study of this West African country, he noted that historically salt was the 'principal object' of commerce there, traded for slaves in Sudan. Brought east in camel caravans, 'On arrival in the Sudan, the bars were deposited and cut according to the contour of the foot of the slave to be traded, the piece taken from the bar representing the price of the slave. It was said that a slave sold himself by the measure of his foot.' Such were the inflationary pressures on the price of slaves – driven upwards by the international trend towards abolition – that by the time the author was writing, a slave of either sex cost an entire camel load of salt, never mind a piece the size of a footprint. Even so, salt was still used to buy everything from slaves to horses, millet to cloth. 'It is said that some trade their children for salt.'[27]

When they were not climbing date palms, risking their lives underground cleaning out wells, satiating their masters' sexual needs, tending to livestock or keeping the house clean, Saharan slaves might also be found collecting gum Arabic from acacia trees. In the 1820s, the French explorer René Caillié, the first European to return alive from Timbuktu (the British officer Major Gordon Laing had pipped him to the post but was murdered in the town in 1826), observed slaves performing this work in Brakna, south-western Mauritania. Each slave was supplied with a milk cow for food, a pair of sandals and a couple of small leather sacs. 'Each morning, the slaves fill their leather sacs with water, and armed with a forked stick, tramp the fields in search of gum,' he wrote. 'The marabout overseer receives a tax which he levies on the gum: the slaves work five days for their master, and the sixth is for the benefit of the overseer.' Travelling in Mauritania a generation later, in 1860, another Frenchman, Antoine-Édouard Bourrel, wrote of a tribal confederation of marabout holy men who sent their slaves to collect gum for six months between January and June. Ostensibly pious and God-fearing, they were also 'very concerned with worldly goods and have many slaves'.[28]

Another man who was similarly concerned with material goods and also owned large numbers of slaves in this part of Africa around this time was the Emir of Kano, a Muslim vassal state in northern Nigeria, formed in 1805 after Fulani jihadists defeated the Hausa-led sultanate of Kano and integrated it into the Sokoto caliphate, the largest Islamic empire in West Africa. One of his slaves, a man called Malam Isyaku, was interviewed by a young researcher, Yusufu Yunusa, in 1975, by which time he was aged ninety.[29]

Isyaku had worked as an overseer in charge of day-to-day operations at the emir's royal estate at Dorayi, a privileged position he had inherited from his father. He was one of seventy slaves cultivating the land – planting locust bean trees and crops like groundnuts, cassava, millet and guinea corn, much of it given to the horses of the royal stable. Isyaku told Yunusa that ordinary slaves who had managed to save enough money could in theory buy their freedom from their master. However, this did not apply to those slaves who worked for the royal family.

Q: They couldn't take money to the Emir and ask for their freedom?
A: No.
Q: They, therefore, remained here forever?
A: They remained here forever, and that is all.

In the town of Kano (northern Nigeria) there was one dominant slave-dealer, his namesake Isyaku. The elderly man told Yunusa that in earlier times many war captives were routinely killed rather than enslaved. Half a century later, you can almost hear the incredulity in Yunusa's next question. 'Why were the victims simply not enslaved?' Isyaku's answer was equally to the point. 'Where will they be enslaved? Slaves were numerous, mister, slaves were numerous.'

His point was that there was a glut of slaves in those days. Isyaku was recalling the period beginning in the 1880s, when the notorious Sudanese warlord and slave-trader Rabih al Zubayr ran amok across a swathe of sub-Saharan Africa, conquering Muslim Borno in 1893, carving out an empire east of Lake Chad and enslaving huge numbers of his fellow Muslim Africans.* Rabih routinely branded slaves, Isyaku explained. 'Such slaves were tied up and an iron instrument placed in the fire to tattoo the slaves.' Royal slaves received three marks on the lower part of their face.

Slaves for sale were generally put in chains and lined up in Kurmi market in groups of about 100, both men and women, having first

---

* Rabih, one of the most brutal slavers of his generation, lived by the sword and died by it. He was killed fighting the French colonial forces of the Central African Mission on 22 April 1900.

A soldier from the Central Africa Mission holds aloft the severed head of Rabih al Zubayr, a notorious African slaver on 22 April 1900.

had ash rubbed on their faces – a sign they were available for purchase. A slave typically cost 200,000 cowries.

Isyaku spoke matter-of-factly about the richest man in Kano, a merchant called Kundila who was the biggest local slave-owner bar none:

> There was no one in Kano with Kundila's wealth. Kundila was very rich and had estates by each of the city gates. When you see him, you see an ordinary person on his horse. But then you are told he is Kundila. He himself did not know precisely how many slaves he had. Hence, he usually asked his slaves questions like: how many are you in that estate of mine? Are you up to a hundred slaves there? In some cases, slaves informed him that, 'Master we are more than that.' You don't ask about the number of slaves in Kundila's house. Slaves were from everywhere. Some were Barawa, some Adamawa. They were all there. There was no ethnic group that was not there. That is Kundila. He bought all his slaves.

Isyaku was interviewed at the same time as a man who occupied a position right at the other end of the social and economic spectrum. Malam Idrisu was then a blue-blooded, seventy-seven-year-old grandee, great-grandson of a powerful Kano royal slave official. A few of his remarks are instructive in revealing attitudes towards slaves and slavery from those who owned them. He also freely acknowledged that the conflicts and slave-raiding which he had lived through pitted Muslims against Muslims:

Q: What was the slave's view or idea on slavery?

A: Slavery was never happily embraced. People were usually forced into bondage. Slaves disliked slavery. Does anyone like slavery?

Q: Was it possible for a slave to prevent his master from selling him?

A: If that was possible, that means no one can sell a slave if a slave was against the act. But that was not possible since it was the master who decided what to do with the slave. The slave is the master's property. Is it possible for a sheep to prevent its owner from selling it?

Idrisu gave short shrift to European interference and the subsequent abolition of the slave trade:

Q: When the Europeans abolished slavery, how did the slaves react?

A: Some were happy, while some were angry and questioned the rationale behind it. The Europeans gave papers to many symbolizing their freedom, and that nobody should be called a slave. They gathered all slaves including the royal ones and gave them their paper of freedom. Yet after collecting the paper some of the slaves said: 'What a useless statement, what business do we have with them?' All the royal slaves were given such paper, including their descendants. They were all given freedom papers by the colonialists.

Q: But the non-native slaves, didn't they go back to their towns?

A: Where will they go? Will a person go back into hardship? Isn't here, where they were slaves, better than their towns?

Q: The slaves' towns?

A: Yes. A person who was in a bad place and brought to the city where he ate what was good; he had no clothing before he came here. Would you then say that such a person should go back to his town? Those who went back were those who knew that they would be better off if they went back. Coupled with the fact that they knew their way back. But would a contented slave go back to his town? That is a joke.

For those African men, women and children who had survived the bloody slaving raids and were forced to cross the Sahara on their way to a new life of servitude, whatever work they were destined to perform in whichever country, the conditions they encountered were harsh beyond belief. Many had to endure torments that, especially for the youngest and weakest, commonly proved fatal.

Again, the sources are overwhelmingly nineteenth-century European travellers, campaigning abolitionists among them. Take the English explorer Dixon Denham, later a short-lived governor of Sierra Leone, who had met George Francis Lyon in London after the latter's unsuccessful attempt to chart the course of the Niger with the late Joseph Ritchie. In 1822, Denham joined the follow-up British mission into Central Africa with Walter Oudney and Hugh Clapperton and the following year the trio became the first Europeans to set eyes on Lake Chad. While in Kuka, capital of Bornu, the impetuous Denham accompanied a slave-raiding mission into Mandara (Cameroon) against the strong advice of his fellow travellers and only narrowly escaped death. Later, during the winter of 1823–4, he travelled with a southbound caravan heading from Tripoli to Bornu. It included thirty freed slaves, one of whom was a deaf woman who had endured unimaginable suffering during her long journey:

> She had left two children behind her; and the third, which was in her arms when she was taken by the Arabs, had been torn from her breast after the first ten days of her journey across the desert, in order that she might keep up with the camels. Her expressive motions in describing the manner in which the child was forced from her, and thrown on the sand, where it was left to perish, while whips were applied to her, lame and worn out as she was, to quicken her tottering steps, were highly eloquent and interesting.[30]

The German Bohemian explorer Ignaz Pallme, who travelled in Kordofan (present-day Sudan) in 1837, observed for himself the aftermath of a slave raid by what he called 'the hard-hearted Turks' in the Nuba Mountains of South Kordofan:

> No pen can describe what cruelties these poor creatures, who were already cast down on account of the loss of their goods, and especially the loss of their liberty, had to suffer on their way. Partly with the heavy *sheba* round their necks, or tied together two and two, with strong leather strings, or their hands fastened within clasps;* these poor negroes

---

* A *shayba* was a forked branch of wood used to yoke two slaves together by their necks.

were driven along like cattle, and treated with far less indulgence, and much more severity. Most of them covered with wounds which they had received in the battle, or from the friction of the *sheba*, the leather strings, or the clasps, had to suffer the most excruciating pains, and if they became too exhausted to keep pace with the others, still greater sufferings awaited them.[31]

The savage reality of this form of desert travel was that those who were unable to keep up with the caravan were left to die where they fell.

A decade after Pallme's travels, the outspoken English explorer and abolitionist James Richardson, who considered the slave trade 'the most gigantic system of wickedness the world ever saw', was travelling by caravan from the southern Libyan oasis of Ghat to Murzuq with a slave-trader called Haj Ibrahim.

On the morning of 11 February 1846, the day after the death of a young female slave who had been ill for a month, he spotted an eleven-year-old slave girl who was also very unwell. Having recommended to Haj Ibrahim that he leave her to be treated, a few moments later Richardson discovered what kind of treatment the slave-dealer had in mind. 'I heard the noise of whipping, and turning round to my great surprise, I saw the Haj beating her not very mercifully,' he wrote. 'He had a whip of bull's hide with which he gave her several lashes.' The sick girl died soon after this whipping. 'If Haj Ibrahim, who is a good master, can treat his slaves thus, what may we not expect from others less humane?' Richardson asked his readers. 'There is no doubt but that the whipping of this poor creature hastened her death. She was, indeed, whipped at the point of death.'

At the end of his first African mission, Richardson returned from Murzuq to Tripoli with a slave-dealer called Essnoussee, witnessing once again the sort of treatment that could be meted out to a defence-less charge by a cruel master:

> I then saw Essnoussee bringing up a slave girl about a dozen years of age, pulling her violently along. When he got her up to the camel, he took a small cord and began tying it round her neck. Afterwards, bethinking himself of something, he tied the cord round the wrist of her right arm. This done, Essnoussee drove the camel on. In a few minutes she fell down, and the slave master, seeing her fallen down, and a man

attempting to raise her up, cried out, 'Let her alone, cursed be your father! You dog.' The wretched girl was then dragged on the ground over the sharp stones, being fastened by her wrist, but she never cried or uttered a word of complaint. Her legs now becoming lacerated and bleeding profusely, she was lifted up by Essnoussee's Arabs. Thus, she was dragged, limping and tumbling down, and crippled all the day, which was a very long day's journey.[32]

Richardson was emotional, irascible and impassioned. A cooler, calmer, more methodical and indeed greater explorer by far was his contemporary Heinrich Barth. The German was an accomplished multilingual scholar and anthropologist, selected to join Richardson's second mission, the Central African Expedition of 1850–55. This was commissioned by Lord Palmerston, the British foreign secretary, to explore sub-Saharan Africa 'in order that a more intimate knowledge may thus be obtained of the state of those Countries, their Production, and commercial Resources and also with a view to substitute legitimate Commerce for the Traffic in Slaves in the Interior of Africa, by encouraging an exchange of the Productions of those Countries for the Production of Europe'.[33]

Britain was already well on its way to extracting such 'intimate knowledge'. In 1840 it had opened a vice-consulate in Murzuq. Between 1843 and 1854, to give one example, Giambattista Gagliuffi, its vice-consul, provided a steady stream of information about the numbers of enslaved men, women and children arriving in the town. The lowest figure for a year was 1,105 (1845), the highest 2,900 (1854). The total was 17,744 over ten years (information was missing in 1850 and 1851), giving an annual average of 1,774. 'To be moved to compassion towards them, one must be an eyewitness, as I am, and see in what state these wretched slaves do arrive from the Interior; certainly they would move to pity even a slave,' he wrote. 'They are naked, and only a small piece of rag, or a skin, covers their genitals.'[34]

After Richardson and then his German colleague Adolf Overweg died near Lake Chad, the Englishman succumbing to heat exhaustion and fever, his fellow traveller likely to malaria, Barth pressed on, eventually travelling an extraordinary 10,000 miles overland. He journeyed across the Sahara, surveyed the country from Lake Chad and Bagirmi on the east to Timbuktu on the west, south as far as Cameroon, and compiled a series of local histories and vocabularies as he journeyed among the ancient sultanates of Bornu, Kano, Sokoto, Gando, Nupe and Timbuktu.

Barth's five-volume, 3,500-page crowning work, *Travels and Discoveries in North and Central Africa*, published in 1857–9, was a masterpiece of historical, geographical, topographical, anthropological, commercial and philological research, enlivened with some magnificent, highly evocative plates. It revealed the inner workings of an intensely humane figure, ahead of his time in the respect shown to the Africans among whom he travelled, the numerous friendships he made among them and his fascination with their history, cultures and languages. Though a stretching read with diminished modern attention spans, it remains an important reference point to this day.*

Barth was an acutely observant eyewitness of the desert slave trade during his long travels. He was particularly affected by the *razzia* raids: 'There can be no doubt that the most horrible topic connected with slavery is slave-hunting; and this is carried on not only for the purpose of supplying the foreign market, but, in a far more extensive degree, for supplying the wants of domestic slavery.' He watched the dividing up of slaves after one raid, noting 'the most heart-rending scenes, caused by the number of young children, and even infants, who were to be distributed, many of these poor creatures being mercilessly torn away from their mothers, never to see them again'. Later he accompanied a Bornu-led raid in which he estimated that 3,000 'pagan' slaves were taken, mostly old women who had not been able to escape the sudden attack. Some were 'so decrepit that they were scarcely able to walk – mere skeletons, who, in their almost total nakedness, presented a horrible sight'. Around 300 adult males who had resisted and been taken prisoner had been slaughtered. The commander of the *razzia* received a third of the slaves captured, prompting Barth to lament 'the endless misery into which the finest and most populous regions of this continent are plunged by the slave-hunting expeditions of their merciless Mohammedan neighbours'.[35]

* Barth is remembered, among other ways, in the Heinrich Barth Institute of Archaeology and Environmental History of Africa at the University of Cologne.

One of the last Europeans to travel in the Libyan Sahara during the final decades of the desert slave trade was Gustav Nachtigal, a German military surgeon and explorer, who reached Murzuq in 1869, sixty-two years after the trade had been legally abolished in London. 'No merchant, to be sure, can any longer enter the towns and visit their markets with hundreds of slaves,' he wrote. 'But the smaller slave troops of the minor merchants can easily be accommodated in the gardens of the towns, whether in Murzuq or Tripoli, and in the neighbouring villages, and disposed of clandestinely.' He estimated the number of slaves passing through Fezzan annually at 1,700–2,700 at most. Although local government officials were frequently directed by Tripoli to stop the trade, such orders were more for foreign than domestic consumption. Poorly paid officials were easy targets for bribes from slave-dealers.

Nachtigal's account of the trade differed from the chronicles of cruelty presented by Denham, Pallme, Richardson and Barth among others and stressed the 'mild administration of the institution of slavery', which the German believed derived both from the precepts of Islam and the good-natured character of the people of Fezzan. 'Slaves are treated quite as members of the family and have nothing to complain of,' he argued.[36]

While there is a debate to be had over the nature of slavery within the Muslim world and a recognition that in some instances within a family it could be relatively benign, Nachtigal's conclusion seems both complacent and hard-hearted. It may be true, too, that Tuareg slave-drivers treated their charges more humanely than did their Tubu counterparts. But a more modern verdict on the desert slave trade is surely closer to the mark than that offered by the German. For many slaves the long and deadly trek across the Sahara involved 'a level of mistreatment in every way comparable with the worst excesses of the Atlantic slave trade'.[37]

'Talking about slavery in Morocco is taboo,' Maha Marouan writes. 'It is not included in educational curricula despite the fact that the trans-Saharan slave trade lasted centuries and has shaped who we are as a people. It is also difficult to talk about slavery because we are a Muslim nation who enslaved other Muslim nations – a practice that is strictly prohibited in Islam.'

Discussing the legacy of slavery in Morocco not only poses distinctly uncomfortable questions about the nation's history and religious discourse but also 'makes us uneasy about our genealogies'.[38]

There is certainly no doubting the longevity or scale of Morocco's involvement in the desert slave trade. 'Moroccan merchants carry with them wool, copper and glassware and bring back gold and captives,' the North African Arab geographer Al Idrisi (1100–65) wrote almost 900 years ago, adding that 'a considerable number' of slaves left for the Maghreb every year.[39]

Marouan, a Professor of African American Studies and Women Studies at Pennsylvania State University, was determined to break the 'systemic silence' surrounding the legacy of the trans-Saharan slave trade in Morocco. In a country where the full magnitude of this trade is still not acknowledged, researching the hushed-up story of her great-grandmother, a slave from Senegal, is 'an act of resistance to forgetting'. With no joy to be had in either historical material or archives, no pictures in family photograph albums, Marouan can only trace the faintest outlines of a life lived on the margins. She cannot even retrieve the woman's name, nor come close to answering questions such as how her great-grandmother came to be separated from her family, whether she married Marouan's great-grandfather by choice and how his pregnant wife managed alone when he divorced her on the orders of his scandalized mother.

Perhaps this unknown woman's most abiding legacy, a century later in a country 'defined by colour lines', is the shame of dark skin which remains 'a thorn in our family's history'. Morocco, Marouan argues powerfully, has yet to come to terms with its history in the Saharan slave trade – as the title of the late Moroccan writer Abd al Karim Ghallab's celebrated 1966 novel has it, *Dafanna al Madi (We Buried the Past)*. Distancing itself from the uncomfortable memory of slavery, Marouan writes, translates into 'a frantic distancing from blackness by all means: whitening creams, facial scrubs, hair straighteners, and a careful construction of ethnic and cultural identity that excludes a large number of our descent: the thousands of sub-Saharan Africans brought to Morocco through the trans-Sahara slave trade'.

In recent years a new generation of scholars is setting about tackling a history that has been not so much contested as almost entirely neglected. In Marouan's words, even discussing slavery is 'taboo'. Chouki el Hamel, author of *Black Morocco*, a groundbreaking study of slavery, race and Islam published in 2013, lifted the lid on this vexed and little-explored territory in an effort to 'recover the silenced histories of slavery in North Africa'.[40] At the centre of his story is his anti-hero, Sultan Moulay Ismail – the captor of, among 25,000 other European slaves, Joseph Pellow, the Cornish lad taken at sea in 1715. That was merely the tip of the iceberg, of course. Ismail enslaved a far larger number of black people – 221,320 according to El Hamel – on the grounds of their skin colour alone, no matter how many of them were free Muslims and therefore protected from enslavement. This colossal enterprise, El Hamel argues, reinforced prejudices towards black people and negatively shaped their image in Morocco up to the present day.

Moulay Ismail's slave-collecting and bloodletting notoriety cannot obscure the wider reality that 'the tragic heroine in Moroccan slavery is female'. For many centuries untold numbers of women like Marouan's great-grandmother – name unknown – were subjected to lives of exploitation, demanding physical labour and sexual violence both within Morocco and far beyond it. Richardson accused Tubu slave-drivers of raping extremely young girls during the forced march across the desert. 'The Tibboos cannot bring a female child over The Desert of the tender age of six or seven, without deflowering her,' he claimed, adding that many Tubu slave-dealers engaged in the trade purely for this purpose:

> A slave-dealer will convey a score or two of female slaves from Mourzuk to Tripoli, and change the unhappy objects of his brutal lust every night. This is, he considers, the *summum bonum* of human existence, and to obtain it, he will continue this nefarious trade, without the smallest gain, or prospect of gain, and die a beggar when his vile passions become extinct.

Johann Ludwig Burckhardt, the Swiss explorer and Arabist, last encountered visiting a castration centre in Upper Egypt in 1813–14, made a similar charge. He had, he wrote, 'frequently witnessed scenes of the most shameless indecency' during his journey to the Red Sea port of Suakin in Sudan. Contrary to what caravan traders in Egypt liked to claim, the slave-dealers did not observe 'the slightest decorum in their intercourse with the slave-girls'. So much so, that 'very few female slaves who have passed their tenth year, reach Egypt or Arabia in a state of virginity'. Such behaviour – rape – was only encouraged by the common saying among Saharan slave-traffickers that the cure for venereal disease was sex with a virgin slave girl.[41]

The Saharan slave trade did not die a natural death. Under unrelenting European pressure, it withered for decades in the nineteenth century before eventually dying in the twentieth. During that long, slow, painful death rattle, as more and more swathes of Africa were passing with violence into European hands, many Arabs found themselves 'wondering if abolitionism was imperialism spelled differently'.[42] For a good deal of them it proved to be two sides of the same coin. Either way, few would have predicted that well into the twenty-first century, and more than 200 years after Britain had abolished the slave trade, modern slavery and people-trafficking across the Sahara would be back with a vengeance.

10

The Ottomans:
A Lordship of Slaves

. . . this is a lordship or republic of slaves . . .
A Venetian *bailo* (ambassador) talking about the
Janissaries and the Ottoman Empire

*The scholarly study of the history of slavery in Ottoman
society – and in Muslim societies as a whole – is characterized
by a deafening silence, which is only seldom broken by lone
voices.*

Ehud R. Toledano, *Slavery and Abolition
in the Ottoman Middle East*, 1998

'I'm a descendant of a slave, I'm one-sixteenth Greek. My great-great-grandfather Ibrahim Edhem Pasha was Greek. In 1822, when he was around three years old, he was captured by Ottoman soldiers on Chios and sold into slavery.'

Edhem Eldem, sixty-something doyen of Turkish historians, is at home in his third-floor apartment in Moda, a fashionable, bar-and-restaurant-thronged district on the Asian side of Istanbul. Through the windows behind him, beyond the historic pier, ferries ply the seagull-crowded waters of the Bosphorus beneath a late-summer sky. We are here to talk about Ottoman slavery.

For almost 500 years, from the mid-fifteenth century to its unhappy demise in the immediate aftermath of the First World War, the Ottoman Empire was the most significant Muslim power on earth. It encompassed a vast body of land stretching across three continents, from southern Poland in the north to Sudan in the south, from the Persian Gulf and the Arabian Peninsula in the east to the shores of North Africa in the western Mediterranean. And it needed slaves.[1]

They came in their thousands. Year after year, from all corners of the empire and far beyond. They came by land and sea, in chains and under the stinging whips of Arab, African and Tatar slavers. They came to the heart of the Ottoman Empire because the transcendent power of the Islamic world had an insatiable appetite for enslaved men, women and children.

African slaves came from Wadai, Bornu and Bagirmi in Central Africa, from Kordofan, Darfur and the White and Blue Nile Basins in Sudan, stumbling across the Sahara in a desert death march that destroyed untold numbers of them. Ethiopian slaves headed north on less dangerous routes by land across the plains and in boats along the Red Sea and up the Nile. Some Africans found themselves struggling along the *hajj* pilgrimage routes across the Arabian Peninsula, still others sailed up the Persian Gulf. More expensive, pale-skinned Circassians and Georgians came south from the Caucasus across the Black Sea and the Mediterranean. From the rugged mountains of the Dinaric Alps on the Dalmatian coast of the Adriatic came a flood tide of Slavs, first enslaved by the Ottomans during their earliest thrust into Bosnia in 1415. Greeks, including Eldem's great-great-grandfather, came in large numbers over several centuries from the Greek islands and mainland. All roads, and sea voyages, led to Istanbul, the City of the World's Desire.[2]

The frequency of manumission, an act of relative mercy, itself stimulated this endless demand for new blood. So too did the legal convention, first, that any child born of a master-slave union was free and not a slave and second, that a slave woman who bore her master a child was herself freed on his death. Thus however 'compassionate' was the Ottoman model of slavery, as its defenders have argued, 'humanity at home inadvertently perpetuated the brutality from without'. The system required the constant replenishment of human capital, and that in turn meant a continuous cycle of brutal slave raids in Africa, Asia and Europe alike, followed by the cruel and often fatal transport of these human cargoes to the heart of empire.[3]

How many came? Easy to ask, the question is largely impossible to answer. Estimating the volume of slave-trafficking into the Ottoman

Empire across several centuries is notoriously difficult for reasons already stated. It is only in the nineteenth century that statistics can start to be treated with a greater degree of credibility. For the most part we must make do with piecemeal figures covering a certain region during a certain period, rather than a universal figure across the entire duration and geography of the empire.

Thus the number of African slaves exported to Ottoman Egypt alone between 1820 and 1900 has been estimated at 362,000. For the entire nineteenth century, the total for those who went across the Red Sea and the Gulf of Aden in a mostly Ottoman trade is reckoned to be around 492,000, with the numbers of Africans taken to Ottoman Algeria, Libya and Tunisia during the same period totalling 350,000. For the Ottoman Empire writ large, across the first seventy years of the same century, which was peak slave trade, the average number of slaves imported annually has been reckoned at 16,000–18,000, giving a rough figure of around 1.2 million.[4]

These are inevitably incomplete, imprecise and unsatisfactory figures. Nevertheless, they powerfully suggest the scale of both the trade and the empire's consumption of slaves. The Ottoman Empire was on the march economically in the nineteenth century and the demand for slaves – whose prices had fallen due to the decline of the Atlantic trade – was correspondingly buoyant. Of course, the Ottoman slave trade in Africa was not the sole operator in the continent. There was, first of all, the larger internal African market and second, the better-known Atlantic trade to the Americas and the Caribbean. And the Ottoman trade, while dominating the Muslim slave trade in Africa, did not account for all the slave exports. The Indian, Iranian and Moroccan markets continued to make their own demands on African human capital.

For Greeks at least, the date of Eldem's ancestor's enslavement lives on in infamy. Up to 20,000 Greeks were slaughtered – hanged, starved and tortured to death – in the 1822 Massacre at Chios, a bloody chapter in the Greek War of Independence which shocked and disgusted Europe. Two years later, the French Romantic artist Eugène Delacroix depicted this inferno of suffering in *Scene of the Massacre at Chios*, a vast, horror-filled painting. Untold numbers of islanders were raped and deported. The island itself was devastated and many of its fine Venetian and Genoese buildings were destroyed. So many Chiots were enslaved during the brutal suppression of the island revolt that Greek captives-turned-slaves were sold for a song, as little as fifty *kuruş*, or around 10 per cent of what a mid-ranking official, such as the warden overseeing Istanbul's slave market, might have earned in a month.[5]

One of them was a Greek Orthodox toddler, name unknown, the future Ibrahim Edhem Pasha. His great-great-grandson picks up the story:

> He was purchased by Husrev Pasha, grand admiral of the Ottoman fleet and a future grand vizier of the Ottoman Empire, who was then a childless man in his late sixties – he was of servile origin, too – and taken into his household. At some point, probably when the boy was in his early teens and by now a Muslim convert called Ibrahim, he was sent, together with three fellow slaves belonging to Husrev, to be educated in France. Years later, having completed his studies at the École des Mines, he returned to Istanbul a qualified engineer – and then he began his steady ascension

Edhem Pasha (1818?–93) in his library, 1880s. Enslaved as a child when the Ottomans took Chios in 1822, Ibrahim Edhem Pasha became an Ottoman statesman of Greek origin, rising to the office of Grand Vizier between 1877–8.

through the state bureaucracy, using his intelligence, knowledge and education to get ahead. He started in the palace as a tutor to the sovereign and his sons and in 1856 was promoted to the rank of vizier with the title of pasha. And then he embarked on this long career as a statesman, first as a governor, then an ambassador to Berlin and Vienna, later as minister of the interior and, in 1877–8, his crowning appointment – grand vizier.[6]

Edhem Eldem, in other words, this urbane Professor of History with a distinguished international chair at the Collège de France, is the descendant of both a slave *and* a grand vizier, the most powerful official within the empire after the sultan – not two different men, but one and the same individual. It is an arresting introduction to the complex, fluid, multifarious and extremely long-lived system of slavery in the Ottoman Empire.

Notwithstanding Eldem's illustrious great-great-grandfather's career and the distinction of some of his descendants – the pasha's son Osman Hamdi Bey was a pioneer of Ottoman modernization, an early painter in the Western tradition and founding father of Ottoman archaeology, while another son, Ismail Galib Bey, is considered the creator of numismatics in Turkey – there is no question of this historian romanticizing or idealizing the rags-to-riches story, or of using it as a representative example of Ottoman slavery. 'For every little Greek boy who was lucky enough to become a pasha, thousands of adults were slaughtered and thousands of other little boys and girls were destined to spend the rest of their lives as domestic slaves or inmates of harems,' he cautions. 'We mustn't forget all those who never made it.'

There is another danger here, too. Turkish historiography, Edhem insists, has tended towards the default setting of denial. Yes there was slavery, the argument goes, but the Ottoman version of it was inherently benign and usually ended through manumission after seven to ten years, conversion to Islam and social and financial elevation. Stories like the unstoppable rise of Ibrahim Edhem Pasha have been used – especially in response to largely Western attacks – to demonstrate the extraordinarily meritocratic nature of Ottoman slavery, its rejection of lineage, its proud position as the very antithesis of aristocracy based on bloodlines, and the spectacular possibilities for promotion it offered:

There's a view that slavery and the harm it caused have been exoticized by Western Orientalism – and Turkish historians have used that to create their own anti-Orientalist histories. So the women in the harem weren't exploited, it wasn't the daily orgy Westerners love to perceive, it was a fully feminine world, run by women, more like an elite finishing school. It's all denial, everything is benign, but at the same time, there's always a half-truth about it, too.

A younger generation of Turkish historians are taking an increasing interest in the story of Ottoman slavery and considering it from a fresh perspective, more challenging of the status quo. Some are finding that old attitudes die hard. 'When I suggested a thesis on state war captives, the professor who would have been my supervisor dismissed the idea immediately,' recalls Nida Nebahat Nalçacı, a historian at Bilkent University in Ankara specializing in the study of slavery. He told me: "Our ancestors treated their slaves very well – don't waste your time with this".'[7] While such attitudes evidently persist, the charge of 'deafening silence' levelled by the historian Ehud Toledano back in 1998, cited at the beginning of this chapter, no longer holds a generation later. Scholars from Turkey and far beyond continue to plough fertile new furrows in the history of slavery in Ottoman society. The silence has become a welcome cacophony.*

It is all too easy to be attracted by the slave-turned-grandee stories, such as those of Ibrahim Edhem Pasha, because they *are* so sensational. They challenge our understanding of the nature of slavery, based so heavily as it is on the American plantation system fed by the Atlantic trade. They completely reverse our notion of the power dynamic inherent in slavery and the total domination and oppression on which it is based. They completely refute what Orlando Patterson, author of a seminal comparative study of slavery, referred to as the 'social death' which servitude inflicted upon its victims. Such

---

* Turkish scholars include Halil İnalcik, Omer Lutfi Barkan, Halil Sahillioglu, Metin Kunt, Ismail Parlatir and Gulnihal Bozkurt. In more recent times there has been a surge of interest, with revisionist accounts by Y. Hakan Erdem, Ceyda Karamursel, Baki Tezcan, Nida Nebahat Nalçacı, Gülay Yılmaz, Betül İpşirli Argıt, Özgür Kolçak, Ayten Kiriş Avaroğulları and Muhammet Avaroğulları. Some writers, such as Ahmet Akgunduz, maintain a traditional apologist line.

Ottoman slave-VIPs, by comparison, were so socially alive that they were more than capable of dominating the societies in which they lived. And they serve as a reminder, too, that the particular and far better-known form of slavery in the Americas is just one among many versions of servitude around the world.

We must acknowledge at the same time that the moth-like histor-ian is also attracted to stories such as the little Greek child slave who became the second most pre-eminent man in the Ottoman Empire for the compelling reason that such celebrated lives are well illuminated and documented. There is no shortage of them, either. Ottoman history teems with Ibrahim Edhem Pashas who stamped their mark across all walks of life. Three centuries before him, a little Christian boy from a small town called Agirnas in central Anatolia was 'harvested' into the army. After years in his chrysalis of professional training, the butterfly that was Mimar Sinan (c.1490–1588) emerged in full glory. He became the greatest Ottoman architect without exception, redefining the built environment and city skylines across the Islamic world, and was the visionary behind a long list of masterpieces scattered across the empire. They included the sky-grazing Suleimaniye and Selimiye Mosques in Istanbul and Edirne, the classically elegant Mehmed Pasha Sokolović Bridge (named after another boy-slave-turned-grand-vizier) across the River Drina in Bosnia and Herzegovina, and the little gem that is the Ayasofya Hurrem Sultan Hamami bathhouse (named after the spell-binding woman who rose from being a slave concubine to a position of preeminence within the Ottoman Empire at the peak of its power).

Then again, there was Mullah Ali, a black African slave-turned-Ottoman judge, who scandalized European ambassadors in Istanbul in 1613 when he threw into prison a Venetian merchant who refused to pay a suddenly imposed poll tax. Who was this 'black Moore' to throw his weight about, wondered Paul Pindar, the ambassador of King James I of England and Scotland? Ali had the last laugh. By 1621 he had been promoted to chief judge and member of the imperial council, a spectacular elevation for a former slave. He took pride in his career and wrote the treatise *Dispelling the Darkness on the Merits of the Ethiopians*, a seventeenth-century Ottoman reprise of the famous essay by Jahiz on the 'Superiority of the Blacks over the Whites'.[8]

The tendency to focus on these counter-intuitive stories, packed with colour and drama, is understandable, though they inevitably distract from all those whose stories have not survived, those who lived their lives, in the title of a recent study, 'as if silent and absent', as though they had never even existed.[9]

All these slaves, whether they scaled the highest peaks of political, social and financial life or trudged anonymously at the lowest levels of society, form an inextricable part of Ottoman history. Slavery, whichever form it took, is a tightly woven thread that runs through and binds together all seven centuries of the Ottoman Empire, from the earliest days of raiding and territorial expansion through its imperial heyday of glorious conquest and on to its final collapse.

Slaves witnessed the birth of the Turkman warrior Osman's (c. 1280–1323/4) great dream of empire in the thirteenth century and slaves were on hand to record its tumultuous death throes in the early twentieth, as the harem eunuchs helped the revolutionaries uncover stashed-away royal loot. If it is an exaggeration to suggest that the Ottoman Empire was a slave state – *au fond*, slavery here was too rarefied a phenomenon to define an entire society and, unlike the plantation version, never underpinned any system of mass production – slavery nevertheless inhered within the Ottoman Empire's very soul. The royal household *kapikulu* system of slavery alone, in which all power-wielding officials, from the most distant governors and military commanders in far-flung places to the viziers in the imperial palace in Istanbul, up to and including men like Ibrahim Edhem Pasha, were the sultan's slave-servants, was completely fundamental to Ottoman rule. It was, in the words of Halil İnalcik, perhaps the greatest Turkish historian of the empire, 'the foundation stone of the Ottoman state'.[10]

It is worth emphasizing, too, that from as early as the mid-fourteenth century the state had a vested financial interest in slavery and the slave trade. Around that time, it was reportedly levying official taxes on slave imports – the famous *pencik* tax, approximately one-fifth of the market value of every slave brought into Ottoman lands. This *ad valorem* tax on imported slaves remained in operation for half a millennium, until 1857. Without the *pencik varakası* title deed a slave could not be legally sold or transported within the empire. The document was also proof of the person's legal enslavement.[11]

The many manifestations of Ottoman slavery – from the refined captive beauties cloistered in the imperial harem, the sharp-elbowed slave-soldiers-turned-political-grandees and the physically tortured, often hugely influential palace eunuchs, to the less celebrated silk-weavers in Bursa and the completely unheralded domestic drudges, rope-makers, shipbuilders, sharecroppers, miners, carpenters, death-defying galley rowers and many more – resist easy generalization. The lives and stories of the great mass of slaves, men, women and children alike, may be virtually impossible to discern, but if we look and listen hard enough, from time to time we can find revealing snapshots of their experiences and, in all too rare instances, the poignant and unmistakable sound of their voices.

Where to begin? How to comprehend this vast terrain, which is both dizzyingly wide-ranging and as long-lasting as the empire itself? It makes sense to start with the rise of the Ottomans, even if the earliest days of the embryonic would-be empire under the expanding rule of its founder, Osman I, are shrouded in uncertainty. Just as the early Muslim Arabs inherited – and later adapted – the system of slavery from their pre-Islamic forebears, not to mention their Persian and Byzantine neighbours, so the Ottomans picked up where Muslim dynasties before them left off. Such examples were by no means confined to the past tense. Rival powers around the rising state, as Ibn Battuta would bear witness, continued to practise their own traditions of slavery.

Carving out a territory in the Anatolian heartland in the thirteenth century and beyond meant raiding, and raiding meant slaving. This was as natural to Osman's Muslim Turkmen warriors as it was to the seventh-century Arabs who brought Islam to the world. Was it not the sacred Quran, after all, which had legitimated holy war plunder? 'Whoever fights in the path of God, whether he be killed or be victorious, on him shall We bestow a great reward,' it promised. Just as the Prophet Mohammed retained a one-fifth share of all booty taken, so Osman and his successors as Ottoman sultan were entitled to the same percentage of the human harvest. Though it wavered over the centuries and was far less prevalent in the later Ottoman Empire than in the early period, slaving through raiding and conquest continued from the time of Osman through to bloody instances of mass enslavement, like the Massacre at Chios in the nineteenth century, and beyond abolition even into the early twentieth century and the empire's final fall.

Life on the frontiers of an emerging state could be extremely capricious. We have a rare European eyewitness from the fifteenth century who had the misfortune – or was it ultimately good fortune? – to experience slavery under the Ottomans and lived to tell his tale. Born sometime between 1430 and 1435, Konstantin Mihailović was a Serbian youth whose first-hand experience of Ottoman conquest and enslavement electrified his much later memoirs. As a soldier of the vassal Serbian state he claimed to have fought in the multi-ethnic army of Sultan Mehmed II which took Constantinople, eastern bastion of Christendom, after the history-changing siege of 1453. Then, in 1455, Mihailović and the fortress town of Novo Brdo in eastern Kosovo found themselves on the wrong end of another forty-day Ottoman siege. Eventually, on 1 June, the town bowed to the inevitable. The immediate consequences of defeat, Mihailović reported, were dire – mass execution and wholesale enslavement:

> After the city surrendered, the Sultan himself had the gates closed, leaving open only one exit. The survivors were told to walk through the gate and on the other side they were separated and placed into groups: boys in one area, girls in another, women in a third, and men in a fourth place. On the spot, he had the important men immediately beheaded. He then selected 320 boys and 704 girls. The girls he gave to his soldiers and took the boys for himself to become his Janissaries. The remainder were allowed to return to the city.[12]

Together with two of his brothers, Mihailović was one of the 'boys' taken to become a slave soldier or Janissary. In time he rose through the ranks and was promoted to a senior command in the cavalry, serving in campaigns against Vlad III 'The Impaler' of Wallachia and in Bosnia before being taken prisoner again, this time by Christian forces under the Hungarian King Matthias Corvinus (r. 1458–90), and finally repatriated. His memoirs, published in the final decade of the fifteenth century before his death in 1500, are as much incident-filled autobiography as an insider's practical manual for the Christian powers on how to defeat the Ottomans. As part of his wide-ranging observations, he noted the entrepreneurial relish with which the Ottomans embarked on slave-raiding:

> The Turkish raiders are voluntary – of their own will they ride on expeditions for their livelihood . . . They live by means of livestock and raise horses . . . If any of them does not want to go on a foray himself, he will lend his horses to others for half of the spoils; if they win some booty they accept it as good, but if they bring nothing, then they say 'We have no gain, but we have great works of piety, like those who toil with us and ride against the Christians, because we support one another.' And whatever they seize or capture, whether male or female except for boys, they will sell them all for money. The emperor himself will pay for the boys.[13]

It was around this time, certainly under the rule of Mehmed II, now revelling in the sobriquet Fatih, the Conqueror, after his brilliant conquest of Constantinople, that slaves began to be employed within the Ottoman bureaucracy for the first time. Before this, native Muslims, especially the *ulema* clergy, had traditionally formed the much smaller pool of talent from which senior officials were chosen.

It is likely that Mehmed had a very personal motivation to introduce reforms along these lines. In 1446, after only two years on the throne, he had been deposed, thanks in large part to the manoeuvrings of the Grand Vizier Çandarlı Halil, who came from a powerful family which had already supplied three grand viziers before him. When Mehmed returned to the throne in 1451 Çandarlı Halil opposed his plans to take Constantinople, arguing that the young sultan was rash and impetuous in his ambitions. Mehmed ignored the advice and stormed the Byzantine capital, a history-changing victory which had eluded would-be Muslim conquerors for almost 800 years. In the sunny afterglow of his do-or-die conquest, he had the elder statesman executed.

Mehmed's next innovation was to throw officialdom wide open to the slave class – so much so that his grand viziers over the next few decades, with a final and fateful exception, were overwhelmingly of slave origin. It set a precedent which quickly became the norm. Mehmed's last grand vizier was a man called Karamani Mehmed Pasha, who came from an old Konya family. The Conqueror's death in 1481 removed the statesman's royal protector, at which point he was murdered by the Janissaries who rose up against him, encouraged by the overlooked and under-promoted pashas of slave origin. In case Sultan Mehmed's successor, Bayezid II (r. 1481–1512), was in any doubt about what his slave soldiers and slave officials were planning, the unfortunate grand vizier's corpse was dragged through the streets to make it clear. Bayezid buckled, agreeing then to promote only men of slave origin to the grand vizierate. Of the first forty-eight grand viziers who served sultans after Mehmed's conquest of 1453, just five were native-born Turks. Little wonder, then, that some Turks referred to the sultan's imperial *divan*, or council, contemptuously as 'the slave market'.[14]

These traditions persisted far longer than might be expected. Four centuries later, the British naval officer Adolphus Slade, a regular visitor to Istanbul, reckoned that 80 per cent of the ministers in the council of the modernizing young Sultan Mahmud II (r. 1808–39) were 'purchased slaves'. Eight hundred miles to the south as the crow flies, it was more of the same in mid-nineteenth-century Ottoman Cairo, which took its lead from the imperial capital. Cairo remained one of the great depots and centres of the slave trade in the Muslim world well into the nineteenth century. When Nassau Senior, the British economist and lawyer, visited the city in the mid-1850s he spoke to Joseph Hekekyan Bey, an Armenian senior official in the administration. The latter went through all the cabinet ministers of Said Pasha (r. 1854–63) who were former slaves one by one and then added: 'In fact, Stephan Bey and Edhem Pasha are the only ministers that occur to me who have *not* been slaves – and I doubt their continuance in power. The *Liberti* will intrigue against the *Ingenui*, and drive them out.'[15]

It should not be a surprise to discover that those enslaved by the Ottomans tended to correlate closely with the trajectory of the expanding empire's conquests. Thus there were mass enslavements of southern Slavs and Greeks during the fourteenth and fifteenth centuries, of Austro-Germans, northern Slavs, Hungarians, Iranians and sub-Saharan Africans in the sixteenth and seventeenth during peak Ottoman power, and Abkhazes, Georgians and other Circassians in the eighteenth and nineteenth.*

---

* The word Circassian refers to a set of diverse ethnic and linguistic groups, including Abkhaz, Chechen, Kabarday, Ossetian, Ubykh and Adyghe, all originating in the Caucasus.

On 29 August 1526, a generation after the death of Konstantin Mihailović, an enormous Ottoman army under Sultan Suleiman the Magnificent (r. 1520–66) faced off against Hungarian and allied Christian forces at the Battle of Mohács. For Hungary, the defeat still represents a national trauma and a humiliating end of the country's greatness, remembered to this day in the popular expression about bad luck that 'more was lost at Mohács'. On a purely individual level, the calamitous defeat threw a page called Bertalan Georgievics, or Bartholomaeus Georgius Pannonius as he styled himself, into slavery. He was tied up or clapped into chains – his various accounts differ, suggesting a degree of unreliability and a canny eye for book sales – and forced to march east for a week before being taken to Macedonia by slave-traders who sold him to his first owner.

Between 1526 and 1539 Georgievics was bought and sold seven times, surviving several escape attempts, enduring regular beatings and remaining for more than a decade in a succession of servile, spirit-testing roles. He was, variously, a water-carrier, shepherd, horseman and farm labourer. He was also a one-man representation of the vicissitudes of Ottoman slavery, beaten one minute, treated kindly the next, launching a doomed escape bid one year, sold off to a new owner the next. During some of his regular attempts to win his freedom he was reduced to eating wild plants, roots and acorns to survive, almost freezing to death while sleeping virtually naked in the Armenian Mountains. Even allowing for the inevitable exaggeration, his time as a slave was an intensely dramatic experience which provided all the ingredients, as it had for Mihailović before him, of a successful book. And it came with a happy ending, too, since eventually he did manage to escape for good – and realized a long-standing dream to visit the Holy Sepulchre in Jerusalem, Santiago de Compostela in Spain and Rome.

Everything looked better in hindsight. 'As with seamen who gladly relate the hardships of a shipwreck afterwards, it is pleasant for me to remember the dangers endured in the Hungarian war, the hardest fetters, a captivity more severe than the Babylonian, a slavery full of all kinds of torture, and the changing fortune of my escape,' he wrote.[16] He died sometime after 1556, his works, which were published in multiple languages, remaining extremely popular for another 120 years.

Slave-taking may never again have reached the heights of these earliest Ottoman centuries, but it emphatically did not go away. In 1683, notwithstanding their defeat by the combined Christian forces of the Holy League at the two-month Siege of Vienna, a moment from when they 'ceased to be a menace to the Christian world', the Ottomans still managed to leave the battlefield, according to one account, with a staggering 81,000 captives – 50,000 children, 25,000 females and 6,000 adult males.[17] This defeat was the Ottoman's Ultima Thule in the north, a decisive turning point in the great 300-year struggle of the Ottoman–Habsburg Wars, a date from which the Holy Roman Empire began to push back against the encroaching tide in Hungary and Transylvania.

Nevertheless, slaving remained firmly on the Ottoman agenda. A century later in 1788, when an Ottoman army under Grand Vizier Koca Yusuf Pasha beat the Austrian forces near Klausenburg, another 50,000 women and children were thrown into slavery. Enslaving war captives was simply part and parcel of the Ottomans' modus operandi, as it had been of successive Arab and Muslim empires before them. And it continued, as evidenced on Chios and beyond, well into the nineteenth century, albeit on a reduced scale from the imperial heyday of the fifteenth and sixteenth centuries.

While prisoners of war represented the bulk of those enslaved by the Ottomans in the fourteenth century, the fifteenth and sixteenth centuries saw the rise of an additional new method of slaving within newly conquered regions. First started during the reign of Murad I (r. 1362–89), the *devshirme* was a 'harvest' or child levy of young, exclusively Christian boys from the Balkans – predominantly Serbs, Greeks and Albanians. Aged ideally between eight and ten but anywhere up to twenty, they were selected for their strength, looks, fitness, intelligence and ability by Ottoman military officers and commissioners. They were then enslaved, circumcised, converted to Islam and educated. Later, after six to eight years' service on Anatolian farms, they were brought to Istanbul to perform a variety of menial roles, from hauling ice and firewood to working on horse-transport ships, as palace gardeners, labourers on the sultan's many construction projects, sailors in the imperial navy or hospital attendants. Only after several more years of manual work would the best of the best be enrolled in the

Yeni Çeri – literally New Army – or Janissaries, initially an elite 7,000–20,000-strong infantry unit designed, through a process of intensive training and indoctrination, to be completely loyal to the sultan. At a less exalted level, those 'harvested' youths who didn't make the cut might be hired out to artisans, often working for years without pay. In time, some might become master artisans themselves.

The Janissaries won their laurels and proved their worth in quick order. With the fate of Constantinople in the balance in the early hours of 29 May 1453, as Mehmed's fortunes wavered on the brink of catastrophe, the Janissaries, 'men who were extremely well armed, daring and brave, and far in advance of the rest in experience and valor', were his final throw. They turned the tables decisively in the young sultan's favour, storming through the city walls, securing Mehmed's position at the head of the Ottoman Empire and winning him the most prestigious place in history. For many years to come, the Janissaries became the spearhead and prize fighting force of the Ottoman army and the terror of Europe. Their powers extended to maintaining security and law and order in Istanbul, patrolling the city's mighty ancient walls, which dated back to the reign of the boy emperor Theodosius II (r. 408–50), garrisoning the Yedikule Hisari, the Fortress of the Seven Towers, and serving as the sultan's fanatically loyal royal bodyguard. They grew steadily in size during the seventeenth century, doubling from 35,000 in 1597 to reach a peak fighting force of just under 70,000 a century later.[18]

Dating back to the reign of Osman's son, Sultan Orhan (r. 1324–62), when they were only several hundred-strong, the slave soldier Janissaries were also the first modern standing army in Europe. Sir Paul Rycaut, the seventeenth-century English diplomat and an astute historian of the Ottoman Empire, identified another aspect of the Janissaries which made them such an attractive force to the sultan. One of his chapters was entitled: 'The Education of young men in the *Seraglio*, out of which those who are to discharge the great Offices of the Empire are elected. It being a Maxime of the Turkish Policy, to have the Prince served by such whom he can *raise without Envy, and destroy without Danger* [my italics].'

Creating a new class of non-native Muslim converts diluted the power of the traditional, pre-Ottoman Turkish elite, many of whom were disaffected by the rapid rise of the dynasty which had displaced them from the centre of authority. As one palace insider wrote: 'There are few native-speaking Turks in the palace because the sultan finds himself more faithfully served by Christian converts who have neither hearth nor home nor parents nor friends. They conceive such an affection for his service that if it were in their power, they would voluntarily expose a thousand lives for the life of his person and the increase of his empire.' Rather than being crushed by their formal servitude, the Janissaries, according to one Venetian *bailo*, positively revelled in it. They 'take great pleasure in being able to say "I am a slave of the Grand Signior"', since they know that this is a lordship or republic of slaves where it is theirs to command'. Overall, Rycaut reckoned, this slave system, 'if well considered and weighed, is one of the most Politick constitutions in the world, and none of the meanest supports of the *Ottoman* Empire'.[19]

Politic it may undoubtedly have been, but whether or not the *devshirme* was strictly legal was another matter entirely. According to Islamic law, the non-Muslim *zimmis* (Turkish version of Arabic *dhimmis*), having acknowledged Muslim authority and in return for their payment of the *cizye (jizya)* tax, were officially protected and free. They certainly could not be enslaved. But the Ottomans were nothing if not pragmatic. Just as generations of Muslim leaders over many centuries could look the other way while droves of young boys were being castrated on the fringes of – sometimes within – their borders for slave service in royal courts, so a degree of post hoc legal sophistry could be deployed to move from treating Christians within Ottoman borders as de facto *zimmis* who paid the poll tax to enslaving them through the *devshirme* and then foregoing the traditional tax.

This was evidently a contentious issue and the Ottoman intelligentsia themselves were divided by such legal contortions. Mustafa Ali, the sixteenth-century writer and official, considered the enslavement of the boys 'at variance with the Divine Law', a verdict echoed half a millennium later by one scholar of Islamic history who thought it a 'flagrant contravention of the law'. Defenders of the system, on the other hand, argued that the very act of conquest of infidel lands turned the local population into slaves, and what could be more 'admissible and reasonable' than making these young men, newly converted to the one true faith, serve in the 'Holy War'?[20]

Legal or not, for many Christian families in the Balkans the *devshirme* was a family-splitting tragedy. In the region of Epirus, which straddles Greece and Albania between the Pindus Mountains and the Ionian Sea, resentment of this human harvest was acute. A popular folk song expressed both the community's pain and its passionate hatred of the Ottoman sultan:

> Be damned, O Emperor, be thrice damned
> For the evil you have done and the evil you do.
> You catch and shackle the old and the archpriests
> In order to take the children as Janissaries.
> Their parents weep and their sisters and brothers too
> And I cry until it pains me;
> As long as I live I shall cry,
> For last year it was my son and this year my brother.[21]

For other families, however, the *devshirme* was the best way out of rural impoverishment. Some parents volunteered their children to the Ottomans, well aware that excellent service in the sultan's military-administrative bureaucracy might lead to the highest status, honours and cold hard cash.

The *devshirme*, whether devastating and controversial or complacently accepted by those in charge and those who wanted out of the provinces, achieved what it set out to perform. It was responsible for around a third of the total number of slaves entering the Ottoman system. Over time its importance declined, however, especially after free Muslims were allowed to enter the ranks, and the system of recruiting through the *devshirme* effectively came to an end in 1648. It was finally abolished during the early years of Sultan Ahmed III's reign (1703–30).[22]

As for the Janissaries, loyalty to the sultan came to be matched, and sometimes eclipsed, by loyalty to the corps. The first revolt of the slave soldiers occurred as early as 1449 and from 1451, starting with Mehmed II, incoming sultans were essentially compelled to distribute rewards and increase the soldiers' pay on their accession – or risk the consequences. In 1622, frustrated that he was to all intents and purposes 'subject to his own slaves', the teenage Sultan Osman II (r. 1618–22) tried to disband the all-powerful Janissaries altogether. Understandable in intention, his effort proved a fatal mistake in its execution: the Janissaries took prisoner the Commander of the Faithful and Successor of the Prophet of the Lord of the Universe, dragged him unceremoniously into the Fortress of the Seven Towers and murdered him there. In 1730 the Janissaries revolted again and forced the abdication of Sultan Ahmed III before their coup was crushed with the slaughter of 7,000 rebels. In 1807 there was another revolt of the Janissaries, this time overthrowing Sultan Selim III (r. 1789–1807), the latest sultan to attempt, and fail, to clip their wings.

The final chapter in the turbulent history of these commanding and temperamental slave soldiers came in 1826. Convinced they had become a reactionary and corrupt force standing in the way of his reforms, especially those that involved the adoption of modern military methods of training, gunnery and other innovations, which were essential against enemies whose armies were moving with the times, the reformist Sultan Mahmud II moved decisively against them. By this time they had evolved into something far beyond the dedicated military force they were intended to be and were routinely flexing their muscles in a peculiarly Ottoman combination of militant trade union, elite social caste and political activist group. Fiercely protective of their inherited privileges – from tax exemption and subsidized meat and bread to a regular salary, annual clothing allowance and cash bonus each time a new sultan arrived – they were not interested in adapting to the changing requirements of battlefield technology.

Mahmud crushed and killed his Janissaries in Istanbul in 1826. In Ottoman-held Baghdad, which was no stranger to tempests of bloodshed and slaughter over the centuries, the abolition of the Janissaries was, for once, less violent. As noted earlier, Daud, Pasha of Baghdad (r. 1816–31) managed to eliminate them with the help of carefully positioned field guns on the parade ground. Wisely they refrained from resistance and agreed on the spot to join his new Nidham Jadid army.

Mahmud had struck at the heart of the Ottomans' traditional military power and the Janissaries were abolished at a stroke – in Istanbul, if not in Baghdad, in a lake of blood.[23]

There are paradoxes within paradoxes here. On the one hand we see a class of formally defined *kul* slaves, on the other a group of rich, power-wielding men who for several centuries dominated both the military and political hierarchies at the heart of a mighty, world-spanning empire. How to reconcile the apparent conflict?

In a sense it was more straightforward than it might first appear. Even in their dazzling ascendancy, the Ibrahim Edhem Pashas and Mimar Sinans of this world remained the property of the sultan. He could, if he felt like it – though it bears saying that this hardly ever happened – kill them on the spot. In theory at least, these prosperous, landed and bejewelled statesmen had fewer rights, even, than a lowly slave who enjoyed the twin protections of Islamic law and social custom. Another important consideration which underlined their *de jure* servile status was the right of inheritance. Even if a slave had been manumitted, as some Janissaries appear to have been, their owner – generally the state, in this case the sultan – retained the right of inheritance. He could, and frequently would, acquire their entire estates on their death in a simple and effective recycling of the slave-grandee's considerable assets.

In practice, however, as the centuries passed, these elite slaves resembled the conventional image of slaves less and less. Their servitude was official and to one uniquely special man only, a lower-level equivalent of the sultan's position as Slave of God, though admittedly more constraining. By the late eighteenth and early nineteenth centuries, whenever senior royal officials fell from favour it was extremely rare for them to receive the sort of humiliating and debilitating punishment typically given to a slave.

To add another apparent paradox, their status as slaves did not preclude these men from owning slaves themselves – the *kuls* of the *kuls* – in some cases immense numbers of them. The *kul* system may have been dominated by, but it was not exclusive to, the sultan's imperial household. While the royal establishment stood resplendent above all others, it was also a model for grandees to emulate on a smaller scale. Viziers, governors, senior statesmen, commanders and high-ranking military officers across the empire – the class of *beyler-beyis*, *sanjak-beyis*, *subashis*, *sipahis* and others – were all expected to maintain retinues in proportion to the income derived from their fiefs.

Ibrahim Pasha, Suleiman's first grand vizier, an all-powerful figure who himself had been enslaved as a child in around 1500, maintained a corps of 1,300 slaves. Ibrahim's prematurely terminated career also highlighted the dangers faced by a slave-turned-grandee at the highest level. His overweening influence during his dozen years as grand vizier grew to the point where he began to boast indiscreetly that he was the real power within the empire, not so much behind the throne as virtually upon it.

His downfall came at the hands of another, even more influential former slave from Ruthenia in what is today Ukraine. In her thirties, she was called Roxelana, the beautiful daughter of an Orthodox priest. In 1533 she had broken her bonds of slavery to become, against all established custom and to the astonishment of Istanbul, Suleiman's lawfully wedded wife Hurrem (Delight). On the night of 5 March 1536, Hurrem had Ibrahim killed in his bedchamber after he had dined with the sultan. In a witty and macabre twist his nickname was changed from Makbul Ibrahim Pasha (the Favourite) to Maktul Ibrahim Pasha (the Executed). Rustem Pasha (1505–61), one of Ibrahim's successors as grand vizier of Suleiman, was a more judicious figure. At the time of his death, the vastly wealthy and all-powerful man, a son-in-law of the sultan, had a retinue of 1,700 slaves.

Strictly speaking, the law was quite clear that slaves could *not* own property, which of course included slaves. A *fetva* (fatwa) from Ebus-suud, the *Şeyhülislam* (Turkish version of *Sheikh al Islam*, the empire's supreme judge) from 1545 to 1574, made this explicit.

> Q: His Excellency the Sultan, the Refuge of the World, sends his wholly-owned slave Zeyd [to a post] outside the palace for a salary. Is it permissible for Zeyd to buy and to have intercourse with slave girls?
> A: It is not possible.[24]

Ebussuud understood, of course, that the sultan's most senior officials – legally speaking slaves – were enormously rich men who could and did own slaves, and did what they liked with them, female and otherwise. But he also appreciated that any answer to the contrary implied that the sultan did not enjoy complete dominion over them. The law was the law, but everyday life didn't always acknowledge it.

We must accept that this sort of practice makes a mockery of any conventional definition of slavery. İnalcik has argued that the translation of the word *kul* as slave is itself 'misleading'. Some suggest that the term servant would be more accurate.

While the legality of the *devshirme* was highly questionable, it was hardly the only, or even the most, problematic aspect of Ottoman slavery. Islamic law was quite clear that no free or manumitted Muslim could be sold into slavery. Executed after a battle by all means, but not enslaved. This was a long-established tenet of slavery within the Muslim world.

The arrival of the Ottomans, and their subsequent expansion into an empire which associated with – and in a number of instances invaded – other Muslim states, saw this tradition tested to breaking point and, in the case of recurring conflicts with Iran in the sixteenth century, completely flouted.

The Ottomans proved extremely willing to enslave their Iranian co-religionists. Different times appeared to call for different measures, and the Ottoman–Safavid War of 1532–55 provided Istanbul with an excuse to break the law repeatedly. There is evidence, for example, that in 1554, the year in which the English Parliament passed the Act for the Marriage of Queen Mary to Philip of Spain, the *Şeyhülislam* Ebussuud issued a legal ruling authorizing the enslavement of Iranians who, he pronounced, could be sold in the same way as infidels.[25] If this looks like another instance of egregious, retrospective justification, it is worth considering that when faced with the dubious alternatives of illegal enslavement or legal execution, had he been consulted, the prisoner of war on a battlefield reeking with blood and slaughter may well have preferred the former. In any case, the Ottomans practised both, massacring captives, as in the aftermath of the Battle of Chaldiran in 1514, and enslaving them, according to the situation. And the evidence from Ebussuud itself is mixed, since in one of his rulings, on the 1554–5 campaign against the Safavids, he prohibited the enslavement of the children of captured Iranians. He also ruled that sexual intercourse with captured women – an overriding concern of the plundering warriors, not to mention a significant percentage of those seeking a definitive ruling from the great jurist – was not licit 'until they accept Islam', meaning that he considered them apostates and not straightforward infidels, who could be enslaved. It was a confusing world.[26]

Only in 1736, almost 200 years after the ruling, did a peace treaty between the two Muslim adversaries formally put an end to illegal Ottoman enslavement, and even then it is clear that in practice some Iranians remained slaves in Ottoman hands. As late as 1767, to give one melancholy example, we hear the plaintive voice of an Iranian slave called Ali petitioning a court for its protection, alleging that his master, a certain Haffaf Haci Mehmed of Ankara, had threatened to sell him and his children, thereby dividing his family after thirty years of loyal service. That Ali's children were also slaves at risk of sale and separation from their family demonstrates that he had been married off to one of Haffaf's female slaves and conveniently provided his master with an additional brood of slaves.

While some Iranians were miserably enslaved by the Ottomans at this time, many others owned slaves themselves and continued to do so until well into the twentieth century. Take the story, a rare instance of first-person testimony, of an Ethiopian concubine in Shiraz called Jamila, who wrote a letter in 1905 summarizing her many trials and tribulations in slavery:

> My name is Jamila Habashi, my father is Lula'd-Din from Saho, my mother Loshabah, and from the Omraniah tribe. I was enslaved when I was a child then was brought to Mecca where I was sold to a broker; the broker took me to Basra from the Jabal, and sold me to an Iranian broker named Mulla Ali, who shipped me from Basra to Muhammara and from there he took me to the Bushihr port and there he sold me to a merchant called Haji Mirza Ahmad Kaziruni who is in Shiraz now, I was his concubine for four years in Bushihr then Haji took me to Shiraz and kept me there for five years; in total, I was with him for nine years and then he sold me to Nasir Nizam the son of 'Ataullah. After one year, Nasir sold me to Haji Muhammad Ali Khan. Now it has been five years that I have been with him.[27]

As upholders of orthodox Sunni Islam, the Ottomans could always justify the enslavement of the Safavid Iranians on grounds that their neighbours were not 'proper' Muslims. No such excuse could be offered in the Ottomans' enslavement of their fellow Ottomans. Here, as ever, profit was the driving motive. While the punishment for this crime was execution in the early days of empire, by the eighteenth and nineteenth centuries this had softened to exile and imprisonment. Thus Ottoman records show that in 1790, a certain Colak Ismail, Ismail the Crippled, and his son Huseyin, who had a track record of convictions for trafficking free Muslim women in Anatolia, were permanently exiled to Bursa from the Ottoman capital for committing the same crime. Some slave-dealers evidently considered the penalty of temporary exile and imprisonment no more than a slap on the wrist. In 1838, less than a decade before the abolition of the Istanbul slave market, a Black Sea ship captain and slaver called Suleiman Reis of Tirebolu, who plied his trade along the shores of Abkhazia and Circassia, got into trouble after bringing his human cargo of captured Muslim pilgrims to the town of Rize, east of Trabzon, on what is today the Turkish Black Sea coast. Suleiman was imprisoned and, after Russian diplomatic intervention, the pilgrims were set free. But that was not the end of the story. Successful slave-dealers tended to have deep pockets and friends in high places. After Suleyman had spent three or four months behind bars, the *vali*, or governor, of Trabzon lobbied Istanbul on the slaver's behalf, arguing that he had been suitably punished. Still, bureaucratic wheels turned slowly, and it was only in early 1840 that the order came to release him.

If fellow Muslims could not always feel safe from enslavement, it is hardly surprising that the officially protected *zimmis* were often seen as fair game. This was neither a rare nor an ad hoc phenomenon. Although illegal, their enslavement was 'a permanent feature of Ottoman society for a considerable time'. While the *devshirme* represented one route into captivity, *zimmis* could also be taken at sea by pirates and corsairs, Muslim and Christian alike. In 1567, the Jewish Duke of Naxos complained to Istanbul that a pirate called Saban Reis had enslaved many *zimmis* from his Aegean island. Marauding soldiers and irregulars could also get in on the act on dry land. In 1815, almost 250 years later, the Armenian Patriarch Bogos was petitioning the imperial capital about Kurdish soldiers' illegal enslavement of Armenian women and children in Diyarbakir and beyond. They were being sold as Yezidi captives. 'We are inhabitants of this and that village,' such petitions would say, 'we are the true Armenian *reayas* [subjects] of the Ottoman state, to sell our wives and children as slaves is contrary to the *Seriat* [sharia] and against the Sultan's will . . .'. In this case, the governor was ordered to stamp out the practice. As far as the Yezidis were concerned, however, both the patriarch's petition and the official response from Istanbul implied that their enslavement was perfectly legal. Certainly, the Ottomans considered them devil-worshippers. They may not have been granted *zimmi* status, or perhaps they had rebelled against the government, or refused to pay the tax. It was an ominous precursor to the enslavement, rape and slaughter of Yezidi women and men by fighters of the so-called Islamic State in 2014.[28]

Prior to the nineteenth century, one of the most fertile hunting grounds for slaves destined for the Ottoman Empire was in the northern Black Sea region. At its heart was the Muslim Crimean khanate, which endured from 1441 to its final annexation by the Russian Empire in 1783 and which was, for most of this time, one of the Ottomans' vassal states. Beginning in 1468, with the first recorded instance of a Crimean Tatar raid, the Slavs living in the northern steppes suffered virtually annual slave-taking raids until the close of the seventeenth century. These attacks were so regular that they came to be known as the 'harvesting of the steppe'. At times the frequency of the raids almost beggared description. In one four-year period alone, 1654–7, Crimean Tatars launched thirty-eight separate attacks into Slavic lands.

Slave-owning in the khanate was so common that, unlike in the Anatolian heartland, it did not denote considerable wealth. Slave-raiding was one of the main sources of livelihoods on the peninsula and, according to the nineteenth-century Ottoman historian Ahmed Cevdet Pasha, Tatar children were told to pray for the rivers to freeze in winter so that their fathers would have an easier time getting their horses across difficult terrain while away on their slave-hunting expeditions. Overall, the capture and enslavement of Russians, Poles and Ukrainians occurred on a phenomenal scale. It has been estimated that approximately 2 million were sold into slavery between 1468 and 1694. Patchy customs records from the sixteenth and seventeenth centuries indicate that Istanbul was the unquestioned leviathan at the centre of this vast ocean of slavery, absorbing as many as 2.5 million European and Caucasian slaves.[29]

Caffa, a Black Sea port, colony and flourishing slave market established by the Genoese in the 1260s, was the heart of this trade.* Here slaves were often bartered for cloth brought to the city by Anatolian merchants. By 1475, a couple of decades after his conquest of Constantinople and hard on the heels of bringing Serbia, Morea, Bosnia, Albania and swathes of Anatolia to heel, Mehmed despatched a fleet north. Caffa, considered one of the gateways to Christendom, was unable to put up much of a resistance in the face of a ruthless bombardment of its city walls. Its fall the same year sent a shudder of fear and loathing across Europe, and the Crimean khanate was forced to accept Ottoman suzerainty in the region. Later in 1475 the Ottomans built the Azov Fortress, their north-easternmost redoubt overlooking the River Don, squeezing the Venetians out of their slave-exporting port of Tana on the Azov Sea just as they had seen off the Genoese. The stage was set for Crimean Tatars to continue their leading role as steppe slave-takers, but now with a new emphasis on the heavy demand coming from Mehmed's burgeoning, muscle-flexing Muslim empire to the south. And Caffa, once it had fallen to the Turks, emerged as *the* Black Sea destination bar none for the purchase of slaves.

Slave-raiding terrorized those who had the misfortune to live on the Eurasian steppe, and it sent shivers down European spines. Sigismund von Herberstein, ambassador of the Holy Roman Emperor to Muscovy in the early decades of the sixteenth century, recorded how in 1521 the Crimean Khan Mohammed Giray (r. 1515–23) launched a devastating slave-taking raid north into the Grand Duchy of Moscow, laying waste to the capital city and plundering without pity:

> He took with him from Muscovy so great a multitude of captives as would scarcely be considered credible; they say the number exceeded

---

* Today the Crimean port is called Feodosia. Previously part of Ukraine, in 2014 it became part of the Russian Federation after Moscow's illegal annexation of Crimea.

eight hundred thousand, part of whom he sold in Kaffa to the Turks, and part he slew. The old and infirmed men, who will not fetch much at a sale, are given up to the Tatar youths, either to be stoned, or to be thrown into the sea, or to be killed by any sort of death they might please.

If the numbers from this account look wildly exaggerated, the 300,000 stated in the *Ostroh Chronicle*, the seventeenth-century Ukrainian version of events, is hardly a source of comfort. Travelling through Caffa in the mid-sixteenth century, a Christian visitor wrote in disgust of the enormous quantities of slaves sold in its market. The city was, he wrote, 'a heathen giant who feeds on our blood'. He was not alone in his horror at this seething entrepot of human flesh. Around the same time, Michalo Lituanus (the pen name for an unknown Lithuanian writer) expressed similar emotions. Caffa, he wrote, was 'not a town, but an abyss into which our blood is pouring'. All this blood was highly profitable, the slave trade swelling imperial coffers in Istanbul to the tune of 100,000 gold ducats per annum by the mid-sixteenth century – the per capita tax on slave sales was four ducats.[30]

The Turkish historian Halil İnalcik calculated that the number of slaves imported into the Ottoman Empire from Poland–Lithuania, Muscovy and Circassia reached over 10,000 a year between 1500 and 1650. Factoring in deaths in transit, another recent study has argued that the population loss of Poland–Lithuania and Muscovy alone between 1500 and 1700 was around 2 million. These are astonishing figures.[31]

On his journey from the Ottoman capital to Vienna in 1555, Ogier Ghiselin de Busbecq, the Flemish diplomat who served as ambassador to Istanbul in the 1550s, came across caravans of European slaves being driven east from Hungary for sale in the empire's great slave market. He wrote about this dismal sight in his memoirs, *Itinera Constantinopolitanum et Amasianum*, published as *Turkish Letters* in 1595:

> ... the beginning of my journey was marked by an evil chance. Just as I left Constantinople I met some waggons of boys and girls who were being carried from Hungary to the slave market at Constantinople; this is the commonest kind of Turkish merchandise, and just as

loads of different kinds of goods meet the traveller's eye, as he leaves Antwerp, so every now and then we came across unhappy Christians of all ranks, ages, and sexes who were being carried off to a horrible slavery; the men, young and old, were either driven in gangs or bound to a chain and dragged over the road in a long file, after the same fashion as we take a string of horses to a fair. It was indeed a painful sight; and I could scarcely check my tears, so deeply did I feel the woes and humiliation of Christendom.[32]

Though his estimate must be treated with the usual caution, the Ottoman traveller and writer Evliya Çelebi, who passed through Crimea in 1665–6, reckoned that its slave population (400,000) was more than double the number of free Muslims (187,000). The last few decades before his visit had been particularly tough on Crimea generally and on Caffa in particular. The combination of fire and disease, and ravaging Cossack and Tatar raids in 1616, 1624 and 1628, brought the city to a low ebb. From the mid-sixteenth to the mid-seventeenth centuries, the non-Muslim population of the province also appears to have plummeted by 70 per cent.[33]

Çelebi is especially interesting on the Crimean and Ottoman slave trade because his writings betray an uncommon combination of the Muslim superiority complex offset by a sense of compassion for the Christian and Jewish suffering he witnessed with his own eyes. On the one hand is his description of how the mighty Muslim Tatars under the Crimean Khan Islam Giray III (r. 1644–54) raided Polish lands seventy-one times through the 1640s and 1650s, taking 200,000 Jews captive and then selling them for the price of a tobacco pipe. This was a source of pride for Çelebi who, not unlike Ibn Battuta, had no great love for the infidels and was himself partial to acquiring the occasional slave from these raids. On the other hand, the Ottoman traveller was a cultured and highly intelligent man. What he saw in the slave market of Karasubazar, the main community for Crimean Jews, must have pulled him up short. It moved him to write: 'A man who had not seen this market, had not seen anything in this world. A mother is severed from her son and daughter there, a son – from his father and brother, and they are sold amongst lamentations, cries of help, weeping and sorrow.'[34]

And still the raids continued, and still the slaves kept coming. In 1769, 300 years after the first recorded Tatar raid, and more than a century after the Crimean visit which aroused such ambivalence in Çelebi, the French military officer Baron de Tott was an eyewitness of the last Tatar raid into Polish and Russian lands. This is what a homeward-bound Tatar horseman and his traumatized human cargo looked like on the move:

> Five or six Slaves of all ages, sixty sheep, and twenty oxen . . . The children with their heads out of a bag at the Pommel of the Saddle, a young Girl sitting before him sustained by his left Arm, the Mother behind, the Father on a led Horse, the Son on another, the Sheep and Oxen before, all are watched, all managed, nothing escapes the vigilant eye of the Conductor. He assembles, directs, provides Subsistence, walks himself to give ease to his Slaves . . . the picture would be truly interesting if Avarice, and the most cruel Injustice, did not furnish the subject.[35]

These Christian perspectives on the sufferings of Christian slaves at the hands of their Muslim captors have their own challenges. Both Michalo Lituanus and Baron de Tott qualify and, in some cases, even contradict their own accounts. Lituanus writes that whereas the Tatars treat their slaves properly and release them after their seven-year servitude is up, Christians keep their slaves forever. The French aristocrat admitted that 'the Europeans, alone, ill-treat their Slaves'. This, he thought, was down to the very different way in which slaves were owned. In the East men amassed wealth to buy slaves. In the West they bought slaves to amass their fortunes. 'In the East they are the enjoyment of Avarice; in Europe its instrument.'[36]

The nineteenth century brought no respite. Fresh agonies awaited the Caucasus and its peoples during the drawn-out Russo–Circassian War of 1763–1864, culminating in waves of expulsions of the Circassians in the 1860s. The Russian military campaign was characterized by 'what one would today call genocide and state terrorism – the systematic burning of villages, wholesale killing of native peoples, and forced deportation'. In May 1864, after the Circassians and their Abkhaz allies had made an unsuccessful last stand at the Battle of Qbaada, twenty-five miles away the Russian officer Ivan Drozdov witnessed terrible scenes around the Black Sea port of Sochi. 'On the road our eyes were met with a staggering image: corpses of women, children, elderly persons, torn to pieces and half-eaten by dogs; deportees emaciated by hunger and disease, almost too weak to move their legs, collapsing from exhaustion and becoming prey to dogs while still alive.'

In all, up to 1.5 million Circassians were either massacred or deported and approximately a million were resettled in Turkish lands to the south in the early 1860s. Even for those men, women and children who survived the slaughter, the outcome of their relocation could still be devastating. Many families found themselves exchanging serfdom in the Caucasus for slavery in the Ottoman Empire, where they faced the breaking up of their households and the sale of their daughters. Increasing numbers started to petition the authorities for their emancipation. Considerably smaller numbers of wealthier, more fortunate men, including expelled Caucasian chieftains, maintained their status as slave-owners in the new territory, albeit facing mounting pressures as the empire to which they had relocated contended with the rising tide of abolition.[37]

The harvest of young boys from the Balkans helped swell the Ottomans' military ranks for several centuries. The plundering of the Eurasian steppe for its human crops fed the Ottoman slave machine for a similar length of time. When it came to the enslavement of girls and women, however, to occupy positions ranging from the lowliest domestic slave to the sultan's favourite concubine in the imperial harem, this lasted far longer – in fact, for the entire lifespan of the Ottoman Empire. The demand was unquenchable.

This sort of slave-taking started early, well before a recognizable empire had even been won. We know that Orhan was taking Christian women from captured Byzantine territory into his household in the early fourteenth century. One of them was Asporca, who may have been Greek. Another was called Nilufer, a florid name – it means water lily in Persian – typically given to slave concubines. One of the most famous foreign eyewitnesses travelling around Anatolia in 1331, at the outset of Orhan's reign, was Ibn Battuta, who would be scandalized by the nudity of the sultan's slave women and daughters in Mali a couple of years later. His famous narrative makes it abundantly clear that Muslim powers were already using Christian women as slaves. In the city of Ladhiq, near the modern city of Denizli in western Turkey, for example, he was disgusted by the local population's use and abuse of Greek girls:

> The inhabitants of this city make no effort to stamp out immorality – indeed, the same applies to the whole population of these regions. They buy beautiful Greek slave girls and put them out to prostitution [illegal under Islamic law], and each girl has to pay a regular due to her master. I heard it said there that the girls go into the bath-houses along with the men, and anyone who wishes to indulge in depravity does so in the bath-house and nobody tries to stop him. I was told that the *qadi* [judge] in this city himself owns slave girls employed in this way.[38]

Ibn Battuta further reported that Sultan Mohammed ibn Aydin, the ruler of Aydin, then a rival power in the central Aegean, maintained a retinue of twenty Greek slaves at the entrance to his palace. They were women 'of surpassingly beautiful appearance', he wrote, 'wearing robes of silk, with their hair parted and hanging loose, and in colour of a resplendent whiteness tinged with red'. Perhaps, given that he evidently liked to sleep with and then dispose of a succession of both wives and slave concubines throughout his travels, he would have been delighted to be given one of these women, but it was not to be. In the end Ibn Battuta had to make do with the still-generous farewell present of 100 *mithqals* of gold, 1,000 silver dirhams, a complete set of clothes, a horse, robes and silver for his entourage, and a Greek male slave called Mikhail. In any case, the Moroccan traveller wasted little time buying what he wanted. Continuing his journey across Anatolia, in Aya Suluq (Ephesus) he bought 'a Greek slave girl, a virgin, for forty dinars' and, a little later in Bala Kasri (Balikesir) on his way to Bursa, which in 1335 would become the first capital of the Ottoman Empire, 'a Greek slave girl named Marghalita'.[39]

The Ottomans, like their contemporaries around them, particularly prized the capture of women from the households of their defeated rivals. For Mehmed II in 1453, the icing on his Constantinople cake was the capture of 'all the [Byzantine] noblewomen and their daughters'. At the Battle of Chaldiran in 1514, when Sultan Selim I overcame the firebrand Iranian Shah Ismail (r. 1501–24), founder of the Safavid dynasty, he revelled in the humiliation inflicted upon his adversary, first seizing his wife, Taclu Khatun, as prisoner and then, even worse, giving her to one of his henchmen in a show that she was not fit for the royal bed. As the Sunni Muslim Akkoyunlu dynasty of eastern Anatolia boasted in a self-serving history indicating the critical importance attached to protecting royal wives and concubines, 'the hand of a conqueror never touched their spouses'.[40]

As far as their women were concerned, Ottoman sultans shifted their domestic arrangements radically over time. Initially, for the first couple of generations under Osman and Orhan, as the dynasty was establishing itself in Anatolia, marriages tended to be contracted as alliances with both Muslim and Christian states. They served the classic purpose of consolidating power and winning supporters. Sultans continued to do this into the fifteenth century, but marriage soon began to be displaced by slave concubinage as the preferred, indeed dominant, form of reproduction. Just as the long-lived Abbasid dynasty had started with blue-blooded royal Arab wives before swiftly shifting to multi-ethnic, frequently non-Arab slave concubines, so the Ottomans followed suit in a move which underlined the primacy of patriarchal power. Queens or sultanas were royal figures in their own right. Slave concubines, no matter how much agency they had and irrespective of their intelligence, were not. A concubine who bore the sultan a male child, his possible heir, would be duly honoured, rewarded and then removed from the Topkapi (New Palace) to the Eski Saray (Old Palace) in what has been described as a 'one-mother-one-son policy'. Her sexual duties to her master were now complete and she was no longer eligible for the sultan's bed. A concubine who gave him a daughter, however, could remain available if so desired. Luigi Bassano, a Venetian from Zadar who was resident in Istanbul in the late 1530s and seems to have worked as a page for Suleiman the Magnificent, described how the women were selected and moved from one palace to the other:

> The Grand Turk has a palace of women at quite a distance from his own. There he keeps a great number of Christian slave girls ... From these the Grand Turk chooses whoever pleases him the most, and keeps her separate for two months, and amuses himself with her as he

pleases; if she becomes pregnant, he takes her as his consort, otherwise he marries her to one of his men . . . .[41]

By this time, less than 200 years after the Osman and Orhan period had ended, the narrative around the 'tradition' of royal reproduction through concubinage had become so firmly established that it was as though Ottoman sultans had never married. Imperial custom, established since time immemorial, the argument went, dictated that a sultan should breed exclusively through his slave concubines and not his royal wives.

This is why Suleiman's decision to marry his favourite concubine Hurrem shook the traditionalists, and the wider public, to the core. 'This week there has occurred in this city a most extraordinary event, one absolutely unprecedented in the history of the Sultans,' the representative of Genoa's Bank of St George reported. 'The Grand Signior Suleiman has taken himself as his Empress a slave-woman from Russia called Roxelana, and there has been great feasting . . . There is great talk about the marriage and none can say what it means.'[42]

Five hundred years later, we can make an attempt. To begin with, Hurrem was abducted by slave-traders from her homeland in Ruthenia when she was fifteen. Later she became the first slave concubine to be freed to become the sultan's lawfully wedded wife. She was the first, too, to hold the title of *haseki*, the sultan's favourite, a title created especially for her. It immediately elevated her over all other women, free or enslaved, and established her position within the imperial dynasty, paving the way for other women to follow her as Haseki Sultan, the Empress Consort. Next, by stealing Suleiman's heart and becoming the chief influencer of his mind, Hurrem had thrown off her slave status and taken her place at the top table of Ottoman authority.

She did not hesitate to use this power. Most lethally she persuaded Suleiman to eliminate Mustapha, his eldest son from his concubine Mahidevran. As the key rival of her own son Mehmed, Mustapha had to go. Ultimately, in this case the scheming was in vain. Hurrem's firstborn died of smallpox in 1543. However, all was not lost. In another radical and scandalous break from tradition, Hurrem was not removed from the sultan when she bore him Mehmed. Instead, she relocated from the residence for the royal women and children and moved into Suleiman's palace. The two became inseparable. What might appear romantic to modern readers horrified many of Suleiman's subjects. Hurrem had transcended the boundaries of what was normal and acceptable behaviour for a woman, particularly a concubine. In the eyes of the dominant men at court, of all the women who resented Hurrem's ascendancy, and of the gossip-hungry public, the concubine-turned-imperial consort had made herself the sultan's master. European diplomats reported that the sultan's subjects reckoned she had 'bewitched' him, resorting to 'love-charms and magic arts' to retain Suleiman's affection.[43] It hardly needs saying that her success in an overwhelmingly male world accounted for her unpopularity.

Hurrem's legacy endured. She bore Suleiman six children, of which her third-born became Sultan Selim II in 1566, ruling until his death in 1574. Her rise to the pinnacle of power ushered in what came to be known as the 'Sultanate of Women', a period which began with her marriage to Suleiman in 1533 and lasted until 1715. Following in her elegant footsteps, a succession of slave concubines transcended their servitude to emerge as strong, free women in their own right, upsetting the patriarchal world of grand viziers, conservative clerics and chief muftis, for whom the proper exercise of power was confined exclusively to men.

Hurrem's startling career is as striking as the barrage of love letters she and Suleiman exchanged while he was away on military campaigns. In one of his most famous verses in his nom de plume of Muhibbi, The Lover, he wrote that she was his 'Sultan', his entire world:

> My Istanbul, my Karaman, the earth of my Anatolia
> My Badakhshan, my Baghdad and Khorasan
> My woman of the beautiful hair, my love of the slanted brow,
>   my love of eyes full of mischief . . .

Her own letters were pitch-perfect. She cleverly deferred to the oversized ego of one of the mightiest men on earth by referring to herself as his humble 'slave', while all the time she maintained an unprecedented influence on the Sovereign of the Sublime House of Osman. She was endlessly inventive, flecking her letters with gold one month, accompanying them with supposedly tear-sodden robes the next. In

1526, around seven years before they married, she wrote of her longing for her beloved:

> I am lost in this universe created by our Lord. I lived my best years
> under your protection, like a pearl in your jewel box.
>
> Please accept this rue from your helpless and miserable slave, suffer-
> ing in your absence.
>
> I only find peace next to you. Words and ink would not be enough to
> tell my happiness and joy, when I am right next to you.[44]

This was a legendary love affair, famous and infamous across the
empire and in Europe. It had more than a tinge of the fairy tale about
it. Hurrem remains, almost 500 years after her death, one of the greatest reversal-of-fortunes stories so recurrent in the history of slavery
within the Islamic world.

Unlike Hurrem, whose life was well documented for her time, we only
have a snapshot of Shemsigul. It provides a much starker example
of the reality of slavery for a concubine. Born around the late 1830s
into an impoverished Circassian family, Shemsigul was purchased in
a slave market in Istanbul by the slave-dealer Deli Mehmed in about
1850. Tantalizing details of her life between 1852 and 1854 emerge
only because she had the courage to bring a lengthy legal case against
Deli Mehmed, the records of which were discovered almost 150 years
later in Egypt's national archives.[45] For a modern reader, the slave-
dealer comes across as a libidinous liar.

By 1852 he had taken her to Cairo, where she was first sold to a
son of Mohammed Ali Pasha, the Albanian Ottoman governor and
founder of the modern state of Egypt (r. 1805–48). At this time the
city's population was around 275,000, including an estimated 10,000–
15,000 slaves. Egypt then received around 5,000 enslaved men and
women annually, most of them black African women destined for
menial domestic work. As a comparison, an estimated 10,000–20,000
enslaved Africans were imported into the Persian Gulf in the early
nineteenth century, many of whom were women going to work in
Iran. As a pale-skinned Circassian, Shemsigul was already in a far
more exclusive category.

The evidence she gave to the police reveals an intelligent, brave and practical woman determined to seek justice against overwhelming odds. It also reveals the powerlessness of a slave who could be bought and sold – and repeatedly, legally raped – by her owner.

On 30 June 1854, Shemsigul provided testimony to police investigators in Cairo. It is clear that the police questioning was another trial in itself. As a female slave in a precarious position, talking to the all-male authorities in a conservative society about intimate personal details, including her sexual activity, missed periods, pregnancy and vicious beating intended to induce a miscarriage, this would have been an appalling experience.

Asked how she had become pregnant, Shemsigul stated that Deli Mehmed was responsible:

> In the boat, on the way here, he forced me to have sexual relations with him. He continued to sleep with me until he sold me. Before the sale, I told him: 'Now you want to sell me, but I have missed my period, and I think that I am pregnant by you.' When I asked him later what would happen, he did not listen, but went away, brought back some medicines, and made me drink them [to induce an abortion]. Finally, he sold me to the palace.

Deli Mehmed was then summoned to the palace, she reported, where she was returned to him, it being illegal to sell a pregnant slave. Later, Deli Mehmed's wife summoned a midwife and ordered her to perform an abortion. Shemsigul was not consulted at any point. The midwife refused because the pregnancy was well advanced, but Deli Mehmed's wife insisted, saying:

> 'I shall put an end to this pregnancy.' Later, her husband, Deli Mehmed, came. She said to him: 'Let us beat this slave and end her pregnancy.' Deli Mehmed stated: 'I am not going to beat her.' But the woman would not stop. She fetched a clothespress, hit me with it several times on my stomach and back, and beat me with a mincing rod.

A neighbour reported the abuse to Selim Bey, a local dignitary, whose wife rescued Shemsigul and took her back to her house where she stayed to have her baby. When the baby boy was born, Deli Mehmed's wife came and took him away from Shemsigul. 'To me she said that he died.'

Three weeks after giving birth, Shemsigul returned to Deli Mehmed's house, where she was not allowed to see her baby. Instead she was given in trust to Timur, another slave-dealer, who tried unsuccessfully to sell her while Deli Mehmed travelled to India and the Hijaz on slave-trading business. Eventually she was sold to Timur in return for a promissory note. The police asked her if she had informed Timur that she had been pregnant and had also been badly beaten. 'As a slave, I was afraid to say anything about my suffering, so I did not tell Timur,' she replied.

The next witness to give evidence was Ali Efendi, head of the slave-dealers' guild. Dealers selling black and white slaves were organized into different guilds and that which Ali Efendi led was formally designated a prestigious merchants' guild within Cairo's Khan al Khalili bazaar. By contrast, the guild which traded in black slaves was listed among the 'cursed and impious' trading associations of low social status.[46]

Ali Efendi appears to have conducted a fairly comprehensive investigation to establish the facts. He told the police that Timur had sent Shemsigul to his house and that he – Timur – had told Ali that the woman 'must be freed after her master's death' because she had borne Deli Mehmed a child. Her sale to Timur was therefore illegal, hence the legal dispute between him and Deli Mehmed. Ali summoned Deli Mehmed, who denied everything.

Ali then listened to Shemsigul's story. Asked if she had any witnesses, she cited Mustapha, his wife and Selim Bey. Finally, Ali questioned Mustapha, who corroborated Shemsigul's story. At this point he took the promissory note from Deli Mehmed, returned it to Timur and detained Shemsigul pending further police investigation.

Deli Mehmed was neither a credible nor an honest witness. He ranged from outright denial of all the accusations to claiming not to remember either Shemsigul or the circumstances of her purchase. He then admitted that he had indeed owned a concubine called Shemsigul. She had borne him a son who had died a few months later, before her own death. Next he changed his story again, admitting that he had brought Shemsigul from Istanbul to Cairo, sold her first to Mohammed Ali Pasha for around 300 Egyptian pounds, later to Timur for half of that sum. He had only taken her back from the palace because she was 'not on friendly terms with the harem ladies'.

Deli Mehmed's transparent unreliability as a witness, combined with Mustapha's damning testimony, helped the police reach their decision. They accepted Shemsigul's story and rejected Deli Mehmed's account outright.

So what happened to Shemsigul? Frustratingly, the final verdict is elusive – no court ruling was ever found. However, since the records show that the matter was referred upwards to the Grand Mufti of Egypt, the most senior Islamic figure in the country, it seems likely that she would have been manumitted – especially since the facts of her having given birth to Deli Mehmed's son had been established, together with the dealer's conduct as a serial liar. The Grand Mufti was unlikely to have gone against a police recommendation based on an exhaustive investigation.

Apart from the shattering personal pain Shemsigul had suffered at the hands of Deli Mehmed, beyond her courage and determination to fight for her rights, her story is powerful because of what it suggests about the great unknown mass of enslaved girls and women and the traumas they must also have experienced without recourse to the law. But Shemsigul's voice sounds loud and clear from a silent mass of suffering.

Hurrem and Shemsigul have much to tell us about the lives of slave concubines. A very different, insider's perspective on female slavery in the Ottoman Empire comes from another remarkable woman called Leyla Hanim (1850–1936), a Turkish composer, writer and poet who spent years within the royal harem of the Topkapi Palace, home to generations of Ottoman sultans. She was the daughter of Dr Ismail Pasha, a man who, like Ibrahim Edhem Pasha from the island of Chios, had Greek parentage, was enslaved as a child and then rose to the very peak of his profession. Sold in the Izmir slave market to a Jewish surgeon, he was instructed in medicine and, decades later, after formal studies at medical school in Istanbul and then Paris, became surgeon-in-chief of the Ottoman Empire under Sultan Abdulmejid I (r. 1839–61), private doctor to the royal family, a vizier, minister of commerce and governor of Crete.

His daughter Leyla Hanim entered the imperial harem as a toddler in around 1853 and spent most of her childhood either there or in the houses of sultanas until the death of Abdulmejid I in 1861. Even after that date she was frequently received by Sultan Abdul Hamid, so maintained a close involvement with the royal family as a maid of honour and then a lady of the palace, living through the reigns of six sultans. The gilded youth extended into a life of privilege and distinction. She married Giritli Sirri Pasha, a senior Ottoman official, poet and later prime minister. She won particular renown when she published her memoirs, translated into English as *The Imperial Harem of the Sultans*.

Reading them a century later, the historian Edhem Eldem's remarks about Turkish denial – the default view that slavery here was a benign institution – come to mind immediately. 'Contrary to what people have sometimes imagined,' she writes, 'slavery in Turkey never presented the horrible characteristics, let us say, of slavery in America, where human cattle were bent under the whip and often died simply to enrich a rapacious and pitiless master.'[47] To say that Ottoman-era slavery was unlike its counterpart in America is one thing, and is indeed true. But to suggest that there was never anything 'horrible' about Ottoman slavery is veering into the territory of denial.

Though her voice and perspective may appear complacent and entitled to today's readers, Leyla Hanim is worth studying both for her considerable store of vivid anecdotes as well as for an understanding of late-empire attitudes towards slaves and slavery. Discussing Circassian slaves, for example, she reveals the domestic tensions that frequently accompanied their arrival in a household:

There were many slaves who were also cruelly mistreated by their mistresses. However, they often brought these punishments and persecutions upon themselves by exciting the jealousy of their mistresses – almost always with considerable justification. In effect, Circassian women had the habit of firmly putting into the heads of their children, from their very cradles, the thought that they would one day marry a pasha, a Prince Charming, and that they would be submerged in every conceivable sort of luxury. These girls imagined this sort of expectation to be their very right and it was while dreaming of this kind of good fortune that they came to Constantinople. When chance, rather than leading them to the lap of a powerful master, left them in the inferior condition of a servant and whenever the master of a house was a bit fickle and enterprising – and which man is not? – they often encouraged him without caring about the rights of his legitimate wife. This always led to a catastrophe. The abandoned or deceived wife, if she was not able to rid herself of the slave by selling her and if she was unable to reconquer the affections of her unfaithful husband, would take vengeance on the girl who had stolen from her the love of her husband. How many private dramas were caused by these Circassian slaves. How many were able to actually supplant their own mistresses![48]

Leyla Hanim states that a Circassian slave's 'legal obligation of servitude was nine years', before which she was not entitled to demand her freedom. In the case of a cruel master, however, she could ask to be resold to another master and, if this request was refused, she might attempt to escape and go to the slave-dealer who had sold her. Once the nine years had passed, the woman would 'automatically receive her certificate or license of liberation'. Some then chose to remain freely with their master, others asked to be married and, depending on the wealth of the family to whom they belonged, would receive a trousseau of earrings, a diamond ring, a gold watch, silver saucers and a coffee set. They might also be given delicate little spoons made of rhinoceros horn, ivory or tortoiseshell, 'along with all the necessary furnishings for a household'. It all seems a long way from Shemsigul's bitter experience.

Leyla Hanim devotes a section of her memoirs to female African slaves, who were 'a class apart' from the others.[49] 'I cannot deny that I like Negresses quite a bit,' she writes. 'Because of their black skin, their white teeth, their kinky hair and their rather clumsy manners, they amuse and please me – very much like an exotic toy.' She goes on to express her 'pity and sympathy' for these 'poor beings' who have been violently torn away from their homeland, refutes the common Turkish saying that 'the intelligence of forty Negresses will hardly fill the seed of a fig' – 'a tasteless witticism contrary to the truth' – and emphasizes that they have been denied an education due to their enslavement.

She also summarizes their horrifying ordeal from the time they were stolen from their families in the African interior to their being gagged, chained and handcuffed for the long march to the coast, put on ships and despatched around the empire. Thanks to the colour of their skin and their language, which no one else in Istanbul could understand, 'they could never hope to become the consort or the concubine of a great personage and were inevitably condemned to the most difficult and hard tasks of the household': working in kitchens in front of the furnace, doing laundry, drawing water from wells, washing and scrubbing floors, 'never given a moment of leisure'.

Later, this well-heeled Turkish woman describes how one day, when she was a younger married woman living in her father's home, the family's slave merchant, a woman called Hatice Hanim, called on her with important news:

> My dear Madam, I have discovered for you a little Negress, who is a love; she is slender and willowy like a young plant, she's black as a crow, her eyes are shining with malice and flash like lightning, her flat nose and thick lips are remarkable – in a word, she is a real devil and jumps around like a mad thing!

Leyla Hanim's father, who she tells us quite openly had an aversion to black girls and women, had to be persuaded to have such a girl in his house. He was soon won over when he saw her – she looked him boldly and directly in the face:

> 'Look at this little rascal,' my father said, 'she is testing me as well. This little one seems to have the looks of an intelligent child – I will buy her and make a present of her to you. Do not give her one of those names so commonly spread around our country such as Full Moon, Face of the Moon, Dawn or Grace; this is not a little Negress that I am giving you but rather a jasmine flower.' Thus the little girl was called Yasemin or Jasmine.

After protracted haggling with the slave-dealer, she was eventually bought for thirty Turkish pounds, 'a very good price in those days, especially for a pickaninny'. Renaming her on the spot was a typical practice for new slave-owners – an immediate assertion of ownership and the abrupt destruction of her identity.

'A name is a destiny,' the American novelist James Salter wrote. 'It is the first of all poems.' We never hear this young girl's original name, but her poem is obliterated and after that short and startling appearance, she disappears, only to return in a tragic postscript a couple of pages later. The following winter, Saz informs us, Yasemin contracted a chill, which ended in severe consumption and her death.

Leyla Hanim's life and times straddled a fascinating period of Ottoman history. It began with a liberalizing reformist movement and ended with the collapse of the 600-year-old empire in 1922 and its replacement by a vastly reduced, territorially speaking, Turkish republic.

Launched by the modernizing Sultan Mahmud II in 1839, the last year of his life, and continuing until 1876, the Tanzimat (reorganization) was a wholesale reordering of the state and its institutions through a series of imperial edicts and decrees. These touched on many, if not most, aspects of Ottoman life. The empire's subjects were granted rights guaranteeing their security and property. The army was restructured and professionalized. A new criminal code was introduced, based on the French model, with European-style courts and equality before the law, irrespective of religion. Tax collection was standardized, again according to the French system, and the traditional *jizya* tax on non-Muslims was ended. New paper currency was launched. Factories replaced guilds, ministries of health and education were established, together with universities, teaching schools, a central bank, stock exchange, post office and Academy of Sciences. Homosexuality was decriminalized in 1858, more than a century before Britain. And a series of restrictions on slavery and the slave trade, introduced over a number of decades and not complete until 1933 (some would argue 1964), transformed the scene of servitude like never before. In this last respect, piecemeal domestic reform coexisted, often uncomfortably, with strong external pressure. Together they coalesced into one word.

Abolition.

11

Abolition I: The Centre

Our holy law permits slavery.

Sultan Abdulmejid I, 1849

It is a shameful and barbarous practice for rational beings to buy and sell their fellow creatures ... Are not these poor creatures our equals before God? Why then should they be assimilated to animals?

Sultan Abdulmejid I, 1851

A frail, grey-haired man, dressed in a black frock coat over a white ruffled shirt, stands before his audience. His right hand leans on the table for support, his left arm is raised aloft in weary exhortation, index finger saluting the heavens. Lame, stoop-shouldered and almost blind, he is pouring the little energy he can still summon into rallying his troops. Around him a sea of 500 faces. Bankers, botanists, booksellers, Baptist missionaries, Quakers, Unitarian preachers and pastors, merchants, lawyers, judges and journalists, poets and publishers, politicians, philanthropists, civil servants, chemists, drapers, diplomats, suffragists and novelists. All the world is here. The overwhelming majority of this expectant gathering is male. Eight women, all in bonnets, are pressed together in a huddle across from the speaker, among them the Romantic novelist Amelia Opie and the poet Lady Byron. Almost everyone in the room is white. One of the very few exceptions is Henry Beckford, a formerly enslaved deacon from Jamaica.

Though their professions are many, these men and women have one purpose in common. They are abolitionists. They have come to

London from all corners, from France, Canada, the United States and Ireland, from Barbados, Jamaica, Haiti, South Africa and Australia. And they are hanging on to every word of the eighty-year-old campaigner. Thomas Clarkson, leading light behind Parliament's 1807 prohibition of the slave trade in the British Empire, is inaugurating the World Anti-Slavery Convention in the heavily swagged Great Room of the Freemasons' Tavern on 61–65 Great Queen Street, the heart of the West End.

The day is 12 June 1840, the beginning of an unusually dry English summer, and this is the very moment when slavery in the Ottoman Empire became, in Britain's view, British business. This landmark on the long path towards abolition was portrayed – rather poorly, most people thought – in a monumental painting by the English artist Benjamin Robert Haydon, which measures three metres by 2.8 metres and which hangs today in London's National Portrait Gallery.*

The goal of the convention, brainchild of the British and Foreign Anti-Slavery Society, which Clarkson had co-founded a year earlier with the Anglican Thomas Fowell Buxton and others, went far beyond Ottoman realms and the Muslim world. As Clarkson told the delegates:

> My dear friends, you have a most difficult task to perform; it is neither more nor less than the extirpation of slavery from the *whole world*. Your opponents who appear the most formidable are the cotton and other planters in the southern parts of the United States; who, I am grieved to say, hold more than two million of their fellow creatures in the most cruel bondage.

Southern planters were undoubtedly forceful adversaries. It would take a four-year civil war costing more than 1 million lives before they were eventually overcome. Ultimately, however, and despite Clarkson's warning, they proved a far less durable opponent to the

---

* The critical response to Haydon's work fell short of his expectations. The *Post* judged it 'a great abortion in historical art'. The Quaker William Lucas dismissed it as 'a waggon-load of heads'. Continually besieged by debt, Haydon committed suicide in 1846. 'No amount of sympathy with him and sorrow for him in his manly pursuit of a wrong idea [being a painter] for so many years . . . ought to prevent one from saying that he most unquestionably was a very bad painter', Charles Dickens wrote.

abolition of slavery than an even more 'formidable' antagonist 6,000 miles to the east: the Ottoman Empire, the most powerful Islamic state on earth.

According to Haydon, who left an impassioned, overwrought and self-important account of the convention's opening session, Clarkson's stirring words triggered a gush of emotion among the delegates. 'The women wept – the men shook off their tears, unable to prevent their flowing; for myself I was so affected and so astonished, that it was many minutes before I recovered,' he wrote.[1]

Try as one might, it is impossible to tell the story of the abolition of slavery within the Ottoman Empire and the wider world without bringing in the British. Though the debate over the role of home-grown Ottoman abolitionists and reformers is as vigorous, heated and contentious as would be expected, energized by the wider context of a cultural clash between Muslim Ottomans and interfering, non-Muslim foreigners, no one nonetheless would suggest that this period in the history of slavery, the slave trade and abolition could be understood without reference to Britain. Like the second-rate painter Benjamin Haydon, the British may have been – and undoubtedly were – impassioned, overwrought and self-important, not to mention calculated, self-interested and bullying as they extended the tentacles of British power ever more tightly around the globe. Equally, they were also enlightened, morally clear-sighted and tenacious in their pursuit of their objective. Whatever one's view of the British intervention, its role at this point in our story was critical.

Although this may not always have been appreciated in foreign capitals, there was a difference between British abolitionists and the British state. Campaigners needed the British government to exert diplomatic pressure where it was felt most keenly. And British governments, however much they deprecated the noisy and overzealous activists, could certainly not ignore a potent anti-slavery lobby which made a deep impression upon the British public and electorate through forceful parliamentary opposition and a freewheeling, vociferous press. The words 'Something must be done' rang regularly through both chambers of the Houses of Parliament and thundered across the front pages of the broadsheets throughout the nineteenth century, at a time when military interventions were regularly urged across the globe, from the mountain passes of Afghanistan, the deserts of Sudan and the Crimean Peninsula to the Burmese jungle, the Gold Coast and the Transvaal. On the question of slavery, British abolitionists and successive governments may have shared a broadly similar world view on abolition, but how they went about achieving it diverged considerably.

The British and Foreign Anti-Slavery Society was the successor organization to The Society for the Mitigation and Gradual Abolition of Slavery Throughout the British Dominions, founded in 1823 to abolish slavery within the limits of the British Empire. With the passage of the Slavery Abolition Act of 1833 that objective had largely been achieved. Abolitionist horizons, as Clarkson told his audience in 1840, were now expanding to 'the whole world'.

During that fortnight-long convention in London, Dr John Bowring, a delegate from Exeter, followed Clarkson on to the stage to deliver a speech on 'slavery in the Mohamedan states'. In it he acknowledged that a slave in 'the East' could rise to 'the highest social elevation' and that fully three-quarters of the *diwan*, or council of ministers, in Istanbul were of slave origin. Nevertheless, he went on, slavery remained 'the great impediment to civilisation' and 'the progress of civil liberty'. With a very deliberate nod to the profit-seeking bankers and merchants in the room, he noted that Egypt produced high-quality cotton which could easily supply the British market. East Africa could likewise supply Britain with its goods if only 'peace and security from the slave hunts could be introduced'. Bowring's address was warmly welcomed. It was agreed that the convention would submit a memorandum to the foreign secretary, Lord Palmerston, calling on the British government to flex its muscles and elicit a declaration from the sultan that would lead to 'the entire suppression of slavery' in the Ottoman Empire.[2]

Though that appeared far-fetched in the extreme, Clarkson's organization, which lives on today as London-based Anti-Slavery International, proved to be an energetic and effective driver of British foreign policy with regard to slavery and the slave trade in the nineteenth century. Its influence in the days following the teary inauguration of the convention in June was felt almost immediately.

The wheels of British officialdom, not typically known for rapid movement, now turned quickly. On 22 August 1840, just two months after the convention had concluded, Palmerston submitted a letter, signed by Clarkson, to Lord Ponsonby, the British ambassador to Istanbul. The letter called on the British government to use its influence with the young and newly enthroned Ottoman Sultan Abdulmejid I by linking British efforts to mediate a peace deal during the Second Egyptian–Ottoman War (1839–41), which was already posing an existential challenge to the empire, to the abolition of slavery.

Under the overall leadership of Mohammed Ali Pasha, the rebellious Ottoman Albanian ruler of Egypt, Egyptian forces under the command of his son Ibrahim Pasha had already seized Syria and marched into the Anatolian interior in 1832, trouncing Ottomans at the Battle of Konya, overcoming much of modern-day Turkey and threatening the heart of the empire. In 1839, after Franco-British intervention had settled that First Egyptian–Ottoman War (1831–3), the armies of the upstart pasha, who had since declared his independence, reappeared in south-eastern Turkey, smashing Ottoman forces at the Battle of Nezib and once again threatening Istanbul. Sultan Mahmud died in the immediate aftermath of the battle, the Ottoman fleet then appeared in the waters off Alexandria not to bombard the rebels but to defect to Mohammed Ali, and the fate of the Ottoman Empire, now bereft of both its army and navy, suddenly rested in the hands of its new, sixteen-year-old sultan, Abdulmejid. With France backing the Egyptians, the Sublime Porte had little option but to turn for support to the Great Powers, whose taking up of the Ottoman cause brought about a hasty switching of sides by the French. By 11 September 1840, a combined Anglo-Ottoman-Austrian fleet was launching a heavy bombardment of Beirut, followed in quick order by similar assaults on Sidon and Acre. Troops were landed and artillery and rifles delivered to the Maronite Christians. The pressure soon told. The Egyptians surrendered in October and Mohammed Ali, after a whirlwind, rumbustious and reforming decade, lost Syria. His consolation prize was to become hereditary ruler of Egypt within the Ottoman realm.

This, then, was the immediate context in which messages made their way between London and the British ambassador's grand, three-storey residence on the Bosphorus at Therapia (today's Tarabya in the

Sariyer district). What did not make it through the diplomatic bag to Lord Ponsonby's desk was just as interesting and revealing as what did. Palmerston had taken a knife to the original draft instructions to his ambassador, prepared by his Foreign Office officials, which he considered uninformed, unrealistic and undiplomatic. In the earlier version, Ponsonby had been directed to convey to the sultan that the Ottomans' seizure of slaves was producing 'a horror of him as a neighbour and a detestation of him as a master', the kind of language, if uttered in an earlier era by someone who did not enjoy diplomatic immunity, that could result in the loss of his head.

The charge sheet against the leader of the world's most powerful Muslim state continued. Abdulmejid was to be reminded of the 1815 Congress of Vienna, in which Turkey alone had refused to declare the slave trade 'a scourge which has so long desolated Africa, degraded Europe and afflicted humanity'. And finally, because, as always, 'Something must be done', the sultan was then expected to issue an edict forbidding 'under the severest penalties of the Mahometan law the unjust practice of procuring humans by force, by cunning, by purchase' – force, cunning and purchase being the sort of practices which Britain would routinely employ around the world as it reached the apogee of its own empire-building from the 1830s.

Palmerston may have shared the spirit of the anti-slavery sentiments contained within the draft but he was castigating in his verdict on the proposed diplomatic approach. 'This is all nonsense,' he wrote of the draft. 'Slavery is so engrained in the social habits of Mahommedans that no Ambassador could with a grave face act upon this draft. It would have been much shorter to tell Lord Ponsonby to ask the Sultan to become a Christian.'[3]

Ponsonby was no naïf. He had sat as an MP in both the Irish and British Parliaments, served as an envoy in Buenos Aires and Rio de Janeiro, and assisted with the accession to the Belgian throne of Prince Leopold of Saxe-Coburg in 1831.* He was familiar with the arts of

---

* King Leopold I's son and heir, Leopold II (r. 1865–1909) went on to found the Congo Free State in 1885. He ran it as a private slave state in tandem with Arab slavers until its annexation as a colony by Belgium in 1908, presiding for several decades over genocidal levels of killing.

British diplomacy. By the time of the 1840 World Anti-Slavery Convention, he had been ambassador in Istanbul for eight years.

After Palmerston's no-nonsense intervention, the ambassador's instructions were heavily diluted in the interests of British pragmatism. The 'continued support of Great Britain', the sultan should be informed, was contingent on favourable popular British sentiment towards the Turkish government. And since the British nation desired above almost everything to end slavery, the Turks would be wise to pursue 'some measure calculated to put an end to the Slave Trade' – not slavery, a critical distinction – within their empire. The intent was clear but allowed enough room to be suitably vague.

From Ponsonby's perspective, however, even these watered-down directives would be completely inappropriate to raise with almost any Turk, let alone the sultan. 'I have mentioned the subject and I have been heard with extreme astonishment accompanied with a smile at the proposition for destroying an institution closely interwoven with the frame of society in this country, and intimately connected with the law and with the habits and even the religion of all classes, from the sultan himself down to the lowest peasant,' he wrote.

Slaves, the ambassador pointed out to Palmerston, echoing the observations made by Bowring at the London convention, regularly enjoyed 'the highest dignities, the greatest power and largest share of wealth of any persons of the Empire'. Besides, as an unnamed Turk had put it to him, 'What would the English Government think of the Sublime Porte if it was to call upon the Sovereign of England and the people of England to alter the fundamental law of their country and change its domestic habits and customs in order to please the taste of the Turks?'

Ponsonby ended with a strong note of caution. 'I think that all attempts to effect your Lordship's purpose will fail, and I fear they might give offence if urged forward with importunity. The Turks may believe us to be their superiors in the Sciences, in Arts, and in Arms, but they are far from thinking our wisdom or our morality greater than their own.'[4]

Diplomats tend towards caution. It is the nature of their calling. Not for them the thunder, zeal and fire of righteous campaigners. Theirs is a steadier course, navigating turbulent seas with care and precision, doing everything possible to avoid storms and keep the ship on an even keel. Yet while few could plausibly deny that Ponsonby knew of what he spoke, that he had attained a thorough understanding of Ottoman society and political culture after a decade in Istanbul, his pessimism and prediction of 'failure' were ultimately not borne out by events.

First, he underestimated, as British diplomats can be wont to do, the persuasive power of British military might and economic clout, sustained over several decades. Again and again this struck ringing blows against the slave trade, reducing it from a flood to a trickle. Second, he completely and forgivably failed to foresee the rise of new generations of Ottoman reformers, some of whom felt much the same way about slavery and the slave trade – albeit without the tears and emotion – as all those abolitionists who had gathered in Freemasons' Tavern in the summer of 1840. The British had a voice, and it was an important, sometimes decisive one. But it was not all about them.

The conflicting statements from Sultan Abdulmejid quoted at the beginning of this chapter reflected a profound ambivalence towards slavery and the slave trade as the nineteenth century wore on. On the one hand, slavery was absolutely permitted by Islamic law, whose screeds of strictures had provided comprehensive regulation from the start. It had been sanctioned by the Prophet, had survived for more than a millennium in Muslim lands from the shores of the Atlantic to the mountains of Afghanistan and beyond, and was deeply rooted in Ottoman and wider Muslim society. It was hardly unique, besides, to the Dar al Islam. Slavery dominated much of African life, Muslim, Christian, pagan and otherwise. It featured everywhere from China, the Eurasian steppes and New Zealand to the plantations of Brazil, the Caribbean and the American South. Yet now the Ottoman Empire found itself under consistent pressure from mostly foreign, occasionally strident and exclusively non-Muslim powers.

On the other hand, and not withstanding that slavery in the Ottoman Empire bore virtually no relation to the specific American model of plantation slavery which brutalized men, women and children and which so horrified and disgusted its critics, slave-seizing and slave-trading looked increasingly at odds with the march of civilization. Or at least that version envisioned by Ottoman reformers, of whom

Abdulmejid's predecessor Sultan Mahmud II had been a vigorous champion. Though his delegates had not joined their European partners in the declaration against the slave trade at the Congress of Vienna, Mahmud had done away with the Mamluk slave soldiers in 1826 and sharply pruned administrative slavery beginning in 1831.

It should be emphasized, too, that the liberalizing, modernizing Tanzimat era, which rewrote the rule books on almost every aspect of Ottoman life, was launched in earnest in 1839, the very year in which Clarkson's British and Foreign Anti-Slavery Society had been founded and lasted almost forty years. The Ottoman state was increasingly likely to take the side of a slave in a dispute with his or her master, for instance over escape or abscondment, whereas before the default setting had invariably been to favour the enslaver. From 1845, to give another example, enslaved men and women were tried in court as free persons.[5] It was a more complicated picture, in other words, than either Palmerston's 'nonsense' note or Ponsonby's 'failure' prediction allowed. Reform may have been piecemeal, limited and unacceptable both to slaves and abolitionists, but the situation nonetheless was changing.

And it was a more convoluted problem than some modern writers have allowed. One eminent British-American has argued that abolition was a wholly Western initiative. 'From a Muslim point of view, to forbid what God permits, is almost as great an offense as to permit what God forbids – and slavery was authorised and regulated by the holy law.'[6] Although based on textual authority, this is an oversimplification which turns the Muslim world into a monolith, ignoring among other things the multiplicity of opinions held, the decades of debates on slavery, the nuances in interpretations of sacred texts, the different approaches to abolition between various sects (the Druze, for instance, abolished slavery in the eleventh century) and the tensions between Muslim faith, cultural tradition and everyday life.

The loud and impassioned Western abolitionist narrative can also easily drown out quieter voices calling for reform. Writing about the fateful British conquest of Egypt in 1882, the English poet and anti-imperialist Wilfrid Blunt recalled a heated correspondence with Charles Allen, the secretary of the Anti-Slavery Society, founded by Clarkson forty years earlier. Blunt, author of *The Secret History of the*

English Occupation of Egypt, had written that Ahmed Urabi Pasha, the short-lived prime minister of Egypt who was deposed in the British invasion that year after only two months in office, was committed to doing away with slavery. His letter, according to Blunt, provoked an 'indignant' reaction in Allen. 'His anger was very much what a master of foxhounds might express at the unauthorised destruction of foxes by a farmer. Mohammedans, he considered, had no business to put down slavery on their own account, or what would become of the Society?'[7]

The heat of nineteenth-century debates between mostly Western opponents and mostly Muslim defenders of slavery is echoed in some scholarly clashes today. The historian Dahlia Gubara, for example, argues that the very histories of slavery and the slave trade in the Middle East are so problematic that they constitute a 'liberal incitement to racial discourse'.* A key problem with such an adversarial approach is that it can easily slide into 'nothing to see here' denial. Some academics, meanwhile, argue that critical discussions in this field are guilty of 'otherizing' Arabs, Muslims and Africans.[8]

As with so many aspects of slavery in the Muslim world, there is no shortage of paradoxes. While Islam was at pains to regulate the institution of slavery from the outset and was outspoken in calling upon the faithful to free their slaves, nevertheless 'Muslim diehards have generally lagged behind those in other faiths in endorsing complete emancipation' and abolition.[9] The persistence of slavery into the twentieth and even twenty-first centuries in parts of the Muslim world from Africa to the Middle East will be addressed in the following chapters.

Returning to the heart of the Ottoman Empire across the long nineteenth century, we find that the situation was no less complex. There is a flow of narrowly focused *firmans* pertaining to the slave trade – a geographically specific suppression here, the outlawing of a specific

---

* Interestingly, Gubara notes that in 2010, the late Libyan leader Colonel Qaddafi publicly apologized to Africa on behalf of Arab states for their role in enslaving Africans. '"On behalf of the Arabs, I condemn, apologise and regret the behavior of Arabs towards their African brothers." He too regretted the by now proverbial culture of silence; it was, he said, "a sensitive issue that has never been tackled before".' 'Al-Azhar and the Orders of Knowledge', p. 28.

category there – and a sense of progress towards a clear yet distant goal; but there is equally a confusing blurring of ostensible reform with decades of contradiction and continuation of both slavery and the slave trade. There is manoeuvring, skulduggery, innovation, conservatism, liberalism and denial. Clarity is hard to come by. Yet, for all the reformist zeal exhibited for so long in so many areas, despite all the *firmans* and the British and other foreign pressure directed at successive sultans, there is one inescapable fact which brings the subject into focus: slavery was never abolished in the Ottoman Empire.

At the time of the empire's final, abject dissolution on 1 November 1922, after 623 years dominating the Middle East, North Africa and swathes of the Mediterranean and south-eastern Europe, slavery still lingered like an unpleasant smell. An intermittently prosecuted campaign of sometimes punitive, sometimes token, strikes against the slave trade may have left this commerce in men, women and children unrecognizable and virtually invisible at the death knell of empire, but slavery itself persisted.

There was another very pragmatic reason for Ottoman ambivalence of the sort expressed in Abdulmejid's remarks at the beginning of this chapter – that, although slavery was permitted by Islam, yet it was 'shameful and barbarous' to buy and sell humans like animals. From Istanbul's perspective, the nineteenth century, especially from the 1830s, was marked by multiple, occasionally long-lasting, conflicts. These were by no means limited to the machinations of Mohammed Ali in Egypt and the Levant. Friends could become enemies in this frenetic century, and enemies friends. The successive sultans Mahmud, Abdulmejid and Aziz (r. 1861–76) found themselves forced to 'secure foreign assistance (usually British, intermittently French, and once or twice Russian) against European foes (usually Russian, intermittently French, and once or twice British) and the latter's three regional surrogates'.[10] There were three wars against the Russians alone, more than a decade fighting the Greek War of Independence (1821–32), conflicts with the Serbs (independent by 1878) and Montenegrins, rebellions in Albania, Bosnia, Bulgaria and Crete. Contracting on-again, off-again alliances with European states, particularly Britain, required creating an impression, at the very least, of moving towards the abolition they called for. By mid-century, when Russian Tsar

Nicholas I likened the Ottoman Empire to 'a very sick man' (leading to the 'sick man of Europe' moniker), Istanbul's economic dependence on European powers, particularly the British and French, was so deeply entrenched that more decisive measures against the slave trade had to be countenanced.

For years Istanbul's central slave market, the largest in the empire, had occupied a sweep of prime property in the heart of the imperial capital between Nuruosmaniye Mosque and Gazi Atik Ali Pasha Mosque in what is today the area of Çemberlitaş around the shop-crowded surroundings of the Grand Bazaar. Its physical presence in the centre of the city symbolized its complete centrality to social and commercial life. In an order of 28 December 1846 – the same year in which the English evangelical and abolitionist James Richardson, a member of the Anti-Slavery Society, witnessed a sick young female slave being whipped to death in Libya – and apparently on his own initiative, Abdulmejid abolished the slave market at a stroke. His motivations, according to the Ottoman nineteenth-century court historian Ahmed Lutfi, were humanitarian. During a meeting about important reforms and the judicial system, the sultan had heard of some 'troubles' in the market – for which read maltreatment of slaves – which contradicted holy law. The closure of the market effectively broke up the Esirci Esnafi, the slave-dealers' guild, the operator and regulator of the trade in the capital, and inevitably and immediately forced the trade underground. By this stage Ottoman slavery was characterized by being predominantly female, African and domestic. The white 'elite' Circassian slavery was, by contrast, a much smaller and more limited affair.

While doing away with the main slave market was a grand gesture, it was certainly not the same thing as abolishing the slave trade. Twenty years after its abrupt closure there were large slave-dealing businesses operating in, among other places, the Tophane quarter of Beyoğlu, Istanbul's first industrial zone, which ran downhill from Galata to the Bosphorus, and across the Golden Horn opposite the Suleymaniye Mosque in the Fatih district, named after the famous Conqueror of Constantinople. That is not to say that the sultan's closure of the main slave market was ineffective. There were pragmatic advantages in putting distance between the government and the slave trade. Abdulmejid was demonstrating to his European allies and domestic reformers that he was moving in the 'right' direction while simultaneously allowing the trade to continue behind closed doors across the capital in a nod to the many millions of his subjects, including conservative clerics who, resenting what they saw as foreign reforms, favoured the status quo.[11]

If the 1846 move against the slave market was Ottoman in motivation, it was British diplomatic pressure which led to the sultan's suppression of the slave trade in the Gulf in 1847, his prohibition of the Circassian slave trade in 1854 and the general outlawing of the black slave trade in 1857.

For most of this period, it was African slavery, the main focus of abolitionist energies, which received the greatest diplomatic attention. At times, however, Circassian slavery also exercised European minds. Thus in August 1854, at the height of the Crimean War, France and Britain both submitted formal notes to the Porte calling for the prohibition of the Circassian slave trade and the sale of these slaves in Istanbul.

Lord Stratford de Redcliffe, the long-standing British ambassador in Istanbul, who served there from 1842 to 1858, did not mince his words. In his letter of 29 August to the Porte, he noted that the enslavement of Muslim Circassians was illegal under Islamic law and that of Christian Georgians was offensive to the allies, 'without whose cooperation the very existence of the Turkish Empire would be endangered'. Far too many 'barbarous practices', such as the shipping of Georgian children on an Austrian steamer to Istanbul, where they had been sold as slaves to a senior Turkish official, had been brought to light. At a time when 'Christian Powers have sent their armies and squadrons into Turkey for its defence, and when those armies and squadrons composed of Christians are fighting side by side with Mussulmans and confounding all differences of religion in the common cause of humanity and national independence, they set at nought every calculation and excite the most unqualified disgust'.[12]

On 18 September, less than three weeks after Stratford's letter, the Council of Ministers met in Istanbul. Mehmed Emin Pasha, then serving the first of his three tenures as grand vizier, reminded the cabinet that the allies' ultimate objective was 'the abolition of slavery'. But a total prohibition of the Georgian and Circassian slave trade would likely result in 'the closing of the gate of slavery', making this, he said, an 'undesirable' policy. An equilibrium had to be sought:

> If we do nothing, there is no doubt that things will compel us to go to the point of total abolition. Thus, we have to find a solution by which we will be able to show, with a new proof, to the two allies that the Ottoman Empire abides by the principles of humanity and in this way we shall be able to secure their goodwill as well as that of the Georgian people.[13]

The carefully calibrated solution was a brace of *firmans*, sent to Mustafa Pasha, commander of the Ottoman army in Batum (Batumi) on Georgia's Black Sea Coast, in mid-October. Both prohibited the export of slaves from Georgia and the Circassian coast respectively, though there were important differences, the most significant being one of religion. As a Muslim people outside his empire, the Circassians could not be prohibited from slave-trading, a major source of income especially during an economically crippling conflict with Russia.

European attention and diplomatic pressure ebbed and flowed like the tide. With the end of the Crimean War in 1856, the allies' pressure on the Ottomans to stamp out 'white slavery' faded correspondingly. While the trade from Georgia virtually ceased, that in Circassian slaves, who continued to be prized by Ottoman buyers at the highest levels of society, continued apace after the war, energetically pursued by Circassian slavers.

Sultan Abdulmejid's 1857 *firman* prohibiting the African slave trade within the empire, with the notable exception of the Hijaz, resulted in a similarly mixed picture. On paper it was a momentous move in the history of Ottoman slavery and abolition, however imperfectly the edict was observed in practice for many years to come. British officialdom at the highest level gave it a cautious, typically pragmatic welcome. The then foreign secretary, Lord Clarendon, writing in 1858, considered its regulations, if executed in good faith, 'sufficient for the purpose for which they are required'. However, officials actually monitoring the slave trade quickly detected the absence of such good faith. Successive British consul generals in Ottoman Tripoli, for example, pronounced the 1857 *firman*, which never had the full weight of law, 'a mere fiction' in 1858 and 'a solemn mockery' in 1863.[14]

Abolition was, as everyone knew, extremely sensitive. In the Hijaz, home of the Holy Places of Medina and Mecca, lodestars of Islam, opposition to Ottoman measures to curb the slave trade tipped into open rioting and rebellion even before the *firman* against the African trade had been announced. By 1855, rumours that such a move was imminent were causing profound unease in the Arabian Peninsula. The flames of insurrection were adeptly fanned by Abd al Muttalib, the sharif of Mecca, who had his own political agenda, which was entirely separate from the question of slavery and its possible abolition: nothing less than the end of Ottoman power in the Hijaz.

A letter, purportedly from the merchants of the port city of Jeddah, an important slave market, was sent to the *ulema* clergy and sharifs of Mecca. It had been prepared, in fact, by Abd al Muttalib and was designed to inflame Arab feelings against the Ottomans. How could 'these infidel regulations be applied to us', the letter asked? How could Muslims tolerate this 'comingling with infidels in everything' when 'in every way, Islam and the religion of the infidels are contrary to one another'? Istanbul learnt of the plot and despatched a senior official to investigate. An order was then given from Kamil Pasha, the Ottoman *wali*, closing the slave markets and prohibiting the slave trade.

When, on 30 October 1855, it was read out in public at the sharia court in front of the *ulema* and sharifs of Mecca, there was uproar. Shaikh Jamal, head of the clerics, issued a fiery fatwa declaring the order void because it violated Islamic law. With this order against the slave trade, he raged, the Turks had revealed themselves as apostates. It was therefore perfectly permissible to kill them with impunity and – with a macabre flourish of irony – even enslave their children. A jihad was declared against the Christians and idolators, which now included Muslim Ottomans. Houses belonging to English and French residents were looted and Ottoman garrisons were attacked by mobs on the rampage. The clerics demanded that Istanbul remove both the judge and the Ottoman garrison from Mecca, insisted on their freedom to continue practising slavery, and called for the expulsion of the consuls and all Christians from the Hijaz. Abd al Muttalib was summarily deposed in response but refused to accept his dismissal. He wrote to the Bedouin chiefs, calling on them to 'rise in the name of Mohammed and the true faith, as the Sultan has become a Christian the same as the Frank'. The rebellion was only suppressed with his arrest seven months later, in June 1856. The truculent Abd al Muttalib was sent into exile, first to Salonica, later to Istanbul. Strangely, considering his brazen disloyalty to the empire, he was reappointed sharif of Mecca in 1880, by which time he was a frail, ineffectual figure on the cusp of ninety – precisely why he had been appointed. His second term did not last long. It ended with his second sacking in 1882, as the Ottomans moved to consolidate direct control over the Hijaz.

All the turbulence had alarmed Istanbul. After this most severe of shocks to the empire in the sacred, deeply conservative epicentre of the faith, it was little surprise that the 1857 *firman* against the African trade made the specific exception for the Hijaz. Reform wasn't for everyone.[15]

The death of Abdulmejid in 1861, after a reign of twenty-two years,

An aristocratic Arab merchant, representative of the Grand Sharif of Mecca, poses with his Circassian slave, c. 1885. The Dutch photographer Christiaan Snouck Hurgronje spent six months living in Mecca and published two volumes about the holy city.

changed the tone of empire. With regard to the slave trade, the accession to the imperial throne of his thirty-one-year-old brother Abdulaziz (r. 1861–76) brought a diminuendo of reform.

Nowhere perhaps was the chasm between official policy and real-world practice most glaringly exposed than in the case of Pertevniyal Valide Sultan (c.1810–83), one of the late Sultan Mahmud II's wives and the redoubtable and influential mother of the new sultan. Romanian, Kurd or Circassian by origin, she was effectively the most powerful woman in the Ottoman Empire and sometimes struggled to live up to her ethereal name. Although literally 'Descended from Radiance', she was equally the steeliest street fighter. She hit the headlines in 1869, during the visit to Istanbul of the French Empress Eugénie, wife of Napoleon III, en route to open the Suez Canal. After a grand banquet in her honour in the Dolmabahçe Palace, Sultan Abdulaziz escorted the empress to meet his mother in the royal harem. Disgusted to see her son walking arm in arm with an unknown European woman – an infidel at that! – in these famously inaccessible quarters, the furious Pertevniyal slapped Eugénie in the face. An international incident was only narrowly avoided.[16]

Breaking protocol was the least of the mother sultan's misdemeanours: breaking the law proved a lucrative speciality during her son's fifteen-year sultanate. The historian Ceyda Karamursel has studied the documentary evidence of almost 100 notes of her slave purchases, bills of sale and related correspondence, which together reveal Pertevniyal to be a relentless dealer in slaves. Although she had a preference for the more expensive Circassian girls between the ages of eight and fourteen, she also exhibited a readiness to buy African slaves wherever she saw the opportunity. Never mind that the trade in both had been banned years earlier.[17]

It was the girls' physical attributes, specifically their perceived beauty or lack of it, and their price that were of most interest to this queen of slaving. Good conduct was, for Pertevniyal, a lower priority. The documents invariably record more information about the white Circassian slaves than they do on the black African girls, whose ethnicity and physical characteristics are rarely mentioned, signifying a general lack of interest on the buyer's part. What was most important for the mother of the empire were the services they could provide, be it as cooks, nannies, wet-nurses or domestics. As presided over by Pertevniyal, this was a racially segregated world with distinct boundaries, with white girls purchased on the whole for sexual service in the harem and black girls bought for domestic duties.

While the sultan personified the full majesty of Ottoman law, Pertevniyal appeared to delight in disregarding it. Far from setting an example of scrupulously law-abiding behaviour, Pertevniyal traded in slaves with impunity, in direct contravention of Ottoman regulations. A decade after the 1857 *firman* she was trading in African slaves, using privileged, publicly unavailable information on incoming shipments to steal an advantage over her less connected competition. Her steward Huseyin, tasked with monitoring Circassian vessels for suitable purchases of young women and girls, found himself on the receiving end of an unwavering stream of orders from the great matriarch.

In 1863, she boldly fired off strict instructions to the governor of Trabzon. He was to intercept ships in his port, seize the girls and specifically reserve 'the good ones' for her. It didn't matter if they were refugees fleeing the humanitarian crisis caused by the violent and ongoing Russian expulsion of Circassians. Early access was essential, she told the governor, because otherwise, by the time the ships reached the Bosphorus in Istanbul, they would be immediately surrounded by a scrum of slave-dealers who would snap up all the best girls in moments.

Consular reports indicate that imports of both African and Circassian slaves were on the rise again from the late 1860s. The flow of Circassian girls destined for the royal and other elite harems continued unabated, many of them shipped across to the Ottoman capital from Trabzon, Samsun and other ports in European steamers, such as those operated by Österreichischer Lloyd (Austrian Lloyd), the largest shipping company in the Habsburg Empire, founded in Trieste in 1833. Its steamers plied a couple of highly profitable routes between Alexandria and Istanbul via a number of Levantine ports and, from their first appearance in the eastern Mediterranean and Aegean from the later 1830s, were highly attractive to those who traded in human cargo. They were chosen by 'dozens (or possibly hundreds) of slave traders to transport thousands (or possibly tens of thousands) of slaves to the Ottoman Empire'.[18]

It fell to foreign officials in particular to monitor this illicit trade, maintaining a typically pragmatic balance between enforcing the law and raising breaches with the Porte. Inevitably, some consular officials were more zealous than others. Robert William Cumberbatch, the British consul in Smyrna (today's city of Izmir, Turkey's third-largest), was at his most vigilant on 3 June 1870, when Austrian Lloyd's 1, 836-ton ship *Mars* steamed into port. By this point in his career he had already made a number of unproven accusations of transporting slaves, all of which had been vigorously denied by the company, which regarded this energetic British official with misgiving and alarm. Records show that some of his colleagues, especially Sir Henry Elliot, the British ambassador in Istanbul from 1867, took a similar view, considering him a loose cannon, whose regular, heavy-handed interventions strained London's carefully managed diplomatic relations with the Porte. Elliot was a faithful servant of empire, dedicated to maintaining British interests at all costs. He was not out to cause an inconvenient brouhaha.

As part of its interventions against the trade, Britain had struck a series of bilateral treaties with a number of countries authorizing the mutual search of each other's ships. One such was the treaty between Britain, Austria, Prussia and Russia, signed in 1841, an agreement which permitted the British consul in Smyrna to subject the Austrian steamship *Mars* to a search. On paper Britain's moves against the slave trade might have appeared clear-cut, as consuls like Cumberbatch saw them, but in practice they were ambivalent and carried a strong dose of pragmatic self-interest. British policy towards policing the slave trade, as clearly expressed in the instructions issued to the Royal Navy in 1866, depended upon maintaining an elaborate fiction: 'the distinction between the export of Slaves to which Great Britain is determined to put an end and the system of Domestic Slavery with which she claims no right to interfere'.[19]

Cumberbatch's regular reporting of illegal slave-trading was threatening this delicate balance. Now, under his eagle eyes, and to the chagrin and horror of its captain Matteo Druscovich, the steamship *Mars* was carefully searched. Several enslaved children were found: an eighteen-year-old boy bought in Egypt for a Turkish pasha in Istanbul; a sixteen-year-old Ethiopian boy; a brother and sister aged between eight and ten; and three young boys who had been captured in a brutal slave raid in Abyssinia.

Cumberbatch, who had already been providing refuge for runaway slaves, to the intense exasperation of Turkish officials, managed to find positions for most of them, but he had stirred up a hornet's nest in the process, flinging ordure on British foreign policy, Austrian diplomats and businessmen and, scandalously, the honour of the Ottoman sultan. Even worse, it soon became apparent that earlier rumours and consular reports were not the imagination of a crusading consul. A good portion of the Austrian Lloyd fleet was indeed engaged on a regular slave shuttle between Alexandria and Istanbul. In Trieste and Vienna there was an irritated and embarrassed shuffling of papers. During the subsequent internal company investigation one of the ship captains protested, not unreasonably, that it was impossible to distinguish a servant from a slave. Slave-dealers and slave-owners routinely claimed that their slaves were their servants. An Austrian Lloyd director complacently agreed. 'The slave trade', he suggested, 'was as much a necessary incident of the Mediterranean trade as the passage of water through the ballast tanks of boats.'[20]

A couple of months later, Elliot was writing to the foreign secretary, Lord Granville, arguing that it was neither possible nor advisable to approach the Porte on abolishing the institution of slavery – as opposed to the slave trade. First and most fundamental, slavery was not illegal in the Ottoman Empire. Second, it was 'sanctioned by immemorial usage' and had 'nothing in it revolting to Turkish feeling'. Finally, it was so woven into the highest reaches of society that any intervention he made against it would inevitably be 'in the highest degree offensive' to his interlocutor. 'With the knowledge not only that the wife of the Grand Vizier had been a Circassian slave, but that the ladies in a still more exalted position had belonged to the same class, Your Lordship will understand that I should have been guilty of gross impropriety if I had gone to Ali Pasha and insisted upon the debasing consequences of an institution, which nobody can think more hateful than I do.'[21]

Elliot achieved the rare feat of annoying both Lord Salisbury and Gladstone. In 1876 he attracted fierce criticism at home after downplaying the brutal Ottoman suppression of a Bulgarian uprising against the empire in which an estimated 12,000–30,000 were killed.[22] British interests in preventing destabilizing change in the 'semi-civilized' Turkish Empire, Elliot wrote at the time, were 'not affected by the question whether it was 10,000 or 20,000 persons who perished in the suppression'. Gladstone, then the leader of the opposition, took a different view. He used the bloody events in Bulgaria for his own political ends – as the basis for a comeback campaign against the Disraeli government – and coined the term 'Bulgarian Atrocities', whipping up a public outcry across Europe against the Ottomans.

In his hard-hitting pamphlet *Bulgarian Horrors and the Question of the East*, Gladstone did not pull his punches. 'They are not the mild Mahometans of India, nor the chivalrous Saladins of Syria, nor the cultured Moors of Spain,' he wrote of the Turks. 'They were, upon the whole, from the black day when they first entered Europe, the one great anti-human specimen of humanity. Wherever they went, a broad line of blood marked the track behind them; and, as far as their dominion reached, civilization disappeared from view.' The Gladstonian view carried the day and, when war began against the Russians the following year, Britain declined to support its Ottoman ally, blaming the public outrage towards the massacres in Bulgaria.

Gladstone's attitudes towards slavery, however, were less unequivocal. He was the fourth son of John Gladstone, the wealthy merchant and politician who, by 1833, had become one of the largest slave-owners in the West Indies, with his various estates there valued at £336,000, the equivalent of more than £30 million today. A year after publishing his inflammatory pamphlet on the Bulgarian atrocities, he wrote of how he was more moved by the sufferings of Bulgarians and Slavs under the Turks than black slaves under their white masters because 'in the case of negro slavery ... it was the case of a race of higher capacities ruling over a race of lower capacities'.[23]

For all the representations from European, especially British, government voices calling for abolition, and for all the agreeably worded Ottoman diplomatic responses, there was no genuine discussion of the subject, no meaningful exchange. It was, to all intents and purposes, a dialogue of the deaf. Both sides regarded the other's position on slavery with withering disdain. On the one hand there was a hectoring, moralizing, self-righteous, hypocritical, opportunist West, on the other the cruel, backward, uncivilized, defensive East, mired in denial.

One of the greatest problems was in the respective understandings of slavery. Here there was no common ground. For the British, slavery was slavery. The African slave toiling beneath the whip of a merciless master on a steaming American plantation had one thing in common with his or her African or Circassian counterpart in the Ottoman Empire. Both were slaves – and Britain was committed to the abolition of slavery. It was that simple. For the Ottomans, comparing the two models of servitude was a monstrous category error. While American slavery was savage, its Ottoman version was humane, benevolent, culturally accepted and religiously sanctioned. There *was* no comparison. It is surely worth stating, too, that slavery was not only a ruling elite pursuit, it was also, quite literally, in the ruling elite's DNA. Sultans, grand viziers and much of the ruling class were either the sons of former slaves or had been slaves at a young age. Why should they see anything wrong with this time-honoured, culturally accepted practice endorsed by their faith? The meddling infidels, who unfortunately held the military and economic trump cards (and therein lay the problem), had got it all wrong.*

Late on the night of 30 May 1876, the Ottoman Empire's stability, which was so prized by Sir Henry Elliot among others, was abruptly shattered. In a shocking coup championed by the reformist Ahmed Sefik Midhat Pasha, former governor of Baghdad, grand vizier and now leader of the constitutional movement, Abdulaziz, who had been on manoeuvres to secure the succession of his eldest son Yusuf Izzedin to the throne, was summarily deposed. He was replaced by his nephew Murad V, an alcoholic who almost immediately succumbed to a mental breakdown and remained on the throne for just ninety-three days before he too was removed, in favour of his half-brother Abdul Hamid II (r. 1876–1909). Abdulaziz was found dead in his apartments in the Feriye Palace on the Bosphorus a few days later in what was pronounced a suicide by nineteen Turkish and foreign

---

* In more recent times, the polarized debate over the supposedly humane treatment of slaves in the Arab world versus the cruelty of the Atlantic slave trade continues. As the Sudanese scholar Yusuf Fadl Hasan once remarked: 'Slavery is slavery and cannot be beautified by cosmetics. It left extreme bitterness in the central parts of the continent against the Arab minority which lived on the coast'. Khair El-Din Haseeb (ed.), *The Arabs and Africa*, p. 33.

physicians – their unanimous verdict doing little to dispel suspicions that he had been the victim of foul play.

At the most prosaic level, Murad's accession to the throne, however short-lived, spelt the end of Pertevniyal's tenure as mother sultan. Her sealed apartments were immediately opened. The results of fifteen years of speculating and wealth accumulation, including all the slave-dealing, were laid out. The concubine Filizten recalled in her memoirs of life in the late-nineteenth-century harem that eight chests of gold and four chests of debentures were discovered. Each chest of gold required eight porters to carry it. Filizten reported that the total weight of the gold recovered, which devolved in theory to the new sultan but in practice to his influential mother, was 5,120 *okkas*, the scarcely credible equivalent of 6,500 kilograms. For the women of the harem it was an extraordinary day, the concubine remembered:

> The harem became a blinding swirl of gold and diamonds. The new Imperial Consorts and the new *hazinedars* [senior female chamberlains], the concubines and the *kalfas* [attendants and supervisors] decked themselves out in the exquisite jewellery lavishly bestowed upon them, so that each of them looked for all the world like a bride on her wedding day.[24]

At a more elevated level, and notwithstanding Murad's very short reign as sultan, the 1876 coup ushered in the empire's first constitution in almost 600 years. According to Midhat's son Ali Haydar Midhat, writing about his famous father from exile in Europe at the turn of the century, Midhat Pasha intervened at the outset of the new sultan's reign to propose the abolition of slavery. As evidence for this claim, Ali Haydar presented the original draft of the accession speech his father had prepared for Sultan Abdul Hamid II:

> The buying and selling of slaves being contrary to the prescriptions of the Sacred Law (Cheri), We hereby enfranchise the slaves and eunuchs of Our Palace, and declare that henceforth all trade in slaves, whether purchase or sale, is hereby formally forbidden in Our Empire, and a date will be fixed for the gradual emancipation of all existing slaves, and special measures will be adopted to prevent any return to slavery.[25]

There are two things to note about this extract. First, as the Turkish historian Yusuf Hakan Erdem has shown, it differed substantially from the Ottoman Turkish version of Ali Haydar Midhat's book, where the draft speech neither condemned the slave trade nor made any reference to measures to prevent the 'return to slavery'. Second, when Abdul Hamid gave his accession speech, he completely omitted the passage referring to slavery and the slave trade altogether.[26]

Drafted by Midhat Pasha and his circle of Young Ottomans, the 1876 constitution, the first fully realized written constitution in the Muslim world, moved towards the separation of legislative, judicial and executive authority in the accelerating spirit of reform. It was grudgingly accepted by Abdul Hamid, who was then facing the same sort of pressure from domestic reformers and foreign powers to liberalize as his immediate predecessors on the throne. Like the accession speech which Abdul Hamid had delivered, however, the constitution did not contain any articles relating either to slavery or its abolition. Instead, there were apparently contradictory sections which potentially brought into play the legality of slavery. Thus, while Articles 9 and 10 granted 'inviolable' freedom to all Ottoman subjects, Article 22 declared the privacy of the home equally 'inviolable'. The result was no move against slavery. Article 113 meanwhile gave the sultan the right to banish anyone from the empire without trial. He wasted little time in exercising it.[27]

Any hopes that Midhat Pasha's appointment for a second term as grand vizier might indicate willingness on the part of Abdul Hamid to embrace a new era of political and social reform were soon snuffed out. Selected to the position just days before the new constitution was declared on 23 December, six weeks later the empire's second most powerful figure found himself exiled in Brindisi. The liberal constitution lasted only a little longer. On Valentine's Day 1878, with the ink barely dry on a truce signed with Russia a fortnight earlier as the Russo–Turkish War entered its final days, and as a British fleet steamed into the Sea of Marmara, Abdul Hamid suspended the constitution and prorogued the first Ottoman parliament before it had even celebrated its first anniversary. Absolute monarchy, not liberal parliamentary democracy, was the order of the day.[28]

Even the most ardent reformers in the Ottoman Empire could send out profoundly mixed messages on slavery. By turns celebrated or distrusted as a reformer, Midhat Pasha, the man who had brought modern schools, hospitals and factories to Baghdad and the Balkans, the visionary who was reinventing the military along modern lines of education and training, was no saint when it came to slavery. He had what the historian Madeline Zilfi calls his 'Jeffersonian moment' during his time as governor of Baghdad, starting in 1869. His first wife, perhaps understandably, had remained in Istanbul during her husband's famously testing hardship posting in Iraq. In her absence he decided to seek a second wife. Yet rather than finding a free woman among the circle of his friends and colleagues, as would have been quite normal in his peer group, he chose instead a Circassian slave girl. His sister scoured the markets and private harems to find the perfect match, eventually choosing a presumably beautiful seventeen-year-old girl called Sehriban for her fifty-year-old brother, purchased for the huge sum of 2,000 gold coins. If, as his son Ali Haydar claimed, Midhat really 'desired to abolish the slave trade, which he considered a scandal and a disgrace to the empire', he had an odd way of showing it. Whatever his abolitionist instincts, it was hardly his finest moment as a liberal reformer.[29]

Nine months after his abrupt dismissal and exile, following a whirlwind tour of European capitals to promote Ottoman reforms, Midhat Pasha was brought in from the cold after British intervention. In November 1878 he was appointed governor of Syria, where, as before in Baghdad and the Balkans, he threw himself into energetic reforms, working hard to improve education, the civil service, infrastructure, minority representation, public transport and the press.

A year after his appointment came news of a rather different Midhat Pasha at work. In what looks like a deliberate attempt to smear him – Sultan Abdulmejid had mistrusted him from the outset and feared him as a potential rival – information was leaked to the British consul in Jeddah that the governor had gifted two female slaves to a religious dignitary. While this sort of patronage would have been par for the course for local power politics in the Ottoman Empire, it was not the sort of behaviour to be expected from the master of abolition, the same man who earlier had encouraged the sultan to set an example by freeing his own palace slaves before abolishing slavery altogether.

In the interests of keeping the peace, and perhaps sensing something underhand, the British chose not to raise the incident with the great modernizer. Things were never as clear-cut as they seemed.[30]

In 1881, Midhat Pasha's fortunes took a final turn for the worse. Arrested and charged with the murder of Sultan Abdulaziz in what looked like decidedly trumped-up allegations, he was sentenced to death by a kangaroo court. The penalty was commuted, following an outcry from the European powers, to life imprisonment in Taif, 1,500 miles away in the heart of the Arabian Peninsula, a place as inimical to reform as could be found in the entire empire. But even this was not enough for Sultan Abdulhamid.

A message was sent from Istanbul impressing upon the local authorities the desirability of an accident. When this failed to materialize, more decisive action was ordered and, on the night of 26 April 1883, Midhat Pasha was strangled to death. In a morbid postscript, it was said that the paranoid sultan required proof that his old adversary, a man widely known as 'the father of the free and the deposer of sultans', was really dead. Midhat Pasha's body was disinterred, the story went, his head cut off and despatched to Yildiz Palace in a box labelled 'Ivoires Japonaises, objets d'art'.[31]

On Sunday, 28 March 1886 readers of the *New York Times* were treated to what is, or used to be, known in the newspaper trade as a 'marmalade dropper'. 'SLAVES SOLD TO THE TURK', the headline proclaimed in eye-catching capitals. 'HOW THE VILE TRAFFIC IS STILL CARRIED ON IN THE EAST. SIGHTS OUR CORRESPONDENT SAW FOR TWENTY DOLLARS – IN THE HOUSE OF A GRAND OLD TURK OF A DEALER.' All that was missing were the exclamation marks!![32]

The newspaper's correspondent in Istanbul, Wolf von Schierbrand, a decorated German war veteran, journalist and author, had a scoop on his hands:

> While a guest at the hospitable board of Dr S. Englander, the chief of Reuter's Agency in the Orient, five days ago, my neighbor, the young Count de Ortega-Morejon, attaché to the Spanish Legation here, remarked quite accidentally: 'By the way, young Aristarchi Pasha has

a young Circassian slave who is said to be as beautiful as the moon – that's his expression. He paid £200 for her – a steep price nowadays. But he had had a windfall and could afford it.'

Von Schierbrand professed astonishment. '"Is the trade in female slaves being carried on right here under the eyes of virtuous England's representative?" I asked.' He had thought that '"this sort of thing belonged in the past"'. His query was met with a howl of laughter, a reaction which encouraged the newspaperman to carry out his own research. A senior British source then told him that the trade in women was 'universally' carried out across the empire, undercover but with the absolute 'knowledge and connivance' of the Turkish authorities, who subsequently denied it when approached by Europeans.

The article said as much, if not more, about the writer as it did about the subject under review. There were stereotypes and sweeping generalizations, along with prejudices typical of their time. There was a typically Western prurience, too, about his discussion of Circassian girls, who apparently possessed the 'Anglo-Saxon' sort of beauty which made them perennial favourites of the Turks:

> The same queenly limbs, the same clear complexion, the same fair skin, blonde, wavy hair, and blue eyes. The Turks themselves being dark, they are naturally attracted to the fair ones of the opposite sex. Thus, since time immemorial it has always been a blonde who has reigned as Sultana Favorita in the Serail.

The Circassian girls, he reported, were the most prized and most expensive, typically costing fifty to 100 Turkish pounds ($220–$400), compared with twenty to thirty pounds for a Syrian girl, the second highest in demand. The latter were 'a little "off color", i.e. their complexions are about as light brown as that of an American quadroon girl,' he continued, warming to his theme of women as commodities defined by the colour of their skin. 'They have generally good figures while young, but age more rapidly than their Circassian sisters.' Finally came the Nubian slave girls, mainly used for domestic service, costing between six pounds and twenty.

There followed a sensationalized account of an undercover expedition. Demonstrating the sort of self-dramatizing enthusiasm which comes naturally to some journalists, he explained how no American newspaperman had ever attempted such a challenge. A visit to one of the 'principal female slave dealers of Stamboul', he added, was fraught with danger.

What could be more essential, then, than a disguise? The German reporter obligingly donned a fez, a fake beard, green glasses and a military sword. Posing as a foreign doctor in the Turkish army who was in the market for a slave girl, he was driven across town, blind-folded, led into a house and hustled into a secret room, where he was introduced to 'a courtly old Turk' by an Armenian middleman. Here a succession of half a dozen Nubian and Syrian girls, aged between twelve and fifteen and led by a 'pompous and fat' black eunuch, were paraded before him as he reclined alongside his white-bearded Turk-ish host, sipping coffee, smoking a *nargileh* water pipe and doing his best to avoid the repeatedly offered sweetmeats. After von Schier-brand said no to this first group another seven young girls, this time Syrian and Circassian, were brought in. Finally, after another dismis-sal, a last group of three was offered, including a Circassian girl of about sixteen, who was 'a beauty, and no mistake'. She was priced at 300 pounds, the dealer said.

Wisely at this point, the German made his excuses before the inter-minable haggling could begin and he became too involved. He told his host he would think about it. Only a week before writing his article, he reported, the same dealer had sold a healthy young slave for £20. 'Truly not even in America's palmiest days of slavery was human flesh held so cheap as it is today in the land of the Crescent!'

But what was most astonishing was that although all the foreign ambassadors of 'civilized' nations knew that slave-trafficking contin-ued, 'nothing is done to check this bestial evil'. Slavery might have been 'mild and rather humane' in Turkey, he concluded, 'but still it is slavery'.

As the nineteenth century drew to a close, while moves against the slave trade were spasmodic and limited, the institution of slavery in the Ottoman Empire continued unabated, notwithstanding a deaf-ening international chorus and less vociferous domestic voices both demanding its abolition.

In 1880, the Anglo–Ottoman Convention for the Suppression of the Black Sea Trade gave both powers the right to search each other's ships there and in the Red Sea, the Gulf and East Africa. The notable and quite deliberate exception was the Mediterranean, the epicentre of the trade, where both Ottoman and probably British-flagged vessels, like those of Austrian Lloyd, were still transporting slaves. As a result of the 1880 convention new laws were required to prosecute those persons found trading in slaves, yet when he was presented with draft legislation against the trade Abdul Hamid dragged his feet for the best part of a decade. Conferences and conventions came and went. In 1885, the Berlin Conference was convened to regulate colonialism and trade across the African continent. In it, Abdul Hamid agreed with his partners to 'strive for the suppression of slavery, and especially the Negro slave trade', but there was still no sign of the missing legislation required to prosecute transgressors. The sultan eventually buckled and signed his assent only under the pressure of the Brussels Anti-Slavery Conference of 1889, a move which took much of the sting out of the abolitionist lobby's tail.[33]

Large numbers of Circassian refugees, both wealthy slave-owners and their downtrodden slaves, arriving in the empire in great numbers from the chaos and conflict in the Caucasus in the later nineteenth century, proved a huge challenge. There were armed riots and rebellions, fuelled by a sense among the enslaved that the tide was turning against slavery worldwide. From their first appearance in the Ottoman Empire during the wave of expulsions at the end of the 1850s, enslaved Circassians started filing petitions and lawsuits demanding their freedom. In so doing they pushed the issue of abolition higher up the public agenda.

One example, to cite a long petition to the Council of State in 1872, were the three slaves from the 'Circassian Mountain' called Haydar, Osman and Zos, who deplored the lack of response from the Ottoman state to their earlier correspondence. 'It must be our poor command of the language and the errors we made in expressing our intention thereof that hindered and delayed the receipt of the answers and just solutions we have been demanding in the last several years,' wrote the aggrieved trio with a touch of sarcasm. Their status as slaves depended on their ancestors having sought protection from local chieftains, they explained in great detail, and now that they were under the protection of the Ottoman state this was no longer valid or just. Serving both their Circassian masters as well as the state, and paying taxes to both, was not viable.

When they finally received their official response, it was a masterpiece of official obfuscation. On the one hand, the letter read, now that the men fell under both *sheri* (sharia) law and civil jurisdiction, their status as slaves should indeed have been invalidated. On the other hand, however, this slave status had been established since time immemorial and the state could not simply reverse it because they had emigrated to a new state. In a spirit of pragmatism and compromise, the Council of State then declared that once male slaves reached the age of forty-five and female slaves thirty-five, they were free. Any children born *before* reaching those landmarks would not be free, however, unless they were manumitted at a cost to be agreed by a commission. Navigating a course through the Scylla of defiant Circassian slave-owners and the turbulent Charybdis of their freedom-seeking slaves tested the Ottoman state to its limits.[34]

For a time at least, the solution most energetically proposed was that outlined in the Council of State's response to Haydar, Osman and Zos. This – *mukatebe*, or manumission – was at the heart of the wider Ottoman approach to slavery in the later nineteenth century. In lieu of abolition, the state alternately suggested and promoted manumission. It was a realistic solution to the destabilizing twin demands of Circassian slaves insisting on their freedom while their masters with equal vigour emphasized their right to own slaves, based on long-established religious law, supported by the Quran and the *Sunna*.

In 1882, Istanbul came up with a novel means to address the situation. Circassian slaves who had already worked on their masters' farms for twenty-five years were immediately manumitted and enlisted in the Ottoman army. Those who had not were exempted from military service for twenty-five years, while any sons they had in the future were to be drafted at the age of twenty. It was a limited move against specifically Circassian agricultural slavery transplanted into the empire, but again there was no question of a strike against slavery as a whole. And, unless there had been flagrant abuse, the religious courts generally sided with the slave-owners in any legal disputes.

For every imperial *firman*, ruling, prohibition or response to a petition, there was a corresponding, larger body of evidence to demonstrate that for many slaves, slave-owners and slave-dealers life simply went on as before, albeit rather less obviously in the public eye. Slaves may no longer have been displayed openly for sale in the markets – as witnessed, among others, by the Habsburg Archdukes Ferdinand Maximilian and Karl Ludwig, younger brothers of Emperor Franz Joseph, on their visit to Smyrna in 1850 – but, as the enterprising newspaperman Wolf von Schierbrand had discovered for himself in 1886, they could easily be procured.

The illicit trade continued to form a commercial thread that ran right through Ottoman society, from the royal women of the harem to street-prowling dealers in the poorer districts of Istanbul and cities across the empire. While elite women such as Pertevniyal could make their fortunes, in 1888 an extraordinary legal case revealed that she was by no means alone in profiting from the trade in overwhelmingly female slaves. Three women called Sidika, Sirin and Kor Nadire were discovered to have been preying ruthlessly on vulnerable Bulgarian refugees in the district of Üsküdar on the Asian side of Istanbul. Court papers and police reports laid bare a sophisticated and merciless operation based on deception.[35]

The women's roles were clearly delineated. First there was Kor Nadire, the initial scout and procurer. She came from Gebze, a city east of Istanbul, where the police reports reveal she had been recruiting girls as well as in the capital. It fell to Kor Nadire to search for and find appropriate families, establish an initial contact with them and then hand over to Sidika to finalize the deal in a follow-up meeting.

Sidika was a Circassian woman who had herself been enslaved in the past. Taken to Istanbul as an eight-year-old, she had been sold into slavery, working for the chief steward of Sultan Abdulmejid's daughter Fatma Sultan before her later manumission and marriage to an Egyptian merchant. By 1888 she was living in Tophane, a district in Istanbul favoured by slave-dealers operating on the quiet. It was Sidika's job to persuade these susceptible parents to part with their daughters, either giving them or selling them to her in the hope that, as Sidika told them, the girls would be given promising positions in the imperial harem. The trio claimed to be palace harem insiders who could take care of everything. The parents, who would be allowed to see their daughters every six months on the condition that they pretended to be their former owners, would be handsomely rewarded by the palace. To cap it all, after a service of around eight years, the girls would be married off to a senior military officer. The family's poverty would be a thing of the past. For impoverished families who had already lost their homes in the Russo–Ottoman War, and who were either waiting to be resettled elsewhere in Anatolia or languishing in urban poverty in the capital, it was an enticing, cynically calibrated proposition.

Finally, the 'negress' Sirin, as she is described in the documents, was another former slave who had been manumitted and now lived, like Sidika, in Tophane. Evidently well connected, she knew a number of the key players required to run a slave-dealing business, from ships' captains transporting slaves to Istanbul to end users and procurers such as senior palace officials and chief eunuchs. It helped that her husband was an Egyptian slaver, too. She bought and sold the girls, charging a 4 per cent commission on each transaction.

Nothing appeared to be off-limits to this enterprising trio. Knowing the market preference for Circassian girls, they freely sold 'white' Muslim Turkish girls, preferably with blue eyes if possible, as Circassian. Thus we hear of a widow called Penbe, a struggling mother of four, who was targeted by the women for her twelve-year-old daughter Muzeyyen in return for 1,500 piastres at a time when the girl was earning a monthly salary of twenty piastres as a servant. Selling slaves was already against the law. Selling Muslims into slavery was piling crime upon crime. Under police interrogation the women, not unsurprisingly, were evasive. Sidika claimed to have only sold slaves on one occasion and admitted instead to recruiting servants. But she was open about how, as soon as she had rebranded a Turkish girl as a more expensive Circassian with a formal bill of sale, she would then sell her 'for commerce, to whoever wanted' her.

This particular example demonstrated how in many cases the trade was almost exclusively female, with the clear exceptions of ships' captains and purchasers. The illegal trafficking depended, of course, on active demand. It is especially revealing, therefore, that the buyers occupied the highest echelons of society. The reports note, for example, that illegally trafficked girls had become the property of men like Mahmud Celaleddin Efendi, son of Sultan Abdulaziz, and Ferhad Aga, chief eunuch of the Beşiktaş royal harem. In so doing these men showed what they thought of the prohibitions on the slave trade.

As far as predators from both sexes were concerned, this was an equal opportunities market. It might have been rare for women to participate so vigorously and profitably in Ottoman commercial life, but compete in slave-dealing they manifestly did. However often official restrictions were issued, for many they fell on deaf ears. Men and women continued to prey, if not freely then with considerable impunity, on African and Circassian women.

The secret and illegal trafficking practised by Sidika, Sirin, Kor Nadire and countless other slavers at all levels of society was *almost* the last gasp of a 600-year history of slavery in the Ottoman Empire.

In the summer of 1908, under pressure both from army mutinies in Macedonia and the relentless march of the Young Turks' Committee of Union and Progress, Abdul Hamid reinstated the 1876 constitution he had suspended thirty years earlier. It was rather too little, far too late, and ultimately not very convincing. The following spring, during a short-lived counter-coup led by conservatives, the autocratic sultan once again suspended the constitution and shut down the parliament. But by April he was gone, deposed and despatched into exile in Salonica. Meanwhile, in a highly symbolic move intended to show the world that they meant to do away with the traditions of the past, the Young Turks freed all Abdul Hamid's harem slaves in the royal palace, calling on Circassian communities across Anatolia to collect their relatives and countrywomen.

Liberation had its limits, though. Cevher Agha, Abdul Hamid's de facto chief eunuch and a man who had enjoyed enormous influence with the sultan, was accused of fomenting Agha to restore the sultan's political power. He was publicly hanged from Galata Bridge in a black coat for all to see. By May, the short-lived chief eunuch Fahreddin Agha, last met in Chapter 6, had been barred from attending state ceremonies and humiliatingly stripped of his title as the Young Turks moved decisively to abolish an official and very senior slave position which had lasted for centuries.[36]

Yet even at this moment, the Young Turks' assault on slavery was considerably less than the sum of its parts. It was a partial and ambivalent

Some of the last concubines and eunuchs of the Ottoman imperial harem, 1909.

strike which looked more like a specific vendetta against Abdul Hamid, the enemy of reform, than abolition per se. The Young Turks did nothing to prevent either Abdul Hamid's successor, the penultimate Ottoman Sultan Mehmed V (r. 1909–18), or other members of the imperial family and senior statesmen from maintaining their own retinues of slaves.

The legislative response was stronger and wider-ranging, if not universal. In 1909, the Young Turks prohibited the Circassian slave trade, though again the strike was not against slavery in general so much as the slave trade in particular.

There were compelling reasons for this. Whatever the reforming, modernizing, liberalizing zeal which animated them, the Young Turks had quickly discovered that their freedom of movement in tackling the legality of slavery was extremely circumscribed. That became apparent during consultations with the *Şeyhülislam* over the Circassian slave trade. One senses that the most senior religious figure in the empire was trying to be as helpful as possible to the new government.

He reaffirmed that the 'basic principle in the House of Islam is liberty' and asserted that whenever there were questions or doubts over a person's status as a slave the decision should be in favour of that person's freedom. But when it came to the legality of an institution which had been endorsed from the earliest days of Islam, the *Şeyhülislam* threw his hands up. There was nothing he could do. The holy law was crystal-clear: 'slavery as an abstract, legal status was inviolable'. There was no question, then, of outright abolition.[37]

Besides, as important as slavery undoubtedly was, it steadily slipped down the reformists' agenda as larger, existential threats started to mount. At this point it was no longer a question merely of the empire's decline, but of fending off its complete destruction.

The Great Powers manoeuvred. Hungary annexed Bosnia and Herzegovina in 1908, Italy helped itself to Ottoman Libya and the Dodecanese in 1911. By 1913, even before the first rumblings of the Great War had sounded across the plains of northern France, the Ottoman Empire had also lost western Thrace, Macedonia and Albania, most of which it had controlled for six centuries. Then, in 1914, a continent went to war, the empire joined forces with the Central Powers against the Allies, and vultures circled. Britain, a friend for so much of the nineteenth century, became an adversary in the twentieth. If victorious, London would not want to miss its share of the carrion.

Suddenly, starting in 1915, came the cataclysm of the Armenian Genocide, a bloodbath which by the end of the war had accounted for the annihilation of between 600,000 and 1 million lives – 90 per cent of Ottoman Armenians. It began in the aftermath of the Battle of Sarikamish, when Ottoman defeat by the Russians triggered a punitive response from the Young Turks against what was seen as Armenian treachery. The killing fields stretched 1,000 miles east from Istanbul. Armenian soldiers were disarmed, demobilized and killed. Armenian intellectuals and politicians in Istanbul followed them to their graves. Of the survivors, hundreds of thousands of Christian women and children suffered forced conversion to Islam and joined the families of Arabs, Turks and Kurds. Many became slaves.

Writing from Kharpert (Harput) in eastern Turkey, amid 'the most thoroughly organised and effective massacre this country has ever seen', the American consul Leslie Davis wrote to Henry Morgenthau, his ambassador in Istanbul, and described what he had witnessed in camps of Armenians deported from Erzerum and Erzinjan:

> A more pitiable sight cannot be imagined. As one walks through the camp mothers offer their children and beg one to take them. In fact, the Turks have been taking their choice of these children and girls for slaves, or worse. In fact, they have even had their doctors there to examine the most likely girls and thus secure the best ones.[38]

Another report, from 1916, on the condition of Armenians who had survived the death march to Syria stated that Armenian girls were being sold into slavery in impromptu slave markets:

> In the track of the Armenians, as they were driven along, female slave markets were established. The price of an Armenian girl from 12 to 14 years of age was from 2 *mejidias* to £1 (Turkish). The writer saw such a market in Damascus, and he was told by his relatives in Aleppo, and by American Missionaries, that thousands of young girls had been sold in open markets.

Girls as young as eight were raped and murdered. Others were freely trafficked and used as sex slaves by Turkish officials.[39]

To this day the Armenian Genocide is officially denied by the Turkish state, which has censored discussion of the subject on the grounds of national security – inexorably connected as it is with the foundation of the republic – and spent millions of dollars lobbying foreign countries not to recognize it, or even use the word genocide. There are parallels between the persistent denial of genocide, widely shared across Turkish society, and the denial about the reality and violence of slavery. There are still many who would prefer not to discuss either.[40]

The mass enslavement of Armenians was the last large-scale flourish of an ancient institution that, like the empire itself, was dying. Anticipating and encouraging its demise, in 1916 the British and French helped themselves – on paper at first, shortly afterwards in practice – to Istanbul's Middle Eastern possessions. London had been working to drive a wedge between Turks and Arabs, sowing the seeds of the Arab Revolt of 1916–18. Unbeknown to the Arabs, who had been promised freedom in return for rising up against the Turks, the secret Sykes–Picot Agreement of 1916 drew a line through these lands and sands, dividing the Ottoman Middle East into spheres of British and French influence and control. There was to be no independence, whatever T. E. Lawrence, the soldier, schemer and would-be statesman, had told his bands of Bedouin guerrillas. It was a colonial dismemberment plain and simple, creating a set of national borders which for the most part have endured to this day.

In 1921, as part of a last-ditch attempt to galvanize international Muslim resistance to Western powers, Enver Pasha, the Young Turk leader, former Ottoman minister of war, one of the principal perpetrators of late-Ottoman genocides against Armenians, Assyrians and Greeks and convicted war criminal, dreamt up the League of Islamic Revolutionary Societies during his short-lived exile in Moscow. He claimed to represent revolutionary organizations from Morocco, Algeria, Tunisia, Tripoli, Egypt, Arabia and India. The choice of words in the league's charter was interesting in its open espousal of the language of slavery and enslavement – portraying Turks and other Muslims as slaves of the West – at a time when the Muslim world was still clinging on to the institution of real, as opposed to metaphorical, slavery. 'The aim of the Society', the charter declared, 'is to make Muslims – who are used like slaves, enslaved and dominated by the imperialists and capitalists – masters of their own fate under the leadership of Turkey ... and to liberate them from captivity.'[41]

The era of the Young Turks ushered in a wider parliamentary debate on reforming civil and family law which pointed towards the end of slavery. That was then delayed successively by the First World War, the tumultuous disintegration of the Ottoman Empire, and the subsequent struggle to form a new republic, eventually achieved, after more years of bloodshed, in 1923. Yet even with the birth of Mustafa Kemal Atatürk's resolutely secular state, announced with such fanfare and based on a profound reversal and rejection of so many Ottoman values and institutions, so much Islamic and Ottoman history, it would still be another decade before slavery disappeared.

Unlike the empire which had nurtured it, on the formal, legal level slavery proved surprisingly resistant to outright abolition. It is tempting to attribute this longevity, at least in part, to the sheer cultural power of religious law and the social custom which flowed from it. For many centuries this had guided Muslims the length and breadth of the Dar al Islam. But that cannot tell the whole story. It is striking that other political and religious icons of Islamic life, hugely important for so many of the faithful, predeceased slavery. It bears repeating that slavery outlived both the sultanate, abolished in 1922, and the caliphate, eliminated in 1924.

By 1923, Mustafa Kemal Atatürk, the revolutionary statesman, field marshal, Gazi (warrior of the faith) and victorious hero of the Turkish War of Independence of 1919–23, was the president of the republic, president of the assembly, president of the cabinet and president of the Republican People's Party. On 15 October 1927, an impeccably dressed Atatürk, resplendent in his trademark Westernized dark suit, wing-collared white shirt, tie and white pocket square, stood in front of the Grand National Assembly of Turkey. Immediately above him was the oversized framed legend *Hakimiyet Milletindir*, 'Sovereignty Belongs to the People'. He then proceeded to give an astonishing thirty-six-hour speech, *delivered over six days*, which indicated that if sovereignty belonged to the people, from now on power would belong to him.

One sympathizes with his audience of parliamentarians, who surely had little idea what a spirit-sapping marathon they were in for. Atatürk's high-flown rhetoric, which dwelt at great length on the concepts of national sovereignty, secularism and republican democracy, and defined the national narrative for many decades to come, contained three fleeting references to slavery – though not what might be expected.*

Focusing on the period from the beginning of the Turkish War of Independence in 1919 to the foundation of the republic in 1923, the founding father of modern Turkey told the members of parliament that the option of becoming the protectorate of a foreign power, as suggested in the 1920 Treaty of Sèvres whose implementation he had

---

* 'The main themes of the speech – and of the official discourse on the Armenian genocide – are silence, denial of the genocide, general amnesia about past violence (unless presenting Turks as the real victims), identifying with the perpetrators, never questioning the great prophetic and infallible leader (Atatürk), and promoting the racial purification of the land in the face of a life-or-death Darwinian struggle with minorities.' See Marc Baer, *Sultanic Saviors and Tolerant Turks: Writing Ottoman Jewish History, Denying the Armenian Genocide* (Bloomington, Indiana, 2020), p. 82.

resisted, had been unacceptable. Unless it enjoyed complete independence, a nation did not deserve to be regarded as anything other than 'a slave in the eyes of civilised humanity'. He went on:

> To accept the protectorate of a foreign power would signify that we admit lack of all human qualities, weakness and incapacity. Indeed, it is impossible to envisage people who have not descended to this degree of abject servitude willingly accepting a foreign master.
>
> But the Turk is both dignified and proud; he is also capable and talented. Such a nation would prefer to perish rather than subject itself to the life of a slave.[42]

National freedom was conspicuously contrasted, in Atatürk's grand national narrative, with personal slavery. But this, it appeared, was not the time to address the question of slavery itself (not even in a speech so long that it was published and sacralized as the 600-page book *Nutuk*, *The Speech*). It would take another six years for his government to do that.

Perhaps it was only appropriate, then, given the empire's long decades of reluctant foot-dragging and equivocation and its ultimate failure to abolish the institution of slavery before its own summary abolition, that the end came not with a bang but a whimper.

There was no patriotic, soul-stirring speech this time, no fine words which would sound through the ages to mark this momentous moment for future generations. It was telling, too, that formal legal abolition was finally achieved not through domestic legislation, not after public protest or a spirited campaign, but in the clinical, bureaucratic prose of an international treaty which Turkey took several years to approve. Only in 1933, when the ten-year-old Turkish Republic finally ratified the 1926 League of Nations Convention on the Suppression of Slavery, was it all over.

But, of course, it was never completely over. That would be far too neat. Just as dictatorships do not die with the death of a dictator but live on in mindsets and mentalities, customs and practices – and all too often the politics and institutions of government – so slavery became, if no longer a lived experience, then a real and living memory for vast numbers of men, women and children from one end of the

Ottoman world to the other. Its spectre cast a long shadow whose darkness can still be discerned today. At the most basic level, this is hardly surprising when one considers it lasted for the entire duration of the empire, from the first clash of Osman's swords in Bithynia on the Byzantine frontier at the dawn of the fourteenth century to its annihilation in the twentieth, and then a little beyond.

Once the era of slavery had given way to abolition and emancipation, from that moment, if not before, slavery was something to be dusted under the carpet. It was swept out of sight, put away and forgotten as though it had never happened. There was nothing to see here. A new post-imperial generation of Turks could be forgiven for not knowing anything about it, as they would know little or nothing of the Armenian Genocide. Instead of a lively discussion in school textbooks and university lecture halls, there was a deafening silence as what has been called the new republican 'project of regulated amnesia' got under way. In the early years of Kemal Atatürk's Turkey, slavery was 'at best forgotten or exoticised and at worst denied, but never confronted'. In some, perhaps many, quarters this selective amnesia and denial has persisted into the twenty-first century, as expressed so clearly by the Bilkent University professor's advice to one among the new generation of Turkish historians at the outset of a career researching new frontiers in Ottoman slavery: 'Our ancestors treated their slaves very well, don't waste your time with this.'[43]

But our story is not about historians. Nor is it a history of history. What about the descendants of slaves in Turkey, specifically that community commonly known as Afro-Turks? Until as recently as 2005, very little was heard from and about them in public discourse in Turkey. Then a writer and activist called Mustafa Olpak that year published his autobiography, *Kenya–Crete–Istanbul: Human Biographies from the Slave Coast*, which told the devastating story of how his Kenyan ancestors had been enslaved and taken to Istanbul. His account gave the lie to the complacent and widespread assumption that Ottoman slavery was invariably benign, that everyone had treated their slaves well. It offered a very different narrative.

First captured in Kenya, an African couple with a young child called Ahmet, Olpak's grandfather, were subsequently put on sale in Crete, bought by a Turkish family and forced to work on the farm. In time, the couple had other children, who were born into slavery. When the father died, the teenage Ahmet, who as a child had been locked in an iron cage after failed attempts to escape, was forced by his owners to marry his stepmother Nuriye, in order to keep the family together under a new patriarch. Ahmet 'from then on had to call "my wife" the same woman whom he considered to be his mother. It's unimaginable, but that is what happened.' Ahmet's ordeal was far from over. In 1918, as the empire teetered towards dismemberment and partition, Nuriye was sold off as a cook to new owners in Istanbul, despite desperate pleas from the couple and their children not to separate them. Once she was gone, the masters announced their new plan to keep the family together. Ahmet was to marry again, this time one of Nuriye's sisters. Again, as a slave, he was unable to refuse and duly married the woman he had known as his sister-in-law. Nuriye never forgave him for this, Olpak wrote, nor for 'allowing' her sale to the family in Istanbul.[44]

Olpak's book caused a stir in a society which had largely glossed over its slaving past and in which the descendants of emancipated African slaves had to contend with 'a near total non-recognition of their unique history as well as discrimination in their daily lives'. That is now changing and there are ongoing efforts to raise awareness of this 'underexposed history'.[45] A year after the publication of his groundbreaking book, the Africans' Culture and Solidarity Association in Turkey, established by Olpak to help put that right, held its first meeting. In the years since then the group has reconnected the Afro-Turks to their heritage by reinstating the *Dana Bayrami*, or Calf Festival, in Izmir. Traditionally, every year the community of African slaves had paraded a decorated calf through the town before slaughtering, cooking and eating it. Donations were sought for the poorest families and food distributed among them. The hugely popular carnival, which could attract thousands of men, women and children singing and dancing to music in the streets, was later banned by Atatürk's government, forcing it underground.

Today, many of the country's estimated tens of thousands of Afro-Turks still live in the Aegean region around Izmir, descendants of the African slaves who had been put to work in the cotton fields near the ancient port city of Smyrna. Slavery may have disappeared in Turkey, but for some members of this community at least, the prejudice and discrimination against them has not. In 2016, a retired tobacco factory worker called Ahmet Dogu described how this affected him. When mothers passed him on the street with their children, he said, they muttered superstitious phrases under their breath. 'Whether you like it or not, it does get to you,' he said bleakly. 'They pray that their children will not turn out so black. They touch wood and look away from me.'

Even today some members of this community still have the surname Zenci, a derogatory word which, like the Arabi Zanj, is an approximate equivalent to the word Negro. Afro-Turks are often casually called 'Arabs' as well, a term Turks have traditionally used for people with darker skin. 'We call ourselves Arab, too,' Ahmet said:

> It is better than 'African', which has such bad connotations – when people think of Africans they think of cannibalism and backwardness. We do not want to be associated with that. These days, we also call ourselves Sudanese or Libyan or whatever, even though we don't know exactly where our families were from.

Never mind that, in so many cases, the raids in which their ancestors had been enslaved were perpetrated by Arab slavers.[46]

Olpak saw himself as part of a natural process of evolving attitudes and approaches to slavery and its enduring legacy. He spelt this out in the first words of his book:

> The first generation lives,
> the second reacts,
> the third researches . . .
> I am Mustafa Olpak. In my family, I am third generation.[47]

Olpak died in 2016, but the research he began continues.

12

Abolition II: Away from the Centre

My grandfather used the edge of his gown to wipe away the tears that had run down his face from laughing so much, and after giving me time to settle myself into the gathering, said, 'By God, that's some story of yours, Wad Rayyes.' This was a cue to Wad Rayyes to continue the story my entrance had interrupted. 'And afterwards, Hajj Ahmed, I put the girl in front of me on the donkey, squirming and twisting, then I forcibly stripped her of all her clothes till she was as naked as the day her mother bore her. She was a young slave who'd just reached puberty – her breasts, Hajj Ahmed, stuck out like pistols and your arms wouldn't meet round her buttocks. She had been rubbed all over with oil so that her skin glistened in the moonlight and her perfume turned one giddy.'

. . .

Her weeping would be made the subject of one of Wad Rayyes' famous stories about his many women with which he regales the men of the village. The rage in my breast grew more savage. Unable to remain, I left; behind me I heard my grandfather calling but I did not turn around.

Tayeb Salih, *Season of Migration to the North*, 1969*

* Quoted in Eve M. Troutt Powell, *Tell This in My Memory: Stories of Enslavement from Egypt, Sudan and the Ottoman Empire*, p. 39.

Slavery, in the East, has little dreadful in it but the name; male slaves are everywhere treated much like the children of the family, and always better than the free servants.

Johann Ludwig Burckhardt, *Travels in Nubia*, 1819

If the nineteenth century was long as far as the persistence of slavery was concerned, it was also wide in its ubiquity. As wide, in fact, as the Muslim world itself, from the shores of the Atlantic right across North Africa, the Sahel and swathes of sub-Saharan Africa, through the Levant, across Anatolia, Iran and the Arabian Peninsula to the steppes and mountains of Central Asia, on into the Indian Subcontinent and beyond to Indonesia, Malaysia and the southern Philippines. Away from the centre of the Ottoman Empire, slavery in the Dar al Islam continued as an essential, mostly unchanged and generally unremarkable feature of daily life – with the exception of market-led surges in demand for productive labour to satisfy international tastes for pearls, ivory, cotton, cloves, dates and other commodities. This was a turbulent century in which peak slavery coexisted and contended with the most potent forces of abolition.

Slavery in Sudan long preceded the Ottomans. It antedated Islam by more than a millennium. One of the earliest references to it comes from Herodotus, writing in the fifth century BCE. Discussing the Persian Great King Cambyses' invasion of Egypt in 525 BCE, the Greek historian recorded that the biennial tribute imposed on the ancient kingdom of Kush (northern Sudan and southern Egypt) included five 'Ethiopian' slave boys. In 652, almost 1,200 years later, the conquering, faith-spreading Muslim Arabs struck their first diplomatic treaty in this region. According to Al Maqrizi, the fifteenth-century Egyptian historian, the *Baqt* treaty, referred to earlier, imposed an annual payment of 360 slaves on the Christian kingdom of Nubia. By the nineteenth century, the semi-industrialized East African slave-processing system which despatched thousands of captive boys, girls, men and women to slave markets in the north, especially Cairo, Istanbul and on the Arabian Peninsula, would make such numbers look quaint. By 1877, when there were said to be upwards of 6,000 slave-traders operating in the region, the British government estimated in

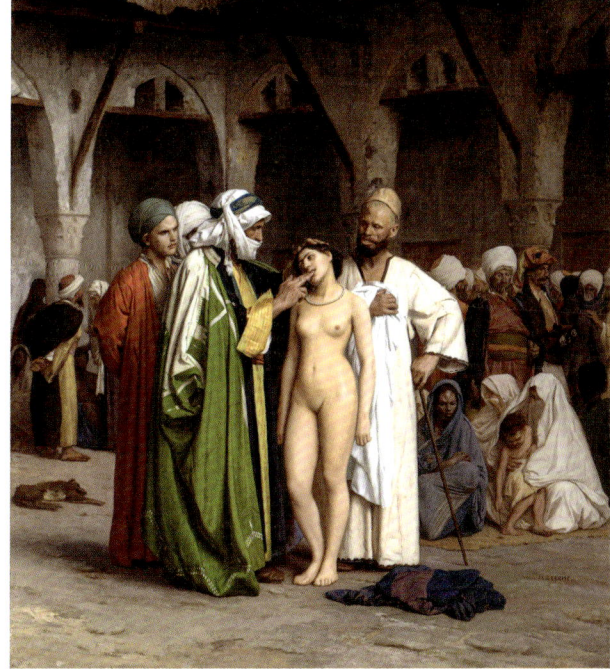

21. *Above:* The massacre of the Mamluks, Cairo, 1811. The Mamluks were the greatest slave soldiers in the history of the Islamic world. They became a dynasty in their own right, ruling over Egypt, the Levant and the Hijaz (1250–1517) and in Iraq from 1704 to 1831.

22. *Right: The Slave Market* by Jean-Léon Gérôme, 1866. This quintessentially Orientalist picture, in which an Arab potential buyer inspects a nude Caucasian slave, pits Western moral supremacy against a cruel and depraved East.

23. Ottoman tortures of Christian slaves in North Africa, as envisaged in Father Pierre Dan's *Historie van Barbaryen, en des zelfs Zee-Roovers*, 1684. It has been estimated that between 1 million and 1.25 million Europeans were enslaved by North African Muslims between 1530 and 1780.

24. Galley slavery was a living hell. Slaves were shackled, barely fed, racked with thirst, sunburnt, whipped and forced to excrete where they sat. An illustration from the Cantigas de Santa Maria, poems attributed to Alfonso X the Wise of Castile (r. 1252–84).

25. Coloured engraving, 1804, of the First Barbary War between the USA and Tripoli (1801–5). In the late eighteenth century, Yusuf Karamanli, pasha of Tripoli, extorted large protection payments from Western nations. Failure to pay resulted in the capture of their ships and the enslavement of their crews.

26. On 16 February 1804, Lieutenant Stephen Decatur led a US boarding party on to the captured American frigate *Philadelphia* in Tripoli harbour, killed the Arab crew and set it on fire. Nelson declared it 'the most bold and daring act of the age'.

27. and 28. All over Europe, Muslim slaves like this captive African in Livorno, *left*, and Janissary in Vienna, *right*, commemorating the unsuccessful siege of the city by the Turks, found themselves sculpted in defeat. It has been estimated that at least 2 million slaves from the Muslim Mediterranean entered Europe between the sixteenth and nineteenth centuries.

29. African warriors try to resist an Arab *razzia* (slaving raid). Africa bore the brunt of the Islamic world's enduring demand for slave labour.

30. Arabs leading enslaved Africans across the Sahara. In 1863, a British official estimated that mortality rates on this lethal route were over 80 per cent.

31. American and European captivity narratives sensationalized the stories of their authors' capture by Muslim pirates and potentates. Captain James Riley's 1817 account of his shipwreck and enslavement was an instant bestseller.

32. *Above left:* The Moroccan sultan Moulay Ismail (r. 1672–1727) enslaved an estimated 221,000 Africans and 25,000 Europeans.

33. *Above right:* In 1840, Said bin Sultan al Busaidi, sultan of Oman (r. 1804–56) moved his capital from Oman to Zanzibar in recognition of the burgeoning trade in African slaves and cloves.

34. In the nineteenth century the British emerged as self-appointed scourge of the slave trade. For many Muslims, abolition was 'imperialism spelled differently'. Here young East African slaves, rescued from an Arab dhow, rest on board HMS *Daphne* in 1868.

35. 'We will conquer your Rome, break your crosses, and enslave your women ...'. The self-styled Sheikh Abu Muhammad al-Adnani, a cheerleader for the Daesh (ISIS) terrorist group's enslavement and rape of Yazidi women, was killed in 2016.

36. Yazidi women protest against Daesh's invasion of Sinjar in August 2015. A UN report concluded that Daesh may have committed 'war crimes, crimes against humanity, and possibly genocide'.

37. and 38. 'Deep down I'm free,' says Hamey, *left*, who escaped his enslavement in Mali in 2018. 'Live or die, I'll never be a slave again.' 'I didn't exist as a human being,' says Habi Rabah, *right*, of her enslavement in Mauritania. 'Now, praise God, I am free.' Hereditary slavery continues in both countries.

39. Slave memorial in Stone Town, Zanzibar, on the site of one of the world's largest slave markets. Those who survived the sea passage to Zanzibar were inspected in pits before being sold. The market closed in 1873.

a report submitted to the Egyptian authorities that around 30,000 slaves per annum were being sent across the Red Sea from the East African coast to the Arabian Peninsula alone.[1]

In the mid-tenth century, the Coptic Bishop of Al Ashmunain, Severus Ibn al Muqaffa (d. 987), reported that Muslims were plundering and enslaving and selling their captives in Egyptian markets, a charge echoed by Nasir Khusraw, the eleventh-century Persian traveller, who wrote of Muslims and others stealing children from the Beja region, a territory ranging from south-eastern Egypt and eastern Sudan into north-western Eritrea, and selling them in Muslim towns and markets. When Muslim states started to be established along the central Nile and Sudanic states from the sixteenth century, they took up where their pagan and Christian predecessors left off, raiding along their borders and enslaving their neighbours. For Arabic speakers along the Nile Valley, both the terms *Nubi* (Nubian) and *Sudani* (Sudanese), meaning black, were synonymous with 'slave'. *Bilad al Sudan*, the Land of the Blacks, referred to all sub-Saharan territories in general, but it is from that Arabic term that the nation of Sudan takes its name. A lasting and painful irony, which has had baleful consequences, is that the northern Arab Sudanese do not consider themselves black, reserving that pejorative term for their dark-skinned Sudanese and South Sudanese compatriots, in addition to Africans from further afield, whom for centuries they enslaved.[2]

The great arterial link between Egypt and Sudan, the enduring commercial thread that bound these two states together in a nexus of slaving as the market and source for enslaved Africans respectively, was the *Darb al Arbain*, as the Arabs knew it, the Forty Days' Road. The easternmost of the great north–south trans-Saharan routes, this was an 1,100-mile road from Kobbei in Darfur to Asyut in Upper Egypt, running through a string of oases so that water was always available within two to three days. Like slavery itself, the *Darb al Arbain* long predated Muslim Arabs and was trodden successively by Egyptian pharaohs, Persian temple-planners, Macedonian invaders, fort-building Romans and Ottoman traders. Caravans of camels – groaning under loads of elephant and hippopotamus ivory, rhinoceros horn, ebony, gold, ostrich feathers and eggs, animal skins, plants, civet, aromatic oils, incense and gum Arabic, salt, alum, natron and cowrie shells – dutifully padded alongside lines of African slaves on foot, often in chains, together with the odd 'exotic' animal destined for a royal court. They plied the tracks towards Egypt, returning south with cargoes of textiles, metals, weapons, semi-precious stones and other luxuries from Europe and the Mediterranean littoral.

Conditions for the slaves along the *Darb al Arbain* varied from humane to appalling. Travelling in Egypt and Sudan in 1813–14, Johann Ludwig Burckhardt, the Swiss explorer and Arabist who witnessed castration operations on young boys near Asyut, described how adult males whose characters and dispositions were not known by the dealers were kept in close confinement and often chained to prevent escape or attack. During the long marches every day, such a male slave was tied by a long pole to a camel, one end tightly forked around the slave's neck; 'his right hand is also fastened to the pole . . . leaving only his legs and left arm at liberty'. At night he was put in chains.[3]

Writing in the mid-nineteenth century, the French General Eugène Daumas described the departure of a slave caravan he was travelling with across the desert. Numbering around 2,100 men, women and children, together with 2,600 camels and other animals, it was a mammoth, horizon-filling assembly, a life-and-death exercise in logistics and, for the slaves, a desperate battle for survival:

> The constant surveillance we needed to exercise over our slaves left us no repose, even though they were chained together like beads on a rosary, the women in two pairs attached by the feet, the men eight or ten together, their necks pushed into iron collars, to which were attached smaller double chains to keep their hands at chest height . . . The signal for departure was given, and . . . a confusion of cries and groans broke out that passed from one slave to the next . . . all were weeping and lamenting, calling to one another, saying their farewells.[4]

The mortality rate on these trans-Saharan slave passages from Sudan and beyond, as discussed earlier, was savage. In 1863, Robert Colquhoun, Britain's then consul general in Cairo, wrote to the foreign secretary, Lord John Russell. In his letter he estimated that for every ten slaves who reached Cairo, fifty 'miserably perished in the transit, which has been described to me as worse than the middle passage in the Cuban slavers'. Colquhoun, like other British officials tasked with monitoring the slave trade at this time, expressed his frustration that while the Egyptian government publicly claimed to be discouraging the trade, Cairo nevertheless maintained large barracoons, or guarded enclosures, in which enslaved Africans were marshalled for government service – the men serving in the Nubian regiments, the women and girls destined for menial work in the harems. The conditions were dire. Smallpox regularly ravaged the barracoons and 'the creatures die like flies', their bodies dumped in large numbers into the Nile.[5]

For those men and women who had survived the hell of the *razzia* slaving raids, who had endured this hideous desert trek and had made it all the way to Cairo, there was little immediate relief to be had in the city's slave markets. Thomas Reade, the acting consul general in Cairo, did not hold back when writing about the slave-traders to Lord Stanley, the foreign secretary, in 1867. 'The cruelties and the abominations perpetrated by the dealers and their agents, who supply the Egyptian market, are not less atrocious than those ever committed by slave traders in any part of the world,' he thundered.[6] These were very British views, of course, partial in their outlook and of their time for the expanding imperial power. They can be discounted, then, but by no means invalidated.

Ottoman-era slavery in Sudan echoed its counterpart in Istanbul in a number of ways. In pre-Ottoman Sudan, slaves were a notable demographic within the military and administrative elite, as well as serving as concubines for noblemen. The most prosperous among what today might be called the aspirational middle class also owned small numbers of slaves in emulation of their grander countrymen. A far larger category were the royal slaves, captured in war and organized into garrisons of slave soldiers as early as the mid-seventeenth century. In the last years of the northern sultanate of Sennar, also known as the Funj sultanate (1504–1821), a territory embracing Sudan, north-western Eritrea and western Ethiopia, the numbers of slave soldiers soared. By 1825, shortly after the Ottoman conquest of Sudan in 1821, the sultan alone commanded 30,000 of them, with many others owned by his most senior officials.

Women enslaved for sexual services were a staple for those who could afford them. And even when a man could not, there were options available. In 1800, short of funds to purchase a concubine individually, a group of religious dignitaries in Khujalab, in what is today northern

Khartoum, clubbed together to buy a woman in common. She was required to sleep with her owners in descending order of precedence, a condition which quickly led to the most senior man making her pregnant, thereby removing her from further circulation. The concubine's outraged co-purchasers wasted no time filing a lawsuit and were ultimately successful in being awarded financial compensation for their loss. The religious men saw nothing wrong or immoral in buying a female concubine for their shared sexual pleasure. History does not record the concubine's views at any point during this 'middle-class parody of noblemen's mores more worthy of the pen of a Molière or Cervantes'.[7]

Where Sudanese slavery departed more significantly from its Ottoman counterpart was in the ruthlessly policed distinctions it created and imposed between ethnic communities. Ancestry, in particular, was everything in Sudan. To be a brown Muslim Arab was to be free. To be a black non-Muslim African was to be a slave. For a Sudanese Arab man, there was no question as to his superiority over someone dismissed disparagingly as 'African', never mind that a Sudanese Arab was, by definition, African. These stark racial views, deeply held by the Arab population, continue in much of Sudan today.[8]

Burckhardt described how the slave-traders generally treated their slaves well during the journey along the *Darb al Arbain*. This was more out of self-interest than general benevolence. 'They are seldom flogged, are well fed, are not over-worked, and are spoken to in a kind manner,' he wrote, 'all this, however, results not from humanity in the traders, but from an apprehension that under different treatment the slave would abscond.'[9]

In 1820, Mohammed Ali, the Ottoman Albanian ruler of Egypt, invaded Sudan. He was clear-sighted about his reasons. 'You are aware that the end of all our effort and this expense is to procure negroes,' he told his son-in-law and senior military commander Mohammed Bey. 'Please show zeal in carrying out our wishes . . .'. In a letter to another commander, who was boasting about how much money he had levied – for which read plundered – from conquered areas, Mohammed Ali stressed that this was not the mission. The value of slaves suitable for army recruitment was 'more precious than jewels . . . hence I have ordered you to raise 6,000 of these slaves'.[10] The invasion was a giant land-grab, but above all it was a mass slave raid, motivated by Mohammed Ali's desire to enslave healthy young men to serve in his fast-expanding army. This force was the foundation of his empire-making adventures in Africa and the eastern Mediterranean, which would last through the 1820s and 1830s.

Mohammed Ali's reign began a long period of Ottoman Egyptian rule in Sudan. It lasted for most of the century, until the Sudanese eventually managed to eject the Egyptians from Khartoum in 1885 at the outset of the Mahdist Revolution – only to discover that in expelling one colonial overlord they had opened the door, several years later, to another. The British, masters of Egypt from 1882 to 1956, would hold sway in Sudan from 1899 until the humiliating debacle of Suez in 1956 ushered in the final chapter of four centuries of British imperial adventures.

The arrival of Ottoman Egyptian forces and new authorities created a huge market for slaves, and a powerful incentive for slave-raiding and slave-trading in Sudan. The new rulers continued the tradition of official slave raids – long a state prerogative – but launched them on a prodigious scale, imposing a tribute of slaves on their new subjects. Orders were given that for every 1,000 soldiers sent south, 3,000 slaves had to be taken, a ratio that proved impossible to satisfy due to the horrifying mortality rates among the slaves despatched north. Huge numbers perished from disease on and after the 800-mile forced march north from Kordofan to Wadi Halfa and then on to Aswan, the Nile town in today's Upper Egypt. 'They died like sheep with the rot,' according to one account. An estimated 20,000 had been sent to Aswan by 1824, of whom fewer than 3,000 – just one in every six to seven men, women and children – survived. Half a century later, mortality rates in this regional trade were reportedly devastating. The numbers of the enslaved who died from malnutrition, disease and savage treatment at the hands of the traders running caravans in Darfur, Kordofan and Bahr al Ghazal between 1875 and 1879 were estimated at between 80,000 and 100,000.[11]

The Ottoman colonial period also fundamentally changed the nature and structure of Sudanese society. Slavery grew from a minority pursuit and entered the mainstream. Voluntarily or otherwise, Muslim pastoralists such as the Shaiqiya north of Khartoum, together with the Rufaa of the Blue Nile and the Baqqara of the White Nile, joined army raids into non-Muslim lands, increasing both the numbers of slaves and their respective functions, so that domestic slavery became commonplace across all sections of society in northern Sudan. From the 1850s, fuelled by regional and European demand for ivory, newly enslaved men, who were cheaper to purchase, feed and maintain than camels, were put to work as porters hauling elephant and hippopotamus tusks to the coast for onward transport to Europe. When they reached their destination they were then sold, often for a profit, together with the consignments of ivory and ostrich feathers which together formed the unholy trinity of nineteenth-century Sudanese trade. The voracious British, European and American demand for luxury goods, from combs and cane handles to folding fans, billiard balls, piano and organ keys and even the ivory inlaid butts of six-shooters for use in the American West, continued to sustain the ivory trade – and the slave trade that was its essential, barely less bloody, partner.[12]

Some Sudanese traders established themselves along the Ethiopian border in response to a high demand for young Ethiopian girls by wealthy northern Sudanese and Egyptians. Here too, many of the various local and Turco-Egyptian administrators were either heavily involved in the trade or were happy – for a price – to look the other way; the Sudanese slave trade was illegal from 1877. They took their lead from the authorities on both sides of the border. The Ethiopian Nagos, Emperor Yohannes IV (r. 1871–1889), the 'Conquering Lion of the Tribe of Judah', extracted the then equivalent of around £21,200 (just under £2 million today) per annum from the traders for granting the slave caravans permission to cross the border from Ethiopia to Qallabat in eastern Sudan.[13]

The market always adapted and the law of supply and demand kicked in. The flooding of the market in slaves under the new Turkish regime predictably caused prices to collapse in the short term. In 1814, the price of a less valuable male slave in Shendi, a key slave market just under 100 miles north-east of Khartoum on the Nile, was eight to ten Spanish dollars, rising to twenty to twenty-five for the most expensive young female. At this time, Burckhardt reckoned, the number of slaves sold annually in the market of Shendi alone was 5,000, half of whom were taken away by merchants from the Red Sea port town of Suakin, with 1,500 carried off by Egyptian traders and the remainder going to Dongola and the Bedouins who lived east of

Shendi. The great majority of the slaves brought to Shendi were aged under fifteen, of which the most desirable and expensive category was between eleven and fifteen.[14]

Data on the price of slaves is so patchy that firm conclusions remain elusive. It is clear during periods of crackdown on the one hand, and slave-raiding during times of extreme instability on the other, that prices rose and plunged accordingly. As the century progressed, the numbers of slaves taken from the mass slaving raids fell significantly. After rising from an estimated 5,000 per annum in the 1850s to 13,000 per annum in the 1860s, the numbers of slaves hunted fell, so that by the 1880s they were in hundreds rather than thousands. Yet here again there are difficulties, since British officials in Egypt observed that prices did not rise during the 1870s, a time of strengthening efforts against the trade, indicating a consistency of supply. To add to the uncertainty, there is evidence that in 1895 slaves could be purchased for as little as one Mahdist *riyal*, a coin worth less than a single Spanish dollar. Clearly there was considerable variation within different territories and within even narrow time frames, so much so that the data available renders any firm pronouncements unwise. To give another example, an eight-year-old boy from the south would sell for forty Spanish dollars in northern Sudan in the early 1870s. By the midpoint of the same decade the cost had risen to sixty to eighty dollars. A male slave in Darfur, meanwhile, could be purchased for around ten Spanish dollars in the 1820s, rising to around three times that figure by 1879.[15] As a rule of thumb, the longer the distances the enslaved had to travel to the markets, the higher their price. In the mid-1870s, for example, boys from southern Sudan aged between twelve and fifteen were sold for fifteen to twenty Spanish dollars. By the time they got to northern Sudan they cost four times that figure. For the dealers, young girls and eunuchs were invariably the most lucrative proposition.[16]

In recent years, the traditional view that slavery in Sudan was generally benign in nature – a view which was never based on the opinions of the slaves themselves – has come under increasing scrutiny. It has been noted that, unlike in other Muslim countries, northern Sudanese slave-owners routinely sold slaves who had been born in their households, undermining the argument that slaves were invariably part of the family and easily assimilated into wider society through manumission and marriage. The Ottoman practice of requiring regular taxes or tributes in slaves weighed heavily against the 'family' tradition, as did the deeply ingrained prejudices of northern Sudanese towards darker-skinned Africans in general. Numerous bills of sale and property transfer documents, in which two and sometimes three generations of slaves were being sold, together with the extreme rarity of *maatuq* (freedmen) referenced in official records, erode the common suggestion that slavery was inherently temporary, institutionally 'part of the family' and compassionate. As interpreted in Sudan, the legal status of a slave offered little in the way of comfort to the enslaved man, woman or child, either:

> Slaves were legally classified as livestock, along with sheep, cattle, horses, and camels, or occasionally as 'talking animals'. They were given peculiar names such as 'Sea of Lusts' (a woman), 'Patience is a Blessing' or 'Increase in Wealth' . . . In at least some districts it was not customary to bury a slave – funerals were expensive. The corpses of slaves were left exposed to scavenging animals or, if inconveniently located, thrown into the river.[17]

The practice of slavery in Sudan was informed by, and intertwined with, age-old attitudes. Nineteenth-century pale-skinned, northern Sudanese Arab Muslims looked upon their dark-skinned, southern Sudanese pagan countrymen, together with their sub-Saharan neighbours, with the same sort of racist contempt Arab writers such as Jahiz, Ibn Qutayba and Masudi had exhibited 1,000 years earlier.

In the words of a nineteenth-century song of the Fur, an ethnic group of Muslims from western Sudan, concentrated in Darfur:

> The people who live in Dar al Fartit* are slaves and yet go free.
> They know nothing at all, neither good nor evil.
> These heathens who eat men are barbarians and go around naked . . .
> We Fur go and bring them among us and teach them our Islam.
> And they live happily among us.[18]

---

* The Fartit was a pejorative catch-all term used by the Fur to describe the communities of the southern lowlands – any people who were not Arab, Fur, Dinka or Luo.

Such attitudes persisted. Babikr Mehdi (1856–1954) was a Mahdist warrior who in later life mellowed into a social activist, the leading exponent among his generation of women's education in Sudan. However, he remained a slave-owner whose posthumously published memoirs reveal the extent of these traditional attitudes towards black Africans. He described how, as soon as he had heard that his cousin, a woman called Al Rawda bint Mohammed, had been married to a black soldier called Bakhit Muwafi, he immediately travelled to Aswan 'to get her away' from the man, marriage of an Arab woman to a black man being considered a family disgrace. When his relative refused to come back with him he was eventually forced to accept defeat. He was then mocked mercilessly by his friend Abdullah Bey, who had predicted that the mission would end in failure:

> 'You're a fool,' said the bey. 'Once the girl has had a taste of the slave's lusty cock, why on earth should she leave it and try yours?'
>
> 'No doubt she was created for the slave's cock,' I said, 'and it for her. What's more, she's young, and was forced to it; so she has her excuses. I've heard worse . . .'[19]

In 2020, this visceral rejection of mixed-ethnicity marriages returned to the fore in the public reaction to the marriage of Issam Abdulraheem, a famous Sudanese footballer, to the make-up artist Reem Khougli. Social media bristled with racial slurs. 'Seriously girl, this is *haram* [Arabic for forbidden] . . . a queen marries her slave,' one commentator posted on Facebook after seeing a photo of the couple. Elsewhere Ihsan Fagiri, the head of a women's rights group called No to Women Oppression, commented on a photo of a black man with a white European wife, saying that the woman might have been looking for 'the creature missing on the evolutionary ladder between humans and monkeys'. Amid the ensuing outcry, Fagiri announced her resignation but No to Women Oppression refused to accept it.[20]

Nineteenth-century abolitionists, who had their own prejudicial attitudes towards Africans and Arabs alike, had to contend with this deeply rooted bigotry – in addition to the vigorous opposition they faced from slave-traders, who rightly feared that their very livelihood was at risk. One of their most obdurate adversaries was Al Zubayr Rahma Mansur Pasha (1831–1913), the entrenched 'king of the

Zubayr Rahma Mansur Pasha, 'king of the slavers', 1900.

slavers', who from the mid-nineteenth century ran his private slave-
and ivory-trading imperium from Deim Zubayr (literally 'Camp
Zubayr'), his headquarters in Bahr al Ghazal, the north-western
region of today's South Sudan.

In 2017, in order to mark its infamous place in the history of slavery
and slave-trading, the government of South Sudan applied to UNESCO
to designate Deim Zubayr a World Heritage Site. It consists of a fort
and the poorly preserved remains of a trench, originally four metres
deep and 3,000 metres long, which served as a wood-and-mud prison
and holding centre for slaves due to be transported along the Nile. The
tree next to the trench, from which slaves who had attempted to escape
were hanged, still stands. In 1871, when Zubayr was at the height of
his powers, presiding over a trading empire stretching across Bahr al
Ghazal and swathes of Chad and the Central African Republic, the
Baltic German botanist Georg Schweinfurth became the first European
to visit Deim Zubayr. He described how all the slaves were subjected
to 'unbelievable degradation and cruelty', including women who were
'passed from hand to hand' as wives, concubines and domestic servants. For Henry Cecil Jackson, the author of *Black Ivory and White,
or The Story of El Zubeir Pasha, Slaver and Sultan, as told by Himself* (1913), Deim Zubayr was simply 'the metropolis and the clearing
house of the slave industry in that part of the world'.[21]

To this day Zubayr still divides opinion, a reflection of the internal
divisions of a country that has split into two. For the Sudanese, he
remains a national hero who fought off the colonial invaders and

successfully established his own state in Bahr al Ghazal without ever dirtying his hands in the slave trade. For the South Sudanese, he is the most infamous slaver of the South Sudanese population – and other Africans – on the greatest scale.

In 2020, Sudanese activists called for the renaming of Zubayr Pasha Street, a main road in downtown Khartoum, which is also home to the British embassy. 'It is disgusting to see that one of the main streets in the Sudanese capital Khartoum bears the name of Zubair Pasha Rahma who was a slave trader,' wrote the writer and journalist Mahmoud Suleiman. 'We demand the change of the street name,' said Hafiz Ibrahim of Justice Africa, 'and an apology from the grandchildren of those who opposed the abolition of slavery in Sudan.'

The street was not renamed and no apology was forthcoming.[22]

At the heart of the Ottoman Empire, as we have seen, abolition was characterized by varying degrees of ambivalence. It was true of pragmatic, progressive, opportunist and empire-building Britain – together with the other European powers – and it was equally true of the alternately reforming, foot-dragging, empire-losing Turkish authorities. A similar dynamic played out in Egypt and Sudan in the later nineteenth century, a period when both slaving and abolitionist activities were at their peak.

Britain's diplomatic offensive here mirrored its efforts in Istanbul, adding military firepower to the mix in the second half of the century. Khedive Ismail came under intensifying pressure from Britain to put 'a stop to this inhuman traffic', as the foreign secretary, Lord John Russell, put it in 1865 in a letter to Sir Henry Bulwer, the ambassador in Istanbul. Ismail's response, according to Bulwer, was promising. He was determined to

> dry up the evil at its source. This source he declared is the Sudan, where various foreigners carry on the most horrible system of negro kidnapping and hunting down . . . we will destroy the whole traffic. I am most desirous to do this, for the negroes now suppose that I sanction the atrocities practised against them which makes my name odious to them, whereas what is done is being done by foreigners against my interest in opposition to my authority.[23]

There were foreigners and then there were foreigners. In 1869, recognizing that suppression of the trade required government annexation of the lands where slaves were being hunted, the khedive hired the Englishman Sir Samuel Baker to extend the government's authority into Bahr al Jabal and suppress the slave trade in the Upper Nile region. Sudan, Baker wrote later in his self-serving account of the expedition, was 'a land sacred to slavery and to every abomination and villainy that man can commit'.[24] Another foreigner, Mohammed al Bulalawi, an adventurer from the Lake Fitri region in today's Chad, was appointed to lead an expedition to Bahr al Ghazal against Zubayr. Al Bulalawi's mission ended in failure and his death at the hands of Zubayr's forces in 1872.

Baker, who had won fame as an explorer of Africa, was an interesting choice to suppress the slave trade. In 1859, while visiting the slave market of Vidin, a Bulgarian port town on the Danube, he had been transfixed by a fourteen-year-old blonde girl with blue eyes who was being put up for auction. Outbid by the Ottoman Pasha of Vidin, Baker bribed the girls' attendants and spirited her away. They later married and she became Florence, Lady Baker.* Appointed major-general in the Ottoman army and governor of Equatoria for four years by Ismail with the rank of pasha, on a huge annual salary of £10,000 (a little shy of £1 million today), Baker led a military expedition into the southern, equatorial regions of Sudan at the head of a force of 1,700 Egyptian troops, many of them freshly released convicts. Today he would be called a mercenary.

The mission, in his own estimation, was a triumph. On 1 April 1873, the day his lucrative four-year term of employment came to an end, he sent a self-congratulatory despatch to his brother from Gondokoro, intending that it should be shared with the press. 'All obstacles have been surmounted. All enemies have been subdued – and the slavers who had the audacity to attack the troops have been crushed. The slave trade of the White Nile has been suppressed – and the country annexed, so that Egypt extends to the equator' – encompassing southern Sudan and parts of northern Uganda.[25]

---

* Although Lady Baker later became a darling of the British public, Queen Victoria refused to receive her at court on the grounds that the couple had had sex before marriage.

Although Baker was being deadly serious, those who understood the reality on the ground might have suspected an April Fools' prank. Baker had not subdued the local leader, Kabarega, who remained a powerful adversary; far from being crushed, the region's slavers had received only a temporary setback; and, as for extending government control, the country had neither been annexed nor had Baker even reached the equator. From a British perspective, the most that could be said was that Baker had done his best and had established some sort of basis for a new equatorial state. From an Egyptian and Sudanese point of view, including the growing numbers of his enemies, he was merely extending British authority in Africa.

In 1874, Baker was replaced as governor of Equatoria, later of Sudan itself, by a man even more celebrated by his countrymen and even more loathed by many Sudanese.

For more than twenty years, General Charles George Gordon has been watching me. He stares out at me now from the wall of my study. It is a head and shoulders portrait, probably Victorian, surrounded by nine smaller illustrations of key moments in a short but startling life full of adventure: 'Gordon's perilous journey across the desert to Khartoum'; 'Gordon shot in the leg in the attack on Kintang'; 'The Crimean trenches bursting of a shell near Gordon'. And within this *Boy's Own* celebration of a favourite imperial servant, the primly moustachioed general gazes out impassively beneath his trademark *tarboosh*, blue and gold striped sash stretched across a chest crammed with medals and frogging. A few lines of text recall his last words to Nubar Pasha, three-time prime minister of Egypt (1878–95), when the Englishman set out on his final, fatal mission to relieve Khartoum in 1884 as the messianic Mohammed Ahmed al Mahdi was setting Sudan on fire in rebellion: 'I will save the honour of Egypt.' An oval border includes the date of his death, 26 January 1885, when he was 'Treacherously killed at Khartoum'. This is classic British Empire myth-making and hero-raising. For the British public, stirred on by a vociferous media – 'Something must be done' again – Gordon was the Victorian era's abolitionist 'white saviour', a one-man scourge of the disgusting African slave trade. A strong dose of Gordon was just what Sudan needed.

There were other, opposing views, of course, even if they were less apparent – or listened to – in London. For many, if not most, Sudanese, the only 'treachery' at play here was that of their Egyptian ruler, Ismail Pasha, khedive (viceroy) of Egypt and Sudan from 1863 to 1879. He was guilty of recruiting a foreign white soldier of fortune, infidel puppet of a country at the forefront of the bloodthirsty Scramble for Africa, to be the governor-general of Sudan. Unlike the country's other invaders, rulers or occupiers, the Mahdi was a home-grown leader of men. He was not Turkish, he was not Egyptian and he certainly was not British. And, unlike these interfering, hypocritical, foreigners, he was not trying to abolish the slave trade, the central pillar of Sudan's domestic agrarian economy.

Gordon's admirers and kindred spirits in the British and Foreign Anti-Slavery Society thought they had their man. But his mission could hardly have been more unrealistic. In the same year Gordon was appointed, Zubayr seized control of Darfur, transforming it into the centre of the slave trade between Egypt and Sudan.

Though Gordon could build a series of stations to monitor and suppress the trade, he could do nothing to staunch the demand. His efforts 'resembled the palliatives of an empiric treating the superficial symptoms of some profound constitutional disease', Lytton Strachey wrote in his excoriating portrait of the Victorian hero. Over time, Gordon came to appreciate that unless you could do away with this demand, there was no chance of eliminating the supply. 'When you have got the ink that has soaked into blotting-paper out of it, then slavery will cease in these lands.'[26]

In the 1870s and 1880s, the British public could have been forgiven for thinking that Sudanese slavery and its abolition depended on just two men: Zubayr and Gordon. Contemporary British writers mythologized Zubayr as 'Sultan and Slaver', 'the black pasha', 'the greatest slaver who ever lived' and 'the richest and worst of them all'.[27]

Gordon and Zubayr were two sides of the same coin. For the messianic Gordon, slavery was 'a thing displeasing to God'. For Zubayr, as he related to Lord Ribblesdale during his later British detention on Gibraltar, slavery in Sudan was considered 'sacred and as belonging to religion'.[28] Gordon saw abolition as an inherent element of Britain's Christian, imperial and civilizing mission on earth. Zubayr, a God-fearing Muslim, considered slaving an equally integral part of his own imperial destiny to civilize his fellow Africans.

The unpalatable truth was that by the later nineteenth century, slave-trading in Sudan was a fundamental pillar of the economy. In 1877, urged on by the British, Khedive Ismail signed the Anglo-Egyptian Convention for the Suppression of the Slave Trade, which, by banning the trade with Sudan, dealt a significant blow to slavery in Egypt. Ismail's attempts to suppress it were considered so damaging and iniquitous by many Sudanese that within four years they had helped tip the country into wholesale revolt under the leadership of the Mahdi.

Ismail had hired foreigners to suppress the slave trade, he had stationed a military force on his southern border to check Arab slave-trading operations and he had started the manumission of slaves. In other words, he had done what the British had asked of him. Yet amid the excesses of his lavish, debt-ridden court, he proved unable or unwilling to set a personal example. 'With 3,000 in his harem, several slave regiments, and lots of gangs on all his sugar plantations, his impudence is wonderful,' wrote Lucie Duff Gordon, the English author who lived in Egypt in the 1860s. 'He is himself the greatest living slave trader as well as owner. My lads are afraid to go out alone for fear of being snapped up by cawasses [policemen] and taken to the army or the sugar works.'[29] The pasha grumbled that slavery in Egypt went back to the time of the pharaohs.

Duff Gordon was writing at a time when Egypt, together with swathes of the Middle East, was becoming enmeshed in an increasingly globalized market. Demand for slave labour in Egypt, particularly on agricultural plantations during the cotton boom unleashed by the US Civil War of 1861–5, was in overdrive.* 'Egypt', she wrote in 1865, 'is

---

* References to enslaved Africans abound in Duff Gordon's letters. She observes the amiable relations between one master and his slaves, takes in an eight-year-old slave girl who was being mistreated, enjoys an impromptu dinner with slave merchants on the banks of the Nile and herself borrows slaves whenever needed. In 1867, she wrote of the 'folly' of abolishing the Circassian slave trade but not its African counterpart. 'The Circassians take their own children to market, as a way of providing for them handsomely, and both boys and girls like being sold to the rich Turks; but the blacks and Abyssinians fight hard for their own liberty and that of their cubs ... I must say that once here the slaves are happy and well off, but the waste of life and the misery caused by the trade must be immense.'

one vast 'plantation' where the master works his slaves without even feeding them. From my window now I see the men limping about among the poor camels that are waiting for the Pasha's boats to take them, and the great heaps of maize which they are forced to bring for their food. I can tell you the tears such a sight brings to one's eyes are hot and bitter. These are no sentimental grievances; hunger, and pain, and labour without hope and without reward, and the constant bitterness of impotent resentment.'[30]

Fuelled by this surging demand for productive labour, the trans-Saharan slave trade rose accordingly as Egypt became the largest slave importer in North Africa. Census data from Egypt in 1848 and 1868, one of the earliest pre-colonial surveys outside the West to include comprehensive household information, including details on slave ownership, has recently been digitized. It is an exceptionally rare source on the slave population of Egypt, and possibly the Middle East, and has revealed how the numbers of agricultural slaves more than trebled from 39,762 (representing 1 per cent of the population) to 144,592 (3 per cent), driven by soaring demand among the rural middle class. Annual imports of enslaved sub-Saharan Africans to Egypt surged from an estimated 3,500 per annum in the 1850s to 10,000 during the 1860s, before plunging down to 2,000 in the 1870s after the end of the cotton boom.

These men, women and children joined local Egyptian workers coerced into plantation work, or 'snapped up', as Duff Gordon put it, by the state. Hundreds were taken to toil on Ismail's sugar plantations. While most slaves in Cairo and other towns tended to be female, and engaged in domestic tasks, a study of four villages in the eastern delta, based on the census data described above, revealed how the slave population shot up from a handful to over 5 per cent of each village's population.[31]

From 1879, the Egypt Ismail notionally ruled, already in mounting debt to his international predator-creditors, was consumed by the Urabi Revolt of 1879–82, a nationalist rebellion against British and French control. London and Paris manoeuvred behind the scenes with Istanbul, Ismail was deposed in 1879 and bundled into exile in the Ottoman capital. British forces then intervened in 1882, occupying

Egypt, suppressing the nationalist revolt, defeating Urabi at the Battle of Tell al Kabir and exiling him to Ceylon. While Ismail drank himself to death with champagne in Istanbul, slavery and the slave trade continued in both Egypt and Sudan. Yet cracks were widening in the ancient institution. In 1881, the Egyptian minister of the interior instructed Cairo's manumission bureau to issue manumission certificates to anyone who applied for one, so that by the middle of that decade the door was open for those enslaved men and women who wanted to be freed.[32]

The British invasion and occupation of Egypt led to the restoration of khedival authority, although all now knew where the real power lay. Originally conceived as a short-term affair, Britain's intervention evolved first into the 'veiled protectorate', which lasted until 1914, when war was declared against the Ottomans, and then a formal protectorate, which ended only in 1956.

In 1884 Britain tightened the noose again, introducing a ban on the import of white enslaved women into Egypt. Yet, just as Ottoman rulers at the highest level blithely disregarded inconvenient laws, so the Khedive Abbas II (r. 1892–1914) was still purchasing Circassian concubines for his harem in 1894. His mother, Princess Amina, outdid him by maintaining a retinue of sixty slaves as late as 1931.[33]

From 1881, Sudan joined its neighbour in the throes of revolution. Growing numbers flocked to the banners of Mohammed Ahmed, the self-proclaimed Mahdi, the promised redeemer of the Muslim world, who had declared jihad against the Turkish oppressors. Armed resistance was also fuelled by widespread anger at foreign attempts to suppress the slave trade, one of the major sources of revenue for the country. The situation became so desperate that by 18 February 1884, fresh from his return to Sudan a decade after his first appointment by Ismail and on the cusp of the ten-month siege of Khartoum, Gordon Pasha, the man who had devoted a decade of his life to suppressing the slave trade, was suddenly thinking the unthinkable.

In a telegram from Khartoum to Evelyn Baring, the British consul general in Cairo, he was absolutely clear on who should govern the country after the Egyptian withdrawal: 'the greatest slave-hunter who ever existed', as he put it. 'H. M. Gov't should select one above all others, namely Zobier [*sic*]. He alone has the ability to rule the Soudan and would be universally accepted by the Soudan. He should be made K.C.M.G and given presents.'[34]

The British government was aghast, the press and public – above all the Anti-Slavery Society – incandescent. Although Queen Victoria, Gladstone, Baring and Nubar Pasha were reluctantly persuaded, the government was unable to stomach it and later reversed the decision. There was little time to ponder the issue. By March Khartoum was under siege by Mahdist forces, and on 26 January 1885 it fell, notwithstanding the best efforts of Gordon to defend it. He was cut down and decapitated, achieving the martyrdom he had long craved. The surviving military garrison, enfeebled by starvation, shattered by months of defence, was eliminated to the last man. Many other men, women and children – with a sinister note of irony – were enslaved. Turco-Egyptian rule in Sudan had been born bathed in blood as Mohammed Ali's slave-raiding forces descended on their neighbour. Its death sixty years later was no less sanguinary.

'At any rate,' Strachey wrote in the blistering conclusion of his essay on Gordon, 'it had all ended very happily – in a glorious slaughter of 20,000 Arabs, a vast addition to the British Empire, and a step in the Peerage for Sir Evelyn Baring.'[35]

Six weeks after Gordon's death, the slaughter of the Khartoum garrison and the massacre or enslavement of its civilian population, Zubayr was detained by the British and spirited off to Gibraltar, where he was imprisoned without trial for over two years. There he gave weekly interviews to Florence Shaw, a rising star of British journalism. During their long conversations he denied any involvement in the slave trade one moment, described his purchase of 20,000 slaves in great detail the next. The abolition of slavery required time and preparation, he argued. In remote territories, where there were virtually no sources of power, he told Shaw, 'The only motive power is slave-power. If you cut off slave-power, the result would be the same as the cutting off of steam and water from England.' It would plunge the country back into 'barbarism'. When Egyptian and Turkish Muslims spoke to European statesmen about the abolition of slavery, she wrote, reporting his view, 'they spoke of what they knew in their hearts to be impossible'. These countries were not ready for such drastic reform.[36]

Zubayr, pink-faced English evangelicals, missionaries and abolitionists notwithstanding, was right. Slavery was too entrenched to be removed in one fell swoop without destabilizing an entire society which had come to depend on slave labour. A national minimum wage would need to be introduced first, and slave-owners properly compensated for the removal of their slaves. 'Taking away the slaves is associated with money . . . a fixed labour wage will have to be made throughout the districts,' Zubayr advised. It would take time – several more decades – before it could be completely extirpated.[37]

The new power in the land had no desire to hasten its demise. On the contrary, the Mahdi, who declared that he had been appointed to rule by the Prophet Mohammed, saw slavery as an Islamic and therefore entirely permissible custom – as long as it was practised in a proper Muslim fashion. Yet although he professed to be opposed to all innovations in Islam, he was perfectly content to enslave his hated co-religionist Turks. This was in direct contravention of holy law, which expressly prohibited Muslims from enslaving fellow Muslims. No matter. The Mahdi simply declared that the Turks themselves were infidels since they were heaping un-Islamic taxes upon the beleaguered population of Sudan.

In late 1883 he wrote a letter giving instructions regarding the division of the spoils of war. 'The booty must be divided into fifths. A fifth is to be deposited into the Bayt al Mal [Public Treasury] and the remainder is to be divided amongst the army . . . Free people should not be enslaved, with the exception of the Turks. Their men and women are booty of war.' The Bayt al Mal doubled up as a slave market.[38]

Yet even here, on the serious question of the legitimacy of enslaving Turkish prisoners, consistency was elusive. The Mahdi's 1883 letter contradicted a fatwa from the previous year in which he had warned 'all of the brothers against the greed for booty . . . Everything you find must be collected save weapons and sent to me. The Muslim women included. If they are captured do not sell them into slavery. For whoever does this is not one of us.'

Why this should be so is suggested in a 1903 history of Sudan by Naum Shuqayr Bey, a senior official in Cairo's War Ministry (whose account should therefore be treated with some caution). According to Shuqayr, the captured women were subsequently shared among the Mahdi and his commanders.[39]

The volte-faces continued. In 1887 Zubayr was freed from British imprisonment and within just a few years 'the greatest slaver who ever lived', the man whom Gordon had first fought and later recommended to rule Sudan, was a trusted adviser to Sir Reginald Wingate, governor of Sudan from 1899 to 1916. Slavery and abolition could make unexpected bedfellows of their respective champions.

It is difficult to imagine that Lytton Strachey, who died in 1932, would have been any less scathing about the following half-century of British rule in Sudan than he had been on the Gordon fiasco which preceded it. By 1899, Herbert Kitchener, nemesis of the Mahdist state – to which he had administered 'a damn good dusting' at the Battle of Omdurman the previous year – was the short-lived governor of Sudan.* It was in this capacity that he issued the following instructions to his provincial officers:

> I leave it to your discretion to adopt the best methods of gradually eradicating the habit of depending upon the slave labour which has so long been part of the religious creed and customs of this country, and which it is impossible to remove without doing great violence to the feelings and injuring the prosperity of the inhabitants.[40]

In the absence of slaves' complaints to the authorities about their mistreatment, non-interference was the order of the day. Concubinage remained untouched and slavery continued under British rule, albeit alongside the abolition of the trade, an end of mass enslavement and an active promotion of emancipation.

Britain was perfectly happy to use the suppression of the slave trade as a justification for imperial expansion. As Joseph Chamberlain, colonial secretary (1895–1903), argued in 1900, 'sooner or later we shall have to fight some of the slave-dealing tribes and we cannot have a better *casus belli* . . . Public opinion here requires that we shall justify imperial control of these savage countries by some serious effort

---

* As Hilaire Belloc wrote in *The Modern Traveller* in 1898: 'Whatever happens, we have got / The Maxim gun, and they have not.'

to put down slave dealing.'[41] A year later, the British had moved on the slaving Sokoto caliphate and by 1903 had conquered it.

Zubayr died in 1913. 'I shall miss the fine old man greatly,' Wingate wrote shortly after his death; 'he was a much misunderstood and much abused man, but ... did more to suppress the slave trade than any of our Anti-Slave Trade people at home – what a shock such a statement would be if made publicly and yet there is a great deal of truth in it.'[42]

As late as the 1940s, despite the formal abolition of slavery in 1924, Kitchener's principle of non-interference remained the prevailing British modus operandi. Despite Britain's earlier efforts, and notwithstanding its official prohibition, expectations that slavery would simply die out altogether, never to return, were not to be borne out. By the dying years of the twentieth century, when Gordon, Zubayr and the Mahdi were all a distant memory, slavery was once again thriving in Sudan.

For the National Islamic Front of Omar al Bashir, the then president of Sudan (in office 1993–2019), it was an effective weapon of war against his black southern Sudanese compatriots. From 1989 to 2011 he presided over the systematic enslavement of Sudanese and South Sudanese from the border region, arming, financing, transporting and supporting slave-taking militia raids into the Nuba Mountains, Abyei and Zubayr's former stronghold of Bahr al Ghazal. Men were routinely killed, women and children enslaved. Boys were trafficked to Libya, Qatar and Saudi Arabia. Non-Muslims were forcibly converted to Islam, and existing Muslims were forcibly Arabized. They were sold into the slave trade, renamed and forced to travel hundreds of miles from home, separated from their families, beaten, abused and forced to work for no pay. Many of the women and children were subjected to sexual abuse and torture. When the country split in 2011, it was estimated that over 35,000 South Sudanese people remained enslaved in Sudan. In Darfur the Janjaweed militia ran amok, committing numerous atrocities. One eyewitness, Neimat al Mahdi, recalled how the Janjaweed would enter the village of an African tribe, kill all the men and rape the women, mocking them afterwards with the age-old racial slur: 'You should celebrate, you slave. You are going to give birth to an Arab.'[43]

The International Criminal Court issued two arrest warrants for Bashir in 2009 and 2010, the first time a sitting head of state had been indicted by the ICC. The court quoted the perpetrators of attacks against civilians, especially from the Fur, Masaalit and Zaghawa tribes, telling their victims: 'the Fur are slaves, we will kill them'; 'You are Zaghawa tribes, you are slaves'; 'we are here to eradicate blacks (*nuba*)'.[44]

Bashir is accused of war crimes, crimes against humanity and genocide in Darfur. At the time of writing, reportedly he remains held in a hospital in Merowe, 200 miles north of Khartoum, and is one of the ICC's longest-running fugitives from justice.

Whichever way you looked across the nineteenth-century Dar al Islam, slavery coolly returned your gaze. Eighteen hundred miles east of Khartoum, across the horizons of the Arabian Peninsula, the mercantile Gulf state of Oman, the oldest independent Arab state in the world, had emerged as a slaving powerhouse.

African slavery in Oman went back at least 1,000 years. One of the earliest known references to it comes from the early tenth century and mentions the sale of an East African king in an Omani slave market. An opportunist Arab sailor called Ismailawayh and his crew were travelling to Sufalah (Mozambique) in 923. When the king of the region stepped on board the ship with a few companions, perhaps for a diplomatic exchange, the captain's greed was triggered. 'I said to myself, "This king would be worth 30 dinars in Oman in the marketplace, and the seven [companions] 160 dinars, and they have clothes worth 20 dinars, so that they would bring us at least 3,000 dirhams, without any risk attached.' They were all sold into slavery in Oman, together with 200 newly captured slaves.[45]

Generations of Omani sultans owned huge numbers of slaves. Saif bin Sultan (r. 1692–1711), nicknamed *Qaid al Ard*, Master of the Land, because he owned one-third of all the date palms in Oman, supposedly had 1,700 slaves. Date cultivation required considerable labour. Saif planted 30,000 date palms and 6,000 coconut palms, in addition to constructing and renovating seventeen *aflaj* irrigation systems. To do it he required slaves, procured from East Africa at the rate of more than 1,000 a year. The buccaneering Sultan bin Ahmad

(r. 1792–1804), who extended trading into Abyssinia and received slave girls and eunuchs as annual gifts, owned 300 slaves at a time when rich Omanis on average owned twenty-five. But figures available can be particularly unreliable. It was said, for example, that Sulayman bin Hamad Al Busaidi, prime minister under Said bin Sultan al Busaidi (r. 1804–56), owned a 'staggeringly unbelievable' 30,000 slaves. They tended 12,000 clove trees for him, providing their master with an annual yield of 210,000lbs of the spice, worth 10,000 Spanish dollars by the late 1840s – a decade which saw soaring prices fuelled by the clove mania of the 1830s come crashing down.[46]

For Oman, which had grown rich on the Indian Ocean slave trade, the nineteenth century began with a troubling warning from its turbulent Arab neighbour. In 1800, a propagandist Wahhabi tract arrived in the capital of Muscat along with the demand to submit to these hard-bitten warriors of the faith.

The Wahhabis were a fundamentalist Sunni Muslim sect who took their name from Mohammed ibn Abdul Wahhab (1703–92), a firebrand and religious reformer from the Arabian Peninsula. He had urged a return to a pure Islam, untainted by modernity, based on the Quran and the *Sunna*, the traditions of the Prophet Mohammed. The religious-political alliance he struck with Mohammed ibn Saud (r. 1727–65), founder of the First Saudi State, had critical consequences which continue to reverberate today. It is thanks to this enduring alliance between the Wahhabi *ulema* clergy and the Al Saud ruling family that the country continues to follow its strict version of Islam. Originally a minority extremist sect, widely regarded by their co-religionists as dangerous heretics, over time and later fuelled by vast quantities of petrodollars, the Wahhabis came to define the 'orthodox' brand of Sunni Islam which Riyadh has energetically championed across the Muslim world. Critics would describe it as an exclusive and intolerant version of Islam, promoting hatred towards other faiths, in addition to inspiring hard-line Islamist ideology and the many terrorist groups around the world, such as Al Qaeda, ISIS and many others, who subscribe to it.

In the minds of the Wahhabis, Oman's rulers, members of the moderate minority Muslim sect known as the Ibadis, were both an affront and a target. An Omani scholar read the tract and suspected the worst. 'The Wahhabi religion calls for Muslims to kill each other and declares other Muslims who do not adhere to its doctrines as polytheists, allowing the plunder of their goods, the enslavement of their women and children, the taking of booty, and the imposition of poll tax and land tax,' he wrote. It was the old trick of branding one's fellow Muslims as infidels in order to enslave them legitimately.

Omani fears were not far-fetched. In 1802, a Wahhabi force of up to 7,000 camels and horses surged north from Arabia and sacked the sacred Shia Muslim city of Kerbala in central Iraq, massacring several thousand inhabitants and looting the gold-filled shrine of Imam Hussain. As Abdullah ibn Saud, the last ruler of the First Saudi State (r. 1814– 18), declared of his neighbours in 1817: 'All these people are our enemies, and by the aid of the Almighty, wherever we may find them or their people we will assuredly slay the one and seize the other.'

The Wahhabis by no means had a monopoly on intra-Muslim prejudice. Mohammed Shah (r. 1834–48), the third Qajar shah of Iran, was scarcely more complimentary about his Omani counterpart, whom he condemned as 'little better than a kafir'. He also dismissed the Ottomans as schismatics and, while defending slavery, told the British minister in Tehran that buying men and women was based on the sharia holy law established by the Prophet Mohammed. There was no question of abolition (an 1868 census in Tehran found that 12 per cent of the civilian population were either African slaves or household servants). 'I cannot say to my people that I am prohibiting something which is lawful,' he told the diplomat.[47]

History does not record the shah's views on the legality of the regular slaving raids Iran suffered at this time at the hands of the Turkmen, an instance of Muslim-on-Muslim bloodshed and enslavement which occurred as close as 100 miles from Tehran. Travelling in Iran with the Anglo-Russian Afghan Boundary Commission in 1884–5, the Scottish artist William Simpson witnessed whole areas which had been entirely depopulated east of Mashhad. 'The raiding of the Turkmens was essentially a slave-dealing system, founded on the assumption of a right of property in human flesh and blood,' he wrote. A raiding party numbering up to 6,000 would approach a selected district under cover of dawn, avoiding all main roads, then pounce 'with a lightning sweep, so as to catch the men or women at work in the fields . . . Young girls, if they were pretty, and children were looked on as the most valuable prizes . . .'.[48]

By the dawn of the nineteenth century, notwithstanding the ominous Wahhabi warning, Oman had established itself as a regional maritime power, a prosperous middleman serving Ottoman, Persian and African markets, together with the emerging European colonies in India and as far east as Indonesia. Having seized Zanzibar from the Portuguese in 1698, Oman's trading empire had steadily expanded, invigorated both militarily and economically by slave labour. The nineteenth-century Omani historian Ibn Ruzayq described how Ahmad bin Said al Busaidi (r. 1744–83), the first Omani ruler of the Busaid dynasty, which has ruled Oman to this day, bought 1,000 Zanj (i.e. East Africans) and 100 Nubian slaves, in addition to hiring 1,000 mercenaries and providing each man with a camel or a horse.[49] Zanzibar even owed its name to the dark skin of its inhabitants. Arabs evolved the Farsi compound word *Zangbar* – literally Zang, black, plus bar, coast – into *Zanjibar*, Land or Coast of the Blacks. It became one of the largest slave markets in the region.

The British had also insinuated themselves into the picture. Towards the close of the eighteenth century, the British 'Resident' in Basra was taking a share for London of import duties on Iraq-bound mocha coffee from Yemen, taken up the Persian Gulf on Omani ships. Merchants spoke the same language of trade and the British were only too happy to hail 'the friendship which subsisted betwixt us and the Muscateers'. Before the abolitionist policy took hold in London, the British were also happy to engage in the Omani slave trade themselves. In 1762, the Bombay Presidency purchased a large number of African slaves for 10,000 rupees via an Indian dealer in Muscat. They were destined for the East India Company, which was then building a new base on Sumatra. Six years later, Bombay hired ships going to Muscat and Africa to buy slaves to work in its marine yard. By the closing decades of the eighteenth century Muscat was turning a brisk trade in East African slaves, satisfying a rising demand from French island-colonies, especially Île de France (Mauritius) and Bourbon (La Réunion).[50]

Trade meant profits, and profits spelt Great Power rivalry. In 1800, Mirza Mahdi Ali Khan, the East India Company's resident at the Iranian port city of Bushire (Bushehr), wrote to Sheikh Sayf bin Mohammed, deputy to the Omani ruler Sultan bin Ahmad. 'Look upon the friendship and esteem of the English government as the Soul by which Muskat breathes and has its being and fly the contamination of French fraternity as you would the plague,' he advised.[51] Beneath the florid diplomatic language lay the suggestion that Britain could throttle Oman if it so pleased. In the later nineteenth century it would threaten to do so with less *politesse*, and by the end of the century it had gobbled up entirely both Oman and Zanzibar as protectorates.

The nineteenth century saw Oman pursue a more expansionist maritime policy, extending its trading empire from Africa's Red Sea coast through Muscat and on across the Indian Ocean along the immense coastline of today's India and Pakistan (Oman only gave up its trading station of Gwadar to Pakistan in 1958).

Trade along the western littoral of the Indian Ocean abounded in high-price goods and commodities. There was gold, together with diamonds, pearls, crystals, silver thread, silk, chinoiserie, chintz, cotton, nankeen, rafia and fine Chinese porcelain. Animals and animal products featured prominently in cargoes, above all ivory, but also leather and exotic skins, tortoise shell, rhinoceros horns, hippopotamus teeth, beeswax, tallow and cowrie shells. Westbound ships from Oman and the Persian Gulf plied the waters with noisy, stinking holds full of horses and donkeys, hunting falcons, dried fish, fish oil, onions and *ghee*. Many dhows boasted more fragrant and colourful cargoes: cumin, cardamom, cinnamon, cloves and cubebs, vanilla, nutmeg, ginger, tamarind, sesame and saffron; ambergris and Arabian dates and raisins, copal resin, copra, castor oil, mocha coffee, Chinese and Tibetan musk, Indian and Socotran aloe, musk rose water, indigo and vermilion. Bales of Persian carpets wobbled in the heaving seas alongside stacks of ebony, sacks of gunpowder, glass beads, opium poppies and almonds, jars of honey and pineapples, pomegranates, guavas, mangoes, lemons and limes, bananas, coconuts, rhubarb and red peppers.[52]

But for the Arabs living in East Africa and for Arab traders sailing along its coast, none of these items was as important as the one live, walking, talking multi-function staple: the African slave.

Nineteenth-century Zanzibar became *the* trading entrepôt of the western Indian Ocean, a major slaving hub for Arab and Swahili traders and a 'symbol of Arab oppression in East Africa'.[53] The two communities formed powerful, violent alliances which extended west into Central Africa – present-day Malawi, Mozambique, Zambia and Tanzania. There were Arab political enclaves in the Lake Nyasa region and alliances with local chiefs of the Bemba, Chewa, Senga and Sena, among others. Destruction, frequently famine and epidemics of cholera and smallpox, followed in their wake. Whole towns and villages were burnt to the ground, entire areas ravaged and depopulated. Political interventions in the interest of the smooth and profitable functioning of the slave trade could also be made when required. Thus in 1872, Arab and Swahili traders helped arrange the assassination of Kazembe Muonga Sunkutu, ruler of the Lunda kingdom of Kazembe (Zambia and south-eastern Congo), ensuring his replacement with a more biddable successor.[54]

Slavery and the slave trade remained the base of Oman's princely fortunes and commercial maritime empire, which was energetically extended during the long reign of Said bin Sultan al Busaidi over the first six decades of the nineteenth century. In the absence of a peasant class, the new plantations springing up in East Africa to supply European demand for sugar cane, copal, rice, vanilla, pepper, cardamom, nutmeg and cloves relied upon slaves to cultivate them. To attempt to suppress the slave trade was tantamount to destroying the time-honoured economic foundations of East Africa and upending political power and local culture. This was precisely what the British set out to do.[55]

Given the paucity of records, estimates for the volume of this regional trade remain imprecise and are regularly revised. In 1811, it was estimated that Zanzibar was sending 10,000 slaves a year, of both sexes and all ages, to the French colonies, Muscat and India. Omani settlers in Zanzibar, who controlled the trade, were reportedly buying slaves for twenty Spanish dollars in the interior and selling them on to the French for double that sum. Export duties and customs revenues levied on the trade lent further lustre. From 1811 to 1873, according to one study, an average of 17,785 slaves were exported annually from the outpost of Kilwa (southern Tanzania), a key staging post on the route to the coast.* Of these men, women and children, 80 per cent were destined for Zanzibar, which by the 1860s was importing just under 19,800 slaves a year, retaining the lion's share (12,000) on the island for labour there and re-exporting the rest of this great human cargo – to Lamu, the Arabian Peninsula, Pemba, Mombasa and Mrima, the section of the coast facing Zanzibar.[56]

Captain Thomas Smee, a British naval officer charting the East African coast in 1811, so often a prelude to colonial conquest, left a description of the Zanzibar slave market. After the slaves were cleaned, he reported, they had their skins burnished with coconut oil, faces painted with red and white stripes ('which is here esteemed elegance') and their hands, feet, ears and noses ornamented with gold and silver rings. They were then paraded through the market, where potential buyers could take a closer look – and more besides:

> The mouth and teeth are first inspected, and afterwards every part of the body in succession, not even excepting the breasts, etc., of the girls, many of whom I have seen examined in the most indecent manner in the public market by their purchasers ... The slave is then made to walk or run a little way to show that there is no defect about the feet ... Women with children newly born hanging at their breasts and others so old they can scarcely walk, are sometimes seen dragged about in this manner. I observed they had in general a very dejected look; some groups appeared so ill fed that their bones seemed as if ready to penetrate the skin.[57]

To take a wider perspective, approaching 500,000 slaves were exported from East Africa across the Red Sea and the Gulf of Aden during the nineteenth century, with a further 300,000 shipped to the Middle East and India. Those figures can only hint at the vast numbers who never made it to their intended destinations – the literally untold human lives lost along the way, during violent slave raids, on the gruelling marches to the coast lasting several months and, for those who survived these

---

* Centuries earlier, Kilwa was a place rich in slaves. Visiting in 1331, Ibn Battuta wrote of the then sultan, Abu al Muzaffar Hasan, making raids into the country of the Zanj. He also claimed to have witnessed this 'virtuous and liberal' sultan and his son giving a beggar twenty slaves and two loads of ivory as a sign of their munificence.

The slave market in Zanzibar, 1860, drawing by the British artist Edwin
R. L. Stocqueler, published in the *Anti-Slavery Reporter* journal in 1877.

ordeals, while sailing onwards in deplorable conditions without food
and with little water. Many of the women had been forcibly separated
from their children and raped during the journey. Some would have
contracted malaria while being cooped up within barracoons at Kilwa.
Average mortality rates on ships carrying slaves from Africa and the
Comoros to La Réunion in the 1850s was reportedly 25 per cent.[58]

The destinations for most of the survivors were the Persian Gulf and
the Arabian Peninsula, with many sold on to Egypt, Syria, the Ottoman
heartland and north-western India. Few went further east than India,
with modest exports there tailing off to a trickle after the 1840s. Prices
varied according to the distance from source as well as the availability of free labour. In 1850, for example, a slave in Zanzibar would be
sold for five to ten dollars, rising to twenty-five in Muscat, forty in the
Iranian port of Bushehr, and as much as 100 in north-western India.[59]

Market forces, shaped by evolving domestic and international consumer tastes for commodities like cotton, cloves, coconuts, copra, oil,
grain and dates, had a direct bearing on the size and composition
of the regional workforce, above all in requiring the development of

extensive plantations. Just as the cotton boom of the 1860s had triggered a rapid escalation in the demand for slave labour in Egypt, so the Gulf boom in date exports from the second half of the nineteenth century required a massive influx of workers. Slave traders worked the routes from Persia, Baluchistan, India, the Arabian Peninsula and, overwhelmingly, from Africa, to satisfy the need for slaves to cultivate the swiftly expanding date plantations of the Gulf.

Perhaps nowhere was the boom so pronounced as in Al Batinah, a swathe of agricultural land stretching almost 200 miles along the northern coast of Oman. International, especially North American, demand for this famously sweet, succulent and filling fruit led to a transfer of human cargo so vast that it has been argued that this region became 'the primary destination for slaves in the late nineteenth and early twentieth centuries', notwithstanding the traditional primacy of Mecca among slave markets on the Arabian Peninsula. American date imports grew from 10 million to 20 million pounds per annum between 1893 and 1903 to 20 million to 30 million pounds from 1903 to 1913, peaking at almost 79 million pounds in 1925.[60] Enslaved Africans were used especially to maintain the *jalibs* (masonry wells) and *qanats* (irrigation channels), both of which required constant maintenance, as well as climbing up and down the date palm trunks in difficult, often painful and dangerous work.

Writing a report on the Omani slave trade in 1927, the English diplomat and explorer Bertram Thomas, who was then serving as finance minister of Sultan Taimur bin Faisal of Muscat and Oman (r. 1913–32), likened the slavery of Africans labouring in Omani date farms to the plantation model of the American South. There was one striking difference. For approximately six months of the year, a typical slave – fed, clothed, lodged and unpaid – would work his master's date plantation before joining the annual migration north to take part, for the rest of the year, in that other great staple of Gulf slavery and indentured labour: pearl-diving.

Here, too, the global commodity market was instrumental in determining models of enslavement. As with cloves in Zanzibar, cotton in Egypt, dates in Oman, so with pearls in the Gulf. The pearling industry, which reached its zenith in the early twentieth century, peaking around 1912, required a sudden surge of divers. The trade in these lustrous ocean stones, destined to garland the necks of wealthy and glamorous women around the world, depended upon a workforce mired in poverty. Although they were not slaves in the traditional sense of owned chattels, these men, who were of African, Asian, Indian and Arab descent, tended to be indentured labourers, so broken by (deliberately fostered) debt to their masters that they were de facto enslaved.

In 1863, Sheikh Mohammed bin Thani, the then ruler of Qatar, ancestor of the fantastically rich dynasty which rules the Gulf state today, spoke for many in the region when he uttered the following words to William Gifford Palgrave, the English Arabic scholar and explorer: 'We are all, from the highest to the lowest, slaves of one master – Pearl.'[61] His form of enslavement, it might be added, was hardly comparable to that of the multinational throng of labourers.

In a recent oral history, Bilal Khamis, a pearl-diver from Jumeirah in Dubai, recalled his career in terms which emphasize that, though romantic in the imagination, the pearl trade was often a living hell on the sea. In boats carrying up to sixty people, divers would spend three to four months away from their families at sea in the height of summer, testing human endurance to the limit.

Rations were meagre, conditions spartan. Fish, rice and dates. A few drops of coffee in the morning and so little water that 'we felt thirsty for the whole day'. Diving lasted from morning to evening, divers treading water on the surface for a few precious minutes to recover between dives before breathing in deeply for a minute and then embarking on another – and another, and another – heart-pumping, lung-bursting descent in waters up to 25 metres deep. Divers wore a *fatam* or nose plug to keep water out, a *diyyin* palm-rope basket around the neck to load the oysters and stone or zinc weights around the ankle. Some wore leather finger-guards and a cotton body suit to protect against jellyfish. It was gruelling work.

Exhaustion was no excuse not to continue. 'We knew we had to go down again. Some of the *nokhadas* [captains and representatives of the expedition's financiers] would beat the people if they didn't go down because the captains had spent a lot of money going diving and they had to bring pearls back. The divers couldn't do anything – they had debts with the captains. They never said no. They had to dive.'

After months at sea with no freshwater for washing, the divers' skin grew rough, cracked and painful. At night, completely shattered, they flopped on to crude mats of date palm leaves thrown across uncomfortable piles of living shells. Fear haunted their waking hours. 'When we were under the water we could see jellyfish or a shark coming near, but we wanted to eat. We were diving for money, for food – to live. It was life.'[62]

In 1905, according to John Lorimer, British Political Resident in the Gulf and author of *Gazetteer of the Persian Gulf, Oman and Central Arabia*, a famous two-volume encyclopedia, the Bahrain pearl-fishing fleet comprised 917 boats and over 17,500 men. There were 410 in Abu Dhabi, 350 at Doha and 335 in Dubai. By 1913, the value of pearls sold by Bahrain alone was around $9 million.[63]

The combination of the First World War, increased availability of cultured pearls from Japan and the global financial crash of 1929 ushered in the ruinous end of Gulf pearling. The boom was now in manumission statements from pearl-divers. On 8 February 1930, 'the slave Naser bin Almas', aged around thirty, appeared at the British Political Agency Bahrain and made the following statement as part of his application for a manumission certificate that would, he hoped, enable him 'to lead a free life'.

> 'My master got me married with one of his slave girls named Asma who gave birth to a daughter who died in her infancy and a son who is about a year old. I am a diver and go for diving in the pearling season and earn for my master. But as my master does not give me sufficient food or clothing and treats me with every possible harshness and severity I have absconded from him even leaving my wife and son.'[64]

Speaking in 2009, Jumaa al Batishi, another retired pearl-diver, gave a similarly baleful verdict on his underwater tribulations more than half a century earlier. 'Diving was a piece of hell,' he said.[65]

While opportunities and profits multiplied, stiff new challenges to Omani fortunes soon materialized. Successive sultans from the Busaid dynasty would find themselves, like Ottoman sultans during the same period, on the receiving end of a sustained diplomatic barrage aimed explicitly at suppressing the slave trade in their dominions – and, less publicly at least, but no less definitely, extending the British Empire. It was a reminder, if one were wanted, that for increasing numbers of Arabs abolitionism was indeed 'imperialism spelled differently'.[66]

In 1822, in a sign of how much had altered from the British perspective (in 1768 Bombay had been procuring slaves from Oman), and how markedly the balance of power between Britain and the 'Muscateers' had shifted, Said was persuaded to sign the Moresby Treaty, named after Fairfax Moresby, the senior naval officer in Mauritius and a future admiral of the fleet. Under the terms of this agreement, the sultan undertook to stop Omanis trading in slaves with the subjects of Christian powers, a move which targeted the Indian Ocean slave trade with British holdings in India. The Moresby Line was also established, starting at Cape Delgado (Mozambique), running north along the East African coast before turning east to the west Indian port town of Diu. Tolerated to the primarily Muslim region west of this line, slave exports were henceforth prohibited to its east. Doubtless exaggerating his financial losses for diplomatic effect, the sultan later said that the Moresby Treaty had cost him 40,000–50,000 Spanish dollars in foregone revenue. Had that been all, Said might have rested easy. It would have been disappointing, but tolerable. Yet this was merely the opening salvo and, for those who could read the runes, it signalled an ominous confrontation ahead.

Arab Omani settlement, in play on Zanzibar from the seventeenth century, had led over time to the development of a plantation system on the island – as well as on the East African mainland – in which mostly Arab and some Asian landowners used, and utterly depended upon, African slave labourers.

By 1839 the African trade in slaves, ivory and spices, especially cloves, had become so fundamental to Omani state fortunes that the then sultan, Said, moved his royal court from Muscat and relocated it 2,500 miles south-west to Stone Town on Zanzibar. In this abrupt continental shift of an Arab dynasty from the heart of the Gulf, so much of which was quintessentially Arabian, to Africa there could be no more eloquent demonstration of political and economic priorities. Said's timing, on the cusp of an export boom in the western Indian Ocean which drove up the demand for slaves from the 1840s to the 1880s, was impeccable.

Under mounting British pressure, however, during the course of the nineteenth century there was an important shift away from the slave trade to an intensifying, export-led focus on plantation slavery. Clearly the Moresby Treaty made an immediate impact. In 1828, Said wrote to his commercial agent in Bombay. 'In consequence of the abolition of the slave trade the collections [revenue] of Zanzibar have been diminished; it has therefore been deemed necessary to make plantations of sugar cane in the islands.' Britain might have been vociferously opposed to the slave trade, but it was not about to try to suppress slavery itself: 'the tender conscience of the British abolitionists was not yet troubled by the consumption of slave-grown spices', as the Tanzanian historian Abdul Sheriff puts it.[67] Or, to put it another way, the unintended consequence of the British-led attack on the slave trade was a significant boost to plantation slavery.

From the mid-nineteenth century, growing quantities of information on the trade became available as a succession of pen-wielding British officials reported back to their masters in Bombay and London. In 1841 Atkins Hamerton, the East India Company representative on Zanzibar and the first British consul there, reported that almost every one of the sultan's subjects owned slaves, 'the poorer about five, and the wealthier from 400 to 1,500'. Tasked with reporting all the sordid details of the trade, he did not hold back. As was so often the case, it was the terrible journeys the captives were forced to make to the slave markets that were singled out for opprobrium:

> I fancy, in no part of the universe is the misery and human suffering these wretched slaves undergo, while being brought here and until they are sold, exceeded . . . They are in such a wretched state from starvation and disease, that they are sometimes not considered worth landing, and are allowed to expire in the boats to save the dollar-a-head duty, and the bodies of these poor people are eaten on the beach by the dogs of the town; none will bury them.[68]

A few miles outside Zanzibar town, surrounded by scented shrubs, breadfruit, rambutan and palm trees, the Mangapwani slave chamber, a dark cell cut into the coral rock beneath a bunker-like roof, is a stark reminder of how the clandestine trade continued illegally during the final two decades of the nineteenth century and the opening years of the twentieth. Slaves were kept here and then led out to the sea through a hidden passage, before being transported by dhow to other markets.

In 1845, another crack appeared in the Zanzibari slaving edifice. Named after Atkins Hamerton, British consul in Zanzibar from 1841 to 1857, the Hamerton Treaty now prohibited slave exports north of Lamu. It was signed by Sultan Said only with enormous reluctance and after considerable resistance. These anti-slavery orders, he argued to the British, were 'the same as the orders of Azrael, the Angel of Death'. The sultan's personal secretary was dumbfounded. 'Arabs have carried on the [slave] trade since the days of Noah,' he exclaimed. 'Arabs must have slaves.'[69] Such pleas fell on deaf ears in London, where the anti-slavery rhetoric had reached messianic levels.

A year later, Lord Palmerston, back for a second time as foreign secretary, wrote to Hamerton, instructing him to impress upon 'these Arabs' that the nations of Europe were destined to eliminate the African slave trade, and that Britain was 'the main instrument in the Hands of Providence for the accomplishment of this purpose'. Resistance would be in vain. The Arabs should 'bow to a superior power'.[70]

London's later intervention in an Omani succession dispute led to the British-sponsored division of Oman into two separate, weaker sultanates in 1861, one on the Arabian Peninsula, the other in East Africa, centred in Zanzibar. The British were on the move.[71]

Although it left life within the sultan's dominions undisturbed, so that slaves could still be used on plantations on Zanzibar, neighbouring Pemba and along the Swahili coast, the Hamerton Treaty still struck a considerable blow to more far-flung commerce. By 1850, Hamerton reckoned it had reduced the volume of the foreign slave trade by 80 per cent.

For the British this was not enough. To go a step further and prohibit the coastal trade in slaves entirely, London wanted to add another article to the treaty, without which it would be 'impossible for the Sultan's officers or the commanders of British cruisers to prevent slaves from being exported from the Zanzibar territory'. Sultan Majid bin Said al Busaidi (r. 1856–70) bridled at the pressure. It was 'too much to expect that I should agree to a measure which must certainly prove my ruin'. Robert Lambert Playfair, the British consul in the early 1860s, agreed. Such a measure, he wrote, 'must inevitably cause the downfall of his House'.[72]

Into this fraught setting strode a tall, straight-backed, black-bearded Afro-Omani merchant-prince called Hamed bin Mohammed al Murjabi (1837–1905). Born in Zanzibar, he was better known as Tippu Tip, a nickname which he claimed referred to the sound of his men's swiftly firing guns during an early, blood-soaked trading expedition into Chungu territory (northern Zambia), but which others said derived from his rapid blinking.

Tippu Tip was the pre-eminent ivory-trader of his generation, a calling which required an intimate connection with slaving and the slave trade. This was not a profession for one afraid of shedding blood. His career started as a precocious teenager in 1855, founded on a number of trading and plundering missions into the interior, burning and slaughtering when he considered necessary. He won both fame and notoriety in Europe, the one for bravely assisting David Livingstone, Henry Morton Stanley and Verney Cameron during their

A silver gelatin print photograph of Tippu Tip, the prolific Afro-Omani slaver and ivory trader, c. 1890.

death-defying explorations in Africa, the other because of the African Arabs' 'appalling reputation for cruelty and violence'.[73] He was a more nuanced character than either of these crude brushstrokes suggest, an energetic, highly intelligent and exceptional leader of men who was capable of both chivalrous hospitality and acts of extraordinary violence. By the time Livingstone met him in 1867, he was at the outset of a twenty-year trading-cum-plundering campaign in the Congo.

In 1881 he explained his opinion on slavery and European attitudes towards it to the Belgian army officer and explorer Jerôme Becker:

> White people have quite false ideas about our customs and habits. Everything which doesn't exist with them – even if it has ended recently – they insist on abolishing immediately everywhere else! ... What is the difference between a slave and a domestic servant? A domestic is free and leaves his master when he feels like it. My slaves wouldn't think of leaving me – they're too content with what they have. If I were unfair to them, perhaps they would run away. But what good would it do them? They'd come under the control of others like themselves, or be sold again, or mistreated, or perhaps killed, or have to work twice as hard as before.[74]

Attitudes varied, depending on where you stood. The hunter tends to take a different view of the hunt than the hunted. The eastern Congolese understandably had a less sanguine view of slaving. They associated men like Tippu Tip and his contemporary Mohamed bin Khalfan, a famous Afro-Omani slave-trader nicknamed Rumaliza (Destroyer), with the most apocalyptic scenes in their homeland: 'the kidnapping of women, cutting off of men's genitals, legs, arms and hands, piercing of noses and ears, burning of villages, scorchings of farms, and killings', as the historian Osumaka Likaka describes the plundering of the Congo.[75]

Tippu Tip proved highly adept in his dealings with predatory Europeans as the land-grabbing Scramble for Africa convulsed the continent. In the mid-1880s, he suggested to Sultan Barghash bin Said (r. 1870–88) that the two men join forces to resist Belgian moves to seize the lucrative territory of the Congo. When a weary Barghash told him that the Europeans were already moving to take Zanzibar from him and that he would no longer have anything to do with the

African mainland, in Tippu Tip's own words, 'I knew that it was all up with us.' Recognizing the arrival of an irresistible force, he manoeuvred accordingly and in 1887 agreed to become governor, on behalf of the Belgians, of the Stanley Falls District of the Congo Free State. His appointment had echoes of Gordon's recommendation of Zubayr, slaver bar none, to rule Sudan.

There was little time to govern, however, because that year he joined Stanley on the disastrous and bloody expedition of 1887–9 to relieve Emin Pasha, Gordon's successor as governor of Equatoria, who was then threatened by Mahdist forces.

After decades of turmoil, conflict and fantastically profitable slaving, in 1891 Tippu Tip finally opted for the quiet life. He retired to Zanzibar, where he dictated his memoirs before his death in Stone Town in 1905.

How to police the maritime slave trade? From the later 1850s the Royal Navy took up the challenge, arrogating to itself the largely unchecked powers to stop, search and frequently destroy vessels sailing from East Africa towards Arabia and beyond. From 1868 to 1870, Philip Howard Colomb, who had already earned his place in posterity by inventing a Morse code system for use at sea, was part of this patrolling fleet in the Indian Ocean. As captain of HMS *Dryad* he captured seven Arab slave dhows with 365 Africans on board. His account of his experiences in the Indian Ocean is a reminder of the great and arbitrary power a Royal Navy captain of the time could deploy. With licence to survey these ships, report them unseaworthy and then scuttle or burn them, British captains were a formidable force. 'The captain of the ship', Colomb wrote in *Slave-catching in the Indian Ocean*, 'is judge, jury, and executioner.'[76]

Delivering justice at sea was not always a pretty sight. For some British officers, the de facto free-for-all proved irresistible. With £5 on offer for each slave rescued, or £4 per ton for ships carrying few slaves, captains and their crew were incentivized to make 'a little more prize money' and wreak havoc on local shipping, 'destroying legitimate trade' in the words of William Cope Devereux, who patrolled the East African coast on HMS *Gorgon* in the early 1860s and sailed up the Zambezi with Livingstone. 'The name of the British sailor is sadly compromised by acts which can come under no other name than piracy,' he confessed in his forthright memoir. 'I believe many a man has been hanged for doing far less.'

Of forty-three Arab dhows captured between 1861 and 1863, thirty-eight were found not to be carrying any slaves. In the years 1868, 1869 and 1870, a total of 109 dhows were captured and 3,172 slaves freed. During that last year, around 400 dhows were boarded, of which just eleven – less than 3 per cent – were carrying slaves. The British stood accused of the indiscriminate destruction of Arab property on the dhows. 'This irregular manner of looting is very disgraceful,' Devereux wrote.[77]

Slavers still pushed their luck, of course, and at the helm of their swift lateen-rigged ships they managed to elude the modest force of ponderous British sloops set against them on the vast Indian Ocean. Decades after the last slave ship had sailed west to the Americas and the West Indies, Arab dhows were still quietly slipping out of Zanzibar, Mombasa and a string of East African ports, their holds tightly crammed with African slaves destined for sale across the Arabian Peninsula, the Persian Gulf, Ottoman Empire and India.[78]

While a maritime version of cat and mouse played out on the high seas, Britain stepped up the pressure. In the opening 1870s, Sultan Barghash found himself caught in a vice between British abolitionists and his fellow Zanzibaris, for whom abolition was complete anathema. His council of sheikhs maintained an unswerving opposition to external interference. But protests to the British consul John Kirk, stationed in Zanzibar from 1870 to 1886, that the Quran sanctioned slavery, and that abolition amounted to force and plunder of local, legally held property, cut little ice.

In 1873, the year in which Sir Samuel Baker completed his four-year mission in Sudan, Barghash consented to a new treaty abolishing the slave trade, closing slave markets and prohibiting British and Indian passport-holders from owning slaves. He did so only under the direct threat of force: sign the treaty or face a naval blockade. When Barghash protested that this was no way to agree a treaty between two friendly nations, Kirk 'bared the teeth of British imperialism' and told the sultan: 'I have not come to discuss but to dictate.' The Stone Town slave market, one of the world's last open markets to trade in humans, closed for the first and last time. Yet once again the treaty was only half-heartedly enforced and the trade, now more covert than ever, refused to disappear altogether.[79]

In his defence of slavery, Barghash was a faithful spokesman for his countrymen – certainly its most prosperous members and especially the Arab and Indian merchant class. His sister, Sayyida Salama bint Said (1844–1924), also called Salme, the youngest of the thirty-six children of the remarkably fecund Said bin Sultan al Busaidi, provided a startling indication of ruling-class views on slavery in her outspoken Zanzibar memoir.

First published in English in 1888, *Memoirs of an Arabian Princess from Zanzibar* was a pioneering autobiography for an Arab woman. It tells the improbably picaresque story of this daughter of a Circassian slave, an exceptional woman who taught herself to write in secret by copying verses from the Quran on to a camel's shoulder blade. In her early twenties she struck up a romantic liaison with a German merchant in Zanzibar's Stone Town, became pregnant, escaped on a British frigate to Aden in 1866, scandalously converted to Christianity and married there in 1867, becoming Emily Ruete. She moved to Hamburg and had four children (her first died soon after birth), before the tragic death of her husband in a tram accident. Having already lost her royal fortune on Zanzibar, she was left in dire financial straits. The memoir was her effort to make ends meet.

'I am perfectly aware that I shall not make any friends by the opinions I hold', her chapter on slavery begins, before sharing her views on abolition and black Africans, whom, like a number of Social Darwinists of this time, she considered biologically inferior and fit for servitude. As a child she witnessed the freeing of slaves owned by British subjects, according to an agreement between Britain and her father the sultan. It distressed 'the upper classes' and Zanzibar suddenly found itself

> saddled with a few thousand idlers, vagabonds, and thieves. These great children thus set free enjoyed their liberty as a release from their bondage, and its inflicted duties, but what was their physical condition in life on waking from their short dream of happiness? They found themselves for the first time in their lives thrown upon their own resources, homeless, and utterly without means of maintenance. The apostles of the anti-slavery

unions, after fighting hysterically for the liberty and rights of citizenship for the slave classes, disappeared on having gained their point, making no more provision for their *protegés* than if they had been lilies of the field, except in so far – and probably to complete the grim farce – that their ladies at home sent woollen socks for the lilies on the burning soil of Africa. Everybody who has lived in the United States, Brazil, or any country where there are negroes, will corroborate the fact that, apart from many good qualities, the black race cannot be induced to work, but only forced.

Taking all this into account, and since there were 'many thieves, drunkards, deserters, and incendiaries among them', there was 'only one expedient – corporal punishment'.[80]

In 2001, 'Princess Salme – Behind the Veil', a touring exhibition of her life and writings, came to the Brunei Gallery of London's School of Oriental and African Studies. Curated by Said al Gheithy, director of the Princess Salme Museum in Stone Town, the exhibition website made no reference to slavery or the princess's attitudes towards Africans. It praised instead her 'visionary' views on healthcare, literacy and education, which were of relevance to the contemporary world and put her 'ahead of her time'. A more recent BBC News story about 'The Tragic Life of Zanzibar's Rebel Princess' likewise made no mention of either slavery on the island or her views of Africans.[81]

Princess Sayyida Salma, who later became Emily Ruete (1844–1924), led a picaresque life which took her from riches in Zanzibar to poverty in Hamburg. Photographed here in her *Memoirs of an Arabian Princess*, 1907.

There were hierarchies of racism in this highly cosmopolitan-colonial setting of East Africa. The British may have deplored the Arabs' merciless attitudes towards, and relentless slaving attacks against, Africans, but they were hardly disinterested in their own outlook towards other races, least of all the Arabs. While the Arabs looked upon Africans with contempt, some British officials regarded the Arabs with scarcely less disdain. On the whole, wrote Sir Charles Eliot, now British consul general in Zanzibar (1900–04), 'they were merely a nation of slave-traders … and illustrated the demoralizing effect of slavery on the slave-owner. For administration, development, even for conquest, they showed a complete apathy. They cared for nothing but the simple right to help themselves to valuables when and how they chose.' One might counter, more than a century later, that the Arabs, though they plundered East and Central Africa with abandon, showed less interest than the British in devouring – and bringing colonial government to – the continent. Hence non-Western, especially Arab, histories typically consider British actions against the slave trade as no more than a 'pretext' for the 'real' mission, in this case the scramble for control of Oman and the Gulf.[82]

In 1890, Britain duly took Zanzibar as a protectorate in the Heligoland–Zanzibar Treaty, an agreement in which Germany gave up its rights in Zanzibar in exchange for Heligoland in the North Sea and a recognition of German East Africa, a vast colony of 1 million square kilometres encompassing Burundi, Rwanda, mainland Tanzania and parts of Mozambique.

Treaties and legislation drafted in distant capitals only went so far. They often meant little in places that remained beyond the reach of the law. In the East African interior, life – and slavery – continued. Alfred Swann, a British missionary-turned-colonial administrator, spent twenty-six years in East Africa between 1882 and 1909 and published his memoir, *Fighting the Slave Hunters in Central Africa*, in 1910. Whatever its shortcomings, it retains considerable value for its eyewitness reporting. Swann includes an extraordinary passage about Ujiji, an important commercial town on the eastern shore of Lake Tanganyika. This was the westernmost point of the 800-mile slave and ivory caravan trade route to the coastal town of Bagamoyo, opposite Zanzibar. His description of the town made famous as the 'Dr Livingstone, I presume?' meeting-place of Stanley and Livingstone in 1871 bears repeating:

Strolling along the sands one evening, I came upon eight dying slaves, who were suffering from smallpox. They were beyond hope, and had been placed close to the water that the crocodiles might carry them off when the sun set. No one was allowed to go near them under penalty of being shot by a soldier who kept guard. I passed three other bodies partly eaten by hyenas. It was the usual manner of getting rid of slaves who were of no value. To a young Arab who accompanied me, I remarked:

'Why don't you endeavour to cure the smallpox and save the life?'

'Oh!' replied he with a shrug of the shoulders, 'it's not worth it. They are Pagans, and we have had all the expense and trouble of bringing them from the Congo for nothing. Who will carry their load of ivory to the coast?'[83]

In 2006, the government of Tanzania applied to UNESCO to designate 'The Central Slave and Ivory Trade Route' from Ujiji to Bagamoyo via Mamboya, Mpwapwa, Kilimatinde and Kwihara a World Heritage site. This would honour the memory of 'millions of Africans . . . captured by slave hunters, chained together and forced to walk sometimes hundreds of kilometres to be sold for example to planters who used them as cheap labour in their fields. Central and East Africa was one of the main areas where the slave hunters and traders, most of them Arabs, made their shade [*sic*] deals.'[84]

Under the terms of the 1890 treaty, Britain had awarded itself the right to approve future candidates for the sultanate. When, in 1896, Barghash's son, Khalid ibn Barghash, acceded to the throne without the British consul's prior approval, London had its *casus belli*. It bombarded the royal palace, sank the royal yacht and won victory within thirty-eight minutes (some reckoned forty-five), making the Anglo–Zanzibari War the shortest recorded conflict in history. The Reuters correspondent reported that the sultan had 'fled at the first shot with all the leading Arabs, who left their slaves and followers to carry on the fighting'.

After the fracas, Sultan Hamoud was installed as a British puppet and agreed to abolish slavery altogether. Yet emancipation, judging by the results, proved no great temptation. Slaves were required to apply for their freedom – it was actually only partial freedom – from the courts. If successful, they would then be liable to taxation and would be considered vagrants unless they could prove both fixed domicile and means of support. Given these requirements, which were both unsympathetic and unrealistic, it was hardly surprising that there was no overwhelming clamour for freedom. After a decade of emancipation, only 17,293 slaves of an estimated 60,000 – less than one in three – had been freed.[85]

The public mood was changing, however, and although conservative voices, such as the Zanzibar chief *qadi*, publicly opposed the ban in 1909, slavery was beginning to fall out of favour here as elsewhere in the Islamic world. These were now the last gasps of the ancient institution. In his 1910 memoir, Swann reached for rhetorical heights as he described how the slaver Rumaliza fought for, and later lost, the Congo to Belgium. 'He was crushed, together with all the vile hordes which for so many years had struck terror into the hearts of Africans. Civilisation had triumphed. Nations whose mottoes were Freedom, Justice, and Protection had planted their standards around the great lake.'[86] They had helped themselves to Africa, in other words.

A black slave was reportedly governing a province in Oman in the 1930s, when Freya Stark, the redoubtable English travel writer, was journeying in Yemen's Hadhramaut. There she learnt that slaves were still sometimes seized by Bedouin and sold on to new masters. Less than a year before her visit, some Omani sailors and Bedouin had collaborated on a cunning operation to procure slaves. 'Mahmud told me how two boys from Calcutta had recently been enticed with the promise of a job by Arabian sailors from Sur in Oman. When they landed, the Arabs sold them for 700 thalers to Se'ar beduin who took them to the northwest and kept them to draw water for two years.' Eventually one of them escaped and the other was bought by a local grandee in Seiyun, immediately freed and sent home.[87]

On the hot and humid night of 10 December 1963, British colonial rule in Zanzibar, a place that many people around the world considered an island paradise, came to an end on a cricket pitch just outside Zanzibar Town. Appearing in his pristine white naval uniform, Prince Philip, the Queen's representative, presided over the four-and-a-half-hour marathon independence celebrations alongside the elegant, blue-robed Jamshid bin Abdullah, sultan of Zanzibar, and Sir George Mooring, the British resident, wearing his white dress uniform complete with pith helmet and egret feathers. As the Union Jack was lowered at midnight to the sound of a police band playing 'God Save the Queen', up rose the new flag of independent Zanzibar – a yellow clove in a green circle on a red background.

The year before the ceremony, a *Reader's Digest* article had extolled the island's attractions in an idle piece of travel journalism. 'Few places on earth are as idyllic,' it declared, praising the island's languid sea, surf and golden equatorial sunshine. The people were 'plump, charming, and exquisitely lazy'. There was nothing to fear here. 'An independent Zanzibar, all agree, will not set the world on fire.'

But the legacy of slavery, particularly the economic divide, and the poisoned Arab–African relations it had engendered, ensured that post-colonial Zanzibar, however charming its people, however languid its climate, might at least set *itself* on fire. There were scores to settle and there was blood to shed. Black Africans remained the poor, put-upon majority, lorded over by a prosperous Arab and Asian minority which routinely benefited from gerrymandered elections. Speaking in parliament around this time, Juma Aley, the finance minister, brazenly expressed his contempt for Africans. He referred to Abeid Amani Karume, the leader of the opposition, as 'the boatman', refusing to answer his questions and wondering aloud at the illiteracy of Africans, who were, he said, incapable of exercising power due to their feeble intellects.

On 12 January 1964, just a month after Prince Philip's cricket-pitch appearance, a bloody revolution was in full swing. Karume 'the boatman' became the president, Aley and other Arab politicians were arrested, and communal hatreds turned to slaughter as waves of African attacks with knives, spears and machetes left thousands of Arabs and many Asians dead – estimates vary wildly from 2,000 to 20,000. To the west of the towering, nineteenth-century Bait al Ajaib, the House of Wonders, built as a palace on Stone Town's seafront for Sultan Barghash, the dhow-crowded waters of the Indian Ocean were as languid as ever. To the east, however, 500 metres away from the old slave market, the elegant clocktower, the tallest structure on Zanzibar, looked down on a newly independent island awash with blood.

There was a last instance of enslavement in 1970, when four under-age Asian girls were forced to marry elderly members of the ruling Zanzibar Revolutionary Council, including President Karume, who was then sixty-four. The girls' outraged relatives were imprisoned and flogged, Arab and Asian protests were lodged at the UN and the international press raged against Africa's latest revolutionary firebrand. Karume was unmoved. 'In colonial times the Arabs took African concubines without bothering to marry them. Now that we are in power, the shoe is on the other foot.'[88] In the same year, a palace coup in Oman, which had controlled Zanzibar from 1698 to 1861, saw the removal of Sultan Said bin Taimur (r. 1932–70) with Britain's blessing. Said was said to have owned 500 slaves, strictly segregated from the wider population and forbidden from marrying and even learning to read and write without royal permission. The sultan also passed a law classifying all people of African descent as slaves. In the 1950s he was reported to have ordered his slaves to swim in the water under his palace balcony and shoot at fish around them for his pleasure. As many as 150 women were said to have been locked up in his palace, while slaves in his palace in the southern city of Salalah were reportedly incarcerated and regularly beaten, as the press discovered after the sultan's ouster.

> Among 12 slaves presented to foreign journalists some had been forced, under pain of beating, not to speak. As a result they had become mutes. Others stood with their heads bowed and eyes fixed on the ground, their necks now paralysed. The slightest glance sideways resulted in a severe beating or imprisonment. Others had incurred physical deformity from similar cruelty.[89]

As a 1975 report put it, this regime of 'tyranny and sadism' could never have survived without Britain's active support.[90] In recent years, historians have subjected British interventions in the Gulf, and the lack of them, to a more critical examination. Some have forcefully challenged the triumphalist British antislavery narrative, arguing that London looked the other way and allowed slavery here to continue since it was seen as critical to the Gulf economy and therefore wider British interests.[91]

As it was, the British-sanctioned coup of 1970, motivated by London's concerns for stability and security in a region critical for oil resources, put the Western-educated Sultan Qaboos (r. 1970–2020) on the throne. Then and only then did Muscat finally and officially put an end to slavery.*

On 4 February 1842, while Atkins Hamerton maintained his steely vigil over slave-trading across the Indian Ocean and the realms of the sultan of Zanzibar, another Muslim monarch, far away on the other side of the continent, wrote a letter to another interfering British consul.

Moulay Abd al Rahman, sultan of Morocco (r. 1822–59), declared:

> Be it known to you that the traffic in slaves is a matter on which all sects and nations have agreed, from the time of the sons of Adam, on whom be the peace of God, up to this day; and we are not aware of its being prohibited by the laws of any sect, and no one need ask this question, the same being manifest to both high and low, and requires no more demonstration than the light of day.

For the Moroccan ruler it was an open-and-shut case. There was nothing to discuss. For John Hay Drummond Hay, the energetic British consul in Tangier, however, this sultanic defence of slavery was not the end of the matter. He may have been a lowly, albeit blueish-blooded, consul and his interlocutor a high-born sultan, but that counted for nothing. He, Drummond Hay, represented Great Britain, so there *was* a need to ask this question – and several more besides.

Had the sultan issued any decrees outlawing the slave trade, he wanted to know? If so, could he see them? Under the rule of Ahmed Bey (r. 1837–55), neighbouring Tunisia was taking its own first steps towards abolition, starting in 1842 with the prohibition of the slave

---

* When it suited, Britain could adopt a remarkably relaxed attitude towards slavery. Slavery in Oman, a British senior civil servant wrote in a 1970 minute for Michael Stewart, the then foreign secretary, 'can be regarded in some respects as the local equivalent of the welfare state'. Abdel Razzaq Takriti, *Monsoon Revolution: Republicans, Sultans, and Empires in Oman, 1965–1976*, p. 163.

trade and culminating in 1846 with a decree making slavery itself illegal, two years before France and nineteen years before the United States. Egypt was moving in the right direction too, Hay continued. While Islamic law of course permitted both slavery and the slave trade, the civilized world could not allow such an institution to continue, which was why both Egypt and Tunisia were following the example of 'Christian governments' on this 'march of beneficence', England foremost among them.

Moulay Abd al Rahman, the flag-bearer of the royal Alaouite family, an Arab sharifian dynasty which proudly traced its lineage back to the Prophet Mohammed, which had ruled Morocco since 1631 and continues in power today, found this intervention unacceptable:

> As to what regards the making of slaves and trading therewith, it is confirmed by our book [the Quran], as also by the *Sunna* of our Prophet, on whom be the blessing and peace of God; and furthermore there is not any controversy between the *Oolamma* [clergy] on that subject, and no one can allow what is prohibited or prohibit that which is lawful.[92]

The British, and later the French, might continue their diplomatic-cum-colonial push against slavery in this westernmost corner of the Dar al Islam, but Morocco proved a challenge. Together with its neighbour Mauritania, an outlier in the Islamic world where hereditary, racialized slavery continues to this day, it managed to withstand the external pressure for abolition longer than most. Had they been asked to explain why this was so, the British would not have been lost for an answer. As James Grey Jackson, one of Drummond Hay's predecessors as a British consul in Morocco, based in the Atlantic port town of Mogador (Essaouira) in the early nineteenth century, put it: 'The pride and arrogance of the Moors is unparalleled; for though they live in the most deplorable state of ignorance, slavery, and barbarism, yet they consider themselves the first people in the world, and contemptuously term all others barbarians.'[93]

This baleful verdict revealed as much about the British as it did about the Moroccans. As recent research has demonstrated, it is simply not the case that strong voices on abolition never emerged within the Muslim world. There were scholars such as the jurist and theologian Jaafar ibn Mohammed al Sadiq (d. 765), Hamdan Qarmat, the ninth-century founder of the Qarmatian Ismaili movement in Iraq, Al Hakim, the Fatimid ruler of Egypt (d. 1021), the Tunisian reformer Mohammed Bayram Khamis (d. 1889), the Moroccan historian Ahmed al Nasiri (d. 1897), the Indian philosopher and modernist Sir Syed Ahmed Khan (d. 1898), Mohammed Abduh, Grand Mufti of Egypt (d. 1905) and the anti-Western Islamic revivalist Rashid Rida (d. 1935), all of whom advanced moral arguments, often based on the Quran, justifying their positions on abolition. Some Muslim writers, including the Indian jurist and historian Syed Ameer Ali (d. 1928) and the Egyptian writer and statesman Ahmad Shafiq (d. 1940), author of *L'esclavage au point de vue Musulman*, also advanced the case that Islam had always meant to abolish slavery but that the institution was so rooted in seventh-century life on the Arabian Peninsula that immediate abolition would have wrecked the Prophet Mohammed's mission to spread the faith before it had started. In this they were echoing some of the arguments made by British and American abolitionists when asked why Jesus had neither condemned nor outlawed slavery.[94]

Such voices, however, tended to be relatively isolated and did not by themselves constitute a fully fledged, indigenous abolitionist movement. This is inevitably contentious territory, and there are some Muslim scholars who have argued, for example, that the Islamic tradition would never have contributed meaningfully to a European-led abolitionist movement, and that sharia holy law lacked an internal mechanism which would have allowed slavery to be abolished. Any analysis also needs to acknowledge that the abolitionist movement arose at a time when Europe was starting to dominate Muslim lands and that it was widely understood as part of a systematic Western effort to undermine and attack the Dar al Islam.[95] As one study has noted, 'the narrative of the West awakening to slavery's inherent evil and then dragging the Orient, Africa and everything else that was not the West into the light by means of inspiration and force has been crucial to the formation of Western identity'.[96]

The fact remained that pale-skinned Moroccans continued – and many would say continue – to harbour racial prejudice towards their dark-skinned compatriots, as well as black Africans more widely.

'Blacks in Morocco have been marginalized for centuries,' writes the historian Chouki el Hamel. They have been defined, among other terms, as *abid* (slaves), *haratin* (freed black persons), *sudan* (black Africans), *gnawa* (black West Africans) and *sahrawa* (from the Saharan region). El Hamel talks of a 'culture of silence' in Morocco, 'the refusal to engage in discussions about slavery, racial attitudes and gender issues'.[97]

Such attitudes continued to find their commercial reflection in a burgeoning trade in black Africans, between 2,000 and 8,000 of whom were imported annually across the nineteenth century, many of them arriving in caravans travelling across the western Sahara via the oases and towns of Tindouf and Tuat in Algeria and Ijil in Mauritania. Many of these enslaved Africans were then covertly trafficked from Morocco to neighbouring Algeria, whose capital, Algiers, had been taken by the French in 1830 at the outset of their long and sanguinary conquest of the country, which was complete only in 1903.

In 1844, a couple of years after Sultan Moulay Abd al Rahman's robust letter to Drummond Hay, the English evangelical, abolitionist and explorer James Richardson, who would be so active in Libya a couple of years later, sat down with the governor of Mogador in a last effort to impress upon him the benefits of abolition. With little sense of irony, he found the Moroccan 'very condescending', according to his *Travels in Morocco*, posthumously published in 1859.* Worse, for this irascible and headstrong Christian missionary, the governor even 'joked about his own slaves, asking me how much I would give him for them'. Clutching at straws, Richardson asked the governor whether it would make a difference if, next time, another British envoy came with better presents and greater powers.

---

* On 4 March 1851, Richardson died of fever and exhaustion at Ungurutuwa, six days' march from Kukawa, west of Lake Chad. 'My way of looking at things was not quite the same as that of my late companion, and we therefore often had little differences,' his companion Heinrich Barth, the German explorer, wrote diplomatically as he paid his respects at the Englishman's grave beneath a fig tree, 'but I esteemed him highly for the deep sympathy which he felt for the sufferings of the native African, and deeply lamented his death.' *Travels and Discoveries in North and Central Africa* (1890), p. 343.

'Not the least whatever,' the Moroccan replied evenly. 'You have done all that could have been done. We look at the subject, not the persons. The Sultan will never listen to anybody on this subject. You may cut off his head but cannot convince him.' Short of full-blown conquest by a Christian country, he went on, it was unthinkable. Richardson then played his last card. 'Sidi, does not the Koran encourage the abolition of slavery, and command it as a duty to all pious Mussulmen?' he asked. The governor shook his head. 'No, it does not command it, but those who voluntarily liberate their slaves are therein commended and have the blessing of God on them.'[98] The interview was over.

Drummond Hay, as the official representative of the British government, did not go in for the fire and brimstone of abolitionists like Richardson. After his early efforts came to naught in the early 1840s, he let things drop during his forty-one-year tenure as British consul in Morocco, from 1845 to 1886. He did not consider it in British interests to intervene directly in this independent nation outside the Ottoman Empire, as successive counterparts of his in Istanbul were wont to do.

In some respects, Drummond Hay was an apologist for slavery in Morocco. His reports back to London repeatedly emphasized its humane aspects while consistently underplaying the volume of the trade. In general, slaves were 'kindly treated by their masters', who frequently emancipated them on their deaths. He described slaves as 'generally the spoiled children of the house'.[99] Similar claims about the treatment of slaves in Iran were made by Charles James Wills, the British medical officer who worked in Hamadan, Isfahan and Shiraz between 1866 and 1881. 'The slaves in Persia have what Americans call a good time; well fed, well clothed, treated as spoiled children, given the lightest work, and often given in marriage to a favourite son, or taken as a "segah," or concubine, by her master himself.'[100]

Other European travellers at the time, free from diplomatic niceties and constraints, offered a more sombre picture. While a number agreed that slaves were typically well treated, were generally in a preferable situation to that of impoverished peasants or paid servants, and often suffered less under a Muslim master's hands than those of a Christian owner, their treatment by slave-dealers was nevertheless 'frightful and abominable'. This was without reckoning the all too often fatal cruelties of the journey across the desert. And it goes without saying that, however humanely slaves were treated once in their master or mistress's possession – as legally defined property – there was nothing benign about their capture (where applicable), enslavement or forced relocation, often without family, to another country.

By the 1880s, consistent pressure from the British and Foreign Anti-Slavery Society, only mildly supported by the British government, had resulted in little change, bar the disappearance of public slave markets in towns and cities along Morocco's long coastline – but even this was scant consolation since the trade continued privately. In 1883, Morocco firmly rejected the British Foreign Office's 'friendly appeal' for it to abolish slavery.[101]

Travellers and abolitionists meanwhile maintained a steady flow of reporting on slavery and the slave trade in the country. In 1892, the British and Foreign Anti-Slavery Society published a twenty-four-page report on *Tripoli, Tunis, Algeria and Morocco* by Henry Gurney and Charles Allen, both Fellows of the Royal Geographical Society. It contained a store of valuable information and statistics about the North African trade, together with some revealing examples.

In Tripoli, the pair observed a refuge house for freed slaves, one of several the Ottoman sultan had commanded to be built to receive freed men and women – the others were in Benghazi and Derna (eastern Libya), Hudaydah (Yemen), Jeddah (Saudi Arabia) and Syria. They also obtained an official manumission document, a facsimile of which appeared in the report. While Tripoli and what is now western Libya were 'free from implication in the Slave-trade', a 'considerable' trade continued in the east of the country, a 'flagrant breach' by the Ottomans of their various treaties and *firmans*. Moving on to the city of Tunis, Gurney and Allen were informed by both British and French senior diplomats that 'the Slave-trade no longer exists', and a similar message was received in Algiers.

On to Morocco, 'a barbarous neighbour, who obstinately resists every attempt to introduce the civilizing influences of commerce and the amelioration of her benighted and barbarous people', where it was a sorrier story. By the closing years of the century Morocco remained the largest slave-owning society in North Africa, and the defiance with which the authorities continued the trade appalled the Europeans. For these two abolitionists, it also rankled that the Moroccan sultan insisted on meeting European ambassadors on horseback, while they were required to remain on foot.

The Gurney and Allen report included a brief summary of the situation in Morocco by a British businessman called Donald Mac-Kenzie, who several years earlier had prepared a report on the Moroccan slave trade for the Foreign Office. MacKenzie noted that there were still 'great' slave markets operating in Marrakesh, Fez, Tetouan and Rabat, together with two annual fairs in the southern region of Sus in which around 1,200 boys and girls were sold. Girls between the ages of ten and thirteen were sold for £16–£24. There was a good deal of slave-trafficking between Morocco and Senegal and French slave-dealers were also in on the action, discreetly bringing in 'pretty girls' from Senegal and selling them on privately to wealthy 'Moors'.

MacKenzie went on to describe how Moroccan chiefs had recently presented Sultan Hassan I (r. 1873–94) and his son with 200 male and female slaves, a present to celebrate the marriage of the heir to the throne. It was an indication, as slavery started, very slowly, to retreat from everyday life in twentieth-century Morocco, that slave-owning would be increasingly confined to the elite, especially royal, sections of society. Gurney and Allen ended with a call to action. The society should consider mobilizing English chambers of commerce to promote to their members the business opportunities available in Morocco, from agriculture and mining to new markets for manufacturers. Legitimate trade would help consign the slave trade and slavery to history, eliminating the 'disgraceful pens for human cattle' in every town where there was no resident European consul and which were 'a scandal to humanity'.[102]

Stephen Bonsal, an American journalist who would go on to win the Pulitzer Prize for History in 1945, visited Morocco in his late twenties. His first book, *Morocco As It Is* (1893), included descriptions of a slave market given a decade earlier by a French traveller and bureaucrat called Dr Adolphe Marcet. The Frenchman described how several auctioneers each led a slave by the hand in this all-female sale, soliciting bids and calling out the prices offered:

> A squatted Moor makes a sign. The slave he indicates is brought to him. She kneels down or stands up as ordered by the intended purchaser, who proceeds to handle her from head to foot, and to examine her eyes, mouth, teeth, and nostrils, inquiring her age and any other particular he requires, after which he makes his bid, or allows her to pass on. The poor creature readjusts her bodice, and the auctioneer continues his tramp, stopping when called to submit his chattel to the further examination of other bidders.
>
> Here is a girl of twelve, with a pretty face and good figure. She is quoted at 6*l.*, and is eagerly sought after . . .
>
> Now comes a young woman with two small children. She carries one of them on her arm, and leads the other, a lovely little girl of three years, by the hand. A small coin hangs from a plaited lock of the little one's hair. The poor mother moves along like a lifeless object, incapable of any effort or will, her face wearing an expression of deep sadness and melancholy. She meekly obeys the auctioneer, who leads her about and exhibits her. Will the lot be sold together, or will the little girl be taken from her mother? There – they are knocked down together for 4*l.*, the children being an objection!
>
> . . . The majority of the youngest are reserved, as is notorious, for the libertine pleasures of a corrupt people. At the age of fourteen or fifteen, the sons of good families possess their slaves. Their parents present them with one for their amusement at an age when we in Europe give our children a pony for exercise . . .
>
> This traffic in human flesh, at the very door of Europe, is monstrous. The spectacle is heart-rending, and there can be no question that moral corruption alone keeps it alive.[103]

This was a reference to the Moroccan male sexual appetite which, Marcet charged, underlay a slave trade which dealt almost exclusively in females.

Although Western, mostly European, voices called the loudest for abolition, they could not claim a complete monopoly on the public discourse against the trade. Ahmad al Nasiri was widely considered the greatest Moroccan historian of the nineteenth century. The author of an epic, multi-volume history of the country from its earliest Muslim days during the seventh-century Arab Conquests to his own time 1,200 years later, Al Nasiri took a dim view of his fellow Moroccans' relentless enslavement of black Africans. The majority of the population across the several Muslim kingdoms of West Africa, he reminded his readers, were the Moroccans' co-religionists:

> Again, even if you suppose that Muslims are not a majority, and that Islam and unbelief claim equal membership there, who among us can tell whether those brought here are Muslims or unbelievers? For the basic assumption in regard to the human species is freedom and lack of any cause for being enslaved. Whoever maintains the opposite is denying the basic principle.

Al Nasiri decried the 'heinousness' of the 'indiscriminate enslavement' of black Africans, the importation of 'droves of them' to be sold in markets 'where men trade in them as one would trade in beasts'. People had grown so accustomed to this trade that many believed that the reason for the Africans' enslavement, according to holy law, was the colour of their skin and their sub-Saharan origin. It was 'one of the foulest and gravest evils perpetrated upon God's religion'.[104]

Ultimately, however, it was neither recalcitrant Moroccan leaders nor impassioned local abolitionists who brought the great edifice of slavery down in this westernmost corner of the Muslim world. It was France. Abolition came in on the coat-tails of colonialism. Paris launched its military conquest of the country in 1907, forcing the beleaguered and heavily indebted Sultan Abd al Hafid (r. 1908–12) to sign the Treaty of Fes in 1912, which turned his proudly independent nation into a French protectorate. French rule, which lasted until 1956, brought an abrupt end to the sovereignty of a nation which had, until then, skilfully evaded European control. It also meant that the days of slavery were numbered, but by no means gone – 'on the eve of decolonization, a French colonial official recorded payments for royal slaves without any remark'.[105]

Just as the British had demonstrated a certain pragmatism – critics would call it hypocrisy – towards the enduring practice of slavery in the Ottoman Empire, France equally maintained a studied ambivalence in its new North African possession. In 1923, Urbain Blanc, senior representative of the resident-general, Hubert Lyautey, issued a circular to French colonial officials abolishing the trade and defining how slaves should be handled by the authorities. Runaway slaves were to be liberated, unless they did not wish to be, a runaway male slave's children would in time likewise be freed and in the case of a female slave escaping with her children it had to be determined whether they were her master's, and therefore free, or conceived by a fellow slave, in which case they were not automatically liberated. Interfering in private households, however, 'to penetrate in the internal life of families', where countless numbers of slaves continued living and working all over the country as 'part of the family', was strictly off-limits.

Blanc's language revealed the French colonial mindset and priorities. Henceforth, a slave was euphemistically called a 'domestic' and official documents referred again and again to 'Muslim policy', an eminently malleable concept which could be made to mean almost anything its proponents desired. As far as domestic servitude was concerned, it indicated that the French would maintain a laissez-faire approach and would tolerate the status quo of slavery behind closed doors. Although criticized as 'toothless and impracticable', the 1923 circular was in fact a model of expediency. As with the British focus on the slave trade over slavery in the Ottoman Empire, so with the French in Morocco. Paris's policy was to satisfy abolitionist expectations at home and internationally while refraining from interfering in the household affairs of the ruling, slave-owning class. A clandestine trade duly continued throughout the protectorate and beyond.[106]

Today, seven decades after Moroccan independence, the legacy of slavery here and across the wider Maghreb makes itself felt in various forms. One of the most enduring, no less real for its widespread denial, is racism towards the dark-skinned population. In 2016, the Algerian writer and journalist Kamel Daoud, a winner of the Prix Goncourt, wrote a withering article for *Jeune Afrique* about the duplicity of public discourse in Algeria and North Africa. Racism, he wrote, is seen as a uniquely Western phenomenon, yet 'arguments worthy of the Ku Klux Klan on the threat posed by Blacks with their incivility, crimes and disease' are freely aired in public. Ahead of a football match between Algeria and Mali, an Islamist news-paper published a photograph of black football supporters beneath the headline: 'Neither hello nor welcome. AIDS behind you, Ebola ahead of you.' Algerians, like Moroccans, Libyans, Tunisians and Egyptians, routinely refer to sub-Saharans as 'Africans' as though they were not part of the same continent, he wrote. Religious con-servatives love to cite the example of the Prophet's slave Bilal, who earned his freedom through conversion to Islam, yet for every Bilal there were millions of other black Africans, including Muslim con-verts, who remained enslaved for generations. 'Arab slavery is still a taboo subject today or is glossed over with judgments against West-ern slavery.'[107]

In Tunisia the era of slavery is painfully remembered in the dread word *abid*, a historical category marking a person out as the descend-ant of a former slave and placing him or her on the lowest rung of the social ladder. Dark-skinned Tunisians routinely encounter severe racism, marginalization and discrimination. In the remote south of Tunisia, a small village called Gosbah is divided by a river. On one side are the all-black population of the *Abid Ghbonton*, descendants of slaves, on the other the lighter-skinned Ghbonton, the descendants of the slave-owners. One section of the community has the choicest farming land, the best olives and the most developed infrastructure, the other has no school, no police and no pharmacy. Marriage between the two communities is strictly prohibited by custom. 'They do not want us to mix with them,' says Samy, a blacksmith from the *Abid Ghbonton*. 'If you walk on the street, you will see blacks with blacks and whites with whites.'[108] Nada Issa, a filmmaker who directed the Al Jazeera documentary 'Tunisia's dirty secret' in 2016, reported wit-nessing Tunisians calling black people *wasif* (servant) or *kahlouch* (blackie), the local equivalent of the 'N' word.[109]

A reckoning with the past is only just beginning. In 2018, having been the first Arab and Muslim country to abolish slavery in 1846, Tunisia became one of the first to criminalize racism. Two years later, a Tunisian court issued a ruling allowing an eighty-one-year-old man to delete from his name the word 'Atig' – meaning 'liberated by', a stigmatizing reference to his personal ancestry.

There is still a long way to go. 'Everyone speaks of the transatlantic slave routes, but no one really speaks of the trans-Saharan slave routes from areas around Burkina Faso, Mali, Niger, Gambia,' says Saadia Mosbah, who runs Mnemty (my dream), an anti-racism organization in Bardo, a suburb of Tunis. 'Why haven't we spoken of these? Principally because it was Arabs and Muslims who enslaved, which makes people reluctant to talk about them.'[110]

Was King Hassan II the last slave-owner in Morocco? We shall probably never know. What we do know is that he set a striking, frequently brutal, example. King of Morocco from 1961 until his death in 1999, Hassan enjoyed the baubles and privileges of power, from sports cars, jet-skis, Arabian horses and multiple palaces to designer clothes, falcon hunting, lucrative business deals and harems teeming with as many as eighty concubines and countless slaves to ease the royal progress through life. Here was a monarch who loved cars and hunting so much he commissioned a one-off convertible, doorless Rolls-Royce off-roader, complete with foldable windscreen and butterscotch leather interior, to indulge one of his favourite passions.[111]

Slaves and concubines in Hassan's royal palaces washed his feet, dressed him in his holiday finery, carried incense, ran his baths, brought him food and drink and, for those who caught his continually roving eye, ministered to his sexual appetites. There was even a separate category, known as 'fire slaves', whose job was to administer corporal punishment to those who had earned the disfavour of a godlike king. This was a monarch whose person was described by the constitution as 'sacred and inviolable'. Hassan himself did nothing to dispel the comparisons with deity. 'Whoever disobeys me, disobeys God,' he declared in 1994, quoting one of the Prophet Mohammed's sayings.

Reading descriptions of palace life under Hassan, it is as though the twentieth century had never arrived. He inherited forty concubines from his father, King Mohammed V (r. 1957–61), and had another forty of his own, which he recruited into the 1970s, none of them older than fifteen. On his father's death in 1961, Hassan received a gift of two girls as concubines from the leading Berber family in the country – one was fifteen, the other thirteen. Hassan married Lalla Latifa, the older of the two.

Malika Oufkir, the daughter of General Mohamed Oufkir, Hassan's minister of the interior, minister of defence and chief of the armed forces, offers a rare window into palace life. After her father's unsuccessful attempt to assassinate the king in 1972 and his immediate execution, she and her remaining family spent most of the next two decades behind bars, much of that time in Tazmamart, a widely feared, purpose-built prison in the Atlas Mountains. More than half of the prisoners who languished in cramped underground cells, starved of heat, light and medical treatment, subjected to torture and executions, died in Tazmamart during the years of its operation.

First published in 1999 and immediately banned in Morocco, *La Prisonnière* was her sensational story of how a fairy-tale palace childhood led to her twenty-year imprisonment in this desert prison. In it she describes a gilded youth in which she had been plucked from the bosom of her family to become the playmate of the king's half-sister Princess Lalla Mina.

Oufkir's memoir is casually populated with royal slaves and concubines, as though this was the most normal thing in the world in the 1960s and 1970s. These customs did not shock her because she had been brought up among them. 'I was too young and too ignorant to be aware that they were medieval.' Many, if not most, of the palace slaves were descendants of those who had been enslaved many generations earlier. In theory they were free to leave. In practice, few did.

Herself the great-granddaughter of a black slave, Oufkir gives the king's royal slaves a series of cameos. There are reminders of the practice of mass slave marriages to accompany a royal wedding, a tradition that consciously echoed Sultan Moulay Ismail's mass forced marriages of his slaves in eighteenth-century Meknes. Oufkir has pious concubines praying on silk mats, showering copper coins on children as a treat and vying with each other to catch the king's attention. There are the singers and drummers of the *aamara* slave choir, together with the seamstresses, cooks and cleaners, nannies and chefs making *hashisha*, hashish-laced jam.

There are also darker moments hinting at the cruelty of a monarch whose human rights abuses during several decades were infamous. Morocco under King Hassan II was an engine room of repression: dissidents were targeted, imprisoned, tortured and summarily executed.

Many were 'disappeared'. There were violent crackdowns on strikers and protesters and purges of the army. Newspapers were closed and books banned. The period from the 1960s through the 1980s was known as *Sanawat al Rusas*, the Years of Lead, which caught the atmosphere of the state's heavy-handed response to any conceivable challenge, real or imaginary.

The slave-owning Hassan was a tyrant. Oufkir remembers one painful punishment administered by the king himself, assisted by a couple of his slaves. She was eight years old and had been playing a prank with the princess. 'Two fire slaves slung each of us across their shoulders, our heads and legs dangling on either side, while the King thrashed the soles of our bare feet with a whip.' When she was fifteen, a poor school report brought a harsher punishment at the hands of the king. Slaves dressed her in a thin *jellabah* gown before she received a savage whipping. 'I still have the scars on my buttocks,' she recalled decades later.[112]

In 1999 Hassan II died. His son and heir, the billionaire Mohammed VI (r. 1999–), one of the richest monarchs in the world, dissolved the royal harem. Racism towards dark-skinned Moroccans and sub-Saharan immigrants is alive and well in this ancient Muslim kingdom but, at the turn of the twenty-first century, slavery had finally run its course.

13

Modern Slavery

Question 4: Is it permissible to have intercourse with a female captive?

It is permissible to have sexual intercourse with the female captive. Allah the almighty said: '[Successful are the believers] who guard their chastity, except from their wives or (the captives and slaves) that their right hands possess, for then they are free from blame Quran 23:5–6.'

Daesh, or the so-called Islamic State, *Sual wa Jawab fi al Sabi wa Riqab (Questions and Answers on Taking Captives and Slaves),* 2014

In an office block in a European city, a senior lawyer hands me a legal brief. It details, in 461 chilling pages, the enslavement of women and children by Daesh, the self-styled Islamic State, in northern Iraq and Syria between 2014 and 2016. It has been compiled by the Commission for International Justice and Accountability (CIJA), a non-governmental organization, in an effort to bring numerous alleged criminals to justice.[1]

There are sections on the background to Daesh's attack on the Yazidis in Mount Sinjar in northern Iraq in August 2014, its policy on enslavement, criminality, and three annexes detailing the names of slave-owners and slave-traders, together with the ninety-one anonymized women interviewed.*

---

* Yazidis are a Kurdish-speaking religious minority spread across Iraq, Syria, Turkey and Iran. They practise an ancient monotheistic and syncretic faith which includes elements of Zoroastrianism, Judaism, Nestorian Christianity and Islam.

The most harrowing material comes from women recounting their ordeals. In Palmyra, where Daesh operated one of its many slave markets – the two principal ones were in Mosul in Iraq and Raqqa in Syria – women describe being forced to walk up and down an aisle in a large hall, holding their children's hands as they walked past laughing fighters who insulted them and bid on those they wanted to buy.

Some slave markets functioned more like brothels, fighters choosing a woman, taking her away for a few days, raping her repeatedly, often beating her, then returning her to the market. Women were constantly told: 'You are our property.' The majority of enslaved women were bought and sold many times. One was sold fourteen times to fourteen different men and was raped by twelve of them.

Resistance took many forms. Some women smeared their baby's excrement on their bodies to avoid being bought, some claimed to have periods, others stopped bathing, some professed to be sick, some fought back. At least one woman killed her owner and escaped. Many received punishment beatings, were separated from their children, locked up in hot, crowded basements amid rising sewage and starved for their refusal to submit to sexual violence. Many did not see daylight for months. Several described the conditions as being like hell.

Flicking through these pages, the words 'beat' and 'raped' occur again and again. Women were beaten with pistols, beaten unconscious and then raped, beaten until they fell down, lashed with cables, gang-raped, forcibly impregnated. They were sold to abusers from Iraq, Syria, Saudi Arabia, Chechnya, Germany, America, Australia, Turkey and Tunisia. There were forced abortions and attempted suicides. One woman was thrown down a set of stairs and hospitalized, another was handcuffed and pulled by a car. One woman's five-year-old daughter was hanged from a window and killed by a fighter for bedwetting. A woman who tried to escape had her feet burnt. The fighter then sold her to a man in Syria who, when asked for water for her children, handed her a bottle of his urine.

For those women who survived this torment, the suffering is not over. Years later, many report extreme psychological trauma and severe health issues, from vaginal infections, scabies and tuberculosis to hepatitis, flashbacks, insomnia, anxiety and pain. Many feel that they are not, in their own words, 'human beings'.

There was nothing ad hoc about enslavement in territory seized and controlled by Daesh. It was official policy, deliberately orchestrated and highly regulated, the revival of an Islamic institution in which taking women as the 'spoils of war' was justified by religious law. The crimes committed, CIJA argues, amount to genocide, crimes against humanity and war crimes.

'This is not "modern slavery", it's the resurrection of chattel slavery, the ownership of humans by others,' William Wiley, the executive director of CIJA, tells me. 'It was also an attempt to annihilate Yazidis by preventing another generation from being born. The evidence is irrefutable and those responsible for the IS slave trade should answer for their crimes.'

In May 2015, Zainab Bangura, the United Nations' special representative on sexual violence in conflict, visited refugee camps in Syria, Iraq, Turkey, Lebanon and Jordan. She listened to horror stories from survivors like those interviewed in the CIJA brief. A detailed international study later that year estimated that 9,900 Yazidis had been kidnapped or killed in August 2014. Of the 3,100 estimated to have been killed, one half were executed (beheaded, shot, burnt alive) and the others, mostly children, died on Mount Sinjar of starvation, dehydration or injuries. A total of 6,800 are thought to have been kidnapped.[2]

Although she had previously worked in several violent conflicts, Bangura said she had never witnessed anything like this. The sadism and inhumanity were incomprehensible. 'We struggled to understand the mentality of people who commit such crimes,' she said.[3]

Only when listening to the perpetrators in their own words, perhaps, does their mentality become easier to comprehend, if not to hear. In their own minds, perverted or not, they were merely following practices allowed by their religion and sanctioned by holy law.

On 3 December 2014, following the international outcry over Daesh's enslavement of Yazidi women in northern Iraq, the 'Research and Fatwa Department' of the self-proclaimed and short-lived caliphate published a pamphlet on social media. *Sual wa Jawab fi al Sabi wa Riqab (Questions and Answers on Taking Captives and Slaves)* justified the enslavement of non-Muslim women on explicitly Islamic grounds and set out the group's rules governing appropriate conduct towards captured women.

Setting aside the horror and revulsion almost everyone in the world felt at this resurgence of mass enslavement, rape and sexual violence amid the slaughter of Yazidi men, what stood out in the text was the laboriously formulated Islamic validation of enslavement followed by sexual abuse:

Question 3: Can all unbelieving women be taken captive?

There is no dispute among the scholars that it is permissible to capture unbelieving women [who are characterized by] original unbelief [*kufr asli*], such as the *kitabiyat* [women from among the People of the Book, i.e. Jews and Christians] and polytheists. However, [the scholars] are disputed over [the issue of] capturing apostate women. The consensus leans toward forbidding it, though some people of knowledge think it permissible. We [ISIS] lean toward accepting the consensus ...

Question 5: Is it permissible to have intercourse with a female captive immediately after taking possession [of her]?

If she is a virgin, he [her master] can have intercourse with her immediately after taking possession of her. However, if she isn't, her uterus must be purified [first] ...

Question 6: Is it permissible to sell a female captive?

It is permissible to buy, sell, or give as a gift female captives and slaves, for they are merely property, which can be disposed of as long as that doesn't cause [the Muslim *ummah*] any harm or damage.

Question 9: If the female captive was impregnated by her owner, can he then sell her?

He can't sell her if she becomes the mother of a child ...

Question 13: Is it permissible to have intercourse with a female slave who has not reached puberty?

It is permissible to have intercourse with the female slave who hasn't reached puberty if she is fit for intercourse; however, if she is not fit for intercourse, then it is enough to enjoy her without intercourse.

The questions and answers continue – there are twenty-seven of them – in a perverse mixture of unrelenting horror and terrible banality. Is it permissible to practise coitus interruptus (yes), to beat one's slave (yes, but only up to a point short of torture and self-gratification and never in the face) and can a female slave meet foreign men without wearing a hijab (yes, she can expose her head, neck, hands and feet as long as there is no 'enticement', in which case it is forbidden to expose these parts). The text is remorselessly bleak – unless, perhaps, the reader happens to be a Muslim man of extremist views who is about to acquire a female slave. There were also female Daesh members and supporters who approved of such rulings. Only at the end is there the briefest glimpse of humanity.

> Question 27: What is the reward for freeing a slave girl?
>
> Allah the exalted said [in the Quran]: 'And what can make you know what is [breaking through] the difficult pass [hell]? It is the freeing of a slave.' And [the Prophet Mohammed] said: 'Whoever frees a believer Allah frees every organ of his body from hellfire.'[4]

Daesh can be dismissed in many terms, but to call the group 'not Islamic', as President Barack Obama did, is to make an important, even dangerous, error – albeit one born of good intentions and wishful thinking. 'The reality is that the Islamic State is Islamic. *Very* Islamic,' writes Graeme Wood, the author of 'What ISIS really wants', an essay for *The Atlantic* in 2015.[5] The Q&As above, like so many of Daesh's official pronouncements and the lexicon of its fighters and supporters, are peppered with Quranic quotations and references to the sayings of the Prophet. It is not in any sense an exercise in secular extremism.

While slavery for almost the entire population of the world was an evil that mercifully had passed into history, for both the leaders and foot soldiers of the caliphate it was a living, breathing component of the idealized twenty-first-century Islamic state. In October 2014, just before Daesh published its rules on slavery, the group's English-language *Dabiq* magazine ran a prominent article on the subject.* 'The Revival of Slavery Before the Hour' consisted of selective quotations from the Quran ('kill the *mushrikin* [polytheists] wherever you find them, and capture them, and besiege them, and sit in wait for them at every place of ambush . . .' 9:4), references to the Yazidis as 'devil worshippers and

---

* *Dabiq* is named after the eponymous town in northern Syria which is mentioned in one of the *hadiths* about Armageddon. Islamist fundamentalists consider it the location of the future, final showdown between Muslim and infidel armies. The inevitable Muslim victory at Dabiq will, it is believed, trigger the apocalypse.

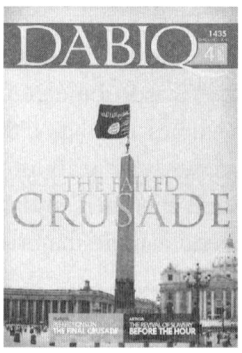

In October 2014, the Daesh (ISIS) terrorist group's English language *Dabiq* magazine ran an article justifying the rape and enslavement of captured women.

Satanists', and an interminable discussion about whether the Yazidis were apostates from Islam, in which case they were to be slaughtered, or pagans, in which event they were ripe for enslavement. The article also favourably compared Daesh fighters selling Yazidi slaves with the Companions of the Prophet selling infidel slaves almost 1,400 years earlier and went on to describe, in terms self-consciously echoing the tone of seventh-century Arab commanders during the great Conquests, how the human spoils of war were to be shared out among the soldiers:

> Yazidi women and children [are to be] divided according to the *Sharia* amongst the fighters of the Islamic State who participated in the Sinjar operations [in northern Iraq] . . . One should remember that enslaving the families of the *kuffar* [infidels] and taking their women as concubines is a firmly established aspect of the *Sharia* that if one were to deny or mock, he would be denying or mocking the verses of the Quran and the narrations of the Prophet . . . and thereby apostatizing from Islam.

Lest there was any confusion about the message, the article included an additional statement from Sheikh Abu Muhammad al Adnani, Daesh's chief spokesman. The enslavement of Yazidis, whose plight had horrified the world, was just the beginning. 'We will conquer your Rome, break your crosses, and enslave your women, by the permission of Allah, the Exalted . . . If we do not reach that time, then our children and grandchildren will reach it, and they will sell your sons as slaves at the slave market.'[6]

This was slavery weaponized as the humiliating consequence of Muslim conquest. Slavery, according to Daesh, should never have been consigned to history. Under the leadership of its self-styled caliph, Abu Bakr al Baghdadi, who claimed to be descended from the Prophet Mohammed's Qurayshi tribe, Daesh was explicitly restoring the Islamic institution of slavery as first practised and regulated in the seventh century. Its leaders did so confident, in their own minds, that they were following classical Islamic doctrine and law.

Irrespective of the published rules, the supposedly ordered system predictably degenerated into a vicious sexual and financial free-for-all in which many fighters raped and abused numerous women and then enriched themselves by extorting money from the girls' and women's families, who were desperate to buy back their children and relatives. It was a human tragedy and atrocity on an incalculable scale.

In November 2014, around the same time as Daesh published its rules on the treatment of enslaved women, a video emerged online of excited young fighters looking forward to their immediate prospects at the next slave market.

'Today is the female sex slave market, God willing. Today it is the market of "what your right hands have possessed". Today is distribution day.'

'Where's my Yazidi girl?'

'You can sell your slave, or give her as a gift . . . You can do whatever you want with your share.'

'Whoever wants to sell, I can buy, my brothers.'

'I will buy her for a pistol.'

'It costs more for one with blue eyes.'

'Check her teeth.'

'Can one take two slave girls? Does that work?'[7]

The bearded young foot soldiers were joshing and joking as their 'caliphate' set out to destroy an entire people.

On 21 June 2016, Nadia Murad, a Yazidi farm girl, student and escaped sex slave, addressed the US Congress in Washington. She had been beaten, burnt by cigarettes and repeatedly raped, had witnessed her six brothers being slaughtered in front of her, had also lost her mother, while her sisters, nieces and aunts were missing presumed dead. She was speaking after a UN report which had alleged that Daesh may have committed 'war crimes, crimes against humanity, and possibly genocide'. Apart from detailing how the group shot, beheaded, bulldozed, burnt alive and threw people off buildings, it also claimed that 3,500 slaves were being held by Daesh.

Murad called on Muslims around the world to do more to denounce Daesh. 'What has been happening has been happening under the name of Islam,' she said. 'The Muslims must be the first ones to resist this . . . We have not seen that Daesh have been labelled as an infidel group within Islam by any Muslim country.'[8]

More than 120 Muslim scholars from around the world had, in fact, written an open letter to Daesh in 2014, denouncing the group as un-Islamic and stating that 'the reintroduction of slavery is forbidden in Islam. It was abolished by universal consensus.'[9]

Given the unspeakable ordeal she had endured, Murad can be forgiven for asking for more. In 2018 she was jointly awarded the Nobel Peace Prize with the Congolese doctor and campaigner Denis Mukwege 'for their efforts to end the use of sexual violence as a weapon of war and armed conflict'. She now lives in Germany and continues to campaign against sexual violence and to bring Daesh to justice for its genocide against the Yazidi community.

Where to end our story of slavery in the Muslim world? Sadly, there are a number of countries in which slavery continues, either in its conventional form or reimagined and adapted in a 'modern' context, where this history could conclude – in Saudi Arabia or Kuwait, the UAE or Yemen, Pakistan or India, Indonesia or Malaysia, Mali, Niger or Nigeria.

Muslim-majority countries were over-represented among the last nations to outlaw slavery. Afghanistan was early, relatively speaking, abolishing it in 1923, in the wake of Dutch Indonesia (1870) and British Malaya and British Borneo (today's Malaysia, 1915). Iran abolished and criminalized slavery in 1929, ahead of Bahrain in 1937. Kuwait abolished it in 1949, triggering a flurry of abolition in the Gulf: Qatar in 1952; then Saudi Arabia and Yemen, both facing strong international pressure, following suit in 1962. Turkey approved legislation specifically outlawing slavery in 1964, by which time Egypt's grandstanding President Nasser was proclaiming himself the leader of the worldwide anti-slavery movement. As a Jordanian delegate to the UN observed in the wake of Saudi Arabian and Yemeni moves on abolition, slavery in the Middle East was now only legal in Britain's Gulf satellites, including the Trucial States (the future United Arab Emirates), and Oman. 'The UK is lined up everywhere with slave owners,' Thomas Fox-Pitt, secretary of the Anti-Slavery Society, fumed.[10] Fox-Pitt might have said the same of the United States when it came to Saudi Arabia. During Washington's earliest engagement with Saudi Arabia in 1945, when President Franklin D. Roosevelt met King Ibn Saud on USS *Quincy* to discuss oil, strategic partnership and the post-war Middle East, the king was surrounded by a throng of his personal slaves. In 1957, 'gigantic Nubian slaves toting jewelled daggers and machine guns' accompanied Ibn Saud on his state visit to Washington. 'The very roots of the American relationship with Saudi Arabia involved the U.S. turning a blind eye to Saudi Arabia's embrace of enslavement.'[11] Oman finally abolished slavery in 1970.

Among the final countries to ratify the 1926 Convention to Suppress the Slave Trade, an international treaty agreed under the auspices of the League of Nations, were a number of Muslim-majority states: Egypt, Syria and Afghanistan in 1954, Iraq and Pakistan in 1955, Kuwait and Algeria in 1963, Azerbaijan in 1996, Kyrgyzstan and Turkmenistan in 1997 and Kazakhstan as late as 2008. It should be added that plenty of non-Muslim countries featured among the later signatories, too.

In 1990, the Organization of Islamic Cooperation (OIC) issued the (non-binding) Cairo Declaration on Human Rights in Islam, widely seen as the Muslim world's response to the UN's 1948 Universal Declaration of Human Rights. Among other things, it denied the legitimacy of slavery – 'Human beings are born free, and no one has the right to enslave, humiliate, oppress or exploit them'. The text was criticized for its conservative, Islamist perspective and the explicit emphasis on sharia law as its sole source. It was revised in 2020, by which time sharia had been replaced by a broader focus on 'Islamic values', and again it rejected slavery. 'Gross and systematic human rights violations, and also slavery, servitude, forced labour and trafficking in persons, shall be prohibited in all forms, and under any circumstances.'[12]

Although it has been formally abolished in almost every country on earth, the systematic practice of slavery still lingers in some parts of the Muslim world and far beyond. For all the treaties and legislation signed internationally, slavery, like the most resilient weeds, has proved especially difficult to root out. In recent years the problem has gone deeper underground, much of it in the Middle East. There is no talk yet in the Arab world, or in Turkey, of reparations. While public debate continues in the West, under pressure from African and Caribbean nations and organizations such as the National Coalition of Blacks for Reparations in America and the American Descendants of Slavery (ADOS) Advocacy Foundation, no such discourse is under way in the Muslim world. Mention the word reparations and a typical response is a raised eyebrow and a look of incomprehension.

Qatar, perhaps, has gone further than most of its neighbours in addressing the historical issue of slavery. In 2015, at a time when Doha was under pressure for reportedly exploiting migrant workers in the build-up to the 2022 World Cup, it opened the government-funded Bin Jelmood House, turning an old whitewashed house, whose courtyard was once thronged with enslaved East Africans waiting to be sold, into a museum commemorating slavery in a global context. The museum puts a positive gloss on the subject: 'The House explores the role Islam played in providing guidance for humane treatment of enslaved people, their integration into society and the eventual abolition of slavery,' it says. 'The story in Qatar begins in enslavement but ends in shared freedom and shared prosperity.'[13]

In recent years, however, the Arab world, especially the Gulf, has become a hub of modern slavery. In its most recent report, *The Global Slavery Index 2023*, which claims to have the world's most comprehensive data set on modern slavery, notes that Arab states have by far the highest prevalence of forced labour in the world when compared with other regions – at 4.8 per 1,000 people. Asia and the Pacific comes second (3.3) with Africa third (2.4). Forced marriages, when measured in the same way, are also highest in Arab states – at 5.3 per 1,000, ahead of Europe and Central Asia (4.4), Asia and the Pacific, and the Americas (both 3.5). Merging the two categories together, Arab states record the highest proportion of their populations in modern slavery – 10.1 per 1,000 people – considerably ahead of Asia and the Pacific (6.8), Europe and Central Asia (6.6) Africa (5.2) and the Americas (5.0).

According to the same report, there were an estimated 1.7 million people living in modern slavery in the Arab world in 2023. Saudi Arabia, with an estimated 740,000, Iraq (221,000), Yemen (180,000), Syria (153,000) and the United Arab Emirates (132,000) together accounted for the great majority of those reported to be trapped in modern slavery in the region.[14] Modern slavery, it should be emphasized, is an international issue which continues to afflict both the USA and UK, among many other countries. The Global Slavery Index records 1.1 million living in modern slavery in the USA and 122,000 in the UK. The countries with the highest estimated number of people in modern slavery in Europe and Central Asia were Russia (1.9 million), Turkey (1.3 million) and Ukraine (559,000).[15]

The problem is particularly acute in parts of the Gulf, one of the most prosperous regions on earth. Migrant workers from poorer Asian countries such as India, Pakistan, Nepal, Bangladesh and the Philippines – the men and women who build the gleaming skyscrapers, drive the taxis, wait in restaurants, care for babies and children, nurse the sick, remove the rubbish, clean houses and endure their employers' abuse – routinely end up in situations 'tantamount to forced labour'. This is due in part to the widespread *kafala*, or sponsorship system, in which workers have traditionally not been allowed to change jobs without their employer's permission, leaving them vulnerable to abuse, exploitation and forced labour. In Saudi Arabia, for example, a particularly serious offender, migrant workers can be subject to 'economic and physical abuse and exploitation [and] the confiscation of passports by employers', leaving them unable to freely terminate their employment. In its 2022 Trafficking in Persons Report for Saudi Arabia, the US State Department stated that, after years of dragging its feet, the government did 'not fully meet the minimum standards for the elimination of trafficking but is making significant efforts to do so'.[16]

In 2019, an undercover investigation into modern slavery in the Gulf revealed that maids and domestic workers were being illegally bought and sold in Saudi Arabia and Kuwait via a number of apps then available from Google Play and Apple's App Store, including Instagram, 4Sale and Haraj. 'What they are doing is promoting an online slave market,' said Urmila Bhoola, the United Nations special rapporteur on contemporary forms of slavery. Posing as a husband and wife newly arrived in Kuwait, the BBC News Arabic team discovered that all would-be purchasers had to do was pick up a smartphone and scroll through thousands of pictures of workers for sale, categorized by race and available to buy for several thousand dollars. Some of the business was transacted on Instagram, helped by algorithm-boosted hashtags – #خادمات للتنازل, or #maidsfortransfer, was a popular one on Facebook – with sales negotiated and finalized via private messages.

The for-sale listings were as brutal as the trade: 'African worker, clean and smiley,' read one. 'Nepalese who dares to ask for a day off,' stated another. The journalists spoke to a policeman who was trying to sell his worker. 'Trust me, she's very nice, she laughs and has a smiley face,' he said. 'Even if you keep her up till 5 a.m. she won't complain.' He went on to describe how domestic workers were regarded and treated as commodities. 'You will find someone buying a maid for 600 KD [Kuwaiti dinars, the equivalent of $2,000] and selling her on for 1,000 KD [$3,300].'

The BBC team was offered Fatou, a sixteen-year-old girl trafficked from the West African nation of Guinea. The seller boasted that during her six months as a domestic worker she had been given no time off, her phone and passport had been confiscated and she had not been allowed to leave the house alone – all of which were illegal in Kuwait. The UN's Bhoola described it as 'the quintessential example of modern slavery. Here we see a child being sold and traded like chattel, like a piece of property.' Fatou (not her real name) was subsequently deported from Kuwait for being a minor. 'They used to shout at me and call me an animal,' she said of her Kuwaiti employers. 'It hurt, it made me sad, but there was nothing I could do.'[17]

Even today, the practice of slavery receives ideological support in certain limited but influential quarters, where belief in slavery as an institution permitted by Islam in the contemporary era also continues. In 2003, the Saudi writer Ali al Ahmed revealed that the Saudi government cleric Sheikh Saleh al Fawzan had offered a trenchant and unequivocal defence of the institution in a secretly recorded lecture. 'Slavery is a part of Islam,' the religious leader declared. 'Slavery is part of jihad, and jihad will remain as long as there is Islam.' He dismissed those who argued that Islam had worked to abolish slavery. 'They are ignorant, not scholars. They are merely writers. Whoever says such things is an infidel.'[18]

It would be tempting to dismiss Sheikh Saleh al Fawzan as a lone voice of extremism. Yet when he made these remarks he stood at the pinnacle of the Saudi religious establishment. Author of *Al Tawheed (Monotheism)*, an uncompromising school textbook, he was a member of the Senior Council of Clerics, the country's highest religious body, a professor at Imam Mohamed Bin Saud Islamic University, the principal Wahhabi centre of learning, a member of the Council of Religious Edicts and Research, and imam of the Prince Mitaeb Mosque in Riyadh. Al Fawzan was many things, but an unsupported Saudi Arabian maverick and lone wolf he was not.

No one would argue that pro-slavery views are either widespread or mainstream in the Muslim world. They are not. Where they do tend to arise, however, is on the deeply conservative or extremist fringe – in lectures or sermons delivered by clerics, either secretly recorded or publicly proclaimed in mosques or via their online channels.

In 2011, the Egyptian newspaper *Youm al Sabeaa* published a lecture given years earlier by the popular Egyptian preacher Abu Ishaq al Huwaini. In it he defended the classical legal rulings on the treatment of persons captured during jihad against an infidel state:

> According to the rules of Islam, all the people in that country become booty and prisoners of war: the women, the men, the children, the money, the homes, the fields ... All these become the property of the Islamic state ...
>
> What is the fate of the prisoners of war according to the shari'a? Since they constitute booty, they should be divided between the mujahideen ...

Let's say that we invaded a country with a population of half a million. What are we supposed to do with them? We check how many mujahideen there were. Let's say there were 100,000. That's it, then. Each mujahid gets five of them. Each one gets five, but there can be a variety. You can take two men, two women, and a child, or the other way around. You divide them up. Great. As soon as this system is in place, there has to be a slave market, where you can sell slaves, slave girls, and children.

Each of these 'heads' comes with a price. Let's say I am entitled to five 'heads'. I don't need any of them but could use a little cash. Am I supposed to hang them just to get rid of them? No, you can sell them in the market. Well, in order for me to be able to sell them there has to be a market.[19]

And so it continued.

One can question the motives of those who publicize these pronouncements, while noting at the same time that those who make them are perfectly happy to defend them.* Thus, on 7 November 2017, the Kuwaiti cleric Saalim bin Saad al Taweel declared on his YouTube channel that slavery was 'one of the virtues of Islam' since it provided infidels with the opportunity to convert to Islam and therefore avoid their otherwise irresistible destiny of hell. Although the Islamic concept of jihad had multiple meanings, 'jihad for the sake of Allah' meant fighting infidels to spread the faith:

> One of the virtues of Islam is that the women and children [of the enemy] are not killed. They are taken as slaves, and they are treated well. They are called upon to convert to Islam. How many Muslim *ulema* were white slaves, who were put to use by Allah as Islamic scholars. If they had died as infidels, they would have been condemned to eternal Hell-fire. Instead, they were taken captive.

Al Taweel's views on whether the Yazidi sex slaves of Daesh fighters were 'treated well' was not recorded. But he had no time for those who argued that there was no slavery in Islam. 'So, this is one of the virtues

---

* Between 2003 and 2020 the American historian and commentator Daniel Pipes, who has frequently been accused of Islamophobia, published a regularly updated collection of such pronouncements on his blog under the headline 'Islamists Endorse Muslims Owning Slaves'.

of Islam, but some people are trying to shrug it off and say: "There is no slavery in Islam." How can you say this? It is in the Quran.'[20]

This history ends in Mauritania, the westernmost African Muslim nation, which in 1981 became the last country in the world to make slavery illegal. Here hereditary racialized slavery, despite its formal abolition, continues. This is not to argue that Mauritania is in any way representative of the status quo regarding slavery in Muslim nations. Clearly it is not. It is an outlier. The country has even been called 'slavery's last stronghold'.[21] Our story ends in Mauritania because this book is about slavery, not its absence.

When Daesh massacred and enslaved the Yazidis, they also stole the headlines. They sought publicity explicitly in order to terrorize, and also because they are narcissists who consider their depravities praiseworthy work in the service of Islam. Their atrocities shocked because it was generally assumed that this brutal and unapologetic form of slavery had long since passed into history. Boko Haram, a terrorist group based in northern Nigeria, did the same in 2014 with its enslavement of 276 mostly Christian schoolgirls – many of whom were subsequently raped.

Yet, far away from the international media lens, slavery stubbornly continues in a number of Muslim-majority countries such as Mali and Mauritania, valiantly monitored and fought against by courageous local activists and campaigners and, from afar, by international human rights and anti-slavery organizations.

That slavery continues in Mauritania almost half a century after its abolition is a calamity which, with some honourable exceptions, makes few waves in the global media. This is not a country that intrudes with any frequency upon Western consciousness. Few in Europe or North America, one suspects, would be able to point to it on a map.

When slavery was first criminalized in Mauritania in 2007, then again in 2015, it was a tacit and reluctant admission, from a government which had long denied that slavery existed in the country, both that the practice continued and that up to that point there had been no sanctions against slave-owners.

Speak to those close to the government in Nouakchott, the

Mauritanian capital, and the sense of denial is still evident today.*
'Slavery doesn't exist in Mauritania,' says Brahim (not his real name),
an analyst working for a government-funded think-tank. 'Europeans
are always writing about slavery here, and the markets where slaves
are supposedly bought and sold, but they don't exist. You don't have
slavery in the West only because you don't need it any more. You have
machines to do the work.'[22]

He goes on, via philosophical digressions on Rousseau, Pascal,
Hume, Kant, Derrida and Shakespeare, to describe Google, Amazon,
Facebook and Apple as 'another form of slavery' and then adds that
the British intelligence officer and writer T. E. Lawrence betrayed the
Arabs. Western hypocrisy is the real problem.

'Do you have slavery in Britain?' he asks. We do, I tell him. Like
many countries, the UK has to confront the horrors of people-
trafficking and modern slavery. But it is difficult to tackle a problem
when you continue to deny that it exists.

'Slavery exists in Mauritania today, and that's intolerable,' says El
Kory Sneiba of SOS Esclaves, a respected anti-slavery organization
in Mauritania.† 'It's hidden these days, it's underground, no one's in
chains or being sold in markets, but you still find it in villages in the
interior. The biggest challenge is the lack of official recognition of
slavery. The biggest slave-owners are those in government. There's no
political will to end it.'

Over at the rundown headquarters of the Initiative for the Resurgence of the Abolitionist Movement (IRA), Hamady Lehbouss, its
secretary-general, has a similar message. If it wished to, he says, the
government could demonstrate its political will by sending some
slave-owners to prison. It would be 'a matter of weeks' to end slavery,
but 'the system isn't ready to change yet'.

---

* The government prefers not to discuss this subject, which remains extremely sensitive. On arrival at Nouakchott airport in 2024, I was questioned by three police
officers separately about the purpose of my visit. Which organization was I working
for, who was I going to speak to, what was I going to talk to them about and why,
what were their telephone numbers, who was I working with, where was I staying,
who did I know, and so on. My Mauritanian colleague and I were subsequently followed by security officials and monitored by informants everywhere we went.
† Its main international partner is Anti-Slavery International.

Broadly speaking, the Mauritanian slave-owning class neatly dove-tails with the country's social, political and financial elite, the dominant caste of pale-skinned Arabic-speaking Arabs and Berbers. They iden-tify as white and refer to themselves as *bidan* – 'white Moors'. It is the *bidan* who, for many centuries, have lorded it over the *haratin*, their darker-skinned Arabic-speaking fellow Muslims – 'black Moors' who today consist of former slaves and their descendants. However, as some *bidan* are keen to emphasize, slavery also exists among the various ethnic groups of what they call the '*Négro-Africaine*' community – the Wolof, Peul, Bambara and Soninke. 'Everyone focuses on the *bidan*,' says Moulaye, my translator, a fifty-something journalist and *bidan*, 'but the Africans also have their own slaves.'

Estimates of the numbers of enslaved men, women and children in Mauritania, a country in which the UN reckons that more than 58 per cent of the population live below the poverty line, vary enor-mously.[23] In its most recent report, for 2023, Global Slavery Index reported that Mauritania had the third-highest prevalence of modern slavery worldwide, estimating that 149,000 men, women and chil-dren were enslaved.* The IRA anti-slavery organization reckons the true figure is much higher – as much as 20 per cent of the country's population, which in 2024 equates to almost 1 million.[24]

The willingness of successive governments in Nouakchott to end slavery has long been questioned. The first successful prosecution under the 2007 anti-slavery legislation came in 2011, when the owner of two enslaved boys was convicted. Any hopes that this might signal genuine change, however, were quickly extinguished both by the leni-ent sentence of two years, and by the owner's subsequent release on bail after only four months. Mauritanian governments have typically preferred to crack down on anti-slavery activists rather than the crim-inal slave-owners.[25]

In recent years, one man in particular has led the fight against slav-ery in Mauritania. On 27 April 2012, shortly after Friday prayers had ended in Nouakchott, Biram Dah Abeid, the charismatic founder

---

* According to Global Slavery Index, the ten countries with the highest prevalence of slavery worldwide were, in order, North Korea, Eritrea, Mauritania, Saudi Arabia, Turkey, Tajikistan, United Arab Emirates, Russia, Afghanistan and Kuwait.

of IRA and a descendant of slaves, held up a handful of books in front of a crowd and then set them alight. The books, a collection of early Islamic Maliki jurisprudence, contained justifications of slavery. Abeid's action, a deliberate provocation to the conservative political and religious establishment, inevitably caused an uproar. He was arrested and quickly branded a heretic by the local media. While he was behind bars, the authorities put it about that he was an Israeli agent. Crowds of demonstrators called for his execution for blasphemy. President Mohammed Ould Abdel Aziz, who had seized power in a coup in 2008, declared that he would administer the death penalty himself. A tribunal found Abeid guilty of apostasy and sentenced him to death.

Such an extreme reaction was no surprise to anti-slavery activists, who regularly report intimidation, harassment and persecution by the authorities. Successive governments in Nouakchott routinely accuse them of an intent to denigrate Islam as part of a worldwide Jewish conspiracy.[26] These are serious and dangerous charges. Arbitrary arrests, imprisonment and torture also concentrate minds and discourage protest.

Eventually, after four months in prison, Abeid, who has been called a Mauritanian Nelson Mandela, was released.[27] It was neither the first nor the last time that he would see the inside of a cell. 'I've been imprisoned five times,' he says, sitting in his office in front of a ceramic lion, the symbol of his latest political bid for the presidency (he came second in the presidential elections of 2014, 2019 and 2024). In 2014, he was arrested for protesting against a court's decision to drop charges against a slave master who had raped his fifteen-year-old slave girl. In a move difficult to comprehend for those unfamiliar with Mauritania, the pregnant girl, Mbeirika Mint M'bareck, was then charged by a public prosecutor with having sex outside marriage, a crime under the prevailing sharia law. While these charges were subsequently dropped, Abeid was only released in 2016, after serving twenty months in prison.[28]

Abeid does not give up easily. He was imprisoned again in 2018, in an attempt to prevent him from running as a parliamentary candidate for the opposition. Extraordinarily, he still managed to be elected from his prison cell. In 2024 he was imprisoned for forty-eight hours, this time accused of terrorism:

I have freed nine-year-old girls from slavery who have already been raped several times by the master or the master's son. Our biggest fight is in the wealthiest districts of Nouakchott. These are the powerful people who still have slaves. The government refuses to do anything about it, the imams refuse, the police officers refuse, the judges refuse.

His critics accuse him of misrepresenting the situation for his own political ends. Serially arrested, detained and allegedly tortured, Abeid is the recipient of numerous international awards, including the 2013 United Nations Human Rights Prize, which in his darker moments must go some way to maintaining his single-minded drive. Nouakchott regularly picks off activists, threatening and intimidating them one minute, luring them into lucrative positions in the public sector the next.

Establishing the prevalence of slavery in a highly impoverished country where a corrupt government does not collect information about it is necessarily difficult and imprecise, often dangerous, but few independent observers doubt that hereditary slavery remains a blight, even if it is in decline.

Before I leave, I meet a twenty-five-year-old man called Said, who tells me he was liberated from his childhood enslavement by IRA in 2011. Today he works in a shop in Nouakchott. We talk together in a flyblown restaurant on the outskirts of the capital while a police informant monitors our conversation at a nearby table.

'I never knew I was living in slavery until I realized the people I considered my family treated me differently to all their other children,' he says. 'I did all the work, the other boys did nothing. They went to school, I never did.'

His eyes shine as he talks of his dreams for the future. 'My only hope now is one day to defend those who have been deprived of their freedom. Unfortunately, I don't have the education to be a lawyer, but I'm studying as hard as I can. I'm never going to give up.'

Epilogue

Nouakchott flashes by beneath the sun. Sand, dust, donkeys, goats, battered cars and roadside sellers burn in the heat. It is over 40 degrees in the Mauritanian capital and summer has not yet arrived.

As we leave the outskirts and turn off the main road, houses become huts, huts become shacks and shacks shelters. There is rubbish everywhere. It is a wasteland of sand and stray dogs, rotting food, squashed plastic bottles, plastic containers, shredded plastic bags, discarded clothes and flip-flops, rubber tyres and occasional power cables siphoning off electricity. The rotting corpse of a donkey adds to the stench. Eventually the ragged road peters out, defeated by deep drifts of sand, and we get out to walk the remaining distance.

This sprawling settlement stretches across the desert outside Riyadh, a suburb twenty miles south-east of Nouakchott. No shops. No roads. No running water. It is a scene of desolation.

Habi Rabah is waiting for us in her home, a small structure built from unfinished concrete breeze blocks beneath a corrugated metal roof. The room we sit in measures three metres by three metres. She sits cross-legged on the floor wearing a blue and pink patterned *melhfa*, the traditional wraparound dress.

She says she does not know how old she is and, because she cannot read, passes her identity card to Moulaye, the translator. It states that she was born in 1974.

She begins by saying that she grew up enslaved in the home of the man she calls her 'master', a *bidan* in Mederdra, a small town 100 miles south of Nouakchott, close to the border with Senegal. Both her parents, enslaved in separate families, died when she was a young child. Life was a punishing and unrelenting routine from as far back as she can remember:

> Early every morning I had to take the goats out and stay with them until sunset. Then I'd bring them back and start milking them after dark, working until one or two in the morning, seven days a week. There were no days off, no holidays, and no school. I wasn't allowed to study and I wasn't allowed to pray because they said I was a slave with the soul of an animal. I also had to look after the family's six children, feed them and wash them. They gave me leftover food when there was some, and when there wasn't any, I had nothing to eat. I slept wherever I could. Often, I slept in the sand with the goats. I knew this was slavery but I had no way of escaping or doing anything about it. The village authorities intimidated me and told me there was no way out.

Physical and sexual violence were an inescapable part of her child-hood. 'The mother was not violent, but he was very severe. He beat me. When I lost a goat, or when he found out that one of the kids had been suckling on its mother and taken the milk, he'd beat me and say, "Why did you allow that?" He also raped me every night when I was still a young girl.'

She got pregnant twice and bore him two children, neither of which he recognized. Yet this was not the worst thing she remembers years later. Her eyes fill when she recalls what she considers the most devas-tating experience of her life. 'Of all the pain I have been through, all the beatings, the rapes and the hopelessness, the deepest evil I suffered was when my mother died. She lived with another family less than three miles away, but my master wouldn't let me go to her. I couldn't even say goodbye to my own mother.'

Sitting next to Habi in a blue *boubou* and white turban is her brother Bilal Ould Rabah, named after the Ethiopian slave-turned-Muslim warrior and hero, Islam's first *muaddin*. He grew up enslaved with another family, cousins of those who kept Habi, about thirty miles away. Then, in 2001, he escaped. 'After Bilal took his freedom, every few months he came to visit me in secret to plan an escape,' says Habi. 'But he had no means to look after me or the ability to confront my powerful master.'

The police, Bilal, says, weren't interested when he reported his sister's case. Later, he had the idea of contacting the anti-slavery activist Biram Dah Abeid and seeking his assistance to free Habi. In 2008, by which time the original master had died and Habi was living with the rest of his family, Biram contacted the *hakim*, a municipal officer, and came to Mederdra with Bilal and a policeman.

'When my brother came to free me, I was against it at first. I didn't want to leave my master. I had heard that Biram could sell me. I even denied I was a slave to the policeman.'

'You were frightened. You were psychologically enchained,' Bilal says gently.

'I didn't know where to go, how I would be able to survive,' Habi continues. 'I was convinced that all my life would be like that, living in slavery. That was my destiny. All my family were slaves for as far back as anyone could remember. It was hereditary slavery. I didn't think there could be a better life.'

After a heated confrontation involving the family, Bilal, Biram and the policeman, Habi finally got into the pickup with her brother and children and was driven away. After thirty-five years of enslavement, she was free.

Her life has since been turned upside down. In 2018, Habi stood for parliament. She stood again in 2023. Although she has not yet been elected – political corruption in Mauritania remains endemic, and the odds are stacked against her – her fight continues. 'I'm proud to be a candidate for the parliament,' she says. The voice is steely and there is fire in her eyes. Nailed to the concrete wall is her election flyer with her portrait. 'I'm proud to have entered this political struggle. I've dedicated the rest of my life to fighting slavery.'

Habi lives in poverty with her husband, with whom she has a son. Sometimes there is little food to eat, but freedom, she says, is the most important thing.

'When I came to Nouakchott, I realized I hadn't been living before. For the first time I started to taste life. Before that I was just an object. I didn't exist as a human being. Now, praise God, I am free.'

Nouakchott, 22 May 2024

Acknowledgements

This book begins in Mali with the harrowing story of Hamey (not his real name), who comes from a family which had been subjected to hereditary enslavement for countless generations. With his escape from slavery in 2018, Hamey broke that chain for himself, his wives and their children forever.

I am grateful to the Sahel researcher Adam Sandor and the journalist Modibo Diallo, both former colleagues in Bamako, for arranging this interview through Temedt, the anti-slavery organization. Thank you to Ibrahim Ag Idbaltanat, its president, and to Alassane Hamza, its representative in Ségou. This interview was held on the sidelines of a challenging communications project in Mali, which somehow continued throughout Covid-19, and during which I benefited from the support of Dan Pimlott, Katya Lvova, Tim Gurney and the Kelenya team, especially Modibo, Aissata Sanogo, Aminata Touré, Sidibé Aboubacar and Nouhoum Traoré. Thank you also to the writer Aminata Dramane Traoré.

During many visits to Libya over the past four decades I have incurred too many debts of hospitality to mention. This was true even during the most dangerous days of the Libyan Revolution of 2011 and the fighting that has continued for too many years since.

While reporting on that conflict, I overheard a group of young rebels call one of the darker-skinned members of their militia a 'slave', an early alert to the history of Arab racism towards black Africans, which I explore in detail in Chapter 3. Several years later, I was working in Libya as a British government-sponsored adviser to the Office of Prime Minster Faiez Serraj when news broke that African migrants were being sold as slaves in secret auctions across Libya, triggering an international furore.

I am especially grateful to Jalal Othman, a close friend and colleague for several years, together with the late Tarek Erwimed, Fadeel Lameen, Serraj Alhammel, Moayed Othman, Hassan al Huni, Mazin Ramadan, Moutaz Ali, Huda Abuzeid, Omar Matoq, Rafaat Belkhair, Ali Sherif and Nayla Muntasser. Thank you to British Ambassadors Peter Millett and Frank Baker and their excellent teams, particularly Iona Thomas, Youcef Marzooq, Helena Owen, Asma Siyala and David True. Thank you to Adel and Rula Dajani for their boundless hospitality in Tunis while I was travelling to and from Tripoli and to Gavin Graham and the Gardaworld team for keeping me safe during repeated visits to Libya.

Professor Matthew Gordon of Miami University, an expert on Middle Eastern and Islamic Studies, has been a generous and insightful guide to early Islamic slavery and I am equally indebted to him for his careful reading of the manuscript, which resulted in a number of changes and additions. I am likewise grateful to another academic at Oxford University for his detailed and very helpful comments on a late draft which have enabled me to amplify various themes and avoid a number of pitfalls.

In Istanbul, thank you to Edhem Eldem, the former International Chair of Turkish and Ottoman History at the Collège de France and a distinguished Professor of History at Boğaziçi University. An interview about Ottoman slavery with Eldem in his Istanbul home begins Chapter 10. Thank you to Professors Çiğdem Kafescioğlu and Faruk Birtek of Boğaziçi University, Professor Felicia Roşu of Leiden University, Professor Baki Tezcan of UC Davis and Professor Hakan Karateke from the University of Chicago. Thanks also to Özalp Birol, head of the Suna and İnan Kıraç Foundation's Pera Museum and the Istanbul Research Institute, Nilay Özlü, Hilmi Kaçar and Agah Karliaga of Bahçeşehir University. I am particularly grateful to Nida Nebahat Nalçacı for setting me off on the right research path, recommending works by Gülay Yılmaz (Janissaries), Betül İpşirli Argıt (female palace slaves), Ceyda Karamürsel (late-Ottoman slavery) and Özgür Kolçak (Habsburg war frontiers and slaves). Likewise I am indebted to Ehud Toledano, Professor of Middle Eastern History at Tel Aviv University, some of whose research I concentrate on in my material on Ottoman-era slavery and abolition.

For the history of slavery in Zanzibar I am grateful to Professor Abdul Sheriff, Emeritus Professor of History at the University of Dar es Salaam and former director of the Zanzibar Indian Ocean Research Institute.

In Oman, thank you to His Excellency Dr Abdulla Al Harrasi, minister of information, Yousef Mohammed Salem Aljabri and Mohammed Albusaidi of the Omani embassy in London, whose hospitality, support and friendship have been second to none.

Staying in London, I salute my agent Georgina Capel, who has shepherded this book through several years, my editors Stuart Proffitt and Eleo Carson at Allen Lane, who have believed in this project and supported it expertly throughout, Vartika Rastogi, Anna Tuck, Imogen Scott, Linden Lawson and Annabel Huxley. Thank you also to the unfailingly helpful staff in the British Library's Rare Books and Music Room, which has been a regular resource.

Through no fault of her own, my long-suffering wife Julia has found herself wedded to this long and controversial project. I am, as ever, grateful for her love and support.

This book concludes in Mauritania, where vestiges of hereditary racialized slavery continue today. For obvious reasons, governments in Nouakchott do not wish this to be investigated or publicly discussed. My research here would not have been possible without a generous research grant from the Pharos Foundation – thank you, Dr David Abulafia and Patrick Nash, its president and executive director respectively – and the courageous support of the journalist and editor Moulaye Najim, who remained undeterred throughout the visit, despite constant pressure from the authorities.

Thank you to Biram Dah Abeid, the founder of the anti-slavery organization IRA, who found time for an interview during his presidential election campaign, Hamady Lehbouss, its secretary-general, El Kory Sneïba of SOS Esclaves, Mauritania's oldest anti-slavery organization, the formerly enslaved young man Said Matt, Yaqub Ahmad Lemrabiet, president of the Kavana youth movement, Aminetou Mint El Mokhtar, president of the Association de Femmes Chef de Famille, the writer Mohammed Salem Yaqubi and the sociologist Yahya Bara, together with those others who prefer to remain anonymous.

Finally, thank you to Habi Rabah, who endured decades of enslavement before her liberation in 2008, assisted by her brother Bilal Ould Rabah and IRA. Habi is now an anti-slavery activist and two-time parliamentary candidate. Her interview brings this book to a close.

Notes

A NOTE ON SOURCES

1. Azraqi, *Kitab Akhbar Makka*, 1:66, quoted in Zayde Antrim, *Routes and Realms: The Power of Place in the Early Islamic World* (Oxford, 2012), p. 44.
2. To understand some of the problems facing historians see Mahmud Ibrahim, *Merchant Capital and Islam*, p. 35; Francis E. Peters, *Mecca: A Literary History of the Muslim Holy Land*, p. 3; Fred M. Donner, 'The Historical Context' in *The Cambridge Companion to the Quran*, p. 33; Patricia Crone, *Meccan Trade and the Rise of Islam*, p. 204; G. H. A. Juynboll, *Studies on the First Century of Islamic Society*, p. 2; Fred Donner, *Muhammad and the Believers: At the Origins of Islam*, p. 51. Summarized in Justin Marozzi, *Islamic Empires: Fifteen Cities That Define a Civilization* (London, 2019), pp. 5–7.
3. For an excellent summary on the challenge of sources see George La Rue, 'Slave Trades and Diaspora in the Middle East, 700 to 1900 CE', *Oxford Research Encyclopedias*, 2021, accessed at https://doi.org/10.1093/acrefore/9780190277734.013.904.
4. See Matthew S. Hopper, *Slaves of One Master: Globalization and Slavery in Arabia in the Age of Empire*, pp. viii–ix.

INTRODUCTION

1. John O. Hunwick and Eve Troutt Powell, *The African Diaspora in the Mediterranean Lands of Islam* (London, 2002), p. ix.
2. James Walvin, *A Short History of Slavery*, cited in Stephanie Cronin, 'Islam, Slave Agency and Abolitionism in the Middle East and North Africa' in *Social Histories of Iran: Modernism and Marginality in the Middle East*, 2021, published online by Oxford University Research Archive, https://

ora.ox.ac.uk/objects/uuid:4935bc32-e8ef-4f68-81b0-9d143a0646cc/
files/m402bc6879defc0142404e28549cbbfc6.

3. Neil Price, *The Children of Ash and Elm: A History of the Vikings* (London, 2020), p. 142; D. R. Banaji, *Slavery In British India* (Bombay, 1933), p. 202.

4. Paul Lovejoy, *Transformations in Slavery*, pp. 72–3.

5. See Hopper, *Slaves of One Master*, p. 6.

6. Benjamin Reilly, *Slavery, Agriculture, and Malaria in the Arabian Peninsula*, p. 126.

7. Ibid., p. 2, p. 3, p. 63.

8. Cronin, 'Islam, Slave Agency and Abolitionism', p. 2.

9. 'Modern Slavery in Saudi Arabia', Walk Free Global Slavery Index/ Country Study, https://www.walkfree.org/global-slavery-index/country-studies/saudi-arabia/.

10. 'Slavery: Historical Survey', Britannica, https://www.britannica.com/topic/slavery-sociology/Historical-survey; Paul Lovejoy, *Transformations in Slavery: A History of Slavery in Africa*, p. xxiv.

11. See John Ralph Willis, 'Jihad and the Ideology of Enslavement' in Willis (ed.), *Slaves and Slavery in Muslim Africa*, Vol. 1, *Islam and the Ideology of Enslavement*, p. x, note 2; see also Yves Beigbeder, *Judging War Crimes and Torture: French Justice and International Criminal Tribunals and Commissions (1940–2005)* (Leiden, 2006), p. 42.

12. Ehud Toledano, *Slavery and Abolition in the Ottoman Middle East*, p. 135; ibid., p. 138; Y. Haken Erdem, *Slavery in the Ottoman Empire and its Demise, 1800–1909*, p. xviii; Bernard Lewis, *Race and Slavery in the Middle East*, cited in John O. Hunwick and Eve Troutt Powell, *The African Diaspora in the Mediterranean Lands of Islam*, p. ix.

13. Scholars such as Chouki El Hamel and Mohammed Ennaji (race and slavery in Morocco), Behnaz A. Mirzai (Iran), Ismael Montana (Tunisia), Yacine Daddi-Adoun (Algeria), Nabil Matar (Mediterranean corsairing), Moulay Belhamissi (Muslim captivity in Europe), Abdulrahman Alebrahim (Gulf slavery), Gülay Yılmaz (Janissaries), Betül İpşirli Argıt, Ceyda Karamürsel and Nida Nebahat Nalçacı (Ottoman slavery), Ayten Kiriş and Muhammet Avaroğulları (Turkish discussion of slavery in Turkish history) continue to break new ground.

14. Murray Gordon, *Slavery in the Arab World*, p. 1; Anthony A. Lee, 'Enslaved African Women in Nineteenth-Century Iran: The Life of Fezzeh Khanom of Shiraz', *Iranian Studies*, Vol. 45, No. 3 (May 2012), p. 422, accessed at https://www.jstor.org/stable/41445217; John Wright, *The Trans-Saharan Slave Trade*, p. xiv; Zeinab Badawi, *An African History of Africa*, p. 215, p. 240.

15. Cronin, 'Islam, Slave Agency and Abolitionism', p. 4.
16. See James Montgomery (trans. and ed.), *War Songs by Antara ibn Shaddad*, p. 151.
17. Ibid., pp. xiv–xv.
18. See, for example, H. T. Norris, *The Adventures of Antar* (Warminster, 1980), p. 1; Remke Kruk, 'Sirat Antar ibn Shaddad' in Roger Allen and D. S. Richards (eds), *Arabic Literature in the Post-Classical Period: The Cambridge History of Arabic Literature* (online summary https://www.cambridge.org/core/books/abs/arabic-literature-in-the-postclassical-period/sirat-antar-ibn-shaddad/B2B4BE56EED470B97FE0F583093C9CEA); see also Montgomery's excellent *War Songs by Antara ibn Shaddad*, p. xviii.
19. Ehud Toledano, *As if Silent and Absent: Bonds of Enslavement in the Islamic Middle East*, p. 33.
20. See 'Enslaved Person: Reparative Description Preferred Term', The National Archives Catalog, https://www.archives.gov/research/catalog/lcdrg/appendix/enslaved-person.

I – FOUR SLAVES AND THE BIRTH OF ISLAM

1. The following account of the life of Bilal is closely based on some of the earliest, most important Muslim sources, as highlighted in 'A Note on Sources'.

Ibn Ishaq (*c.*704–*c.*767) was one of the earliest biographers of Mohammed. His narrative treatment offered a new approach after the earlier episodic and fragmentary accounts, the *Sirat Rasul Allah* (*Life of the Messenger of God*), which survived most fully in the version edited by the Iraqi historian Ibn Hisham (d. 833). For his account of Bilal see *The Life of Muhammad*, pp. 143–4.

Mohammed ibn Saad (*c.*784 845) was the author of *Kitab al Tabaqat al Kabir* (*The Major Book of Classes*), a collection of biographies of the most famous Muslim figures, above all the Prophet Mohammed and his Companions and Helpers, together with the Followers, the next generation of Muslims who succeeded them. For Ibn Saad's description of Bilal see *Kitab al Tabaqat al Kabir*, Vol. 3, *The Companions at Badr*, pp. 177–83.

Tabari (839–923), a key primary source for early Muslim history, compiled his magisterial history using a number of sources, including historians such as Urwa ibn al Zubayr, the seventh-century Muslim traditionist and a founding father of Islamic history, Wahb ibn Munabbih, the seventh-century Yemeni traditionist, Ibn Ishaq, the Prophet's biographer, the early Iraqi historians Abu Mikhnaf and Hisham ibn al Kalbi, the eighth-century historians Al Waqidi and Awana ibn al Hakam, among others, in addition to a large number of oral accounts in circulation during his life. For his account of Bilal see *The History of al-Tabari*, Vol. 39, *Biographies of the Prophet's Companions and Their Successors*, p. 44, p. 290.

For more modern accounts and interpretations of Bilal see W. Arafat, 'Bilal ibn Rabah' in *Encyclopedia of Islam* 2, Vol. 1, p. 1215; M. A. J. Beg, *Brief Lives of the Companions of the Prophet Mohammed*; H. A. L. Craig, *Bilal*.

2. *Sahih al Bukhari*, Hadith 1149, accessed at https://sunnah.com/ bukhari:1149. This highly valued collection of *hadiths*, the reported sayings of the Prophet Mohammed, is widely considered by Muslims to be the most authentic.

3. For the life of Zayd see Tabari, *The History of al-Tabari*, Vol. 39, pp. 6–10, p. 65, pp. 171–2, p. 180–81; Ibn Ishaq, *The Life of Muhammad*, pp. 141–2; Ibn Saad, *Kitab al Tabaqat al Kabir*, Vol. 3, pp. 28–33; David S. Powers, *Zayd*.

4. Tabari, *The History of al-Tabari*, Vol. 39, pp. 8–9.

5. Ibn Saad, *Kitab al Tabaqat al Kabir*, Vol. 3, p. 32.

6. Ibid., p. 33.

7. For the life of Salman see Tabari, *The History of al-Tabari*, Vol. 39, p. 66, p. 99; Ibn Ishaq, *The Life of Muhammad*, pp. 95–8, p. 121; G. Levi della Vida, 'Salman al Farisi' in *Encyclopedia of Islam* 2, Vol. 12, pp. 701–2; Al Majlisi, *Bihar al Anwar*, Vol. 22, p. 348; Sarah Bowen Savant, 'Muhammad's Persian Companion, Salman al-Farisi' in *The New Muslims of Post-Conquest Iran: Tradition, Memory, and Conversion*, pp. 61–89.

8. G. Levi della Vida, 'Salman al Farisi' in *Encyclopedia of Islam* 2, Vol. 12, pp. 701–2.

9. See Ibn Ishaq, *The Life of Muhammad*, p. 95.

10. Ibid., p. 96.

11. Bowen Savant, 'Muhammad's Persian Companion, Salman al-Farisi', p. 82.

12. Al Majlisi, *Bihar al Anwar*, Vol. 22, p. 348. Quoted in Sayyid Saeed Akhtar Rizvi, *Slavery: Islamic & Western Perspectives*, p. 24.

13. For more on Hind see Ibn Ishaq, *The Life of Muhammad*, p. 548, p. 371.

14. Ibid., p. 548.

15. This account of Sumayya comes from Ibn Saad, *Kitab al Tabaqat al Kabir*, Vol. 3, p. 77, p. 178; *Volume 8: The Women of Madina*, pp. 185–6; Ibn

Ishaq, *The Life of Muhammad*, p. 145; Tabari, *The History of al-Tabari*, Vol. 39, pp. 29–30, pp. 116–17; M. A. J. Beg, *Brief Lives of the Companions of the Prophet Mohammed*, p. 77.

16. Ibn Ishaq, *The Life of Muhammad*, p. 304.

2 – SLAVERY 101: BLUEPRINTS AND FOUNDATIONS

1. Jonathan E. Brockopp, *Early Maliki Law: Ibn Abd Al-Hakam and His Major Compendium on Jurisprudence*, p. 138; Lewis, *Race and Slavery in the Middle East*, pp. 6–7.

2. For two versions of this story see Kecia Ali, *Marriage and Slavery in Early Islam*, pp. 12–13.

3. Jonathan Brown, *Slavery and Islam*, p. 68.

4. Ibid., pp. 68–9.

5. Brockopp, *Early Maliki Law*, pp. 148–53.

6. Philip Hitti, *The Origins of the Islamic State. Being a translation from the Arabic, accompanied with annotations, geographic and historic notes of the Kitab Futuh al-Buldan of al-Imaam abu-l 'Abbas Aḥmad ibn Jabir al-Baladhuri*, p. 165.

7. Tabari, *The History of al-Tabari*, Vol. 12, *The Battle of al-Qadisiyyah and the Conquest of Syria and Palestine*, p. 70.

8. Daniel Pipes, *Slave Soldiers and Islam: The Genesis of a Military System*, p. 140; Philip Hitti, *History of the Arabs*, p. 235 (1974).

9. Figures for Musa ibn Nusayr's slaving operations cited in Brockopp, *Early Maliki Law*, p. 146. Atlantic slave trade statistics from https://www.slavevoyages.org/assessment/estimates and https://www.statista.com/statistics/1143207/slaves-brought-from-africa-to-americas-1501-1866/#:~:text=The%20transatlantic%20slave%20trade%20reached,each%20year%20between%20these%20dates.

10. For Al Maqrizi's full text of the treaty see Yusuf Fadl Hasan, *The Arabs and the Sudan: From the Seventh to the Early Sixteenth Century*, pp. 22–4.

11. *Sunan al-Tirmidhī 1566*, Daily Hadith Online, The Teachings of Prophet Mohammed, accessed online at https://www.abuaminaelias.com/dailyhadithonline/2014/01/15/separating-children-parents/.

12. Like so much of the literature on early Islam, dating the canonization of the Quran is highly contentious. For a recent summary of the discussion see Herbert Berg, 'The Collection and Canonisation of the Qur'Ān' in *Routledge Handbook on Early Islam* (2017), pp. 37–48, accessed at https://www.routledgehandbooks.com/doi/10.4324/9781315743462.ch3.

13. Daniel Pipes, 'Mawlas: Freed Slaves and Converts in Early Islam' in Willis, *Slaves and Slavery in Muslim Africa*, Vol. 1, p. 221, accessed at https://www.danielpipes.org/documents/8230.pdf.

14. For *mawlas* and *wala* see Matthew S. Gordon, 'Slavery in the Islamic Middle East (c.600–1,000 CE)' in *The Cambridge World History of Slavery*, Vol. 2, *AD 500–AD 1420*, pp. 348–9.

15. See Roy Mottahedeh, 'The Abbasid Caliphate in Iran' in *The Cambridge History of Iran*, Vol. 4, *The Period from the Arab Invasion to the Saljuqs*, p. 57.

16. Ibid., pp. 179–80.

17. See N. Levtzion and J. F. P. Hopkins (eds), *Corpus of Early Arabic Sources for West African History*, pp. 347ff.

3 – RACE, RACISM AND REVOLT

1. Cited in Joseph E. Harris (ed.), *Global Dimensions of the African Diaspora*, p. 316.

2. 'Daily life in Libya's rebellion', NBC News, 26 August 2011, https://www.nbcnews.com/slideshow/news/daily-life-in-libyas-rebellion-44281439.

3. 'Libyans don't like people with dark skin, but some are innocent', *Independent*, 30 August 2011, https://www.independent.co.uk/news/world/africa/libyans-dont-like-people-with-dark-skin-but-some-are-innocent-2345859.html; 'Libya's spectacular revolution has been disgraced by racism', *Guardian*, 30 August 2011, https://www.theguardian.com/commentisfree/2011/aug/30/libya-spectacular-revolution-disgraced-racism; 'Libyans turn wrath on Dark-skinned Migrants', *New York Times*, 5 September 2011, https://www.nytimes.com/2011/09/05/world/africa/05migrants.html; Izza Leghtas, '"Death Would Have Been Better": Europe Continues to Fail Refugees and Migrants in Libya', Refugees International report, 15 April 2018, accessed at https://static1.squarespace.com/static/506c8ea1e4b01d9450dd53f5/t/5ad3ceae03ce641bc8ac6eb5/1523830448784/2018+Libya+Report+PDF.pdf).

4. See 'People for sale: Where lives are auctioned for $400', CNN, 14 November 2017, https://edition.cnn.com/2017/11/14/africa/libya-migrant-auctions/index.html and '"Where is the world?": Libya responds to outrage over slave auctions', CNN, 23 November 2017, https://edition.cnn.com/2017/11/23/africa/libya-reaction-slave-trade/index.html.

5. On Jahiz see Alexandre Popović, *The Revolt of African Slaves in Iraq in the 3rd/9th Century*, p. 21.

6. On Ibn Qutayba see Lewis, *Race and Slavery in the Middle East*, p. 46.

7. On Masudi see Willis, *Slaves and Slavery in Muslim Africa*, Vol. 1, p. 68.

8. On Ibn Sina see Jakob Rosenthal, *Political Thought in Medieval Islam: An Introductory Outline*, pp. 154–5.

9. On Ibn Butlan see Bernard Lewis, *Islam from the Prophet Mohammed to the Capture of Constantinople*, Vol. 2, pp. 243–51.

10. On Ferdowsi, Saadi and other Persian examples see Minoo Southgate, 'The Negative Images of Blacks in Some Medieval Iranian Writings', *Iranian Studies*, Vol. 17, No. 1 (Winter, 1984), pp. 3–36.

11. On Ibn Khaldun see his *Muqaddimah*, Vol. 1, p. 301.

12. See Abduh Badawi, *Al-Shu'ara' al Sud wa Khasa'isuhum fi al Shi'r al Arabi*, cited in Bernard Lewis, 'The Crows of the Arabs', *Critical Inquiry*, Vol. 12, No. 1 (Autumn 1985), pp. 88–97.

13. For a discussion of these poets see Nicholas C. McLeod, 'Race, Rebellion, and Arab Muslim Slavery: The Zanj Rebellion in Iraq, 869–883 CE', *Electronic Theses and Dissertations*, Paper 2381, pp. 94–8, accessed at https://ir.library.louisville.edu/cgi/viewcontent.cgi?article=3436&context=etd.

14. On the curse of Ham see David M. Goldenberg, *The Curse of Ham: Race and Slavery in Early Judaism, Christianity, and Islam*, p. 1, p. 350, note 11; John B. Boles, review of Stephen R. Haynes, *Noah's Curse: The Biblical Justification of American Slavery*, *The American Historical Review*, Vol. 108, No. 4 (October 2003), pp. 1150–51; Masudi's comments in Levtzion and Hopkins, *Corpus of Early Arabic Sources for West Africa*, p. 34.

15. On Benjamin of Tudela see A. Asher (trans. and ed.), *The Itinerary of Rabbi Benjamin of Tudela*, Vol. 1, pp. 145–6.

16. For Jahiz's 'Superiority of the Blacks over the Whites' see Charles Pellat (ed.), *The Life and Works of Jahiz*, pp. 195–8; see also Akbar Muhammad, 'The Image of Africans in Arabic Literature' in Willis, *Slaves and Slavery in Muslim Africa*, Vol. 1, pp. 47–74.

17. On Ibn al Jawzi see Willis, ibid., p. 52.

18. See Tabari, *The History of al Tabari*, Vol. 36, *The Revolt of the Zanj*, p. xvii; Vol. 37, *The Abbasid Recovery*.

19. Tabari, Vol. 36, p. 126.

20. Al Masudi, *Les Prairies d'Or*, Vol. 8, p. 59; Popović, *The Revolt of African Slaves*, p. 64.

21. See James Montgomery, 'Scenes of Violence in Arabic Literature' in *Cambridge World History of Violence*, Vol. 2, *500–1500 CE*, pp. 617–18.

22. Popović, *The Revolt of African Slaves*, p. 131.

23. Ibid., p. 132.

24. See Nigel D. Furlonge, 'Revisiting the Zanj and Re-Visioning Revolt: Complexities of the Zanj Conflict (868–883 AD)', *Negro History Bulletin*, Vol. 62, No. 4 (December 1999), pp. 7–14.

25. Quran 109:1–6; Popović, *The Revolt of African Slaves*, p. 74.

26. Tabari, *The History of al-Tabari*, Vol. 37, p. 102.

27. For the poets' reaction to the crushing of the Zanj Revolt see Tabari, Vol. 37, pp. 140–43.

28. Ibid., p. 152.

4 – SEX AND SINGING: THE CONCUBINES

1. Julia Ashtiany (ed.), *Abbasid Belles Lettres: The Cambridge History of Arabic Literature*, Vol. 2, p. 216.

2. Masudi, *The Meadows of Gold: The Abbasids*, pp. 43–5; Baron Mac Guckin de Slane (trans.), *Ibn Khallikan's Biographical Dictionary*, Vol. 1, p. 208.

3. For Jahiz's portrait of a singing slave girl see Pellat, *The Life and Works of Jahiz*, pp. 265–7.

4. For the harrumphing Al Tawhidi see Fuad Matthew Caswell, *The Slave Girls of Baghdad: The 'Qiyān' in the Early Abbasid Era*, p. 58.

5. For Al Washsha see ibid., pp. 39–40.

6. Quoted in Hugh Kennedy, *When Baghdad Ruled the Muslim World: The Rise and Fall of Islam's Greatest Dynasty*, pp. 177–8.

7. Herodotus, *The Histories* (London, 2003), p. 3.

8. For a summary of Inan's life and career see Ibn al Sa'i, 'Inan, Daughter of Abd Allah, "Restraint", Slave of Al Natifi' in Shawkat M. Toorawa and Julia Bray (eds), *The Consorts of the Caliphs: Women and the Court of Baghdad*, pp. 11–19. See also Caswell, *The Slave Girls of Baghdad*, pp. 56–81; for the first exchange with Abu Nuwas see Eric Ormsby, 'Questions for Stones: On Classical Arabic Poetry', *Parnassus: Poetry in Review*, Vol. 25, No. 1 and No. 2, p. 30. For a good general study see also Nadia Maria El Cheikh, 'Revisiting the Abbasid Harems', *Journal of Middle East Women's Studies*, Vol. 1, No. 3 (2005), pp. 1–19, accessed at http://www.jstor.org/stable/40326869.

9. Taef El-Azhari, *Queens, Eunuchs and Concubines in Islamic History, 661–1257*, p. 77.

10. For accounts of Arib see Ibn al Sa'i, 'Arib al-Ma'muniyah, "Ardent", Member of the household of the caliph al-Ma'mun' in *The Consorts of the Caliphs*, pp. 24–32; Abu al Faraj al Isfahani, *Kitab al Aghani (Book of Songs)*, Vol. 22, pp. 348–59; Matthew Gordon, 'Arib

al-Ma'muniyah (797–890)' in *Arabic Literary Culture, 500–925*, pp. 85–90, *Dictionary of Literary Biography*, Vol. 311 (New Haven, Conn., 2005); on Ibn al Asakir see Steven Judd and Jens Scheiner (eds), *New Perspectives on Ibn 'Asākir in Islamic Historiography*, p. 124; for the singing competition staged by Abu Isa ibn al Mutawakkil see Matthew S. Gordon, 'The Place of Competition: The Careers of 'Arib al-Ma'muniya and 'Ulayya bint Almahdi, Sisters in Song', 2002, accessed at https://www.academia.edu/358518/The_Place_of_Competition_Arib_and_Ulayya_Sisters_in_Song; see also Agnes Imhof, 'Traditio vel Aemulatio? The Singing Contest of Samarra, Expression of a Medieval Culture of Competition', *Der Islam*, 90 (2013), pp. 1–20, accessed at https://goedoc.uni-goettingen.de/bitstream/handle/1/10792/Traditio%20vel%20Aemulatio.pdf?sequence=1; for the Al Tanukhi anecdote see Al Tanukhi, *Table Talk of a Mesopotamian Judge*, pp. 144–6; 'a hard prick and a sweet breath', Caswell, *The Slave Girls of Baghdad*, p. 112.

11. Cited in Dominic P. Brookshaw, 'Palaces, Pavilions and Pleasure-gardens: The Context and Setting of the Medieval Majlis', *Middle Eastern Literatures*, 6 (2) (2003), pp. 199–223.

12. For accounts of Mahbuba see Masudi, *Meadows of Gold*, pp. 264–6; Ibn al Sa'i, 'Mahbubah, "Beloved", Slave of the Caliph al-Mutawakkil' in *The Consorts of the Caliphs*, pp. 77–83. See also Deborah Schlein, 'The Talent and The Intellect: The Qayna's Application of Skill in the Umayyad and 'Abbasid Royal Courts', 2013, accessed at https://etd.library.emory.edu/concern/etds/5h73pw11p?locale=en; for the legendary Mahbuba see Richard F. Burton (trans.), *The Book of the Thousand Nights and a Night* (London, 1885), Vol. 4, pp. 291–2, accessed at https://www.gutenberg.org/files/53254/53254-h/53254-h.htm#c291.

13. See Amikam Elad, 'An Epitaph of the Slave Girl of the Grandson of the Abbasid Caliph al-Ma'mun', *Le Museon*, Vol. 111 (1998), pp. 227–44, accessed as PDF.

5 – SLAVE SOLDIERS

1. For the death of Mutazz see Masudi, *Meadows of Gold*, p. 300; for the death of Muhtadi see Tabari, *The History of al Tabari*, Vol. 36, p. 94; for his summary of the Samarra period see Tabari, *The History of al Tabari*, Vol. 35, *The Crisis of the Abbasid Caliphate*, p. 10.

2. David Ayalon, *Eunuchs, Caliphs and Sultans: A Study of Power Relationships*, p. 44, p. 30.

3. Cited in Matthew Gordon, *The Breaking of a Thousand Swords: A History of the Turkish Military of Samarra 815–889*, p. 17.

4. See Jahiz, 'The Merits of the Turks and the Imperial Army as a Whole' in Pellat, *The Life and Works of Jahiz*, pp. 91–7. Ibn Hawqal's verdict on the Turks is cited in Reuven Amitai, 'The Mamluk Institution: 1000 Years of Military Slavery in the Islamic World' in Philip Morgan and Christopher Brown (eds), *Arming Slaves: From Classical Times to the Modern Age*, p. 46.

5. Yaaqubi cited in Gordon, *The Breaking of a Thousand Swords*, p. 17; on the *ghilman* see Kennedy, *When Baghdad Ruled the Muslim World*, p. 214.

6. For the process of making a slave soldier see the seminal study by Patricia Crone, *Slaves on Horses: The Breaking of a Thousand Swords*, p. 79.

7. For an attempt to determine the size of the Turkish forces in Samarra see Hugh Kennedy, 'Military Slaves' in *The Armies of the Caliphs: Military and Society in the Early Islamic State*, pp. 126–7.

8. On Ibn Tulun and Al Qatai see Thierry Bianquis, 'Autonomous Egypt from Ibn Tulun to Kafur, 868–969' in *The Cambridge History of Egypt*, Vol. 1, pp. 86–119. On the Ibn Tulun Mosque see Tarek Swelim, *Ibn Tulun: His Lost City and His Great Mosque*; see also Doris Behrens-Abouseif, 'Early Islamic Architecture in Cairo' in *Islamic Architecture in Cairo: An Introduction*, 1989, pp. 47–57.

9. Cited in Lewis, *Race and Slavery in the Middle East*, p. 66.

10. Ibid.

11. For a summary of the Battle of the Blacks see Jere L. Bacharach, 'African Military Slaves in the Medieval Middle East: The Cases of Iraq (869–955) and Egypt (868–1171)', *International Journal of Middle East Studies*, Vol. 13, No. 4 (1981), pp. 487–9, accessed at http://www.jstor.org/stable/162910; Michael Brett, *The Fatimid Empire*, pp. 171–2, p. 292; Lewis, *Race and Slavery in the Middle East*, pp. 66–8.

12. Cited in Yehoshua Frenkel, 'Some Notes Concerning the Trade and Education of Slave-Soldiers During the Mamluk Era' in Reuven Amitai and Christoper Cluse (eds), *Slavery and the Slave Trade in the Eastern Mediterranean (c.1000–1500 CE)*, p. 187.

13. See Robert Irwin, *The Middle East in the Middle Ages: The Early Mamluk Sultanate, 1250–1382*, pp. 21–3; Amitai, 'The Mamluk Institution', p. 56.

14. Orlando Patterson, *Slavery and Social Death*, p.171.

15. For an unusual look at the life and career of Razia Sultan see Alyssa Gabbay, 'In Reality a Man: Sultan Iltutmish, His Daughter, Raziya, and Gender Ambiguity in Thirteenth Century Northern India', *Journal of*

Persianate Studies, Vol. 4, Issue 1 (January 2011), pp. 45–63, accessed at http://libres.uncg.edu/ir/uncg/f/a_gabbay_reality_2011.pdf#page4.

16. See Kurt Franz, 'Slavery in Islam: Legal Norms and Social Practice' in Reuven Amitai and Christopher Cluse (eds), *Slavery and the Slave Trade in the Eastern Mediterranean*, p. 118.

17. Cited in Amitai, 'The Mamluk Institution', p. 62.

18. See Amalia Levanoni, *A Turning Point in Mamluk History: The Third Reign of al-Nasir Muhammad Ibn Qalawun (1310–1341)*, p. 3.

19. See Amitai, 'The Mamluk Institution', p. 67.

20. On the pejorative response to the arquebus see *The Cambridge History of Islam*, Vol. 1, p. 229; on the advent of gunpowder and its effect on the Mamluk state see David Ayalon, *Gunpowder and Firearms in the Mamluk Kingdom: A Challenge to Medieval Society*; on the creation of the corps of black slave arquebusiers and Ibn Iyas's critical comments see Shaun Marmon, 'Black Slaves in Mamluk Narratives: Representations of Transgression', *Al Qantara*, Vol. 28, No. 2, July–December 2007, pp. 456–64.

21. Gary L. Rashba, *Holy Wars: 3000 Years of Battles in the Holy Land*, p. 140.

22. See Dr Edward Ives, *A Voyage from England to India, in the Year 1754 … Also a Journey from Persia to England by an Unusual Route*, note, p. 273; William Heude, *A Voyage up the Persian Gulf, and a Journey Overland from India to England, in 1817*, pp. 145–6.

23. Ives, *A Voyage from England to India*, p. 282.

24. Heude, *A Voyage up the Persian Gulf*, p. 149.

25. Ives, *A Voyage from England to India*, pp. 286–7.

26. Caroline Finkel, *Osman's Dream: The Story of the Ottoman Empire 1300–1923*, p. 435.

6 – GUARDIANS OF SACRED SPACES: THE EUNUCHS

1. 'Adel Quraishi: The Guardians', *Meer*, 3 November 2015, accessed at https://www.meer.com/en/18131-adel-quraishi-the-guardians.

2. Xenophon, *Cyropedia*, 7.5.60–66, accessed at http://www.perseus.tufts.edu/hopper/text?doc=Xen.%20Cyrop.%207.5&lang=original. See N. M. Penzer, *The Harem*, pp. 137–8. For the history of eunuchs in Persia see also 'Eunuchs', *Encyclopaedia Iranica*, 2012, accessed at https://iranicaonline.org/articles/eunuchs#:~:text=According%20to%20Xenophon%2C%20Cyrus%20the,3f.%2C%20par.

3. Sunan an-Nasa'i 4736, *Kitab al Qasamah (The Book of Oaths)*, accessed at https://sunnah.com/nasai:4736; see also Taef El-Azhari, *Queens, Eunuchs*

and Concubines, p. 30. The two verses in the Quran are as follows: 'So direct your face toward the religion, inclining to truth. [Adhere to] the fitrah of Allah upon which He has created [all] people. No change should there be in the creation of Allah. That is the correct religion, but most of the people do not know.' (30:30). '"I will certainly mislead them and delude them with empty hopes. Also, I will order them and they will slit the ears of cattle and alter Allah's creation." And whoever takes Satan as a guardian instead of Allah has certainly suffered a tremendous loss.' (4:119).

4. El-Azhari, *Queens, Eunuchs and Concubines*, pp. 44–5.

5. See Ayalon, *Eunuchs, Caliphs and Sultans*, pp. 218–20.

6. P. C. Remondino, *History of Circumcision from the Earliest Times to the Present – Moral and Physical Reasons for its Performance*, pp. 99–100. See also Raoul du Bisson, *Les Femmes, les Eunuques, et les Guerriers du Sondan*.

7. Jan Hogendorn, 'The Hideous Trade. Economic Aspects of the "Manufacture" and Sale of Eunuchs', *Paideuma*, Vol. 45 (1999), pp. 137–60, accessed at http://www.jstor.org/stable/40341768.

8. Jan Hogendorn, 'The Location of the Manufacture of Eunuchs' in Miura Tora and John Edward Philips (eds), *Slave Elites in the Middle East and Africa: A Comparative Study*, pp. 44–5, accessed at https://www.artsrn. ualberta.ca/amcdouga/Hist349/resources/making%20eunuchs%20 hogendorn.pdf.

9. El-Azhari, *Queens, Eunuchs and Concubines*, p. 146. There are different versions of the terminology for eunuchs. The fourteenth-century jurist Abd al Wahhab al Subki, for instance, designated three categories of eunuchs: *mamsuh*, who had both penis and testicles removed; *khasi*, who had testicles only removed; *majbub*, who had penis only removed.

10. A. Ezgi Dikici, 'The Making of Ottoman Court Eunuchs: Origins, Recruitment Paths, Family Ties, and "Domestic Production"', *Archivum Ottomanicum* 30 (2013), p. 131.

11. 'Al Aghawat had vowed themselves to the service of the two Holy Shrines', *Al Riyadh*, Rajab 29th, 1443 AH, 6 March 2022, privately translated by Manaf al Damluji.

12. Quoted in Kennedy, *When Baghdad Ruled the Muslim World*, pp. 71–2.

13. See El-Azhari, *Queens, Eunuchs and Concubines*, p. 156; Tabari, *The History of al Tabari*, Vol. 31, *The War Between Brothers*, p. 58.

14. Yacov Lev, 'The Ruling Circles' in *State and Society in Fatimid Egypt*, 1991, accessed at https://sourcebooks.fordham.edu/med/lev.asp; Ayalon, *Eunuchs, Caliphs and Sultans*, pp. 16–18.

15. For the life of Munis al Khadim see Hugh Kennedy, 'Mu'nis al Muzaf-far: An Exceptional Eunuch' in Almut Höfert, Matthew Mesley and Serena Tolino (eds),*Celibate & Childless Men in Power: Ruling Eunuchs and Bishops in the Pre-modern World*, pp. 79–91; see also El-Azhari, *Queens, Eunuchs and Concubines*, p. 126.

16. Ayalon, *Eunuchs, Caliphs and Sultans*, p. 161.

17. For a discussion of Mutanabbi and his tortured relationship with Kafur see Margaret Larkin, *Al- Mutanabbi: Voice of the 'Abbasid Poetic Ideal*, pp. 63–78.

18. D. S. Richards (ed.), *The Chronicle of Ibn Al-Athir for the Crusading Period from Al-Kamil Fi'l-Ta'rikh. Part 1. The Years 491–541/1097–1146: The Coming of the Franks and the Muslim Response*, p. 29.

19. Montesquieu, *The Persian letters of Montesquieu*, p. 13.

20. Ibn Jubayr in R. J. C. Broadhurst (trans. and ed.) *The Travels of Ibn Jubayr*, p. 52.

21. For a discussion of the use of eunuchs as guardians of royal tombs in Egypt see Shaun Marmon, *Eunuchs and Sacred Boundaries in Islamic Society*, pp. 16–29.

22. Thomas Dallam, *Early voyages and travels in the Levant*, pp. 79–80.

23. See Jane Hathaway, *Beshir Agha: Chief Eunuch of the Ottoman Imperial Harem*, p. 52. See also Tobias P. Graf, *The Sultan's Renegades: Christian-European Converts to Islam and the Making of the Ottoman Elite, 1575–1610*, pp. 167–8.

24. Dikici, 'The Making of Ottoman Court Eunuchs', p. 113.

25. Cited in Jane Hathaway, *The Arab Lands Under Ottoman Rule, 1516–1800*, pp. 11–12.

26. Behnaz A. Mirzai, *A History of Slavery and Emancipation in Iran, 1800–1929*, pp. 104–7, p. 111.

27. Ibid., p. 111.

28. Toledano, *Slavery and Abolition in the Ottoman Middle East*, p. 44.

29. For a meticulously reconstructed life of this hugely influential eunuch see Hathaway, *Beshir Agha*, p. 21, p. 107.

30. Marmon, *Eunuchs and Sacred Boundaries in Islamic Society*, pp. 33–4, note 264, p. 146; George H. Junne, *The Black Eunuchs of the Ottoman Empire: Networks of Power in the Court of the Sultan*, p. 142.

31. Penzer, *The Harem*, p. 135; Sir Richard F. Burton, *Personal Narrative of a Pilgrimage to Al-Madinah and Mecca*, Vol. 2, p. 256; Vol. 1 (Leipzig, 1884), p. 81; Penzer, *The Harem*, p. 135.

32. Junne, *The Black Eunuchs of the Ottoman Empire*, pp. 124–5.

33. Jane Hathaway, *The Chief Eunuch of the Ottoman Harem: From African Slave to Power-Broker*, pp. 139–40.

34. Hathaway, *Beshir Agha*, pp. 88–9.

35. Ibid., p. 105.

36. Sema Ok, *Harem Dünyasi, Harem Agalari*, pp. 75–6, quoted in Junne, *The Black Eunuchs of the Ottoman Empire*, p. 259.

37. Toledano, *Slavery and Abolition in the Ottoman Middle East*, p. 12.

38. Noel Barber, *The Sultans*, p. 200, quoted in Junne, *The Black Eunuchs of the Ottoman Empire*, p. 249.

39. The accounts of the last chief black eunuchs are based on the summary in Junne, ibid., pp. 259–72. See also Hathaway, *The Chief Eunuch of the Ottoman Harem*, pp. 242–5; Francis McCullagh, *The Fall of Abdul-Hamid*, pp. 274–6; for more on the life of Nadir Agha see 'Son Dönem Harem Ağalarından Nadir Ağa', *TESAD*, 4 January 2021, accessed at https://www.tesadernegi.org/son-donem-harem-agalarindan-nadir-aga.html; for more on Fahreddin Agha see Erdem, *Slavery in the Ottoman Empire and Its Demise*, p. 150; Gnammankou Dieudonné, 'Hayrettin Effendi, the last Black Eunuch of Turkey', *Black Men*, August 2000, accessed at https://www.thecoli.com/threads/interview-with-the-last-ottoman-black-eunuch.252548/.

40. Erdem, *Slavery in the Ottoman Empire and Its Demise*, loc. cit.

7 – ROGUES AND RENEGADES: SLAVERY IN THE MEDITERRANEAN

1. Suraiya Faroqhi, *The Ottoman Empire and the World Around It*, p. 125; Nabil Matar, *Mediterranean Captivity Through Arab Eyes, 1517–1798*, p. 256.

2. Adrian Tinniswood, *Pirates of Barbary: Corsairs, Conquests and Captivity in the 17th-Century Mediterranean*, pp. 30–31.

3. Joseph Morgan, *A Compleat History of the Piratical States of Barbary*, pp. iv–v, translated from Jacques Philippe Laugier de Tassy, *Histoire du royaume d'Alger*. See also 'Countering Islamophobia in the early eighteenth century', Voltaire Foundation blog, 16 July 2020, accessed at https://voltairefoundation.wordpress.com/tag/jacques-philippe-laugier-de-tassy/.

4. Charles Sumner, *White Slavery in the Barbary States*, p. 84.

5. For estimates of the numbers of Muslim slaves in the Mediterranean see Nabil Matar, 'Piracy and Captivity in the Early Modern Mediterranean: The Perspective from Barbary' in Claire Jowitt (ed.), *Pirates? The*

Politics of Plunder, 1550–1650, p. 57; see also Salvatore Bono, *Les Corsairs en Méditerranée*, pp. 215–16. On Malta see Humphrey J. Fisher, *Slavery in the History of Muslim Black Africa*, p. 31.

6. For Muslim galley slaves see Gillian Weiss, 'Ransoming "Turks" from France's Royal Galleys', *African Economic History*, Vol. 42 (2014), pp. 37–57, accessed at http://www.jstor.org/stable/44329666. For an absorbing discussion of 'Esclaves Turcs in European Sculpture' see Matar, *Mediterranean Captivity*, pp. 233–52.

7. Roger Crowley, *Empires of the Sea: The Final Battle for the Mediterranean, 1521–1580* pp. 123–4.

8. See Salvatore Bono, 'Slave Histories and Memoirs in the Mediterranean World' in Maria Fusaro, Colin Heywood and Mohamed-Salah Omri (eds), *Trade and Cultural Exchange in the Early Modern Mediterranean: Braudel's Maritime Legacy*, p. 105, accessed at https://www.academia.edu/28681791/pdf_228_Slaves_Histories_and_Memoirs_in_the_Mediterranean_World_pdf. See also Daniel Hershenzon, "'[P] Ara Que Me Saque Cabesea Por Cabesa …": Exchanging Muslim and Christian Slaves across the Western Mediterranean', *African Economic History*, Vol. 42 (2014), pp. 11–36, accessed at http://www.jstor.org/stable/44329665. For a brief summary of recent research on this subject see Felicia Roşu, 'Muslim Slaves in Early Modern Europe: A Forgotten History of Slavery', Leiden Islam blog, accessed at https://www.leidenislamblog.nl/articles/muslim-slaves-in-early-modern-europe-a-forgotten-history-of-slavery. For his figures on major corsair slave-taking activity between 1516–1798 and an estimated overall total see Robert C. Davis, *Christian Slaves, Muslim Masters: White Slavery in the Mediterranean, The Barbary Coast, and Italy, 1500–1800*, pp. xiv–xvi, p. 23. For another critique of Davis's methodology see M'Hamed Oualdi, 'D'Europe et d'Orient, les approches de l'esclavage des Chrétiens en terres d'Islam', *Annales. Histoires, Sciences Sociales*, 63e année (4), pp. 829–43, accessed at https://shs.cairn.info/revue-annales-2008-4-page-829?lang=fr.

9. See Daniel J. Viktus and Nabil Matar (eds), *Piracy, Slavery, and Redemption: Barbary Captivity Narratives from Early Modern England*, pp. 9–11. See also Jerry Brotton, *This Orient Isle: Elizabethan England and the Islamic World*.

10. See William Zammit, *Slavery, Treason and Blood: The 1749 Plot of the Slaves in Malta*.

11. Mario Klarer (ed.), *Piracy and Captivity in the Mediterranean 1550–1810*, p. 14.

12. Paul Baepler, 'The Barbary Captivity Narrative in American Culture', *Early American Literature*, Vol. 39, No. 2 (2004), pp. 217–46, accessed at http://www.jstor.org/stable/25057349.

13. Samuel Pepys, *The Diary of Samuel Pepys*, 8 February 1661, accessed online at https://www.pepysdiary.com/diary/1661/02/08/.

14. Hugh Bicheno, *Crescent and Cross: The Battle of Lepanto 1571*, p. 277.

15. Virginia Lunsford-Poe, *Piracy and Privateering in Golden Age Netherlands*, p. 233.

16. Tinniswood, *Pirates of Barbary*, p. 34.

17. Fernand Braudel, *The Mediterranean and the Mediterranean World in the Age of Philip II*, Vol. 2, p. 885; Davis, *Christian Slaves, Muslim Masters*, p. 8. See also Mario Klarer (ed.), *Barbary Captives: An Anthology of Early Modern Slave Memoirs by Europeans in Africa*.

18. Joseph Morgan, *A Complete History of Algiers*, pp. 670–71.

19. For a brief summary of Barbary corsairing against England see Ben Johnson, 'Barbary Pirates and English Slaves', Historic UK, accessed at https://www.historic-uk.com/HistoryUK/HistoryofEngland/Barbary-Pirates-English-Slaves/; Diego de Haëdo cited in Davis, *Christian Slaves, Muslim Masters*, p. 35.

20. For a fascinating discussion of the raid and its lasting effect on the Icelandic psyche see Thorsteinn Helgason, 'Historical Narrative as Collective Therapy: The Case of the Turkish Raid in Iceland', *Scandinavian Journal of History*, Vol. 22, No. 4 (1997), pp. 275–89, accessed at https://www.academia.edu/36985804/Historical_narrative_as_collective_therapy_The_case_of_the_Turkish_raid_in_Iceland.

21. See Adam Nichols, 'The Barbary Corsair Raid on Iceland, 1627', 20 February 2017, accessed at https://jddavies.com/2017/02/20/the-barbary-corsair-raid-on-iceland-1627/. For more on Egilsson's remarkable story see Karl Smari Hreinsson and Adam Nichols (trans.), *The Travels of Reverend Olafur Egilsson: The Story of the Barbary Corsair Raid on Iceland in 1627*, p. 17.

22. For an important challenge to Davis's methodology see Nabil Matar, *British Captives from the Mediterranean to the Atlantic 1563–1760*, pp. 8–10, pp. 33–4.

23. For more on this extraordinary Dutchwoman see Maria ter Meteelen, 'Miraculous and Remarkable Events of Twelve Years of Slavery' in Klarer, *Barbary Captives*, pp. 255–79. See also Judith E. Tucker, 'She Would Rather Perish: Piracy and Gendered Violence in the Mediterranean', *Journal of Middle East Women's Studies*, Vol. 10, No. 3 (2014), pp. 19–20, accessed at https://www.jstor.org/stable/10.2979/jmiddeastwomstud.10.3.8.

24. See Klarer, *Barbary Captives*, pp. 357–68.

25. Thomas Pellow, *The Adventures of Thomas Pellow, of Penryn, Mariner, Three and Twenty Years in Captivity among the Moors*, p. 54. For the following passages see p. 196, p. 327, p. 78, p. 75, p. 329. See also Giles Milton, *White Gold: The Extraordinary Story of Thomas Pellow and North Africa's One Million European Slaves*.

26. Milton, *White Gold*, p. 78.

27. The following passages are taken from Robert Daborne, *A Christian Turn'd Turk: Or, The Tragicall Lives and Deaths of the two Famous Pirates, Ward and Dansiker*, accessed at https://crrs.ca/wp-content/uploads/2016/02/A-Christian-turnd-turk-short-scenes.pdf.

28. Nabil Matar, *Turks, Moors and Englishmen in the Age of Discovery*, p. 61.

29. 'Venice: November 1607' in Horatio F. Brown (ed.), *Calendar of State Papers Relating to English Affairs in the Archives of Venice, Volume 11, 1607–1610* (London, 1904), pp. 53–69, *British History Online*, accessed at http://www.british-history.ac.uk/cal-state-papers/venice/vol11/pp53-69. See also 'Venice: June 1608' in ibid., pp. 137–43, *British History Online*, accessed at http://www.british-history.ac.uk/cal-state-papers/venice/vol11/pp137-143.

30. Matar, *Turks, Moors and Englishmen*, pp. 61–2.

31. William Lithgow, *The Totall Discourse of The Rare Adventures & Painefull Peregrinations of long Nineteene Yeares Travayles from Scotland to the most famous Kingdomes in Europe, Asia and Affrica* (1906 reprint of 1632 original), p. 349.

32. Nabil Matar, *Europe Through Arab Eyes, 1578–1727* (New York, 2009), p. 41.

33. Matar, *Mediterranean Captivity*. For more on Al Qaysi see pp. 44–50; for Abd al Nabi Suleyman see pp. 100–101; for Ahmad ibn Mahdi al Ghazzal see pp. 193–206.

34. Cited in ibid., p. 232.

8 – THE UNITED STATES GOES TO WAR

1. Sumner, *White Slavery in the Barbary States*, p. 53.

2. John Foss, *A journal, of the captivity and sufferings of John Foss; several years a prisoner at Algiers: together with some account of the treatment of Christian slaves when sick, and observations of the manners and customs of the Algerines*, p. 17. For a critique of Foss's account and the captivity genre more widely see Saad Boulahnane, 'Barbary Mahometans in Early American Propaganda: A Critical Analysis of John Foss's Captivity Account', *AWEJ for Translation & Literary Studies*, Vol. 2,

No. 1 (February 2018), accessed at https://papers.ssrn.com/sol3/papers.cfm?abstract_id=3127190.

3. 'From Thomas Jefferson to Horatio Gates, 13 December 1784', *Founders Online*, National Archives, accessed at https://founders.archives.gov/documents/Jefferson/01-07-02-0411.

4. 'From John Adams to Thomas Jefferson, 17 February 1786', *Founders Online*, National Archives, accessed at https://founders.archives.gov/documents/Adams/06-18-02-0083.

5. See James Parton, *Life of Thomas Jefferson: Third President of the United States*, p. 299; see also Joseph Wheelan, *Jefferson's War: America's First War on Terror, 1801–1805*, p. 41.

6. Paul Baepler (ed.), *White Slaves, African Masters: An Anthology of American Barbary Captivity Narratives*, pp. 71–2.

7. Circular from James L. Cathcart to Agents and Consuls of the United States, 15 May 1801, *Naval Documents Related to the United States with the Barbary Powers*, Washington, US Govt. Print. Off., 1939–44, Vol. 1 pp. 454–5, accessed at https://babel.hathitrust.org/cgi/pt?id=uva.x004116176&view=1up&seq=508&skin=2021.

8. See CPI Inflation calculator, https://www.officialdata.org/.

9. 'To John Adams from Yusuf Karamanli, 25 May 1800', translated extract from a letter of the bashaw of Tripoli to the president of the United States, 25 May 1800, *Founders Online*, National Archives, accessed at https://founders.archives.gov/?q=Author%3A%22Karamanli%2C%20Yusuf%22&s=1111311111&r=1.

10. On the size of Tripoli's corsair fleet at the dawn of the nineteenth century see Ronald Bruce St John, *Libya: From Colony to Independence*, p. 36. For Yusuf's boasting see Spencer C. Tucker (ed.), *The Encyclopedia of the Wars of the Early American Republic, 1783–1812: A Political, Social and Military History*, p. 433.

11. Wheelan, *Jefferson's War*, p. 70. See also Ian W. Toll, *Six Frigates: The Epic History of the Founding of the U.S. Navy*.

12. Wheelan, *Jefferson's War*, p. 175.

13. For the American accounts of their captivity in Tripoli see John Wright, *Travellers in Turkish Libya 1551–1911*, pp. 68–71.

14. Joshua London, *Victory in Tripoli: How America's War with the Barbary Pirates Established the U.S. Navy and Shaped a Nation*, p. 165; Frank Lambert, *The Barbary Wars: American Independence in the Atlantic World*, p. 144.

15. Tucker, *The Encyclopedia of the Wars of the Early American Republic*, p. 433; Alexander Slidell Mackenzie, *Life of Stephen Decatur, a Commodore in the Navy of the United States*, p. 122.

16. Mordecai Manuel Noah, *Travels in England, France, Spain, and the Barbary States in the Years 1813–14 and 15*, p. 144.

17. 'From James Madison to the Dey of Algiers, 21 August 1816', *Founders Online*, National Archives, accessed at https://founders.archives.gov/documents/Madison/03-11-02-0323.

18. Edwin John Brett, *Brett's Illustrated Naval History of Great Britain: From the Earliest Period to the Present Time*, pp. 315–16.

19. Thomas Otte, 'Slavery in the Middle East', 'History Reclaimed' webinar, 3 February 2023, accessed at https://historyreclaimed.co.uk/slavery-in-the-middle-east/?mc_cid=16fd974053&mc_eid=36abb8b3c7.

20. John Wright, *Libya, Chad and the Central Sahara*, p. 62.

21. M. H. Cherif, 'Algeria, Tunisia and Libya: The Ottomans and their heirs' in B. A. Ogot (ed.), *General History of Africa*, Vol. 5, *Africa from the Sixteenth to the Eighteenth Century*, p. 260.

22. James McDougall, 'Savage Wars? Codes of Violence in Algeria, 1830s–1990s', *Third World Quarterly*, Vol. 26, No. 1 (2005), pp. 117–31, accessed at http://www.jstor.org/stable/3993767. See also Peter Lamborn Wilson, *Pirate Utopias: Moorish Corsairs and European Renegadoes*, p. 36.

23. Matar, *Mediterranean Captivity*, p. 256.

9 – THE SAHARAN SLAVE TRADE

1. Captain G. F. Lyon, *A Narrative of Travels in Northern Africa in the Years 1818–20*. On the condition of the slaves in the caravan see pp. 120–22; Murzuq slave market, pp. 267–9; on the slaves' resilience pp. 341–3.

2. John Wright, *The Trans-Saharan Slave Trade*, p. 60.

3. Ahmed Hassanein Bey, *The Lost Oases*, pp. 180–81.

4. See Marina Tolmacheva, 'Concubines on the Road: Ibn Battuta's Slave Women' in Matthew S. Gordon and Kathryn A. Hain (eds), *Concubines and Courtesans: Women and Slavery in Islamic History*, pp. 163–89.

5. Lyon, *A Narrative of Travels*, p. 78.

6. Said Hamdun and Noël King, *Ibn Battutah in Black Africa*, p. 59.

7. Ross Dunn, *The Adventures of Ibn Battuta*, p. 306.

8. For a summary of the statistics see Lovejoy, *Transformations in Slavery*, p. 25; for the 'vast exodus' see J. O. Hunwick, 'Black Slaves in the Mediterranean World: Introduction to a Neglected Aspect of the African Diaspora' in Elizabeth Savage, *The Human Commodity: Perspectives on the Trans-Saharan Slave Trade*, p. 5.

9. Wright, *The Trans-Saharan Slave Trade*, p. 85.

10. Quoted in Savage, *The Human Commodity*, pp. 3–4.

11. Rudolph T. Ware III, 'Slavery in Islamic Africa 1400–1800' in David Eltis and Stanley L. Engerman (eds), *The Cambridge History of World Slavery*, Vol. 3, *1420–1804*, p. 50.

12. Suzanne Miers and Igor Kopytoff (eds), *Slavery in Africa: Historical Perspectives*, p. 160. See also Alessio Iocchi, *Living Through Crisis by Lake Chad: Violence, Labor and Resources*.

13. See, for example, Joshua Hammer, *The Bad-Ass Librarians of Timbuktu and Their Race to Save the World's Most Precious Manuscripts* and Charlie English, *The Book Smugglers of Timbuktu: The Quest for This Storied City and the Race to Save Its Treasures*.

14. See Al Hasan ibn Muhammad al-Wazzan al-Fasi, *The History and Description of Africa*, modern translation taken from Professor Paul Brians, 'Leo Africanus: Description of Timbuktu from The Description of Africa (1526)', accessed at https://brians.wsu.edu/2016/11/04/leo-africanus-description-of-timbuktu-from-the-description-of-africa-1526/.

15. John Hunwick and Fatima Harrak (trans. and annot.), *Mira'j al Su'ud: Ahmad Baba's Replies on Slavery*, p. 27.

16. Cited in Ware, 'Slavery in Islamic Africa 1400–1800', p. 64.

17. See Camille Lefebvre, 'Hausa Diasporas and Slavery in Africa, the Atlantic, and the Muslim World', *Oxford Research Encyclopedias*, 22 March 2023, https://doi.org/10.1093/acrefore/9780190277734.013.917; Murray Last, 'The Sokoto Caliphate' in Peter Fibiger Bang, C. A. Bayly and Walter Scheidel (eds), *The Oxford World History of Empire*, Vol. 2, *The History of Empires* (2021), pp. 1082–110; Paul Lovejoy, *Slavery, Commerce and Production in the Sokoto Caliphate of West Africa*; Paul Lovejoy, *Slavery in the Global Diaspora of Africa*, p. 5; see also Roger B. Beck, 'Africa, the Ottoman Empire, and the New Imperialism 1800–1914' in Merry E. Wiesner-Hanks, Patricia Buckley Ebrey, Roger B. Beck, Jerry Davila, Clare Haru Crowston and John P. McKay (eds), *A History of World Societies: Combined Volume*, p. 1567.

18. For the story of Ali Eisambi Gazirmabe see Lefebvre, 'Hausa Diasporas and Slavery'; see also Richard Anderson and Henry B. Lovejoy, *Liberated Africans and the Abolition of the Slave Trade, 1807–1896*, p. 148. On the Ansante see Boniface Obichere, 'The Social Character of Slavery in Asante and Daomey', *Ufahamu: A Journal of African Studies*, Vol. 12, Issue 3 (1983), https://escholarship.org/uc/item/72k2n7m2; Badawi, *An African History of Africa*, p. 298, p. 336. On Dahomey see, for example, S. Daget, 'The Abolition of the Slave Trade' in J. F. Ade Ajayi (ed.), *General History of Africa VI, Africa in the Nineteenth Century until the 1880s*, p. 75.

19. Ware, 'Slavery in Islamic Africa 1400–1800', p. 55. See also Richard Brent Turner, 'African Muslim Slaves and Islam in Antebellum America' in Juliane Hammer and Omid Shafi (eds), *The Cambridge Companion to American Islam*, p. 31. For more on enslaved Muslims in the United States see also Sylviane A. Diouf, *Servants of Allah: African Muslims Enslaved in the Americas*.

20. See Terry Alford, *Prince among Slaves: The True Story of an African Prince Sold into Slavery in the American South*.

21. Turner, 'African Muslim Slaves and Islam in Antebellum America', pp. 39–40. See also The Library of Congress Omar ibn Said Collection, https://www.loc.gov/collections/omar-ibn-said-collection/about-this-collection/#text2.

22. See Al Hasan ibn Muhammad al-Wazzan al-Fasi, *The History and Description of Africa*, p. 825.

23. Alida Jay Boye and John Hunwick, *The Hidden Treasures of Timbuktu: Historic City of Islamic Africa*, p. 37.

24. For details of this absorbing correspondence see Bruce Hall and Yacine Daddo Addoun, 'The Arabic Letters of Ghadames Slaves in the Niger Bend, 1860–1900' in Alice Bellagamba, Sadra E. Greene and Martin A. Klein (eds), *African Voices on Slavery and the Slave Trade*, Vol. 1, *The Sources*, pp. 485–502.

25. Griga's powerful story was originally told by Fernand J. G. Mercadier in *L'Esclave de Timimoun* (1971). These extracts are taken from Hunwick and Powell, *The African Diaspora in the Mediterranean Lands of Islam*, pp. 199–215. On the foggara irrigation system see also Tayeb Otmane and Yaël Kouzmine, 'Timimoun, évolution et enjeux actuels d'une oasis Saharienne Algérienne', *Insaniyat*, 51–52 (2001), accessed at https://journals.openedition.org/insaniyat/12686.

26. See E. Ann McDougall, 'Salt, Saharans, and the Trans-Saharan Slave Trade' in Savage, *The Human Commodity*, pp. 61–4.

27. Ibid., p. 71.

28. Ibid., p. 74.

29. Yusufu Yunusa's interviews with Malam Isyaku and Malam Idrisu are extracted in Mohammed Bashir Salau, 'Slavery in Kano Emirate of Sokoto Caliphate as Recounted: Testimonies of Isyaku and Idrisu' in Bellagamba, Greene and Klein, *African Voices on Slavery and the Slave Trade*, pp. 88–104.

30. Dixon Denham, Hugh Clapperton, Walter Oudney and Abraham V. Salamé, *Narrative of Travels and Discoveries in Northern and Central Africa in the Years 1822, 1823, and 1824*, Vol. 1, p. 188.

31. Hunwick and Powell, *The African Diaspora in the Mediterranean Lands of Islam*, p. 67.

32. On Haj Ibrahim see James Richardson, *Travels in the Great Desert of Sahara*, Vol. 2, pp. 265–6. On Essnoussee see p. 364.

33. Cited in Justin Marozzi, *South from Barbary: Along the Slave Routes of the Libyan Sahara*, pp. 161–2.

34. See Wright, *The Trans-Saharan Slave Trade*, p. 73ff.

35. For his observations on slave-raiding see Heinrich Barth, *Travels and Discoveries in North and Central Africa*, Vol. 2, pp. 386–418.

36. Gustav Nachtigal, *Sahara and Sudan*, Vol. 1, p. 122.

37. Wright, *The Trans-Saharan Slave Trade*, p. 5.

38. Maha Marouan, 'Incomplete Forgetting: Race and Slavery in Morocco', *Islamic Africa*, Vol. 7, No. 2 (2016), pp. 267–71, accessed at https://www.jstor.org/stable/pdf/90017603.pdf?refreqid=excelsior%3Ac5086f774501 47a2714c4b97b484737c&ab_segments=0%2Fbasic_search_gsv2%2Fco ntrol&origin=&acceptTC=1.

39. Mohammed Ennaji, *Serving the Master: Slavery and Society in Nineteenth-Century Morocco*, pp. 2–6.

40. For the following section see Chouki El Hamel, *Black Morocco: A History of Slavery, Race and Islam*, pp. 297–307.

41. Richardson, *Travels in the Great Desert of Sahara*, Vol. 2, p. 312, p. 348; Johann Ludwig Burckhardt, *Travels in Nubia*, pp. 300–301.

42. Eve M. Troutt Powell, 'Slaves or Siblings? Abdallah al-Nadim's Dialogues about the Family' in Terence Walz and Kenneth M. Cuno (eds), *Race and Slavery in the Middle East: Histories of Trans-Saharan Africans in Nineteenth-Century Egypt, Sudan, and the Ottoman Mediterranean*, p. 220.

10 – THE OTTOMANS:
A LORDSHIP OF SLAVES

1. Ehud Toledano, 'Enslavement in the Ottoman Empire in the Early Modern Period' in David Eltis and Stanley L. Engerman (eds), *The Cambridge History of World Slavery*, Vol. 3, *AD 1420–AD 1804*, p. 25.

2. Toledano, *Slavery and Abolition*, p. 7.

3. Loc. cit.

4. See Ralph Austen, 'The Mediterranean Islamic Slave Trade out of Africa: A Tentative Census', *Slavery & Abolition*, Vol. 13, Issue 1 (1992), p. 226; Toledano, *Slavery and Abolition*, p. 8.

5. Alexander Mikaberidze (ed.), *Atrocities, Massacres, and War Crimes: An Encyclopedia*, Vol. 2, p. 741; Erdem, *Slavery in the Ottoman Empire and Its Demise*, p. 26, p. 96.

6. Interview with author, Istanbul, 6 September 2022. For more on Ibrahim Edhem Pasha see Edhem Eldem, 'The Story of the Little Greek Boy Who Became a Powerful Pasha: Myth and Reality in the Life of İbrahim Edhem Pasha, c. 1818–1893', Athens Dialogues, Stories and Histories, Period Two, 2010, accessed at http://athensdialogues.chs.harvard.edu/cgi-bin/WebObjects/athensdialogues.woa/wa/dist?dis=51.

7. Interview with author, 4 November 2022.

8. See Baki Tezcan, 'Dispelling the Darkness of the Halberdier's Treatise: A Comparative Look at Black Africans in Ottoman Letters in the Early Modern Period' in Helga Anetshofer, Erdem Çıpa, and Hakan Karateke (eds), *Disliking Others: Alterophobia in Pre-Modern Ottoman Lands* (Boston, 2018), pp. 43–74.

9. Toledano, *As if Silent and Absent*.

10. Halil İnalcik, *The Ottoman Empire, The Classical Age, 1300–1600*, p. 77.

11. Erdem, *Slavery in the Ottoman Empire and Its Demise*, p. 19.

12. Konstantin Mihailović, ed. Zeljko Zidaric, *Memoirs of a Janissary*, p. 5, accessed at https://www.academia.edu/50960067/Memoirs_of_a_Janissary_or_T%C3%BCrkish_Chronicle.

13. Halil İnalcik, 'Servile Labour in the Ottoman Empire' in Abraham Ascher et al. (eds), *The Mutual Effects of the Islamic and Judeo-Christian Worlds: The East European Patterns*, pp. 36–7.

14. İnalcik, *Ottoman Empire*, pp. 77–8; Philip Mansel, *Constantinople: City of the World's Desire*, p. 18.

15. Toledano, *Slavery and Abolition in the Ottoman Middle East*, p. 27.

16. See Lajos Tardy, *Beyond the Ottoman Empire: 14th–16th Century Hungarian Diplomacy in the East*, pp. 142–7.

17. Walter Leitsch, '1683: The Siege of Vienna', *History Today*, Vol. 33, Issue 7 (July 1983). The numbers of captives are reported in Erdem, *Slavery in the Ottoman Empire and Its Demise*, p. 30.

18. On the Janissaries' role in the 1453 conquest of Constantinople see Kritovoulos, *History of Mehmed the Conqueror*, pp. 68–9; on the Janissaries see Gábor Ágoston, 'Firearms and Military Adaptation: The Ottomans and the European Military Revolution, 1450–1800', *Journal of World History*, Vol. 25, No. 1 (2014), pp. 85–124, accessed at http://www.jstor.org/stable/43286061. See also Ágoston, 'Janissaries' in Kate Fleet, Gudrun Krämer, Denis Matringe, John Nawas and

Everett K. Rowson (eds), *Encyclopaedia of Islam – Three*, Vol. 2, pp. 146–50.

19. Sir Paul Rycaut, *The Present State of The Ottoman Empire*, p. 25, p. 42; Mansel, *Constantinople*, p. 18.

20. Erdem, *Slavery in the Ottoman Empire and Its Demise*, p. 2, p. 6.

21. Daniel Goffman, *The Ottoman Empire and Early Modern Europe*, p. 55.

22. I. Metin Kunt, *The Sultan's Servants: The Transformation of Ottoman Provincial Government 1550–1650*, p. 32; Rhoads Murphey, *Ottoman Warfare 1500–1700*, p. 223.

23. Finkel, *Osman's Dream*, p. 435.

24. For a discussion on the legality and practice of slaves owning property in the Ottoman Empire see Colin Imber, *Ebu's-su'ud: The Islamic Legal Tradition*, p. 79.

25. For this section on illegal Ottoman enslavement see Erdem, *Slavery in the Ottoman Empire and Its Demise*, pp. 20–26.

26. Imber, *Ebu's-su'ud*, p. 88.

27. Quoted in Anthony A. Lee, 'Enslaved African Women in Nineteenth-Century Iran: The Life of Fezzeh Khanom of Shiraz', *Iranian Studies*, Vol. 45, No. 3 (May 2012), p. 422, accessed at https://www.jstor.org/stable/41445217.

28. Ibid., pp. 24–5.

29. Firat Yasa, 'Between Life and Death: Slaves and Violence in Crimean Society in the Last Quarter of 17th Century', Selçuk University Journal of Studies Turcology, Vol. 47 (2019), pp. 433–43, accessed at http://sutad.selcuk.edu.tr/sutad/article/view/1486/976; *The Cambridge World History of Slavery*, Vol. 3, *AD 1420–AD 1804*, p. 145.

30. See Eizo Matsuki, 'The Crimean Tatars and their Russian-Captive Slaves: An Aspect of Muscovite-Crimean Relations in the 16th and 17th Centuries', *The Mediterranean World*, Vol. 28 (2006), pp. 171–82. See also Mikhail Kizilov, 'Slave Trade in the Early Modern Crimea from the Perspective of Christian, Muslim, and Jewish Sources', *Journal of Early Modern History*, Vol. 11, No. 1–2 (2007), pp. 1–31, accessed at https://www.researchgate.net/publication/233710745_Slave_Trade_in_the_Early_Modern_Crimea_From_the_Perspective_of_Christian_Muslim_and_Jewish_Sources; Brian Davies, *Warfare, State and Society on the Black Sea Steppe, 1500–1700*, pp. 24–5; İnalcik, *Ottoman Empire*, p. 131.

31. See Dariusz Kołodziejczyk, 'Slave Hunting and Slave Redemption as a Business Enterprise: The Northern Black Sea Region in the Sixteenth to Seventeenth Centuries', *Oriente Moderno*, Vol. 25 (86), No. 1 (2006), pp. 149–59, accessed at http://www.jstor.org/stable/25818051.

32. Ogier Ghiselin de Busbecq, *The Life and Letters of Ogier Ghiselin de Busbecq*, Vol. 1, p. 162.

33. See Alan Fisher, 'The Ottoman Crimea in the Mid-Seventeenth Century: Some Problems and Preliminary Considerations', *Harvard Ukrainian Studies*, Vol. 3/4, Part 1 (1979–1980), pp. 215–26, accessed at https://www.jstor.org/stable/41035828.

34. Kizilov, 'Slave Trade in the Early Modern Crimea', pp. 23–4.

35. Ibid., p. 10.

36. Ibid., p. 14.

37. Charles King, *The Ghost of Freedom: A History of the Caucasus*, p.16; figures from 'The Circassian Genocide', Unrepresented Nations and Peoples Organisation, 14 December 2004, accessed at https://unpo.org/article/1639, cited in Walter Richmond, *The Circassian Genocide*, p. 2. See also Ceyda Karamursel, *'In the Age of Freedom, in the Name of Justice': Slaves, Slaveholders and the State in the Late Ottoman Empire and Early Turkish Republic, 1857–1933*, Publicly Accessible Penn dissertations, 2015, pp. 62–3, accessed at https://repository.upenn.edu/edissertations/1803.

38. Ibn Battuta, *The Travels of Ibn Battuta*, Vol. 2 (1961), pp. 425–6.

39. See Leslie Peirce, *The Imperial Harem: Women and Sovereignty in the Ottoman Empire*, pp. 36–7; see Ibn Battuta, *The Travels of Ibn Battuta*, Vol. 2, pp. 442–9.

40. Peirce, *The Imperial Harem*, p. 37.

41. Ibid., p. 42, pp. 120–21.

42. Ibid., p. 61.

43. Ibid., p. 63.

44. See 'Newly published letter reveals Hürrem Sultan's love for Süleyman the Magnificent', *Daily Sabah*, 15 February 2019, accessed at https://www.dailysabah.com/history/2019/02/15/newly-published-letter-reveals-hurrem-sultans-love-for-suleyman-the-magnificent; see also Simon Sebag Montefiore, *Written in History: Letters that Changed the World*, p. 29 (ebook).

45. For more on Shemsigul's extraordinary story see Ehud Toledano, 'Shemsigul: A Circassian Slave in Mid-Nineteenth-Century Cairo' in Edmund Burke III (ed.), *Struggle and Survival in the Modern Middle East*, pp. 59–74.

46. Gabriel Baer, 'Slavery in Nineteenth Century Egypt', *The Journal of African History*, Vol. 8, No. 3 (1967), p. 428, accessed at http://www.jstor.org/stable/179829.

47. The following extracts are taken from Leyla Hanim, *The Imperial Harem of the Sultans: Daily Life at the Çiragan Palace During the 19th Century*.

48. Ibid., pp. 65–6.
49. Ibid., pp. 70–71, p. 77.

11 – ABOLITION I: THE CENTRE

1. Thomas Clarkson, *Speech of Thomas Clarkson, Esq.: As Originally Pre-pared by Him in Writing, and Intended to Have Been Delivered at the Opening of the General Anti-Slavery Convention : Distinguishing Those Passages Which Were Omitted, but Which Are Now Published at Mr. Clark-son's Request*, 1840, accessed at https://jstor.org/stable/60227906; Benjamin Robert Haydon, *Description of Haydon's Picture of the great meeting of Delegates at the Freemasons' Tavern, June 1840, for the aboli-tion of Slavery and the Slave Trade*, p. 10.
2. For Bowring's intervention see Erdem, *Slavery in the Ottoman Empire and Its Demise*, pp. 69–70.
3. Ibid., p. 71; Alison Frank, 'The Children of the Desert and the Laws of the Sea: Austria, Great Britain, the Ottoman Empire, and the Mediterra-nean Slave Trade in the Nineteenth Century', *The American Historical Review*, Vol. 117, No. 2 (April 2012), p. 419, accessed at https://www.jstor.org/stable/23310742.
4. Toledano, *Slavery and Abolition in the Ottoman Middle East*, pp. 116–17.
5. Ehud R. Toledano, 'Abolition and Anti-slavery in the Ottoman Empire: A Case to Answer?' in W. Mulligan and M. Bric (eds), *A Global History of Anti-slavery Politics in the Nineteenth Century*, p. 120.
6. Lewis, *Race and Slavery in the Middle East*, p. 78.
7. Wilfrid Scawen Blunt, *Secret History of the English Occupation of Egypt: Being a Personal Narrative of Events*, p. 184.
8. Dahlia El-Tayeb Gubara, 'Al-Azhar and the Orders of Knowledge', PhD dissertation, p. 192, accessed at https://doi.org/10.7916/D8Z036C8; pri-vate comments to the author, February 2025.
9. William Gervase Clarence-Smith, *Islam and the Abolition of Slavery*, pp. 16–21. Clarence-Smith's book provides a broad-ranging summary of abolition across the Muslim world.
10. Madeline C. Zilfi, *Women and Slavery in the Late Ottoman Empire*, p. 97.
11. Erdem, *Slavery in the Ottoman Empire and Its Demise*, p. 95; Zilfi, *Women and Slavery in the Late Ottoman Empire*, pp. 216–17.
12. Candan Badem, 'The Ottoman Crimean War (1853–1856)' in Suraiya Faroqhi and Halil İnalcik (eds), *The Ottoman Empire and its Heritage: Politics, Society and Economy*, p. 350.

13. Erdem, *Slavery in the Ottoman Empire and Its Demise*, pp. 102–3.

14. Frank, 'The Children of the Desert and the Laws of the Sea', p. 424.

15. For accounts of the 1855–6 rebellion see Michael Christopher Low, *The Mechanics of Mecca: The Technopolitics of the Late Ottoman Hijaz and the Colonial Hajj*, pp. 98–102, accessed at https://doi.org/10.7916/D8W95880; William Ochsenwald, 'Muslim-European Conflict in the Hijaz: The Slave Trade Controversy, 1840–1895', *Middle Eastern Studies*, Vol. 16, No. 1 (1980), pp. 115–26, accessed at http://www.jstor.org/stable/4282774.

16. John Freely, *Inside the Seraglio: Private Lives of the Sultans in Istanbul*, p. 273.

17. The following passage on Pertevniyal is based on Karamursel, '*In the Age of Freedom, in the Name of Justice*', pp. 116–30.

18. Frank, 'The Children of the Desert and the Laws of the Sea', p. 416.

19. 'Instructions for the guidance of Her Majesty's Naval Officers employed in the suppression of the Slave Trade', p. 7, Royal Navy, 1844, accessed at https://www.google.co.uk/books/edition/Instructions_for_the_guidance_of_Her_Maj/OEZcAAAAcAAJ?hl=en&gbpv=1.

20. For the Cumberbatch and Druscovich episode see Frank, 'The Children of the Desert and the Laws of the Sea', pp. 422–7.

21. Quoted in Toledano, *Slavery and Abolition in the Ottoman Middle East*, p. 33; Frank, 'The Children of the Desert and the Laws of the Sea', p. 423.

22. Alexis Heraclides and Ada Dialla, 'Chapter 8: The Bulgarian Atrocities: A Bird's Eye View of Intervention with Emphasis on Britain, 1875–78' in *Humanitarian Intervention in the Long Nineteenth Century: Setting the Precedent*, pp. 150–51, accessed at https://www.jstor.org/stable/pdf/j.ctt-1mf71b8.13.pdf?acceptTC=true&coverpage=false.

23. Malcolm MacColl, *The Eastern Question: Its Facts and Fallacies*, p. 412; William Ewart Gladstone, *Bulgarian Horrors and the Question of the East*, pp. 12–13. See also R. Quinault, 'Gladstone and Slavery', *The Historical Journal*, Vol. 52, No. 2 (June 2009), pp. 363–83.

24. Douglas Scott Brookes (trans. and ed.), *The Concubine, the Princess and the Teacher: Voices from the Ottoman Harem*, p. 41.

25. For Ali Haydar Midhat's version of the original speech drafted for Sultan Abdul Hamid II's accession by his father see Ali Haydar Midhat, *The Life of Midhat Pasha: A Record of His Services, Political Reforms, Banishment, and Judicial Murder*, pp. 106–9.

26. Erdem, *Slavery in the Ottoman Empire and Its Demise*, pp. 126–8.

27. See Michael Ferguson, 'Abolitionism and the African Slave Trade in the Ottoman Empire (1857–1922)' in Gwyn Campbell and Alessandro

Stanziani (eds), *The Palgrave Handbook of Bondage and Human Rights in Africa and Asia*, p. 220.

28. Finkel, *Osman's Dream*, pp. 489–91.

29. See Zilfi, *Women and Slavery in the Late Ottoman Empire*, pp. 229–30; see also Ali Haydar Midhat, *The Life of Midhat Pasha*, p. 112.

30. See Ferguson, 'Abolitionism and the African Slave Trade', p. 218; Erdem, *Slavery in the Ottoman Empire and Its Demise*, pp. 131–2.

31. Peters, *Mecca*, p. 338.

32. 'Slaves sold to the Turk', *New York Times*, 28 March 1886, accessed at https://timesmachine.nytimes.com/timesmachine/1886/03/28/10630 0694.pdf.

33. Clarence-Smith, *Islam and the Abolition of Slavery*, p. 107; Michael Ferguson and Ehud Toledano, 'Ottoman Slavery and Abolition in the Nineteenth Century' in *The Cambridge History of World Slavery*, Vol. 4, *AD 1804–AD 2016*, p. 210.

34. Karamursel, '*In the Age of Freedom, in the Name of Justice*', pp. 99–103.

35. The following section is based on ibid., pp. 108–15.

36. McCullagh, *The Fall of Abd-ul-Hamid*, p. 275.

37. Erdem, *Slavery in the Ottoman Empire and Its Demise*, p. 150; Toledano, 'Abolition and Anti-slavery in the Ottoman Empire', p. 126.

38. Donald E. Miller and Lorna Touryan Miller, *Survivors: An Oral History of the Armenian Genocide*, p. 21.

39. 'Report by a resident of Syria on the condition of Armenian deportees, November 27, 1916', *Foreign Office 371/2783/24258*, accessed at https://www.armenian-genocide.org/br-11-27-16-text.html; Taner Akcam, *The Young Turks' Crime Against Humanity: The Armenian Genocide and Ethnic Cleansing in the Ottoman Empire*, pp. 313–14.

40. See, for instance, Fatma Muge Gocek, *Denial of Violence: Ottoman Past, Turkish Present and Collective Violence Against the Armenians, 1789–2009*, p. 2.

41. See Martin Kramer, *Islam Assembled: The Advent of the Muslim Congresses*, p. 175.

42. Mustafa Kemal Atatürk, *The Speech*, p. 30 (ebook).

43. Murat Ergin, '"Is the Turk a White Man?" Towards a Theoretical Framework for Race in the Making of Turkishness', *Middle Eastern Studies*, Vol. 44, No. 6 (November 2008), p. 837, accessed at https://www.jstor.org/stable/40262624. See Karamursel, '*In the Age of Freedom, in the Name of Justice*', p. 248.

44. Eve M. Troutt Powell, *Tell This in My Memory: Stories of Enslavement from Egypt, Sudan and the Ottoman Empire*, pp. 144–5.

45. Ferguson, 'Abolitionism and the African Slave Trade', p. 226. For awareness-raising initiatives see, for example, 'The coffee reading: Tales of the Afro Turkish diaspora', visual podcast, https://www.foam.org/articles/the-coffee-reading-tales-of-the-afro-turkish-diaspora.

46. Alev Scott, 'The Turks who lost their language', BBC Travel, 8 September 2016, accessed at https://www.bbc.com/travel/article/20160829-turkeys-little-known-africans.

47. Toledano, *As if Silent and Absent*, p. 51. See also Michael Ferguson and Aysegul Kayagil, 'Mustafa Olpak obituary', *Guardian*, 11 November 2016, accessed at https://www.theguardian.com/world/2016/nov/11/mustafa-olpak-obituary.

12 − ABOLITION II: AWAY FROM THE CENTRE

1. Alice Moore-Harell, 'Slave Trade in the Sudan in the Nineteenth Century and Its Suppression in the Years 1877-80', *Middle Eastern Studies*, Vol. 34, No. 2 (April 1998), p. 121, p. 124, accessed at https://www.jstor.org/stable/4283940.

2. For early examples of Arab slave-raiding in Sudan see Yusuf Fadl Hasan, 'Some Aspects of the Arab Slave Trade from the Sudan 7th–19th Century', *Sudan Notes and Records*, Vol. 58 (1977), p. 89, accessed at http://www.jstor.org/stable/44947358; see also Douglas H. Johnson, *The Root Causes of Sudan's Civil Wars: Old Wars and New Wars*, p. 2.

3. Burckhardt, *Travels in Nubia*, p. 335.

4. Translated from Eugène Daumas, *Le Grand Désert, ou Itinéraire d'une Caravane du Sahara au Pays des Nègres* (Paris, 1848), pp. 265–7.

5. Robert G. Colquhoun to Earl Russell, 17 August 1863, *British and Foreign State Papers 1863–1864*, Vol. 54, 1869, pp. 458–9.

6. Thomas F. Reade to Lord Stanley, 9 August 1867, *British and Foreign State Papers 1867–1868*, Vol. 58, 1873, p. 949.

7. Jay Spaulding, 'Slavery, Land Tenure and Social Class in the Northern Turkish Sudan', *The International Journal of African Historical Studies*, Vol. 15, No. 1 (1982), note 29, p. 8, accessed at https://doi.org/10.2307/218446.

8. For a discussion of this subject see G. P. Makris, 'Slavery, Possession and History: The Construction of the Self among Slave Descendants in the Sudan', *Africa: Journal of the International African Institute*, Vol. 66, No. 2 (1996), pp. 159–82, accessed at https://doi.org/10.2307/1161315. See also William Fant, 'Slavery and the Search for Belonging in Modern Sudan', *History in the Making*, Vol. 2, Article 4 (2009), accessed at https://scholarworks.lib.csusb.edu/history-in-the-making/vol2/iss1/4.

9. Burckhardt, *Travels in Nubia*, pp. 332–3.

10. P. M. Holt and M. W. Daly, *A History of the Sudan: From the Coming of Islam to the Present Day*, p. 39; Khaled Fahmy, *All the Pasha's Men: Mehmed Ali, His Army and the Making of Modern Egypt*, p. 87.

11. Henry Dodwell, *The Founder of Modern Egypt: A Study of Muhammad Ali*, pp. 64–5; Moore-Harell, 'Slave Trade in the Sudan', p. 115.

12. R. W. Beachey, 'The East African Ivory Trade in the Nineteenth Century', *The Journal of African History*, Vol. 8, No. 2 (1967), p. 288, accessed at http://www.jstor.org/stable/179483. See also Johnson, *The Root Causes of Sudan's Civil Wars*, p. 5.

13. Moore-Harell, 'Slave Trade in the Sudan', p. 115.

14. Burckhardt, *Travels in Nubia*, pp. 324–5.

15. Alice Moore-Harell, *Gordon and the Sudan: Prologue to the Mahdiyya, 1877–1880*, p. 129.

16. For an insight into the sparse and contradictory evidence on the fluctuating prices of slaves see Spaulding, 'Slavery, Land Tenure and Social Class', pp. 10–11; Moore-Harell, 'Slave Trade in the Sudan', p. 124.

17. Spaulding, 'Slavery, Land Tenure and Social Class', p. 12.

18. Elizabeth Isichei, *A History of African Societies to 1870*, p. 317.

19. Babikr Bedri, *The Memoirs of Babikr Bedri*, pp. 117–18.

20. 'Viewpoint from Sudan – where black people are called slaves', BBC News, 26 July 2020, accessed at https://www.bbc.co.uk/news/world-africa-53147864.

21. Judith Schaefer, 'Jihad in 19th Century Sudan, Part II', *Smithsonian Libraries Unbound*, 3 March 2017, accessed at https://blog.library.si.edu/blog/2017/03/03/jihad-19th-century-sudan-part-ii/#.ZABoEezPokh; Henry Cecil Jackson, *Black Ivory and White, or The Story of El Zubeir Pasha, Slaver and Sultan, as told by Himself*, p. 109.

22. 'Deim Zubeir – Slave route site', UNESCO website, accessed at https://whc.unesco.org/en/tentativelists/6275/; 'Decolonise and rename' streets of Uganda and Sudan, activists urge', *Guardian*, 1 July 2020, accessed at https://www.theguardian.com/global-development/2020/jul/01/decolonise-and-rename-streets-of-uganda-and-sudan-activists-urge. Mahmoud Suleiman, 'A Slave Trader Al-Zubair Pasha cannot be a Representative of the Sudanese People's Streets', *Sudan Jem*, 30 August 2021, accessed at https://sudanjem.com/2021/08/a-slave-trader-al-zubair-pasha-cannot-be-a-representative-of-the-sudanese-peoples-streets/.

23. Reda Mowafi, *Slavery, Slave Trade, and Abolition Attempts in Egypt and the Sudan, 1820–1882*, p. 61.

24. Samuel White Baker, *In the Heart of Africa*, p. 155.

25. Robert O. Collins, *The Southern Sudan in Historical Perspective*, p. 20.

26. Lytton Strachey, *Eminent Victorians: The Illustrated Edition*, p. 147.

27. See Lawrence Mire, 'Al-Zubayr Pasha and the Zariba-Based Slave Trade in the Bahr al-Ghazal 1855–1879' in John Ralph Willis, *Slaves and Slavery in Muslim Africa*, Vol. 2, *The Servile Estate*, p. 101; see also Jeanie Lang, *The Story of General Gordon*, p. 74 (London, 1906).

28. Henry William Gordon, *Events in the Life of Charles George Gordon: from its beginning to its end* (London, 1886), p. 329; Lord Ribblesdale, 'Conversations with Zobeir Pasha at Gibraltar', *Nineteenth Century*, Vol. 63 (1908), p. 941, accessed online at https://books.google.com.ua/books?redir_esc=y&id=OjhaAAAAYAAJ&q=sacred#v=snippet&q=%22sacred%20and%20as%22&f=false.

29. Christopher de Bellaigue, *The Islamic Enlightenment: The Modern Struggle Between Faith and Reason*, p. 193.

30. Lucie Duff Gordon, letter to Mrs Austin, 9 January 1865, in *Lady Duff Gordon's Letters from Egypt*, accessed online at https://www.gutenberg.org/files/17816/17816-h/17816-h.htm.

31. For a study of slavery in nineteenth-century Egypt, see Mohammed Saleh, 'Trade, Slavery, and State Coercion of Labor: Egypt during the First Globalization Era', *The Journal of Economic History*, Vol. 84, No. 4 (2024), pp. 1107–41, accessed at https://eprints.lse.ac.uk/121130/3/trade-slavery-and-state-coercion-of-labor-egypt-during-the-first-globalization-era.pdf; see also Kenneth M. Cuno, 'African Slaves in 19th-Century Rural Egypt', *International Journal of Middle East Studies*, Vol. 41, No. 2 (2009), pp. 186–8, accessed at http://www.jstor.org/stable/40206097; Mowafi, *Slavery, Slave Trade and Abolition Attempts*; La Rue, 'Slave Trades and Diaspora in the Middle East, 700 to 1900 CE', *Oxford Research Encyclopedias*, 2021, accessed at https://doi.org/10.1093/acrefore/9780190277734.013.904.

32. Cronin, 'Islam, Slave Agency and Abolitionism', p. 28.

33. Kenneth Cuno, *Modernizing Marriage: Family, Ideology, and Law in Nineteenth- and Early Twentieth-Century Egypt*, p. 42.

34. Quoted in Zachary S. Berman, 'Owing and Owning: Zubayr Pasha, Slavery, and Empire in Nineteenth-Century Sudan', *CUNY Academic Works*, 2017, p. 304, accessed at https://academicworks.cuny.edu/gc_etds/1779.

35. Strachey, *Eminent Victorians*, p. 192.

36. Flora L. Shaw, 'The Story of Zebehr Pasha As Told by Himself', *Contemporary Review*, Vol. 52 (1887), p. 581.

37. Berman, 'Owing and Owning', p. 319.

38. Kim Searcy, 'The Sudanese Mahdi's Attitudes on Slavery and Emancipation', *Islamic Africa*, Vol. 1, No. 1 (Spring 2010), p. 73, accessed at www.jstor.org/stable/42656316.

39. Ibid., p. 77.

40. Lovejoy, *Transformations in Slavery*, p. 270.

41. Ibid., p. 271.

42. Berman, 'Owing and Owning', p. 319.

43. See 'Children in Sudan: Slaves, Street Children and Child Soldiers', Human Rights Watch report, 1 September 1995, accessed at https://www.hrw.org/report/1995/09/01/children-sudan/slaves-street-children-and-child-soldiers; see also Randall Fegley, 'Sudan and South Sudan' in Junius P. Rodriguez, *Slavery in the Modern World: A History of Political, Social, and Economic Oppression*, pp. 504–7; Max Elgot, 'Slavery in South Sudan', Humanitarian Aid Relief Trust, 27 March 2020, accessed at https://www.hart-uk.org/blog/slavery-in-south-sudan/. See also Nesrine Malik, 'Sudan's outsider: how a paramilitary leader fell out with the army and plunged the country into war', *Guardian*, 20 April 2023, accessed at https://www.theguardian.com/world/2023/apr/20/sudan-outsider-hemedti-mohamed-hamdan-dagalo-leader-militia-army-war-conflict.

44. See 'Prosecutor's Application for a Warrant of Arrest under Article 58 against Omar Hassan Ahmad Al Bashir', International Criminal Court, 4 March 2009, p. 9, accessed at https://www.icc-cpi.int/sites/default/files/NR/rdonlyres/64FA6B33-05C3-4E9C-A672-3FA2B58CB2C9/277758/ICCOTPSummary20081704ENG.pdf .

45. George F. Hourani and John Carswell, *Arab Seafaring in the Indian Ocean in Ancient and Early Medieval Times*, pp. 81–2.

46. Patricia Risso, *Oman and Muscat: An Early Modern History*, pp. 197–200; Mohamed Reda Bhacker, *Trade and Empire in Muscat and Zanzibar: Roots of British Domination*, p. 131.

47. Clarence-Smith, *Islam and the Abolition of Slavery*, p. 179, p. 115. See also Lee, 'Enslaved African Women in Nineteenth-Century Iran'.

48. See Robert Salisbury, *William Simpson and the Crisis in Central Asia 1884–85*, pp. 73–4, p. 85.

49. ḥamid ibn Muḥammad Ibn Ruzayq, *History of the Imâms and Seyyids of 'Omân*, p. 165.

50. David Abulafia, *The Boundless Sea: A Human History of the Oceans*, p. 795 (ebook); Risso, *Oman and Muscat*, p. 82.

51. Risso, ibid., p. 154.

52. Beatrice Nicolini, *Makran, Oman and Zanzibar: Three-Terminal Cultural Corridor in the Western Indian Ocean (1799–1856)*, p. xix.

53. Donald Petterson, *Revolution In Zanzibar: An American's Cold War Tale* (Boulder, Col., 2009), p. 7.

54. See A. F. Isaacman, 'The Countries of the Zambezi Basin' in J. F. Ade Ajayi (ed.), *General History of Africa VI, Africa in the Nineteenth Century until the 1880s*, pp. 185–97.

55. See Nicolini, *Makran, Oman and Zanzibar*, pp. 116–22.

56. Risso, *Oman and Muscat*, pp. 126–7; Abdul Sheriff, *Slaves, Spices & Ivory in Zanzibar: Integration of an East African Commercial Empire into the World Economy, 1770–1873*, p. 226, p. 231.

57. Thomas Smee, 'Observations during a Voyage of Research, on the East Coast of Africa, from Cape Gardafui south to the Island of Zanzibar, in the H. C's cruizers Ternate, Capt. T. Smee, and Sylph schooner, Lieut. Hardy', *Transactions of the Bombay Geographical Society*, Vol. 6 (1844), p. 46.

58. William Gervase Clarence-Smith (ed.), *The Economics of the Indian Ocean Slave Trade in the Nineteenth Century*, p. 15.

59. See Ralph A. Austen, 'The 19th Century Islamic Slave Trade from East Africa (Swahili and Red Sea Coasts): A Tentative Census', *Slavery & Abolition*, Vol. 9, Issue 3 (1988), pp. 21–44, accessed at https://doi.org/10.1080/01440398808574960; Clarence-Smith, *The Economics of the Indian Ocean Slave Trade*, p. 5.

60. Hopper, *Slaves of One Master*, p. 64, p. 58.

61. Mark Hobbs, 'Divers are a Pearl's Best Friend: Pearl Diving in the Gulf 1840s–1930s', *Qatar Digital Library*, 18 December 2014, accessed at https://www.qdl.qa/en/divers-are-pearl%E2%80%99s-best-friend-pearl-diving-gulf-1840s%E2%80%931930s.

62. Bilal Khamis' story is told in his own words in Julia Wheeler and Paul Thuybaert, *Telling Tales: An Oral History of Dubai* (Dubai, 2006), pp. 22–5.

63. Hobbs, 'Divers are a Pearl's Best Friend'.

64. IOR/R/15/2/1367, f. 10. India Office Record, cited in Mark Hobbs, 'Twilight of Pearl Trade Sees "Slave" Divers Seek Freedoms', *Qatar Digital Library*, accessed at https://www.qdl.qa/en/twilight-pearl-trade-sees-%E2%80%98slave%E2%80%99-divers-seek-freedoms.

65. For Jumaa al Batishi's recollections see 'The Perils of the Pearl Divers', *The National*, 21 June 2009, https://www.thenational.ae/uae/the-perils-of-the-pearl-divers-1.559014.

66. Troutt Powell, 'Slaves or Siblings?', p. 220.

67. Sheriff, *Slaves, Spices & Ivory in Zanzibar*, p. 48.

68. Cited in Alastair Hazell, *The Last Slave Market: Dr John Kirk and the Struggle to End the East African Slave Trade*, p. 21 (ebook).

69. Bhacker, *Trade and Empire in Muscat and Zanzibar*, p. 167, pp. 129–30.

70. Viscount Palmerston to Captain Hamerton, Foreign Office, 18 December 1846, *British and Foreign State Papers 1846–1847*, Vol. 35, p. 639.

71. Bhacker, *Trade and Empire in Muscat and Zanzibar*, p. 167. See also Mohamed Reda Bhacker, 'Family Strife and Foreign Intervention: Causes in the Separation of Zanzibar from Oman: A Reappraisal', *Bulletin of the School of Oriental and African Studies*, University of London, Vol. 54, No. 2 (1991), p. 269, accessed at https://www.jstor.org/stable/619135.

72. Sheriff, *Slaves, Spices & Ivory in Zanzibar*, p. 223.

73. Stuart Laing, *Tippu Tip: Ivory, Slavery and Discovery in the Scramble for Africa*, p. 4.

74. Ibid., p. 281.

75. Osumaka Likaka, *Naming Colonialism: History and Collective Memory in the Congo, 1870–1960*, p. 104.

76. Captain Colomb, *Slave-catching in the Indian Ocean: A Record of Naval Experiences*, p. 74.

77. W. C. Devereux, *A Cruise in the 'Gorgon', Or Eighteen Months on H. M. S. 'Gorgon', Engaged in the Suppression of the Slave Trade on the East Coast of Africa*, p. 412, p. 129; figures from Sheriff, *Slaves, Spices & Ivory in Zanzibar*, p. 224.

78. Murray Gordon, *Slavery in the Arab World*, p. 4.

79. Sheriff, *Slaves, Spices & Ivory in Zanzibar*, p. 237.

80. See Emily Ruete, *Memoirs of an Arabian Princess: An Autobiography*, pp. 218–20.

81. 'Princess Salme – Behind the Veil', accessed at https://www.soas.ac.uk/about/event/princess-salme-behind-veil; 'Sayyida Salme: The tragic life of Zanzibar's rebel princess', BBC News, 1 June 2019, https://www.bbc.co.uk/news/world-africa-47556607.

82. Heinrich Brode, *Tippu Tip: The Story of His Career in Zanzibar and Central Africa, Narrated from his own accounts by Dr Heinrich Brode*, pp. ix–x; Nasser Hashim As-Saadi, 'The Impact of the Abolition of the Slave Trade on Oman in the Late 19th Century (1856–1913)', *PalArch's Journal of Archaeology of Egypt/Egyptology*, Vol. 17, No. 6 (2020), p. 16693, accessed at https://archives.palarch.nl/index.php/jae/article/view/9954.

83. Alfred J. Swann, *Fighting the Slave Hunters in Central Africa*, p. 76.

84. 'The Central Slave and Ivory Trade Route', UNESCO website, 20 February 2006, accessed at https://whc.unesco.org/en/tentativelists/2095/.

85. Ian Hernon, *Britain's Forgotten Wars: Colonial Campaigns of the 19th Century*, p. 402; Mohammed Ali Bakari, *The Democratisation Process in Zanzibar: A Retarded Transition*, pp. 49–50.

86. Swann, *Fighting the Slave Hunters in Central Africa*, pp. 273–4.

87. See Freya Stark, *The Southern Gates of Arabia: A Journey in the Hadhramaut*, pp. 280–81.

88. This summary of the Zanzibar Revolution is based on accounts in Anthony Clayton, *The Zanzibar Revolution and Its Aftermath*, p. 63, p. 124; Petterson, *Revolution In Zanzibar*, pp. xvi–xvii.

89. 'The Struggle for Liberation in Oman', *MERIP Reports*, No. 36 (1975), p. 11, accessed at https://doi.org/10.2307/3011444.

90. Loc. cit.

91. See, in particular, Matthew S. Hopper, *Slaves of One Master: Globalization and Slavery in Arabia in the Age of Empire*.

92. El Hamel, *Black Morocco*, pp. 243–4.

93. James Grey Jackson, *An Account of the Empire of Marocco*, pp. 135–6.

94. For a short summary on whether abolition is indigenous to Islam see Brown, *Slavery and Islam*, pp. 203–12.

95. El Hamel, *Black Morocco*, p. 306.

96. Brown, *Slavery and Islam*, p. 214.

97. Brahim El Guabli, an interview with Chouki El Hamel, *Jadaliyya*, 24 April 2013, accessed at https://www.jadaliyya.com/Details/28480.

98. For an account of the exchange see James Richardson, *Travels in Morocco*, Vol. 2, pp. 194–7.

99. El Hamel, *Black Morocco*, p. 249.

100. C. J. Wills, *In the Land of the Lion and Sun*, p. 326.

101. Lovejoy, *Transformations in Slavery*, p. 286.

102. See H. Gurney and C. Harris Allen, *Tripoli, Tunis, Algeria and Morocco: Report to the committee of the British and Foreign Anti-Slavery Society*, 1892, accessed at https://babel.hathitrust.org/cgi/pt?id=nnc2.ark:/13960/t5s823z13&view=1up&seq=20.

103. Stephen Bonsal, *Morocco As It Is*, pp. 330–32.

104. Hunwick and Powell, *The African Diaspora in the Mediterranean Lands of Islam*, pp. 44–5.

105. R. David Goodman, 'Expediency, Ambivalence, and Inaction: The French Protectorate and Domestic Slavery in Morocco, 1912–1956', *Journal of Social History*, Vol. 47, No. 1 (2013), p. 101, accessed at https://www.jstor.org/stable/43306047.

106. See François-Paul Blanc and Albert Lourde, 'L'esclavage au Maroc au temps du protectorat' in Tanguy Le Marc'hadour and Manuel Carius

(eds), *Esclavage et Droit: Du Code Noir à nos Jours*, pp. 91–124; Goodman, 'Expediency, Ambivalence, and Inaction', p. 107, p. 101.

107. Kamel Daoud, 'Être noir en Algérie', *Jeune Afrique*, 17 May 2016, accessed at https://www.jeuneafrique.com/mag/323695/societe/etre-noir-algerie-kamel-daoud/.

108. Marta Scaglioni, 'A History of Slavery in the Village of El Gosbah', *Nawaat*, 19 May 2016, accessed at https://nawaat.org/2016/05/19/a-history-of-slavery-in-the-village-of-el-gosbah/. See also Marta Scaglioni, '"She is not a Abid": Blackness Among Slave Descendants in Southern Tunisia', *Open Democracy*, 14 February 2018, accessed at https://www.opendemocracy.net/en/beyond-trafficking-and-slavery/she-is-not-abid-blackness-among-slave-descendants-in-southern-tunisia/.

109. Nadia Issa, 'Tunisia's Dirty Secret', Al Jazeera online report and film, 17 March 2016, accessed at https://www.aljazeera.com/program/people-power/2016/3/17/tunisias-dirty-secret.

110. Simon Speakman Cordall, 'What's in a name? How the legacy of slavery endures in Tunisia', *Guardian*, 7 November 2020, accessed at https://www.theguardian.com/global-development/2020/nov/07/whats-in-a-name-how-the-legacy-of-slavery-endures-in-tunisia.

111. See, for example, Marvine Howe, *Morocco: The Islamist Awakening and Other Challenges*, p. 6; 'ROYAL ROLLER: Unique £200,000 off-road Rolls-Royce built for a Moroccan KING is for sale – and he had a bizarre use for it', *Sun*, 20 June 2022, https://www.thesun.co.uk/motors/18943030/unique-royce-built-for-a-moroccan-king-for-sale/.

112. See Malika Oufkir and Michele Fitoussi, *La Prisonnière: Twenty Years in a Desert Gaol*, p. 65, p. 77, pp. 79–80.

13 – MODERN SLAVERY

1. 'Enslavement of Women and Children by Islamic State in Northern Iraq and Syria August 2014 to May 2016', legal brief compiled by the Commission for International Justice and Accountability, author visit and interview, May 2024.

2. See V. Cetorelli, I. Sasson I, N. Shabila and G. Burnham, 'Mortality and Kidnapping Estimates for the Yazidi Population in the Area of Mount Sinjar, Iraq, in August 2014: A Retrospective Household Survey', *PLoS Medicine*, Vol. 14(5): e10022972017, accessed at https://doi.org/10.1371/journal.pmed.1002297.

3. James Reinl, 'Q&A: Probing Islamic State's sex atrocities with the United Nations: *Middle East Eye* speaks with Zainab Bangura, the UN envoy on sexual violence in conflict, about the latest IS crimes', *Middle East Eye*, 27 May 2015, accessed at https://www.middleeasteye.net/news/qa-probing-islamic-states-sex-atrocities-united-nations.

4. Kenneth Roth, 'Slavery: The ISIS rules', *New York Review of Books*, 24 September 2015, accessed at https://www.nybooks.com/articles/2015/09/24/slavery-isis-rules/.

5. Graeme Wood, 'What ISIS really wants', *The Atlantic*, March 2015, accessed at https://www.theatlantic.com/magazine/archive/2015/03/what-isis-really-wants/384980/.

6. 'The revival of slavery before the hour', *Dabiq*, 14 October 2014. For the full text of the article see David Cook, *Understanding Jihad*, pp. 237–42. See also Wood, 'What ISIS really wants'.

7. 'Islamic State: Yazidi women tell of sex-slavery trauma', BBC News, 22 December 2014, accessed at https://www.bbc.co.uk/news/world-middle-east-30573385. Transcript also adapted from Commission for International Justice and Accountability legal brief, 'Enslavement of Women and Children by Islamic State in Northern Iraq and Syria August 2014 to May 2016', pp. 61–2, accessed by author May 2024.

8. Ryan Browne, 'Escaped ISIS sex slave tells Congress of horrors', CNN, 21 June 2016, accessed at https://edition.cnn.com/2016/06/21/politics/escaped-yazidi-slave-isis-us-fight/; see also 'ISIS holding 3,500 slaves in Iraq, U.N. says', CBS News, 19 January 2016, accessed at https://www.cbsnews.com/news/un-isis-slaves-iraq-yazidi-women-children-civilian-death-toll/.

9. 'Muslim scholars release open letter to Islamic State meticulously blasting its ideology', *Huffington Post*, 24 September 2014, accessed at https://www.huffpost.com/entry/muslim-scholars-islamic-state_n_5878038.

10. Suzanne Miers, *Slavery in the Twentieth Century: The Evolution of a Global Problem*, p. 360.

11. Nicholas DeAntonis, 'Joe Biden is making clear that Saudi human rights violations won't be ignored', *Washington Post*, 11 March 2021, accessed at https://www.washingtonpost.com/outlook/2021/03/11/joe-biden-is-making-clear-that-saudi-human-rights-violations-wont-be-ignored/.

12 For the original text of the 1990 declaration, see https://www.oic-iphrc.org/en/data/docs/legal_instruments/OIC_HRRIT/571230.pdf. For a balanced critique of the declaration and its subsequent evolution, see Turan Kayaoglu, 'The Organization of Islamic Cooperation's declaration on human rights: Promises and pitfalls', Brookings report, 28 September 2020 https://www.brookings.edu/articles/the-organization-of-islamic-

cooperations-declaration-on-human-rights-promises-and-pitfalls/#
:~:text=In%20the%201990%20Cairo%20Declaration,and%20med
ical%20and%20social%20care

13. 'Bin Jelmood House', Msheireb Museums website, accessed at https://
msheirebmuseums.com/en/about/bin-jelmood-house/.

14. The Global Slavery Index 2023, p. 100, accessed at https://cdn.walkfree.
org/content/uploads/2023/05/17114737/Global-Slavery-Index-2023.pdf.

15. Ibid., p. 90, p. 132.

16. *Global Estimates of Modern Slavery: Forced Labour and Forced Marriage*,
a report by International Labour Organization, Walk Free, and International Organization for Migration, September 2022, p. 57, accessed at
https://cdn.walkfree.org/content/uploads/2022/09/12142341/GEMS-
2022_Report_EN_V8.pdf; see also '2022 Trafficking in Persons Report:
Saudi Arabia', US Department of State, accessed at https://www.state.gov/
reports/2022-trafficking-in-persons-report/saudi-arabia/#:~:text=The%20
government%20prosecuted%2090%20individuals,and%20six%20
for%20sex%20trafficking.

17. 'Maids for sale: Silicon Valley's online slave market', BBC television
report, 1 November 2019, https://www.youtube.com/watch?v=Qxz-
vmbFXd4; see also 'Slave markets found on Instagram and other apps',
BBC News Arabic, 31 October 2019, https://www.bbc.co.uk/news/
technology-50228549.

18. Ali al Ahmed, 'Author of Saudi Curriculums Advocates Slavery', Saudi
Information Agency, 7 November 2003, accessed at https://swap.stan-
ford.edu/was/20090418061718/http://www.arabianews.org/english/
article.cfm?qid=132&sid=2.

19. 'Egyptian cleric Abu Ishaq Al-Heweny explains enslavement of people
captured in jihad: they all become booty (archival)', Middle East Media
Research Institute (MEMRI), 8 June 2011, accessed at https://www.
memri.org/tv/egyptian-cleric-abu-ishaq-al-heweny-explains-enslavement-
people-captured-jihad-they-all-become.

20. 'Kuwaiti cleric Saalim At-Taweel: jihad for the sake of Allah means
fighting the infidels to make them convert to Islam; enslaving infidels
is one of the virtues of Islam', MEMRI, Special Dispatch No. 7253,
Kuwait, 29 December, 2017, accessed at https://www.memri.org/reports/
kuwaiti-cleric-saalim-taweel-jihad-sake-allah-means-fighting-infidels-
make-them-convert.

21. 'Slavery's last stronghold', a CNN special report by John D. Sutter and
Edythe McNamee, March 2012, https://edition.cnn.com/interactive/
2012/03/world/mauritania.slaverys.last.stronghold/index.html#:~:

text=If%20that's%20not%20unbelievable%20enough, Proclamation%20in%20the%20United%20States.

22. All interviews in Nouakchott by author, May 2024.

23. United Nations Development Programme, *Multidimensional Poverty Index 2023*, p. 2, https://hdr.undp.org/sites/default/files/Country-Profiles/MPI/MRT.pdf.

24. See Global Slavery Index 2023, p. 78, accessed at https://cdn.walkfree.org/content/uploads/2023/05/17114737/Global-Slavery-Index-2023.pdf.

25. 'Haratines', *World Directory of Minorities and Indigenous Peoples*, Minority Rights Group International website, accessed at https://minorityrights.org/minorities/haratin/.

26. Alexis Okeowo, 'Freedom fighter: A slaving society and an abolitionist's crusade', *New Yorker*, 8 September 2014, accessed at https://www.newyorker.com/magazine/2014/09/08/freedom-fighter.

27. 'Mauritania: The thorn in the side of President Aziz digs deeper', *Middle East Eye*, 13 February 2015, https://www.middleeasteye.net/features/mauritania-thorn-side-president-aziz-digs-deeper.

28. 'UNPO appeals MEPs to sign letter for urgent action against slavery case', Unrepresented Peoples and Nations Organization website, 12 September 2014, accessed at https://unpo.org/article/17515.

Bibliography

GENERAL READING

Atiyah, Edward, *The Arabs* (London, 1955)

Badawi, Zeinab, *An African History of Africa: From the Dawn of Humanity to Independence* (London, 2024)

Bennison, Amira, *The Great Caliphs: The Golden Age of the Abbasid Empire* (London, 2009)

Brown, Jonathan, *Slavery and Islam* (London, 2020)

Chafik, Ahmed, *L'esclavage au point de vue Musulman* (Cairo, 1938)

Chinweizu, *The West and the Rest of Us: White Predators, Black Slavers, and the African Elite* (New York, 1975)

Clarence-Smith, William Gervase, *Islam and the Abolition of Slavery* (London, 2020, reprint of 2006 original)

Dawood, N. J. (trans.), *The Koran* (London, 2000)

Fay, Mary Ann, *Slavery in the Islamic World: Its Characteristics and Commonality* (Basingstoke, 2019)

Gordon, Matthew, 'Slavery in the Islamic Middle East (*c*.600–1000 CE)' in *The Cambridge History of World Slavery*, Vol. 2, AD 500–1420 (Cambridge, 2021)

Gordon, Murray, *Slavery in the Arab World* (London, 1998)

Haseeb, Khair El-Din (ed.), *The Arabs and Africa* (Abingdon, 2012, reprint of 1985 original)

Hitti, P. K., *History of the Arabs* (New York, 1937)

Hourani, Albert, *A History of the Arab Peoples* (London, 2013, reprint of 1991 original)

Ibn Khaldun, *The Muqaddimah: An Introduction to History* (London, 1958 & 1978)

Lewis, Bernard, *The Arabs in History* (Oxford, 2002, reprint of 1950 original)

– *Race and Slavery in the Middle East: An Historical Enquiry* (New York, 1990)

459

Lovejoy, Paul, *Slavery on the Frontiers of Islam* (Princeton, N.J., 2004)

– *Transformations in Slavery: A History of Slavery in Africa* (Cambridge, 2011, reprint of 1983 original)

Mackintosh-Smith, Tim, *Arabs: A 3,000-Year History of Peoples, Tribes and Empires* (New Haven, Conn., 2019)

Marmon, Shaun, *Slavery in the Islamic Middle East* (Princeton, N.J., 1998)

The New Cambridge History of Islam, 6 vols (Cambridge, 2010)

Rizvi, Sayyid Saeed Akhtar, *Slavery: Islamic & Western Perspectives* (Cape Town, 2001, reprint of 1972 original)

Robinson, Chase, *Islamic Historiography: Themes in Islamic History* (Cambridge, 2003)

Rogan, Eugene, *The Arabs: A History* (London, 2012, reprint of 2009 original)

Segal, Ronald, *Islam's Black Slaves: The Other Black Diaspora* (New York, 2001)

Toledano, Ehud, *As if Silent and Absent: Bonds of Enslavement in the Islamic Middle East* (New Haven, Conn., 2007)

Willis, John Ralph, *Slaves and Slavery in Muslim Africa*, Vol. 1, *Islam and the Ideology of Enslavement* (Abingdon, 2014, reprint of 1985 original)

I – FOUR SLAVES AND THE BIRTH OF ISLAM

Arafat, W., 'Bilal ibn Rabah' in *Encyclopedia of Islam 2*, Vol. 1 (Leiden, 1986)

Armstrong, Karen, *Muhammad: A Prophet for Our Time* (New York, 2006)

Beg, M. A. J., *Brief Lives of the Companions of the Prophet Muhammad: The Sahabah in Islamic History* (Cambridge, 2002)

Bostom, Andrew G. (ed.), *The Legacy of Jihad: Islamic Holy War and the Fates of Non-Muslims* (Amherst, N.Y., 2008)

Bowersock, Glen, *Crucible of Islam* (Cambridge, Mass., London, 2017)

Bukhari, *Sahi Bukhari*, https://www.sahih-bukhari.com

Craig, H. A. L., *Bilal* (London, 1977)

Crone, Patricia, *Meccan Trade and the Rise of Islam* (Princeton, New Jersey, 1987)

Donner, Fred M., 'The Historical Context', *The Cambridge Companion to the Quran* (Cambridge, 2006)

– *Muhammad and the Believers: At the Origins of Islam* (Cambridge, Mass., 2010)

Hoyland, Robert G., *Arabia and the Arabs: From the Bronze Age to the Coming of Islam* (London, 2001)

Ibn Ishaq, *The Life of Muhammad*, trans. A. Guillaume (London, 1955)

Ibn Saad, *Kitab al Tabaqat al Kabir*, Vol. 3, *The Companions at Badr*, trans. A. Bewley (London, 2013)

– Vol. 8, *The Women of Madina*

Ibrahim, Mahmud, *Merchant Capital and Islam* (Austin, Tex., 1990)

Juynboll, G. H. A., *Studies on the First Century of Islamic Society* (Carbondale, Ill., 1982)

Kennedy, Hugh, *The Great Arab Conquests: How the Spread of Islam Changed the World We Live In* (Cambridge, Mass., 2007)

Levi Della Vida, G., 'Salman al Farisi', *Encyclopedia of Islam 2* (online edn, 2015)

Montgomery, James (trans. and ed.), *War Songs by Antara ibn Shaddad* (N.Y., 2018)

Peters, Francis E., *Mecca: A Literary History of the Muslim Holy Land*, (Princeton, N.J., 2017, reprint of 1994 original)

– *Muhammad and the Origins of Islam* (Albany, N.Y., 1994)

Powers, David S., *Zayd* (Philadelphia, Penn., 2014)

Robinson, Chase, 'Slavery in the Conquest Period', *International Journal of Middle East Studies*, Vol. 49, Issue 1 (February 2017), pp. 158–63 (accessed online)

Sardar, Ziauddin, *Mecca: The Sacred City* (London, 2014)

Savant, Sarah Bowen, 'Muḥammad's Persian Companion, Salman al-Farisi' in *The New Muslims of Post-Conquest Iran: Tradition, Memory, and Conversion* (Cambridge, 2013)

Tabari, *The History of al-Tabari*, Vol. 39, *Biographies of the Prophet's Companions and Their Successors* (New York, 1998)

Watt, Montgomery W., 'Mecca – The Pre-Islamic and Early Islamic Periods', *Encyclopedia of Islam*, Vol. 5 (Leiden, 2008)

– and McDonald, M. V., *The History of al-Tabari, Volume VI, Muhammad at Mecca* (Albany, New York, 1988)

2 – SLAVERY 101: BLUEPRINTS AND FOUNDATIONS

Ali, Kecia, *Marriage and Slavery in Early Islam* (Cambridge, Mass., 2010)

Berg, Herbert, 'The Collection and Canonisation of the Qur'Ān' in *Routledge Handbook on Early Islam* (online edn, 2018)

Brockopp, Jonathan E., *Early Maliki Law: Ibn Abd Al-Hakam and His Major Compendium on Jurisprudence* (Leiden, 2000)

Brown, Jonathan, *Slavery and Islam* (London, 2020)

Brunschvig, R., 'Abd' in *Encyclopaedia of Islam I*, pp. 24–40 (Leiden, 1960)

The Cambridge History of Islam, 2 vols (Cambridge, 1970, 1978)

Franz, Kurt, 'Slavery in Islam: Legal Norms and Social Practice' in Amitai, Reuven and Cluse, Christopher (eds), *Slavery and the Slave Trade in the Eastern Mediterranean (c.1000–1500 CE)* (Turnhout, 2018)

Freamon, Bernard, *Possessed by the Right Hand: The Problem of Slavery in Islamic Law and Muslim Cultures* (Leiden, 2019)

Hasan, Yusuf Fadl, *The Arabs and the Sudan: From the Seventh to the Early Sixteenth Century* (Edinburgh, 1967)

Hitti, Philip, *The Origins of the Islamic State. Being a translation from the Arabic, accompanied with annotations, geographic and historic notes of the Kitab Futuh al-Buldan of al-Imaam abu-l 'Abbas Aḥmad ibn Jabir al-Baladhuri* (New York, 1916)

Levtzion, N. and Hopkins, J. F. P. (eds), *Corpus of Early Arabic Sources for West African History* (Cambridge, 1981)

Lewis, Bernard, *Race and Slavery in the Middle East: An Historical Enquiry* (New York, 1990)

Mottahedeh, Roy, 'The Abbasid Caliphate in Iran' in *The Cambridge History of Iran*, Vol. 4, *The Period from the Arab Invasion to the Saljuqs* (Cambridge, 1975)

Pipes, Daniel, 'Mawlas: Freed Slaves and Converts in Early Islam' in Robert Hoyland (ed.), *Muslims and Others in Early Islamic Society* (Abingdon, 2017, reprint of 2004 original)

3 – RACE, RACISM AND REVOLT

Asher, A. (trans. and ed.), *The Itinerary of Rabbi Benjamin of Tudela*, Vol. 1 (London, 1840)

Furlonge, Nigel D., 'Revisiting the Zanj and Re-Visioning Revolt: Complexities of the Zanj Conflict (868–883 AD)', *Negro History Bulletin*, Vol. 62, No. 4 (December 1999), pp. 7–14.

Goldenberg, David M., *The Curse of Ham: Race and Slavery in Early Judaism, Christianity, and Islam* (Princeton, N.J., 2003)

Gordon, Matthew, 'Preliminary Remarks on Slaves and Slave Labor in 9th century Abbasid Empire' in Culbertson, Laura, *Slaves and Households in the Near East* (Chicago, Ill., 2010) (accessed online)

Harris, Joseph E. (ed.), *Global Dimensions of the African Diaspora* (Washington DC, 1993)

Jahiz, 'Superiority of the Blacks over the Whites' in Pellat, Charles, *The Life and Works of Jahiz*, (Berkeley and Los Angeles, Cal., 1969), pp. 195–8

Lewis, Bernard, 'The Crows of the Arabs', *Critical Inquiry*, Vol. 12, No. 1 (Autumn 1985), pp. 88–97

– *Islam from the Prophet Mohammed to the Capture of Constantinople*, Vol. 2 (New York, 1987)

– *Race and Slavery in the Middle East: An Historical Enquiry* (New York, 1990)

Masudi, *Les Prairies d'Or*, Vol. 8 (Paris, 1861)

McLeod, Nicholas C., 'Race, Rebellion, and Arab Muslim Slavery: The Zanj Rebellion in Iraq, 869–883 C.E.' (2016) (accessed online)

Montgomery, James, 'Scenes of Violence in Arabic Literature' in *Cambridge World History of Violence*, Vol. 2, *500–1500 CE* (Cambridge, 2020)

Muhammad, Akbar, 'The Image of Africans in Arabic Literature' in Willis, John Ralph (ed.), *Slaves and Slavery in Muslim Africa*, Vol. 1, *Islam and the Ideology of Enslavement* (Abingdon, 2014, reprint of 1985 original)

Pellat, Charles (ed.), *The Life and Works of Jahiz* (Berkeley and Los Angeles, Cal., 1969)

Popović, Alexandre, *The Revolt of African Slaves in Iraq in the 3rd/9th Century* (Princeton, N.J., 1999)

Reilly, Benjamin, *Slavery, Agriculture, and Malaria in the Arabian Peninsula* (Athens, Ohio, 2015)

Rosenthal, Jakob, *Political Thought in Medieval Islam: An Introductory Outline* (Cambridge, 1958)

Southgate, Minoo, 'The Negative Images of Blacks in Some Medieval Iranian Writings', *Iranian Studies*, Vol. 17, No. 1 (Winter 1984), pp. 3–36.

Tabari, *The History of al Tabari*, Vol. 36, *The Revolt of the Zanj* (Albany, N.Y., 1992)

– Vol. 37, *The Abbasid Recovery* (Albany, N.Y., 1987)

Talhami, Ghada Hashem, 'The Zanj Rebellion Reconsidered', *The International Journal of African Historical Studies*, Vol. 10, No. 3 (1977), pp. 443–61 (accessed online)

Urban, Elizabeth, *Conquered Populations in Early Islam: Non-Arabs, Slaves, and the Sons of Slave Mothers* (Edinburgh, 2020)

Willis, John Ralph (ed.), *Slaves and Slavery in Muslim Africa*, Vol. 1, *Islam and the Ideology of Enslavement* (Abingdon, 2014, reprint of 1985 original)

4 – SEX AND SINGING: THE CONCUBINES

Ahsan, Muhammad Manazir, *Social Life Under the Abbasids* (London, 1979)

Ali, Sayed Amir, *The Spirit of Islam: A History of the Evolution and Ideals of Islam with a Life of the Prophet* (London, 1922)

Ashtiany, Julia (ed.), *Abbasid Belles Lettres: The Cambridge History of Arabic Literature*, Vol. 2 (Cambridge, 1990)

Awde, Nicholas, *Women in Islam: An Anthology from the Quran and Hadiths* (New York, 2000)

Bray, Julia, 'Men, Women and Slaves in Abbasid Society' in Brubaker, Leslie and Smith, Julia M. H., *Gender in the Early Medieval World: East and West 300–900* (Cambridge, 2004)

Brookshaw, Dominic P., 'Palaces, Pavilions and Pleasure-gardens: The Context and Setting of the Medieval Majlis', *Middle Eastern Literatures*, Vol. 6, Issue 1 (2003), pp. 199–200.

Caswell, Fuad Matthew, *The Slave Girls of Baghdad: The 'Qiyān' in the Early Abbasid Era* (London, 2011)

Clot, André, *Harun al-Rashid and the World of the Thousand and One Nights*, trans. John Howe (London, 2005)

Coke, Richard, *Baghdad: The City of Peace* (London, 1927)

de Slane, Baron Mac Guckin (trans.), *Ibn Khallikan's Biographical Dictionary* (London, 1842–71)

Duri, A. A., 'Baghdad', *Encylopaedia of Islam 2*, Vol. 1 (Leiden, 1965)

Elad, Amikam, 'An Epitaph of the Slave Girl of the Grandson of the Abbasid Caliph al-Ma'mun', *Le Museon*, Vol. 111 (1998), pp. 227–44

El Cheikh, Nadia Maria, 'Revisiting the Abbasid Harems', *Journal of Middle East Women's Studies*, Vol. 1, No. 3 (2005), pp. 1–19

Gordon, Matthew, ''Arib al-Ma'muniyah (797–890)' in Cooperson, M. and Toowara, S. M. (eds), *Arabic Literary Culture, 500–925* (Detroit, Mich., 2005), pp. 85–90

– 'The Place of Competition: The Careers of 'Arib al-Ma'muniya and 'Ulayya bint Almahdi, Sisters in Song' (2002) (accessed online)

– and Hain, Kathryn A. (eds), *Concubines and Courtesans: Women and Slavery in Islamic History* (Oxford, 2017)

Gruendler, Beatrice, *Medieval Arabic Praise Poetry* (London, 2002)

Ibn al Sa'i, ''Arib al-Ma'muniyah, "Ardent", Member of the Household of the Caliph al-Ma'mun' in *The Consorts of the Caliphs*, pp. 24–32

– 'Inan, Daughter of Abd Allah, "Restraint", Slave of Al Natifi' in Toorawa, Shawkat M. and Bray, Julia (eds), *The Consorts of the Caliphs: Women and the Court of Baghdad* (New York, 2015), pp. 11–19

– 'Mahbubah, "Beloved", Slave of the Caliph al-Mutawakkil' in *The Consorts of the Caliphs*, pp. 77–83

Imhof, Agnes, 'Traditio vel Aemulatio? The Singing Contest of Samarra, Expression of a Medieval Culture of Competition', *Der Islam*, 90 (2013) (accessed online)

Irwin, Robert, *The Arabian Nights: A Companion* (London, 2004)

Isfahani, Abul Faraj, *Kitab al Aghani* (Cairo, 1905)

Jahiz, 'Portrait of a Singing Slave-girl' in Pellat, Charles (ed.), *The Life and Works of Jahiz* (Berkeley and Los Angeles, Cal., 1969), pp. 265–7

Judd, Steven and Scheiner, Jens (eds), *New Perspectives on Ibn ʿAsākir in Islamic Historiography* (Leiden, 2017)

Kennedy, Hugh, *When Baghdad Ruled the Muslim World: The Rise and Fall of Islam's Greatest Dynasty* (Cambridge, Mass., 2005; US edn of *The Court of the Caliphs*, London, 2005)

Le Strange, Guy, *Baghdad During the Abbasid Caliphate* (Oxford, 1900)

Lyons, Malcolm (trans.), *The Arabian Nights: Tales of 1,001 Nights*, 3 vols (London, 2008)

Marozzi, Justin, *Baghdad: City of Peace, City of Blood* (London, 2014)

Masudi, *The Meadows of Gold: The Abbasids*, trans. and ed. Paul Lunde and Caroline Stone (London, 1989)

Moukheiber, Karen Raif, *Slave Women and Free Men: Gender, Sexuality and Culture in Early Abbasid Times* (Beirut, 2015) (accessed online)

Ormsby, Eric, 'Questions for Stones: On Classical Arabic Poetry' in *Parnassus: Poetry in Review*, Vol. 25, No. 1 and No. 2 (2001), p. 30

Peirce, Leslie, *The Imperial Harem: Women and Sovereignty in the Ottoman Empire* (New York, 1993)

Prince-Eichner, Simone, 'Embodying the Empire: Singing Slave Girls in Medieval Islamicate Historiography', 28 April 2016 (accessed online)

Richardson, K., 'Singing Slave Girls (Qiyan) of the ʿAbbasid Court in the Ninth and Tenth Centuries' in Campbell, Gwyn, Miers, Suzanne and Miller, Joseph C. (eds), *Children in Slavery Through the Ages* (Athens, Ohio, 2009)

Schlein, Deborah, 'The Talent and The Intellect: The Qayna's Application of Skill in the Umayyad and ʿAbbasid Royal Courts' (2013) (accessed online)

Tanukhi, *Nishwar al-Muhdhara wa Akbar al-Muthakara (Table Talk of a Mesopotamian Judge)*, ebook, http://www.al-mostafa.com, privately translated by Manaf al Damluji

Wiet, Gaston, *Baghdad: Metropolis of the Abbasid Caliphate* (Norman, Okla., 1971)

5 – SLAVE SOLDIERS

Amitai, Reuven, 'The Mamluk Institution: 1000 Years of Military Slavery in the Islamic World' in Morgan, Philip and Brown, Christopher (eds), *Arming Slaves: From Classical Times to the Modern Age* (New Haven, Conn., 2006)

Ayalon, David, *Eunuchs, Caliphs and Sultans: A Study of Power Relationships* (Jerusalem, 1999)

– *Islam and the Abode of War: Military Slaves and Islamic Adversaries* (Aldershot, 1994)

– *Gunpowder and Firearms in the Mamluk Kingdom: A Challenge to Medieval Society* (London, 1978, reprint of 1956 original)

Bacharach, Jere L., 'African Military Slaves in the Medieval Middle East: The Cases of Iraq (869–955) and Egypt (868–1171)', *International Journal of Middle East Studies*, Vol. 13, No. 4 (1981), pp. 471–95 (accessed online)

Behrens-Abouseif, Doris, 'Early Islamic Architecture in Cairo' in *Islamic Architecture in Cairo: An Introduction*, pp. 47–57 (Cairo, 1989)

Bianquis, Thierry, 'Autonomous Egypt from Ibn Tulun to Kafur, 868–969' in *The Cambridge History of Egypt*, Vol. 1 (Cambridge, 2008), pp. 86–119

Brett, Michael, *The Fatimid Empire* (Edinburgh, 2017)

Crone, Patricia, *Slaves on Horses: The Evolution of the Islamic Polity* (Cambridge, 1980)

Fay, Mary Ann, 'Gender Race and Slavery in the Mamluk Households of Eighteenth-Century Egypt' in *Slavery in the Islamic World: Its Characteristics and Commonality* (Basingstoke, 2019)

Finkel, Caroline, *Osman's Dream: The Story of the Ottoman Empire 1300–1923* (London, 2005)

Frenkel, Yehoshua, 'Some Notes Concerning the Trade and Education of Slave-Soldiers During the Mamluk Era' in Amitai, Reuven and Cluse, Christoper (eds), *Slavery and the Slave Trade in the Eastern Mediterranean (c.1000–1500 CE)*

Gabbay, Alyssa, 'In Reality a Man: Sultan Iltutmish, His Daughter, Raziya, and Gender Ambiguity in Thirteenth Century Northern India', *Journal of Persianate Studies*, Vol. 4, Issue 1 (January 2011), pp. 45–63 (accessed online)

Gordon, Matthew, *The Breaking of a Thousand Swords: A History of the Turkish Military of Samarra 815–889* (Albany, N.Y., 2001)

Heude, William, *A Voyage up the Persian Gulf, and a Journey Overland from India to England, in 1817* (London, 1819)

Irwin, Robert, *The Middle East in the Middle Ages: The Early Mamluk Sultanate, 1250–1382* (Beckenham, 1986)

Ives, Dr Edward, *A Voyage from England to India, in the Year 1754 … Also a Journey from Persia to England by an Unusual Route* (London, 1773)

Jahiz, 'The Merits of the Turks and the Imperial Army as a Whole' in Pellat, Charles (ed.), *The Life and Works of Jahiz* (Berkeley and Los Angeles, Cal., 1969), pp. 91–7

Kennedy, Hugh, 'Military Slaves' in *The Armies of the Caliphs: Military and Society in the Early Islamic State* (Abingdon, 2001)

Levanoni, Amalia, *A Turning Point in Mamluk History: The Third Reign of al-Nasir Muhammad Ibn Qalawun (1310–1341)* (Leiden, 1995)

Marmon, Shaun, 'Black Slaves in Mamluk Narratives: Representations of Transgression', *Al Qantara*, Vol. 28, No. 2 (July–December 2007), pp. 456–64

Masudi, *The Meadows of Gold: The Abbasids*, trans. and ed. Paul Lunde and Caroline Stone (London, 1989)

Miura, Toru and Philips, John E. (eds), *Slave Elites in the Middle East and Africa: A Comparative Study* (London, 2000)

Patterson, Orlando, *Slavery and Social Death* (New Haven, Conn., 2018, reprint of 1982 original)

Pipes, Daniel, *Slave Soldiers and Islam: The Genesis of a Military System* (New Haven, Conn., 1981)

Rashba, Gary L., *Holy Wars: 3000 Years of Battles in the Holy Land* (Havertown, Penn., 2011)

Swelim, Tarek, *Ibn Tulun: His Lost City and His Great Mosque* (Cairo, 2015)

Tabari, *The History of al Tabari*, Vol. 35, *The Crisis of the Abbasid Caliphate* (Albany, N.Y., 1985)

– *The History of al Tabari*, Vol. 36, *The Revolt of the Zanj* (Albany, N.Y., 1992)

Yılmaz, Gülay, 'Becoming a Devshirme: The Training of Conscripted Children in the Ottoman Empire' in Campbell, Gwyn, Miers, Suzanne and Miller, Joseph C. (eds), *Children in Slavery Through the Ages* (Athens, Ohio, 2009) (accessed online)

6 – GUARDIANS OF SACRED SPACES: THE EUNUCHS

Alquraishi, Adel, *The Guardians* (Astar Publishing, 2020)

Ayalon, David, 'The Eunuchs in the Mamluk Sultanate' in *Studies in Memory of Gaston Wiet* (Jerusalem, 1977), pp. 267–95

– *Eunuchs, Caliphs and Sultans: A Study of Power Relationships* (Jerusalem, 1999)

Broadhurst R. J. C. (trans. and ed.), *The Travels of Ibn Jubayr* (London, 1952)

Dallam, Thomas, *Early voyages and travels in the Levant* (London, 1893)

Dieudonné, Gnammankou, 'Hayrettin Effendi, the Last Black Eunuch of Turkey', *Black Men*, August 2000 (accessed online)

Dikici, A. Ezgi, 'The Making of Ottoman Court Eunuchs: Origins, Recruitment Paths, Family Ties, and "Domestic Production"', *Archivum Ottomanicum* 30 (2013), pp. 105–36 du Bisson, Raoul, *Les femmes, les eunuques, et les guerriers du Sondan* (Paris, 1868)

El-Azhari, Taef, *Queens, Eunuchs and Concubines in Islamic History, 661–1257* (Edinburgh, 2019) (accessed online)

Graf, Tobias P., *The Sultan's Renegades: Christian-European Converts to Islam and the Making of the Ottoman Elite, 1575–1610* (Oxford, 2017)

Hathaway, Jane, 'Eunuchs and the State in the Mamlūk Sultanate and the Ottoman Empire: A Comparison' in Castiglione, Frank, Menchinger, Ethan and Şimşek, Veysel (eds), *Ottoman War and Peace: Studies in Honor of Virginia H. Aksan* (Leiden, 2019)

– *The Arab Lands Under Ottoman Rule, 1516–1800* (Abingdon, 2008)

– *Beshir Agha: Chief Eunuch of the Ottoman Imperial Harem* (London, 2005)

– *The Chief Eunuch of the Ottoman Harem: From African Slave to Power-Broker* (Cambridge, 2018)

Hogendorn, Jan, 'The Hideous Trade. Economic Aspects of the "Manufacture" and Sale of Eunuchs', *Paideuma*, Vol. 45 (1999), pp. 137–60 (accessed online)

– 'The Location of the Manufacture of Eunuchs' in Tora, Miura and Philips, John Edward (eds), *Slave Elites in the Middle East and Africa: A Comparative Study* (London, 2000), pp. 44–5 (accessed online)

Junne, George H., *The Black Eunuchs of the Ottoman Empire: Networks of Power in the Court of the Sultan* (London, 2016)

Kennedy, Hugh, 'Mu'nis al Muzaffar: An Exceptional Eunuch' in Höfert, Almut, Mesley, Matthew and Tolino, Serena (eds), *Celibate and Childless Men in Power: Ruling Eunuchs and Bishops in the Pre-modern World*, pp. 79–91 (Abingdon, 2018)

Larkin, Margaret, *Al- Mutanabbi: Voice of the 'Abbasid Poetic Ideal* (London, 2013, reprint of 2008 original), pp. 63–78

Lev, Yacov, 'The Ruling Circles' in *State and Society in Fatimid Egypt* (Leiden, 1991), pp. 65–81 (accessed online)

Marmon, Shaun, *Eunuchs and Sacred Boundaries in Islamic Society* (New York, 1995)

Matar, Nabil, *Turks, Moors and Englishmen in the Age of Discovery* (New York, 1999)

McCullagh, Francis *The Fall of Abd-ul-Hamid* (London, 1910)

Meinardus, Otto, 'The Upper Egyptian Practice of the Making of Eunuchs in the XVIIIth and XIXth Century', *Zeitschrift für Ethnologie/Journal of Social and Cultural Anthropology*, Bd. 94, H. 1 (1969), pp. 47–58 (accessed online)

Mirzai, Behnaz A., *A History of Slavery and Emancipation in Iran, 1800–1929* (Austin, Tex., 2017)

Montesquieu, *The Persian Letters of Montesquieu* (New York, 1929)

Penzer, N. M., *The Harem* (London, 2005, reprint of 1936 original)

Richards, D. S. (ed.), *The Chronicle of Ibn Al-Athir for the Crusading Period from Al-Kamil Fi'l-Ta'rikh. Part 1. The Years 491–541/1097–1146: The Coming of the Franks and the Muslim Response* (Farnham, 2010) (accessed online)

Remondino, P. C., *History of Circumcision from the Earliest Times to the Present – Moral and Physical Reasons for its Performance* (Philadelphia, Penn., 1891)

Tabari, *The History of al Tabari*, Vol. 31, *The War between Brothers* (Albany, New York, 2015)

Toledano, Ehud R., 'The Imperial Eunuchs of Istanbul: From Africa to the Heart of Islam', *Middle Eastern Studies*, Vol. 20, No. 3 (July 1984), pp. 379–90 (accessed online)

7 – ROGUES AND RENEGADES: SLAVERY IN THE MEDITERRANEAN

Auchterlonie, Paul, *Encountering Islam: Joseph Pitts: An English Slave in 17th-Century Algiers and Mecca. A critical edition, with biographical introduction and notes of Joseph Pitts of Exeter's 'A Faithful Account of the Religion and Manners of the Mahometans' 1731* (London, 2012)

Baepler, Paul, 'The Barbary Captivity Narrative in American Culture', *Early American Literature*, Vol. 39, No. 2 (2004), pp. 217–46 (accessed online)

– *White Slaves, African Masters: An Anthology of American Barbary Captivity Narratives* (Chicago, 1999)

Bamford, Paul W., *Slaves for the Galleys of France, 1665 to 1700* (Minneapolis, Minn., 1965)

Bicheno, Hugh, *Crescent and Cross: The Battle of Lepanto 1571* (London, 2003)

Blunt, Wilfrid, *Black Sunrise: The Life and Times of Mulai Ismail, Emperor of Morocco 1646–1727* (London, 2022, reprint of 1951 original)

Bono, Salvatore, 'Slave Histories and Memoirs in the Mediterranean World' in Fusaro, Maria, Heywood, Colin and Omri, Mohamed-Salah (eds), *Trade and Cultural Exchange in the Early Modern Mediterranean: Braudel's Maritime Legacy* (London, 2010) (accessed online)

– *Les Corsairs en Méditerranée* (Rabat, 1998)

Braudel, Fernand, *The Mediterranean and the Mediterranean World in the Age of Philip II*, Vol. 2 (Berkeley and Los Angeles, Cal., 1995)

Brotton, Jerry, *This Orient Isle: Elizabethan England and the Islamic World* (London, 2016)

Brown, Horatio F. (ed.), *Calendar of State Papers Relating to English Affairs in the Archives of Venice*, Vol. 11, *1607–1610* (London, 1904) (accessed online)

Colombo, Emanuele, 'Baldassare Loyola de Mandes (1631–1657), Prince de Fez et Jésuite' in Dakhlia, Jocelyne and Vincent, Bernard (eds), *Les musulmans dans l'histoire de l'Europe* (Paris, 2011), pp. 159–93

Corrales, Eloy Martín, *Muslims in Spain, 1492–1814* (Leiden, 2020)

Cortés, Manuel Lomas, 'L'esclave captif sur les galères d'Espagne (XVIe-XVIIIe siècles)', *Cahiers de la Méditerranée* 87 (2013), pp. 17–31

Crowley, Roger, *Empires of the Sea: The Final Battle for the Mediterranean, 1521–1580* (London, 2009)

Daborne, Robert, *A Christian Turn'd Turk: Or, The Tragicall Lives and Deaths of the two Famous Pirates, Ward and Dansiker* (London, 1612) (accessed online)

Dakhlia, Jocelyne and Vincent, Bernard (eds), *Les musulmans dans l'histoire de l'Europe* (Paris, 2011)

Davis, Robert C., *Christian Slaves, Muslim Masters: White Slavery in the Mediterranean, The Barbary Coast, and Italy, 1500–1800* (Basingstoke, 2003)

– *Holy War and Human Bondage: Tales of Christian-Muslim Slavery in the Early-Modern Mediterranean* (Santa Barbara, Cal., 2009)

Faroqhi, Suraiya, *The Ottoman Empire and the World Around It* (London, 2005)

Fisher, Humphrey J., *Slavery in the History of Muslim Black Africa* (London, 2001)

Fynn-Paul, Jeff, 'Empire, Monotheism and Slavery in the Greater Mediterranean Region from Antiquity through the Early Modern Era', *Past and Present*, 205 (2009), pp. 3–40

Helgason, Thorsteinn, 'Historical Narrative as Collective Therapy: The Case of the Turkish Raid in Iceland', *Scandinavian Journal of History*, Vol. 22, No. 4 (1997), pp. 275–89 (accessed online)

Hershenzon, Daniel, '"[P]Ara Que Me Saque Cabesea Por Cabesa …": Exchanging Muslim and Christian Slaves across the Western Mediterranean', *African Economic History*, Vol. 42 (2014), pp. 11–36 (accessed online)

– *The Captive Sea: Slavery, Communication, and Commerce in Early Modern Spain and the Mediterranean* (Philadelphia, 2018)

Hreinsson, Karl Smari and Nichols, Adam (trans.), *The Travels of Reverend Olafur Egilsson: The Story of the Barbary Corsair Raid on Iceland in 1627* (Keflavík, 2016)

Hunwick, J. O. and Powell, Eve Troutt, 'Islamic Law and Polemics Over Race and Slavery in North and West Africa, Sixteenth to Nineteenth Century', *Princeton Papers, Interdisciplinary Journal of Middle Eastern Studies*, Vol. 7 (1999), pp. 43–68

– *The African Diaspora in the Mediterranean Lands of Islam* (Princeton, N.J., 2002)

Jamieson, Alan G., *Lords of the Sea: A History of the Barbary Corsairs* (London, 2012)

Klarer, Mario (ed.), *Piracy and Captivity in the Mediterranean 1550–1810* (London, 2018)

– *Barbary Captives: An Anthology of Early Modern Slave Memoirs* (New York, 2022)

Laugier de Tassy, Jacques Philippe, *Histoire du royaume d'Alger* (Paris, 1750)

Lunsford-Poe, Virginia, *Piracy and Privateering in Golden Age Netherlands* (New York, 2005)

Malcolm, Noel, *Agents of Empire: Knights, Corsairs, Jesuits and Spies in the Sixteenth-Century Mediterranean World* (London, 2015)

Matar, Nabil, 'Piracy and Captivity in the Early Modern Mediterranean: The Perspective from Barbary' in Jowitt, Claire (ed.), *Pirates? The Politics of Plunder, 1550–1650* (Basingstoke, 2007)

– 'The Renegade in English Seventeenth-Century Imagination', *Studies in English Literature 1500–1900*, Vol. 33, No. 3 (1993), pp. 489–505 (accessed online)

– *Britain and Barbary, 1589–1689* (Gainesville, Fla., 2005)

– *British Captives from the Mediterranean to the Atlantic 1563–1760* (Leiden, 2014)

– *Mediterranean Captivity Through Arab Eyes, 1517–1798* (Leiden, 2021)

Maxwell-Stewart, Hamish, ' "Like Poor Galley Slaves . . .": Slavery and Convict Transportation' in Fernandes-Dias, Maria-Suzette (ed.), *Legacies of Slavery: Comparative Perspectives* (Newcastle, 2007), pp. 48–61

Milton, Giles, *White Gold: The Extraordinary Story of Thomas Pellow and North Africa's One Million European Slaves* (London, 2003)

Morgan, Joseph, *A Complete History of Algiers* (London, 1728)

Nichols, Adam, 'The Barbary Corsair Raid on Iceland, 1627', J. D. Davies blog, 20 February 2017 (accessed online)

Oualdi, M'hamed, *A Slave Between Empires: A Transimperial History of North Africa* (New York, 2020)

Palmer, Russell 'Slavery, Captivity and Galley Rowing in Early Modern Malta', *Antiquity*, Vol. 95, Issue 383 (2021), pp. 1280–97

Peabody, Sue, *'There Are No Slaves in France': The Political Culture of Race and Slavery in the Ancien Régime* (Oxford, 1996)

Pellow, Thomas, *The Adventures of Thomas Pellow, of Penryn, Mariner, Three and Twenty Years in Captivity among the Moors* (London, 1751)

Pepys, Samuel, *The Diary of Samuel Pepys*, 8 February 1661 (accessed online)

Rosu, Felicia, 'Muslim Slaves in Early Modern Europe: A Forgotten History of Slavery', Leiden Islam blog, 16 June 2016 (accessed online)

Salzmann, Ariel, 'Migrants in Chains: On the Enslavement of Muslims in Renaissance and Enlightenment Europe', *Religions*, Vol. 4 (2013), pp. 391–411

Sears, Christine E., '"Tyran[n]ical Masters Are the Turks": The Comparative Context of Barbary Slavery' in Fay, Mary Ann, *Slavery in the Islamic World: Its Characteristics and Commonality* (Basingstoke, 2019)

Sumner, Charles, *White Slavery in the Barbary States* (Boston, 1847)

Ter Meetelen, Maria, 'Miraculous and Remarkable Events of Twelve Years of Slavery' in Klarer, Mario (ed.), *Barbary Captives: An Anthology of Early Modern Slave Memoirs by Europeans in Africa* (New York, 2022), pp. 255–79

Tinniswood, Adrian, *Pirates of Barbary: Corsairs, Conquests and Captivity in the 17th-Century Mediterranean* (London, 2010)

Tucker, Judith E., 'She Would Rather Perish: Piracy and Gendered Violence in the Mediterranean', *Journal of Middle East Women's Studies*, Vol. 10, No. 3 (2014), pp. 19–20 (accessed online)

Viktus, Daniel J. and Matar, Nabil (eds), *Piracy, Slavery, and Redemption: Barbary Captivity Narratives from Early Modern England* (New York, 2001)

Webb, Simon, *The Forgotten Slave Trade: The White European Slaves of Islam* (Barnsley, 2021)

Weiss, Gillian, 'Ransoming "Turks" from France's Royal Galleys', *African Economic History*, Vol. 42 (2014), pp. 37–57 (accessed online)

– *Captives and Corsairs: France and Slavery in the Early Modern Mediterranean* (Stanford, Cal., 2011)

White, Joshua M., *Piracy and Law in the Ottoman Mediterranean* (Stanford, Cal., 2018)

Zammit, William, *Slavery, Treason and Blood: The 1749 Plot of the Slaves in Malta* (Kalkara, Malta, 2022)

8 – THE UNITED STATES GOES TO WAR

Boulahnane, Saad, 'Barbary Mahometans in Early American Propaganda: A Critical Analysis of John Foss's Captivity Account', *AWEJ for Translation & Literary Studies*, Vol. 2, No. 1 (February 2018), pp. 106–16 (accessed online)

Brett, Edwin John, *Brett's Illustrated Naval History of Great Britain, From the Earliest Period to the Present Time* (London, 1871)

Cherif, M. H., 'Algeria, Tunisia and Libya: The Ottomans and their heirs' in Ogot, B. A. (ed.), *General History of Africa*, Vol. 5, *Africa from the Sixteenth to the Eighteenth Century* (Paris, 1992)

Foss, John, *A journal, of the captivity and sufferings of John Foss; several years a prisoner at Algiers: together with some account of the treatment of Christian slaves when sick, and observations of the manners and customs of the Algerines* (Newburyport, Mass., 1798)

Lambert, Frank, *The Barbary Wars: American Independence in the Atlantic World* (New York, 2005)

London, Joshua, *Victory in Tripoli: How America's War with the Barbary Pirates Established the U.S. Navy and Shaped a Nation* (Hoboken, N.J., 2005)

Mackenzie, Alexander Slidell, *Life of Stephen Decatur, a Commodore in the Navy of the United States* (Boston, 1846)

McDougall, James, 'Savage Wars? Codes of Violence in Algeria, 1830s–1990s', *Third World Quarterly*, Vol. 26, No. 1 (2005), pp. 117–31 (accessed online)

Noah, Mordecai Manuel, *Travels in England, France, Spain, and the Barbary States in the Years 1813–14 and 15* (New York, 1819)

Otte, Thomas, 'Slavery in the Middle East', 'History Reclaimed' webinar, 3 February 2023 (accessed online)

Parton, James, *Life of Thomas Jefferson: Third President of the United States* (Boston, Mass., 1874)

St John, Ronald Bruce, *Libya: From Colony to Independence* (London, 2008)

Toll, Ian W., *Six Frigates: The Epic History of the Founding of the U.S. Navy* (New York, 2008)

Tucker, Spencer C. (ed.), *The Encyclopedia of the Wars of the Early American Republic, 1783–1812: A Political, Social and Military History* (Santa Barbara, Cal., 2014)

Wheelan, Joseph, *Jefferson's War: America's First War on Terror, 1801–1805* (New York, 2004)

Wilson, Peter Lamborn, *Pirate Utopias: Moorish Corsairs and European Renegadoes* (New York, 2003)

Wright, John, *Libya, Chad and the Central Sahara* (London, 1989)

–*Travellers in Turkish Libya 1551–1911* (London, 2011)

9 – THE SAHARAN SLAVE TRADE

Africanus, Leo, *The History and Description of Africa*, Vol. 2 (London, 1896)

Al Fasi, Al Hasan ibn Muhammad al Wazzan, *The History and Description of Africa*, a modern translation taken from Professor Paul Brians (accessed online)

Alford, Terry, *Prince Among Slaves: The True Story of an African Prince Sold into Slavery in the American South* (New York, 2007, reprint of a 1977 original)

Anderson, Richard and Lovejoy, Henry B., *Liberated Africans and the Abolition of the Slave Trade, 1807–1896* (Rochester, N.Y., 2020)

Barth, Heinrich, *Travels and Discoveries in North and Central Africa*, Vol. 2 (London, 1857)

Beck, Roger B., 'Africa, the Ottoman Empire, and the New Imperialism 1800–1914' in Wiesner-Hanks, Merry E., Ebrey, Patricia Buckley, Beck, Roger B., Davila, Jerry, Crowston, Clare Haru and McKay, John P. (eds), *A History of World Societies: Combined Volume*, 11th edn (New York, 2018)

Boahen A. A., 'The Caravan Trade in the Nineteenth Century', *The Journal of African History*, Vol. 3, No. (1962), pp. 349–59

Boye, Alida Jay and Hunwick, John, *The Hidden Treasures of Timbuktu: Historic City of Islamic Africa* (London, 2008)

Brett, M. 'Ifriqiya as a Market for Saharan Trade from the Tenth to the Twelfth Century A.D.', *The Journal of African History*, Vol. 10, No. 3 (1969), pp. 347–64

Cordell, Dennis D., *Dar-Al-Kuti and the Last Years of the Trans-Saharan Slave Trade* (Madison, Wis., 1984)

Daget, S., 'The Abolition of the Slave Trade' in Ajayi, J. F. Ade (ed.), *General History of Africa VI, Africa in the Nineteenth Century until the 1880s* (Paris, 1998)

Denham, Dixon, Clapperton, Hugh, Oudney, Walter and Salamé, Abraham V., *Narrative of Travels and Discoveries in Northern and Central Africa In the Years 1822, 1823, and 1824*, Vol. 1 (London, 1828, reprint of 1826 original)

Diouf, Sylviane A., *Servants of Allah: African Muslims Enslaved in the Americas* (New York, 1998)

Dunn, Ross, *The Adventures of Ibn Battuta* (Berkeley, Cal., 2012, reprint of 1989 original)

El Hamel, Chouki, *Black Morocco: A History of Slavery, Race and Islam* (Cambridge, 2013)

English, Charlie, *The Book Smugglers of Timbuktu: The Quest for This Storied City and the Race to Save Its Treasures* (London, 2017)

Ennaji, Mohammed, *Serving the Master: Slavery and Society in Nineteenth-Century Morocco* (Basingstoke, 1999)

Hall, Bruce and Addoun, Yacine Daddo, 'The Arabic Letters of Ghadames Slaves in the Niger Bend, 1860–1900' in Bellagamba, Alice, Greene, Sandra E. and Klein, Martin A. (eds), *African Voices on Slavery and the Slave Trade*, Vol. 1, *The Sources* (Cambridge, 2013), pp. 485–502

Hamdun, Said and King, Noël, *Ibn Battutah in Black Africa* (Princeton, N.J., 2009)

Hammer, Joshua, *The Bad-Ass Librarians of Timbuktu and Their Race to Save the World's Most Precious Manuscripts* (New York, 2016)

Hassanein Bey, Ahmed, *The Lost Oases* (London, 1925)

Hunwick, J. O., 'Black Slaves in the Mediterranean World: Introduction to a Neglected Aspect of the African Diaspora' in Savage, Elizabeth, *The Human Commodity: Perspectives on the Trans-Saharan Slave Trade* (London, 1992)

– and Harrak, Fatima (trans. and annot.), *Mira'j al Su'ud: Ahmad Baba's Replies on Slavery* (Rabat, 2000)

Ibn Battuta, *The Travels of Ibn Battutah*, Vols 1–4, trans. H. A. R. Gibb (Cambridge, 1971)

Iocchi, Alessio, *Living Through Crisis by Lake Chad: Violence, Labor and Resources* (Abingdon, 2023)

Jumare, Ibrahim M., 'The Ideology of Slavery in the Context of Islam and the Sokoto Jihad', *The Islamic Quarterly*, Vol. 40, No. 1 (1996), pp. 31–8

Last, Murray, 'The Sokoto Caliphate' in Bang, Peter Fibiger, Bayly, C. A. and Scheidel, Walter (eds), *The Oxford World History of Empire*, Vol. 2, *The History of Empires* (Oxford, 2021), pp. 1082–110

Lefebvre, Camille, 'Hausa Diasporas and Slavery in Africa, the Atlantic, and the Muslim World', *Oxford Research Encyclopedias*, 22 March 2023 (accessed online)

Le Gall, M., 'The End of the Saharan Slave Trade in Tripoli', *Princeton Papers in Near Eastern Studies*, No. 2 (1993), pp. 25–55

Lovejoy, Paul, *Slavery, Commerce and Production in the Sokoto Caliphate of West Africa* (Trenton, N.J., 2005)

– *Slavery in the Global Diaspora of Africa* (London, 2019)

– *Transformations in Slavery: A History of Slavery in Africa* (Cambridge, 2000)

Lyon, Captain G. F., *A Narrative of Travels in Northern Africa in the Years 1818–20* (London, 1985, reprint of 1821 original)

Marozzi, Justin, *South from Barbary: Along the Slave Routes of the Libyan Sahara* (London, 2001)

McDougall, E. Ann, 'Salt, Saharans, and the Trans-Saharan Slave Trade' in Savage, Elizabeth, *The Human Commodity: Perspectives on the Trans-Saharan Slave Trade* (London, 1992), pp. 61–4

Mercadier, Fernand J. G., *L'esclave de Timimoun* (Paris, 1971)

Miers, Suzanne and Kopytoff, Igor (eds), *Slavery in Africa: Historical Perspectives* (London, 1977)

Nachtigal, Gustav, *Sahara and Sudan*, Vol. 1, trans. Fisher, Allan G. B. and Fisher, Humphrey J. (London, 1974)

Obichere, Boniface, 'The Social Character of Slavery in Asante and Daomey', *Ufahamu: A Journal of African Studies*, Vol. 12, Issue 3 (1983) (accessed online)

Otmane, Tayeb and Kouzmine, Yaël, 'Timimoun, évolution et enjeux actuels d'une oasis Saharienne Algérienne', *Insaniyat*, 51–52 (2001) (accessed online)

Richardson, James, *Travels in the Great Desert of Sahara in the Years of 1845 and 1846*, 2 vols (London, 1848)

Salau, Mohammed Bashir, 'Slavery in Kano Emirate of Sokoto Caliphate as Recounted: Testimonies of Isyaku and Idrisu' in Bellagamba, Alice, Greene, Sandra E. and Klein, Martin A. (eds), *African Voices on Slavery and the Slave Trade*, Vol. 1, *The Sources* (Cambridge, 2013), pp. 88–104

Tolmacheva, Marina, 'Concubines on the Road: Ibn Battuta's Slave Women' in Gordon, Matthew S. and Hain, Kathryn A. (eds), *Concubines and Courtesans: Women and Slavery in Islamic History* (Oxford, 2017)

Troutt Powell, Eve M., 'Slaves or Siblings? Abdallah al-Nadim's Dialogues about the Family' in Walz, Terence and Cuno, Kenneth M. (eds), *Race and Slavery in the Middle East: Histories of Trans-Saharan Africans in Nineteenth-Century Egypt, Sudan, and the Ottoman Mediterranean* (Cairo, 2011), pp. 217–28

Turner, Richard Brent, 'African Muslim Slaves and Islam in Antebellum America' in Hammer, Juliane and Shafi, Omid (eds), *The Cambridge Companion to American Islam* (Cambridge, 2013), pp. 28–44

Ware, Rudolph T. III, 'Slavery in Islamic Africa 1400–1800' in Eltis, David and Engerman, Stanley L. (eds), *The Cambridge History of World Slavery*, Vol. 3, *1420–1804* (Cambridge, 2011), pp. 47–80

Wright, John, *The Trans-Saharan Slave Trade* (London, 2007)

10 – THE OTTOMANS: A LORDSHIP OF SLAVES

Ágoston, Gábor, 'Firearms and Military Adaptation: The Ottomans and the European Military Revolution, 1450–1800', *Journal of World History*, Vol. 25, No. 1 (2014), pp. 85–124 (accessed online)

– 'Janissaries' in Fleet, Kate, Gudrun, Matringe, Denis, Nawas, John and Rowson, Everett K. (eds), *Encyclopaedia of Islam – THREE*, Vol. 2, pp. 146–50 (Leiden, 2007)

Argıt, Betül İpşirli, *Life After the Harem: Female Palace Slaves, Patronage and the Imperial Ottoman* Court (Cambridge, 2020)

Austen, Ralph, 'The Mediterranean Islamic Slave Trade out of Africa: A Tentative Census', *Slavery & Abolition*, Vol. 13, Issue 1 (1992), pp. 214–48 (accessed online)

Avaroğulları, Ayten Kiriş and Avaroğulları, Muhammet, 'An Example of Distortion in Turkish Social Studies and History Textbooks: Slavery' in *World Journal of Education*, Vol. 8, No. 6 (2018) (accessed online)

Baer, Gabriel, 'Slavery in Nineteenth Century Egypt', *The Journal of African History*, Vol. 8, No. 3 (1967), pp. 417–41 (accessed online)

Busbecq, Ogier Ghiselin de, *The Life and Letters of Ogier Ghiselin de Busbecq*, Vol. 1 (London, 1881)

Dávid, Géza and Fodor, Pál (eds), *Ransom Slavery Along the Ottoman Borders (Early Fifteenth–Early Eighteenth Centuries)* (Leiden, 2007)

Davies, Brian, *Warfare, State and Society on the Black Sea Steppe, 1500–1700* (London, 2007)

Eldem, Edhem, 'The Story of the Little Greek Boy Who Became a Powerful Pasha: Myth and Reality in the Life of İbrahim Edhem Pasha, *c.*1818–1893', *Athens Dialogues*, Stories and Histories, Period Two, 2010 (accessed online)

Erdem, Y. Hakan, *Slavery in the Ottoman Empire and Its Demise, 1800–1909* (Basingstoke, 1996)

Finkel, Caroline, *Osman's Dream: The Story of the Ottoman Empire 1300–1923* (London, 2005)

Fisher, Alan, 'The Ottoman Crimea in the Mid-Seventeenth Century: Some Problems and Preliminary Considerations', *Harvard Ukrainian Studies*, Vol. 3/4, Part 1 (1979–1980), pp. 215–26 (accessed online)

– 'The Sale of Slaves in the Ottoman Empire: Markets and State Taxes on Slave Sales, Some Preliminary Considerations', *Boğaziçi Üniversitesi Dergisi 6* (1978), pp. 149–74 (accessed online)

Goffman, Daniel, *The Ottoman Empire and Early Modern Europe* (Cambridge, 2002)

Hanim, Leyla, *The Imperial Harem of the Sultans: Daily Life at the Çiragan Palace During the 19th Century* (Istanbul, 1994)

Imber, Colin, *Ebu's-su'ud: The Islamic Legal Tradition* (Edinburgh, 1997)

İnalcik, Halil, 'Servile Labour in the Ottoman Empire' in Ascher, Abraham et al. (eds), *The Mutual Effects of the Islamic and Judeo-Christian Worlds: The East European Patterns* (New York, 1979)

– *The Ottoman Empire, The Classical Age, 1300–1600* (New York, 1989, reprint of 1973 original)

Karamursel, Ceyda, '*In the Age of Freedom, in the Name of Justice': Slaves, Slaveholders and the State in the Late Ottoman Empire and Early Turkish Republic, 1857–1933*, Publicly Accessible Penn dissertations, 2015 (accessed online)

– 'Ottoman Slavery as a Tool for Historical Analysis: A Review of Recent Literature' (Cambridge, 2016) (accessed online)

– 'The Uncertainties of Freedom : The Second Constitutional Era and the End of Slavery in the Late Ottoman Empire', *Journal of Women's History*, Vol. 28, No. 3 (2016), pp. 138–61

Kołodziejczyk, Dariusz, 'Slave Hunting and Slave Redemption as a Business Enterprise: The Northern Black Sea Region in the Sixteenth to Seventeenth Centuries', *Oriente Moderno*, Vol. 25 (86), No. 1 (2006), pp. 149–59 (accessed online)

King, Charles, *The Ghost of Freedom: A History of the Caucasus* (Oxford, 2008)

Kizilov, Mikhail, 'Slave Trade in the Early Modern Crimea from the Perspective of Christian, Muslim, and Jewish Sources', J*ournal of Early Modern History*, Vol. 11, No. 1–2 (2007), pp. 1–31 (accessed online)

Kritovoulos, *History of Mehmed the Conqueror* (Westport, Conn., 1970)

Kunt, I. Metin, *The Sultan's Servants: The Transformation of Ottoman Provincial Government 1550–1650* (New York, 1983)

Lee, Anthony A., 'Enslaved African Women in Nineteenth-Century Iran: The Life of Fezzeh Khanom of Shiraz', *Iranian Studies*, Vol. 45, No. 3 (May 2012), pp. 417–37 (accessed online)

Leitsch, Walter, '1683: The Siege of Vienna', *History Today*, Vol. 33, Issue 7 (July 1983), pp. 37–40

Mansel, Philip, *Constantinople: City of the World's Desire* (London, 1998, reprint of 1995 original)

Matsuki, Eizo, 'The Crimean Tatars and their Russian-Captive Slaves: An Aspect of Muscovite-Crimean Relations in the 16th and 17th Centuries', *The Mediterranean World*, Vol. 28 (2006), pp. 171–82

Mihailović, Konstantin, ed. Zeljko Zidaric, *Memoirs of a Janissary*, 2021 (accessed online)

Mikaberidze, Alexander (ed.), *Atrocities, Massacres, and War Crimes: An Encyclopedia*, Vol. 2 (Santa Barbara, Cal., 2013)

Montefiore, Simon Sebag, *Written in History: Letters that Changed the World* (London, 2018)

Murphey, Rhoads, *Ottoman Warfare 1500–1700* (London, 2006, reprint of 1999 original)

Nebahat, Nalçacı, Nida, 'Inherited Institution: Ottoman State Slavery and War Captives in the Early Modern Era', *Bulletin of the Institute of Classical Studies*, 2021 (accessed online)

– 'Slavery in Ottoman Istanbul', History of Istanbul From Antiquity to the 21st Century project (2020) (accessed online)

Peirce, Leslie, *The Imperial Harem: Women and Sovereignty in the Ottoman Empire* (New York, 1993)

Richmond, Walter, *The Circassian Genocide* (New Brunswick, N.J., 2013)

Rycaut, Sir Paul, *The Present State of The Ottoman Empire* (London, 1668)

Tardy, Lajos, *Beyond the Ottoman Empire: 14th–16th Century Hungarian Diplomacy in the East* (Szeged, 1978)

Toledano, Ehud, 'Enslavement in the Ottoman Empire in the Early Modern Period' in Eltis, David and Engerman, Stanley L. (eds), *The Cambridge History of World Slavery*, Vol. 3, *AD 1420–AD 1804* (2011), pp. 25–46

– 'Shemsigul: A Circassian Slave in Mid-Nineteenth-Century Cairo' in Burke, Edmund (ed.), *Struggle and Survival in the Modern Middle East* (Berkeley, Cal., 1993), pp. 59–74

– *The Ottoman Slave Trade and its Suppression: 1840–1890* (Princeton, N.J., 1982)

– *Slavery and Abolition in the Ottoman Middle East* (Seattle, Wash., 1998)

Wagner, Veruschka, 'Lives in Pieces: Female Slaves and Mobility in Early Modern Istanbul in Klein, Denise and Vlachopoulou, Anna, *Transottoman Biographies, 16th–20th Centuries* (Göttingen, 2023), pp. 77–104

Yasa, Firat, 'Between Life and Death: Slaves and Violence in Crimean Society in the Last Quarter of 17th Century', *Selçuk University Journal of Studies in Turcology*, Vol. 47 (2019), pp. 433–43 (accessed online)

Yermolenko, *Roxolana in European Literature, History and Culture* (Farnham, 2010)

11 – ABOLITION I: THE CENTRE

Akcam, Taner, *The Young Turks' Crime Against Humanity: The Armenian Genocide and Ethnic Cleansing in the Ottoman Empire* (Princeton, N.J., 2013)

Atatürk, Kemal, *The Speech (Nutuk)*, trans. Köhler, Kurt (Cromwell, Conn., 2020, accessed as e-book)

Badem, Candan, 'The Ottoman Crimean War (1853–1856)' in Faroqhi, Suraiya and İnalcik, Halil (eds), 'Servile Labour in the Ottoman Empire' in Ascher, Abraham et al. (eds), *The Mutual Effects of the Islamic and Judeo-Christian Worlds: The East European Patterns* (New York, 1979)

– *The Ottoman Empire and its Heritage: Politics, Society and Economy* (Leiden, 1994)

Blunt, Wilfrid Scawen, *Secret History of the English Occupation of Egypt: Being a Personal Narrative of Events* (New York, 1922, reprint of 1895 original)

Brookes, Douglas Scott (trans. and ed.), *The Concubine, the Princess and the Teacher: Voices from the Ottoman Harem* (Austin, Tex., 2008)

Clarence-Smith, William Gervase, *Islam and the Abolition of Slavery* (London, 2020, reprint of 2006 original)

Clarkson, Thomas, *Speech of Thomas Clarkson, Esq.: As Originally Prepared by Him in Writing, and Intended to Have Been Delivered at the Opening of the General Anti-Slavery Convention : Distinguishing Those Passages Which Were Omitted, but Which Are Now Published at Mr. Clarkson's Request* (London, 1840) (accessed online)

Ergin, Murat, '"Is the Turk a White Man?" Towards a Theoretical Framework for Race in the Making of Turkishness', *Middle Eastern Studies*, Vol. 44, No. 6 (November 2008), pp. 827–50 (accessed online)

Ferguson, Michael, 'Abolitionism and the African Slave Trade in the Ottoman Empire (1857–1922)' in Campbell, Gwyn and Stanziani, Alessandro (eds), *The Palgrave Handbook of Bondage and Human Rights in Africa and Asia* (New York, 2020)

– and Ehud Toledano, 'Ottoman slavery and abolition in the nineteenth century' in *The Cambridge History of World Slavery*, Vol. 4, *AD 1804–AD 2016* (Cambridge, 2017)

Frank, Alison, 'The Children of the Desert and the Laws of the Sea: Austria, Great Britain, the Ottoman Empire, and the Mediterranean Slave Trade in the Nineteenth Century', *The American Historical Review*, Vol. 117, No. 2 (April 201), p. 419 (accessed online)

Freely, John, *Inside the Seraglio: Private Lives of the Sultans in Istanbul* (London, 2000)

Gladstone, William Ewart, *Bulgarian Horrors and the Question of the East* (London, 1876)

Gocek, Fatma Muge, *Denial of Violence: Ottoman Past, Turkish Present and Collective Violence Against the Armenians, 1789–2009* (Oxford, 2015)

Gubara, Dahlia El-Tayeb, 'Al-Azhar and the Orders of Knowledge', PhD dissertation, 2014 (accessed online)

Haidar, HRH Princess Musbah, *Arabesque: An Account Of Harem Life* (London, 1968, reprint of 1944 original)

Haydon, Benjamin Robert, *Description of Haydon's Picture of the great meeting of Delegates at the Freemasons' Tavern, June 1840, for the abolition of Slavery and the Slave Trade* (London, 1844)

Heraclides, Alexis and Dialla, Ada, 'Chapter 8: The Bulgarian Atrocities: A Bird's Eye View of Intervention with Emphasis on Britain, 1875–78' in *Humanitarian Intervention in the Long Nineteenth Century: Setting the Precedent* (Manchester, 2015), pp. 148–68 (accessed online)

Kramer, Martin, *Islam Assembled: The Advent of the Muslim Congresses* (New York, 1986)

Low, Michael Christopher, *The Mechanics of Mecca: The Technopolitics of the Late Ottoman Hijaz and the Colonial Hajj*, PhD dissertation, Columbia University, 2015, pp. 98–102 (accessed online)

MacColl, Malcolm, *The Eastern Question: Its Facts and Fallacies* (London, 1877)

Midhat, Ali Haydar, *The Life of Midhat Pasha: A Record of His Services, Political Reforms, Banishment, and Judicial Murder* (London, 1903)

Miller, Donald E. and Miller, Lorna Touryan, *Survivors: An Oral History of the Armenian Genocide* (Berkeley, Cal., 1993)

Ochsenwald, William, 'Muslim-European Conflict in the Hijaz: The Slave Trade Controversy, 1840–1895', *Middle Eastern Studies*, Vol. 16, No. 1 (1980), pp. 115–26 (accessed online)

Peters, Francis E., *Mecca: A Literary History of the Muslim Holy Land* (Princeton, N.J., 2017)

Quinault, R., 'Gladstone and Slavery', *The Historical Journal*, Vol. 52, No. 2 (June 2009), pp. 363–83

Shaarawi, Huda, *Harem Years: Memoirs of an Egyptian Feminist 1879–1924* (New York, 1987)

Toledano, Ehud R., 'Abolition and Anti-slavery in the Ottoman Empire: A Case to Answer?' in Mulligan, W. and Bric, M. (eds), *A Global History of Anti-slavery Politics in the Nineteenth Century* (Basingstoke, 2013)

– *As if Silent and Absent: Bonds of Enslavement in the Islamic Middle East* (New Haven, Conn., 2007)

– 'Late Ottoman Concepts of Slavery (1830s–1880s)', *Poetics Today*, Vol. 14, No. 3, *Cultural Processes in Muslim and Arab Societies: Modern Period I* (Autumn 1993), pp. 477–506

– *Slavery and Abolition in the Ottoman Middle East*

Troutt Powell, Eve M., *Tell This in My Memory: Stories of Enslavement from Egypt, Sudan and the Ottoman Empire* (Stanford, Cal., 2012)

Zilfi, Madeline C., *Women and Slavery in the Late Ottoman Empire* (Cambridge, 2010)

12 – ABOLITION II: AWAY FROM THE CENTRE

Abulafia, David, *The Boundless Sea: A Human History of the Oceans* (London, 2019)

Addoun, Yacine Daddi, '"So That God Frees the Former Masters from Hell Fire": Salvation Through Manumission in Nineteenth Century Ottoman Algeria' in Araujo, Ana Lucia, Candido, Mariana P. and Lovejoy, Paul E. (eds), *Crossing Memories: Slavery and African Diaspora* (Trenton, New Jersey, 2011), pp. 249–60 (accessed online)

– 'L'Abolition de l'esclavage en Algerie 1816–1871', PhD dissertation, 2010 (accessed online)

Alebrahim, Abdulrahman, 'Glimpses of an Untold History of the Gulf: Notable Slaves as an Example', *Arabian Humanities*, Vol. 16 (2022), accessed at https://doi.org/10.4000/cy.8343.

Ali, Abbas Ibrahim Muhammad, *The British, the Slave Trade, and Slavery in the Sudan, 1820–1881* (Khartoum, 1982)

As-Saadi, Nasser Hashim, 'The Impact of the Abolition of the Slave Trade on Oman in the Late 19th Century (1856–1913)', *PalArch's Journal of Archaeology of Egypt/Egyptology*, Vol. 17, No. 6 (2020), pp. 16687–97 (accessed online)

Baer, Gabriel, 'Slavery and its Abolition' in Baer, Gabriel (ed.), *Studies in the Social History of Modern Egypt* (Chicago, 1969), pp. 161–89

Bakari, Mohammed Ali, *The Democratisation Process in Zanzibar: A Retarded Transition* (Hamburg, 2001)

Baker, Samuel White, *In the Heart of Africa* (Westport, Conn., 1970, reprint of 1884 original)

Beachey, R. W., 'The East African Ivory Trade in the Nineteenth Century', *The Journal of African History*, Vol. 8, No. 2 (1967), pp. 269–90 (accessed online)

Bedri, Babikr, *The Memoirs of Babikr Bedri* (London, 1969)

Belhamissi, Moulay, *Alger, l'Europe et la guerre secrète (1518–1830)* (Algiers, 2009)

– *Les captifs algériens et l'Europe chrétienne (1518–1830)* (Algiers, 1988)

Berman, Zachary S., 'Owing and Owning: Zubayr Pasha, Slavery, and Empire in Nineteenth-Century Sudan', *CUNY Academic Works*, 2017 (accessed online)

Bhacker, Mohamed Reda, 'Family Strife and Foreign Intervention: Causes in the Separation of Zanzibar from Oman: A Reappraisal', *Bulletin of the*

School of Oriental and African Studies, University of London, Vol. 54, No. 2 (1991), pp. 269–80 (accessed online)

– *Trade and Empire in Muscat and Zanzibar: Roots of British Domination* (London, 2002, reprint of 1994 original)

Blanc, François-Paul and Lourde, Albert, 'L'esclavage au Maroc au temps du protectorat' in Le Marc'hadour, Tanguy and Carius, Manuel (eds), *Esclavage et Droit: Du code noir à nos jours* (Arras, 2021), pp. 91–124

Bonsal, Stephen, *Morocco As It Is* (London, 1893)

Boubrik, Rahal, 'Nineteenth Century Slave Markets: The Moroccan Slave Trade', *Al Muntaqa*, Vol. 4, No. 2 (December 2021/January 2022), pp. 63–79 (accessed online)

Brode, Heinrich, *Tippu Tip: The Story of His Career in Zanzibar and Central Africa, Narrated from his own accounts by Dr Heinrich Brode* (London, 1907)

Burckhardt, Johann Ludwig, *Travels in Nubia* (London, 1819)

Clarence-Smith, William Gervase (ed.), *The Economics of the Indian Ocean Slave Trade in the Nineteenth Century* (London, 1989)

Clayton, Anthony, *The Zanzibar Revolution and Its Aftermath* (London, 1981)

Collins, Robert O., *The Southern Sudan in Historical Perspective* (New Brunswick, N.J., 2006)

Colomb, Captain P. H., *Slave-catching in the Indian Ocean: A Record of Naval Experiences* (London, 1873)

Cooper, Frederick, 'Islam and Cultural Hegemony: The Ideology of Slave-owners on the East African Coast' in Paul Lovejoy (ed.), *The Ideology of Slavery in Africa* (London, 1981), pp. 271–307

– *Plantation Slavery on the East Coast of Africa* (London, 1977)

Cordall, Simon Speakman, 'What's in a name? How the legacy of slavery endures in Tunisia', *Guardian*, 7 November 2020 (accessed online)

Cronin, Stephanie, 'Islam, Slave Agency and Abolitionism in the Middle East and North Africa' in *Social Histories of Iran: Modernism and Marginality in the Middle East* (Oxford, 2021) (accessed online)

Cuno, Kenneth, *Modernizing Marriage: Family, Ideology, and Law in Nineteenth- and Early Twentieth-Century Egypt* (Syracuse, N.Y., 2015)

Daoud, Kamel, 'Être noir en Algérie', *Jeune Afrique*, 17 May 2016 (accessed online)

de Bellaigue, Christopher, *The Islamic Enlightenment: The Modern Struggle Between Faith and Reason* (London, 2017)

Devereux, W. C., *A Cruise in the 'Gorgon', Or Eighteen Months on H. M. S. 'Gorgon', Engaged in the Suppression of the Slave Trade on the East Coast of Africa* (London, 1869)

Dodwell, Henry, *The Founder of Modern Egypt: A Study of Muhammad Ali* (Cambridge, 2011, reprint of 1931 original)

Fahmy, Khaled, *All the Pasha's Men: Mehmed Ali, His Army and the Making of Modern Egypt* (Cairo, 2002, reprint of 1997 original)

Fant, William, 'Slavery and the Search for Belonging in Modern Sudan', *History in the Making*, Vol. 2, Article 4 (2009) (accessed online)

Fegley, Randall, 'Sudan and South Sudan' in Rodriguez, Junius P., *Slavery in the Modern World: A History of Political, Social, and Economic Oppression* (Santa Barbara, Cal., 2011), pp. 504–7

Goodman, R. David, 'Expediency, Ambivalence, and Inaction: The French Protectorate and Domestic Slavery in Morocco, 1912–1956', *Journal of Social History*, Vol. 47, No. 1 (2013), pp. 101–31 (accessed online)

Gurney, H. and Allen, C. Harris, *Tripoli, Tunis, Algeria and Morocco: Report to the committee of the British and Foreign Anti-Slavery Society*, (London, 1892) (accessed online)

Harms, Robert, Freamon, Bernard K. and Blight, David W. (eds), *Indian Ocean Slavery in the Age of Abolition* (New Haven, Conn., 2013)

Hasan, Yusuf Fadl, 'Some Aspects of the Arab Slave Trade from the Sudan 7th–19th Century', *Sudan Notes and Records*, Vol. 58 (1977), pp. 85–106 (accessed online)

Hazell, Alastair, *The Last Slave Market: Dr John Kirk and the Struggle to End the East African Slave Trade* (London, 2011)

Hernon, Ian, *Britain's Forgotten Wars: Colonial Campaigns of the 19th Century* (Stroud, 2003)

Holt, P. M. and Daly, M. W., *A History of the Sudan: From the Coming of Islam to the Present Day* (Harlow, 2000, reprint of 1961 original)

Hopper, Matthew S., *Slaves of One Master: Globalization and Slavery in Arabia in the Age of Empire* (New Haven, Conn., 2015)

Hourani, George F. and Carswell, John, *Arab Seafaring in the Indian Ocean in Ancient and Early Medieval Times* (Princeton, N.J., 1995)

Howe, Marvine, *Morocco: The Islamist Awakening and Other Challenges* (Oxford, 2005)

Ibn Ruzayq, ḥamid ibn Muḥammad, *History of the Imâms and Seyyids of 'Omân*, trans. and ed. George Percy Badger (London, 1871)

Isaacman, A. F., 'The Countries of the Zambezi Basin' in Ajayi, J. F. Ade (ed.), *General History of Africa VI, Africa in the Nineteenth Century until the 1880s* (Paris, 1998), pp. 185–97

Isichei, Elizabeth, *A History of African Societies to 1870* (Cambridge, 1997)

Issa, Nadia, 'Tunisia's Dirty Secret', Al Jazeera online report and film, 17 March 2016 (accessed online)

Jackson, Henry Cecil, *Black Ivory and White, or The Story of El Zubeir Pasha, Slaver and Sultan, as told by Himself* (Oxford, 1913)

Jackson, James Grey, *An Account of the Empire of Marocco* (Philadelphia, Penn., 1810, reprint of 1809 original)

Johnson, Douglas H., *The Root Causes of Sudan's Civil Wars: Old Wars and New Wars* (Rochester, N.Y., 2016, reprint of 2003 original)

Laing, Stuart, *Tippu Tip: Ivory, Slavery and Discovery in the Scramble for Africa* (Surbiton, 2017)

Likaka, Osumaka, *Naming Colonialism: History and Collective Memory in the Congo, 1870–1960* (Madison, Wis., 2009)

Lovejoy, Paul, *Transformations in Slavery: A History of Slavery in Africa* (Cambridge, 2011)

Makris, G. P., 'Slavery, Possession and History: The Construction of the Self among Slave Descendants in the Sudan', *Africa: Journal of the International African Institute*, Vol. 66, No. 2 (1996), pp. 159–82 (accessed online)

Marouan, Maha, 'Incomplete Forgetting: Race and Slavery in Morocco', *Islamic Africa*, Vol. 7, No. 2 (2016), pp. 267–71 (accessed online)

Mire, Lawrence, 'Al-Zubayr Pasha and the Zariba-Based Slave Trade in the Bahr al-Ghazal 1855–1879' in Willis, John Ralph, *Slaves and Slavery in Muslim Africa*, Vol. 2, *The Servile Estate* (London, 1985)

Montana, Ismael Musah, *The Abolition of Slavery in Ottoman Tunisia* (Gainesville, Fla., 2013)

Moore-Harell, Alice, 'Slave Trade in the Sudan in the Nineteenth Century and Its Suppression in the Years 1877–80', *Middle Eastern Studies*, Vol. 34, No. 2 (April 1998), pp. 113–28 (accessed online)

– *Gordon and the Sudan: Prologue to the Mahdiyya, 1877–1880* (Abingdon, 2001)

Mowafi, Reda, *Slavery, Slave Trade, and Abolition Attempts in Egypt and the Sudan, 1820–1882* (Stockholm, 1981)

Nicolini, Beatrice, *Makran, Oman and Zanzibar: Three-Terminal Cultural Corridor in the Western Indian Ocean (1799–1856)*, trans. Penelope-Jane Watson (Leiden, 2004)

Oufkir, Malika and Fitoussi, Michele, *La Prisonnière: Twenty Years in a Desert Gaol* (London, 2000)

Richardson, James, *Travels in Morocco*, 2 vols (London, 1860)

Risso, Patricia, *Oman and Muscat: An Early Modern History* (London, 2016)

Rosenthal, Franz, *The Muslim Conception of Freedom Prior to the Nineteenth Century* (Leiden, 1960)

Ruete, Emily, *Memoirs of an Arabian Princess: An Autobiography* (New York, 1888)

Salisbury, Robert, *William Simpson and the Crisis in Central Asia 1884–85* (London, 2020)

Scaglioni, Marta, 'A History of Slavery in the Village of El Gosbah', *Nawaat*, 19 May 2016 (accessed online)

– '"She is not a Abid": Blackness Among Slave Descendants in Southern Tunisia', *Open Democracy*, 14 February 2018 (accessed online)

Schaefer, Judith, 'Jihad in 19th Century Sudan, Part II', *Smithsonian Libraries Unbound*, 3 March 2017 (accessed online)

Searcy, Kim, 'The Sudanese Mahdi's Attitudes on Slavery and Emancipation', *Islamic Africa*, Vol. 1, No. 1 (Spring 2010), pp. 63–83 (accessed online)

Shaw, Flora L., 'The Story of Zebehr Pasha As Told by Himself', *Contemporary Review*, Vol. 52 (1887) pp. 333–49; 564–85; 658–83

Sheriff, Abdul, *Slaves, Spices & Ivory in Zanzibar: Integration of an East African Commercial Empire into the World Economy, 1770–1873* (Athens, Ohio, 1987)

Smee, Thomas, 'Observations during a Voyage of Research, on the East Coast of Africa, from Cape Gardafui south to the Island of Zanzibar, in the H. C's cruizers Ternate, Capt. T. Smee, and Sylph schooner, Lieut. Hardy', *Transactions of the Bombay Geographical Society*, Vol. 6 (1844)

Spaulding, Jay, 'Slavery, Land Tenure and Social Class in the Northern Turkish Sudan', *The International Journal of African Historical Studies*, Vol. 15, No. 1 (1982), note 29, pp. 1–20 (accessed online)

Stark, Freya, *The Southern Gates of Arabia: A Journey in the Hadhramaut* (London, 1936), pp. 280–81

Strachey, Lytton, *Eminent Victorians: The Illustrated Edition* (London, 1989, reprint of 1918 original)

Swann, Alfred J., *Fighting the Slave Hunters in Central Africa* (London, 1910)

Takriti, Abdel Razzaq, *Monsoon Revolution: Republicans, Sultans, and Empires in Oman, 1965–1976* (Oxford, 2013)

Wills, C. J., *In the Land of the Lion and Sun* (London, 1883)

13 – MODERN SLAVERY

Ahmed, Ali al, 'Author of Saudi Curriculums Advocates Slavery', Saudi Information Agency, 7 November 2003 (accessed online)

BBC, 'Islamic State: Yazidi women tell of sex-slavery trauma', BBC News, 22 December 2014 (accessed online)

– 'Maids for sale: Silicon Valley's online slave market', television report, 1 November 2019 (accessed online)

Browne, Ryan, 'Escaped ISIS sex slave tells Congress of horrors', CNN, 21 June 2016 (accessed online)

Campbell, Gwyn and Elbourne, Elizabeth (eds), *Sex, Power and Slavery* (Athens, Ohio, 2014)

Cetorelli, V., Sasson I., Shabila, N. and Burnham, G., 'Mortality and Kidnapping Estimates for the Yazidi Population in the Area of Mount Sinjar, Iraq, in August 2014: A Retrospective Household Survey', *PLoS Medicine*, Vol. 14(5): e10022972017 (accessed online)

Commission for International Justice and Accountability, 'Enslavement of Women and Children by Islamic State in Northern Iraq and Syria August 2014 to May 2016', legal brief viewed privately by the author, 2024

Cook, David, *Understanding Jihad* (Berkeley, Cal., 2015, reprint of 2005 original)

Craemer, Thomas, 'International Reparations for Slavery and the Slave Trade', *Journal of Black Studies*, Vol. 49, No. 7 (October 2018), pp. 694–713

Huffington Post, 'Muslim scholars release open letter to Islamic State meticulously blasting its ideology', 24 September 2014 (accessed online)

International Labour Organization, Walk Free, and International Organization for Migration, *Global Estimates of Modern Slavery: Forced Labour and Forced Marriage*, September 2022 (accessed online)

Middle East Media Research Institute (MEMRI), 'Egyptian cleric Abu Ishaq Al-Heweny explains enslavement of people captured in jihad: They all become booty (Archival)', 8 June 2011 (accessed online)

– 'Kuwaiti cleric Saalim At-Taweel: Jihad for the sake of Allah means fighting the infidels to make them convert to Islam; Enslaving infidels is one of the virtues of Islam', Special Dispatch No. 7253, Kuwait, 29 December, 2017 (accessed online)

Miers, Suzanne, *Slavery in the Twentieth Century: The Evolution of a Global Problem* (Walnut Creek, Cal., 2003)

Okeowo, Alexis, 'Freedom Fighter: A slaving society and an abolitionist's crusade', *New Yorker*, 8 September 2014 (accessed online)

Reinl, James, 'Q&A: Probing Islamic State's sex atrocities with the United Nations: *Middle East Eye* speaks with Zainab Bangura, the UN envoy on sexual violence in conflict, about the latest IS crimes', *Middle East Eye*, 27 May 2015 (accessed online)

Roth, Kenneth, 'Slavery: The ISIS rules', *New York Review of Books*, 24 September 2015 (accessed online)

Sutter, John D. and McNamee, Edythe, 'Slavery's last stronghold', a CNN special report, March 2012 (accessed online)

Wood, Graeme, 'What ISIS really wants', *The Atlantic*, March 2015 (accessed online)

Index

Page references in *italics* indicate images.